Betsy Sholl, *Genealogy* 66
A. E. Stallings, *Another Lullaby for Insomniacs* 335
Dylan Thomas, *Do Not Go Gentle into That Good Night* 117
Brian Turner, *What Every Soldier Should Know* 217

Nonfiction

Brian Arundel, *The Things I've Lost* 216
Brian Doyle, *Two Hearts* 340
Amy Fusselman, From *The Pharmacist's Mate* 76
Dylan Landis, *In My Father's Study upon His Death* 161
Brenda Miller, *Swerve* 118
Dinty W. Moore, *Son of Mr. Green Jeans: An Essay on Fatherhood, Alphabetically Arranged* 305
Jack Ridl and "Repairing the House," *The Poem and I Have a Little Conversation* 396
Vincent Scarpa, *I Go Back to Berryman's* 65
Karissa Womack, *I Remember All of You* 398

Drama

Charlotte Glynn, Excerpt from *Duct Tape Twins* (screenplay) 218
Jenifer Hixson, *Where There's Smoke* (monologue) 162
Peter Morris, *Pancakes* (play) 274
Marco Ramirez, *I am not Batman.* (play) 70

Comic

Scott McCloud, Excerpt from *Understanding Comics* 422
Jarod Roselló, *The Neighbor* 27

Flash/Micro

Brian Arundel, *The Things I've Lost* 216
Brian Doyle, *Two Hearts* 340
Carolyn Forché, *The Colonel* 185
A. Van Jordan, *af•ter•glow* 67
Rod Kessler, *How to Touch a Bleeding Dog* 250
Dylan Landis, *In My Father's Study upon His Death* 161
Brenda Miller, *Swerve* 118
Pamela Painter, *The New Year* 69
Jarod Roselló, *The Neighbor* 27
George Saunders, *Sticks* 304
Vincent Scarpa, *I Go Back to Berryman's* 65

THE PRACTICE OF CREATIVE WRITING

A GUIDE FOR STUDENTS

THIRD EDITION

HEATHER SELLERS

University of South Florida

bedford/st.martin's
Macmillan Learning

Boston | New York

For Bedford/St. Martin's

Vice President, Editorial, Macmillan Learning Humanities: Edwin Hill
Editorial Director, English: Karen S. Henry
Executive Editor: Vivian Garcia
Senior Developmental Editor: Jill Gallagher
Assistant Production Editor: Erica Zhang
Senior Production Editor: Jessica Gould
Editorial Assistant: Julia Domenicucci
Production Supervisor: Carolyn Quimby
Associate Marketing Manager: Sophia Latorre-Zengierski
Copy Editor: Linda McLatchie
Director of Rights and Permissions: Hilary Newman
Permissions Editor: Kalina Ingham
Senior Art Director: Anna Palchik
Text Design: Jerilyn Bockorick
Cover Design: John Callahan
Cover Art: Peter Goldlust
Composition: Cenveo Publisher Services
Printing and Binding: RR Donnelley and Sons

Manufactured in the United States of America.

1   0   9   8   7   6
f   e   d   c   b   a

For information, write: Bedford/St. Martin's, 75 Arlington Street, Boston, MA 02116 (617-399-4000)

ISBN 978-1-319-04016-1

Acknowledgments

Text acknowledgments and copyrights appear at the back of the book on pages 504–506, which constitute an extension of the copyright page.

PREFACE
FOR INSTRUCTORS

For many years, I taught creative writing the way it had been taught to me. I took my students through lessons on developing character, deepening theme, and measuring out meter. And as I did so, I felt like a fraud (a well-intentioned fraud) in the classroom; my own writing process bore no resemblance to the approach I offered my students.

In my writing room, I always began—and still do—as many writers do: with *an image*. Considering literary terms never entered into the generative phase of my writing process as I concentrated on a kind of movie in my mind's eye; in fact, I would have been hidebound and blocked as a new writer if I had consciously thought about metonymy or diction. We work as writers not from literary terms but by exploring a specific, grounded moment in time on a very physical level. Then, as now, I delay genre decisions until I know more about what it is I have on the page.

As writers, we devote a lot of energy to what is called "creative concentration." What trips us up often isn't line breaks or thematic considerations or genre conventions—not at first—it's actually getting to the writing desk and staying there. To improve as writers, we have to learn how to create and sustain productive focus. Making art is in large part a head game, and teaching a course that enables students to create a meaningful writing practice requires us to study what writers actually do with their attention and their purpose when they are creating. The course of study begins there, with process, and then moves, step-by-step, through the strategies writers use, regardless of genre, to develop and enhance their efforts. Preparing well, starting smarter, and learning how to spend more time on one's writing, in the face of great doubt—practicing those techniques helped me grow most as a writer, and enabled me, quite a way down the road, to at last understand why on earth I needed to know a pyrrhic foot from a spondee.

I used to teach my creative writing classes as though they were literature courses with some creative writing assignments mixed in. But in truth, writing poetry and plays and narrative was a lot more like going for a long run, dreaming, watching a movie. After I took a life-changing class with Lynda Barry, I came to understand how to teach writing as deep play, akin to the kind of focused imaginative state of mind we sustained for hours on end when we played as kids. In interviews with artists and writers, we hear this same sort of "dreaming deep" method described again and again. As I studied creativity and method, my teaching transformed. My students—spending more time learning about the nature of imagination, the way humans tell stories, and the psychology of concentration—wrote more and they wrote *better*. As my writing life and my teaching practice came into better alignment, I wanted to create a textbook for students that foregrounded the creative writing process and presented the specific ways writers read. We read differently in creative writing courses than we do in literature courses, and I wanted my textbook to teach sophisticated and nuanced reading skills in an approachable, welcoming way.

The Practice of Creative Writing teaches writing students how to seriously play. Like athletes, they warm up, they work out, they learn how to locate their weak areas, and they practice a little every day. Wind sprints. Scales. Exercises. And as students practice, they get better at what they're good at, and they develop a capacity for awareness based on a habit of *looking more closely*. They build skills that help them become fearless observers of the world and people around them, all in the service of the reader's experience—they learn how to take readers, with words, through emotions and feelings that really matter. This approach to the creative writing classroom privileges the writer's way of knowing and seeing and makes it possible for a wide range of students to come into the room and discover what it is they have to say and how best to say it.

The Practice of Creative Writing has always presented three overarching goals for students. First, a good creative writing class is always a course in reading more closely. Students leave with more sophisticated reading skills and exposure to a wide range of innovative literature. Second, literature both shapes and reflects human experience, and this book invites students and teachers into an ongoing conversation about art, language, and meaning-making endeavors. Third, this book is for student writers both beginning and advanced. Making a move from personal expression to powerful creative writing is demanding. The book assures students: *It takes time to learn to write well. It's a weirdly maddening mix of fun and difficulty. You can do this, and it's worth the trouble.*

NEW IN THE THIRD EDITION

Based on feedback from students and instructors, this edition of *The Practice of Creative Writing* contains five new features.

In-depth instruction on close reading. An entire chapter is devoted to using literature in the creative writing classroom. Chapter Two, Creative Reading, empowers students to read closely, to apprehend more difficult texts with less fear and more confidence, and, above all, to read intentionally, with an eye toward learning specific skills that they can use in their own writing.

New focus on short forms. For instructors pressed for time or those wanting to meet student demand for **flash fiction and micro-memoir** forms, this edition has a sequence of flash/micro readings and assignments, as well as expanded coverage of these agile, portable forms.

Expanded presentation of the genres. Part Three, Genres, now offers even more types of genres, with coverage of forms including lists and monologues.

Detailed discussion of the revision process. Chapter Nine, Revision, now includes two new case studies of student writers revising their work so that students are able to see a model revision process, step-by-step. Additional examples and revision narratives are also available in the Instructor's Manual.

Instructor support in an updated Instructor's Manual. The new Instructor's Manual includes lesson plans and detailed sample syllabi, as well as specific instruction on using *The Practice of Creative Writing* to teach a genre-based course. Additional resources, writing prompts, alternative reading suggestions, and revision strategies are included as well.

This new edition also introduces outstanding, student-favorite new authors—Dylan Landis, Brian Doyle, Natalie Diaz, and George Saunders—alongside classic authors such as Ernest Hemingway and Gwendolyn Brooks. Work in translation is presented, along with suggestions for a translation unit in the Instructor's Manual. Fresh voices, such as Ely Shipley, bring gender issues and experience to the page, while Jericho Brown urges readers to attend to race in America in his brilliant poem "Iustle."

In addition to the changes to the new edition, the hallmark features of *The Practice of Creative Writing* all remain in the book.

A flexible, process-based approach for writers in every genre. *The Practice of Creative Writing* shows students that things they already know how to do—observe, concentrate, practice—are the very skills they can use to become better writers. Throughout the book, students produce generative seed material and learn how to mine that material for images that will live and breathe in any genre.

In Part One, students begin to look at the world as subject matter, to see on the sensory, visual, imagistic level. Chapter One, Finding Focus, introduces students to the work that practicing, published writers do—attending to focus and concentration, using daily practice and rituals, and learning to manage doubt, fear, distraction, and procrastination. All writers have to deal with these psychological aspects of the writing process, and *The Practice of Creative Writing* provides practical advice for handling challenges to creative concentration.

In Chapter Two, Creative Reading, students study how great writers draw readers in, hold their attention, and transport them to another world. Student writers have to learn to shift from focusing on the *self* to focusing on the *reader*. The reader's experience of the text is what counts. Creative writing isn't "personal expression." It's *for* the reader, and it exists to activate *her* feelings, her emotions. As students read published authors and their own peers, they develop a vocabulary that lets them talk about technique. As they become more articulate about what creative writing can do, how it works, and why, their own writing ability improves. Throughout the text, guided examples show students exactly how writers accomplish their goals; students then apply this instruction to the reading selections, paying close attention to how language works in multiple genres.

Chapter Three, Building Blocks, presents the basic vocabulary and principles of structure that are key to good writing. The chapter shows that poems, stories, and plays are put together with similar shapes. Conflict in a narrative is parallel to tension in a poem; the climax in a short story equates to the turn in a sonnet, or the "reveal" in reality television. By following close examinations of Raymond Carver's classically structured "Cathedral" and clear, straightforward poems, students learn and practice the building blocks of creative writing, one by one.

A focus on six strategies common to all good writing. Part Two of *The Practice of Creative Writing* teaches students to focus on the essentials: vigor, depth, freshness, language, movement, the revelation of something interesting and important, sharp clear observations, and a good ear. The six strategies addressed in Part Two (images, energy, tension, pattern, insight, and revision) are the nuts and bolts of all good writing, regardless of genre. Successful writing is always grounded in images and always has energy and tension. It suggests patterns that lead to insights, and revision makes it more powerful and alive. These central chapters show how the strategies work individually and together to produce good creative writing: writing that is rewarding to create and rewarding to read and reread. Strategies are presented in order of difficulty so that students can build facility with them and layer the techniques to produce more sophisticated pieces as the course progresses. In each strategy chapter, a concept essential to good creative writing is introduced, and specific examples of what to do and what *not* to do are provided.

Then students read—a poem, a short story, part of a screenplay, a short nonfiction piece—in order to increase awareness of how the strategy functions, what technique a writer uses to deepen the power of the work. For example, in Chapter Five, students learn that creating work that has energy requires attention to time, language, leaps and gaps, and the shape of actual experience (rather than rendering thoughts and passive observations). In the chapter on tension, students learn how to manipulate the elements of writing to intensify their power; in the pattern chapter, students practice layering techniques used by professionals as they work with more sophisticated subject matter.

For instructors wishing to teach by genre, the chapters are arranged in an order that lends itself to moving through nonfiction/fiction and poetry units in a smooth flow, adding drama or flash units if the course allows.

The Practice of Creative Writing presents revision as something writers do throughout the writing process, not an activity they tack on at the end. Revision *is* writing. Revision is a skill built on close reading, so students are referred back to the early chapters on reading as writers as they learn to assess their own work and that of their peers. The section on student revision now includes longer works by student writers and close examinations of students at work, taking chances, developing patience and skill, and ending up with radically changed texts.

All along the way, in every chapter, practical prompts and checklists aid students in distinguishing between revising and editing and encourage higher levels of reader awareness.

Writing in the genres. Part Three, Genres, focuses on genre as a method for helping writers at any stage of their process discover what they have to say. These forms challenge students to flex creative muscles they don't usually use, a process that helps them imagine new possibilities in their writing. Fiction writers learn image and concision by studying poetry. Playwrights hone dialogue skill by reading short fiction. All writers can learn structure by studying comics and graphic forms, and it's fun.

Instructors might ask students to tackle longer, more formal genre-based projects late in the course, after the six strategies have been mastered. Or instructors may wish to organize their course around the genres, referring to the strategies as students work their way through a series of assignments and move toward a portfolio of complete projects. Examples of each form presented in Chapter Ten appear throughout the text, including journeys, graphic narratives, sonnets, and villanelles.

Imaginative writing activities. Practice activities throughout the book—suitable for in-class writing, small groups, journaling, writing groups, or homework assignments—help students try a wide range of approaches and build new skills. These activities can also be a source for rough drafts for pieces that will be developed and extended. Practices build on each other, and the student is encouraged to work as professional writers do, returning to practices from previous weeks, combining and layering. Students learn to use image listing as a way to generate their own writing prompts; other practices give direction for writing better dialogue, increasing the tension in lines of poetry, and using the senses to create depth in nonfiction. Longer, classroom-tested projects—suitable for workshops, portfolios, and larger assignments—ask students to relate and link what they have learned in previous chapters and guide them through full-length pieces. Workshop sections in each strategy chapter provide guidance for peer response and take students through the revision process, step-by-step. Writers' tips and checklists also help students revise their own work and make constructive suggestions to peers. Thus, practices can become projects, which can ultimately be revised to create a portfolio, a chapbook, or a live reading at the end of the course.

In sum, the practices, projects, workshops, writers' tips, and checklists throughout the book provide opportunities for writing at every stage in the process. They help students develop productive writing habits and work with the strategies. They also give students the experience and confidence to build up to finished pieces for publication or public reading.

Lively readings in all genres. The readings in the book are vibrant, fresh, and popular among students and include works by contemporary authors such as Raymond Carver, Michael Cunningham, Rick Moody, Akhil Sharma, Kim Addonizio, George Saunders, Gwendolyn Brooks, and E. E. Cummings. A wonderfully wide range of work is presented, including short stories, flash fiction, essays, memoir, poems, prose poems, comics, monologue, and drama. Most important, every piece included represents aspects of the six strategies; each piece can be used to illustrate image, energy, tension, pattern, insight, and revision, and each chapter automatically encourages review of previously introduced concepts. Always, the focus in *The Practice of Creative Writing* is on helping students focus tightly on what makes good writing good, no matter what form the writer chooses.

In the introductory course, students benefit from seeing a wide range of voices, possibilities, themes, and styles. And for many students, a concept is made clear only when presented in several forms—after they read for images or tension or energy in a play, a poem, and a story, the technique becomes crystal clear. Cross-training works, and students like it. Studying formal poetry strengthens the fiction writer's ear for rhythm; prose writers can create better dialogue by reading monologues and plays; and observing a nonfiction writer's use of insight helps student writers see the world more astutely. Students love the quotations from famous artists, scientists, thinkers, and writers that appear throughout the book, while instructors use them as reflective writing prompts and discussion starters, with the hope that the quotations will spark new ideas.

Once again, I've paid special attention to both screenplays and graphic narratives. *The Practice of Creative Writing* looks at screenplays, plays, and graphic/comic works as ways to practice the strategies of good writing: tension, pattern, and especially images, which help fiction writers and poets greatly. For example, if you simplify your short story or memoir to its bare bones by turning it into a four-panel cartoon, you can address issues of plot, structure, and characterization much more easily.

ACKNOWLEDGMENTS

Karissa Womack has been my editorial assistant for this project at the University of South Florida; she contributed countless hours and fantastic suggestions for every chapter, and her background as a high school English teacher proved invaluable. Annalise Mabe and Melanie Griffin, also at USF, offered insight and wisdom along the way. Thanks to Imani Lee and April Manna for technical support. Nancy Serrano, Jennifer Bosson, Kate Small, Suzanne Finney, Amanda Geerts, Lauren Bull, Erin Gilbert, Marina Kiriakou, Brian Lessing, Colin Jenkins, Felicity Jenkins, Wendy Durand, Debbie Maller, Nancy Rutland, Nora Conant, and Catherine Cox provided support and beauty, as did Jacob DeZwaan and Adele Sellers.

I am most deeply indebted to my writing partner, Dylan Landis, and my extended writing community: Jane Bernstein, Sy Safransky, Claire Whitcomb, Helen Pruitt Wallace, Enid Shomer, Don Morrill, Lisa Birnbaum, Silvia Curbelo, Elaine Smith, Susanna Childress, Stephanie Vanderslice, Amelia van Conant, Beth Trembley, Gianna Russo, Jesse Lee Kercheval, Dinty Moore, Elaine Sexton, and Robin Messing. Janice Shapiro and Michele Brafman contributed fresh ideas to this project; Ellen Darion helped immensely early on.

My generous colleagues at the University of South Florida, especially Kevin Yee, Jarod Roselló, Rita Ciresi, John Fleming, Ira Sukrungruang, Karen Brown, Dianne Donnelly, Hunt Hawkins, and Jay Hopler, inspire my writing and my classroom daily. In the MFA program at the University of South Florida, I learn from a particularly fine group of graduate students, and I'm privileged to teach a diverse body of undergraduates who have inspired and influenced many of the updates in this new edition, along with students at Kripalu, Bronx Manhattan Community College, New York University, St. Lawrence University, and Hope College.

Hope College supported this project in numerous ways for many years, and I remain ever grateful to friends, students, and colleagues there. I'm especially indebted to Dave Myers, Jackie Bartley, and my colleagues in the English Department at Hope.

At Bedford/St. Martin's, editors Sarah Macomber and Jill Gallagher provided feedback and support during all stages of the writing and revision process. Joan Feinberg, Denise Wydra, Karen Henry, and Steve Scipione all provided invaluable guidance and encouragement. Special thanks to Leasa Burton's and Vivian Garcia's leadership during this edition. Erica Zhang and Jessica Gould skillfully handled production, while Julia Domenicucci helped with countless details, Sophia Latorre-Zengierski and Joy Fisher Williams coordinated marketing efforts, and Kalina Ingham and Elaine Kosta managed permissions. I also want to thank John Callahan, who designed the cover.

Many thanks to the following reviewers, who helped shape *The Practice of Creative Writing* with their excellent feedback and suggestions:

Rebecca Balcaral, Tarrant County Community College; Kim Blaeser, University of Wisconsin–Milwaukee; Jill Boettger, Mount Royal University; Gregory Byrd, St. Petersburg College; Marlys Cervantes, Cowley College; Aviva Cristy, University of Wisconsin–Milwaukee; Dan Crocker, Kirkland Community College; Rachelle Cruz, University of California, Riverside; Jeanne DeQuine, Miami Dade College; Rebecca Dunham, University of Wisconsin–Milwaukee; Nancy Edwards, Bakersfield College; Heid Erdrich, University of St. Thomas; Patrick Finn, Chandler-Gilbert Community College; Geoffrey H. Forsyth, University of Iowa; Laura Fox, Harford Community College; Timothy Geiger, University of Toledo; Pamela Gemin, University of Wisconsin–Oshkosh; Karen B. Golightly, Christian Brothers University; Racquel Goodison, Borough of Manhattan Community College; Bunny Goodjohn, Randolph College; Nancy Gorrell, Morristown High School; Barbara Griest-Devora, Northwest Vista College; Kurt Gutjahr, University of Iowa; Martha Hayes, Gateway Community College; Ashley Hogan, Meredith College; Honoree Fannone Jeffers, University of Oklahoma; Emily Johnston, University of Nevada–Reno; Kirk K. Jones, SUNY Canton; Sara Kaplan, Del Mar College; Lynn Kilpatrick, Salt

Lake Community College; Leslie Kreiner-Wilson, Pepperdine University; Barry Lawler, Oregon State University; Martha Benn Macdonald, York Technical College; Martha Marinara, University of Central Florida; Teresa C. Mayle, Halifax Community College; Micheline Maylor, Mount Royal University; Paul Miller, Davidson College; Michael Minassian, Broward Community College; Rebecca Mooney, Bakersfield College; Jefferson Navicky, Southern Maine Community College; Lisa Norris, Central Washington University; Jeffrey Oaks, University of Pittsburgh; Wendy Oleson, University of Nebraska–Lincoln; Randy Phillis, Mesa State College; Neil Plakcy, Broward College, South Campus; Christopher Ransick, Arapahoe Community College; Vincent J. Reusch, University of Michigan; Michelle Rogge-Gannon, University of South Dakota; Matthew Roth, Messiah College; Jean Rukkila, Coconino Community College; Karyn Smith, Housatonic Community College; Gabrielle Stauf, Georgia Southwestern; Steve Stewart, Brigham Young University–Idaho; Anne Dyer Stuart, Bloomsburg University; Isaac Sullivan, University of Iowa; Stephanie Swartwout, Southeast Missouri State; Peter Telep, University of Central Florida; Michael Theune, Illinois Wesleyan University; Stephanie Vanderslice, University of Central Arkansas; John Walser, Marion College of Fond du Lac; Eliza Warren, University of Maryland, University College; and Karen J. Weyant, Jamestown Community College.

Heather Sellers
Saint Petersburg, Florida

ADDITIONAL RESOURCES FOR *THE PRACTICE OF CREATIVE WRITING*

Accompanying *The Practice of Creative Writing* are student and instructor resources that enable you to tailor the book to your course, inspire and improve your teaching, and connect with a community of teachers and writers.

Instructor's Manual for Teaching with The Practice of Creative Writing, Third Edition

Written by Heather Sellers, this teaching resource offers detailed advice about how to make the most of the book. Sample student work and syllabi, along with detailed support for teaching the course by genre, are included. In addition, the Instructor's Manual offers suggestions on what to do on the first day of class, how to organize peer feedback groups, and resources for instructors seeking to improve their craft. For high school teachers, Common Core guidelines are included. To download a PDF, go to **macmillanlearning.com/practicecreativewriting/catalog**.

The Macmillan English Community

The Macmillan English Community offers numerous professional resources, including *LitBits*, the popular blog site offering new ideas for your course. Converse with teachers, pedagogy scholars, and creative writers. In addition, you can

- Sign up for webinars
- Download resources from our professional resource series
- Start a discussion or ask a question
- Follow your favorite members

Visit **community.macmillan.com** to join the conversation with your fellow teachers.

LaunchPad Solo for Literature: The Online, Customizable Guide to Close Reading

The customizable online course space for creative writing and literature classes. To get the most out of *The Practice of Creative Writing*, assign it with *LaunchPad Solo for Literature*, which can be packaged at a significant discount. In this course space, you can build interactive, collaborative assignments around your favorite reading selections and video content—and draw on the content we offer there, too.

Students and instructors have access to an additional 200 literary selections, more than 500 reading comprehension quizzes on commonly taught literary selections, and several engaging videos by well-known authors on literary elements such as character, dialogue, and voice. Visit **macmillanhighered.com /launchpadsolo/literature** for more information.

LaunchPad Solo
macmillan learning

Pairing *The Practice of Creative Writing* with *LaunchPad Solo for Literature* helps students succeed.

Available for free when packaged with *The Practice of Creative Writing*, *LaunchPad Solo for Literature* provides a customizable online space to host conversations around writers' works and create interactive multimedia assignments for your creative writing and literature courses.

To package *LaunchPad Solo for Literature*, use ISBN 978-1-319-09537-6.

How can you use *LaunchPad Solo for Literature* to enhance your creative writing course? Here are a few ideas:

Enrich craft lessons with instructor-led close readings. Upload a favorite reading selection to *LaunchPad Solo for Literature*, and then annotate it with notes or questions to help students identify craft moves and learn to read like writers. Students can also respond to each other, further collaborating and deepening their understanding of a text.

Take the writing workshop online. Prior to an in-class workshop, upload student work to *LaunchPad Solo for Literature* and ask students to critique it using the Notes feature and highlighting tools. Encourage students to take advantage of the collaborative environment and engage their peers' comments as they add their own. The student whose work is up for review can access the entire class's feedback in a single, handy location, and you can use this preliminary discussion to foreground a deeper, more targeted workshop conversation in person.

Upload author readings and interviews. Know of a great video of an author reading one of the selections in your textbook? An interview with a writer about his or her craft process to which you'd like to have students respond? Embed videos, including those from YouTube, into your course space and use *LaunchPad Solo for Literature*'s video tools to build conversation and assignments around them. *LaunchPad Solo for Literature* also offers a growing library of author videos, including the one with Ha Jin shown here.

To explore *LaunchPad Solo for Literature*, visit **macmillanhighered.com/launchpadsolo/literature**.

CONTENTS

Preface for Instructors   *iii*

Additional Resources for *The Practice of Creative Writing*   *xii*

Teaching with *LaunchPad Solo for Literature*   *xiii*

INTRODUCTION: WHY CREATIVE WRITING? *OR* HOW TO EXPLAIN TO OTHERS WHAT IT IS YOU'RE DOING IN THIS CLASS   *1*

What Creative Writers Do   *2*

Questions Creative Writers Ask   *3*

The Four Parts of Creative Writing   *4*

Creative Writers Write   *4*

Writing for Yourself   *5*

Writing for Others   *5*

Images   *5*

Energy   *6*

Tension   *6*

Pattern   *6*

Insight   *6*

Revision   *6*

Creative Writers Read   *7*

Creative Writers Work with Other Writers   *7*

Creative Writers Share Their Work   *7*

PART ONE

BASICS   *9*

1 FINDING FOCUS   *11*

The Mind's Eye   *11*
   Write What You See   *12*
   Moving Images   *13*

Subject: Focus on What?   *16*
   Write What You Know   *16*
   Explore What Really Makes Us Who We Are   *17*

Practicing Focus   *18*
   The Writing Habit   *19*
   Writing Rituals   *20*
   Flow   *21*

Lack of Focus   *22*
   Writer's Block   *22*
   Distraction   *23*
   Procrastination   *24*
   Judgment   *25*

WRITING PROJECTS   *26*

READING   *27*
     ■ Jarod Roselló, *The Neighbor*   *27*

2 CREATIVE READING   *35*

The Nature of a Creative Reader's Personality   *36*
   Curious   *36*
   Tolerant of Discomfort   *37*

Creative Reading Is Close Reading   *38*
   Close Reading Your Own Work   *39*
     Read from Hard Copy   *39*
     Read Aloud   *39*
   Close Reading Work by Peers   *40*
   Close Reading Literature   *41*
     Read Multiple Times   *41*
     Read Aloud   *42*
     Practice Copywork   *42*
     Memorize   *43*
     Annotate   *43*

Reading across the Genres: A Field Guide to Creative Writing   *45*
  Fiction   *45*
  Creative Nonfiction: Memoir and Literary Essay   *47*
  Poetry and Prose Poetry   *48*
  Drama: Spoken Word, Monologue, Play, and Screenplay   *50*
  Comics, Graphic Works, and Experiments   *52*

Imitation: Reading to Write   *54*
  Imitation: Guided Practice   *54*
  Types of Imitation   *56*
  Scaffolding: Writing between the Lines   *56*
    Scaffolding a Poem   *57*
    Narrative Scaffolding   *60*

WRITING PROJECTS   *62*

READINGS   *65*
  ■ Vincent Scarpa, *I Go Back to Berryman's*   *65*
  ■ Betsy Sholl, *Genealogy*   *66*
  ■ A. Van Jordan, *af•ter•glow*   *67*
  ■ Adam Scheffler, *Woman and Dogs*   *67*
  ■ Pamela Painter, *The New Year*   *69*
  ■ Sebastian Matthews, *Buying Wine*   *69*
  ■ Marco Ramirez, *I am not Batman.*   *70*
  ■ Bob Hicok, *A Primer*   *74*
  ■ Amy Fusselman, From *The Pharmacist's Mate*   *76*

3 **BUILDING BLOCKS**   *83*

Parts of Narrative   *84*
  Sentences   *85*
  Conflicts   *86*
  Scenes   *87*
  Building Narratives Using Conflict-Crisis-Resolution   *90*
  Pulling It All Together: Writing Scenes for Narratives   *93*

Parts of Poems   *95*
  A Word on Words   *96*
  Lines   *99*
    ■ Gwendolyn Brooks, *We Real Cool*   *101*
  Turns   *103*
  Stanzas   *107*
  Playing with Form   *108*

WRITING PROJECTS   *109*

BUILDING BLOCKS WORKSHOP   *111*

READINGS   *112*

- Kim Addonizio, *First Poem for You*   *112*
- Jericho Brown, *Hustle*   *112*
- Terrance Hayes, *Liner Notes for an Imaginary Playlist*   *113*
- Gregory Corso, *Marriage*   *114*
- Dylan Thomas, *Do Not Go Gentle into That Good Night*   *117*
- Brenda Miller, *Swerve*   *118*
- Raymond Carver, *Cathedral*   *119*

PART TWO

STRATEGIES   *131*

4 IMAGES   *133*

The Principles of Images   *133*
Images Are Active   *134*
Reading Is Image Viewing   *134*
Images Are the Opposite of Thought   *137*
Generating Images   *140*

Creating with Images   *142*
Focus on People in Action   *142*
Think from within Images   *143*
Use Specifics   *145*
Move Around in Images   *147*
One Sentence, One Action   *148*
Summary Images   *151*
Sliding   *152*

A WORD ON IDEAS   *154*

WRITING PROJECTS   *156*

IMAGES WORKSHOP   *157*

READINGS   *158*

- Katie Ford, *Still-Life*   *158*
- Jay Hopler, *That Light One Finds in Baby Pictures*   *158*
- Natalie Diaz, *My Brother at 3 a.m.*   *159*
- Ely Shipley, *Magnolia*   *160*
- Dylan Landis, *In My Father's Study upon His Death*   *161*

■ Jenifer Hixson, *Where There's Smoke*   162
■ Mary Robison, *Pretty Ice*   166
■ Akhil Sharma, *Surrounded by Sleep*   171

5 ENERGY   *183*

The Principles of Energy   *183*
    Subject: Focus on What's Fascinating   *184*
      ■ Carolyn Forché, *The Colonel*   185
    Guidelines for Increasing Energy   *187*
      Provide Interesting Information   *187*
      Avoid the General   *188*
      Write about Lively, Particular Subjects You Know Intimately   *188*
    Leaps: The Power of Gaps   *189*
    Words   *193*
      Specificity   *193*
      Verbs   *195*

Manipulating Energy   *199*
    Pace   *199*
      Slow Down to Increase Energy   *201*
      Vary Pace to Sustain Energy   *202*
    Camera Work   *202*
    Too Much Energy?   *207*

TROUBLESHOOTING ENERGY   *208*

WRITING PROJECTS   *209*

ENERGY WORKSHOP   *210*

READINGS   *212*
    ■ Rick Moody, *Boys*   212
    ■ Brian Arundel, *The Things I've Lost*   216
    ■ Brian Turner, *What Every Soldier Should Know*   217
    ■ Charlotte Glynn, Excerpt from *Duct Tape Twins*   218

6 TENSION   *222*

The Principles of Tension   *222*
    Desire + Danger = Tension   *222*
    Setting the Thermostat: The Four Elements of Tension   *225*

Maintaining Tension   *228*
    Work with Two or Three Characters   *228*
    Match Your Opponents   *229*

Stay Specific   *230*
Write from Close Up   *231*

Manipulating Tension   *232*
Thermostat Control: Adjusting the Temperature   *233*
Layers: Adding Dimension   *237*
Layering Images   *238*
Layering with Triangles   *238*
Layering Dialogue and Action   *240*
Façade   *242*

WRITING PROJECTS   *246*

TENSION WORKSHOP   *248*

READINGS   *250*
■ Rod Kessler, *How to Touch a Bleeding Dog*   *250*
■ Marisa Silver, *What I Saw from Where I Stood*   *251*
■ Jessica Shattuck, *Bodies*   *263*
■ Peter Morris, *Pancakes*   *274*

7 PATTERN   *280*

Pattern by Ear   *281*
Rhyme and Echoes   *281*
Consonants and Vowels   *283*
Word Order   *285*
■ E. E. Cummings, *(Me up at does)*   *287*
Rhythm   *288*
Meter   *289*
Iambic Pentameter   *289*
Free Verse   *291*

Pattern by Eye   *292*
Objects   *292*
Gestures   *295*
Pattern on the Page   *296*

LAYERING PATTERNS   *298*

WRITING PROJECTS   *299*

PATTERN WORKSHOP   *300*

READINGS   *302*
■ Gregory Orr, *The River*   *302*
■ Randall Mann, *Pantoum*   *302*
■ Laure-Anne Bosselaar, *Stillbirth*   *303*

■ George Saunders, *Sticks*   304
■ Dinty W. Moore, *Son of Mr. Green Jeans: An Essay on Fatherhood, Alphabetically Arranged*   305

8 INSIGHT   311

Principles of Insight   314
  Accuracy   314
    Gestures   315
    Dialogue   315
  Generosity   316

Cultivating Insight   317
  Use Experience   318
  Trust Images   320
  Ask Questions   320
  Go Cold   322
  Reverse Course   325
  Go Big   326
  Surprise Yourself   326
  Create Subtext   327

THREE TIPS   329

WRITING PROJECTS   331

INSIGHT WORKSHOP   334

READINGS   335
  ■ Jessica Greenbaum, *A Poem for S.*   335
  ■ A. E. Stallings, *Another Lullaby for Insomniacs*   335
  ■ Naomi Shihab Nye, *Wedding Cake*   336
  ■ Ernest Hemingway, *Cat in the Rain*   337
  ■ Brian Doyle, *Two Hearts*   340
  ■ Michael Cunningham, *White Angel*   341

9 REVISION   355

Revision Is Seeing Again   357
  Look Closer   357
  Conquer Common Writing Blocks   359
    What If in Revising I Make It Worse?   359
    I Love My Piece / I Hate My Piece. Why Revise? It Seems Overwhelming.   360
    What If I Don't Want to Change My Writing?   361

Revising Effectively   *362*
  1. Limit Your Time   *363*
  2. Sketch, Then Write   *363*
  3. Read to Get Unstuck   *365*
  4. Work by Hand   *366*
  5. Choose Where to Begin   *366*
  6. Delete It; Don't Fix It   *367*
  7. Ask Your Writing Questions   *367*

Revision Step-by-Step   *369*
  Revising Fiction   *370*
  Revising Poetry   *375*
  Revising Nonfiction   *379*

EDITING AND PROOFREADING   *390*

WRITING PROJECTS   *392*

REVISION WORKSHOP   *393*

READINGS   *395*
  ■ Jack Ridl, *Repairing the House*   *395*
  ■ Jack Ridl and "Repairing the House," *The Poem and I Have a Little Conversation*   *396*
  ■ Karissa Womack, *I Remember All of You*   *398*

PART THREE

GENRES   *403*

10 FORMS   *405*

Writing in the Genres   *407*
  Table of Forms   *407*
  Experiment   *407*
  Finished Forms   *408*
  A Note on Poetry   *408*

Abecedarius   *409*
  Reading Abecedarii   *410*
  Writing an Abecedarius   *412*

Anaphora   *413*
  Reading Anaphora   *413*
  Writing an Anaphora   *415*

Braid   *416*
    Reading Braids   *417*
    Writing a Braid   *418*

Graphic Narrative and Comics   *420*
    Reading Comics and Graphic Narratives   *420*
    Writing a Comic or Graphic Narrative   *423*

Flash   *426*
    Reading Flash Fiction and Micro-Memoir   *427*
    Writing Flash Fiction   *428*
    Writing Micro-Memoir   *428*

Ghazal   *430*
    Reading Ghazals   *430*
    Writing a Ghazal   *432*

Journey   *433*
    Reading Journeys   *433*
    Writing a Journey   *434*

List   *436*
    Reading Lists   *436*
    Writing a List   *437*
        ▪ Danielle Kraese, From *Apologies and a Few Things
          I'm Sorry About*   *438*

Monologue   *439*
    Reading Monologues   *440*
    Writing a Monologue   *441*

Play/Screenplay   *442*
    Reading Plays   *442*
    Writing a Play   *443*

Pantoum   *446*
    Reading Pantoums   *446*
    Writing a Pantoum   *448*

Sestina   *450*
    Reading Sestinas   *450*
    Writing a Sestina   *452*

Sonnet   *453*
    Reading Sonnets   *454*
        ▪ David Livewell, *Fatigues*   *455*
    Writing a Sonnet   *456*

Villanelle   *458*
  Reading Villanelles   *459*
  Writing a Villanelle   *460*

PART FOUR

THE WRITING LIFE   *461*

11 REACHING READERS   *463*

Public Readings   *465*

Literary Magazines: Print and Digital   *469*
  Online Resources   *469*
  Research a Wide Range of Publications   *471*
  Submit Your Work   *472*
    Decide Where to Send Your Work   *472*
    How to Send Your Work Out   *473*
  Embrace Rejection   *474*

Chapbooks and Portfolios   *475*
  Creating a Chapbook   *476*
  Writing an Artist's Statement   *478*

WRITING PROJECTS   *480*

12 GOING FURTHER   *481*

Smart Searching   *482*

Social Media   *484*
  Facebook Groups   *485*
  Twitter Accounts   *485*
  Mobile Apps   *486*

General Resources   *486*
  Creativity and Inspiration   *486*
  Images: Seeing More Closely   *487*
  Self-Expression and Personal Writing   *488*
  Literary News   *489*

Instruction in Specific Genres   *490*
  Fiction   *490*
  Flash Fiction and Micro-Memoir   *491*

Poetry   *492*
Form Poetry   *494*
Spoken Word   *494*
Nonfiction   *495*
Plays and Screenplays   *496*
Children's Books   *496*
Graphic Narratives and Comics   *497*
Teaching Creative Writing   *497*
The Business of Writing: Agents, Freelancing, Book Proposals, and
   Publishing   *499*

Appendix: Terminology for Creative Writers   *501*

Acknowledgments   *504*

Index   *507*

WHY CREATIVE WRITING? *OR* HOW TO EXPLAIN TO OTHERS WHAT IT IS YOU'RE DOING IN THIS CLASS

Creative writing—like relationships, sports, music, or dance—makes life more meaningful and interesting. Recent neuroscience provides proof for what you may have suspected all along: The pursuit of creative writing measurably increases a person's ability to observe, intuit, empathize, impose structure on chaos, read closely, and understand nuance. These skills will serve you well not just in your writing life but also in college and in every job you will ever have.

Creative writing was interdisciplinary long before "interdisciplinary" became a buzzword. In composing our writing, we writers combine elements of architecture, psychology, philosophy, language, and scientific observation. In our careful attention to detail, creative writers and scientists share a similar and complementary approach to the world: We increase our skill in our field by dipping into these complementary inquiries. In designing and sustaining a creative writing life, writers have a lot in common with athletes and musicians, who know how to spend large blocks of time focused on one activity. And on top of all that, creative writing helps us become more thoughtful, discerning, and articulate.

WHAT CREATIVE WRITERS DO

As creative writers, we practice a process, a way of working with our intellect and our feelings to make art objects that people learn from and enjoy. It's a mixture of individual hard work (focused time we spend at our desks, composing and shaping) and group work (listening to other writers and reading their work).

Creative writing is like photography. Photographers care about shape, emotion, pattern, human experience—all that meets the eye. It's not a hobby; it's a commitment to understanding all that is inside and outside oneself. Lots of people take selfies—selfies are wonderful for documenting the celebrations and daily moments of our lives. Photographers aren't just shooting selfies. They are artists. And like a good piece of writing, a good photograph is a composed image, which stops us, makes us enter a place and observe more closely. Good photographs and good writing have another key quality in common: They make the reader or viewer feel. A selfie might do those things. But it might do them only for the people who *know* the subject and love him or her dearly (or not so much).

The practice of creative writing—like the practice of soccer, or playing the piano, or kissing, or ballroom dancing—helps train your mind and enrich your soul. You become more able to concentrate, to sort out and understand emotions and information, to read people more clearly, to take a broader view, to make finer distinctions. The practice of creative writing is useful in itself—you don't need to publish it or do anything else with it—to allow writing to enhance who you are, right now.

Creative writing is *not*:

- an easy way to get rich or famous
- a way to vent personal feelings
- for only a few talented geniuses
- rarefied, difficult, "artsy," special
- dark, creepy, emo
- just for English majors

Creative writers are everywhere. CEOs write stories about the life lessons they've learned. Stay-at-home dads keep journals about their days' pains, weirdnesses, and joys. Video game creators go to graduate school, writing new games. Lawyers write poetry, ministers lead fiction-writing groups, schoolteachers create comics, grandmothers blog. Students, travelers, novelists, grocery store clerks, and regular Joes and Janes create poetry, stories, graphic novels, and screenplays. Creative writing isn't for a chosen few. You don't have to be good at Shakespeare to succeed at creative writing. You just have to learn *how* to practice, and that's what this textbook teaches you.

Some writers publish. Some do not. Some have lifelong writing groups, meeting in person once a month or online. This book introduces you to the range of experiences a successful creative writer needs to practice—generating material, conquering typical writing fears and blocks, entering the community of creative writers, productively revising work. The purpose of this class is to offer you time to practice and to present some tools for making your creative writing more interesting to readers.

Creative writing is:

- learning to pay closer attention to the world and to human experience
- practicing rendering, with words, those experiences, in a way that makes them alive in the reader's mind
- using writing and words—both yours and others—to expand who you are and what you can know

QUESTIONS CREATIVE WRITERS ASK

The literary arts—art forms using words as their medium instead of paint or musical notes or movement or clay—take up the same questions you study in your philosophy, psychology, anthropology, religion, sociology, and communications classes:

- What is interesting, puzzling, hilarious about human nature?
- What is it like to be a particular human person, with a particular set of problems?
- What does it feel like and look like to attempt to be good, to do the right thing, to make a mistake, or to fail utterly, given a person's set of circumstances?

Creative writing increases your ability to ask the questions that are important to you—hard, interesting, delightful questions—and come up with answers that both teach you and inform others in a wholly original way.

Creative writers also wonder about process:

- Should you wait to write until you are inspired?
- Should you write your fantasy novel now or learn the short story form first?
- If you hate sitting alone in a room, can you really be a writer?
- What happens if someone criticizes your work and then you no longer want to write?

This book helps you answer these questions, deal with doubts, work with other writers, get unstuck, and, most of all, write.

Do you want to know the secret—the one true secret—to becoming a creative writer? Learn how to deal with frustration. If you get one thing from this textbook that will serve you in all of your education, it's this key lesson. In her book on creativity, *Big Magic*, global superstar writer Elizabeth Gilbert talks about learning to cope with the frustration of writing:

> Back in my early twenties, I had a good friend who was an aspiring writer, just like me. I remember how he used to descend into dark funks of depression about his lack of success, about his inability to get published. He would sulk and rage. . . . But I remember thinking that learning how to endure your disappointment and frustration *is* part of the job of a creative person. If you want to be an artist of any sort, it seemed to me, then handling your frustration is a fundamental aspect of the work—perhaps the single most fundamental aspect of the work. Frustration is not an interruption of your process; frustration *is* the process. . . . You don't just get to leap from bright moment to bright moment. How you manage yourself *between* those bright moments, when things aren't going so great, is a measure of how devoted you are to your vocation, and how equipped you are for the weird demands of creative living. (148–49)

THE FOUR PARTS OF CREATIVE WRITING

Many people mistakenly believe that creative writers disappear to the writing desk and come out some moments or hours or days later with fabulous creative writing. While that magical kind of lucky break happens to some people, and only once in a while, nothing could be further from the reality of what it is like to be a creative writer, for real, over an extended period of time.

Creative writers do four different things with the time they devote to creative writing—writing, reading, revising, and publishing. Writing, of course, is the central part, but it is only one part. Creative writers also need to know how to read, work with other writers in order to learn techniques and revise, and take their work to the next level by reading it aloud to an audience or submitting it to a literary publication.

Creative Writers Write

This textbook breaks writing into two categories: writing you do for yourself, such as journaling, and writing you do for other people, such as creative writing. Writing for yourself is often made up of feelings, emotions, opinions, and anything else you want. Creative writing is made up of five components—images, energy, tension, pattern, and insight—and a process, revision.

Writing for Yourself. You may have written poems to express certain personal feelings. Maybe the poem was for one other person, but mostly it was written just for you. Some writing—venting, journaling, freewriting, keeping a diary, composing stories in your notebook—you do for yourself, just for fun or practice, not necessarily to share with anyone else, or maybe to share with a trusted friend. The writing you do to seduce, please, or impress a lover is similarly private. Texting, tweeting, posting, and other kinds of writing that you do for close friends as much as for yourself is valuable writing, of course, but usually you do it for pleasure or necessity, and it doesn't need to be "good" or "artistic."

Writing for Others. But some writing you do expressly for other people to read. Poems, stories, plays, comics, novels—these pieces of writing aren't about expressing your personal feelings. Rather, they are designed to create an experience in your reader. They are *for* the reader. They may have lots of your own feelings in them, but the pieces of creative writing we will work on this semester are designed not to express your experience but to create an experience in the reader. **Creative writing is for your reader, not for you.**

Creative writing is the art of crafting language—designing words on a page—so that a reader (a stranger!) will have a specific kind of emotional experience. *Design* is the key word. Creative writing is essentially a service industry. We use our emotions, but expression of them isn't the goal.

Writing for others is a lot harder than writing for yourself. Writing for yourself is often pleasurable, fun, therapeutic—with instant results. You reflect on and gain insight into who you are and what you are doing. Writing for others involves delayed gratification. You have to be patient. It takes a lot longer to transform your raw emotions, the stuff of life, into a piece of art.

If we carefully study great creative writing from other centuries and other cultures (and I have), we can find six elements or qualities of good work. If we include everyone from Shakespeare to Aristotle to Amy Tan to J. R. R. Tolkien to Stephenie Meyer to J. K. Rowling, from the creators of great screenplays and comics and memoirs, we identify six elements or qualities of writing that show up again and again. To make sure your creative writing is effective when you are writing for others, you can (must!) use these six strategies: **images, energy, tension, pattern, insight,** and **revision.**

As you learn these strategies, it can be helpful to practice each of them in more than one genre. Poems, plays, stories, creative essays, memoirs, screenplays, and comics all share the same six core craft elements. As a beginner, the "cross-training" you receive by practicing in several genres serves to strengthen your abilities as you focus, perhaps, on one genre, such as poetry or fiction.

Images. Images are the living pictures, the "movie in the reader's mind," that your writing creates on the reader's mental screen. Images are real. When you dream, you "see" things. The same is true with reading: When you read a great piece of writing, your imagination (notice that *image* is the root of the word) is activated; you can see, and smell, and hear, and touch.

Energy. Energy is the spark that makes a reader pay attention. Hemingway's taut, terse sentences emit a lot of energy. George R. R. Martin's plots are packed with energized movement. James Joyce's inventive prose style is infused with life. Screenplays and graphic novels crackle with crisp characters and tight plot points. Good creative writers pay attention to words that are energetic (compound abstractions like *ponderous sensation* or *evocative impediment* absorb rather than reflect energy), sentences and lines that are energetic (placing the strongest words at the beginning and the end), and paragraphs and stanzas that are strung together so the reader feels momentum, pleasing leaps, interesting gaps and pauses. Energy is pacing, intensity, heat, excitement, and interest.

Tension. Tension is the underlying push-pull, conflict, juxtaposition, or *what will happen next?* in all good creative writing. The reader has to have something to wonder about, though you should remember that while mystery is good, confusion isn't. To create tension, you push energy in two opposing directions. Readers *want* to figure things out. They don't want you as the writer to show off, overexplain, perform, or have more fun than they are having. Tension is like the bass line in a song—it's something you modulate as a writer, turning the volume up and down. To create energy, you vary the levels of tension. This book shows you how.

Pattern. Pattern attracts the human eye, and repetition pleases us. From babyhood, you liked games that repeated: patty-cake, peekaboo, jump rope. Creative writing is a sensory art form, and pattern is part of how creative writing makes its meanings. Through repetition of images, words, or sounds, readers will pay attention to what you want them to notice.

Insight. We read to be entertained but also to learn, to see the world from the perspective of others. One of the reasons we read creative writing is to learn in a pleasurable way. We don't want our creative writing to lecture us or sermonize; we want our art forms to show wisdom, to illuminate insight, so that we can come to our own conclusions. Good creative writing asks questions and provides insights through careful attention to human experience—wisdom is *in specific moments, actions, and objects.*

Revision. When we look at the word *revision*, we quickly see the word *vision.* Rewriting creative work does not have to be a laborious, horrible process.

Instead, what most professional writers do when they revise is simply to return to the first strategy, *images*. Revision means reseeing. And the best way to revise is by looking—really looking again—more closely at what's being created for readers in their mind's eye. Revision often involves drawing— physically drawing or redrawing your scene or poem or essay. After you learn how simple and clear reseeing is, revision is no longer a chore. It's the heartbeat of the writing process.

Creative Writers Read

Creative writers read closely, to see how various literary effects create sparks in their mind's eye. We read to learn what kind of energy drives good writing, and what kinds of shapes readers are hungry for. What's this writer doing, and how can I pick up some of his or her technique to make my own work stronger? We're a little greedy, we creative writers, when we read. More than anything, we want to learn how to write better.

Most writers are voracious readers—they read widely, they attend live readings, they watch poets and writers deliver performances of their work online, and they surround themselves with words.

Writers read three kinds of work: professional creative writing—stories, poems, drama, and creative nonfiction—published by expert writers; the writing about the writing process (like this book) that provides guidance and insight into the craft of creative writing; and work by fellow students in the class. See Chapter Twelve for more suggestions to help you keep learning your craft.

Creative Writers Work with Other Writers

Some of your work this semester will focus on how to read work written by other student writers and how to learn the same kinds of things from your classmates' early triumphs and failures that you do from polished, published texts. Learning how to offer meaningful, helpful observations on a work-in-progress is an art in itself, and a very useful skill for anyone entering the job market, in any profession. Learning how to form bonds with members of the writing community, how to create a writing community where one doesn't yet exist, and how to nurture supportive writing relationships are essential to your sustained growth as a writer. Most writers have a writing group in place after their coursework in creative writing ends. This book helps you learn how to be a sought-after contributor to such an endeavor.

Creative Writers Share Their Work

Working with other writers naturally leads to that next step: taking your writing to the next level by testing it out in front of an audience or in a publication.

Most creative writers focus on practice—writing for themselves, writing for others, working with other writers, reading—for about 90 percent of their writing time. But then comes a time when you may want or need to show your work to a larger community. The audience might be your entire class, a trusted friend, a teacher, a supportive reader, or a small critique group. It might be your friends at a coffee shop. The audience grows as your confidence grows. To observe for yourself what works in your writing and what falls flat, nothing is more helpful than reading it in front of a live audience, even if that audience consists of only one person.

Focusing on publication—whether that's publishing in a hot new online journal or simply submitting work to your school's literary magazine—helps you learn to revise skillfully and efficiently and compels you to develop the crucial skills of editing and proofreading, those final stages of the revision process.

Welcome to the practice of creative writing.

BASICS

I never knew anyone who had a passion for words who had as much difficulty saying things as I do.
MARIANNE MOORE

Without craft, art remains private. Without art, craft is merely homework.
JOYCE CAROL OATES

Follow your inner moonlight; don't hide the madness.
ALLEN GINSBERG

CHAPTER ONE

FINDING FOCUS

You are reading a wonderful book. Time drops away, you forget where you are sitting, you no longer hear the sounds around you. When you are totally absorbed in a great piece of writing, you are *transported* to another time and place—the words create a new reality, and you, the reader, inhabit another world. Not only do you see a kind of movie play out in your head as you read, but you also experience, with all your senses, another world. And that world is just as real and fully formed as this one.

THE MIND'S EYE

When you read creative writing, the kind of writing we will attempt in this course, you are meant to experience this very specific mental state, marked by visual images, sounds, and sensory experience—you can feel, taste, touch, and move around in this world. It's not fake. It's real.

In Shakespeare's play, when Hamlet says he is seeing his father "in [his] mind's eye," Hamlet's friend Horatio worries he is going mad. Horatio tells Hamlet his father is dead—he isn't seeing him. But Hamlet insists, and he is right. He *is* seeing his father. (If you close your eyes now and imagine your father, do you see an actual person? Try it. What do you see?)

The image Hamlet sees in his mind is *just as real* as breakfast, his girlfriend, the castle walls. It talks. It moves. The primary goal of creative writing is to create and link images—real, live moving images—in your reader's mind's eye.

Art is a sensory experience, and creative writing—the making of art objects using language—appeals first to that sensory experience. We don't read creative writing to be told about other worlds. Learning about other worlds through the knowing, thinking brain is important, and it's the vital work of historians, philosophers, and scientists. In creative writing, in literature, we read in order to have an experience, to actually feel what it is like to be in another world, another body, another soul, another point of view. When it comes to creative writing, readers want to forget they are reading. Take me somewhere, the reader says. Anywhere. But don't remind me — with too much description or analysis or thinking or interruptions — that I'm reading.

Think about how you tell the story of something that happened to you on a bad day when you tell it well versus when you tell it poorly. When you retell how hard it was for you to find a parking space this morning, if you are fully involved in your storytelling, some part of you is still sitting behind the steering wheel, trolling around, stressed out. Notice how we all do that: We relive the experience — in order to tell it well. Your stories and your jokes come out best when you *reexperience the original sensations* as you retell. You transport yourself into the scene you are trying to re-create. And thus you create it for your listener or reader. Weak writers, like weak storytellers, don't transport themselves back into the moment. They tell *about* the experience. And it's usually boring. "I looked all over for a parking space," they report, generalizing, distancing. "I can never find a place to park. It took like forever."

> *Get out of the blocks, run your race, stay relaxed. If you run your race, you'll win. Channel your energy. Focus.*
> — CARL LEWIS

Notice the difference in the good teller's rendition:

> I was creeping down that back lane of Siberia, you know, by those bashed-in Dumpsters, heading into the sun, when I look at my watch — it was 8:02, I have the 8:00 class, and all of a sudden I hear, I hear this hissing. I was banging on the steering wheel, and this guy was coming toward me, almost running, pointing at my front passenger-side tire.

To put you, the reader/listener in the scene, the writer must focus all mental attention inside the very scene or image, to tell it in a way that makes it real for the reader/listener.

Write What You See

Think for a moment of flipping through cable channels, and landing, on Saturday afternoon, on one of those programs with a title like *Learn to Paint Oceans!* or *Perfect Flowers in One Minute!* A guy in a windowless television studio with a canvas, a lot of blue paint, a lot of white paint — and no ocean, no flowers — explains to viewers how to rotate the brush for a wavelike swoop, how to dollop more white for crests of waves, and ta-da! — a very cool little wrist motion that will create the perfect expanse of sand. Use pink paint and the same exact wrist motion to do roses!

At no point is it suggested that we look at an actual ocean, wave, or beach, rose, pansy, or peony. At no point is the viewer's experience of the painting considered. This kind of approach to art is based on tricks instead of looking closely at the real world. Fooling the eye, these shortcuts usually produce bad paintings that look like everyone else's bad paintings.

Techniques for making fresh art of high quality involve the artist's experience and, more important, focusing on the viewer's experience. The bad paintings don't really create a world; they suggest a shorthand for The Beach, The Ocean, Nice Garden Scene, Floral Medley. When you look at a bad painting, you see the painting. When you look at a good painting, not only do you see the painting, but you are transported to your own childhood memories of sweet afternoons at the shore, Grandma's rose bed, the peonies you grew last summer.

You want to avoid the kind of "quick trick" techniques that keep you from *really looking closely at the real world* and focusing on the people in it. "How to Plot Your Novel in Thirty Days," "Create Fabulous Characters in an Hour!"—these shortcuts do not usually produce very good work. What produces good writing is accurately noticing specific, real, living individuals and instances. Focus on the things you notice, and focus on the very small things you notice—the things other people, nonwriters, pass right over.

Creative writers work from life. They improve by *noticing* the tiny movements and gestures and details—a torn sock, a hangnail, nervous hair-tugging, the blue light reflected on a friend's face as she reads a disturbing text—and they build from the ground up using the true observed stuff of real life.

PRACTICE

Think of an "idea" for writing. The bigger and broader and the less firsthand experience you have with this idea the better. For example, write about life, love, death, homelessness, or illness in *general*. Write fast. Ramble. Think, *don't try to see any one thing in particular*. Put in lots of your feelings and ideas. Avoid images and specifics. Think out loud on the page. Don't focus your mind's eye on anything. Now, read over what you wrote. Will your reader have a visual experience?

Moving Images

Imagine a child swinging on a swing set at a playground.

Okay, do you have in your mind a picture of a kid, in motion?

Did you invent a kid, or is the image hovering in your mind's eye of a real kid, someone you know, perhaps yourself when you were six? Look closer. Can you see what the kid is wearing? Where the kid stands? His hair, his arms, his hands, his face?

Pause for a moment, and using the power of your mind's eye, look at this kid, noticing anything small, anything interesting. Notice how you can make him swing faster. Slower. Notice how you can make him jump off the swing—seeing this in your mind's eye all the while—and make him run across the park, over to a dog.

The point of this example is that your mind can create all of these things—real, live, moving images. You don't need a lot of description to have this experience; your reader doesn't either. In fact, the more information you give, the harder it is for the reader to see what you are talking about:

> The kid was born in Orlando in 1982, to very poor parents who had worried constantly about everything for years. The hospital was really run-down, and the kid was always worrying and whining. He suffered from hemochromatosis later in life and made straight A's, but not without a struggle.

Notice what happened to the image of the kid in your mind's eye. In the wordy description, where as reader you are overloaded with information, you don't really get an image in your mind's eye. You see words, you think, you remember, you consider—all valuable activities. But art is about apprehending a *sensory emotional experience*. Very different.

Even if you could keep a strong visual image alive in your mind during the general description above, you were working hard. Too hard. Readers can't be expected to work that hard; they need clear images to focus on. The reader wants to see her own kid, her own banana, her own house. She is fully capable of doing so all on her own. That's the central lesson of this chapter: If you write from a focused place—seeing the exact kid you want the reader to picture, in Prospect Park on 15th Street—your reader will see. If you see, in your mind's eye, the fruit, the animal, the breakup scene—your reader will see it, too.

Be specific (*banana*, not *fruit*; *kid*, not *person*). Name what you see. But most important of all, as you write, keep part of your mind in focus on the live scene, the image.

Many writers mistakenly believe that scene painting is good writing, and they include adjectives and adverbs to decorate and enrich the writing. In creative writing, don't spend lots of time "painting" the perfect fruit: "The glowing red orb pocked with holes made by denizens of the humble earth" is really hard to see. Just say *old apple*.

In tennis, baseball, football, the coaches constantly remind you to "keep your eye on the ball." Same for writers. Keep your eye on what you are writing.

Bring in one of your favorite pieces of creative writing—a poem, a few paragraphs of a short story, a part of a memoir. You might use something you loved from childhood or a published story or a piece from another class. Read aloud from your piece. After you are finished, interview your listener. Did your partner "see" something on the "screen" in her brain? What? What parts of the piece did or did not activate this moving picture or live image? Compare your favorite published pieces to the purposely unfocused writing you created (for the Practice on p. 13). What are the differences? What launches a reader into the scene, and what blocks a reader from a *sensory* experience?

As you practice creative writing in this course, notice when you are aware of an image, a movie, in your head, when you read and when you write. When you aren't transported into an alive, moving image, what *does* happen in your mind when you read? Paying this kind of close attention is tricky, but you will get better at it as you practice. Not every sentence or line in a piece of creative writing has to feed the moving picture, but most probably do. And it's important to notice what *is* happening on the page when you aren't "in the moment" as a reader.

Practice noticing what you like to read, what moves you, what affects you. When are you "lost" in the reading, totally unaware of this world because you are in the author's creation? Try to articulate to yourself what makes a piece memorable and powerful for you, and your own writing technique will improve.

Create a list of moving images you can use to generate creative writing in this course. Number from one to twenty-five. Play the story of your life, from about age five to now, so that item number one is the first image you see. Don't strain too hard—you are just practicing noticing how your image-making mind works. What's the first little movie of yourself you can see? Climbing onto a tractor? Running to catch the school bus? Slugging your brother? Write down a minititle: Tractor. Bus. Joey. Move through your life, naming the little movies that star you. Don't work from photographs or memories of photographs and don't use the Official Frequently Told Stories. Capture real images that show you in action. Swing Set Heather. New Skateboard Day. Disney World with Mom. If you think of something but can't see it, you can't put it on your list. Insignificant little flashes of image are what you are looking for: Include only mental movies. Reread your list. Which entries seem the most interesting for writing? Which create an image in your mind's eye? Place a star by those.

SUBJECT: FOCUS ON WHAT?

> *A playwright knows that what is most private in her heart of hearts is also the most astonishing.*
> — TINA HOWE

"What do I look at?" That's a question writers ask all throughout their writing careers. "What makes a good subject for my creative writing?" "What should I write about?"

You can write about anything you want as long as you (1) focus on what you see and (2) write as truthfully and honestly and accurately as possible. As you look for good subjects (no matter how fantastical, made-up, or imagined your work is), keep in mind two considerations: Write about what you know, and write about what defines us as human.

Write What You Know

Your job as a writer is to report from the world you know, to bring the news of that world to us. What is there, how do people act, what do people yearn for? What are the rules in that world? What happens when they are broken? How do people act? Why? Any worlds to which you have behind-the-scenes access are going to be excellent choices for writing topics this semester.

Remember: This "knowing" we are speaking of is a *visual sensory knowing*. Write what you see, not what you know in your head.

"I have an idea for a poem," writers often say. It's better to have an *image* for a poem. And instead of making up fanciful images or chasing ephemeral ideas, start with a concrete sensory detail from a world you have special access to. If you know a lot about the prep schedule at the Windmill Restaurant, how Terry likes the eggs to be set up, how the bread is made fresh, how the delivery guy spits outside the door every single morning, then start with those images, the specifics you know really well. If you haven't ever been in a war, but you want to write a war poem, you will need to get some specific insider images—things only someone who has seen combat would have visual access to.

For now, as a beginner, as you are training in this craft, write what only *you* can write. It's going to take some practice to get a feel for how that works. How can your boring apartment in Rockaway Beach, your boring parents, your boring little sister be the stuff of art? How can your dumb wedding plans in your dumb small town make a novel? Your ridiculous middle-class life in your homogeneous suburb? The great writers of the world—Abigail Thomas, Julia Alvarez, Jhumpa Lahiri, Xu Wei, Edwidge Danticat, Jesmyn Ward, Ross Gay, Miranda July, Junot Díaz, Haruki Murakami, Willa Cather, Alison Bechdel—have used the simple material of their plain lives to create great art simply by looking closely at what was in front of their eyes.

You do not need to write autobiography, but you do need to choose topics on which you are an expert. Fortunately, you are an expert on many, many things. Hamster owning, work, your great-aunt Madge who was a roller-skating star— you know *a lot*. Your passions, your hobbies, your work environments, and the interesting lives of those around you are probably the topics you will choose from for your creative writing assignments. Start five lists. Add to them over the next few weeks. Using each of these categories— such as jobs, relatives and parents, summer, sports/hobbies, and trips/journeys— come up with fifteen items in each category:

Jobs: McDonald's, babysitting, working in the lab, raking for Mrs. Jones, living with multiple sclerosis . . .

Relatives' jobs: accountant, stay-at-home mom, homeschooler, Uncle Joe the mortician in Jersey, jobs they held before you were born . . .

Summer activities: camps, archery, fort building, falling in love, dog, swimming, school, building a house for Habitat for Humanity . . .

Sports/hobbies: knitting, Nintendo, roller derby, transgender support group, Saturday night Pancake House gathering at 2 a.m. during the fall semester . . .

Trips/journeys: confirmation, Japan to meet family I did not know I had, the mall with Darcy, Haiti, the Grand Canyon . . .

You now have an additional seventy-five potential writing topics. Next time you are stuck or blocked, force yourself to choose an item and use this list to spark new images.

Make a list of ten secret worlds you have or have had access to. Places no one else in this class has ever been— ever. Except for you. Burger King, 24th Street, the kitchen, summer 2014, when Marcie was managing. Under your little sister's bed the year she had the secret illegal pet snake. Your mother's office on Division Avenue the afternoon you saw the boss kissing her. Your soccer team in the locker room after a loss. Keep your list with your other lists from this chapter— you are generating terrific writing images to feed your work.

Explore What Really Makes Us Who We Are

A famous writer has said that when you have someone special over to your house, you break out the best whiskey, the stuff you keep in the back for special occasions. And, he says, when you have readers, they must be treated in the same way as that special visitor, the one for whom you break out the good stuff. Your subjects must not be bottom-shelf, generic, unimportant. They must come from the place where you keep your very best, most treasured items—dark, potent, intense. Stuff you've saved up.

Discipline in art is a fundamental struggle to understand oneself, as much as to understand what one is drawing.

— HENRY MOORE

How humans interact with each other, with human emotions—love, fear, hatred, lust, joy—in tiny, real moments—that's what art is made of. By focusing tightly on your visual experience, the elements essential to our humanity will come forward.

When you compose creative writing, unlike a sermon or a police report, focus on a mixture of qualities. Let your good guys be a little bad, and they will be more human to your reader. Give your villains some appealing qualities, and readers will feel more engaged with the writing, more distraught at the outcome. Creative writing is a lot like a psychology course in action: Writers are always asking, Why do people act like this? Why do we keep making the same mistakes? Why do we keep ourselves from getting what we want? How do we fall in love with whom we fall in love with? Your list of questions can point you toward your best material. You can change the players and mix and match the histories and settings and motivations, but staying close to the essence of the questions that trouble, delight, intrigue, and keep you up late at night is part of the secret to focusing on good subjects.

PRACTICE

Make a list of twenty things that confuse or concern you about how people treat one another. The questions can be large (Why do women fall in love with men who treat them badly?), but it's better if you make them small, and specific. Why does Aunt Ruthie live with a man thirty years her junior, and why does the whole family get annoyed and judgmental and weird about it? Why does my roommate go home every single weekend, when she never has a good time and just complains about the town and her high school friends and how immature they are? Why did I break up with Lori?

PRACTICING FOCUS

Writing from this place of visual, mental focus is a skill, and as you practice it you get better at it. Sometimes, our old writing habits—writing *about* things in general, using "head" and "thought" words like *it seemed*, or *she remembered*, or *realizing*—block the reader's experience of a real visual image. In addition to the technique of "being there" when you write, it's useful to look at several practical and physical ways to support and increase your ability to focus.

> *I practice every day. You have to stay on good speaking terms with your piano. Or the piano will rebuff you.*
> — HANK JONES

The Writing Habit

Becoming a writer means being creative enough to find the time and the place in your life for writing. A physical place and a committed block of time become habits you can count on. To the basic platform you learned above (how to use your mind's eye to focus on mental pictures in order to do creative writing), we will add another mental state: the focus that comes from establishing and sustaining a writing habit. Most beginning writers work best if they do a little creative writing every day, at the same time of day, in the same place, for the same amount of time. Without a writing habit, something reassuring you can count on, it's asking too much of your imagination and your confidence to write fabulous stuff on demand, just because you feel like it. If you don't have a writing habit, you aren't being fair to yourself. You might even be setting yourself up for failure. If you write only when you are "in the mood" or when you "have some time," you will never be able to write enough material to see what you are good at and what needs work. Good writers write whether they are in the mood or not. They practice whether they feel like it or not. It's the only way. Everyday practice. That's how you get better.

> *I never could have done what I have done without the habits of punctuality, order, and diligence, without the determination to concentrate myself on one subject at a time.*
>
> — CHARLES DICKENS

Writers are simply people who have figured out how to spend enough time in the writing room every day in order to create enough work so that some of it is good.

Remember: You will want to *avoid* writing. All writers struggle with procrastination, writer's block, distraction, or laziness. All successful writers develop strategies to deal with these issues. Conquering not-writing is probably half the battle when you are taking a writing class. Almost everyone struggles with this.

One strategy for overcoming not-writing is to simply schedule your daily writing session for the same time and same place every day. Some writers write in bed, first thing in the morning, before they are awake enough to get too freaked out and intimidated by the writing process. Others go to the basement of the library after work every night. Others like the white noise of a crowded coffee shop or restaurant during lunch hour. That's when they focus best.

Another way to ease yourself into a productive daily writing habit, where you can focus your mind on practicing various writing skills and techniques, is to use rituals.

PRACTICE

In your calendar, block out a period of time for writing each day, just as you do for your classes and work commitments. Usually, writers hook their writing time onto another activity. It's very easy to do all your other homework first and save the writing for last (and then not get to it). Will you write when you first get up? During lunch? Try to make your writing slot the same time each day.

> *The problem of creative writing is essentially one of concentration and the supposed eccentricities of poets are usually due to mechanical habits or rituals developed in order to concentrate.*
> — STEPHEN SPENDER

Writing Rituals

Rituals help us achieve and intensify focus.

Writing rituals are the key to keeping your writing habit in place. Most athletes warm up. They run a few slow laps, do push-ups, stretch hamstrings. Most people don't pull into the parking lot, leap out of the car, and start jogging around the track in their business suits. Think about the other activities in which you engage every day. Are there rituals that go along with those activities? Pre-study rituals? Pre-dinner rituals? Rituals guide our brains into successful practice. The more you repeat a ritual, the smoother your practice is. You know the athlete who can't compete without his lucky shirt, or race without a specific pair of sneakers? Writers aren't weird—they're just human. Rituals let your body and your creating mind know it's time to work. It's unrealistic to rush home, bang out a poem, and then revise it as you make dinner, get your chemistry lab under way, and talk on the phone to Joey. Create a regular time for your daily writing, a block in your schedule when you go to a certain place, with specific tools. One writer I know, Bob Vivian, lights a candle when he starts, and blows it out when he is finished. Every time. Another writer I know walks her dog for forty-five minutes, and then together they climb up to her attic studio and she works for three hours. (She admits to some napping. The dog naps the whole time.) It doesn't matter what your rituals are; what is important is that you pay attention to what you do right before your writing sessions—and repeat what works for you.

Rituals teach your creative brain how and when to focus. Rituals save you valuable time. If you are a busy student, you might not have time to *not* rely on rituals.

PRACTICE

Take a few minutes to write out what your dream writing life looks like. If you had all the time in the world, didn't have to work to pay for school, didn't have a car payment or any other classes, what would your writing days look like? Would you write in the morning? At night? Pretend you can shape your writing life to look like anything you want. The only catch: You have to do it every day. How long would you want to spend? What would be in your writing room? What would this room look like? What do you have on your desk? Include a sketch if you like, and a list of your prewriting routine— what do you do to get in the mood? Share in class, and on the board keep track of the rituals that show up most often in people's dream lives. Are there some things that writers really do need to do in order to get to—and stay at—the writing desk? Next, make a list of three to five writing rituals that you would like to use during this course in order to establish a healthy daily writing practice. An example list: Light a candle, set a timer, read a poem to warm up, tune my ear, and, when finished, blow out the candle.

Flow

When you are "in the zone" on the basketball court, the basket looks enormous. You can't hear the fans in the stands. Things take place almost as if in slow motion. When you are in the zone as a writer, you lose all sense of time, too. You are *in* the scene or moment you are writing — you aren't sitting in your writing room at all. You can't hear your roommate's conversation. You are in the writing zone.

> *Ninety percent of my game is mental. It's my concentration that has gotten me this far.*
> — CHRIS EVERT

Some researchers call this state of creative concentration **flow** — when you are involved in an activity and you go into a kind of focused trance. Susan Perry, a psychologist who studies creativity, describes it this way in her book *Writing in Flow*:

> Flow is a relatively new term for an essential and universal human experience. You know you've been in flow when time seems to have disappeared. When you're in flow, you become so deeply immersed in your writing, or whatever activity you're doing, that you forget yourself and your surroundings. You delight in continuing to write even if you get no reward for doing it — monetary or otherwise — and even if no one else cares whether you do it. You feel challenged, stimulated, definitely not bored. Writing in flow, you're often certain you're tapping into some creative part of yourself — or of the universe — that you don't have easy access to when you're not in this altered state. Sports figures call this desired condition being "in the zone."

Psychologists who study the creating brain identify the state in which work happens, almost effortlessly, as flow. You know flow. You play for hours at pastimes that absorb you — video games, lacrosse, cycling, knitting, talking with friends — whatever your passion. You fall out of time and become lost in a narrative. You create and sustain another world because you do it all the time. When you're in chemistry class, dreaming about your weekend with your friends, you are *in* that world, and probably in flow, if you don't hear a single word your professor is saying.

Practice paying attention to when you are utterly absorbed by a task. How did you get into that state? What brought you out of it?

When you write creatively, your task is to get yourself into that state.

PRACTICE

When were you last in flow? How do you know when you are in it? Have you had a flow experience as a writer? In any other parts of your life?

LACK OF FOCUS

Nothing interferes with my concentration. You could put on an orgy in my office and I wouldn't look up. Well, maybe once.
— ISAAC ASIMOV

Every single writer faces difficulties with focus such as writer's block or procrastination. **Writer's block** can be best defined as the inability to focus, the loss of creative concentration. Often what gets labeled "writer's block" is actually distraction—external or internal distraction. You probably say you have a problem with procrastination, but actually you may want to consider all of these issues—writer's block, distraction, and procrastination—as various manifestations of *the loss of focus*.

As a writer, you will need strategies for combating lack of focus. To develop such strategies, it may help to learn a bit more about the nature of writer's block, distraction, and procrastination. After all, the known enemy is easier to defeat than the unknown enemy.

Writer's Block

Writers sometimes say they are blocked when they cannot write. They feel disconnected from their own work. The blocked writer feels tapped out, completely devoid of imaginative energy. The blocked writer can't envision the scenes and moments and images that transport *the writer*, much less a reader!

To cure a block, most experts recommend you try a five-part approach:

- Begin at least five new pieces—just start things. Multiple things.
- Write for a set amount of time each day, say ten or fifteen minutes only.
- Allow yourself to write poorly without judging the writing.
- Study the psychology and process of writing (your teacher can recommend some books on blocks).
- Have a friend call out a random number between one and ten. Using one of your lists from this chapter, force yourself to write for three minutes, using the list topic corresponding to that number.

Expect to get stuck at unpredictable times. Plan on getting stuck just when things are going well; that is very common. Good writers are good learners—they pay attention to what it is that led them to being stuck. They also pay attention to what exactly—mentally, physically, emotionally—preceded a great writing session. Good writers are self-aware. Like excellent scientists, beginning writers study their own processes in order to prepare for and work through blocks.

Writer's block is the greatest side effect of boredom.
— JASON ZEBEHAZY

WRITERS' TIPS: Getting Unstuck

Here's a checklist of methods for getting unstuck—some of the most popular tricks writers use to break through inevitable blocks.

1 Set the timer. Write for ten minutes at a time.

2 Stay in the moment. Stay present by focusing just on what you *see*.

3 Write a smaller chunk: Take some writing you already have and slow it down, move closer, really go blow-by-blow.

4 When voices of doubt plague you, write down what the voices are saying. Or banish the judge/critic by swearing at it.

5 Write every day for at least ten minutes. Don't worry if today doesn't go well. There's always tomorrow. (If you miss a day, remember that the next three will be harder than you think they ought to be.)

6 Write by hand when you are stuck. Slowing down often helps the mind focus. Try writing in all capital letters.

7 Go back to the last thing you wrote that you liked. Use it as a jumping off point for new work.

8 Take another try at an assignment you liked, one that went well. Doing more of what you are good at is a great way to get unstuck.

9 Make your own list of "ways to get unstuck" based on what has worked in the past; notice what gets you stuck and how you work through blocks.

10 Plan on getting stuck, and don't beat yourself up. Writers get stuck. It's part of writing. Stop, start up again later.

Most writing blocks are actually manifestations of fear: fear of not being good enough, fear of being cheesy, fear of hurting someone with your words. Most writing fears are common, normal, and realistic: You probably *do* want to be a better writer than you are now. You might write some clichéd pieces, especially when you are just starting out. And words are extraordinarily powerful: It's wise to be aware of your intentions and sensitive to how your work might affect others. Perhaps you will create a list of writing "rules" that work best for you.

Distraction

There are two kinds of distraction: internal—where the thoughts in your head keep you from staying focused—and external. External distractions include your roommate, your three-year-old, your dog, your boyfriend, your feelings about your boyfriend, the radio, the temperature of the room. Distraction destroys flow.

Writers are often distracted by external circumstances, and smart writers work hard to set up their writing life (using rituals) so that they have uninterrupted time each day to work. Libraries, empty classrooms, and very early or very late hours are what writers gravitate toward. Trying to write ten minutes before dinner with a living room full of hungry friends and the television playing is unlikely to produce good writing or teach you much about focus.

When you do get interrupted, notice how you get back into your piece. Next time you are writing along happily about your sister and the way she was cutting the gum out of your hair and the phone rings — the real phone — what do you do? Take the call, talk, and get back to work. Notice what your mind does. When you come back to the piece, and you can't remember — Where was I going with this? — what do you usually do? Many writers reread their last few sentences, or start at the beginning, reading and fiddling with the words until they get caught back up in the piece. Notice how you get seduced back into your work, reoriented in the "moving picture," simply by *reading*.

External distractions are easy to manage when you believe your writing practice is important. You deserve a quiet, comfortable place to work, and the time to work. Make sure you set yourself up for success. You will be interrupted. Notice how you concentrate and recover.

Procrastination

Procrastination is simply internal distraction. You want to write, you intend to write, but some force inside you keeps you from doing it.

Many students say they procrastinate. They suspect they are lazy. They wrongly assume there are "real" writers out there, working around the clock, on schedule, happily scooting along, churning out poem after poem.

> *Procrastination is fear of success. People procrastinate because they are afraid of the success that they know will result if they move ahead now. Because success is heavy, carries a responsibility with it, it is much easier to procrastinate and live on the "someday I'll" philosophy.*
> — DENNIS WAITLEY

Psychological research on creativity proves that we work better when there is a limited amount of time — some time pressure — in which to complete a task. Many students, and many writers, constrict the amount of time they have so they can jump-start their ability to focus. T. S. Eliot once said that not having as much time for his writing as he would like allowed him to concentrate better. Perhaps this is why we procrastinate instead of doing the work for our classes.

Having a limited amount of time forces us to concentrate. In that state, where we are passionate about getting the project done, we concentrate with our full creative powers. You can use that human instinct to your advantage: Always set a time limit for your writing session (limit the time to ten or fifteen minutes at first), and set micro-deadlines for yourself. Use the compression and intensity of a deadline to jump-start flow.

When you catch yourself being distracted — unfocused on an image or a scene or your writing topic, or avoiding the writing altogether — instead of beating yourself up as a lowly procrastinator, listen to what is going on. You are probably nervous about writing. Writing is hard, and scary, and daunting. That never really changes; expert and published writers describe this state as a daily part of the writing life.

You need strategies. You need ways to get your focus back on the *image*. You need to catapult yourself into the scene at hand. Find out what works for you by practicing. How do you get out of procrastinating and into work-flow mode? Run around the block? Draw a sketch of the scene at hand? Start a new, different piece? Start by copying over or revising what you worked on yesterday? Experiment. Repeat what works for you.

Procrastination is a lack of focus caused by internal distraction. Learning how your mind works and repeating productive behaviors is your best line of defense, and your best way back into focus. However, if you are using procrastination itself as a focusing tool, and it works for you, perhaps procrastination isn't the worst thing. If you have plenty of extra time in your life, procrastination doesn't hurt anything. If you are pressed for time, you will need to develop more efficient strategies.

Often, the secret to breaking through a procrastination habit is to become more aware of the inner voices of judgment that are holding you back from working to your greatest potential.

Judgment

To avoid loss of focus, you need strategies for nipping it in the bud, when it first crops up. Psychologists who study creativity theorize that blocks, distractions, and procrastination — all the things we do to sabotage ourselves — are caused by judgment, that unhelpful critical voice.

On page 23, you tried to write down all the judging voices that crop up when you sit down to work — the parents, teachers, or friends who may have said negative things about your creative efforts, and the negative comments you've directed toward yourself.

But judgment doesn't have to be negative to be distracting. If you are thinking how great you are, how much money you will make, how profound you are, how beautiful the words will sound when you read them aloud at your Pulitzer Prize acceptance, you are distracted. You aren't focused on the reader's experience. And chances are that the writing won't be nearly as powerful as it could be.

If you go to your writing session to beat yourself up or to feel really brilliant and poetic, it's going to be hard to focus. When you write from your center self and keep in mind that moving picture, you are focused, and there isn't room for judging the work: You *are* the work.

Your question isn't "Is this going well?" or "Is this bad?" because you can never really know that. When you are at work, your question is "What else interesting do I see, do I experience, what interesting thing is my character about to do?" And you watch. And follow.

What a strange endeavor, this writing business. You don't know how it's going. Well, remember our main concept: It's not about you. It's about your reader. You are a sort of middleperson, a channel. Your job as a writer is to reach down and scoop up the stuff that is buried at the image level inside you—in your body, not in your head. You bring it up to the light, trying not to overanalyze the emotions or explain what's going on—just show your readers the movie in your mind.

WRITING PROJECTS

1. Write a dialogue between you and the critical voice in your head. Give the voice a name. Discuss your writing life with the critical voice; argue with it. Format the piece like a play.

2. Write a poem or narrative piece about becoming a writer or being a writer-at-work, but use another activity (baseball, cooking, making your bed) that you know well to describe the steps, pitfalls, or processes. Use images. Don't write *about* what you see. Write the actions and images, experiencing them on the sensory level as you write.

3. Rewrite the Practice you did on page 13, translating the feelings and thoughts and ideas and analyses into images so that the reader sees people, action, and real objects.

4. Draw your personal creative history in the form of a tree. Some limbs are your teachers, others are your creative pursuits. What feeds you creatively? Music? Favorite authors you read again and again? Maybe these are your creative roots. Bring your tree to class to share.

5. Read the comic by Jarod Roselló (p. 27). Reflect on what he's saying about the creative process. Then take a sheet of paper and divide it into four equal parts by drawing a line down the center and a line across the middle. In these four squares, draw the story of you taking a creative risk.

Jarod Roselló

The Neighbor

It was last Wednesday when I found the hole in the backyard.

I thought, something must have done this during the night. I was certain it hadn't been there the day before.

I mentioned the hole to the neighbor, but he seemed disinterested or distracted, as though he had better things to worry about than a hole in my backyard.

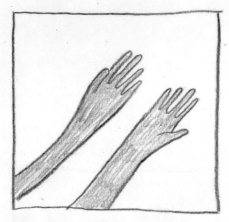

I asked if I might borrow his shovel to fill the hole. He hesitated, then agreed, and handed it to me over the fence.

I think this was when he walked back into his home. I didn't see him, but I heard the swooshing of the sliding glass door, and then a silence I associate with absence.

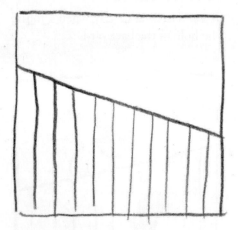

But this is the story of the hole, not the neighbor.

The hole was perfectly round. At first I believed something had fallen from the sky, or been shooting through space and hit here with such velocity it dug itself straight into the ground, compacting the dirt beneath it.

And because the grass around the hole appeared to be burned, it must have been moving with great speed.

Something small that fell from a tremendous height.

But it didn't matter what caused it, only that it was here and that I needed to do something about it. So I used the neighbor's shovel to fill the hole with loose soil and rocks from around the fence that separated our properties.

After an hour, and once I'd depleted my own soil and rocks and loose plant matter, I carefully scooped some from the neighbor's yard just underneath the fence, but it still wasn't enough to completely fill the hole.

While contemplating what to do next, a gust of wind brushed against my leg.

Startled, I shifted my body and the shovel slipped from my hand, falling into the hole.

I scrambled to retrieve it, but I was not quick enough.

I sat down beside the hole and tried to think of a new plan. The shovel was lost. The neighbor would be angry. I could think of nothing else to do.

Just before the sun set, I went to the neighbor's house to tell him about the fate of his shovel, but before I could knock on his door, I heard the sound of a person crying: a deep, low sobbing.

I placed my hand on the hot wood of the neighbor's door and waited.

There are times when it is appropriate to interrupt someone while they are crying, and though I did not know the reason the neighbor was crying, the manner, duration, and intensity allowed me to deduce that this was not a crying that came from the momentary pain of injury.

It was not a sadness associated with a heartbreaking commercial or the penultimate scene of a family drama.

Instead, it was the kind of crying that comes only with deep, enduring sadness: the kind that courses its way through one's entire body, tingling the fingertips, warming the face, and twisting the stomach.

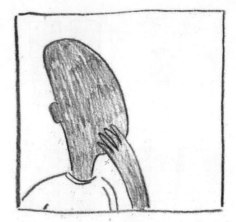

This, I believed, was the kind of grief that rerouted entire lives, altered trajectories of one's existence. Or else, this was the kind of sadness that made it impossible to continue on: the pain that renders a life unlivable.

At a lull, I knocked on the door and waited.

The trees above my head rustled in a gentle wind.

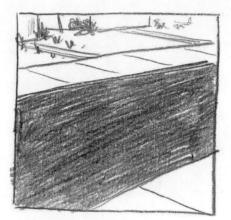

Somewhere a cat hissed.

A siren dissolved with distance.

I tapped my foot on the ground, then knocked again.

The door opened and my neighbor appeared: eyes bloodshot, face red, fists clenched.

For a few seconds we stared at one another and then I said, "Something's happened to your shovel."

And he said, "I know."

And like that, the hole was never filled.

CHAPTER TWO

CREATIVE READING

Creative writers read differently than do literature students or casual bookstore shoppers or beach readers. We're reading for pleasure, of course. But we're also intent on developing our craft. By reading closely and strategically, with a very specific and perhaps somewhat selfish agenda, we read to pick up new techniques we can use in our own creative efforts.

Writers approach reading as musicians do live shows: for enjoyment, yes, but also to expose ourselves to new moves, to learn more of what's possible, to get inspired. Just as musicians often listen to thousands of hours of music, obsessively, writers read voraciously.

We aren't able to confine ourselves to one section of the library or to one specific type of book in a bookstore. Creative writers are free-range readers, roaming from new works by young authors hot off the press over to poetry, perhaps dabbling in the classics before grazing over to science fiction, eagerly hunting down novels, comics, plays, and pieces that defy genre classification written by authors of all ages, from the ancients to the postmodernists, and from all over the globe. We tend to be delightfully undisciplined and radically inclusive in our choices: We'll read pretty much *anything*. We read and read and read. Because there is so much to learn about the craft of writing, our reading lives are driven by a particular hunger: We read to live, artistically. We learn to write—and continue to improve—by reading. As a writer, literature is our most valuable teacher—an especially wallet-friendly kind of education—for years to come.

THE NATURE OF A CREATIVE READER'S PERSONALITY

Curious

Creative writers are a bold and brave group: intrepid readers. Rarely do we quickly glance at a new work and say "I don't like it," walk away, and head back to what's safe and familiar (*Harry, where are you?*). We don't stick with what's "relatable" because we are eager to know about the worlds we *haven't* experienced. Instead of focusing on how a piece of writing connects to our own, perhaps limited experience, we like to extend ourselves boldly and discover how we relate to the new, the strange, the unexpected, the different.

We tend to be more patient readers than the general population because our curiosity overrides our irritation, confusion, or boredom. When put off by a text, instead of giving up and going back to an easier read we tend to see difficulty as a challenge, a problem to be solved. When stymied while reading, we try to burrow in, asking ourselves:

- Why is the writer doing it this way?
- Why have other readers found this useful or interesting?
- What might I be missing?

A hallmark of the writer reading is his or her ability to reread a difficult poem or passage until it unlocks. An interviewer once asked William Faulkner what he, the interviewer, should do—he had read Faulkner's novel three times and still didn't understand it. Faulkner said, famously, "Read it four times." Some pieces just aren't going to be meaningful to you. We all have reading blocks and literary blind spots. But staying with a difficult or strange piece, really working to understand it, and then having it open up for you is nothing short of amazing. Literature, read closely, can truly be life-changing.

Creative reading is, in part, the ability to postpone settling hastily into likes/dislikes and to lead with curiosity. In fact, as creative readers, often we don't even care very much if we like or dislike a piece of writing. Usually we're much more interested in figuring out what the author is trying to do, how exactly she's creating the effect she's creating, whether it's successful, and why it is or isn't successful.

Describe your reading life to date. What have you typically gravitated toward as a reader? Was there a time in your life you read a lot? Not at all? How do you decide what to read next? Do you read a lot of works that are in the genres you wish to write in? What's your favorite piece of writing of all time? Least favorite? Why?

Tolerant of Discomfort

Creative reading is about going to new places and hanging out, even when it's strange, uncomfortable, and really far from home. Just like travelers, creative readers know in advance they are going to get lost, confused, and overwhelmed. Some degree of trepidation and crankiness is inevitable on any trip. Difficulty and discomfort are, by definition, part of travel.

In *Beautiful and Pointless*, his book on why to write poetry and how to read it, David Orr discusses this very topic:

> The comparison may seem ridiculous at first, but consider the way you'd be thinking about Belgium if you were planning a trip there. You might try to learn a few useful phrases, or read a little Belgian history, or thumb through a guidebook in search of museums, restaurants, flea markets, or promising-sounding bars. The important thing is that you'd know you're going to be confused, or at least occasionally at a loss, and you'd accept that confusion as part of the experience. What you wouldn't do, however, is become paralyzed with anxiety because you don't speak fluent Flemish. . . . Nor would you decide in advance that you'd never understand Belgians because you couldn't immediately determine why their most famous public statue is a depiction of a naked kid peeing in a fountain (which is true). You'd probably figure, hey, that's what they like in Belgium; if I stick around long enough maybe it will make sense. (p. xv)

We read to travel across the human experience, to save ourselves from our own limits, to extend the range of what we can know and understand and feel and love. We don't expect every part of the trip to be comfy, familiar, and easy—that's just not how travel works. Creative reading means we like going places we haven't been before, and to do so we know we're going to develop a tolerance for not getting the whole thing at once, an ability to be lost and not get frustrated and retreat to familiar ground.

Some readers are naturally bolder than others by nature. Some readers easily tolerate not knowing / not getting it: Oh, kid peeing in fountain, makes no sense, gotta love it. Others find strange things (A kid peeing in a fountain? Seriously?) more off-putting.

But steering toward what is comfortable and familiar isn't creative. It's safe, to the point of numbing. Writers are rarely the kind of people who want everything spelled out, simplified, familiar. When someone wants to improve as a writer, the ability to diversify one's tastes, to go on harder, more challenging trips as a reader, is essential. Just as rock climbers continue to seek more difficult vertical ventures and just as gym rats keep increasing the resistance even though it's frustrating and sometimes even painful, creative writers crave works that challenge them anew.

Frustration with not knowing, not getting it—this isn't a problem. It's another word for learning.

The most efficient way to improve as a creative writer is (1) to read works you would not *naturally* read and not worry if you are frustrated because frustration isn't really a problem; (2) to practice strategies for noticing the aspects of a piece of writing that will most help you with your own writing; and (3) to cast a wide net, seeking out writing that will spark new inspiration and creativity.

To find new and interesting things to read, consult Chapter Twelve. There you'll find suggestions for resources on social media and how to search online for new literary magazines and current writers. For example, you can subscribe to the *Los Angeles Times Review of Books* and find lively, fresh reading suggestions delivered to your phone weekly. Many literary magazines are on Facebook and Twitter, and in addition to tweets from *The Believer*, *The Offing*, and *Tin House*, don't forget to troll your local bookstore for zines and local literary journals. Ask other students in your creative writing program who they are reading and where they find the best recommendations. Google "best new writers under forty." Go to Powells.com and peruse their Staff Picks and "Twenty-Five Books to Read Before You Die." Your instructor will have suggestions for you as well. Perhaps you will start a real or virtual bulletin board in your department where others can post their top picks for best new authors to read.

PRACTICE

Scan the readings at the end of this chapter. Which two pieces would you be most likely to read, in full, first? Note why. There's no right or wrong answer here—you're just trying to get to know your tastes better so that you can expand intentionally. Which two pieces are you least likely to read on your own, unless assigned? Why? Try to notice your assumptions about each piece as you scan it and to put your tastes, biases, and preferences into words.

CREATIVE READING IS CLOSE READING

Creative writers read three different kinds of writing: (1) professional works and published texts, (2) their own works-in-progress, and (3) the work of peers—in class or in writing groups.

Before we look at how to read professional work as a writer, let's pause for a moment and consider the reading you do of your own work-in-progress. Revision is, in large part, a reading process. Most writers don't draft, smoothly revise, and then declare

> *There is creative reading as well as creative writing.*
> — RALPH WALDO EMERSON

"I'm done." Writers read their pieces—over and over, and for different purposes at different stages. Writers read their work and wonder: What is confusing? What's wordy or awkward? What could be more interesting, more vivid? They make adjustments on the page and read, deeply, again. And again. And again.

Another kind of close reading you'll do with your own work, much later in the process, is reading to edit: You'll straighten out clunky sentences, fact-check, adjust line breaks, and correct grammar.

Lastly, the final close read an author does is proofreading. These three separate kinds of reading constitute revision skills and are presented in depth in Chapter Nine.

Close Reading Your Own Work

For now, you should focus on two key strategies when reading your own work as you generate new pieces: reading from hard copy and reading aloud.

Read from Hard Copy. At regular intervals during your writing session, print your pages and read with your pencil in hand. Composing entirely on your phone or laptop can distort your impressions of what you have on the page and what your writing will be like for the reader to read.

Devices, by their very nature, allow us to write quickly and erase quickly. Professional writers try to find a pace that is more like the pace of a reader actually reading. Get in the habit of printing, and reading slowly, and making your revisions with a pencil on hard copy and then entering those corrections into the text on-screen.

Read Aloud. Many students find that the best way to improve their writing is to read it aloud. Some students record into their phone and play back their own work while others read aloud alone to themselves. Still others find that the best way to capture mistakes, cull out rough patches, and adjust the voice is to read their work to a trusted writing partner or to read to their sofa and imagine that this is a live audience.

Print a copy, and read it out loud. Your ear will catch many inconsistencies, rough passages, and parts that just aren't clear, things your eye tends to gloss over. Get in the habit of reading your piece aloud, making the revisions by hand as you go, and then entering those into the electronic document later.

QUESTIONS TO ASK: Reading Your Own First Drafts Aloud

After you draft a piece, print out a hard copy. Read it out loud. Focus on these aspects of the piece to help yourself choose where to revise.

1   What parts are most transporting? Where might a reader be able to "see" images?

2   Are certain sections unclear?

3   Which places have the greatest energy? The least energy?

4   What is/are the essential tension(s) in the piece?

5   Is the dialogue realistic and interesting?

6   Did I stumble in certain places when I read?

7   Did some places sound wordy? Awkward?

Close Reading Work by Peers

Look at the acknowledgments for this book (p. ix). So many people helped it come into being. Look at the acknowledgments page of any book on your shelf. Artists—including writers—rarely work alone. We rely on one another for feedback: Is this piece doing what I want it to do?

Learning how to effectively close read the work of peers, in order to offer friendly and useful comments on their works-in-progress, is a vital part of any creative writing course, and it's a skill set that has rich benefits for you as a writer and as a future professional in a number of fields. When you read a work-in-progress by a classmate and you're tasked with articulating what that piece of writing accomplishes, how it does so, and where the piece might be unclear or ineffective, you are actually teaching yourself how to write better.

> *Easy reading is damn hard writing.*
> — MAYA ANGELOU

Writers can be prickly, strong-willed, certain of their point of view, overly blunt, or overly anxious about saying something that could be taken the wrong way. But learning how to read peer work thoughtfully, and to talk about work-in-progress to others who, like you, perhaps hope to continue writing in the future, is one of the most valuable parts of this course. Because if you pursue a career in creative writing or in any of the other arts (or in business and science as well), you'll need to be able to talk effectively with others about work-in-progress—yours as well as theirs.

Earn the respect of your peers by reading carefully, asking questions, and trying to figure out what the writer is trying to do *before* suggesting changes. There are some ground rules for reading other people's work; strategies for giving feedback in workshops, in small groups, or to a writing partner are covered earlier in this chapter.

In class, remember what kinds of reading reactions and comments are helpful to you as a writer, and model your own responses after those. You are often most helpful when you present your reactions to other works as those of a fellow beginner, another artist trying to do the same hard things. The goal is for the members of the class to always leave *wanting* to write more, not less.

Close Reading Literature

When we read literature, we pay attention to the effect the whole piece has on us emotionally. And we pay close attention to how the words, lines, sentences, scenes — the parts — work together to create the whole effect. Because a piece of literature — whether it's a poem, a play, a micro-memoir, or a short story — is very complex, we usually focus on one set of concerns at a time. As writers, we want to appreciate each piece as fully as we can, and we also want to come up with useful observations we can then apply to our own work. We read literature to *write* it. To read creatively, writers use five strategies.

> *Literature is a game, but it's a game one can put one's life into.*
>
> — JULIO CORTÁZAR

Read Multiple Times. We read a piece more than once before we weigh in with judgments or commentary. Most instructors suggest that you read a piece three times before you decide whether you like it or not. With more difficult texts, most of us read certain passages many times, and often we discover rich rewards.

The first read is a drive-by, a chance to get the lay of the land, to notice what looks interesting, to notice any trouble spots. If we love the piece, great. There's more pleasure ahead. If we're stymied or put off, we don't freak out. (We just arrived in Belgium. We don't speak the language. It's too soon to say if we like it or not.) On the first read, we might jot down a note or two on what is most confusing, just as on a trip we might jot down things we want to follow up on — what's the name of that cool pub on the corner, is there a shopping district nearby? On the first read, we pay attention to what orients us in the piece. What information do we get from the title? Where does the piece take place? Who is talking? Is the piece serious or funny?

Researchers have studied how people behave in art museums. The average viewer spends five seconds — five *seconds* — in front of a painting or sculpture before moving on. Professionals know that it takes five *minutes* of looking before a viewer can really start to appreciate the basics of what's going on in a painting, and more time is needed to appreciate the subtleties of meaning and craft. Don't be the tourist who says, grumpily, "My kid could do that." Take time. It's often worthwhile to go more slowly, look longer, stare quietly. You'll be amazed at what you can see when you *look*.

Or, in our field, when you read and listen.

Read Aloud. The second read is usually best performed aloud. (Note: For poetry and drama, we always read aloud.) Hearing creative work read out loud, in your own voice or someone else's, makes a significant difference in your ability to appreciate subtle aspects of a piece as well as to understand the piece, which is especially true for poetry. The ear can pick up things the eye doesn't. Having someone else read a piece aloud to you while you read along on the page is another good way to embark on a successful second read. Whether you are listening or speaking, reading aloud forces you to go more slowly, and in doing so, you have the chance to notice more of what's going on behind the scenes, under the surface.

PRACTICE

Silently read to yourself the poem "Another Lullaby for Insomniacs" by A. E. Stallings (p. 335). What do you notice? What's puzzling? Jot down a few initial impressions. Now read the poem aloud, slowly. What do you hear — if anything — that you didn't notice in the silent reading? Finally, have someone else read the poem aloud to you. What do you notice on the third read? Do you see any patterns or repeated images you missed on the first two reads? Could you hear things you didn't see? Talk about it with a partner or in class. What's going on in the poem?

Practice Copywork. Another way writers like to close read is to practice what we call copywork. Robert Louis Stevenson and Jack London, a self-educated writer, both famously taught themselves to write by copying out, by hand, long passages from their favorite books. Copywork teaches you to read closely because it forces you to pay attention to every word. Working by hand has proven cognitive benefits as well. Copying favorite passages teaches you about word choice and opens up possibilities for sentences and style, dialogue and pacing, structure and detail. When writers are stuck, many will use the technique of copywork to get their groove back.

PRACTICE

Take any one of the poems or a paragraph of prose from this textbook. Choose something that looks appealing to you but is unfamiliar — something you haven't read before. Read the piece. Then retype the words or copy them over by hand. Now read the poem or paragraph aloud. What do you notice when you reread the piece that you didn't notice before you copied it over?

Memorize. Actors memorize, and so do writers. Poets often memorize poems. Poet Beth Ann Fennelly is well known for "My One Hundred," a notebook of one hundred poems she keeps at hand on her writing desk. She tries to have one hundred poems memorized, ready to recite, at all times. This kind of mental copywork, the act of memorizing a poem, demands the kind of close reading that allows creative writers to grow and thrive as they internalize more sophisticated pieces of literature. When working on a monologue or play, you will learn the lines in order to memorize them, to say them aloud, to ensure they "track" for both the audience and the performer. Spoken word and rap artists memorize huge swaths of material, uploading it into their brains so they can infuse their performances with passion and heart.

PRACTICE

Listen to "Where There's Smoke" by Jenifer Hixson online, easily found on YouTube or The Moth's Web site. How is *hearing* creative writing different for you than reading it on the page? Do you prefer one over the other? Do you think you could memorize a piece of this length?

PRACTICE

Memorize a short poem. You can find short poems that work well for this kind of close reading on pages 112, 158, and 302 in this textbook and online at the Poetry Foundation or Poetry Daily. Copying the poem a number of times will aid your memorization process. Recite your poem. Notice what you learned about the poem by memorizing it.

Annotate. A very popular type of close reading involves annotating the physical text. Annotations are reading notes, comments a creative writer makes about the elements of a piece. Like a scientist, the creative writer labels the parts of a text, commenting on how the parts are working, noting patterns, asking questions.

We perform this type of close reading with a pencil in hand, as we observe and note, very consciously, the very same techniques we're trying to improve in our own work. Throughout the course, you'll want to annotate the readings you are studying, labeling and examining the finer points of each piece.

When annotating, you'll focus on specific techniques in turn.

Creative writers use five overarching categories of techniques when they make a piece of writing. Think of these parts of creative writing as different lenses you can look through—filters—so you can focus on one part of the process at a time. When you are reading closely in order to annotate, you'll look at the following elements of creative writing, one at a time.

1. Images: These are the various concrete actions, details, and pieces of dialogue that create "movies" in your mind as you read. What do you "see" or experience as you read?
2. Energy: What moves does the writer make that give the piece its particular flavor? What keeps you reading?
3. Tension: All creative writing has tension or conflict. What does the writer do, exactly, on the page that makes the piece taut, complex, interesting, readable?
4. Pattern: Art relies on pattern to create meaning. When you close read for pattern, your annotations will focus on rhythm, repetition, rhyme, echoes, layers, and syntax.
5. Insight: Good creative writing continues to feed the reader more, even after a second, third, or fourth reading. How does the piece of writing get its meaning across to the reader? When you close read for depth, you'll try to peer behind the curtain — under the surface of the piece — in order to teach yourself how to deepen your own work and increase its power and reach. In literature courses, this is often called *theme*.

A. Van Jordan
af • ter • glow

> Based on the title, I predict that this poem will explore the light of late evening, full of lightning bugs.

> Instead of talking about skies in general, we see the specific sky light in Ohio. The setting grounds the poem.

> *Phosphorescent* means that something glows without getting hot.

> The entire workweek is encapsulated in this line, lending a tone of timelessness.

> These slashes break up the prose poem and make me pause. The lines end on the most important words that tie back to *afterglow*, like "light" and "ablaze."

af•ter•glow \≈\ n. **1.** The light esp. in the Ohio sky after sunset: as in the look of the mother-of-pearl air during the morning's afterglow. **2.** The glow continuing after the disappearance of a flame, as of a match or a lover, and sometimes regarded as a type of phosphorescent ghost: This balm, this bath of light / This cocktail of lust and sorrow, / This rumor of faithless love on a neighbor's lips, / This Monday morning, this Friday night, / This pendulum of my heart, / This salve for my soul, / This tremble from your body / This breast aflame, this bed ablaze / Where you rub oil on my feet, / Where we spoon and, before sunrise, turn away / And I dream, eyes open, / swimming / In this room's pitch-dark landscape.

< The structure imitates a dictionary entry and creates a new, emotive definition for the word *afterglow*.

< A pendulum is a weight that swings freely.

< How does this line fit in with the others? It is sensual with the word *oil*, but the mention of feet surprised me.

< My prediction expressed my personal connection to the word *afterglow*. I think this poem similarly explores the narrator's personal connection to the word.

PRACTICE

Annotate Sebastian Matthews's "Buying Wine" (p. 70) by making three to five comments in the margins about the strategies you see in the poem. Look for and label (1) repeated sounds and (2) images that you see in your mind's eye when you read. Then make a comment about the closure at the end of the poem: What happens in the last lines?

You can use numerous strategies for close reading, including reading aloud, reading slowly, reading and annotating, and memorizing. With close reading, you take the skills you are learning as a writer and examine pieces of writing to see how those same skills are deployed in various ways. Close reading is sort of like studying and sort of like falling in love, at the same time. Close reading is your bread and butter as a writer.

READING ACROSS THE GENRES: A FIELD GUIDE TO CREATIVE WRITING

Genre means "kind" or "sort" and refers to the various subcategories of creative writing. There are genres of form (poetry, fiction, plays) and genres of subject (fantasy, science fiction, romance). Your class will likely focus on some of the following kinds of writing: fiction, poetry, creative nonfiction (memoir, literary essay), and drama. Creative writers thrive on cross-training: If you want to be a fiction writer, learning imagery and depth by writing poetry will greatly assist your short story technique. If you want to be a spoken word artist, learning narrative skill from fiction and sound work technique from poetry will allow your performances to soar and will help you hold your audiences' interest.

In the beginning, stay open to experimentation; don't pigeonhole yourself as The Poet or Master Playwright too quickly. Who knows? You might be like one of those athletes who letter in cross-country, basketball, and tennis—an all-star writer who excels in prose poetry, comics, and screenplays. Because all the genres of creative writing rely on the same core strategies (images, energy, tension, insight, pattern, and structure), you'll learn the basic strategies for good creative writing, one at a time, as they relate to the genres. You'll be able to compose in any genre you choose.

Fiction

Fiction is an invented story, of course, and these narratives can take the form of short stories, flash fiction, short-shorts, novellas, comics or graphic works, or novels. Speculative fiction (Kelly Link, Karen Russell, George Saunders) has supernatural, fantastic, or futuristic elements. Realistic fiction is exactly that. In either case, a story usually consists of two or more characters in a situation that forces one of them to undergo some kind of change or realization, and the secondary character serves as the catalyst for the primary character's change. For this reason, stories with just one character may be very hard to pull off.

Additionally, contemporary narrative is often built out of scenes, as in cinema, based on slices of real time, so the reader sees events play out on a kind of stage in the mind's eye. Fiction is like a play in the reader's head. It's not a report or a summary of events—we experience the events as the characters do, in "real time." Short stories typically run from a couple of pages in length up to forty or more pages.

Micro-fiction, flash fiction, and short-shorts are very short stories—a paragraph or a page in length. A novella is a short novel, and the length varies greatly, but fifty to one hundred pages is typical. Novels may run two hundred to six hundred pages long and can focus on more characters and perhaps cover more time—years instead of moments—than we typically see in a short story.

Creative writing classes often use the short story as a training ground for writers learning to write fiction because it can be read in one sitting, is complete in and of itself, and provides many instructive challenges—you have to do everything quickly.

Many writers practice short stories first, to get comfortable with how narrative works, honing their skills in the shorter form. And they read. Reading widely—all kinds of fiction, long, short, funny, serious, fantastic, realistic—is the fastest way to improve fiction-writing technique.

Fiction includes genres such as fantasy (George R. R. Martin and J. R. R. Tolkien), science fiction (Robert Heinlein), horror (Stephen King),

QUESTIONS TO ASK: Responding to Fiction

Focus on these aspects when reading works-in-progress or published writing in this genre.

1. What do you see in your mind's eye when you read?
2. What is interesting? Visually? Emotionally?
3. Whom is the story about?
4. What details reveal the most about character?
5. Where does the story take place?
6. What is "versus" what in this story? What is the nature of the conflict?
7. Comparing the last page to the first page (or, for a short-short, comparing the last sentence to the first sentence), what has changed? What is different?

romance, western, detective, gay/lesbian, young adult, and middle-grade (ages nine through twelve). These subcategories have very specific publishing conventions, and many students who are interested in gaining expertise in one of these genres turn to specific resources that lay out the conventions. Some writers have success tweaking these conventions, combining and reinventing the rules. Regardless of your publishing goals or genre interests, learning the basic building blocks of fiction — character, dialogue, scene, and conflict — will serve you extremely well in crafting everything from sonnets to screenplays.

PRACTICE

Read George Saunders's short story "Sticks" (p. 304) and answer the questions on page 46.

Creative Nonfiction: Memoir and Literary Essay

It's interesting — perhaps somewhat annoying, too — when a vocabulary term defines something it is *not*. Nonfiction is a broad category that includes history, guides on caring for your new pet kookaburra, sociology, and books on winemaking and cycling and weather. This kind of writing uses summarizing, instruction (as does the book you are reading now), reporting, and telling to get its points across. *Creative* nonfiction is writing that is 100 percent factual and based squarely in the real, true, known world. However, it refers specifically to a special subcategory of nonfiction writing that uses the conventions of fiction to tell a true story. Essays rely on reporting, analyzing, explaining, and describing — that's what you study in nonfiction- or essay-writing courses (and probably what you studied in your first-year expository writing course). By contrast, creative nonfiction relies heavily on the techniques of fiction writing: scene making, or letting the reader *see* the story, instead of being *told* about it. Creative nonfiction uses drama, storytelling, characterization, beautiful language, detail, development, and theme, just as fiction does. But instead of invented material, everything in creative nonfiction is absolutely true. In creative nonfiction, the reader is *transported* visually and emotionally — the reader is in the scene. The story plays out as a movie in the reader's mind's eye, instead of appealing to the reader's intellect alone.

Creative nonfiction includes two subcategories: memoir, or a personal story; and the literary essay, in which you research a topic or write about another person, not yourself. In both forms, you use images, scenes, metaphors, dialogue, and pattern. Creative nonfiction allows you to expand and question perceptions, to learn more about the world and the self. In memoir, you tell a story from your own life in order to help the reader see his or her own life in a new, richer way.

Researched work (sometimes called **new journalism**) combines facts and imagination to create scenes. Robert Kurson, for example, in *Shadow Divers* (2004), leads his reader through a deep-sea shipwreck with professional scuba divers; when they enter the wreck of a German submarine, you feel as though you are right there, gasping for air. Kurson's research (reading and extensive interviews with professional wreck divers) allowed him to create scenes so real that when you read them, you feel as though you are actually having the experience.

Lyric essays are a subgenre of creative nonfiction. Composed more the way poetry is composed, using sections of highly imagistic, detailed prose and relying on structures such as braid or collage, lyric essays tend to have less plot, less story, and highly resonant language.

As with fiction, creative nonfiction can be almost any length, from a paragraph-long micro-essay to a book. And, as with fiction, there are graphic and comic versions, ranging from history to memoir. If you are interested in graphic memoir, you might take a look at *Fun Home* by Alison Bechdel and *Stitches* by David Small.

Poetry and Prose Poetry

Poetry could be defined as creative writing in which the lines don't go all the way to the right side of the page. But that visual definition doesn't *really* get at the nature and range of poetry. A poem is often compressed, but there are long

QUESTIONS TO ASK: Responding to Creative Nonfiction

Focus on these aspects when reading works-in-progress or published writing in this genre.

1. What do you see in your mind's eye when you read?
2. What is interesting? Visually? Emotionally?
3. Whom is the story about? How do you come to know the people in the piece?
4. Where does the story take place?
5. What is the conflict in this story?
6. What information do you learn? What insights do you gain?
7. Comparing the last page to the first page, what has changed? What is different?
8. So what? What makes you care about what happens?

poems that could be formatted differently and called prose poems or flash fiction. Poems are short and also rich with language and emotion; regardless of length, readers are expected to read a poem several times, allowing the nuances to unfurl. There are two basic kinds of poetry: narrative and lyric. You will study these subcategories in depth in Chapter Three. Narrative poetry uses some of the same tools that novels and short stories use: character, conflict, and story. Lyric poetry doesn't necessarily tell a story; instead, it presents a brief (sixty lines or fewer), concentrated feeling or emotion. Dramatic poetry, a third type of poetry, could also be called monologue, spoken word, or a play. Emily Dickinson defined poetry this way: "If I feel physically as if the top of my head were taken off, that is poetry." Here is one way to define "what is poetry": a piece of writing, usually short, with distinctive rhythms, and with images that reveal one thing while also pointing to another. Narrative reels in the reader, invites him on a ride. Poetry often doesn't reel us in. *Stop!* it says. *Pay close attention.*

PRACTICE

Read Sebastian Matthews's poem "Buying Wine" (p. 70) and A. E. Stallings's poem "Another Lullaby for Insomniacs" (p. 335). Which one tells more of a story? Which one focuses more on evoking a single emotion in the reader, concentrating on a very particular effect? Support your answer with specific references to each of the poems.

Prose poems are poems in blocks of type, usually one paragraph or sometimes two. The prose poem looks like prose (prose is fiction and creative non-fiction, work that is formatted in traditional paragraphs). Sometimes prose poems have characters, but not always; a prose poem can be all description. It has to be read with the same amount of concentration as a poem because the stage setup we can expect in fiction — scenes, characters, images playing out in our mind's eye in real time — may not exist. A prose poem may feature strange, surprising, or surreal situations. A prose poem may not be a story at all; it might be pure emotion and feeling and description. It usually employs the heightened language of poetry: images, sounds, and feelings, with more overt rhythm to the words.

QUESTIONS TO ASK: Responding to Poetry and Prose Poems

Focus on these aspects when reading works-in-progress or published work in these genres.

1. Who is speaking?
2. Where is the poem taking place?
3. What are the images?
4. What is the structure of the poem?
5. What happens in the poem? What's the "story"?
6. What do you see in your mind's eye?
7. What feelings are evoked?
8. What sounds in the poem emphasize the visuals, the feelings?
9. What gives the poem its energy?
10. What makes you, the reader, interested in the poem?

PRACTICE

Read A. Van Jordan's "af•ter•glow" (p. 67), Vincent Scarpa's "I Go Back to Berryman's" (p. 65), and Jay Hopler's "That Light One Finds in Baby Pictures" (p. 158). Read them a second time, aloud. Which one focuses most on story: the sequence of events? Which focuses most on images and emotions?

Drama: Spoken Word, Monologue, Play, and Screenplay

Spoken word, monologues, plays, and screenplays are all forms that are designed for presentation on the stage or screen. Spoken word, because it is performed live, uses inventive rhythm and rhyme (to make it easier to memorize and to heighten the musicality) and embraces improvisation, free association, and wordplay. Sometimes associated with hip-hop, spoken word could be considered the original creative writing genre, long predating the written word. Contemporary spoken word has roots in jazz, blues, and folk music as well as in oral story-telling and epic and narrative poetry, and it's related to experimental performance and monologue theater.

A monologue is a play for one person, or any work of literature in which one person speaks alone, to the audience (as opposed to a soliloquy, in which one person is speaking aloud to him- or herself).

Plays and screenplays are designed to be performed or filmed. They exist on the page in two forms: One form, which you will practice this semester, is formatted for readers. The second is formatted for an entire theater company or movie production. If you are interested in writing for stage or screen, numerous books discuss the specific conventions for formatting and submitting your work. In this course, we will focus primarily on how to write strong scenes, evoke clear conflicts, and deploy fresh, energetic dialogue in plays or screenplays. Later, you may choose to take a more in-depth course focused exclusively on scriptwriting.

Playwriting and screenwriting are storytelling in images. Too many hopeful screenwriters get so distracted by the cool things they can do with cameras that they forget about what the writer must still do: create a story, with images, that moves readers/viewers. Like fiction and creative nonfiction, plays (in all their forms, including monologues and spoken word) must be clear and evocative in order to appeal to readers/viewers. Obviously, writing in this genre helps your dialogue skills if you are a fiction or creative nonfiction writer. But a play also uses sound, music, and rhythm, just as a poem does.

Like a poem, a play is compressed, focused, and intense. The play, however, relies on dialogue to tell the story and illustrate the conflict. Reading aloud takes much longer than reading to yourself, but you will be amazed at how fast a few pages of dialogue are used up. Drama is intensely concentrated, with the dialogue hyper-focused, fast-moving, and multilayered. Conflict (as in fiction) is the mother of drama, and the challenge for the author of a play is to make sure the words the character or characters are speaking reveal conflicts, layers, tension, and action. In poetry, the author has to play with sound and meaning; in a play, the author has to present several things that are going on simultaneously on the visual and verbal levels, even in monologues, in which only one person is talking.

> *Without tradition, art is a flock of sheep without a shepherd. Without innovation, it is a corpse.*
> — WINSTON CHURCHILL

PRACTICE

Read "I am not Batman." by Marco Ramirez (p. 71). Answer the questions on the following page.

QUESTIONS TO ASK: Responding to Monologues, Plays, and Screenplays

Focus on these aspects when reading works-in-progress or published writing in any of the dramatic genres.

1. Where is this taking place? When?
2. Who talks?
3. What is the psychology of the person or people in the play?
4. What are the conflicts that come through in the dialogue?
5. What conflicts come through in the action?
6. What conflicts come through via the setting?
7. What changes over the course of the play?
8. What images do you see in your mind as you listen to the dialogue?

Comics, Graphic Works, and Experiments

Creative writing is not limited to the four basic genres discussed above (fiction, creative nonfiction, poetry, and drama). For centuries, creative writers have resisted rules and boxes, consistently reinventing and redefining what can be done with black marks on white sheets of paper. The graphic novel, a particularly fertile genre for new young writers, has a long and sturdy history. A graphic novel or memoir is a comic that works like a prose novel or memoir, and while some are as short as fifty pages, others are long enough to take up multivolume sets. Besides graphic novels and memoirs, graphic literature includes graphic instruction manuals and graphic histories.

Comics and graphic novels have always attracted some of the world's wisest and most adventurous artists; you may know Art Spiegelman's *Maus* or the work of Matt Groening (creator of *The Simpsons*, who originally wrote a comic strip appearing in college and alternative newspapers). Cartoons and comics provide excellent training in the essentials of storytelling because the author has to construct a clear, compelling narrative that proceeds step-by-step. Because the artwork carries a lot of the information, the writing itself is often pared down and simplified, making the form fascinating and rewarding to study. Like a play, graphic literature uses words to render dialogue, and images to render action and setting. Just as the playwright has to coordinate the visual line with the aural (spoken) line, the graphic artist works the visual and verbal in tandem. The graphic writer, then, has to be expert at every single genre, every single technique available to creative writers. Graphic novels are currently experiencing a surge in popularity, just as they did in the nineteenth century, the 1930s, and the 1960s. In Chapter Twelve, you will find a list of guidebooks on how to create your own comics.

Experimental creative writing is also fertile ground for new writers. Realize that the more difficult your work is to read, and the more off-putting your subject matter, the fewer readers you will have. One rule to consider (and possibly break): The author should never have more fun than the reader. The more you stray, as a writer, from a strong, clear narrative story line, the harder your reader has to work to understand what is going on and stay involved in the piece. If the writing provides a great payoff—in terms of humor or insight—the reader may rise to the occasion. Think about what you love to read, and try to give your readers the same kinds of pleasure. The longer your experiment, the harder it is to sustain. Ultimately, creative writers *are* lovers of experiment and play. Try new things. Risk failing. Read work you wouldn't normally be drawn to. If you are working at the edge of what is comfortable for you, you are very likely growing as a writer.

> *Everything has been said before but since nobody listens, we have to keep going back and beginning all over again.*
> — ANDRÉ GIDE

PRACTICE

Read the pieces at the end of this chapter. Rank them from your favorite to your least favorite. For the ones you really like, what is it about them that attracts you? For the pieces you like least, what specifically turns you off? Were you surprised by any of your preferences? Is it the genre itself you like or don't like, or is it the specific piece? Why?

QUESTIONS TO ASK: Responding to Graphic Novels, Comics, and Experimental Pieces

Focus on these aspects when reading works-in-progress or published writing in these genres.

1. What is the work about?
2. What's the story the piece is telling?
3. What emotions are covered in this piece?
4. Is the dialogue accurate, lively, and interesting?
5. What does each panel, section, or line do that is different from the other panels, sections, or lines?
6. What keeps you interested in reading this work?
7. How does the artwork (if included) amplify the power of the story?
8. What does the experiment (if included) ask the reader to do? Is it worth it?

> *Reading is equivalent to thinking with someone else's head instead of with one's own.*
>
> — ARTHUR SCHOPENHAUER

IMITATION: READING TO WRITE

When you were little, you learned to walk, talk, and make friends by watching other people do these things and then copying them. You copied, you learned; life was good.

Imitation is a time-honored way to understand more deeply and to get more proficient at any art or skill, whether it's writing, cooking, painting, dancing, composing, acting, or designing clothes, furniture, or houses. At first, beginning chefs copy the recipe closely, getting their techniques down. Then they start to add more and more of their own special touches, finally inventing not just recipes but techniques and concepts of their own (which are then imitated, taught in culinary school, and on and on).

A similar process is at work in writing. By carefully examining, from the inside out, how other writers work—by copying, in essence—you become a better writer. And nothing forces you to read more closely, more carefully, than imitation.

Most writers find they have to practice every day, just like athletes and musicians and painters. The imitation practices in this chapter are useful for writers who need a jump start, who want to have "something to do" for their daily practice, or for stuck writers who want to limber up, stretch old muscles, and strengthen new ones. The imitation process is flexible, and you can bend it to fit your needs. You can imitate a whole piece or just an *aspect* of a piece.

Imitation is a great way to hone your reading skills, to deepen your creative thinking skills, to increase your confidence, and to help you find your way to your own best material. It's like dancing on someone else's feet. It might feel awkward, but it's a quick, direct path, like copywork, to internalizing the basic moves that separate the amateur from the pro.

Imitation: Guided Practice

Some students feel shy about imitation at first. They feel as though they are stealing. Or they fear that people will think they are too dim to come up with their own ideas. Most writers want to be original. But when you hear a great new band cover a classic song, you don't think to yourself, "Gosh, they can't come up with anything new. They've turned into mindless copiers!" No. You think, "Cool version. I didn't ever hear it that way before." Interesting. To cover a song, or to imitate a published piece of creative writing, is to pay homage.

The writer Voltaire put it this way: "Originality is nothing but judicious imitation. The most original writers borrowed from one another. The instruction we find in books is like fire. We fetch it from our neighbors, kindle it at home, communicate it to others, and it becomes the property of all."

When you imitate, you aren't copying or stealing. You're performing a training exercise, one that has a long and respected tradition in the arts. Of course you always acknowledge the imitation. It's against the law to take someone else's words or ideas or creations and pass them off as your own, and it's embarrassing to pretend your work is original when clearly it is not. That's not what you are doing. Here, in this class, you are not going to try to publish your imitations, or pass them off as your own totally inspired personal invention. You're practicing. Imitation is training, development. You are trying to block out your normal thinking habits and force yourself into some new patterns and new moves. Imitation works.

Stevie Wonder told me that he heard me coming in on the radio from Windsor [Ontario], that I had influenced some of his pieces. It wasn't like he copped the lick or anything like that, but basically he went in a more adventurous chordal direction than he would have had I not existed. That's the kind of influence that I like. It is not copying.

— JONI MITCHELL

You are imitating, unconsciously, whenever you write. All writers are influenced by the works they have read, what they watch, what they know about literature. Stories you learned as a child are stuck in your head. Phrases and rhythms of works you read last semester lodge in your writing mind and come out in your work. This is a good thing! Successful writers enjoy embedding subtle references to other pieces of literature in their works. We pass on, translate, adore, and keep alive the writers who influence us, consciously and unconsciously. Every time we sit down to write, we're all imitating to some extent. The more widely you read, the more texture your own writing has—artist as melting pot. If you slavishly read only one or two writers, your work may suffer from a poverty of influence.

Some students worry that if they imitate, they will lose their own personal stamp. To *truly* imitate another writer is almost as impossible as imitating another person. When you do impressions of your roommate, her accent and mannerisms, everyone knows it's you, not her. You can get close to taking on someone else's voice and tone; maybe over the telephone you can fool people. You heighten some aspects of her personality and leave out others entirely. But we know it's *you*—it's *you* being *her*. That's what intentional literary imitation is, too. It's you, but dressed in the clothes of someone else—someone who has really learned how to shop! Someone with style that's better than or different from your own. Imitation doesn't decrease creativity. It strengthens and feeds creativity.

Young musicians usually have extensive collections of music by other musicians. They attend performances in weird warehouses and in the garages of friends of friends. Up-and-coming musicians have deep knowledge about who is playing what, with whom, and how well. Do musicians immerse themselves in the music scene in order to steal ideas, chord combinations, clever lyrics? No. They do it because they know that surrounding themselves with other practitioners of their chosen art *feeds their work*. When you are a working artist, you can't *not* be obsessed with what everyone else is doing. It's how you learn how to do what you do better.

Writers are like musicians. Our versions of garage bands are often little magazines, zines, and blogs. Our shows are live readings. We follow poets to community centers, colleges, parks, and theaters to see what they have. In the same way that musicians go to see their favorite live bands again and again, we writers drive hours to see our favorite fiction writer for the fifth time. Our favorite writers are those who have something to teach us. We learn by following them, sometimes word by word.

When you imitate, remember that you are experimenting. It's just for practice. Stay loose, stay open. When you go back to your own ways of writing, you'll be a better writer. You'll have new tools, new approaches, a whole new range. Imitation is a way to practice writing.

Types of Imitation

For their experiments, writers use two basic types of imitation: scaffolding (writing between the lines) and fill-in-the-blank (like Mad Libs). Each one allows your front brain, your thinking/planning/knowing mind, to step aside so that the back of your mind, the creative part, dormant for much of daily life, can come forward and *play*. Gaps, leaps, nonsense, surprise, discomfort, weirdness—all these are welcome aspects of imitation. Remember: This is for practice, not necessarily for publication. You are learning new dance steps to increase the range of what you can do.

Scaffolding: Writing between the Lines

Scaffolding is the use of another writer's text, line by line, to create your own piece. Call to mind a building under construction. You know the system of platforms constructed *around* the building site, as the new floors are built? That's scaffolding, and scaffolding is the function of the text we use to launch our imitations. Then, when the new piece is completed, the scaffolding is removed. The building stands. We forget all about the scaffolds. The original text provides the inspiration and supports the new work.

When you imitate in this way, don't worry about fitting everything together or making absolute sense. You are after a sense of play. It might feel awkward. But it can be fun, like when you were a kid, and you danced standing on someone else's feet.

Scaffolding a Poem. Choose a poem you enjoy but perhaps do not completely "get." Copy the poem on a sheet of paper, skipping three blank lines in between each line of the poem. That's your scaffold. You will build your own poem in between the existing lines, the supports. Here's an example of how the technique works, using a poem by Bob Hicok. (The poem "A Primer" appears in its original form on p. 75.)

Imitating Bob Hicok
A Primer

I remember Michigan fondly as the place I go
I remember _____ _____ *as the place I go*
  (*your home town, state, or place of significance*) (*adverb*)

to be in Michigan. The right hand of America
to be in _____ . *The* _____ _____ *of America*
  (*repeat place name*) (*locate your place with a body part*)

waving from maps or the left
_____ _____ _____ _____ _____ _____
  (*six words to describe your place as though it's alive*)

pressing into clay a mold to take home
_____
  (*another image for how your place looks—comparison that spills onto next line*)

from kindergarten to Mother. I lived in Michigan
_____ _____ . *I lived in* _____
  (*conclude physical comparison of your place*) (*your place name*)

forty-three years. The state bird
_____ . *The* _____ *bird*
  (*how long you lived there*) (*repeat your place name or synonym*)

is a chained factory gate. The state flower
is a _____ . *The state flower*
  (*a surprising leap: compare your place to a symbol for something negative about your place*)

is Lake Superior, which sounds egotistical
_____ *which sounds* _____

> (*fill in the blank with something that isn't a flower, but names a specific aspect of the place that is positive, and then make a sarcastic comment*)

though it is merely cold and deep as truth.
though it is merely cold and _____ *as* _____.

> (*fill in blanks with surprising leaps*)

A Midwesterner can use the word "truth,"
A _____-*er can use the word* _____,

> (*Using a term that describes the people from your place, Kansans, or Dutch-ers, fill in the second blank by repeating the last word from the line above.*)

can sincerely use the word "sincere."
can sincerely use the word "sincere."

> (*copy this line as it is*)

In truth the Midwest is not mid or west.
In truth the _____ *is not* _____ *or* _____.

> (*repeat the name of your place in blank one, and break the word into two parts: i.e., Florida becomes "Flori" or "da"*)

When I go back to Michigan I drive through Ohio.
When I go back to _____ *I* _____ *through* _____.

> (*name your place again, and show how you get there*)

There is off I-75 in Ohio a mosque, so life
_____, *so life*

> (*describe the features of the landscape as you approach your place*)

goes corn corn corn mosque, I wave at Islam,
goes _____ _____ _____ _____, *I wave at*
_____,

> (*fill in with repeated words and specifics from your place*)

which we're not getting along with
which we're not getting along with

> (*repeat this line as is*)

on account of the Towers as I pass.
on account of _____ *as I pass.*

> (*fill in source of conflict in your place*)

Then Ohio goes corn corn corn
Then _____ *goes* _____ _____ _____

> (*fill in with the specifics from your place, repeating the words as Hicok does*)

billboard, goodbye Islam. You never forget

_____, *goodbye* _____. *You never forget*

   (*fill in using specific images from your place*)

how to be from Michigan when you're from Michigan.

how to be from _____ *when you're from* _____.

   (*fill in your place, twice*)

You can end your poem here, or continue scaffolding, creating "blanks" in Hicok's poem and filling in your own specific details. To begin, list the neighborhoods, towns, and places you have lived. After you write lines of your own *built from Hicok's lines*, copy out just your poem, on a new sheet of paper. As you copy, tinker with your lines. Delete and add words to make them connect to each other. If a particular line really interferes with your new poem, leave it out; or add lines as you need to.

Read the poems out loud to the class. Do you notice the scaffolding? Are the poems alike or different? Did you make any new moves that you would not have thought of without Hicok as the trigger?

If you decide to submit the piece to a literary magazine or a class anthology, you can simply put "After Bob Hicok's 'A Primer'" under the title if you feel it is still very closely related to the original. Poets and writers often talk to each other in this complimentary fashion; it's not unusual at all. Imitation is, after all, the highest form of flattery.

PRACTICE

Try the above experiment again, on your own. Choose one of the poems in this book, such as "Buying Wine" by Sebastian Matthews (p. 70) or "Genealogy" by Betsy Sholl (p. 66). Your teacher may provide alternate examples for you to work from: Emily Dickinson, Tomas Tranströmer, Robert Hass, and Rumi work well — poets who are slightly opaque, surreal.

To begin, copy the poem you will imitate, triple-spacing it on the page. Print the page. Cover up the lines with a second sheet of paper so you can see only one line at a time. Then, using each line as a prompt and guide, write your own lines, leaving out some of the poet's words and replacing them with your own.

Variation 1: Scaffold off a classmate's imitation of Hicok, using the student's new poem as your prompt poem.

Variation 2: Use one of the poems a classmate wrote for this course. Copy the student's lines, triple-spacing, and write your own lines.

Variation 3: Your instructor or a partner gives you the lines from a poem you have never read before, one at a time. You write your own line in response to each line.

Narrative Scaffolding. Creative nonfiction and fiction—the narrative genres—provide excellent opportunities for increasing your creative techniques by imitation. To practice, we will work with an excerpt from writer Amy Fusselman's memoir. In Fusselman's *The Pharmacist's Mate*, she writes about herself and her family. The book's arc traces her unique journey: As she mourns the death of her father, she is also on a quest to have a child. Because she writes in short, deft sections, she provides a good model for creating a prose piece of your own using the scaffolding method. Instead of relying on (perhaps clichéd) random ideas or spending hours staring off into space hoping for a good idea, you work the muscles of inspiration by paying close attention to how writers like Fusselman work, what they write about, and how they braid and relate disparate topics to generate more interest and create fresh meanings. This is how imitation helps us be less predictable and bolder and more original.

PRACTICE

Read the excerpt from the opening portion of Amy Fusselman's memoir, *The Pharmacist's Mate* (p. 76). Then answer the questions for creative nonfiction on page 48.

When you imitate something (or someone), you study it closely. You learn how it moves. What its habits are. To get ready to write, reread the Amy Fusselman selection. Examine it closely. Notice the different layers of her text. Fusselman braids together three kinds of information. What categories of information do her various sections contain?

> stories about her body, trying to get pregnant
> excerpts from her father's journals, kept when he was young
> stories about her father, her brother, her family

What order does she put the sections in? Can you detect a pattern? Reread her work. How does she start her sections? End them? Why are they numbered? As we closely read, we find the three subjects of her writing— becoming a mom, her father's journals, and her father's death—intertwine in a pattern that adds up to more than the sum of its parts. Reading a piece in order to imitate it encourages you to identify its parts. It's like inventing a recipe from a cooked dish that you really like. What's in it? How might the cook/author have assembled the parts? In what order?

Imitating is a lot like reading through a microscope. Look more closely. What makes a section a section in Fusselman's piece? What kind of unit does she use? Are these sections ministories? Does each one have a particular insight? Or do all these units have something else in common? Are there several types of units?

When you scaffold off Fusselman's prose, think of the sections as stanzas in a poem, and the paragraphs—the groups of sentences separated by white space within her numbered sections—as lines.

You will do the same thing you did for "A Primer" by Bob Hicok (p. 57): Launch your own "lines" based on Fusselman's.

Before you begin, you want to be oriented in time and space on the image level. To orient yourself, choose three braids, or *types* of information, to include in your personal memoir, your rendition of *The Pharmacist's Mate*.

When imitating, fill in the blanks as quickly and intuitively as you can. This may feel very uncomfortable and forced—you are improvising. Try it again with Betsy Sholl's poem "Genealogy" (p. 66). Write an imitation, based on your parents or grandparents.

> *Imitation gave me room to operate with my own scalpel in someone else's scrubs. To use a style that I wasn't used to connected some circuits in my head, and I felt more freedom to explore different directions with the tools I already had. I could discover rhythm and ride the wave all the way to shore.*
>
> — STUDENT WRITER CHRISTIAN PIERS, ON IMITATING AMY FUSSELMAN

Imitating Betsy Sholl
Genealogy

One of my parents was a _____, the other a _____.

One was a _____, the other a _____.

In the night I'd wake to _____ and the faint smell of _____.

The _____ tattooed on my lower back is the one for _____.

One of my parents was a _____,
the other a _____ I carried into the night,
convinced it was _____.

One of my parents I drank, the other I dreamed.

In the revolving door of my becoming,

one _____ and one _____ .
Thus, my troubled birth, my endless _____ .

One was an _____, the other a _____ .
How they amused each other.

One was a _____, the other a _____ . I was ashamed
of _____, embarrassed I couldn't _____ .

I was a girl/boy calling across the _____ to a _____
she/he didn't have.

PRACTICE

Try a variation on this exercise, using the same poem. Instead of writing about your
parents, write about two roommates, two coaches, two exes, two siblings, or two
friends. Try to capture the essential quirks of each with contrasting concrete images.

WRITING PROJECTS

1. Write a poem of about sixteen to eighteen lines about your father's house or
   the home of someone older—a coach, a grandparent, an uncle—someone
   who lives very differently than you do; perhaps it seems as though this person is living in a different time period. Include an image in every line. In the
   last line, have the person describe you or react to you.

2. Write a short-short story. Limit yourself to one page (about 250 words).
   Working from the lists you created in Chapter One, choose a slice of time
   and write a fictional story—perhaps simply one complete scene—in which
   two characters struggle against something difficult, strange, or surprising.

3. Compose a short memoir (250–1,000 words). Focus your mind's eye on an
   important feature of the landscape or city where you live now or lived in the
   past. Title the piece "I Go Back to _____." Walk through this place you
   know well, and list what you see, smell, and hear as you walk. You will
   notice people, but also look at specific aspects of the weather, architecture,
   plant life, and soundscape. Consider writing in the second person: "If *you*
   walk down Buckwood Drive, *you'll* be shaded by live oaks . . ."

4. Of the two main types of poetry, what kind of poetry do you prefer, lyric or
   narrative? Do you focus tightly on one image or topic, or are you more of a
   storyteller? Write a poem, just for practice, in the mode you like best, lyric
   or narrative.

5. Write a narrative poem or a micro-memoir, one or two pages long, in which you create a scene that presents the defining moment when you realized something interesting but confusing about a parent or caregiver. Or create a scene, as Adam Scheffler does in his poem "Woman and Dogs" (p. 67), in which you watch your friend or partner by actually writing about the person's pets / office space / photographs. Include unexpected objects in your portrait.

6. Write a definition poem. Choose a simple word, like *beds* or *green* or *water*. Take the reader through images from various aspects of your life so that the entire dictionary entry is a micro-memoir about interesting, odd things from your world. Notice how A. Van Jordan includes a symbol in his poem "af•ter•glow" (p. 67) and also how the definition "breaks" into a poem (the slash marks in the text indicate where line breaks would be if the piece were formatted as a poem).

7. Write a short dialogue scene in which two characters in a busy location (designated clearly by you) are talking. Each character wants something but doesn't want to say so. For example, Person A wants to buy herself an engagement ring (she has no fiancé), and the clerk, Person B, wants to ask her out.

8. Write a three-page play about a superhero.

9. Take one of the pieces you have written this semester and recast it in play form. Do you need to change the location to make it more visually interesting? Write the dialogue, seeing your characters' actions as you write. For example, if you wrote a narrative poem about a tricky parental conflict, after Sebastian Matthews's "Buying Wine" (p. 70), you could recast that piece as a micro-play, focusing on the dialogue from that scene.

10. Rewrite any of the pieces you drafted from the scaffolding assignments, growing, stretching, honing your lines, cutting out what you don't like, and adding more of what you do like. Keep the best lines, while elaborating, clarifying, and cutting. Bring your piece to class, and with a partner or in a group, discuss the questions for responding to a piece of poetry on page 50. After discussing the questions, will you make any further changes?

11. Try building a prose poem or a short story using the scaffolding technique. Use Pamela Painter's story "The New Year" (p. 69) or Vincent Scarpa's piece "I Go Back to Berryman's" (p. 65). Or choose another short-short story that you like or one that your instructor assigns. Cover each physical page of the story with a blank sheet of paper so you see only one line at a time. Write your own sentences, inspired by the ones you are reading, and, working one step at a time, slowly slide your cover sheet down the page. Read your story aloud to a partner. Does anything in it surprise you? Were you prompted to come up with things you wouldn't have come up with otherwise?

12. Choose three parts of your life to work from. If you can use another person's texts for one of your sections, as Fusselman uses her father's journal entries, your work will be even easier. Students have used texts from old friends, parents' letters, family histories, Tumblr, Facebook, and their own high school diaries. The other two parts of your memoir will be inspired by Fusselman's work: Choose wisely. For one of your topics, you might use the struggle to make a team, fight an illness, begin a relationship, or conquer a difficult project. The third topic, Fusselman's dealing with the death of her father, for you might be the fallout after a death in your own family, the loss of a friendship, a grandparent's illness, or a sibling's trouble. Working one section at a time, tell your three stories, piece by piece, sticking closely to the Fusselman model. When she writes dialogue, you write dialogue. When she writes what "the big problem" is, you state your big problem. When she has a theory, you write a theory of your own. And so on, until you have twelve short sections.

READINGS

Vincent Scarpa
I Go Back to Berryman's

All of the streets in the trailer park are named for fruits or for dead presidents—Cherry, Lincoln, Peach, Garfield—and if you walk them and peer through windows with parted curtains, you will see love being made, hate being made, bodies being discovered, bodies being forgotten, smoking and drinking and swearing and Bible reading, you will see people doing their best, and you will see that sometimes their best is *not that good,* and you will see rooms where welfare mothers rock babies and sing *If I needed you I would you come to me?,* and you will see double-wide lawns where men like my best friend's father try to exorcise the gay out of their sons by placing a bat in their hands and lobbing underhanded tosses when what their sons really want is to bring the stereo on the front porch and choreograph intricate and well-intentioned routines to top 40 pop, and you will see Renee apply tanning oil to her frail leather body as she sprawls across the driveway from where she has moved her dented pick-up pocked with bullet scars, you will see her repositioning her beach chair to follow the sun in a circle and rotate 20-20 front and back, her body so crisp and even in next week's open casket, you will see sober fathers and drunk fathers and belt-bearing fathers and fathers who hide child pornography in secret folders on their computer, you will see mothers like mine knocking over patio furniture in fits of manic rage, or mothers who hang confederate flags alongside American flags, or mothers who pray for drunk drivers and who pray for terrorists and who pray for their own recovery from afflictions of the mind and heart and body and soul, mothers who erect roadside memorials across town for sons and daughters squished between liquored tires, you will see old women whose children do not call or do not call often on hold with phone psychics from whom they seek guidance and answers but also sheer company, you will see old men who think of the rifles in their closets when a black or a Puerto Rican walks by but also when they catch themselves in the mirror or have too much time to think or drink, you will see motherless children riding rusted bikes and scooters and falling on cracked pavement, their knees and elbows scuffed and skinned like the scratch-off lottery tickets their fathers allow them at the liquor store checkout, you will see teenagers who consider themselves to be much older pass loosely rolled joints in the woods, the girls flashing their tits to the guys who ask nicely or who only ask or who simply insist, guys with acne on their backs which you could connect to resemble an outline of the continental forty-eight,

65

guys who claim they're allergic to latex, and you will see their younger brothers and younger sisters who sneak through the woods trying to find the hiding spot, and you will hear the older siblings yell, *Get outta here you retards, go home,* and you will see a pool the size of a postage stamp in the middle of the park where children are taught to swim, to dive, to walk don't run walk don't run walk don't run, where these children compete to see who can hold their breath the longest but also to see who has the most bruises, kid fears, war stories, dead cousins, and you will see me leaving the pool despite having just arrived because I'll never be comfortable taking my shirt off in front of anyone who isn't a doctor, and even then, and you will see me walk back to my trailer on Lot 252, my dry towel dragging behind me like a tail that collects gravel and cigarette butts, and you will follow me into my house where my mother is having sex with her boyfriend, you will see their door close as I take off my sandals, you will see me contemplate going to the fridge—I am so thirsty—and decide against it because the kitchen is too close to my mother's bedroom, and I don't want to prevent her or interrupt her or make her think of me, and so instead you will see me walk into my room, where I will write in my journal on a blank page: *I feel homesick but I'm writing this at home.*

Betsy Sholl
Genealogy

One of my parents was a flame, the other a rope.
One was a tire, the other a dial tone.

In the night I'd wake to a hum and the faint
smell of burnt rubber.

One of my parents was a flag, the other a shoe.

The ideogram tattooed on my lower back
is the one for dog trying to run on ice.

One of my parents was a star already gone out,
the other a cup I carried into the night,
convinced it was fragile.

One of my parents I drank, the other I dreamed.

In the revolving door of my becoming,

one pushed from inside, one from without.
Thus, my troubled birth, my endless stammer.

One was an eyebrow, the other a wink.
How they amused each other.

One was a candle, the other a bird. I was ashamed
of not burning, embarrassed I couldn't fly.

I was a girl calling across the ice to a dog
she didn't have.

A. Van Jordan
af • ter • glow

af • ter • glow \≈\ *n.* **1.** The light esp. in the Ohio sky after sunset: as in the look
of the mother-of-pearl air during the morning's afterglow. **2.** The glow continuing after the disappearance of a flame, as of a match or a lover, and sometimes
regarded as a type of phosphorescent ghost: This balm, this bath of light / This
cocktail of lust and sorrow, / This rumor of faithless love on a neighbor's lips, /
This Monday morning, this Friday night, / This pendulum of my heart, / This
salve for my soul, / This tremble from your body / This breast aflame, this bed
ablaze / Where you rub oil on my feet, / Where we spoon and, before sunrise,
turn away / And I dream, eyes open, / swimming / In this room's pitch-dark
landscape.

Adam Scheffler
Woman and Dogs

My girlfriend's dog is small and fat and neurotic
and smells at night like an African meat flower.
It loves her more than some people love anyone
in a riddle of love it worries at, lying there on the floor.
As she writes it makes strange sounds:
lickings, sighings, suckings, shiftings
like the worrying-tide of the world, like the vast
dog-tide of the world in its love of the moon
and of fetching sticks. My girlfriend is very quiet
and very white like the moon, and some people think
she is cold and uncaring just like it.
But her dog knows better, it knows she is quiet
like the sun as she writes her stories
tapping them quietly with her fingers, shaping
the messages she has heard of painful warmth
and love, quietly as a tree repeating the hard message
of the sun in its devotion of leaves and listening.

I have listened carefully to the dog. I have stolen
the dog's secret about her. I have figured it out.
She is quiet and so she writes long stories
and I am loud and so I write quick poems
tiring myself out more quickly to look up at her
as lovingly and neurotically as the dog
perhaps never as lovingly as the dog
who unlike me has nothing to prove
who does not write poems except the thought-poems
of the chase, the sky, the walk, the meal.
Sick of the dog, I have had too much also of poems
petulant, filled with strange achings,
I think of my navel which is too deep like a mine,
I send my finger into it like a canary and feel sad
and weird and know I will die. But sometimes
she tells me she likes my chest and I take her
in my arms and feel for once superior to the dog.
Before this dog she had another dog I never met, a
golden retriever, who was not at all neurotic
who swallowed her childhood happily
like a white spiral fossil and brought it back
covered with a fine varnish, fine slobber of evening
and died, and now is only a picture in a cheap frame
on the top of her desk as she writes. It makes me think
of all I can't see: the long list of books she gave me
how they existed all my life and before it
and her story right now invisible to her too
like the idea of a flower to all the roots underneath
their gossipy brags and worries: how their flowers
go blue as a nun's lips in winter, grow tall as
the spine of a young boy, unless the earth goes
upwards forever unbroken — but there she is
at least, complete, watched by the dog who is dead
watched by the dog who smells bad and is alive
watched by me, who is sick of poems and of life too maybe
but is alive and glad to look at her, at the tiny mark
on her cheek where the clamp brought her forth kicking
from the womb, to sit one day quietly in the
wound and fury of writing before the three of us
who cannot help, who wait in aches and shiftings
for her to turn round and speak gently our names.

Pamela Painter

The New Year

It's late Christmas Eve at Spinelli's when Dominic presents us, the waitstaff, with his dumb idea of a bonus—Italian hams in casings so tight they shimmer like Gilda's gold lamé stockings.

At home, Gilda's waiting up for me with a surprise of her own: my stuff from the last three months is sitting on the stoop. Arms crossed, scarlet nails tapping the white satin sleeves of her robe, she says she's heard about Fiona. I balance the ham on my hip and pack my things—CDs, weights, a vintage Polaroid—into garbage bags she's provided free of charge. Then I let it all drop and offer up the ham in both hands, cradling it as if it might have been our child. She doesn't want any explanations—or the ham.

Fiona belongs to Dominic, and we are a short sad story of one night's restaurant despair. But the story's out and for sure I don't want Dominic coming after my ham.

Under Gilda's unforgiving eye, I sling my garbage bags into the trunk of the car and all Christmas day I drive with the radio off except when I call Gilda from a phone booth by the side of the road. Bing Crosby and me singing "White Christmas" means nothing to her, so I head west, the ham glistening beside me in the passenger's seat. Somewhere in Indiana I strap it into a seat belt.

I stop to call again, but Gilda hangs up every time. After the next state, I send her pictures of my trip instead: The Ham under the silver arch of St. Louis; The Ham at the Grand Canyon; The Ham in Las Vegas. I'm taking a picture of The Ham in the Pacific when a big wave washes it out to sea. I send the picture anyway: The Ham in the Pacific Undertow. In this picture, you can't tell which of us is missing.

Sebastian Matthews

Buying Wine

When we were boys, we had a choice: stay in the car or else
follow him into Wine Mart, that cavernous retail barn,

down aisle after aisle—California reds to Australian blends
to French dessert wines—past bins loaded like bat racks

with bottles, each with its own heraldic tag, its licked coat
of arms, trailing after our father as he pushed the ever-filling cart,

bent forward in concentration, one hand in mouth stroking
his unkempt mustache, the other lofting up bottles like fruit

then setting them down, weighing the store of data in his brain
against the cost, the year, the cut of meat he'd select at the butcher's:

a lamb chop, say, if this Umbrian red had enough body to marry,
to dance on its legs in the bell of the night; or some scallops maybe,

those languid hearts of the sea, a poet's dozen in a baggy,
and a Pinot Grigio light enough not to disturb their salty murmur.

Often, we'd stay in the car until we'd used up the radio
and our dwindling capacity to believe our father

might actually "Just be back," then break free, releasing
our seatbelts, drifting to the edges of the parking lot like horses

loosed in a field following the sun's endgame of shade; sometimes
I'd peer into the front window, breath fogging the sale signs,

catching snippets of my father's profile appearing and disappearing
behind the tall cardboard stacks. Once I slipped back into the store,

wandering the aisles, master of my own cart, loading it to bursting
for the dream party I was going to throw. But mostly, like now,

as I search for the perfect $12 bottle, I'd shuffle along, dancing bear
behind circus master, and wait for my father to pronounce, tall

in his basketball body, wine bottles like babies in his hands, "Aha!"

Marco Ramirez

I am not Batman.

Sudden drumming, then quiet. Lights up on a BOY, *maybe 7, maybe 27, wearing a hooded sweatshirt. He looks out directly before him, breathing nervously. A* DRUMMER *sits behind a drum set placed in the middle of the stage, in some kind of silhouette. The* BOY *is excited, but never gets ahead of himself.*

BOY. It's the middle of the night and the sky is glowing like mad radioactive red. And if you squint you could maybe see the moon through a thick layer of cigarette smoke and airplane exhaust that covers the whole city, like a mosquito net that won't let the angels in.

(LIGHT SNARE DRUMMING.)

And if you look up high enough you could see me. Standing on the edge of a eighty-seven story building,—

(Thick steam shoots out of some pipes behind him—)

—And up there, a place for gargoyles and broken clock towers that have stayed still and dead for maybe like a hundred years—up there is *me.*

(DRUMS.)

And I'm freakin' *Batman.*

(CYMBAL.)

And I gots Bat-mobiles and Bat-a-rangs and freakin' Bat-caves like for real, and all it takes is a broom closet or a back room or a fire escape, and Danny's hand-me-down jeans are gone.

(BOOM.)

And my navy blue polo shirt?—

(—BOOM—)

—The-one-that-looks-kinda-good-on-me-but-has-that-hole-on-it-near-the-butt-from-when-it-got-snagged-on-the-chain-link-fence-behind-Arturo's-but-it-isn't-even-a-big-deal-'cause-I-tuck-that-part-in-and-it's-like-all-good?—

(—BOOM—)

—*that* blue polo shirt?—

(—BOOM—)

—It's gone too. And I get like, like transformation-al.

(BOOM. SNARE.)

And nobody pulls out a belt and whips Batman for talking back—

(SNARE—)

—Or for *not* talking back,—

(—SNARE, CRASH—)

And nobody calls Batman simple—

(—SNARE—)

—Or stupid—

(—SNARE—)

—Or skinny—

(—CYMBAL—)

—And *nobody* fires Batman's brother from the Eastern Taxi Company 'cause they was making cutbacks, neither, 'cause they got nothing but respect, and not like *afraid*-respect. Just like *respect*-respect. 'Cause nobody's afraid of you.

'Cause Batman doesn't mean nobody no harm.

>   *(BOOM.)*

Ever.

>   *(SNARE, SNARE.)*

'Cause all Batman really wants to do is save people and maybe pay Abuela's bills one day and die happy and maybe get like mad famous. For real. . . . And kill the Joker.

>   *(DRUMS.)*

Tonight, like most nights, I'm all alone. And I'm watching . . . And I'm waiting . . . Like a eagle. Or like a—no, yea, like a eagle.

>   *(The DRUMS start low but constant, almost tribal.)*

And my cape is flappin' in the wind ('cause it's freakin' long), and my pointy ears are on, and that mask that covers like half my face is on too, and I got like bulletproof stuff all in my chest so no one could hurt me and nobody—*nobody*—is gonna come between Batman,

>   *(CYMBAL.)*

and Justice.

>   *(The SLOW KICKS continue, now there are SHORT hits randomly placed on the drum set. They somehow resemble city noises.)*

From where I am I could hear everything.

>   *(The DRUMS build, then STOP.)*

Eyes glowing white, cape blowing softly in the wind.

>   *(HIT. HIT.)*

Bulletproof chest heaving. My heart beating right through it in a Morse code for "fuck with me, just once, come on, just try."

>   *(HIT. HIT. HIT.)*

And the one good-for-nothing left standing, the one with the handgun, he laughs, he lowers his arm, and he points it at me and gives the moon a break, and he aims it right between my pointy ears, like goalposts and he's special teams.

>   *(The BOY stands, frozen, afraid.)*

And JanitorMan is still calling Saint Anthony but he ain't pickin' up,

>   *(Silence.)*

And for a second it seems like . . . *maybe I'm gonna lose.*

    (The BOY *takes a breath. Sudden courage.)*

Naw.

    (—SNARE. The BOY *mimes the fight.)*

SHOO—SHOO! FUACATA!—

    (—SNARE—)

—"Don't kill me mannn!!"—

    (—CYMBAL—)

—SNAP!—

    (—SNARE—)

—Wrist CRACK—

    (—SNARE—)

—Neck—

    (—SNARE—)

—SLASH!—

    (—CYMBAL—)

—Skin—meets—acid—

    (—SNARE—)

—"AHH!!"—

    (—SNARE.)

And he's on the floor. And I'm standing over him. And I got the gun in MY hands now. And I hate guns, I hate holding 'em cause I'm Batman, and— ASTERICKS: Batman don't like guns 'cause his parents got iced by guns a long time ago—but for just a second, my eyes glow white, and I hold this thing, for I could speak to the good-for-nothing in a language he maybe understands,

    (He aims the gun up at the sky.)

. . . CLIC—CLIC . . .

    (The BASS DRUM.)

And the good-for-nothings become good-for-disappearing into whatever toxic-waste-chemical-sludge-shit-hole they crawled out of.

    (A pause.)

And it's just me and JanitorMan.

And I pick him up.

And I wipe sweat and cheap perfume off his forehead.

And he begs me not to hurt him and I grab him tight by his JanitorMan shirt
collar and I pull him to my face, and he's taller than me, but the cape helps,
so he listens when I look him straight in the eyes and I say two words to
him:

"Go home."

And he does, checking behind his shoulder every ten feet.

And I SWOOSH from building to building on his way there, 'cause I know
where he lives. And I watch his hands tremble as he pulls out his keychain
and opens the door to his building.

And I'm back in bed before he even walks in through the front door.

> *(SNARE.)*

And I hear him turn on the faucet and pour himself a glass of warm tap water.
And he puts the glass back in the sink.

> *(SNARE.)*

And I hear his footsteps,

> *(BOOM. BOOM.)*

And they get slower as they get to my room.

> *(BOOM.)*

And he creaks my door open like mad slow.

> *(Silence.)*

And he takes a step in, which he never does.

> *(BOOM.)*

Bob Hicok

A Primer

I remember Michigan fondly as the place I go
to be in Michigan. The right hand of America
waving from maps or the left
pressing into clay a mold to take home

from kindergarten to Mother. I lived in Michigan
forty-three years. The state bird
is a chained factory gate. The state flower
is Lake Superior, which sounds egotistical
though it is merely cold and deep as truth.
A Midwesterner can use the word "truth,"
can sincerely use the word "sincere."
In truth the Midwest is not mid or west.
When I go back to Michigan I drive through Ohio.
There is off I-75 in Ohio a mosque, so life
goes corn corn corn mosque, I wave at Islam,
which we're not getting along with
on account of the Towers as I pass.
Then Ohio goes corn corn corn
billboard, goodbye, Islam. You never forget
how to be from Michigan when you're from Michigan.
It's like riding a bike of ice and fly fishing.
The Upper Peninsula is a spare state
in case Michigan goes flat. I live now
in Virginia, which has no backup plan
but is named the same as my mother,
I live in my mother again, which is creepy
but so is what the skin under my chin is doing,
suddenly there's a pouch like marsupials
are needed. The state joy is spring.
"Osiris, we beseech thee, rise and give us baseball"
is how we might sound were we Egyptian in April,
when February hasn't ended. February
is thirteen months long in Michigan.
We are a people who by February
want to kill the sky for being so gray
and angry at us. "What did we do?"
is the state motto. There's a day in May
when we're all tumblers, gymnastics
is everywhere, and daffodils are asked
by young men to be their wives. When a man elopes
with a daffodil, you know where he's from.
In this way I have given you a primer.
Let us all be from somewhere.
Let us tell each other everything we can.

Amy Fusselman

From *The Pharmacist's Mate*

1.

Don't have sex on a boat unless you want to get pregnant. That's what my friend Mendi's sailor ex-boyfriend used to tell her.

I want to get pregnant. Or maybe more accurately, I don't want to die without having had children.

I was a child once, with a dad. My dad is dead now. He died two weeks ago. I have never had anyone so close to me die. I am trying to pay attention to what it feels like.

I know it's early, but I keep thinking he's still here. Well, not here, I know he's not here, but on his way here. On his way back here from somewhere. Coming here.

Of course, I don't think it's my old dad in his old body coming here. It's my old dad, in a new form.

Thinking your dad might be coming in a new form is not so bad. It's like you're always excited, and getting ready, and listening for the door.

2.

The big problem I have had in trying to get pregnant is that I don't ovulate. Thus, I don't get my period. I mean, I can go six months.

I don't know why this is. And after a million tests at the gyno, they don't seem to know why either. Everything looks OK.

My theory is that I am stopping myself from having my period. I am doing this with my brain. I don't know how I am doing it, but I am doing it. And I am doing it because as much as I want to get pregnant, I am also very afraid.

3.

Before my dad was a dad, he was a guy on a boat in a war. This was World War II.

My dad had been studying pre-med at Virginia Military Institute. He had enlisted in the Army in 1944, but after a few months they discharged him because, my dad told me, "They didn't know what they were doing with medical students." So my dad went back to school for a while, until my grandfather called him up from Ohio and said people at home were starting to talk, and they were saying my dad was studying pre-med just to get out of serving. My dad told me that's when he said the hell with it, and signed up for the Merchant Marine. This was in the fall of 1945. He was twenty-one.

My dad was the Purser-Pharmacist's Mate on the Liberty Ship *George E. Pickett*. He kept a log from his first eight months at sea. He wrote a lot about his work.

Sample:

> Chief Steward came to me today with a possible case of gonorrhea. I'm going to wait until tomorrow to see how things turn out. Had him quit handling the food, at least.

It's funny to read things like that, because my dad never became a doctor. After the war, he went back to school and got his MBA.

4.

Sometimes I think this problem with children is something that runs in my family. My brother, who lives in Houston and is ten years older than me, had a problem with children fifteen years ago. He was in Ohio visiting my parents (I was away at school), when all of a sudden the phone rang. It was his live-in girlfriend, telling him she had just had two babies, a boy and a girl. Twins.

My parents didn't even know she was pregnant. My brother flew back to Houston. The next thing my parents heard, they had given the infants up for adoption.

The whole thing was so shrouded in weirdness and secrecy that several years after it happened I called my brother just to make sure that it was true. Because all I knew was what I had heard from my parents.

And my brother had said yes, it was true. He sounded pained. My brother and I are not very close. I didn't ask him more than that.

Another thing: my brother has a job selling high-tech sonar equipment to clients like the Navy, equipment they use to do things like search for John F. Kennedy Jr.'s plane.

And another: I have always wondered if someday these kids might show up on our doorstep.

5.

I am trying to get pregnant with Frank. Frank is my husband. He is 6'4". My dad was 5'7". Frank and my dad got along. Even though Frank's full name is Frank, my dad always gave his name two extra syllables, and said it sing-song, "Frank-a-lin."

Frank and my dad were both born and raised in Youngstown, Ohio. When they got together they liked to talk about the town landmarks, Market Street and Mill Creek Park, places I didn't know because I grew up around Cleveland.

And it never came up in conversation, but long ago, even before I was born, my dad had made arrangements to be buried in the cemetery at the end of Frank's street: Forest Lawn.

6.

I want to talk to my dad, but my dad is dead now. I know we can't have a regular conversation so I am trying to stay open to alternatives. I am trying to figure out other ways we can communicate.

Right after my dad's funeral, I came back to New York for a week of visits to the high-end fertility doctor. I had just started with the high-end fertility doctor, after nine months of getting nowhere with the low-end one.

I needed a week of visits to have my follicles monitored. I had just taken five days' worth of clomiphene citrate, a drug that tricks your pituitary gland into producing extra FSH (follicle stimulating hormone) and LH (luteinizing hormone), two natural gonadotropins that encourage follicle growth.

A follicle-monitoring appointment at the high-end fertility doctor involves the following: getting there between seven and nine a.m.; putting your name on a list; waiting until the nurse calls your name; going and getting your blood taken; returning to the waiting room with your arm bent around a cotton ball; waiting for the nurse to call your name again; and when she does, going to the examination room to lie on the table with your pants off so one of the ever-changing array of attractive, resident physicians can stick the ultrasound probe in your vagina to measure how big the follicle is. You need a follicle to get to eighteen millimeters before they will give you the shot of hCG (human chorionic gonadotropin) to make the follicle burst and release the egg.

After four mornings of this, a resident told me that one follicle, on my left side, had hit eighteen. So they gave me the shot, and then the next day, I was inseminated.

And I was sure when it was over that I was pregnant, because unlike all the other times I had taken clomiphene citrate, and been shot with hCG, and been inseminated, this time I was doing it with my dad being dead. And I was sure my dad would be trying to help me out.

But the morning I was supposed to take my pregnancy test, I got my period.

7.

1/31/46: Eight days have now been spent in port at Pier 15 Hoboken, NJ. Ship still remains unassigned and unloaded. Vessel is of the Liberty type and called the *George E. Pickett*. It is manned and operated by the Waterman SS Co AT 0625. On 1/26 an adjoining vessel struck us and wrecked the No. 4 lifeboat davit. Hell of a racket. The crew is not a bad lot, but always clamoring for advances on their wages. The "Old Man," A. C. Klop, a Hollander by birth, is as tight with money as they come. There are many bets being made among the crew as to our port of destination, but it still remains a secret.

The ship is undergoing repair now, which it badly needs. Has been dry-docked, scraped and painted. All guns and mountings have been removed.

The previous voyage was to Yokohama, Japan, and lasted seven months. Some of the original crew remained for this voyage, but very few.

I am determined to learn to navigate, and study a little geography. Knowledge of both these subjects very poor.

8.

Before my dad died I saw the world as a place. By place I mean space. Fixed. Space did not move, but people moved in space. People and space could touch each other, but not very deeply.

After he died, I saw that people and space are permeable to each other in a way that people and people are not. I saw that space is like water. People can go inside it.

9.

My dad loved guns, loved them. My mom told me that when she and my dad were dating, he drove with a Luger lying in the space between their seats. Part of me chalks this up to the fact that my dad went to military school, then war. Part of me thinks he was living in a different time. Part of me isn't sure.

My father was in the hospital for six weeks before he died. When it became clear that his condition was really serious, my brother came home. One of the first things my brother did was roam around the house, searching for the guns. My mother had never wanted anything to do with them, and didn't even know where they all were stored.

My brother found three automatics, a revolver, and two rifles. He couldn't find the old Luger, though he said he knew my dad still had it.

He unloaded the guns. Then he laid them all out in a long row, on my dad's dresser:

one stainless steel Walther PPK .380 caliber automatic
one stainless steel Seacamp .32 caliber automatic
one blued steel Colt .380 caliber automatic
one titanium Smith & Wesson .22 caliber revolver with laser target
one Armalite .22 caliber survival rifle
one .30 caliber M-1 carbine

When I saw all the guns like that, rounded up from their hiding places and disassembled, the semi-automatics and rifles separated from their clips, the revolver emptied of its bullets, that's when I started to know that my dad wasn't going to live much longer.

10.

2/16/46: Well, I'm as salty a sailor as they come now. We have had the worst possible weather these last three days. It can't get any worse. As far as seasickness, I guess I'm immune to it. My stomach felt a little squeamish the first two days but it is all over now. I can eat just as regularly as on land. It is good to feel the roll of the ship under your feet, and these Liberties roll more than any cargo ship afloat, since they are almost flat on the bottom. We were having a 36° roll last night.

Had a fellow receive two nail punctures in his foot in the steering engine room. Couldn't do much about it. Opened it up and put sulfathiazole creme in it, and gave him a tetanus shot. I couldn't remember whether to give it subcutaneous or intravenous. Gave it sub-q and hoped for the best. At least I got it in. Looked it up in *Christopher's Minor Surgery* later and found out I gave it right. It's just an accident that I happened to have the antitoxin with me. I was so darn busy in port that I was going to let it go and take a chance by not having it. I just happened to be down near the WSA warehouse so I took the time to pick it up. It's a good thing.

11.

What is it about my dad being dead that I can't say it enough? That I feel like My Dad Is Dead would be a good name for my son?

That I can picture myself saying, "I can't talk right now, I have to pick My Dad Is Dead up from hockey?"

Singing, "Happy birthday to you, happy birthday to you, happy birthday dear My Dad Is Dead"?

I look My Dad Is Dead up on Yahoo! and discover that there is a band with that name. And they're from Ohio, like my dad, like me. And I can listen to their song right now, a noisy, static-y MP3 called "Don't Look Now."

12.

My dad is invisible. Everything invisible is interesting to me now. Like when I sit in the apartment we just moved into, and play guitar. When I sit here and am aware, as I play and sing, that the music is invisible. And I imagine what I would look like to a deaf person. That I would look like someone opening and closing her mouth and sliding one hand along some wood and using the other to touch some strings. And how that doesn't look like much. Just someone sitting, making little movements. Little patterns with the mouth, open close, open close, little patterns with the hand, up and down, up and down. And how the only way a deaf person would know what I was doing is because the movements are creating vibrations. And how even though the vibrations are invisible, I can feel them in the air. I can feel them, they are there, they are as there as I am.

I have always thought that seeing a band play in a bar is more interesting theater than most plays in theaters. The guitarist standing there, wiggling the fingers, and making the giant vibrations, is about hundred times more poetic and mysterious than someone in a costume saying words they memorized, words that are supposed to be About Something.

But I say that and then I also have to admit that when I am at home playing guitar and singing, I am playing and singing a song I wrote when I was in college, in a band that played in bars. And the song is called "I Love My Mom," and we played it loud and fast:

I love my mom
I love my mom
She's no sex bomb
But she's my mom
She sends me food
When I am gone
She's old, she's cool, my mom rules

I love my dad
I love my dad
I am so glad
That he's my dad

He sends me money
Even though I'm bad
He's old, he's cool, my dad rules

And on one level the song was supposed to be funny, because even though it had sweet lyrics, we played it like a rant. But on another level it wasn't funny at all, because at the time I wrote it I was mad as hell at my mom and dad, and the song was like an imitation of how I was loving them then, through clenched teeth.

And now, when I sing the song, I remember specifically how I held my dad's hand and sang it to him in the hospital, two days before he died.

CHAPTER THREE

BUILDING BLOCKS

So far, we've looked at the key habits writers cultivate in order to create their work—practicing daily, reading widely, and focusing on the image. We've examined the genres creative writers work with: poetry, fiction, flash fiction, plays, prose poems, and graphic narrative. Through imitation, you used the scaffolding, or support, provided by an existing piece in order to structure your own creations. Up until now, we have been working with whole pieces. Here, we're going to look at structure: the arrangement of the parts of creative writing that add up to a whole.

> *Dreaming is a form of planning.*
> — GLORIA STEINEM

Each finished piece of writing is made up of parts—words, sentences, lines, scenes, and stanzas. These building blocks can be combined in many different ways to create different effects. How the writer chooses to arrange the building blocks is called the **structure**. Think about what you enjoy reading the most, and you'll find you likely prefer some structures over others. Do you love long, dense, formless rants? Spoken word? Short snappy character-driven plots? Poetry that rhymes? Paying attention to the parts of a piece—the building blocks—allows you to expand your technique as a creative writer. Learning a little bit about each of the parts helps you create inventive, workable structures for your own readers. The more you know about the building blocks of creative writing, the *more* you can create.

Structure in creative writing, as in building, does its work mostly invisibly— *behind* the scenes. Structure is in walls, in the ceiling, underneath the floors. It's the framework that holds the building together, and then when we enter the grand hall, or your poem or story, our attention as readers is carried by the details, the feelings, the emotions of the experience. Structure doesn't constrain your writing; rather, it lets you create an experience for the readers so they can move around in your piece easily. In fact, if the writer has done a good job putting the building blocks together, many times readers will not even notice the structure.

> *Style and structure are the essence of a book; great ideas are hogwash.*
> — VLADIMIR NABOKOV

The chart below provides a general overview of structure in both narrative (which includes stories—both fiction and nonfiction—plays, and graphic works) and poetry. Note that many pieces you read or write don't use *all* the building blocks. But good writers consider them all as they work, deciding what they need and what they don't. And creative writers sometimes mix and match the parts, as Dinty W. Moore does in his essay "Son of Mr. Green Jeans" (p. 305) or Carolyn Forché does in her prose poem "The Colonel" (p. 185).

Parts of Narratives (Fiction, Memoir, Creative Nonfiction, Graphic Narratives, Plays, Screenplays)	Parts of Poems
Sentences	Lines
Conflicts	Turns
Scenes	Stanzas

PARTS OF NARRATIVE

Narratives are composed of three parts: sentences, conflicts, and scenes. You will need a beginning piece and an end piece of course, and a middle and stuff to happen along the way, but all the components of your narrative are built using sentences, conflicts, and scenes. Just as a house is built from boards, nails, and windows, you can arrange the parts in endless combinations. You can experiment, and not use some parts at all—there are windowless dwellings and scene-free narratives. But be aware that when you experiment (a house with no roof, no windows, no walls) some people might choose not to hang out in your creation for very long.

> *It's not how life works, I know, but I think that it is the writer's most basic job to pick specific things out of the chaos of real life and structure them in a meaningful way for the reader.*
> — DEBRA WIERENGA

We'll start our discussion with a straightforward, traditional structure, one that isn't unusual or intimidating. The short story "Cathedral" by Raymond Carver (p. 119) is a brilliant example of a well-constructed narrative effectively using the three basic narrative building blocks.

PRACTICE

Read Raymond Carver's "Cathedral" (p. 119). What are the building blocks of this story? What parts make up the story? Then read Sebastian Matthews's poem "Buying Wine" (p. 70). What are the parts of this poem?

Sentences

Sentences are the basic building block of narrative (and often of poetry, too). They are the cells of the body of your piece. Each sentence matters; each sentence needs a reason to be in your story. When you tell a story, you use sentences. When you tell about your horrible day, you use sentences to show what you have gone through. Sentences are the vehicles for the images: They show us

> *You want to write a sentence as clean as a bone. That's the goal.*
> — JAMES BALDWIN

who the people in your piece are and what they are doing. Because we are trying to help readers experience our story visually, using the five senses, creative writers rely on action-oriented sentences; action sentences are the lifeblood of narrative, the tiny pieces of mosaic that contribute to the whole.

You can use four basic kinds of sentences to reveal a narrative:

Character Sentence	Shows, through behavior, the character of a person
Relationship Sentence	Shows, through actions and reactions, who people are by how they interact with each other
Plot Sentence	Presents an action step that is going to have some consequences
Backstory Sentence	Provides information from the character's past actions and previous hopes that sheds light on the present situation

The opening sentence might reveal something about a character (how she orders a drink, plays pinball). The next sentence might exist in order to establish relationships (a mother needles her daughter about gaining weight; a young boy is kicked out of the playground by his buddies). Another sentence might move the plot forward (your character loads boxes into her car and drives off with her best friend's child; a teenager is wrongly arrested) so that the reader *has to keep reading in order to find out what happens next.* Lastly, backstory sentences are carefully chosen images from the past that give your story depth and context.

These four kinds of sentences are your most basic narrative building blocks. They are active, and they almost always make a single point. However, in a good story, the sentences may have one main focus (plot) and also be, secondarily, revelatory of character. Just as in a well-built home, the stair-rail is both beautiful and functional.

Here is an example of each of the four types of narrative sentences, taken from Raymond Carver's story "Cathedral":

CHARACTER SENTENCE:	She was at the draining board doing scalloped potatoes.
RELATIONSHIP SENTENCE:	I reached to draw her robe back over her, and it was then that I glanced at the blind man. What the hell! I flipped the robe open again.
PLOT SENTENCE:	"Get us a pen and some heavy paper. Go on, bub, get the stuff," he said.
BACKSTORY SENTENCE:	She'd seen something in the paper: HELP WANTED—Reading to Blind Man, and a telephone number. She phoned and went over, was hired on the spot.

PRACTICE

Find examples of each of the four types of sentences in Raymond Carver's story "Cathedral" (p. 119). Then revisit the excerpt from Amy Fusselman's *The Pharmacist's Mate* (p. 76). Find an example of each type of sentence in this excerpt from her memoir.

Conflicts

> *I learned that you should feel when writing, not like Lord Byron on the mountain top, but like a child stringing beads in kindergarten: happy, absorbed, and quietly putting one bead after another.*
>
> — BRENDA UELAND

Without **conflict**, there's no story. If, for instance, you tell me about your day, and it was a pleasant sunny day and things went well, and food tasted so super good, and Joey was friendly as he always is, and you got your homework done a bit early, and you found a parking place right in front of your apartment; then you got to bed early and slept quite well . . . Why are you even telling me this? There is absolutely no story. You have created *an account*. It's like reading a diary entry. It's lovely. Really, really lovely. But it's not a story.

Why? No conflict. *Narrative is a container for conflict.* Conflicts are the essential "what happens" moments, the blow-by-blow account of the complicated active emotional track of the story. You must have problems to have a story. And the problems must matter, somehow, very much. In "Cathedral," a man who is limited in his ability to be comfortable around others is forced to confront his fears when the blind man, a good friend of his wife's, visits his home overnight. There's going to be a story that arises from a highly charged encounter like that. Or when a pregnant teenager decides to take the decisions about her baby's future into her own hands—you've got a story. In Pamela Painter's "The New Year" (p. 69), an adulterous affair has serious consequences (especially for the ham). There's a story there because there's inherent conflict.

> *Learning to use that intuitive, emotional thing is important. But to understand dramatic structure, to learn what literature really is; those things are valuable, too.*
> — JIMMY SMITS

Conversely, imagine your four-year-old niece, reporting her dream. The dragons were chasing her and she fed them. And then they were chasing her. And they turned purple. And then she was hungry and she was chasing them. And she turned green! And they went to the store and there were dragons there, too. And she got chased . . . Conflicts? Well, sort of. But they don't matter because there are no implications. One event just rolls right into the next. There is no cause and effect. There is no shape. Things go on and on and on!

Conflicts are cause-and-effect situations, rendered in image, with implications for the character who, because of this situation, now has to deal. So, in a conflict, the *direction of the story changes*. There's a "so what."

In all forms of creative writing that are story based, you want to create a narrative made up of moments that give the reader/viewer a dramatic story experience, focused on forward motion.

The building block writers use in order to give a meaningful shape to any conflict is called **scene**. The four-year-old's story has no scenes—it's one long dream. Scene is the building block you use to:

- render conflict in image
- link cause and effect
- reveal the implications of these events (the "so what")
- keep the reader engaged
- contain the drama and shape the impact

Scenes

Conflicts combine to make up scenes. A scene is essentially a moment in time when people are in conflict with each other. To write a scene, you have to have three essential ingredients: time (a clock ticking),

> *Art is not what you see, but what you make others see.*
> — EDGAR DEGAS

place (an intriguing, interesting setting), and action (two or more characters involved with troubles).

We know a scene by its shape: It's a box containing a series of dramatic conflicts, delimited by time. A scene starts at a certain point in time—2:00 p.m. at Sally's Boutique—and it presents multiple points of conflict:

a. Sally is ticked off because she dyed Bob's hair green, which is what he asked for, but he doesn't like it;
b. Bob's wife is flirting with Sally's fifteen-year-old son;
c. Sally refuses to refund Bob. The scene stops at, say, 2:20, when Bob and his adorable wife . . .
d. . . . storm out of the salon yelling, "We will ruin your business!"

When you change your location—the parking lot in front of Sally's—you start a new scene, and that new scene will need its own conflicts. When you change *time*—picking up the story the next day, for example—you change scenes, and that scene needs its own conflict. Prose writers work *exactly as filmmakers and playwrights* do: envisioning their work as a series of scenes. Time change? New scene. Location change? New scene.

A scene, then, is a dramatic unit. A scene is confined to a sequence of little conflicts that build to a larger issue. The scene starts at a specific *time of day* and moves through time, ending at or just after the moment of greatest intensity. The scene usually doesn't change locations—it plays out, just like in a movie, in a specific place and time.

Let's look closely at the structure of Raymond Carver's story "Cathedral," beginning on page 119. The first two pages of the story are made up of backstory sentences. As the narrator waits for the blind man's arrival, he reflects on his wife's relationship with this man, their shared history. There is a *conflict* in the backstory—the narrator almost hears what the blind man really thinks of him, but the tape cuts off! The first two pages are not in scene—we aren't told when this reflecting begins exactly—it's just generally before the arrival of the blind man. And we aren't given a stage set. Without time and place specified, we know we aren't in a scene yet.

To find the first scene in "Cathedral," look for the place and time that holds the opening conflict. It occurs when the husband says, cruelly, that he could take the blind man bowling. The scene establishes the ordinary world of their relationship—about to be radically changed forever by Robert. Notice the conflict: This man is not connected to his wife, or himself. He is pretending to be funny, and really, he is scared to death—of alive things, of blindness, of closeness. But he doesn't know any of this. That's a powerful conflict. A lot is at stake. Is this guy, the narrator, going to ruin the visit? Is the blind man seriously going to have to interact with this rude dude? Is this guy going to live the rest of his life *blind* to the feelings of others?

That we are reading a new scene, scene two, is signaled by the words on page 122: "So when the time rolled around, my wife went to the depot to pick him up." There is a time change. The narrator watches his wife assist the blind man. And then they enter, and already the scene is saturated with conflict: The narrator criticizes, internally, Robert's beard. He hasn't even met him yet, but he already dislikes him. The wife is laughing and happy out there in the driveway. So when the door opens, there is a lot at stake. The wife is happier than the narrator imagined she would be. This is going to be much, much worse than he thought. We see he is jealous. As readers, maybe we feel something like pity or empathy for "Bub." Again, there are implications. There are things that could really go wrong here. Good authors always move us closer to unstable moments, moments of conflict, pain, or intensity. Track time and place to see where this scene ends. It's on page 123, when the blind man fills the ashtray, and his wife empties it. The narrator is realizing he knows nothing about blind people.

The new scene, scene three, begins on page 123, with the words "When we sat down at the table for dinner . . ." New time. New place. The scene runs until the space break on page 125. The climax of the scene is when the narrator turns on the television. His wife is "heading toward a boil." The blind man is very comfortable.

PRACTICE

Label each of the scenes in Carver's story by listing the conflicts in each scene: for example, "husband confronts blind man," "tense dinner with the three of them." How many scenes are there in the story? Note the start time and stop time, the setting, and the main conflict in each remaining scene.

A sketch can really help you see your scene. A sketch is your visual outline for what you want to accomplish on the page, and it can save you a lot of wasted time. Examine student writer Meghan Wilson's sketch of a scene on page 364. Notice how she blocks out the main action, labels the main character, and clarifies her setting before she begins writing the scene. Much as an actor prepares to perform a scene, a writer "gets into character" before setting pencil to paper.

There's something about free play within an ordered and disciplined structure that resonates for readers. And there's something about complete caprice and flux that's deadening.

— DAVID FOSTER WALLACE

If you choose *not* to write the bulk of your story in scenes, you risk losing your reader. Scenes break your narrative into manageable chunks. Like periods in a basketball game, or innings in baseball, scenes give the piece structure so your reader knows where he is and where things stand. And, just as in a game, where many points or only a few are scored in a given period, a scene may contain one conflict or a series of conflicts. You will want to practice writing simple one-conflict scenes, as well as more complex multi-conflict scenes.

PRACTICE

Read Brenda Miller's "Swerve" (p. 118), Pamela Painter's "The New Year" (p. 69), and Gregory Corso's "Marriage" (p. 114). Try turning each piece into a four-panel comic. You can use just stick figures since this isn't a drawing class. Divide a sheet of paper into four squares; then divide the story or poem into four key scenes. For each of the four key scenes in the piece, show the central conflict in that scene. Now try doing a four-panel sketch for a story or poem you might write.

Building Narratives Using Conflict-Crisis-Resolution

To build a series of scenes into a successful narrative, many writers turn to the classical three-part **conflict-crisis-resolution** structure.

Reread Pamela Painter's short prose piece "The New Year" (p. 69). Notice the classic story beats of conflict, crisis, resolution. Painter keeps the reader engaged with her narrative by holding tightly to the time-tested conflict model.

Here are some tips for using conflict-crisis-resolution:

1. **Start with conflict right away.** Don't start with a character alone with her thoughts. Don't warm up, wander around, or muse. Start with a battle: one character's strong unmet desire set against, and directly opposing, another equally viable character's strong unmet desire. A battle takes place when two characters have conflicting agendas. The characters must each want something, and the wants must conflict, which means something in *one person's action* blocks the desire of the other. Notice how Painter starts the story immediately with problem, after problem, after problem. Readers aren't interested in the buildup—how the family came to be, what it was like to wake up that morning. Don't preface, set up, or introduce. Plunge into problems. Throw us into the midst! Readers are interested in how the conflict plays out, and *beginnings always contain the first stage of the high-stakes conflict.*

CRISIS: Gilda kicks her
husband out. In this
flash fiction, the
crisis is in the
second sentence.

RESOLUTION: The holiday
ham—Dominic's gift—washes
out to sea. After a series of
attempts to reconnect to
Gilda, the husband
realizes he's lost.
Just like the ham.

CONFLICT: Gilda versus her husband
versus Fiona, his lover (who happens
to be his boss's wife)

Conflict Diagram for "The New Year," by Pamela Painter

2. **Build to crisis.** Start with conflict, and then show conflicts that keep increasing in intensity. The most significant conflict in your narrative is called the crisis.

A crisis is when the battle is at its very, very worst. When the loser loses, things can't get any worse in the narrative. In some large, significant, or subtle and moving way, the world as these characters know it seems to have come to an end. In "The New Year," the opening conflict is clearly between a husband and wife. The husband is the speaker in the piece, and the news of his affair with Fiona, the boss's wife, has gotten back to his wife. His wife is no wallflower. She wears shiny gold stockings—maybe she's a dancer. We know she's not a slouch. And she's pissed: Even though it's Christmas Eve, she's put all his stuff on the stoop.

Note how the crisis occurs in the second paragraph. In a longer story, like "Cathedral," the crisis comes later, when the blind man helps the narrator come to realize some important blindnesses of his own. In flash fiction and micropieces, the crisis comes early. The rest of "The New Year" is devoted to the list of all his belongings, which tells us what kind of person he is, and the backstory on how the affair with Fiona was a one-night stand, and the development of loading the car, and driving west with the ham. He tries to call Gilda. She doesn't take his calls. He sends her photos. He loses the ham. It's bad. All of it. But none of this is as drastic as his stuff on the stoop—the most drastic moment in your story is the crisis.

> *The more restrictions you have, the easier anything is to write.*
>
> — STEPHEN SONDHEIM

3. End with resolution. Do you have to have a resolution? Well, yes. The story has to stop somewhere. Art is not life. Art demands that you deliver significance to the reader. In her classic textbook *Writing Fiction*, Janet Burroway suggests thinking about resolution in this way. She lays out six choices for writers looking for ways to resolve the crises in their works:

- The two fighting forces call a truce.
- The two fighters call a truce and agree to fight again later.
- Declaring victory, the hero lives happily ever after, and the loser suffers.
- Losing, the main character offers insight into life with loss.
- The two fighters both realize no one will ever win.
- Each side thinks it has won.

Essential with any of these six choices for resolution is your ability to show *the newly changed life* of your main character (or in a poem, the speaker). Usually, in contemporary creative writing, the change is small, interior, subtle, psychological, well-observed. Also remember that you don't have to resolve the conflict itself (stating a clear winner and loser—usually that isn't how life works). You just have to resolve the *story line*.

With these concepts in mind, how do you see Painter's ending? Does the conflict have a resolution? How does the *story* resolve? Some readers see the husband as defeated. And certainly the last line can be read as a loser's insight into the nature of his loss: "In this picture, you can't tell which of us is missing." The ham washed away. Maybe this marriage's love washed away. Certainly the husband has disappeared from his partner's life. At the end, perhaps he realizes he wasn't present, in some pretty significant ways, to his wife's life. The resolution isn't overtly presented in a scene or an image but is implied. We imagine a plucky, righteous Gilda: *I sent that asshole packing.* And other readers see Gilda as the loser. She needs to forgive: People make terrible mistakes. Answer the phone, at least. Don't let your husband wash out to sea. Your personal feelings about the resolution may change as you read and reread.

Good artists make their resolutions complex, but not murky. It's good for your ending to provoke discussion, which is different from confusion. When in doubt, look back to your opening, be sure it links clearly and logically to your crisis, and let your resolution reverse something already established in the piece. Focus on the *point of the change*. Focus on the psychology of your characters, watching the impact of the battle, the conflict, in their lives. That's the key to writing resolution.

Mystery, yes. Confusion, no.

PRACTICE

Reread Vincent Scarpa's "I Go Back to Berryman's" (p. 65) and "White Angel" by Michael Cunningham (p. 335). Locate the conflict, crisis, and resolution. Now do the same for a narrative poem of your choosing, such as "Buying Wine" by Sebastian Matthews (p. 70) or Adam Scheffler's "Woman and Dogs" (p. 67).

PRACTICE

Plan out three narratives, using conflict-crisis-resolution. Always start in the middle of the trouble, bring it to its highest point (crisis), and for each of your three stories, choose a different resolution. You don't need to write the narratives; just practice building. You can plan narrative structures using words, diagrams, or three-panel comics.

PRACTICE

Get in the habit of paying attention to conflict-crisis-resolution by creating a "beat sheet." Watch any television show or movie in a format that lets you rewind and review. Create a "beat sheet"—a list of the emotional turning points. Simply make a list of the point or purpose of each scene. For example:

1. Joey leaves with hot chick; Ross jealous.
2. Chandler lies to Monica; she doesn't realize.
3. Cake flops; Phoebe distraught.

Film and television writing is highly structured, and you can learn a lot about narrative structure watching television with pen and paper in hand.

Pulling It All Together: Writing Scenes for Narratives

To write a scene, it helps to prepare. House building requires blueprints, the ordering of materials, and staging. Just as an actor prepares before she goes onstage, a writer can plan and save writing time.

Before you write, you will want to make some notes on each of the following aspects of scene. Here's a recipe you can use throughout this class:

1. **Draw the problem.** Conflict drives scenes and gives them shape and dramatic interest. (The four-year-old's dream story lacks conflict—things happen freely, randomly, with no opposing force.) As you already know, weak characters without strong agendas (desires, needs) will not generate much conflict—or much reader interest. Your main character needs a clear problem, and he or she must be *opposed* by a worthy opponent. As in football, a

blowout is not much fun for the audience; readers want a fair fight between equally matched characters. So do a little sketch on notebook paper. What, visually, will your readers watch on the movie screen in their minds when they are reading this scene? Artistic talent does not matter. But it does matter that you can see people, in action, and that the action is intriguing. For some examples of scene sketches, see pages 364, 371, and 373 in Chapter Nine.

2. **Consider polarity.** Polarity is the *direction* the fight goes, the impact of the solution to the problem, the energy of the scene. Every scene has to move from one point to another point (or else it is static and not effective). To find out the polarity of a scene (think of a battery, with the + and the − on either end), ask yourself how it starts, up or down. And then where does it go? Do things get better, or worse?

   As you sketch your scene, consider the effects you can create. Will your scene be more creative and interesting if it has a POSITIVE polarity? Or will it be more surprising and original if it has a NEGATIVE polarity? You don't want neutral scenes. You want juice. You want scenes that spark. "The New Year" moves from something very positive, the gift of a ham, to something superbly negative: That ham washes away to sea, leaving its owner the loneliest of men.

3. **Tighten up the time.** You must be clear on when the scene starts—right down to the minute. Note that time, and the day, and the season, on your sketch. You want to know when the scene ends, too. Jot down that time. Scenes in which there is time pressure—the boss is coming, the rent is due, you're late getting home and the fairy godmother is going to freak out—are stronger than scenes where time is *not* a factor. Dark is falling, the clock is ticking, capture is imminent: Consider ways to tighten the time around your scenes. Every scene starts at a certain precise time, but there should be a kind of time pressure, too. If your characters are blithely wandering through their lives, you're going to lose your reader's interest. Imagine, in each scene, there is a scoreboard at the end of the field, and the clock is ticking. Before you start writing, add a clock to your sketch: What's the time pressure going to be? "The New Year" and "Cathedral" both take place in very short time frames.

4. **Pick a place.** Scenes take place in specific, boundaried settings: a kitchen, a park, a car, a living room, a cliff. The writer must be able to see, in her or his mind's eye, every detail of the setting before she or he writes the scene. Good scenes take place in tight spaces. Your trip down Route 1 to Key West—that's not a scene, it's *a saga*, and sagas are often *boring*. The tighter

> *Structure is more important than content in the transmission of information.*
> — ABBIE HOFFMAN

the "walls" of your scene, the more interesting the scene is. The hallway, the rooftop garden, the bathroom, the walk-in freezer—as you practice, you will develop an eye for what makes an exciting scene location. To tell the story of your Key West trip, what are the three most interesting scenes you could use? Make a list of potentials, and choose the most vibrant three. You are looking for space limitations, and also keeping in mind *conflict*: At what point are the problems between people most interesting? That's how you find the scenes you need to write. The rest? You don't need it.

> *I think that as a director you have to at the very least shape the script; structure it. Otherwise you're not really doing your job.*
> — JOHN BOORMAN

PRACTICE

Read the opening scene in the story "White Angel" by Michael Cunningham (p. 341). Notice where the first scene starts—when the author writes "Here is Carlton," locating the characters in space, starting the movie. Now we see the boys in action. What's the polarity? The scene starts with "cold" and "shocks" and drugs and terror; it ends, right before the space break on page 343, with "how real everything is" and Carlton as a source of deep comfort and security. It goes from negative (death) to positive (life and heightened sensory experience).

PRACTICE

Plan out four different scenes. Using the four-pronged recipe above, do a sketch, determine polarity, anchor time and space, and list out the small conflicts that will build to the larger conflict that ends the scene. Choose your favorite and write it as a play, graphic, story, or memoir.

PARTS OF POEMS

Many poems use narrative structure and tell a story—so the work you have done in learning story structure will surely inform your poetry writing. But poems are made up of three special components: lines, turns, and stanzas. As in stories, essays, and plays, the components themselves are made up of images.

For the purposes of this course, there are two basic types of poetry: **lyric poetry**, which is image based, expressing the feelings and observations of the speaker; and **narrative poetry**, which uses images but places them in a clear story, or narrative format. In lyric poetry, stanzas may be crafted to reveal different approaches to the feeling, mood, or emotion being portrayed. Wallace Stevens's lyric poem "Thirteen Ways of Looking at a Blackbird" doesn't tell a story;

it presents a variety of ways of considering nature and life. (Some lyric poems in this book include A. Van Jordan's "af•ter•glow" on page 67, Katie Ford's "Still-Life" on page 158, and Ely Shipley's "Magnolia" on page 160.) On the other hand, a narrative poem moves through a sequence of events, while a lyric poem circles, hovers, dwells, intensifies, presenting a variety of angles or points of view. (Narrative poems, in which there is a clear beginning-middle-end in a story, included in this book are "Buying Wine" by Sebastian Matthews on page 70 and Adam Scheffler's "Woman and Dogs" on page 67.)

The parts of poems, in either case, lyric or narrative, can be put together in very free and open ways, or the poet may choose to use a formal structure, or recipe, for putting together the parts—the lines, turns, and stanzas. A poem can tell a story or can create an overall impression or feeling for the reader. The beginning writing student will want to produce free, open forms of poetry as well as formal, structured poems.

The sonnet, lullaby, limerick, and haiku are examples of formal structures you may already be familiar with. At any point, you can turn to Part Three, the Forms section of this book, for easy quick-start guides for creating complex structures in a variety of genres. Part of the purpose in practicing sophisticated structures, such as sonnet, sestina, pantoum, and villanelle, is so that you can bring more architecture and intrigue to any poem you write.

But before you begin your pursuit of poetry, it's a good practice to take a close look at the three building blocks poets use to make a well-crafted poem: lines, turns, and stanzas. These building blocks will help you write *any* poem.

A Word on Words

Place a single word on a sheet of paper. It draws a lot more attention than the page you are reading right now, covered with words. Poetry is the one place in the world where we return our focus to *words*. Tiny, simple, dangerous, mighty words. There are forbidden words. Words for which we must apologize or atone, and to do so we use . . . words.

> *I always felt if we were going in to do an album, there should already be a lot of structure already made up so we could get on with that and see what else happened.*
> — JIMMY PAGE

Words start battles and stop them. Words are very nearly as vital to us as oxygen, food, love. (Try being silent for an entire day.) And words are the essential building blocks of poetry.

In a poem, just as in a narrative, *every single word* matters. Because there are usually fewer words in poetry than in prose (stories, essays, memoir), each word has a great deal of reader attention on it and carries *visible* weight on the page because of the way poetry is formatted. The words at the ends of lines and at the beginnings of lines jump out at the reader; the words are especially chosen with deliberate care by the poet.

In a poem, every single word is handpicked by the poet to create a certain effect. Every word counts. When selecting words to place in a poem, the poet takes into account:

- the sound of the word (in a lullaby-like poem, you might not want the harsh-sounding word *ratchet*; in a hate poem, you might avoid the cute *snickerdoodle*)
- its history and connotations (*reception* has a different ancestry than the word *party*, and *crap* is quite, quite different from *defecation*; consider *television* versus *idiot box* versus *tube*; and *man-child, homie, boy,* and *dude*)
- the feel of the word in the reader's mouth (the word *spatula* is different in the mouth than the word *murmur* and creates different feelings in the reader)
- how a word interacts with the other words in the poem, especially in terms of echoes (a poem with a string of "s" sounds is going to play differently than a poem made of "t" and "d" words)

All these word choices create a profound effect on the reader—whether or not the reader is able to consciously articulate why. The effects of each word choice can be powerful. Words *always* matter.

In a poem, words provide the foundation for your piece. Each word has to be purposefully selected, individually, by the poet, just as a bricklayer laying a path chooses or rejects individual bricks based on how well they will fit the overall pattern and how sturdy and perfectly formed they are.

Beginning writers in all genres must work to avoid word packages—words that come in groups mostly through habit. *Tears rolling down her cheeks, shuddering with fear, nervous with anticipation, pleasantly surprised*—words that frequently travel in little packs together usually need to be broken up and reconsidered when structuring a poem. They're prefabricated, these packages, and so they leave the reader flat. Especially in poems, each word is to be carefully and individually selected. Poets are the most economical of writers, and any word you want that is anticipated by the reader *is already in the reader's head*. So it need not be written and, in fact, must not be. Therefore, poetry is a wonderful genre for all writers to practice, as it teaches economy, specificity, and attention to language—goals every writer seeks to master.

> *When forced to work within a strict framework the imagination is taxed to its utmost—and will produce its richest ideas. Given total freedom the work is likely to sprawl.*
>
> —T. S. ELIOT

No matter what genre you are writing in, your practice with poetry, with its emphasis on words, will serve you well. Words are the atoms of literature.

Every word counts. Look at the following lines from Naomi Shihab Nye's poem "Wedding Cake" (p. 336):

> Gold studs glittered
> in the baby's ears.
> She wore a tiny white dress
> leafed with layers
> like a wedding cake.

Clever word choices here by Nye. When you read the lines, you have a strong image of this dressed-up little baby. When you read again, aloud, and again, you notice the alliteration of "gold" and "glittered." You notice how each of those words starts with a hard "g" and ends with a "d." The sounds fairly shine in your mouth as you read. When you read "tiny white," the words rhyme inside—the long "i" sound blends the two words together. Notice "leafed" and "layers" also link through alliteration. Each word is carefully chosen to blend with other nearby words. This is called a soundscape, a landscape created out of words. We have strong images for the eye in these lines because the words are clear and concrete and simple. And we have a strong and pleasing soundscape for the ear. Each word contributes to its line.

Terrance Hayes's sestina "Liner Notes for an Imaginary Playlist" (p. 113) is a sestina which showcases a vibrant vocabulary: *DJ's PJs, hipsters, shell-toe sneakers, dope video, shambles, bullshit, jam, cove, melanchonic.* Nearly every single word is a surprise and it's the words that make this poem thrum with energy. Poets literally make music with words.

Read the end words—the words that appear at the end of each line—aloud in a poem and you'll find the spine of the poem. Some poets use only strong, hard words for their end words. Notice how Hayes chooses his end words carefully: *shambles, music, mystique, battle.* (Can you identify the pattern in his end words throughout the poem? See Sestina on page 450.) Other poets, like Sharon Olds, prefer articles—*the, an, a*—in order to push the reader on to the next line.

PRACTICE

If you can predict the next word in a poem, chances are you may be experiencing a word package. Try this: Fill in the blanks for the following prompts. If what you fill in is what most other people would fill in, that's a word package, and you should avoid placing those words together in your poetry.

Shining _____.
Eyes like _____.
_____ _____ hair.
_____ mist.
A _____ moon.
Joy and _____.
Nice and _____.
Crying like a _____.
Jumping _____.

Choosing good, crisp words is just as important in narrative as it is in poetry, but in poetry the words show up as though each one is in boldface. Words in poetry are absolutely as important *as sentences* in prose. Each must sing. Each word must stand on its own. Each word in a poem must *earn* its keep. Many poets keep in their notebook a special section where they collect favorite words for use in future poems.

PRACTICE

Read the poem "Do Not Go Gentle into That Good Night" by Dylan Thomas (p. 117). Underline the words that are fresh, beautiful, intense, sparky, interesting. How many words—what percentage—in the poem carry weight? Now read Jericho Brown's poem "Hustle" (p. 112). Underline the most interesting words. Did you need to look up any words or names in order to understand the meaning of the line? Which poem do you like better? Which one has more fresh, interesting words per square inch, in your opinion?

PRACTICE

Make a list of words you used to love when you were a kid (*infrared, Lollapalooza, TimberSkan, Donatello*) and continue to add to the list. What are some words that you have enjoyed from the readings in this textbook so far? Find ten to fifteen words this week—from your childhood, your daily life, your friends' creative conversations, literature you love—and create a poem from them.

Lines

In poetry, a **line** is all the words on one line of text. The poetic line may be a full sentence, but many poems are broken up into lines, with the sentences cut into pieces. The word that the line ends on is called the **line break**. A line that ends in punctuation is called **end-stopped**:

Strange inclusion, I know, but sometimes lyrics wear a blindfold.

A line that has only part of a sentence on it is called **enjambed**. Enjambment looks like this:

> *1945, after everyone got hip to the blues, this is the code*
> *The hipsters devised. This is what they call a mean*

Notice that a line in a poem is not the same thing as a sentence. In Terrance Hayes's sestina, reprinted in full on page 113, notice that the first three lines in the poem are made out of two sentences. The end of the sentence is not automatically the end of the line. In stanza 3 of his poem, each line is end-stopped. Compare the difference, when you read the stanzas aloud, to the feel of stanza 4, which uses enjambment in the first four lines.

Lines in poetry, like the scenes in a story, make up the basic rhythm of the piece. If words are the cells in poetry, lines are the bones. In a poem, the line has to accomplish a lot—as much as a whole paragraph in an essay or a whole scene in a narrative! In a graphic novel, each pane of action is equivalent to a whole line in a poem. Lines have to work hard. Lines have to be tight, well-constructed, and power-packed.

Lines have a polarity, too, just like a scene does. Each line has to *move* in a specific direction. Poets avoid lines that simply recast or repeat what came before or what comes after; poetry is compressed. Each line in a poem is a micro-moment. Unlike sentences in a paragraph, which can link and build and clarify and explain, a poem's lines must move from point A to point B, every time.

If a narrative is like a house, a poem is like a tree fort or a houseboat. Every line, like a board, matters. Every word, like a nail, is serving at least one purpose. Poetry isn't prose with shorter margins. A poem is a terrific, tight, beautifully crafted piece of art. And many early poem drafts are baggy, sloppy, or bulky because of a lack of attention to the line: Each line has to work hard to earn its right to stay in the poem.

PRACTICE

Take one of your pieces of narrative composed this semester and type it up, breaking the sentences into pieces. Try to choose end words that are significant to you. Try to create lines that stand on their own in some interesting way. But don't make any grammatical changes—simply break a piece of prose into lines. Which version do you like better? Does the poem version accomplish anything the prose version does not?

A line in a poem can be as short as one word (or even one letter: *O* and *I* being the shortest words we have available to us). A poet can also choose to run the lines all the way to the right-hand side of the page. Reread A. Van Jordan's poem "af•ter•glow" (p. 67). Often, this style of formatting lines is called **prose poetry**. Every word has been chosen very carefully, and the piece is not written using sentences, conflicts, and scenes. It's formatted like a narrative, yet using the building blocks of poetry: words and lines. Hence, prose poetry. How does a poet decide how long to make the lines? In free verse, short lines often make the poem read faster and longer lines slow the reader down. Poets may place the lines justified evenly along the left margin, or they might place the lines on the page in a visually interesting format. Usually, the poet is counting syllables, and attending to the rhythm of the poem. Formal verse dictates specific rhythms for many poem forms and the line is controlled by the number of beats; iambic pentameter lines are ten syllables long; the line might be made up of ten one-syllable words or a few multiple-syllable words, varying in visual length, but sounding, to the ear, quite beautiful and rhythmic.

PRACTICE

Retype A. Van Jordan's poem "af•ter•glow" (p. 67) and make the long lines into short bits only two, three, or four syllables long. What changes when you read the new version aloud? When you look at it on the page, what is most striking to you, compared to the prose version? Does the meaning of any of the lines change?

Read the following poem by Gwendolyn Brooks. As you examine the line lengths, pay special attention to the emotional beat—what *happens*—in the line.

Gwendolyn Brooks
We Real Cool

The Pool Players.
Seven at the Golden Shovel.

We real cool. We
Left school. We
Lurk late. We
Strike straight. We

Sing sin. We
Thin gin. We

Jazz June. We
Die soon.

What do you notice about these short lines? And the strong breaks after *We* in each line? How does having the same word as the end word for each line underscore the poet's meaning? *We* occurs more than any other word in the poem. It must be very important. It's likely the poet is making a statement about how important the group identity is for a young gang member. There isn't really an "I" or a self. The self is subsumed by the group. And whatever the group does—*sing* or *strike* or *sin* or *jazz*—the I is automatically doing it. The group operates as its own entity. The emphasis on *We* is so strong, so powerful, that you can almost hear a fist banging a table, or a beat of some kind. *We* matters. *We* rules. The reader may sense some of the power and excitement that comes from being part of a very tight group, and also some of the weirdness when you aren't making your own decisions anymore. In fact, your very life is shortened, harshly and suddenly, because you don't have strength of self—you gave your soul to the group. You might read the poem another way, but any reading is going to have to take into account those insistent hard lines that end in *We* after *We*. Interestingly, there is no *We* at the end. That line ends short, just like the lives of the kids described, yes? It's missing a beat. It's missing a pronoun. It's over.

PRACTICE

Retype Gwendolyn Brooks's lines into long, long lines and read the new version aloud. What's different?

Short lines can be very effective and hard-hitting. The longer the line, the more attentive the poet must be to the principles of structure discussed above, in Parts of Narrative. In particular, the poet using long lines needs to keep in mind conflict and scene, which will help keep the reader's attention engaged with the poem. In a poem with long lines, the poet typically takes on an epic journey or a philosophical quest, and/or the poet packs the poem with action and images that demand the reader's attention and reward the reader with well-observed, crafty detail and scintillating word choices.

PRACTICE

Read "Marriage" by Gregory Corso (p. 114). Why does the poet choose long lines? If Corso had written "Marriage" in short lines, what would be lost? Gained? Where do you see principles of narrative in this poem? What word choices stand out as particularly poetic, handpicked by the poet especially for this poem? Also, analyze Corso's line breaks. Are there places he ends the line that seem particularly significant to you?

"Marriage" is a young man's vibrant philosophical freak-out about relationships. He wants a lover, but he fears turning into his parents. He is horrified by the conventions that govern weddings and the whole lawnmower/apple pie/ have-a-baby trajectory. The "pleasant prison dream" that is celebrated in magazines like *American Bride* terrifies him. He wants love; he just isn't sure about marriage. The poem is a rant against marriage, a sort of purging of all his fears. Corso, the poet, doesn't hold back! He tells you everything. His fears are huge, the institutions freaking him out are looming, and the long lines—and long length of the poem—necessarily expand, greatly. Form follows function. But things aren't random. Look closely at the line breaks. Corso's end words, if you read them straight down along the right margin of the poem, give the reader a very clear sense of the beats that are most important: *fence, sky, him, dust, snow, worn, man, crib, bib, Parthenon, father, window, city.* What does this soundtrack of key words underscore? A man, torn between greatness and openness and destiny and the quotidian, domestic world of cribs and bibs and babies. In the lines, the poet is able to play out the tensions that matter most. Gwendolyn Brooks, on page 101, is concerned with lives shortened by gang membership and group identity. Corso, on the other hand, is concerned with the possibilities for individual identity, going against the norm, breaking out of social conventions. What better way to break out than to write a poem whose lines won't be contained? Also, he is worried about the deadening length of being yoked to one person, forever—what is marriage if not a *long line*?

Notice that in the lines, whether short or long, there is usually more than one thing happening. In Gwendolyn Brooks's poem, the kids act, but that hard *We* at the end points to the cost of their actions. In Corso's poem, he usually juxtaposes at least two elements in each long line—"Should I get married?" precedes a surprising follow-up question, "Should I be Good?" so that the line sparks with friction. Poets want their lines to work hard, harder than sentences. Look at the next three lines: *girl next door* is contrasted with *crazy pretentious English major clothing*; in line 3, *movies* is juxtaposed with *cemeteries*; and in the next line, the poet really packs the line with *werewolf bathtubs and forked clarinets.* A good poet attends to each line as a kind of miniature poem.

PRACTICE

Read Kim Addonizio's "First Poem for You" (p. 112) and Katie Ford's "Still-Life" (p. 158), and write a brief paragraph analyzing how the length of the lines affects the poem, and what happens in the lines—is more than one thing going on in each line?

Turns

Poetry is often called **verse**; the word *verse* actually means "turn." A key part of poetry, often overlooked by novices, is the building block called **turning**. Narratives are built out of a series of conflicts culminating in a climax; a poem is a series of turns.

When you write a poem, you don't want to go in a straight line. You must *turn* or change directions in your poem. If your poem goes like this:

I love Joey.
Joey is fantastic, adorable, and hot.
Joey and I will always be together.
Joey is great and we were meant to be.

you are not really writing poetry. You're gushing. You're kind of just blabbing. You are going, in this poem, in only one direction: You love Joey. We get it. The sentiment — your love for young Joseph — is stated clearly, but in order for it to be a poem, you need to send the reader in a *different direction*. At least once.

Notice the difference:

I love Joey.
Joey is adorable and hot.
Joey and I were meant to be.
His wife will see this someday soon.

Pay attention only to the form; emotion will come spontaneously to inhabit it. A perfect dwelling always finds an inhabitant.
— ANDRÉ GIDE

The turn takes place in the last line. The word choices in this poem are really basic and un-lovely. The lines are not well thought out — they're random. Notice how the poet just ends each line where the sentence ends. And the lines do only one thing, never two things. A lot of weaknesses! But there is a turn. The turn is an essential building block of poetry. Using turns will increase the power of your poetry.

You can turn the poem in every line:

I love Joey my baby baloney
head. And I hate like freak
him too. He has a perfect
wife. "Veronica." Ver-
onica, Hair-onica, snake woman.
I hate her more. Joey —
love me. You are bald but
you deserve more!

No great word choices. Some interesting line breaks. But it turns. Turns add drama and life to your poetry. You must employ turns. Don't write straight-line poems. Verse is twist!

To study a *good* example of a series of turns in a well-crafted poem, one where word choices and lines are also employed to great effect, read "First Poem for You" by Kim Addonizio (p. 112). Notice how the poet uses strong narrative building blocks—she sets us in a specific place, and her sentences move through time, step-by-step, as she traces her lover's tattoos. The list of steps—how she loves the tattoos—is all written in images. Each sentence is structured with *I—I like, I'm sure of where, . . . I pull you to me, . . .* and *I love . . .* Until—you guessed it—the turn. The words *They'll last* five lines from the end of the poem indicate a change in direction and call our attention to, perhaps, a double meaning. The tattoos will last until death—but will, perhaps the poet wonders, the lovers? From the "I" list that drove the first two-thirds of the poem, there's a strong shift. She uses two *theys: They'll last* and *they will still be there.* Then there's another turn: *Such permanence is terrifying.* That sentence doesn't go with any of the others. It's a long pull back, up, and out from the lover's bed. It's a strong, large philosophical statement, an insight into our complicated craving for love that lasts forever and the overwhelming idea of "forever." Cool turn. In the last line, this graceful, nimble poet pirouettes yet again—*So I touch them in the dark . . .* hooks right back up to the opening line, where she told us she liked touching tattoos in the dark. Turn, turn, turn again, and come full circle. Turns are a powerful poetic tool, one you'll want to practice each time you write a poem.

Reread "Marriage" by Gregory Corso (p. 114). Look closely at the first line of each of the first three stanzas.

> Should I get married?
> When she introduces me to her parents . . .
> Should I tell them?

In these three stanzas, Corso is asking questions about how he will interact with his proposed future in-laws. Although it's wild and ridiculous and overblown (you might look on YouTube for a terrific video of this poem being read aloud), the poem is going pretty much in a straight line so far in these first three stanzas—*should I get married, what will the parents be like, will they hate me, should I tell them the truth, that I am completely unready for this?*

The first turn comes in stanza 4:

> Oh God, and the wedding!

Up until now, the imagined horrors have been manageable, but in stanza 4, Corso *turns* up the volume. He goes over the top imagining his discomfort in a church, on a honeymoon, in a hotel. When you hear this stanza aloud, you notice that there has been a kind of key change, a new direction — Corso was worried in the first three stanzas. Now he is screaming, ranting — he's lost it. He has turned from unhappy, to freaked, to catastrophic.

Notice the next turn, in the first line of stanza 5:

But I should get married I should be good.

It's as though the music stops. He's calm again. A completely new tone of voice. A turn in a whole new direction. In spite of my irrational fears, *it'd be nice to come home to her.* Twist, turn: *Marriage sounds like death but maybe (turn) I will love it.*

There are some key words poets use regularly to indicate turns, as in this stanza and the four that follow. Words that signal turns include:

But
Yet
No, I doubt
Because . . .
Ah, yet, well. . . .

Usually a poem has at least one turn, and most often this turn is toward the end of the poem. Often there will be small turns leading up to the big turn toward the end. Practice reading to notice where the poem changes direction. It might be a direction in tone, voice, subject matter, energy level, or type of imagery. The line lengths might shift radically, or the kinds of word choices could change. In songs, we hear key changes indicating turns. In poetry, words, lines, imagery, and tone indicate turns. You can practice your turning technique by looking for similar moves in prose, too. A turn is simply a change in direction. It's an essential building block, and once you know it exists, it's often very easy to locate.

Reread the poems "Buying Wine" (p. 70), "Woman and Dogs" (p. 67), and Kim Addonizio's "First Poem for You" (p. 112). For each, find one small turn and one large turn. Compare these poems to Jericho Brown's "Hustle" (p. 112), which is a form known as ghazal. In the ghazal, there's a turn after each stanza. Do you see the turns after each couplet — each two-line stanza — in his poem?

Look carefully at each of the turns in Gregory Corso's poem "Marriage" (p. 114). What does he "turn" from, toward what? How many turns do you find in the poem? Are there any that are such strong turns, you might call them 180s? 360s?

PRACTICE

Reread Raymond Carver's "Cathedral" (p. 119). Locate three significant turns in the narrative. Then reread Brenda Miller's short essay "Swerve" (p. 118). Where are the turns? How are they signaled in this prose piece? How does the title indicate this piece will be *about* a very specific kind of turn in real life?

Stanzas

When lines are grouped together, separated from other lines, with spaces, we use the word **stanza**. In songwriting, stanzas are called **verses**. Stanzas may come in groups of two lines, groups of three, groups of four, or more. Stanzas can be huge and vary in the number of lines, as in Corso's "Marriage" (p. 114). Or the pattern of stanzas can be perfectly even, as in Terrance Hayes's sestina on page 113, in which every stanza has six lines except for the last stanza, which has only three lines. Notice how the stanzas take on different topics. In Corso, each stanza takes up a different stage of the courtship/marriage process. In Hayes, the sestina is a mix-tape created for someone (we only know the recipient of the play-list has the initial "R.") and each song means something important to both the speaker and, presumably, R. The "liner notes" for each song create the stanzas.

Stanzas, which comes from the word for "stopping place" in Italian, are like scenes in a story or paragraphs in a composition. A stanza gathers together an image or images that relate closely. Stanzas serve an important purpose: to out-line and emphasize a step in the sequence the author is presenting. Stanzas slow the reader down, help her, and guide her through complex ideas. Stanzas are the final key building block of poetry.

PRACTICE

Compare Bob Hicok's "A Primer" (p. 75) with "That Light One Finds in Baby Pictures" by Jay Hopler (p. 158). How does Hopler's use of stanzas affect your reading? What if Hopler didn't use any stanzas?

Think of the poem as a dresser where you store your clothes in the various drawers, and the stanzas are the drawers. When you put together the structure that holds your poem together, you may have to sort out what you have and then organize it. Just as you put all your socks in one drawer and your T-shirts in another drawer, in a poem each stanza holds things on one topic. You may choose to establish a pattern so that your stanzas match in terms of content and also visually on the page. Or some of your "dresser drawers"—the stanzas—might be quite large and others very slender or narrow. Some poem forms, or recipes, dictate how to set up the stanzas; you may have noticed a pattern in Dylan Thomas's "Do Not Go Gentle into That Good Night" (p. 117) and Jericho Brown's sophisticated ghazal "Hustle" (p. 112). For detailed instruction on how to write a poem in a specific form, see the Ghazal, Sestina, and Villanelle sections in Chapter Ten. The preset guidelines for how to create stanzas can actually make it easier, much easier, to write a poem.

> *The one overall structure in my plays is language.*
> — EDWARD BOND

Some poets choose to invent their own reasons for dividing the poem into stanzas and invent guidelines for stanza organization anew for each poem. You can use your training as a student of narrative to increase your poetic powers. If there is a scene or location change, or a new idea, or you are coming into your topic from a different angle, it's a good idea to consider a new stanza.

But you can play with these principles of organizing stanzas. They are not hard-and-fast rules, just opportunities. For example, if you are writing about losing someone very close to you, maybe you will decide to chop your poem up into stanzas, breaking it right in the middle of key moments because you might decide reading it, with unexpected breaks like that, perfectly replicates the experience of losing someone you love—what is more of an unexpected break than death?

Often stanzas in narrative poems are arranged in a structure that parallels classic story structure, the sequencing of conflicts moving toward a big conflict, which you studied earlier in this chapter when you looked closely at narrative. Often the stanzas build an idea by (1) introducing the central conflict or tension; (2) deepening and intensifying, complicating that central idea; and (3) building toward the climax, the highest, most intense moment in the story.

Playing with Form

Now that you have a working sense of the parts of poems, words, lines, stanzas, and turns, you can play with the basic building blocks in all sorts of combinations. While many student poets enjoy free verse, or simply writing without giving too much thought to structure, others find that having a predetermined structure actually makes it easier to come up with exciting and original poems.

Turn to Chapter Ten and explore some of the form poems there. The villanelle, pantoum, ghazal, sestina, and sonnet are wonderful forms with rich histories of experimentation that will give you hours of poetic pleasure. When you play with form poems, keep in mind that it's always difficult to read about the structure, and much easier to simply begin writing—the building blocks come together as you work on the poem.

A number of the forms in Part Three will allow you to practice the techniques presented in this chapter in depth. For narrative, take a look at Braid, Graphic, Journey, Play, and Sonnet. For poetry, play with Sonnet (especially good for practicing turns), Villanelle, Sestina (especially good for honing skills with word and line), and Ghazal (helpful for practicing stanza skills).

WRITING PROJECTS

Here are additional suggestions for ways to practice working with the building blocks.

1. Craft a scene (play, graphic, screenplay, memoir, or short story) with a positive-negative-positive conflict structure. Your main character is winning, then losing, then winning. For example, he asks a girl out, and she says she has seen him around a lot. She smiles. This is a "positive" charge for the bit. Write a negatively charged bit to follow (using this example to start, or your own) and end on a positively charged exchange, creating a scene with strong movement.

2. Write a story or dramatic scene that takes exactly the same amount of time to read as is played out on the page.

3. Watch and listen to Corso read his rant poem "Marriage" online; then write an imitation. Rant against something you are expected to hold in high value, but secretly, inside, you have a lot of doubts and conflict about this institution or value. Rant and rave about your own fears about marriage, faith, graduation, having children, getting a full-time job, or committing to someone you've been dating a short time. Freak out. Explode. Expand. Take up three pages and write long, long lines, packing them with juxtapositions. Use strong turns and group lines into stanzas by topic. Read your poem aloud to the class.

4. Write a story structured in three scenes. Use three different locales. Use a short amount of time, and keep the time of each scene brief. Each scene should have three to six little conflicts.

5. As a class, create a list of as many clichés and word packages as you can: *Lips as red as a rose, heart beating like a drum, put the pedal to the metal, busy as bees in a tarbucket,* and *hit this one out of the park.* Then craft a poem, using all of the clichés, busting them apart, and mixing and matching to create the most surprising word un-packages you can. Title your poem and share it with the class. (For example, "Her lips beat like bees as she put the rose to

the drum.") Don't try to make sense — simply play with language and surprising combinations.

6. Write a poem of exactly 100 words (delicious words) and keep it to one stanza.

7. Write a poem using only one-word lines. Make your poem at least thirty lines or longer, but not longer than one page. Choose a subject that fits this staccato structure — breakups, endings, anything that is harsh, cutoff, quick. Choose words that stand out; avoid mundane, predictable, flat words. As always, create images even with just these deft, short strokes; avoid abstract words like *love* and *freedom*.

8. Take one of your stories from this semester and translate it into a narrative poem, substituting words as needed to emphasize sound, meaning, clarity, and interest. Does each scene in your story need to be its own stanza, or do you prefer to structure the stanzas differently? Be ready to discuss your choices.

9. Read Terrance Hayes's "Liner Notes for an Imaginary Playlist" (p. 113) and write an imitation, creating a playlist for someone who is very close to you. Follow the rules for writing a sestina on page 452. *McSweeney's* literary magazine has a fabulous trove of sestinas online.

10. Make a list of the rules for narrative presented in this chapter. Then write a scene or short-short or one-act play that violates every single one of those rules.

11. Write an imitation of Brenda Miller's "Swerve" (p. 118) in which you create a scene based on apologies. Don't forget to turn.

12. Write a sestina using one-word lines. (See the Sestina section, p. 450, in Chapter Ten.) Search online for "Sestina" by Ciara Shuttleworth to use as inspiration. The formula for the order of the words is on page 451.

13. Read Dylan Thomas's "Do Not Go Gentle into That Good Night" (p. 117) aloud. Try writing a villanelle. (See Villanelle, p. 458.)

14. Write a ghazal of five to twelve stanzas — each stanza in a ghazal has two lines. Read the section on Ghazal on page 430 of Chapter Ten. Using Jericho Brown's ghazal "Hustle" (p. 112) as your model, write about a topic in which you have a lot of emotion invested — problems in your family, mistreatment, or the urgent need for change in your life — and include your name in the final stanza. Remember: There's a turn after each stanza — writing a ghazal is like writing a series of beads that go on a string. Each stanza stands on its own.

BUILDING BLOCKS WORKSHOP

If you choose to do one of the writing projects on pages 109–10, you may bring your work to class or to a group of readers. The following prompts will help you constructively discuss your classmates' work. You can use them to keep your discussion on track. Or use these prompts to create a written response for another writer's work.

1. Identify a place in the student's piece where the writing could be made more vivid by condensing the section into a bit (prose) or a single word (if you are reading a peer poem) — by doing more with less.

2. Label the parts of the strongest scene or stanza in the piece. Bracket the section off, and tell the writer what you like best about it.

3. Create a list of the conflicts in this piece, noting what happens at each pulse point (beat) in the piece. What are the three strongest, most vivid, transporting moments or lines? Which three are the weakest? Say why you believe those three points to be weak. Is it because they are not in image? Repetitive? Not presenting a new emotional hit or turn?

4. Circle all the words that you consider "packaged" — words with which you would be able to fill in the blank, given the preceding word or words. Underline the vivid, sparkly, fresh, interesting words and phrases.

5. Does each line or scene have a polarity — a movement from positive to negative, or vice versa? Label each line that does with a + or a −, and use a ? to indicate that you aren't sure or that the line does not have enough energy to move the reader from a negative emotion or feeling to a positive one (or the reverse).

6. Does each scene or stanza connect to the one before and also add new emotion or new information?

READINGS

Kim Addonizio
First Poem for You

I like to touch your tattoos in complete
darkness, when I can't see them. I'm sure of
where they are, know by heart the neat
lines of lightning pulsing just above
your nipple, can find, as if by instinct, the blue
swirls of water on your shoulder where a serpent
twists, facing a dragon. When I pull you
to me, taking you until we're spent
and quiet on the sheets, I love to kiss
the pictures in your skin. They'll last until
you're seared to ashes; whatever persists
or turns to pain between us, they will still
be there. Such permanence is terrifying.
So I touch them in the dark; but touch them, trying.

Jericho Brown
Hustle

They lie like stones and dare not shift. Even asleep, everyone hears in prison.
Dwayne Betts deserves more than this dry ink for his teenage years in prison.

In the film we keep watching, Nina takes Darius to a steppers ball.
Lovers hustle, slide, and dip as if none of them has a brother in prison.

I eat with humans who think any book full of black characters is about race.
A book full of white characters examines insanity—but never in prison.

His whole family made a barricade of their bodies at the door to room 403.
He died without the man he wanted. What use is love at home or in prison?

We saw police pull sharks out of the water just to watch them not breathe.
A brother meets members of his family as he passes the mirrors in prison.

Sundays, I washed and dried her clothes after he threw them into the yard.
In the novel I love, Brownfield kills his wife, gets only seven years in prison.

I don't want to point my own sinful finger, so let's use your clean one instead.
Some bright citizen reading this never considered a son's short hair in prison.

In our house lived three men with one name, and all three fought or ran.
I left Nelson Demery III for Jericho Brown, a name I earned in prison.

Terrance Hayes

Liner Notes for an Imaginary Playlist
(For R.)

1. "Wind Solo" by the Felonious Monks
From the album *Silense* © 1956

1945, after everyone got hip to the blues, this is the code
The hipsters devised. This is what they call a mean
Horn. High on something, the sax man wades beyond the shallow
End of a stormy sea. You can almost see him gathering mist.
The album cover's got nothing but the contours of his body
And a dangerous language you comprehend even if you can't read.

2. "The DJ's PJs" by SGP (The Stank Gangsta Prankstas)
From the album *Loot the Joker* © 1992

This is for shell-toe sneakers and warmups dyed the hottest red
I ever saw. So red it was cool. So cool it was a permanent cold.
You can almost hear Negroes freed of the ghetto, the mint
Spewing greenbacks in this song. Who wouldn't want to shampoo
In Benjamins? Even one hit and a dope video makes a mystic
Of the pauper. At the end of the track you can hear spit in a bottle.

3. "Mood Etude # 5" by Fred Washington Sr.
From the album *Blassics* © 1985

Strange inclusion, I know, but sometimes lyrics wear a blindfold.
How many violins, harps, and grand pianos constitute a jazz reed?
This is Bach according to a young man born on the Carolina coast.
This is Bach according to a man whose favorite word is "Amen."
This is Bach according to a man whose childhood was a shambles.
What if Keats heard Jazz, what if Bach heard the Blues. It's all music.

4. "Metal Face" by Glad Battle Wounds
From the album *New Battle* © 2004

Remember the Mute Trout album, Empty MT? The mystique
Of this jam won't puzzle you if you do. The way the battle
For hearts and minds sounds like the same old bullshit. A newsreel
Of tanks crushing corpses and a brave soldier in a coat
Of medals. Remember those old war songs about the Age of Man?
Maybe like those cuts this one is about being bold and shackled.

5. "Oh, You" by Marvin & the Gay Ghosts
From the album *Baby, Don't Won't* © 1987

Everything that needs to be said here is contained in a shadow.
Whenever I fell asleep listening to this song, I woke drenched in music,
The CD on repeat, my mouth filled with the meat of the bitter-
Sweet. I'd dream of my first love, then find none of it was real.
Some songs are like that, I suppose. Like being clothed
In sweat and wistfulness. Sigh. It's a tune to make you moan.

6. "Mythic Blues" by Big Bruise Guitar
From the album *The Devil's Angel* © 1924

If you're happy, skip this one. It's definitely not meant
To make you dance. Yes, the previous track was also slow. Use the shuffle
Mode if you don't want to walk the path I've left you. Called "The Mythic
Blues," this track has a way of reminding you how sin does battle
With the good in you. Saltwater is all a listener can reap.
You can see nothing but the blues even when your eyes are closed.

dear r, if anything, this cd tells you how I am sometimes willing
to shuffle into the cove of the melancholic, ready to live
among the men music continuously baffles . . . t.

Gregory Corso
Marriage

Should I get married? Should I be Good?
Astound the girl next door with my velvet suit and faustaus hood?
Don't take her to movies but to cemeteries

tell all about werewolf bathtubs and forked clarinets
then desire her and kiss her and all the preliminaries
and she going just so far and I understanding why
not getting angry saying You must feel! It's beautiful to feel!
Instead take her in my arms lean against an old crooked tombstone
and woo her the entire night the constellations in the sky—

When she introduces me to her parents
back straightened, hair finally combed, strangled by a tie,
should I sit knees together on their 3rd degree sofa
and not ask Where's the bathroom?
How else to feel other than I am,
often thinking Flash Gordon soap—
O how terrible it must be for a young man
seated before a family and the family thinking
We never saw him before! He wants our Mary Lou!
After tea and homemade cookies they ask What do you do for a living?
Should I tell them? Would they like me then?
Say All right get married, we're losing a daughter
but we're gaining a son—
And should I then ask Where's the bathroom?

O God, and the wedding! All her family and her friends
and only a handful of mine all scroungy and bearded
just waiting to get at the drinks and food—
And the priest! He looking at me if I masturbated
asking me Do you take this woman for your lawful wedded wife?
And I trembling what to say say Pie Glue!
I kiss the bride all those corny men slapping me on the back
She's all yours, boy! Ha-ha-ha!
And in their eyes you could see some obscene honeymoon going on—

then all that absurd rice and clanky cans and shoes
Niagara Falls! Hordes of us! Husbands! Wives! Flowers! Chocolates!
All streaming into cozy hotels
All going to do the same thing tonight
The indifferent clerk he knowing what was going to happen
The lobby zombies they knowing what
The whistling elevator man he knowing
The winking bellboy knowing
Everybody knowing! I'd be almost inclined not to do anything!
Stay up all night! Stare that hotel clerk in the eye!
Screaming: I deny honeymoon! I deny honeymoon!

running rampant into those almost climatic suites
yelling Radio belly! Cat shovel!
O I'd live in Niagara forever! in a dark cave beneath the Falls
I'd sit there the Mad Honeymooner devising ways to break marriages, a
    scourge of bigamy a saint of divorce —
But I should get married I should be good
How nice it'd be to come home to her
and sit by the fireplace and she in the kitchen
aproned young and lovely wanting my baby
and so happy about me she burns the roast beef
and comes crying to me and I get up from my big papa chair
saying Christmas teeth! Radiant brains! Apple deaf!
God what a husband I'd make! Yes, I should get married!
So much to do! like sneaking into Mr Jones' house late at night
and cover his golf clubs with 1920 Norwegian books
Like hanging a picture of Rimbaud on the lawnmower
like pasting Tannu Tuva postage stamps all over the picket fence
like when Mrs Kindhead comes to collect for the Community Chest
grab her and tell her There are unfavorable omens in the sky!
And when the mayor comes to get my vote tell him
When are you going to stop people killing whales!
And when the milkman comes leave him a note in the bottle
Penguin dust, bring me penguin dust, I want penguin dust —

Yet if I should get married and it's Connecticut and snow
and she gives birth to a child and I am sleepless, worn,
up for nights, head bowed against a quiet window, the past behind me,
finding myself in the most common of situations a trembling man
knowledged with responsibility not twig-smear not Roman coin soup —
O what would that be like!
Surely I'd give it for a nipple a rubber Tacitus
For a rattle bag of broken Bach records
Tack Della Francesca all over its crib
Sew the Greek alphabet on its bib
And build for its playpen a roofless Parthenon

No, I doubt I'd be that kind of father
not rural not snow no quiet window
but hot smelly New York City
seven flights up, roaches and rats in the walls
a fat Reichian wife screeching over potatoes Get a job!
And five nose running brats in love with Batman

And the neighbors all toothless and dry haired
like those hag masses of the 18th century
all wanting to come in and watch TV
The landlord wants his rent
Grocery store Blue Cross Gas & Electric Knights of Columbus
Impossible to lie back and dream Telephone snow, ghost parking—
No! I should not get married and I should never get married!
But—imagine if I were to marry a beautiful sophisticated woman
tall and pale wearing an elegant black dress and long black gloves
holding a cigarette holder in one hand and highball in the other
and we lived high up a penthouse with a huge window
from which we could see all of New York and even farther on clearer days
No I can't imagine myself married to that pleasant prison dream—

O but what about love? I forget love
not that I am incapable of love
it's just that I see love as odd as wearing shoes—
I never wanted to marry a girl who was like my mother
And Ingrid Bergman was always impossible
And there maybe a girl now but she's already married
And I don't like men and—
but there's got to be somebody!
Because what if I'm 60 years old and not married,
all alone in furnished room with pee stains on my underwear
and everybody else is married! All in the universe married but me!

Ah, yet well I know that were a woman possible as I am possible
then marriage would be possible—
Like SHE in her lonely alien gaud waiting her Egyptian lover
so I wait—bereft of 2,000 years and the bath of life.

Dylan Thomas

Do Not Go Gentle into That Good Night

Do not go gentle into that good night,
Old age should burn and rave at close of day;
Rage, rage against the dying of the light.

Though wise men at their end know dark is right,
Because their words had forked no lightning they
Do not go gentle into that good night.

Good men, the last wave by, crying how bright
Their frail deeds might have danced in a green bay,
Rage, rage against the dying of the light.

Wild men who caught and sang the sun in flight,
And learn, too late, they grieved it on its way,
Do not go gentle into that good night.

Grave men, near death, who see with blinding sight
Blind eyes could blaze like meteors and be gay,
Rage, rage against the dying of the light.

And you, my father, there on the sad height,
Curse, bless me now with your fierce tears, I pray.
Do not go gentle into that good night.
Rage, rage against the dying of the light.

Brenda Miller

Swerve

I'm sorry about that time I ran over a piece of wood in the road. A pound of marijuana in the trunk and a faulty brake light—any minute the cops might have pulled us over, so you were edgy already, and then I ran over that piece of stray lumber without even slowing down. *Thunk, thunk,* and then the wood spun behind us on the road. Your dark face dimmed even darker, and you didn't yell at first, only turned to look out the window, and I made the second mistake: *What's wrong?* That's when you exploded. *You're so careless, you don't even think, what if there had been a nail in that damn thing,* you yelled, your face so twisted now, and ugly. *And I'm always the one that has to fix it whenever something breaks.*

I'm sorry, I said, and I said it again, and we continued on our way through the desert, in the dark of night, with the contraband you had put in our trunk, with the brake light you hadn't fixed blinking on and off, me driving because you were too drunk, or too tired, or too depressed, and we traveled for miles into our future, where eventually I would apologize for the eggs being over-cooked, and for the price of light bulbs, and for the way the sun blared through our trailer windows and made everything too bright, and I would apologize when I had the music on and when I had it off, I'd say sorry for being in the bathroom, and sorry for crying, and sorry for laughing, I would apologize, finally, for simply being alive, and even now I'm sorry I didn't swerve, I didn't get out of the way.

Raymond Carver
Cathedral

This blind man, an old friend of my wife's, he was on his way to spend the night. His wife had died. So he was visiting the dead wife's relatives in Connecticut. He called my wife from his in-laws'. Arrangements were made. He would come by train, a five-hour trip, and my wife would meet him at the station. She hadn't seen him since she worked for him one summer in Seattle ten years ago. But she and the blind man had kept in touch. They made tapes and mailed them back and forth. I wasn't enthusiastic about his visit. He was no one I knew. And his being blind bothered me. My idea of blindness came from the movies. In the movies, the blind moved slowly and never laughed. Sometimes they were led by seeing-eye dogs. A blind man in my house was not something I looked forward to.

That summer in Seattle she had needed a job. She didn't have any money. The man she was going to marry at the end of the summer was in officers' training school. He didn't have any money, either. But she was in love with the guy, and he was in love with her, etc. She'd seen something in the paper: HELP WANTED — *Reading to Blind Man*, and a telephone number. She phoned and went over, was hired on the spot. She'd worked with this blind man all summer. She read stuff to him, case studies, reports, that sort of thing. She helped him organize his little office in the county social-service department. They'd become good friends, my wife and the blind man. How do I know these things? She told me. And she told me something else. On her last day in the office, the blind man asked if he could touch her face. She agreed to this. She told me he touched his fingers to every part of her face, her nose — even her neck! She never forgot it. She even tried to write a poem about it. She was always trying to write a poem. She wrote a poem or two every year, usually after something really important had happened to her.

When we first started going out together, she showed me the poem. In the poem, she recalled his fingers and the way they had moved around over her face. In the poem, she talked about what she had felt at the time, about what went through her mind when the blind man touched her nose and lips. I can remember I didn't think much of the poem. Of course, I didn't tell her that. Maybe I just don't understand poetry. I admit it's not the first thing I reach for when I pick up something to read.

Anyway, this man who'd first enjoyed her favors, the officer-to-be, he'd been her childhood sweetheart. So okay. I'm saying that at the end of the summer she let the blind man run his hands over her face, said goodbye to him, married her childhood etc., who was now a commissioned officer, and she moved away from Seattle. But they'd kept in touch, she and the blind man. She made the first contact after a year or so. She called him up one night from an Air Force base in Alabama. She wanted to talk. They talked. He asked her to send him a tape and tell him about her life. She did this. She sent the tape. On the tape, she told the blind man about her husband and about their life together in the military. She told the blind man she loved her husband but she didn't like it where they lived and she didn't like it that he was a part of the military-industrial thing. She told the blind man she'd written a poem and he was in it. She told him that she was writing a poem about what it was like to be an Air Force officer's wife. The poem wasn't finished yet. She was still writing it. The blind man made a tape. He sent her the tape. She made a tape. This went on for years. My wife's officer was posted to one base and then another. She sent tapes from Moody AFB, McGuire, McConnell, and finally Travis, near Sacramento, where one night she got to feeling lonely and cut off from people she kept losing in that moving-around life. She got to feeling she couldn't go it another step. She went in and swallowed all the pills and capsules in the medicine chest and washed them down with a bottle of gin. Then she got into a hot bath and passed out.

But instead of dying, she got sick. She threw up. Her officer—why should he have a name? he was the childhood sweetheart, and what more does he want?—came home from somewhere, found her, and called the ambulance. In time, she put it all on a tape and sent the tape to the blind man. Over the years, she put all kinds of stuff on tapes and sent the tapes off lickety-split. Next to writing a poem every year, I think it was her chief means of recreation. On one tape, she told the blind man she'd decided to live away from her officer for a time. On another tape, she told him about her divorce. She and I began going out, and of course she told her blind man about it. She told him everything, or so it seemed to me. Once she asked me if I'd like to hear the latest tape from the blind man. This was a year ago. I was on the tape, she said. So I said okay, I'd listen to it. I got us drinks and we settled down in the living room. We made ready to listen. First she inserted the tape into the player and adjusted a couple of dials. Then she pushed a lever. The tape squeaked and someone began to talk in this loud voice. She lowered the volume. After a few minutes of harmless chitchat, I heard my own name in the mouth of this stranger, this blind man I didn't even know! And then this: "From all you've said about him, I can only conclude—" But we were interrupted, a knock at the door, something, and we didn't ever get back to the tape. Maybe it was just as well. I'd heard all I wanted to.

Now this same blind man was coming to sleep in my house.

"Maybe I could take him bowling," I said to my wife. She was at the draining board doing scalloped potatoes. She put down the knife she was using and turned around.

"If you love me," she said, "you can do this for me. If you don't love me, okay. But if you had a friend, any friend, and the friend came to visit, I'd make him feel comfortable." She wiped her hands with the dish towel.

"I don't have any blind friends," I said.

"You don't have *any* friends," she said. "Period. Besides," she said, "goddamn it, his wife's just died! Don't you understand that? The man's lost his wife!"

I didn't answer. She'd told me a little about the blind man's wife. Her name was Beulah. Beulah! That's a name for a colored woman.

"Was his wife a Negro?" I asked.

"Are you crazy?" my wife said. "Have you just flipped or something?" She picked up a potato. I saw it hit the floor, then roll under the stove. "What's wrong with you?" she said. "Are you drunk?"

"I'm just asking," I said.

Right then my wife filled me in with more detail than I cared to know. I made a drink and sat at the kitchen table to listen. Pieces of the story began to fall into place.

Beulah had gone to work for the blind man the summer after my wife had stopped working for him. Pretty soon Beulah and the blind man had themselves a church wedding. It was a little wedding—who'd want to go to such a wedding in the first place?—just the two of them, plus the minister and the minister's wife. But it was a church wedding just the same. It was what Beulah had wanted, he'd said. But even then Beulah must have been carrying the cancer in her glands. After they had been inseparable for eight years—my wife's word, *inseparable*—Beulah's health went into a rapid decline. She died in a Seattle hospital room, the blind man sitting beside the bed and holding on to her hand. They'd married, lived and worked together, slept together—had sex, sure—and then the blind man had to bury her. All this without his having ever seen what the goddamned woman looked like. It was beyond my understanding. Hearing this, I felt sorry for the blind man for a little bit. And then I found myself thinking what a pitiful life this woman must have led. Imagine a woman who could never see herself as she was seen in the eyes of her loved one. A woman who could go on day after day and never receive the smallest compliment from her beloved. A woman whose husband could never read the expression on her face, be it misery or something better. Someone who could wear makeup or not—what difference to him? She could, if she wanted, wear green eye-shadow around one eye, a straight pin in her nostril, yellow slacks and purple shoes, no matter. And then to slip off into death, the blind man's hand on her hand, his blind eyes streaming tears—I'm imagining now—her last thought maybe this: that he never even knew what she looked like, and she on an express to the grave. Robert was left with a small insurance policy and half of a twenty-peso Mexican coin. The other half of the coin went into the box with her. Pathetic.

lowered his head. My wife looked at me, her mouth agape. "Pray the phone won't ring and the food doesn't get cold," I said.

We dug in. We ate everything there was to eat on the table. We ate like there was no tomorrow. We didn't talk. We ate. We scarfed. We grazed that table. We were into serious eating. The blind man had right away located his foods, he knew just where everything was on his plate. I watched with admiration as he used his knife and fork on the meat. He'd cut two pieces of meat, fork the meat into his mouth, and then go all out for the scalloped potatoes, the beans next, and then he'd tear off a hunk of buttered bread and eat that. He'd follow this up with a big drink of milk. It didn't seem to bother him to use his fingers once in a while, either.

We finished everything, including half a strawberry pie. For a few moments, we sat as if stunned. Sweat beaded on our faces. Finally, we got up from the table and left the dirty plates. We didn't look back. We took ourselves into the living room and sank into our places again. Robert and my wife sat on the sofa. I took the big chair. We had us two or three more drinks while they talked about the major things that had come to pass for them in the past ten years. For the most part, I just listened. Now and then I joined in. I didn't want him to think I'd left the room, and I didn't want her to think I was feeling left out. They talked of things that had happened to them — to them! — these past ten years. I waited in vain to hear my name on my wife's sweet lips: "And then my dear husband came into my life" — something like that. But I heard nothing of the sort. More talk of Robert. Robert had done a little of everything, it seemed, a regular blind jack-of-all-trades. But most recently he and his wife had had an Amway distributor-ship, from which, I gathered, they'd earned their living, such as it was. The blind man was also a ham radio operator. He talked in his loud voice about conversations he'd had with fellow operators in Guam, in the Philippines, in Alaska, and even in Tahiti. He said he'd have a lot of friends there if he ever wanted to go visit those places. From time to time, he'd turn his blind face toward me, put his hand under his beard, ask me something. How long had I been in my present position? (Three years.) Did I like my work? (I didn't.) Was I going to stay with it? (What were the options?) Finally, when I thought he was beginning to run down, I got up and turned on the TV.

My wife looked at me with irritation. She was heading toward a boil. Then she looked at the blind man and said, "Robert, do you have a TV?"

The blind man said, "My dear, I have two TVs. I have a color set and a black-and-white thing, an old relic. It's funny, but if I turn the TV on, and I'm always turning it on, I turn on the color set. It's funny, don't you think?"

I didn't know what to say to that. I had absolutely nothing to say to that. No opinion. So I watched the news program and tried to listen to what the announcer was saying.

"This is a color TV," the blind man said. "Don't ask me how, but I can tell."

"We traded up a while ago," I said.

The blind man had another taste of his drink. He lifted his beard, sniffed it, and let it fall. He leaned forward on the sofa. He positioned his ashtray on the coffee table, then put the lighter to his cigarette. He leaned back on the sofa and crossed his legs at the ankles.

My wife covered her mouth, and then she yawned. She stretched. She said, "I think I'll go upstairs and put on my robe. I think I'll change into something else. Robert, you make yourself comfortable," she said.

"I'm comfortable," the blind man said.

"I want you to feel comfortable in this house," she said.

"I am comfortable," the blind man said.

After she'd left the room, he and I listened to the weather report and then to the sports roundup. By that time, she'd been gone so long I didn't know if she was going to come back. I thought she might have gone to bed. I wished she'd come back downstairs. I didn't want to be left alone with a blind man. I asked him if he wanted another drink, and he said sure. Then I asked if he wanted to smoke some dope with me. I said I'd just rolled a number. I hadn't, but I planned to do so in about two shakes.

"I'll try some with you," he said.

"Damn right," I said. "That's the stuff."

I got our drinks and sat down on the sofa with him. Then I rolled us two fat numbers. I lit one and passed it. I brought it to his fingers. He took it and inhaled.

"Hold it as long as you can," I said. I could tell he didn't know the first thing.

My wife came back downstairs wearing her pink robe and her pink slippers.

"What do I smell?" she said.

"We thought we'd have us some cannabis," I said.

My wife gave me a savage look. Then she looked at the blind man and said, "Robert, I didn't know you smoked."

He said, "I do now, my dear. There's a first time for everything. But I don't feel anything yet."

"This stuff is pretty mellow," I said. "This stuff is mild. It's dope you can reason with," I said. "It doesn't mess you up."

"Not much it doesn't, bub," he said, and laughed.

My wife sat on the sofa between the blind man and me. I passed her the number. She took it and toked and then passed it back to me. "Which way is this going?" she said. Then she said, "I shouldn't be smoking this. I can hardly keep my eyes open as it is. That dinner did me in. I shouldn't have eaten so much."

"It was the strawberry pie," the blind man said. "That's what did it," he said, and he laughed his big laugh. Then he shook his head.

"There's more strawberry pie," I said.

"Do you want some more, Robert?" my wife said.

"Maybe in a little while," he said.

We gave our attention to the TV. My wife yawned again. She said, "Your bed is made up when you feel like going to bed, Robert. I know you must have had a long day. When you're ready to go to bed, say so." She pulled his arm. "Robert?"

He came to and said, "I've had a real nice time. This beats tapes, doesn't it?"

I said, "Coming at you," and I put the number between his fingers. He inhaled, held the smoke, and then let it go. It was like he'd been doing it since he was nine years old.

"Thanks, bub," he said. "But I think this is all for me. I think I'm beginning to feel it," he said. He held the burning roach out for my wife.

"Same here," she said. "Ditto. Me, too." She took the roach and passed it to me. "I may just sit here for a while between you two guys with my eyes closed. But don't let me bother you, okay? Either one of you. If it bothers you, say so. Otherwise, I may just sit here with my eyes closed until you're ready to go to bed," she said. "Your bed's made up, Robert, when you're ready. It's right next to our room at the top of the stairs. We'll show you up when you're ready. You wake me up now, you guys, if I fall asleep." She said that and then she closed her eyes and went to sleep.

The news program ended. I got up and changed the channel. I sat back down on the sofa. I wished my wife hadn't pooped out. Her head lay across the back of the sofa, her mouth open. She'd turned so that her robe had slipped away from her legs, exposing a juicy thigh. I reached to draw her robe back over her, and it was then that I glanced at the blind man. What the hell! I flipped the robe open again.

"You say when you want some strawberry pie," I said.

"I will," he said.

I said, "Are you tired? Do you want me to take you up to your bed? Are you ready to hit the hay?"

"Not yet," he said. "No, I'll stay up with you, bub. If that's all right. I'll stay up until you're ready to turn in. We haven't had a chance to talk. Know what I mean? I feel like me and her monopolized the evening." He lifted his beard and he let it fall. He picked up his cigarettes and his lighter.

"That's all right," I said. Then I said, "I'm glad for the company."

And I guess I was. Every night I smoked dope and stayed up as long as I could before I fell asleep. My wife and I hardly ever went to bed at the same time. When I did go to sleep, I had these dreams. Sometimes I'd wake up from one of them, my heart going crazy.

Something about the church and the Middle Ages was on the TV. Not your run-of-the-mill TV fare. I wanted to watch something else. I turned to the other channels. But there was nothing on them, either. So I turned back to the first channel and apologized.

"Bub, it's all right," the blind man said. "It's fine with me. Whatever you want to watch is okay. I'm always learning something. Learning never ends. It won't hurt me to learn something tonight. I got ears," he said.

We didn't say anything for a time. He was leaning forward with his head turned at me, his right ear aimed in the direction of the set. Very disconcerting. Now and then his eyelids drooped and then they snapped open again. Now and then he put his fingers into his beard and tugged, like he was thinking about something he was hearing on the television.

On the screen, a group of men wearing cowls was being set upon and tormented by men dressed in skeleton costumes and men dressed as devils. The men dressed as devils wore devil masks, horns, and long tails. This pageant was part of a procession. The Englishman who was narrating the thing said it took place in Spain once a year. I tried to explain to the blind man what was happening.

"Skeletons," he said. "I know about skeletons," he said, and he nodded.

The TV showed this one cathedral. Then there was a long, slow look at another one. Finally, the picture switched to the famous one in Paris, with its flying buttresses and its spires reaching up to the clouds. The camera pulled away to show the whole of the cathedral rising above the skyline.

There were times when the Englishman who was telling the thing would shut up, would simply let the camera move around over the cathedrals. Or else the camera would tour the countryside, men in fields walking behind oxen. I waited as long as I could. Then I felt I had to say something. I said, "They're showing the outside of this cathedral now. Gargoyles. Little statues carved to look like monsters. Now I guess they're in Italy. Yeah, they're in Italy. There's paintings on the walls of this one church."

"Are those fresco paintings, bub?" he asked, and he sipped from his drink.

I reached for my glass. But it was empty. I tried to remember what I could remember. "You're asking me are those frescoes?" I said. "That's a good question. I don't know."

The camera moved to a cathedral outside Lisbon. The differences in the Portuguese cathedral compared with the French and Italian were not that great. But they were there. Mostly the interior stuff. Then something occurred to me, and I said, "Something has occurred to me. Do you have any idea what a cathedral is? What they look like, that is? Do you follow me? If somebody says cathedral to you, do you have any notion what they're talking about? Do you know the difference between that and a Baptist church, say?"

He let the smoke dribble from his mouth. "I know they took hundreds of workers fifty or a hundred years to build," he said. "I just heard the man say that, of course. I know generations of the same families worked on a cathedral. I heard him say that, too. The men who began their life's work on them, they never lived to see the completion of their work. In that wise, bub, they're no different from the rest of us, right?" He laughed. Then his eyelids drooped again. His head nodded. He seemed to be snoozing. Maybe he was imagining himself in Portugal. The TV was showing another cathedral now. This one was in Germany. The Englishman's voice droned on. "Cathedrals," the blind man said. He sat up and rolled his head back and forth. "If you want the truth, bub, that's about all I know. What I just said. What I heard him say. But maybe you could describe one to me? I wish you'd do it. I'd like that. If you want to know, I really don't have a good idea."

I stared hard at the shot of the cathedral on the TV. How could I even begin to describe it? But say my life depended on it. Say my life was being threatened by an insane guy who said I had to do it or else.

I stared some more at the cathedral before the picture flipped off into the countryside. There was no use. I turned to the blind man and said, "To begin with, they're very tall." I was looking around the room for clues. "They reach way up. Up and up. Toward the sky. They're so big, some of them, they have to have these supports. To help hold them up, so to speak. These supports are called buttresses. They remind me of viaducts, for some reason. But maybe you don't know viaducts, either? Sometimes the cathedrals have devils and such carved into the front. Sometimes lords and ladies. Don't ask me why this is," I said.

He was nodding. The whole upper part of his body seemed to be moving back and forth.

"I'm not doing so good, am I?" I said.

He stopped nodding and leaned forward on the edge of the sofa. As he listened to me, he was running his fingers through his beard. I wasn't getting through to him, I could see that. But he waited for me to go on just the same. He nodded, like he was trying to encourage me. I tried to think what else to say. "They're really big," I said. "They're massive. They're built of stone. Marble, too, sometimes. In those olden days, when they built cathedrals, men wanted to be close to God. In those olden days, God was an important part of everyone's life. You could tell this from their cathedral-building. I'm sorry," I said, "but it looks like that's the best I can do for you. I'm just no good at it."

"That's all right, bub," the blind man said. "Hey, listen. I hope you don't mind my asking you. Can I ask you something? Let me ask you a simple question, yes or no. I'm just curious and there's no offense. You're my host. But let me ask if you are in any way religious? You don't mind my asking?"

I shook my head. He couldn't see that, though. A wink is the same as a nod to a blind man. "I guess I don't believe in it. In anything. Sometimes it's hard. You know what I'm saying?"

"Sure, I do," he said.

"Right," I said.

The Englishman was still holding forth. My wife sighed in her sleep. She drew a long breath and went on with her sleeping.

"You'll have to forgive me," I said. "But I can't tell you what a cathedral looks like. It just isn't in me to do it. I can't do any more than I've done."

The blind man sat very still, his head down, as he listened to me.

I said, "The truth is, cathedrals don't mean anything special to me. Nothing. Cathedrals. They're something to look at on late-night TV. That's all they are."

It was then that the blind man cleared his throat. He brought something up. He took a handkerchief from his back pocket. Then he said, "I get it, bub. It's okay. It happens. Don't worry about it," he said. "Hey, listen to me. Will you do me a favor? I got an idea. Why don't you find us some heavy paper? And a pen. We'll do something. We'll draw one together. Get us a pen and some heavy paper. Go on, bub, get the stuff," he said.

So I went upstairs. My legs felt like they didn't have any strength in them. They felt like they did after I'd done some running. In my wife's room, I looked around. I found some ballpoints in a little basket on her table. And then I tried to think where to look for the kind of paper he was talking about.

Downstairs, in the kitchen, I found a shopping bag with onion skins in the bottom of the bag. I emptied the bag and shook it. I brought it into the living room and sat down with it near his legs. I moved some things, smoothed the wrinkles from the bag, spread it out on the coffee table.

The blind man got down from the sofa and sat next to me on the carpet.

He ran his fingers over the paper. He went up and down the sides of the paper. The edges, even the edges. He fingered the corners.

"All right," he said. "All right, let's do her."

He found my hand, the hand with the pen. He closed his hand over my hand. "Go ahead, bub, draw," he said. "Draw. You'll see. I'll follow along with you. It'll be okay. Just begin now like I'm telling you. You'll see. Draw," the blind man said.

So I began. First I drew a box that looked like a house. It could have been the house I lived in. Then I put a roof on it. At either end of the roof, I drew spires. Crazy.

"Swell," he said. "Terrific. You're doing fine," he said. "Never thought anything like this could happen in your lifetime, did you, bub? Well, it's a strange life, we all know that. Go on now. Keep it up."

I put in windows with arches. I drew flying buttresses. I hung great doors. I couldn't stop. The TV station went off the air. I put down the pen and closed and opened my fingers. The blind man felt around over the paper. He moved the tips of his fingers over the paper, all over what I had drawn, and he nodded.

"Doing fine," the blind man said.

I took up the pen again, and he found my hand. I kept at it. I'm no artist. But I kept drawing just the same.

My wife opened up her eyes and gazed at us. She sat up on the sofa, her robe hanging open. She said, "What are you doing? Tell me, I want to know."

I didn't answer her.

The blind man said, "We're drawing a cathedral. Me and him are working on it. Press hard," he said to me. "That's right. That's good," he said. "Sure. You got it, bub. I can tell. You didn't think you could. But you can, can't you? You're cooking with gas now. You know what I'm saying? We're going to really have us something here in a minute. How's the old arm?" he said. "Put some people in there now. What's a cathedral without people?"

My wife said, "What's going on? Robert, what are you doing? What's going on?"

"It's all right," he said to her. "Close your eyes now," the blind man said to me.

I did it. I closed them just like he said.

"Are they closed?" he said. "Don't fudge."

"They're closed," I said.

"Keep them that way," he said. He said, "Don't stop now. Draw."

So we kept on with it. His fingers rode my fingers as my hand went over the paper. It was like nothing else in my life up to now.

Then he said, "I think that's it. I think you got it," he said. "Take a look. What do you think?"

But I had my eyes closed. I thought I'd keep them that way for a little longer. I thought it was something I ought to do.

"Well?" he said. "Are you looking?"

My eyes were still closed. I was in my house. I knew that. But I didn't feel like I was inside anything.

"It's really something," I said.

STRATEGIES

Exercise the writing muscle every day, even if it is only a letter, notes, a title list, a character sketch, a journal entry. Writers are like dancers, like athletes. Without that exercise, the muscles seize up.

JANE YOLEN

Night-time is when I brainstorm; last thing, when the family's asleep and I'm alone, I think about the next day's writing and plan a strategy for my assault on the blank page.

ATHOL FUGARD

Writing has laws of perspective, of light and shade just as painting does, or music. If you are born knowing them, fine. If not, learn them. Then rearrange the rules to suit yourself.

TRUMAN CAPOTE

CHAPTER FOUR

IMAGES

Creative writing relies on **images**: three-dimensional mental pictures that inspire thoughts and feelings, movies in the reader's mind. As writers, that's what we are always trying to make happen in our reader's brain — a sustained *moving picture* that's real, visual, sensory, and alive, just like a dream is.

THE PRINCIPLES OF IMAGES

We all access these images — the alive, moving picture in our mind's eye — when we read, play, write creatively, or dream. When we listen to our friend tell a story, we may be able to see, in our mind's eye, the people and situation she's talking about. When children play, they are hooked into a live image. They are not pretending they are riding a horse. They *are* riding a horse; they can feel its reins, sense its warmth, hear it whinny. The story as it plays out on our mental movie screen is physical; it's entirely real. Using images — creating live mini-movies for your reader — is your most essential go-to strategy as a writer.

Your most powerful images will be those that *activate* the five senses. If asked, you could tell me what the desk chair you are sitting in right now feels like, what it smells like, what sound it makes when you drag it across a tile floor. You could actually feel what it's like to touch the horse if you wanted to. Your images will have sound, dialogue, visuals, textures, tastes, and smells. And your reader will experience your work as though it's alive.

> *The book is a thing in itself, and it is not me. There is no ego in it. I am glad that you sense that while I am in it and of it, I am not the book. It is much more than I am. The pictures have come to me out of some hugeness and sometimes they have startled me. But I am glad of them.*
> — JOHN STEINBECK

Images Are Active

Creative writing, at its core, uses people in action to create a powerful moving picture made inside another person's head when that person simply *reads words on a page*. Images are bundles of memory, emotion, action, physical details, and dialogue, put together smoothly for the reader to experience being transported fully into your world. In an image, everything happens at once, providing a rich, seamless experience. The reader is *there*. This is the essential difference — moving images — between what we call "creative" writing and other kinds of writing. Creative writing is writing that triggers a living, moving picture in your audience's brain.

PRACTICE

Listen to Jenifer Hixson read aloud her memoir, "Where There's Smoke," easily found online at The Moth. As you listen, notice what you see in your mind's eye. Now go through the piece, which begins on page 162, and see what you can determine about how she creates the moving image. What does she do or not do to enable her audience to *see*, to "be there"?

> *My task is to make you hear, feel, and see. That and no more, and that is everything.*
> — JOSEPH CONRAD

When we read history or criticism or a book on how to rebuild our engine block, we respond with very different mental strategies. History and other kinds of writing require intellectual work on the part of the reader; the writing is abstract, analytical, and thought-based. In creative writing, we dwell in the sensory, moving, living image. Art makes meaning not with ideas and concepts, but with pictures.

Reading Is Image Viewing

Read the following excerpts, or, if you can, have someone read them aloud to you while you close your eyes. As you read, concentrate on the picture in your head. What do you see? When there isn't a picture in your head, what *is* happening? Can you break down the different ways in which parts of your mind are activated? Can you isolate the "thinking" mind versus the "seeing" mind versus the "experiencing" mind?

Go slowly. Reading this way takes a lot of focus and a little practice. You are trying to watch what happens in your mind as you read.

1

I've never met, or personally known, anyone who was blind. This blind man was late forties, a heavy-set, balding man with stooped shoulders, as if he carried a great weight there. He wore brown slacks, brown shoes, a light-brown shirt, a tie, a sports coat. Spiffy. He also had this full beard. But he didn't use a cane and he didn't wear dark glasses. I'd always thought dark glasses were a must for the blind. Fact was, I wished he had a pair. At first glance, his eyes looked like anyone else's eyes. But if you looked close, there was something different about them. Too much white in the iris, for one thing, and the pupils seemed to move around in the sockets without his knowing it or being able to stop it. Creepy.

— RAYMOND CARVER, "Cathedral"

2

Will was on the station platform, leaning against a baggage truck. He had a duffle bag between his shoes and a plastic cup of coffee in his mittened hand. He seemed to have put on weight, girlishly, through the hips, and his face looked thicker to me, from temple to temple. His gold-rimmed spectacles looked too small.

My mother stopped in an empty cab lane, and I got out and called to Will.

— MARY ROBISON, "Pretty Ice"

3

In the cul-de-sac shaded
by trees, Marissa and I
played all summer where magnolias
hung, hands withering over us

— ELY SHIPLEY, "Magnolia"

4

He sat cross-legged, weeping on the steps
when Mom unlocked and opened the front door.
  O God, he said. *O God.*
    He wants to kill me, Mom.

— NATALIE DIAZ, "My Brother at 3 a.m."

Which of the passages above created the most vivid moving picture in your mind? What or whom do you remember "seeing"? One of the best ways to read as a writer is to actively notice: What *did* you see as you read?

Read again. Read the four passages a second or third or fourth time. Watch, again, for any images to flash in your mind's eye. Practice reading with an awareness of what it is you are "flashing on" as you read. This takes concentration: the exact same kind of concentration you will practice as you write.

Practice reading to try to notice the difference between *knowing* and *seeing*. They are two different

> *You can observe a lot by just watching.*
> — YOGI BERRA

ways for the mind to apprehend information. Report writing explains: "My mother confronted me about the drinking" or "My kid's coach was an amazing lecturer." Most writing tells or reports information. Nothing wrong with that at all, but it's very different from what we do. We create images, and creative writing shows instead of telling. A mother walks her daughter down to the pond. It's a beautiful day. The daughter has a hangover; she is practically tiptoeing. The mother brings up the forbidden topic; this is the day she says out loud what no one has said out loud: "You have a drinking problem." Boom. There's an image, and it's alive, moving. "You can't teach speed," the coach told our family. We were all huddled in the cold. My little brother was zipping down the field, truly that kid was a blur of blue. "*You can't teach speed.*" Creative writing works—and powerfully so—in images.

PRACTICE

Try tracking images. Write out what you see in your mind's eye when you read the four excerpts on pages 134–35. Be as careful and specific as you can—jot down what you flash on as you read. Either in class or at home, compare responses with a partner. If there is a lot of variety in what's seen in these images by other readers, discuss why.

An image is a container with action inside it. Notice that all of the image examples on pages 134–35 have a few ingredients in common:

- Two people (a man meeting a blind man, a girlfriend picking up her boyfriend, two childhood friends playing together, a mother confronting a son in trouble)
- People (entities) doing things, active things. If they are thinking, the thoughts are active, rich, specific, detailed, and action-oriented. (The girlfriend notices her boyfriend has changed *a lot* since she last saw him.)
- A specific moment in time that bounds, or frames, the image—a living room, a train station platform, a lawn, a doorstep

Every mind is different. Each person's set of experiences is different, so the picture you see will vary from your teacher's, your friend's, the author's. Reading is viewing, and every viewer is a little bit different; we all come from different families, different backgrounds, different cultures, different experiences. If you grew up in the southern United States, you may have a very specific image of those magnolia trees and their creepy hands. If you have picked people up at a train station or been in a long-distance relationship, you'll view "Pretty Ice" slightly differently than will someone who hasn't had those experiences. If you have never seen a blind man or thought much about blindness, you may not "see" clear-cut images when you read Raymond Carver's passage. You may only have a general sense of what he is talking about. Our job as writers is to create a living, moving image and to trust that what comes to life in the reader's mind is fairly close to what we had in mind.

Try to notice this—when you are skimming over a passage, and when your brain is working in image mode. You want to notice the writing techniques that make you *see in images as you read*.

The more you read, though, the more wide-ranging your transporting experiences will be. If you don't see a lot right away, keep practicing. The more images you expose your brain to, the more perceptive you will become. A side benefit of this practice: You will see more nuances in real-life situations, too. Dating, job interviews, interactions with teachers and parents—you'll be reading them all as a writer does, alert and attentive to the little gestures and actions and specifics that reveal the inner lives and fascinating aspects of your subjects.

> *The culture is telling you to hurry, while the art tells you to take your time. Always listen to the art.*
> — JUNOT DÍAZ

Images Are the Opposite of Thought

Let's define *thought* as any nonvisual mental activity. Images are the *opposite* of thought.

Most beginning writers *overwrite* the thoughts in their first drafts and *underwrite* the images. Not surprising. Writing instruction in school, up until now, usually has been limited to a focus on essays—thinking pieces. Many of us haven't had encouragement or support or training in trusting our eyes and writing what is seen, *not* what is thought or felt. Many new writers don't trust their eyes to get the job done; they forget how potent reading is and how creative the human brain is—your reader *is* going to see it, and get it, and understand many layers of feeling and thought, without your interrupting the flow to explain. In fact, most students who have been trained to use their eyes are athletes and visual artists. But using your vision is extremely vital for your work as a creative writer as well; images are your most essential strategy.

You might try to exaggerate in the opposite direction. Try to *overwrite* the images. Try to be too visual, too sensory. Get your audience to say to you, "I can see this too clearly! This is too vivid!"

You are likely very, very good at writing thoughts; most anyone who survived high school has been trained to write this way—telling instead of showing, explaining and reporting instead of creating word pictures and movies with language. It might even feel uncomfortable to *not* write thoughts. Creative writers constantly have to work against that comfort zone. In all your other classes this year, you

> *Nothing exists in the intellect that has not first gone through the senses.*
> — PLUTARCH

should be *thinking.* But not when you sit down to write creatively. In this class, in this kind of writing, you work with your eyes. Here, you are practicing *transporting yourself to another place and seeing.* Thoughts suck the drama and the richness out of your writing. They keep everything juicy and hot offstage. Thoughts are filters, middlemen. The writer's job is to make it easy for the reader to see.

There is an enormous difference between thinking "My mother is sitting" and seeing your mom, plunked down in the old red chair. Practice now. Do it as a thought. Mother in chair. Pure intellect, just the concept—do not let your mind see a picture. Then do it as an image. See your mother in a specific chair, in a room, with light coming in the window, right in her eyes . . . see the difference? We are trying to avoid the first mental action and focus our attention and energy on the second. The second practice, that's the real thing.

The basic unit for creative writing is this image, this alive word picture. The

> *It is not sufficient that what one paints should be made visible. It must be made tangible.*
> — GEORGES BRAQUE

ability you have as a writer to create these living word pictures in your reader's head is where the magic and transformative power of our craft resides. As creative writers, we don't want our readers to just sit back and hear our thoughts. We want them to see and feel. If your work comes from thoughts, it might be great writing, but it won't be what we call creative writing.

For example, in an essay (writing that may well be creative but isn't what we are doing in this course), you might write, "The Pueblo method of divorce can be as simple as this: A woman leaves her husband's moccasins on the doorstep. And it's over." In creative writing, using images, you want your reader to have the weight of those shoes, to be able to imagine the house, the marriage, the sky, the pain of the divorce for both parties—all that. And more. Images let you trigger whole worlds of consciousness in your reader.

When you write, put yourself there physically. Don't think, "Okay, my character is feeling really angry with her husband." *See something*:

> She brushed her skirt and sat on the bed with his shoes next to her. His toes seemed to be always in these shoes, in all his shoes—there were five dimples at the tops of each shoe, shiny, where the suede was worn away. She picked one of the moccasins up. They were always heavier than they appeared to be. She threw the shoe at the door.

Your images shouldn't be about describing; they shouldn't be *about* anything at all. They should *be the thing.* Experience the musty leather as you write; if you experience, your reader will, too. When you fully imagine that house, that marriage, the bedspread, the smells of the field, all you have to do as a writer is to paint some deft strokes, outline a few items, an emotion, the palm of a hand—and your reader will fill in the entire town. Eventually, as you gain practice using images, you can make your images so powerful that by describing a front porch, your reader will see the whole county and feel as though he or she has been there before.

So. Don't write what you think. Write what you see. If you can't see it, you can't write it. If you rely on explanation, prefacing, concluding, analyzing, musing, reflecting, thinking—you deny your reader a large part of the pleasure and impact of creative writing, of what we do.

Instead, give yourself over to the experience of image. Go where it goes. Don't think it out.

Determine if the following is an image or a thought:

I was really into boys. All I thought about was boys, boys, boys.

It's a thought. Essentially this writer is thinking out loud on the page, an approach we might use for writing essays, journals, letters, notes to the self. It's perfectly fine writing, but it's not exactly creative writing. The writer/speaker is looking back at her life, making a conclusion. It's a thought about a thought—and that kind of approach to creative writing is dangerous. Your reader is basically on pause here. No mental image occurs. The disk spins, but the reader, like the writer, is not engaged. The two sentences above are not alive. They're fine, they're not wrong, they're just not *doing* anything. (You may wish to look at student writer Karissa Womack's essay on p. 398 for a profound example of showing these two sentences about boys.)

If you focus on thought, you, as a writer, have wasted an opportunity to make something happen in your reader's brain. You must use that opportunity; you cannot waste it. Creative writing isn't about simply knowing. It's about knowing *through seeing and experiencing something alive.* Thoughts kill that process. They pierce the experience, like light coming into a darkened movie theater.

Thoughts interfere with the reader's ability to see the image for herself. Try to avoid thoughts in your writing, and instead work on noticing what people say and do. *Thoughts* include the following:

CONCLUSIONS   "Ultimately, I really did love him."

"Class wasn't so bad."

"I ended up in the emergency room."

"The summer I turned eight my mom decided I was spending too much time in front of the television and ruining my eyes."

EMOTION DESCRIPTIONS	"Hannah hated hearing her brother Brian complain about Mrs. Danch when he was in seventh grade."
	"She was speechless."
	"I wished I hadn't quit."
THOUGHT REPORTS	"I figured it was a good way to get out of karate."
	"I knew she was an idiot."
EXPLANATIONS	"To be clear, my mother was mad. Real mad."
	"Once I am out of a relationship, I am really ready to get back in one."

Most thought sentences are actually images waiting to be born. Your writing will be instantly and dramatically improved as you translate thoughts into images.

PRACTICE

Read the short story "Surrounded by Sleep" by Akhil Sharma (p. 171). With a highlighter (or by taking notes and making a list), mark every passage that is an image (where you see, or could see, a scene play out in your mind). Focus on where you see people in action. What percentage of the story is images?

Generating Images

To create a live image to work from as a writer, you answer a set of questions. Ground yourself in space and time in order to generate images.

Grounded in images, your work will be instantly alive. Oriented in place and time, you hit the ground running. Trust your reader and trust the power of images—they will provide the second half of the equation. Write from this deeply experiential point of view. Instead of doing a rough draft, practice anchoring yourself in time and space before you write. You will save *hours* of revision time.

Instead of writing, "Hannah hated hearing her brother Brian complain . . . ," which is a conclusion about a memory—all thought, no action, no image— translate the thought into an image.

PRACTICE

Read the poem "Still-Life" by Katie Ford (p. 158). Is there any thinking in this poem, or is it entirely in image? Try a "still-life" poem of your own, in which you go outside and stare at a scene and write down only what you see.

Before you write, every single time, be securely in the moment you are writing. It doesn't matter if it's poetry, fiction, nonfiction, or a play. Know exactly where your character/self is in time and space. It doesn't matter if your work is based on your life or totally made up. Become the person you are writing and jot down: Where are you? Where is the other person in this poem or memoir or story? What can you hear? What meal was just eaten? What clothes are you (as your character)

> *I want to reach that state of condensation of sensations which constitutes a picture.*
> — HENRI MATISSE

wearing? Get in the habit of writing anchored in space and time. The drawing technique presented earlier is extremely useful. When you slip out of the image, practice translating your thoughts back into pictures: full-blown moving images.

Deciding *where and when* you are going to point your vision, and staying tightly in that one space and time, is the secret to powerful image-based creative writing.

PRACTICE

Read Dylan Landis's "In My Father's Study upon His Death" (p. 161). This is a list essay. Which images do you "see" in your mind's eye as you read? What is the time and place she chose to write? Does she veer from her chosen time and place in this piece?

QUESTIONS TO ASK: Orienting Yourself in Images before Writing

Before you write, always locate yourself with an image. Use these questions to locate yourself, your writing eye, deeply within the image before you start writing. *Answer the orienting questions before beginning any piece of creative writing.*

1 Where are we? What room, neighborhood, town, county, place?

2 What time is it? What minute, hour, day, month, year?

3 What is the weather outside like? What's the atmosphere inside like (lighting, hot/cold, smoky, comfortable, etc.)?

4 Who is there, "onstage"? Who just left? Who is nearby?

5 Who is expected?

6 What just happened?

7 How old is each person "onstage"?

8 What are people wearing? What do they have in their hands?

9 What is in the room/location? What "stuff" is around?

10 What is the dominant smell?

11 What is (or are) the dominant sound (or sounds)?

12 As you gaze around the image, what else do you notice?

PRACTICE

To prepare to write an image, draw a sketch that answers the orienting questions on page 141, or make a list of your answers (or your character's answers) to those orienting questions. Let the answers launch you into an image. Write a paragraph, a few lines of dialogue, or a few lines of poetry, about the same length as the excerpts above (pp. 139–40). Stay in the image. Follow the action/speech; don't scene-set.

PRACTICE

Read Jay Hopler's poem "That Light One Finds in Baby Pictures" (p. 158). Do a quick sketch: Where is the poem's image taking place? When? Who is there? What are the images you see most clearly as you reread?

CREATING WITH IMAGES

Focus on People in Action

Now that you know how to launch an image, begin working with images by focusing on two essential components of the image: people (or beings of some kind) and action (meaningful movement by the people or beings).

Few creative works are purely abstract—no people, no action, nothing we can see. Even poems about beautiful sunsets or perfect, still fields often *imply* people and action.

Noncreative writing begins with ideas, principles, or theories. Creative writing begins with Joe, in a tree, watching his grandmother's front yard, where a fight is breaking out.

> *Seeing is polysensory, combining the visual, tactile, and kinesthetic senses.*
>
> — ROBERT McKIM

Creative writing is rooted in individuals, struggling and interacting with the physical world, and others in that world. It's easiest to create pictures your reader can see when you have two or more entities. People alone are often thinking. Thoughts aren't usually interesting enough on their own to sustain creative writing. But two or more people—that attracts the eye. These ingredients—two people, something happening—give you the spark you need to ignite images.

Read Mary Robison's short story "Pretty Ice" (p. 166) slowly, out loud. Read it a second time, carefully noticing where the story shows people in action. The entire story is in images, isn't it? Belle balances her accounts, reckoning her bank balance and the amount of love she has to give. Notice how the image of a person in action also points to what's going on inside the character's psyche. When Belle makes her way across the frozen pond that is her yard (life?), water seeps in her shoes. Does someone have "cold feet"? Yes. By focusing on people in action, the author creates, with images, a complex, fascinating portrait of two women, frozen, stunted by grief. Notice how, after the opening scene, the characters spark because there's conflict between the mother and daughter, and then when the triangle is introduced, there's conflict between all three characters: Belle, her mother, and Will. The entire story is in real time, in action, in scene, in image. When Robison describes setting, it's never as background—it's because Belle's mother, an awful driver, plows into the cab lane, or her cigarette smoke blends with the acrid, yellow smoke of the dying midwestern town.

PRACTICE

Choose six of the thought examples on pages 139–40 to translate into images. Take each thought and translate it into an image, a moving picture, that will create something alive in the reader's mind. Do the anchoring activity each time, using your sketch or floor plan, so you are firmly in the room, in the image, before you start to write. Read a few of these short passages out loud either in class or on your own. Ask your group to tell you what else they can see in your picture. Do they guess any of the items from your jotted list correctly? Do they see things you didn't even mention in your writing but had in mind when you wrote? In your group, rank your most successfully vivid images from most to least effective.

PRACTICE

Collect your creative writing pieces—all your drafts—from the course so far. Using a marker, go through your writing and underline and label as many conclusions, emotion descriptions, thought reports, and explanations as you can. Do you tend to rely on one of these four image killers more than others? Write a brief analysis of your particular image-killing habits, and list a few of your strongest images.

Think from within Images

How do writers use thoughts, then, in their work? Sparingly. And only when firmly, deeply anchored in the image. Make sure you have an image up and running, with action and moving pictures, *before* you offer the reader a thought, an insight, a conclusion, or a comment.

> *Merely to see is not enough. It is necessary to have a fresh, vivid, physical contact with the object you draw through as many of the senses as possible—and especially through the sense of touch.*
>
> — KIMON NICOLAÏDES

Read the following passages. Which ones are more grounded, providing a flash or a moving picture in your mind? Which rely on reporting or present generalized thought and not images?

1

I love my freedom. My relationships, especially the one with Dana, were always really strained, especially after the deadly three-month period. There is no reason for people to try to control each other so totally.

2

I am mad at you
But you make me laugh
I'm still mad at you
But now I'm laughing
We are the same.
Our hair, our eyes, our interests.

3

BOB: This party sucks.
JEN: I know. It is so ridiculous.
BOB: Why did we even come?
JEN: You wanted to talk to you know who.
BOB: I just can't stop thinking about him, you know?
JEN: I do know.

4

I'd peer into the front window, breath fogging the sale signs,

catching snippets of my father's profile appearing and disappearing
behind the tall cardboard stacks. Once I slipped back into the store,

wandering the aisles, master of my own cart, loading it to bursting
            — SEBASTIAN MATTHEWS, "Buying Wine"

Which of these passages engages you most fully, really makes something happen for you in your mind's eye? What *causes the image to pop into your head*?

PRACTICE

Place the passages above, numbered one through four, in order from the most thought-oriented (you process the writing through the analytical part of your brain) to the most imagistic (you see a picture of something in your mind's eye).

Remember that different readers experience images differently. You may not "see" the same images as your classmates. It depends, in part, on the quality of the writing, but also on your life experiences, your tastes as a reader, and how experienced a reader you are. It's useful for you to practice sensitizing yourself to the experiential qualities of creative writing. As you do so, always keep this in mind: Thoughts distance us from images. In creative writing, in art, be careful with thoughts. Be generous with images. The thoughts will take care of themselves; readers are more interested in their *own* thoughts and conclusions, not yours. Trust your reader; trust your material. If you are faithful to the image, the truth—and better ideas than you could ever "think" of—will come out.

PRACTICE

Write a scene containing a moment you show to the reader as an image, completely free of any telling or explaining or thinking. Then do the reverse, taking the most imagistic of the passages on page 144 and summarizing it into a thought. Keep the reader from seeing anything.

If the reader's brain sees a picture—blue ocean, hot white sand, your old worn flip-flops—you have activated an image. If the reader is *thinking about* what it would be like to be at the beach but not *picturing it in real time*, you have created a thought; that's not exactly what creative writing is trying to accomplish. You do not have complete control—literature isn't brainwashing material. Some of your readers will be distracted. Others won't have strong muscles of concentration. Still others will have had so many similar experiences that images flood in as they read. Finally, the stock-in-trade of creative writing is creating images—that's what we do. We try to put on paper words that will create a vivid, continuous sensory dream in our readers' brains. If the dream is really compelling, we may stop the film, talk briefly, explain something. But that is dangerous. When the film isn't running, the reader is likely to stop reading. We don't want that. If that happens, we are out of a job. Our goal is to keep readers from thinking and force them to experience the image as a moving, real-time film, running in their brains. Created by us.

Use Specifics

Specific words—concrete nouns, place names, proper nouns, active verbs—are the fuel that feeds the image, keeping it alive and sparkly.

It's not enough for writers to "be descriptive." In fact, you have probably heard readers say, "The description goes on too long; you can skip it." It's very likely you have done some skipping or skimming yourself; most of us have.

Sentences that billow with very formal language and flowery word choices might seem specific. These kinds of sentences may draw praise from some teachers, friends, or parents not trained as creative writers. Actually, lots of *words* may block your reader's engagement with the piece:

The pulsating rivers plunged toward their ultimate and terrible death!

This is the story of heartache and heartbreak, of tumultuousness and terror and I want you to always remember, this is true, and real!

The joy of holding hands,
You are in my mind always
My heart beating and yours
Beating beating as one heart.

It's unlikely you really see any specific images in the passages above. What's blocking the image? Not thoughts this time, but language. General or over-blown language is as ineffective as thoughts when you are trying to get your reader fully absorbed in your writing.

In fact, more simple writing activates the brain's image-making machine most often. Instead of worrying about adjectives and beautiful word-picture-painting — "writerly things" — concentrate on where *you* are, in your mind's eye, when you write. Creative writing isn't about the writer. It's about the reader, having an experience, being somewhere, seeing through someone else. You don't report your emotions and thoughts; you activate those of your reader. Creative writing serves readers. It's not a stage for show-offs.

When writing in images, name the simple, actual things in the world. Instead of writing *missing you*, you place your lover and yourself in your car, your last Friday night together, ever. Instead of *car,* you write *Angel's old Cadillac* or *the sedan with the human teeth marks.* Instead of writing *fruit*, write *five strawberries*. See the difference for the reader? See how *fruit* makes you think? You may or may not picture a fruit — you think *fruit* as a concept. That's absolutely contrary to the goals and pleasures of creative writing. Write *five strawberries*, and you've got them. Your mouth might even water. When you are in the image, writing what you see, write really, truly what you see. Be specific by looking carefully, naming the small parts, and keeping it simple.

PRACTICE

Make a list of every single specific word choice in three of the poems at the end of this chapter (Natalie Diaz's poem "My Brother at 3 a.m.," Jay Hopler's "That Light One Finds in Baby Pictures," and Ely Shipley's "Magnolia"). For each poem, count how many words are specific and how many are abstract. Does one poem have a higher percentage of specific words than the other poems? In which poem do you "see" the images most clearly? Is it because of the specific word choices, or for another reason?

When a photograph is out of focus, we adjust the lens to sharpen the image. Sharpening the focus of your written image means choosing more specific words. Specific concrete nouns and clear action verbs *intensify* images. Professional, published writers go over their work many, many times, to sharpen every single word, to make sure every single syllable is contributing to, not distracting from, the moving live picture in the reader's head. Poets do this, of course, but so do narrative writers in their creative nonfiction and fiction.

PRACTICE

Reread Akhil Sharma's short story "Surrounded by Sleep" (p. 171). Scan through the story using your highlighter (or making a list) to capture every single specific word in the story. This is going to be a long list! *Isocal, Hindi women's magazine,* It's a Wonderful Life, *chaplain, Clark Kent, Three Musketeers, Harlem Globetrotters, Budweiser, dark dress pants, mouth, lungs, stomach, mini-mall, pizzeria, Reese's Peanut Butter Cups, 7 train, fat as a heel,* and so on. Estimate what percentage of the story is made up of specifics.

Move Around in Images

Images are alive, which means that things move in that picture inside the reader's head. Action takes place. Whether it's a poem, play, nonfiction piece, or story, the image has movement in it.

Amateur videographers tend to make one common mistake. They stand in one place when they shoot Freddy's soccer game or Bitsy's first Christmas. No matter what is happening — Freddy scoring a point, or Bitsy biting the dog — we the viewers watch the action but are forced to remain in a fixed location. Amateur videographers have a hard time following the image to where it is most alive. *America's Funniest Home Videos* is a collection of videos by amateurs who happened to get lucky — they captured something amazing on film. Most of the time, however, hours of footage are shot, and nothing happens. The photographer holds the camera at eye level, pointing it straight ahead. The real action, the lively images, take place off-camera, somewhere else.

We tend not to watch other people's Freddy and Bitsy videos because *nothing very interesting happens.* The image is moving, but we aren't moving anywhere interesting as we watch. When you create an image (using your checklist from p. 141), you create a solid starting point. Once you have launched the image, you need to *move.*

Move to where, to look at what? What's interesting. It will feel funny at first, just as it does to walk around with a video camera, filming *but not looking through the camera.* Keep your eye on what's interesting, what's dramatic, what tiny specifics you can see that will reveal so much more about this person than words ever could.

If you started your image in the living room, where your mom is sitting in her favorite chair, but she is just sleeping, you need to move your camera. You need to get really, really close up so that we can see the pores of her skin, *or* you need to go somewhere else to capture something that is *more interesting*. Leave the room. No need to write boring. Film your way into the kitchen. Your dad fighting with your obnoxious older brother who refuses to lift a finger around the house? That could be good. Move in close. Really close. Read the story "Boys" by Rick Moody (p. 212). Notice how there is always action, always lots of movement—the boys run around, in and out of the house, year after year, shooting a dog, itching and scratching, breaking out into pimples, calling names, torturing their sister. Notice where the camera is in each of these image flashes: positioned over the neighborhood, then, *whoosh*, down into a backyard, then in a church pew, right over the shoulder of one of the boys, then at the bathroom mirror, close up on a boy's face, then the camera, *whoosh*, is on a dolly, tracking down the upstairs hallway as the boys chase their sister. The camera is *always moving. The distance between the camera and the subject is constantly changing.*

At first, it feels awkward to walk around and film simultaneously. As you practice writing this way, focused on the moving image, you will feel more comfortable.

PRACTICE

Examine Akhil Sharma's "Surrounded by Sleep" (p. 171). Make a list of at least ten moving images. Where are you transported (where do you see the full image play out on the movie screen in your head)? Notice where the camera is positioned, and how close the writer is to the image. How much movement is there? Which images are close-ups? Which are filmed from farther back? Compare these to the moving images in "Pretty Ice" by Mary Robison (p. 166).

Amateurs tend to stay back. It's weird and intrusive and uncomfortable to get in people's faces. But that is what artists do. The amateur stands stock-still, and everything is filmed from the same distance. Excellent filmmakers vary the distance. They open with a long shot, and we see the whole world. Then, for high impact, they close in. Then they pull out a little. Then they zoom in, and all we can see is part of a face. Part of a life. A secret inside view. Keep moving. Keep changing your angles. That's how you get the good stuff, the alive parts of your image.

One Sentence, One Action

Action feeds the image. Action keeps it alive. But often, while tracking actions and gestures, we get all tangled up.

> Nancy was rushing to get to class on time and she stumbled and fell while picking up her books from the sofa to get out the door on time.

What's wrong here is that the author thinks she is writing in the image, using action, nouns, and verbs. But she isn't. Because the human brain reads English sentences in a linear fashion, from left to right, we take in the order of events sequentially. If your image sequence is off, if your sentences try to handle too many actions, the reader won't be transported. He or she may be able to muscle through, and *think* out what is happening, but that isn't what you want as a writer. You want the reader *to not work too hard.* The reader wants to just see what's happening. The reader doesn't want to have to sort out all the stage directions. That involves thinking, heavy lifting. Creative writing is all about *seeing*.

> *We live on the leash of our senses.*
>
> — DIANE ACKERMAN

So an important aspect of manipulating images is remembering the limitations of the sentence. Do only one thing at a time:

Harry grabbed the gin and tonic. He rushed down the driveway, spilling.

As opposed to:

Harry, coming in the door, grabbed his drink and got undressed and changed into his soccer shorts.

It's physically impossible to come in a door and grab a drink *and* get undressed. This is summary. It's not a real image. It's a list of events. Good writers break down what they see and render what's important for the reader to notice.

Notice how in the readings in this chapter most of the sentences are devoted to one action, one thing. Readers are reading lines, in a linear fashion, from left to right. Sentences that try to do two things — "She walked in and put down her coat, and he read the comic book to his brother" — are not as effective as sentences that devote themselves to a single action, a single concept. Simplify your sentences and make them into straight lines, simple, sharp, clearly aimed at their target. You can still write complex sentences with complex actions. It's just a matter of tightly focusing your logic and lining it up with your tightly focused camera work. Isolate the action one thing at a time, and the sentence breaks the action down into bite-size pieces.

Kim Addonizio's "First Poem for You" (p. 112) illustrates this point perfectly.

I like to touch your tattoos in complete
darkness, when I can't see them. I'm sure of
where they are, know by heart the neat
lines of lightning pulsing just above

A complex argument, a lot going on in this moment. But Addonizio lets her sentences do one thing at a time. I was going to do X. Instead I did Y, which caused Z.

Compare Addonizio's lines to typical non-image sentences:

I'm crazy about him. He is my soul mate.
I know everything about him.

Wait. One sentence at a time. One image, one step, and one line at a time. What happens first here? The speaker likes to touch her lover's tattoos when the room is dark, "when I can't see them." What happens next? She feels certain of where the tattoos are—she really knows her lover, and the lover's skin—it's a map she can read in the dark. What do we see next? A tattoo: lightning bolts. One thing at a time so that we, the readers, actually participate in the act! Instead of writing "I know everything about him" or "he is my soul mate," Addonizio, a skillful poet, shows, in real time, how she loves him and how he matters. When we write general sentences like "he makes my heart sing," we aren't really looking at our subject. When we write feelings and thoughts, we often aren't transporting the reader into our image—we're shutting the reader out. Before you write, and when you rewrite, get grounded in your image. Answer the questions on page 141. What does the room look like? What do the two lovers look like? Where are the tattoos, what are they of? Who says what? Who does what? What's the light like in this room, what kind of darkness are they in? When is this happening? What's the address, the building, the city, the place? The answers won't all be in your poem, essay, story, or play. But you need to be fully grounded in the image you are writing *before* you write it. See it before you say it, and let each sentence or line do one thing at a time, in sequence.

New writers often make mistakes relating to image focus in transitions. For some reason, we get all hung up in transitions, when people move from house to car, or driveway to party. Try to remove awkward transitions—people getting into and out of cars, leaving rooms, saying good-bye—and use white space instead, skipping two double lines.

His father said, "One minute," and they climbed out of the car.
They went up wooden steps into the bar. Inside, it was dark and smelled of cigarette smoke and something stale and sweet.

Look again at the way Sharma keeps his images moving, alive, thrumming. He uses physicality, action, gesture, movement. He describes actions—what his characters are doing, how they are moving, what tasks they are involved in; emotions and statements are used sparingly, and only when the image is very strong, very alive, so its momentum will keep playing out in the reader's mind while he pauses to give you information, say something he just really wants to say. When writing a transition, simplify the image. Write what you see. Stay focused on what's alive, and practice cutting out unnecessary logistical explanations.

Summary Images

In a short piece—a poem or a short-short, for example—you can sustain an image, and that can be your entire piece. In a longer work, a more complex short story—Akhil Sharma's "Surrounded by Sleep" (p. 171), for example—you have to build bridges between the images. There are two kinds of bridges. One is quick and slides the reader from one place and time to another in a single sentence, a transition from image to image. We'll look at *slides* in a moment. The second type of bridge, or transition, is a *summary image*.

In creative writing, summary passages are just as important as image-based sections. Summary provides the connective tissue so that the images work together. Summary also lets you cover a lot of time deftly and vividly. And summary highlights images so that they show up, framed, emphasized. The difference between a summary and a slide is that the summary is bigger, fuller, richer. It's like grout. It fills in the spaces between the image tiles with information, drama, or backstory.

Summary images help the reader understand the relationship of the parts to each other and to the larger themes of the piece. *However, on the other hand,* and *Following up on that point* are the cues that an essay writer uses when adding more information to counter or develop a previous point. In creative writing, all this work is done with the mental movie intact. A summary image gives a sweeping overview, a look at the big picture. The camera is much farther back. It may present snapshots of numerous typical moments, skidding over time to get to the next important point in the piece, which of course will be presented in a full-blown image.

In Sharma's story, trying to show the entire life of Ajay's family after the accident *in images* would fill many volumes! Sharma has to pick: He shows some things in full-blown images—the key moments. He shows the reader other moments in a different way—through summary images.

Summary images have to be interesting, active, and vibrant but are presented in less detail. Signal phrases that announce a summary image often have to do with time. *That summer* or *For five weeks it went on* are the kinds of cues that let the reader know how things generally went over the next chunk of time.

Notice that in paragraph two of "Surrounded by Sleep," Sharma gives a summary, the backstory, an overview of how Ajay's family arrived at the pool that August afternoon. During this summary, what happens in your mind's eye? Does the screen go blank? Do you reason your way through this passage, as in a chemistry textbook? Do you *see* as you learn more information about the family?

A period of weeks is covered, and in the reader's mind these weeks probably play out in a series of brief flashes, glimpses—the mother's attempt to manipulate the doctors, the call from the insurance company, the father's visits to the hospital. You imagine, just below the level of "movie," what this *felt like, looked like*. It's different from a police report. It's different from reading sociology. Art appeals to our emotions and the physical senses, and so does summary—we are aware of these actual people moving through their real lives. We keep hold of the image in summary as we get more necessary information. We don't leave the playing field. The writer doesn't break the movie-dream.

The same rules apply to summary images as to regular images: As you write, make sure that you *experience* the moment; don't just write about it. Stay close up, use concrete nouns and action verbs. And keep your focus on the actions.

Sliding

To move from summary to real-time image and back again, or to move from place to place, from image to image, in your poem or story or play, you learn to slide. **Sliding** is like smooth camera work, when you gently shift the image focus, moving your reader's attention slowly from the park swing set, where two kids are playing, gently over to the mall parking lot across the street. Moving the "camera" is called sliding. You slide in fiction, poetry, nonfiction, and plays.

Writers who don't learn sliding frequently commit two writing sins. If you whip the camera around, you make your reader sick or dizzy or, worse, confused. (Your point might be that these characters are sick, crazy, unfocused. In that case, you might *choose* to jump from one thing to the next.) Too many locations, not enough depth, and no transitions might result in this type of scatter-shot, slideless writing:

> Joey ate his sandwich. The diner was crazy. When he was talking to Clara later at her house, he picked yet another fight with the girl. On the dance floor, she wouldn't talk to him.

The other outcome of not using the slide is boring writing. Many writers—unsure of how or when to move the camera, the focus, the action—simply keep writing. They have something going, and because so much can go wrong, they just stay with it. They write a long paragraph, maybe the whole first page of a story, about waking up. Turning off the alarm. Getting ready. Next page, leaving the apartment, driving to work. There's no slide—*everything is explained*. This approach is difficult for the reader. Everything is presented at exactly the same level of intensity. It's like a security camera. Lots and lots of hours of footage. Very rarely something interesting to look at.

If you don't use the slide, your reader will have trouble entering the image and moving around in your piece.

Marisa Silver, author of "What I Saw from Where I Stood" (p. 251), is a master of the slide. Examine this short excerpt from her story, which you will read in full later, and simply notice the sliding action:

> I drove Dulcie's car to work the next day. When I got home that night, Dulcie had moved our mattress from our bed into the living room, where it lay in the middle of the floor, the sheets spilling over onto the carpet.

Silver slides from the narrator's workday into the scene that follows, where the couple discovers, and argues over, the rat. The reader doesn't need the workday, the car ride, or the character's entrance into the apartment:

> "It's the rat," she said. "He's back."

The reader knows we have slid into the apartment scene. The reader has space in the image to move the narrator from his car up into the apartment—no need to spell that out in a full-blown scene. The slide is an efficient summary that uses action, location, and an anchored image to slide over time, covering a large amount quickly. A slide is a bridge, different from pure summary, in that the slide moves us scenically to a new location and time. The reader needs these slides—and the spaces between them—in order to engage actively with the piece.

| PRACTICE |

Find an example of a slide from summary to scene in any of the pieces you've read so far in this textbook.

Examine the following passage from Sharma's story, and notice where the slide from summary to scene occurs:

> Sometimes when Ajay arrived his mother was on the phone, telling his father that she missed him and was expecting to see him. . . . Ajay had thought of his parents as the same person: MummyDaddy. Now . . . Ajay sensed that his mother and father were quite different people. After his mother got off the phone, she always went to the cafeteria to get coffee for herself and Jell-O or cookies for him. He knew that if she took her coat with her, it meant that she was especially sad. . . .
>
> That day, while she was gone, Ajay stood beside the hospital bed and balanced a comic book on Aman's chest. He read to him very slowly. Before turning each page, he said, "Okay, Aman?"

Sharma uses *image* summary to make us experience how it is when someone is in the hospital. A bunch of days are all alike. These days blur together. Sharma,

> *Every picture I paint is*
> *a three-way struggle*
> *between what I know, what*
> *I see, and what I want.*
> — THOMAS BUECHNER

in summary-image mode, can stop and tell us Ajay's new insights into his parents, how he is seeing them as people, as more than just entities designed to meet his needs. Sharma doesn't stop and lecture to us, though. He stays deep in the moment by calling out the four main physical images from those days: coffee, Jell-O, cookies, and his mother and her coat.

That's the key: Anchor summary in specific images — moving ones. When you have your specific images in place, you can hang insights and conclusions on them. Without the images, the summary becomes too heavy, it ceases to be art, and it becomes an essay. Nothing wrong with essays. It's just not what we are doing here as creative writers. When we read creative writing, *imaginative* writing, we expect to have pictures play out in our minds. That's part of the deal.

So, with the summary passage engaged, alive, and made out of the stuff that transports a reader to a time, mood, and place simultaneously, notice how Sharma slides from the generalized summary image to the full-blown "this is happening right now" image. The change happens so smoothly. Sharma freezes the frame on one day. In summary time, the mother walks outside. "That day, while she was gone . . ." is the line where Sharma hits the pause button. See how he does that? We've been seeing her come and go, do her coffee-and-coat routine, and one day, while she is out, Sharma anchors us firmly in real time, in an image we are going to be in for a while. We're going in for a closer look. And voilà — she goes out, and we are given Ajay. Real time.

We are in a full-blown scene, an image with a floor, a ceiling, walls — it's not a blur. We're going to stay here. Something is going to happen. Time slows down, the comic book's pages are turned slowly, and we are up against Aman's chest — see how much closer we are? Notice where the camera is, and what happens in your mind as you read. Sharma writes this by imagining what it's like to see through Ajay's eyes. He doesn't write *about* the boy; he writes *from* the boy. And so we follow this image-moment, the reading of the comic book, with an extended close-up focusing on Aman's physicality, his equipment, his injuries. Notice how this description is never laid on top of the skin of the story — it's part of the story. We are in Ajay's body. We see how he sees. His brother reminds him of that terrible melted bowl. The images aren't decorative. The images are how a character sees, feels, exists, moves in the world.

A WORD ON IDEAS

Ideas are giant super-thoughts. A lot of nonwriters think that what writers do is Have Great Ideas. Nothing could be further from the truth. Writers See Great Images. In fact, ideas can potentially be bad for writers. When Dylan Landis wanted to write about her father's death, she didn't want to emote. She didn't want to fall into clichés about grief. She very much wanted to mark the occasion of his passing and reveal how powerfully affected she was by sitting in his study. As she went through his office that night, she was stunned by what she

People have to go out of their minds before they can come to their senses.

— TIMOTHY LEARY

found there. She'd known her father, and she had not, at all. Both were true. Instead of trying to tell the reader that, and risking the writing falling flat, she set out to create a movie view of his office, by focusing on only the *things she found*. No thoughts. No feelings. Just the list of actual things. She trusted, absolutely, that her reader would "get it" by simply seeing the images. She didn't need to explain. She didn't need to share her feelings. The reader would know.

Many writers have ideas for writing. When the idea is a *picture in the brain*, when the idea isn't in words yet, it is viable. But many "ideas" for writing are dead on arrival—the thought demons have already fed, and all you really have is a carcass. For example, you have an idea for a poem about your grandmother. Often, starting from the thought—Grandma was beautiful, even in old age—is more difficult, more distancing. Better to start with a description of you and her, in a room, on a particular day, what her toes looked like, what she said. Get in the habit of working from images. The ideas will take care of themselves, and your writing will be fresher, richer, more original. And smarter.

Don't think. Write. Don't make this work cerebral. Keep it sensory (and sensual). Don't save up ideas. Instead of thinking in ideas for stories and poems and plays, collect images, details, specifics, and overheard bits of real-world dialogue. Jot those things down in your journal, and avoid ideas, such as "homeless man" or "war story." Get in the habit of writing in images instead of putting down all your thoughts, hoping to translate them into images later. Try to have the experience while writing—even when you are at the very, very earliest note-taking stage—that you want your reader to have while reading.

Instead of asking "idea" questions to generate writing topics and creative projects, ask "sense" questions: What did it feel like to the touch? What was the taste in your mouth? What were the visual images from that day? Get grounded in your body, and in the scene, and write from the five senses rather than thinking, remembering, or drawing from other writers' images, such as those you encounter on television or in film. Your key to success as a creative writer rests inside your sense memory.

As a creative writer, one of the most powerful prompts for you to launch yourself into the image is to rely on your sense of smell. Smell triggers memory and the emotions attached to those memories; the neuroscience on this effect is well documented.

Doubtless, you've also been transported by smells—scent memories lodge deep in our brains. Practice keeping track of your body's reactions to things.

A woman's perfume launches you back to kindergarten and your love for Mrs. Vander K. When you notice the way a friend organizes the stuff under her kitchen sink, your mom's drinking problem comes flooding back to you—those bottles of alcohol hidden among the bottles of cleaning supplies. The way the sky looks right before it snows, and whoosh, there's childhood, the night your sister left, pregnant, the last night you ever saw her. It was that sky. Use these triggers for creative writing, rather than ideas.

PRACTICE

Working from your own childhood, make four lists of about twenty items apiece: What did childhood smell like? What did childhood taste like? What did childhood look like? What did childhood sound like? Use this rich bank of images to feed your stories, poems, plays, and essays.

WRITING PROJECTS

1. Break the rules. Write a piece that is all thoughts, commentary, no images. How do you engage, transport the reader?

2. Using Dylan Landis's piece on page 161 as your inspiration, write a list piece that is a detailed inventory of the things you find in a friend's car, in a cousin's living room, on the back counter at Chipotle where you work. No thoughts or commentary allowed. Illegal snooping? You're on your own.

3. Take an image from any previous piece of your writing and extend it, moving in closer with your camera and slowing time down, so that you expand this single moment, this glimpse, into five pages of prose or twenty lines of poetry.

4. Pick an image from Akhil Sharma's short story "Surrounded by Sleep" (p. 171) to serve as a launching point, and write an imitation, using a similar scene from your own life—for example, a sibling's accident, a hospital scene, an outing with a parent. Use at least three of the same techniques for achieving presentness that Sharma does. Your piece may take the form of a play, short story, or memoir.

5. Write a piece that involves a slide from summary image into full-blown scene, and a slide from full-blown scene into summary image. Avoid clichés: waking up, falling asleep, drifting into reflection.

6. From your own collection of photographs, choose a few photos of the same person, someone you are close to, at different points in life. Write paragraph

sections inspired by the images in the photographs, very directly, as well as images from your life with this person. Avoid thoughts! You can make each section a photograph section if you have enough photos. Make your essay four to seven sections in length.

7. Write a 250-word micro-memoir showing the story of your life in smells. No thinking, commenting, analyzing, summary, or telling allowed.

8. Using Jenifer Hixson's piece on page 162 as your model, write a monologue about an encounter with a stranger. To begin, use the drawing technique, and make lists of all the five senses.

9. Read Jay Hopler's poem "That Light One Finds in Baby Pictures" on page 158. Locate a series of your family's baby photos and notice what they have in common. Or look back at all your selfies from freshman year in high school, and examine the images carefully. What can you see now that you couldn't see then? What do the selfies or baby photos all have in common? Find at least four things, and create a poem modeled on Hopler's in four sections.

IMAGES WORKSHOP

The following prompts will guide your discussion of your classmates' work.

1. In the student piece you are reading, highlight the places you truly see as "moving images," the alive parts of the piece, where you aren't reading words on a page as much as experiencing something, seeing.

2. Identify three to five places in the student piece where an image could be made more powerful, alive, and focused. Look for passages that rely on thoughts, feelings, explanations, or description. Circle these.

3. Identify a place in the piece where the student writer uses summary images effectively. Label it "good summary."

4. Find a passage in the student piece where there is a transition from one real-time image to another, a slide. Box it. Label it by naming the locations: "kitchen to bedroom" or "parking lot to lobby." Find another section in the piece where the transition from one moment to another is rough, not an image, or confusing. Box it. Make a suggestion for improving the flow so that the reader stays focused on the moving image and is never jolted out of the present.

5. Identify your favorite image in this piece.

READINGS

Katie Ford
Still-Life

Down by the pond, addicts sleep
on rocky grass half in water, half out,
and there the moon lights them
out of tawny silhouettes into the rarest
of amphibious flowers I once heard called *striders*,
between, but needing, two worlds.
Of what can you accuse them now,
beauty?

Jay Hopler
That Light One Finds in Baby Pictures

1/

$\qquad\qquad\qquad$ Being born is a shame —

But it's not so bad, as journeys go. It's not the worst one
We will ever have to make. It's almost noon

And the light now clouded in the courtyard is
Like that light one finds in baby pictures: old

And pale and hurt —

2/

When all roads are low and lead to the same
Place, we call it *Fate* and tell ourselves how

We were born to make the journey. Who's
To say we weren't?

3/

$\qquad\qquad$ The clouded light has changed to rain.
$\qquad\qquad$ The picture —. *No, the baby's blurry.*

4/

That's me—, the child playing in the sand with a pail
And shovel; in the background, my mother's shadow

Is crawling across a soot-blackened collapse of brick
And timber, what might have been a bathhouse once.

The tide is coming in—. Someone has written HELL
On its last standing wall.

Natalie Diaz

My Brother at 3 a.m.

He sat cross-legged, weeping on the steps
when Mom unlocked and opened the front door.
    O God, he said. *O God.*
        He wants to kill me, Mom.

When Mom unlocked and opened the front door
at 3 a.m., she was in her nightgown, Dad was asleep.
    He wants to kill me, he told her,
        looking over his shoulder.

3 a.m. and in her nightgown, Dad asleep,
What's going on? she asked. *Who wants to kill you?*
    He looked over his shoulder.
        The devil does. Look at him, over there.

She asked, *What are you on? Who wants to kill you?*
The sky wasn't black or blue but the green of a dying night.
    The devil, look at him, over there.
        He pointed to the corner house.

The sky wasn't black or blue but the dying green of night.
Stars had closed their eyes or sheathed their knives.
    My brother pointed to the corner house.
        His lips flickered with sores.

Stars had closed their eyes or sheathed their knives.
O God, I can see the tail, he said. *O God, look.*
    Mom winced at the sores on his lips.
        It's sticking out from behind the house.

O God, see the tail, he said. *Look at the goddamned tail.*
He sat cross-legged, weeping on the front steps.
     Mom finally saw it, a hellish vision, my brother.
          O God, O God, she said.

Ely Shipley
Magnolia

In the cul-de-sac shaded
by trees, Marissa and I
played all summer where magnolias
hung, hands withering over us
as we wove

between them. In her backyard
we circled the empty,
dirty pool where petals and leaves
floated, where insects waded. We came to a shed
hidden in the back

corner of her yard; jars held pale, slick
shapes, cylindrical and bulbed, only
later I learned were preserved
vegetables. Marissa swore they were

testicles and a penis, and when I didn't believe her, no—
they were fingers, eyes, and tongues
her step-father collected, who later that day
I met by mistake. He'd come home early,

liquor on his breath, speaking
slowly, quietly, and only
in Spanish, though I was also in that congested
room where every curtain was
closed and the air thick

with heat, whispering. And Marissa's face
stiffening into a mask, glazed
with sweat, her eyes cast
down as he punched

the air, each syllable a balled-up
fist. Marissa told me then

I wasn't allowed inside her
house anymore. Outside, as if
to apologize, she picked me

a magnolia blossom. And I carried it
carefully in my sweating
hands, not yet understanding
by the time I got home

the petals would no longer be
white but darkening everywhere
they'd been touched.

Dylan Landis
In My Father's Study upon His Death

An article on Vincent Van Gogh, explaining that one year to the day before Van Gogh was born, his mother gave birth to another son, also named Vincent. The infant died and was upheld as a kind of angel, the most perfect and most adored son. The article suggests that Vincent, in second place, despaired of ever earning his mother's love and approval, and fell into life-long depression.

A painting by my father of himself sitting with his own father — two thin men with somber, distracted faces, staring into separate distances, leaning away from each other in art as they did in life.

A file marked "Courage" containing clippings and book reviews in which my father has underlined *imperturbability, intention* and *fixed resolve.*

A file marked "Breathing and Emotions" containing my father's writings and a slip of paper on which he has tightly handwritten:

> *She takes your breath away*
> *You can breathe freely around him*
> *He suffocates me*
> *I gasped when I saw how she changed*
> *It knocked the wind out of me*
> *I'd like some breathing room*

An unlabeled file containing patient notes from my father's days as a psychoanalyst. The patient, now deceased, was a famous man, and the notes are faded and nearly illegible, but two phrases stand out as the shredder sucks in the pages: "The idiocy of fear." "I feel I ought to be better."

A photograph of my mother in her thirties, wearing a two-piece leopard-print bathing suit, vamping for the camera. (One room away, my mother now sleeps on the sofa, a tracheostomy tube jutting from her throat, a feeding tube snaking from her stomach.)

A fake book stamped *Main Street* and *Sinclair Lewis* in gold on the spine. It is hollow and contains an envelope on which my father has written "Emergency $300." The envelope holds a twenty-dollar bill. At one point it held $300. At another point it held $80, but an aide needed money for parking in New York City. My father was convinced that aides were stealing from him over the months of his long neurological illness. It is possible. Items not found in my father's study, or anywhere else: an ivory carving; a zippered money belt in which he kept a thousand dollars tucked away for decades.

78 artist's paint brushes, most stained blue and green, one fan-shaped and never used, arranged in several dense bouquets.

His final painting, made on a square of corrugated cardboard, a field of darkest blues and greens penetrated by a meandering white line.

Two files marked "Dylan," containing every letter I ever wrote my father.

Jenifer Hixson
Where There's Smoke

I reached over and secretly undid my seat belt. And when his foot hit the brake at the red light, I flung open the door, and I ran. I had no shoes on. I was crying. I had no wallet. But I was okay because I had my cigarettes. And I didn't want any part of freedom if I didn't have my cigarettes.

When you live with someone who has a temper—a very bad temper—a very, very bad temper—you learn to play around that. You learn, *This time, I'll play possum, and next time I'll just be real nice, or I'll say yes to everything.*

Or you make yourself scarce, or you run. And this was one of the times when you just run.

And as I was running, I thought, *This was a great place to jump out*, because there were big lawns and cul-de-sacs.

Sometimes he would come after me and drive and yell at me to "get back in, get back in!"

And I was like, *No, I'm outta here. This is great.* And I went and hid behind a cabana, and he left.

And I had my cigarettes.

I started to walk around this beautiful neighborhood. It was ten-thirty at night, and it was silent and lovely. There was no sound, except for sprinklers. And I was enjoying myself. Enjoying the absence of anger, and enjoying these few hours I knew I'd have of freedom.

Just to perfect it, I thought, *I'll have a smoke.* And then it occurred to me, with horrifying speed, *I don't have a light!*

Just then, as if in answer, I see a figure up ahead. *Who is that? It's not him. Okay. They don't have a dog. What are they doing out on this suburban street?*

And the person comes closer, and I can see it's a woman. Then I can see she has her face in her hands. Oh, she's crying. And then she sees me, and she composes herself. And she gets closer, and I see she has no shoes on. She has no shoes on, and she's crying, and she's out on the street.

I recognize her, though I've never met her.

And just as she passes me, she says, "You got a cigarette?"

And I say, "You got a light?"

And she says, "Damn, I hope so."

And then she digs into her cutoffs in the front. Nothing. Then digs in the back. And then she has this vest on that has fifty million little pockets on it, and she's checking and checking, and it's looking bad. It's looking very bad. She digs back in the front again, deep, deep, and she pulls out a pack of matches that have been laundered at least once.

We open it up, and there is *one match* inside.

Oh my God, it's like NASA now. *How we gonna do it?* And we hunker down. We crouch on the ground. *Where's the wind coming from?* We're stopping. I take out my cigarettes. *Let's get the cigarettes ready.*

"Oh, my brand," she says. Not surprising.

We both have our cigarettes at the ready. She strikes once. Nothing. She strikes again. *Yes!* Fire. Puff. Inhale. Mmmm. The sweet kiss of that cigarette.

And we sit there, and we're loving the nicotine, and we both need this right now, I can tell. The night's been tough.

Immediately we start to reminisce about our thirty-second relationship:

"I didn't think that was gonna happen."

"Me neither."

"Oh, man, that was close."

"I'm so lucky I saw you."

"Yeah."

Then she surprises me by saying, "What was the fight about?"

And I say, "What are they all about?"

And she says, "I know what you mean. Was it a bad one?"

And I say, "You know like, medium."

"Oh."

And we start to trade stories about our lives. We're both from up north. We're both kind of newish to the neighborhood (this is in Florida). We both went to college—not great colleges, but, man, we graduated.

And I'm actually finding myself a little jealous of her because she has this really cool job washing dogs. She had horses back home, and she really loves animals, and she wants to be a vet.

And I'm like, "Man, you're halfway there!"

I'm a waitress at an ice cream parlor. I don't know where I want to be, but I know it's not that.

And then it gets a little deeper, and we share some other stuff about what our lives are like. Things that I can't ever tell people at home. This girl, I can tell her the really ugly stuff, and she understands how it can still be pretty. She understands how nice he's gonna be when I get home, and how sweet that'll be.

We are chain-smoking off each other. "Oh, that's almost out. Come on . . ."

We go through the entire pack until it's gone.

Then I say, "You know what? This is a little funny, but you're gonna have to show me the way to get home." Because although I'm twenty-three years old, I don't have my driver's license, and I just jumped out right when I needed to.

And she says, "Well, why don't you come back to my house, and I'll give you a ride?"

"Okay, great."

We start walking. And we get to this corner with lots of lights, and the roads are getting wider and wider, and there are more cars. I see lots of stores—you know, Laundromats and dollar stores and EmergiCenters.

And then we cross over US-1, and she leads me to some place, and I think, *No.*

But, yes.

Carl's Efficiency Apartments. This girl lives here.

And it's horrible, and it's lit up so bright, just to illuminate the horribleness of it. It's the kind of place where you drive your car right up, and the door's right there, and there are fifty million cigarette butts outside. There are doors one through seven, and you just know behind every single door there's some horrible misery going on. There's someone crying or drunk or lonely or cruel.

And I think, *Oh, God, she lives here. How awful.*

We go to the door—door number four—and she very, very quietly keys in. As soon as the door opens, I hear the blare of a television, and on the blue light of the television, the smoke of a hundred cigarettes in that little crack of light.

I hear a man, and he says, "Where were you?"

She says, "Never mind. I'm back."

And he says, "You all right?"

And she says, "Yeah, I'm all right."

And then she turns to me and says, "You want a beer?"

And he says, "Who the *fuck* is that?"

And she pulls me over, and he sees me, and he says, "'Oh. Hey."

I'm not a threat.

Just then he takes a drag off of his cigarette, a very hard drag—the kind that makes the end of it really heat up hot, hot, hot. And long. And it's a little scary. And I follow the cigarette down, 'cause I'm afraid of that head falling off. And I'm surprised when I see, in the crook of his arm, a little boy, sleeping. A toddler. And I think, [*gasps*].

And just then the girl reaches under the bed and takes out a carton, and she taps out the last pack of cigarettes in there. On the way up, she kisses the little boy, and then she kisses the man.

And the man says again, "You all right?"

And she says, "Yeah. I'm just gonna go out and smoke with her."

And so we go outside and sit amongst the cigarette butts and smoke.

I say, "Wow. That's your little boy?"

"Yeah, isn't he beautiful?"

"Yeah, he *is*. He is beautiful."

"He's my light. He keeps me going," she says.

We finish our cigarettes. She finishes her beer. I don't have a beer, 'cause I can't go home with beer on my breath. She goes inside to get the keys. She takes too long in there getting the keys, and I think something must be wrong.

She comes out, and she says, "Look, I'm really sorry but, um, like, we don't have any gas in the car. It's already on 'E,' and he needs to get to work in the morning. I'm gonna walk to work as it is. So what I did was, here, look, I drew out this map for you. You're like a mile and a half from home. If you walk three streets over, you'll be back on that pretty street, and you just take that and you'll be fine."

She also has wrapped up, in toilet paper, seven cigarettes for me—a third of her pack, I note. And a new pack of matches.

And she tells me, "Good-bye," and "that was great to meet you," and "how lucky," and "that was fun," and, you know, "let's be friends."

And I say, "Yeah, okay." And I walk away.

But I kinda know we're not gonna be friends. I might not ever see her again. And I kinda know I don't think she's ever gonna be a vet. And I cross, and I walk away.

And maybe this would have seemed like a visit from my possible future, and scary, but it kinda does the opposite. On the walk home I'm like, *Man, that was really grim over there. And I'm going home now to my nice boyfriend, and he's gonna be so extra-happy to see me. And we have a one-bedroom apartment. And we have two trees, and there's a yard. And we have this jar in the kitchen where there's loose money that we can use for anything. We would never, ever run out of gas. And I don't have a baby, you know? So I can leave whenever I want.*

I smoked all seven cigarettes on the way home. And people who have never smoked cigarettes just think, *Ick, disgusting and poison.* But unless you've had them and held them dear, you don't know how great they can be, and what friends and comfort and kinship they can bring.

It took me a long time to quit . . . that boyfriend. And then to quit smoking. But sometimes I still miss the smoking.

Mary Robison

Pretty Ice

I was up the whole night before my fiancé was due to arrive from the East—drinking coffee, restless and pacing, my ears ringing. When the television signed off, I sat down with a packet of the month's bills and figured amounts on a lined tally sheet in my checkbook. Under the spray of a high-intensity lamp, my left hand moved rapidly over the touch tablets of my calculator.

Will, my fiancé, was coming from Boston on the six-fifty train—the dawn train, the only train that still stopped in the small Ohio city where I lived. At six-fifteen I was still at my accounts; I was getting some pleasure from transcribing the squarish green figures that appeared in the window of my calculator. 'Schwab Dental Clinic,' I printed in a raveled backhand. 'Thirty-eight and 50/100.'

A car horn interrupted me. I looked over my desktop and out the living-room window of my rented house. The saplings in my little yard were encased in ice. There had been snow all week, and then an ice storm. In the glimmering driveway in front of my garage, my mother was peering out of her car. I got up and turned off my lamp and capped my ivory Mont Blanc pen. I found a coat in the semidark in the hall, and wound a knitted muffler at my throat. Crossing the living room, I looked away from the big pine mirror; I didn't want to see how my face and hair looked after a night of accounting.

My yard was a frozen pond, and I was careful on the walkway. My mother hit her horn again. Frozen slush came through the toe of one of my chukka boots, and I stopped on the path and frowned at her. I could see her breath rolling away in clouds from the cranked-down window of her Mazda. I have never owned a car nor learned to drive, but I had a low opinion of my mother's compact. My father and I used to enjoy big cars, with tops that came down. We were both tall and we wanted what he called 'stretch room.' My father had been dead for fourteen years, but I resented my mother's buying a car in which he would not have fitted.

'Now what's wrong? Are you coming?' my mother said.

'Nothing's wrong except that my shoes are opening around the soles,' I said. 'I just paid a lot of money for them.'

I got in on the passenger side. The car smelled of wet wool and Mother's hair spray. Someone had done her hair with a minty-white rinse, and the hair was held in place by a zebra-striped headband.

'I think you're getting a flat,' I said. 'That retread you bought for the left front is going.'

She backed the car out of the drive, using the rear-view mirror. 'I finally got a boy I can trust, at the Exxon station,' she said. 'He says that tire will last until hot weather.'

Out on the street, she accelerated too quickly and the rear of the car swung left. The tires whined for an instant on the old snow and then caught. We were knocked back in our seats a little, and an empty Kleenex box slipped off the dash and onto the floor carpet.

'This is going to be something,' my mother said. 'Will sure picked an awful day to come.'

My mother had never met him. My courtship with Will had all happened in Boston. I was getting my doctorate there, in musicology. Will was involved with his research at Boston U., and with teaching botany to undergraduates. 'You're sure he'll be at the station?' my mother said. 'Can the trains go in this weather? I don't see how they do.'

'I talked to him on the phone yesterday. He's coming.'

'How did he sound?' my mother said.

To my annoyance, she began to hum to herself.

I said, 'He's had rotten news about his work. Terrible, in fact.'

'Explain his work to me again,' she said.

'He's a plant taxonomist.'

'Yes?' my mother said. 'What does that mean?'

'It means he doesn't have a lot of money,' I said. 'He studies grasses. He said on the phone he's been turned down for a research grant that would have meant a great deal to us. Apparently the work he's been doing for the past seven or so years is irrelevant or outmoded. I guess "superficial" is what he told me.'

'I won't mention it to him, then,' my mother said.

We came to the expressway. Mother steered the car through some small windblown snow dunes and down the entrance ramp. She followed two yellow salt trucks with winking blue beacons that were moving side by side down the center and right-hand lanes.

'I think losing the grant means we should postpone the wedding,' I said. 'I want Will to have his bearings before I step into his life for good.'

'Don't wait too much longer, though,' my mother said.

After a couple of miles, she swung off the expressway. We went past some tall high-tension towers with connecting cables that looked like staff lines on a sheet of music. We were in the decaying neighborhood near the tracks. 'Now I know this is right,' Mother said. 'There's our old sign.'

The sign was a tall billboard, black and white, that advertised my father's dance studio. The studio had been closed for years and the building it had been in was gone. The sign showed a man in a tuxedo waltzing with a woman in an evening gown. I was always sure it was a waltz. The dancers were nearly two stories high, and the weather had bleached them into phantoms. The lettering—the name of the studio, my father's name—had disappeared.

'They've changed everything,' my mother said, peering about. 'Can this be the station?'

We went up a little drive that wound past a cindery lot full of flatbed trucks and that ended up at the smudgy brownstone depot.

'Is that your Will?' Mother said.

Will was on the station platform, leaning against a baggage truck. He had a duffle bag between his shoes and a plastic cup of coffee in his mittened hand. He seemed to have put on weight, girlishly, through the hips, and his face looked thicker to me, from temple to temple. His gold-rimmed spectacles looked too small.

My mother stopped in an empty cab lane, and I got out and called to Will. It wasn't far from the platform to the car, and Will's pack wasn't a large one, but he seemed to be winded when he got to me. I let him kiss me, and then he stepped back and blew a cold breath and drank from the coffee cup, with his eyes on my face.

Mother was pretending to be busy with something in her handbag, not paying attention to me and Will.

'I look awful,' I said.

'No, no, but I probably do,' Will said. 'No sleep, and I'm fat. So this is your town?'

He tossed the coffee cup at an oil drum and glanced around at the cold train yards and low buildings. A brass foundry was throwing a yellowish column of smoke over a line of Canadian Pacific boxcars.

I said, 'The problem is you're looking at the wrong side of the tracks.'

A wind whipped Will's lank hair across his face. 'Does your mom smoke?' he said. 'I ran out in the middle of the night on the train, and the club car was closed. Eight hours across Pennsylvania without a cigarette.'

The car horn sounded as my mother climbed from behind the wheel. 'That was an accident,' she said, because I was frowning at her. 'Hello. Are you Will?' She came around the car and stood on tiptoes and kissed him. 'You picked a miserable day to come and visit us.'

She was using her young-girl voice, and I was embarrassed for her. 'He needs a cigarette,' I said.

Will got into the back of the car and I sat beside my mother again. After we started up, Mother said, 'Why doesn't Will stay at my place, in your old room, Belle? I'm all alone there, with plenty of space to kick around in.'

'We'll be able to get him a good motel,' I said quickly, before Will could answer. 'Let's try that Ramada, over near the new elementary school.' It was odd, after he had come all the way from Cambridge, but I didn't want him in my old room, in the house where I had been a child. 'I'd put you at my place,' I said, 'but there's mountains of tax stuff all over.'

'You've been busy,' he said.

'Yes,' I said. I sat sidewise, looking at each of them in turn. Will had some blackish spots around his mouth — ballpoint ink, maybe. I wished he had freshened up and put on a better shirt before leaving the train.

'It's up to you two, then,' my mother said.

I could tell she was disappointed in Will. I don't know what she expected. I was thirty-one when I met him. I had probably dated fewer men in my life than she had gone out with in a single year at her sorority. She had always been successful with men.

'William was my late husband's name,' my mother said. 'Did Belle ever tell you?'

'No,' Will said. He was smoking one of Mother's cigarettes.

'I always like the name,' she said. 'Did you know we ran a dance studio?'

I groaned.

'Oh, let me brag if I want to,' my mother said. 'He was such a handsome man.'

It was true. They were both handsome — mannequins, a pair of dolls who had spent half their lives in evening clothes. But my father had looked old in the end, in a business in which you had to stay young. He had trouble with his eyes, which were bruised-looking and watery, and he had to wear glasses with thick lenses.

I said, 'It was in the dance studio that my father ended his life, you know. In the ballroom.'

'You told me,' Will said, at the same instant my mother said, 'Don't talk about it.'

My father killed himself with a service revolver. We never found out where he had bought it, or when. He was found in his warm-up clothes — a pullover sweater and pleated pants. He was wearing his tap shoes, and he had a short towel folded around his neck. He had aimed the gun barrel down his mouth, so the bullet would not shatter the wall of mirrors behind him. I was twenty then — old enough to find out how he did it.

My mother had made a wrong turn and we were on Buttles Avenue. 'Go there,' I said, pointing down a street beside Garfield Park. We passed a group of paper boys who were riding bikes with saddlebags. They were going slow, because of the ice.

'Are you very discouraged, Will?' my mother said. 'Belle tells me you are having a run of bad luck.'

'You could say so,' Will said. 'A little rough water.'

'I'm sorry,' Mother said. 'What seems to be the trouble?'

Will said, 'Well, this will be oversimplifying, but essentially what I do is take a weed and evaluate its structure and growth and habitat, and so forth.'

'What's wrong with that?' my mother said.

'Nothing. But it isn't enough.'

'I get it,' my mother said uncertainly.

I had taken a mirror and a comb from my handbag and I was trying for a clean center-part in my hair. I was thinking about finishing my bill paying.

Will said, 'What do you want to do after I check in, Belle? What about breakfast?'

'I've go to go home for a while and clean up that tax jazz, or I'll never rest,' I said. 'I'll just show up at your motel later. If we ever find it.'

'That'll be fine,' Will said.

Mother said, 'I'd offer to serve you two dinner tonight, but I think you'll want to leave me out of it. I know how your father and I felt after he went away sometimes. Which way do I turn here?'

We had stopped at an intersection near the iron gates of the park. Behind the gates there was a frozen pond, where a single early-morning skater was skating backward, expertly crossing his blades.

I couldn't drive a car but, like my father, I have always enjoyed maps and atlases. During automobile trips, I liked comparing distances on maps. I liked the words *latitude, cartography, meridian.* It was extremely annoying to me that Mother had gotten us turned around and lost in our own city, and I was angry with Will all of a sudden, for wasting seven years on something superficial.

'What about up that way?' Will said to my mother, pointing to the left. 'There's some traffic up by that light, at least.'

I leaned forward in my seat and started combing my hair all over again.

'There's no hurry,' my mother said.

'How do you mean?' I asked her.

'To get William to the motel,' she said. 'I know everybody complains, but I think an ice storm is a beautiful thing. Let's enjoy it.'

She waved her cigarette at the windshield. The sun had burned through and was gleaming in the branches of all the maples and buckeye trees in the park. 'It's twinkling like a stage set,' Mother said.

'It is pretty,' I said.

Will said, 'It'll make a bad-looking spring. A lot of shrubs get damaged and turn brown, and the trees don't blossom right.'

For once I agreed with my mother. Everything was quiet and holding still. Everything was in place, the way it was supposed to be. I put my comb away and smiled back at Will — because I knew it was for the last time.

Akhil Sharma
Surrounded by Sleep

One August afternoon, when Ajay was ten years old, his elder brother, Aman, dove into a pool and struck his head on the cement bottom. For three minutes, he lay there unconscious. Two boys continued to swim, kicking and splashing, until finally Aman was spotted below them. Water had entered through his nose and mouth. It had filled his stomach. His lungs collapsed. By the time he was pulled out, he could no longer think, talk, chew, or roll over in his sleep.

Ajay's family had moved from India to Queens, New York, two years earlier. The accident occurred during the boys' summer vacation, on a visit with their aunt and uncle in Arlington, Virginia. After the accident, Ajay's mother came to Arlington, where she waited to see if Aman would recover. At the hospital, she told the doctors and nurses that her son had been accepted into the Bronx High School of Science, in the hope that by highlighting his intelligence she would move them to make a greater effort on his behalf. Within a few weeks of the accident, the insurance company said that Aman should be transferred to a less expensive care facility, a long-term one. But only a few of these were any good, and those were full, and Ajay's mother refused to move Aman until a space opened in one of them. So she remained in Arlington, and Ajay stayed too, and his father visited from Queens on the weekends when he wasn't working. Ajay was enrolled at the local public school and in September he started fifth grade.

Before the accident, Ajay had never prayed much. In India, he and his brother used to go with their mother to the temple every Tuesday night, but that was mostly because there was a good *dosa* restaurant nearby. In America, his family went to a temple only on important holy days and birthdays. But shortly after Ajay's mother came to Arlington, she moved into the room that he and his brother had shared during the summer and made an altar in a corner. She threw an old flowered sheet over a cardboard box that had once held a television. On top she put a clay lamp, an incense-stick holder, and postcards depicting various gods. There was also a postcard of Mahatma Gandhi. She explained to Ajay that God could take any form; the picture of Mahatma Gandhi was there because he had appeared to her in a dream after the accident and told her that Aman would recover and become a surgeon. Now she and Ajay prayed for at least half an hour before the altar every morning and night.

At first she prayed with absolute humility. "Whatever you do will be good because you are doing it," she murmured to the postcards of Ram and Shivaji, daubing their lips with water and rice. Mahatma Gandhi got only water, because he did not like to eat. As weeks passed and Aman did not recover in time to return to the Bronx High School of Science for the first day of classes, his mother began doing things that called attention to her piety. She sometimes held the prayer lamp until it blistered her palms. Instead of kneeling before the altar, she lay face down. She fasted twice a week. Her attempts to sway God were not so different from Ajay's performing somersaults to amuse his aunt, and they made God seem human to Ajay.

One morning as Ajay knelt before the altar, he traced an Om, a crucifix, and a Star of David into the pile of the carpet. Beneath these he traced an *S*, for Superman, inside an upside-down triangle. His mother came up beside him.

"What are you praying for?" she asked. She had her hat on, a thick gray knitted one that a man might wear. The tracings went against the weave of the carpet and were darker than the surrounding nap. Pretending to examine them, Ajay leaned forward and put his hand over the *S*. His mother did not mind the Christian and Jewish symbols—they were for commonly recognized gods, after all—but she could not tolerate his praying to Superman. She'd caught him doing so once several weeks earlier and had become very angry, as if Ajay's faith in Superman made her faith in Ram ridiculous. "Right in front of God," she had said several times.

Ajay, in his nervousness, spoke the truth. "I'm asking God to give me a hundred percent on the math test."

His mother was silent for a moment. "What if God says you can have the math grade but then Aman will have to be sick a little while longer?" she asked.

Ajay kept quiet. He could hear cars on the road outside. He knew that his mother wanted to bewail her misfortune before God so that God would feel guilty. He looked at the postcard of Mahatma Gandhi. It was a black-and-white photo of him walking down a city street with an enormous crowd trailing behind him. Ajay thought of how, before the accident, Aman had been so modest that he would not leave the bathroom until he was fully dressed. Now he had rashes on his penis from the catheter that drew his urine into a translucent bag hanging from the guardrail of his bed.

His mother asked again, "Would you say, 'Let him be sick a little while longer'?"

"Are you going to tell me the story about Uncle Naveen again?" he asked.

"Why shouldn't I? When I was sick, as a girl, your uncle walked seven times around the temple and asked God to let him fail his exams just as long as I got better."

"If I failed the math test and told you that story, you'd slap me and ask what one has to do with the other."

His mother turned to the altar. "What sort of sons did you give me, God?" she asked. "One you drown, the other is this selfish fool."

"I will fast today so that God puts some sense in me," Ajay said, glancing away from the altar and up at his mother. He liked the drama of fasting.

"No, you are a growing boy." His mother knelt down beside him and said to the altar, "He is stupid, but he has a good heart."

Prayer, Ajay thought, should appeal with humility and an open heart to some greater force. But the praying that he and his mother did felt sly and confused. By treating God as someone to bargain with, it seemed to him, they prayed as if they were casting a spell.

This meant that it was possible to do away with the presence of God entirely. For example, Ajay's mother had recently asked a relative in India to drive a nail into a holy tree and tie a saffron thread to the nail on Aman's behalf. Ajay invented his own ritual. On his way to school each morning, he passed a thick tree rooted half on the sidewalk and half on the road. One day Ajay got the idea that if he circled the tree seven times, touching the north side every other time, he would have a lucky day. From then on he did it every morning, although he felt embarrassed and always looked around beforehand to make sure no one was watching.

One night Ajay asked God whether he minded being prayed to only in need.

"You think of your toe only when you stub it," God replied. God looked like Clark Kent. He wore a gray cardigan, slacks, and thick glasses, and had a fore-lock that curled just as Ajay's did.

God and Ajay had begun talking occasionally after Aman drowned. Now they talked most nights while Ajay lay in bed and waited for sleep. God sat at the foot of Ajay's mattress. His mother's mattress lay parallel to his, a few feet away. Originally God had appeared to Ajay as Krishna, but Ajay had felt foolish dis-cussing brain damage with a blue god who held a flute and wore a dhoti.

"You're not angry with me for touching the tree and all that?"

"No. I'm flexible."

"I respect you. The tree is just a way of praying to you," Ajay assured God.

God laughed. "I am not too caught up in formalities."

Ajay was quiet. He was convinced that he had been marked as special by Aman's accident. The beginnings of all heroes are distinguished by misfortune. Superman and Batman were both orphans. Krishna was separated from his par-ents at birth. The god Ram had to spend fourteen years in a forest. Ajay waited to speak until it would not appear improper to begin talking about himself.

"How famous will I be?" he asked finally.

"I can't tell you the future," God answered.

Ajay asked, "Why not?"

"Even if I told you something, later I might change my mind."

"But it might be harder to change your mind after you have said something will happen."

God laughed again. "You'll be so famous that fame will be a problem."

Ajay sighed. His mother snorted and rolled over.

"I want Aman's drowning to lead to something," he said to God.

"He won't be forgotten."

"I can't just be famous, though. I need to be rich too, to take care of Mummy and Daddy and pay Aman's hospital bills."

"You are always practical." God had a soulful and pitying voice, and God's sympathy made Ajay imagine himself as a truly tragic figure, like Amitabh Bachchan in the movie *Trishul*.

"I have responsibilities," Ajay said. He was so excited at the thought of his possible greatness that he knew he would have difficulty sleeping. Perhaps he would have to go read in the bathroom.

"You can hardly imagine the life ahead," God said.

Even though God's tone promised greatness, the idea of the future frightened Ajay. He opened his eyes. There was light coming from the street. The room was cold and had a smell of must and incense. His aunt and uncle's house was a narrow two-story home next to a four-lane road. The apartment building with the pool where Aman had drowned was a few blocks up the road, one in a cluster of tall brick buildings with stucco fronts. Ajay pulled the blanket tighter around him. In India, he could not have imagined the reality of his life in America: the thick smell of meat in the school cafeteria, the many television channels. And, of course, he could not have imagined Aman's accident, or the hospital where he spent so much time.

The hospital was boring. Vinod, Ajay's cousin, picked him up after school and dropped him off there almost every day. Vinod was twenty-two. In addition to attending county college and studying computer programming, he worked at a 7-Eleven near Ajay's school. He often brought Ajay hot chocolate and a comic from the store, which had to be returned, so Ajay was not allowed to open it until he had wiped his hands.

Vinod usually asked him a riddle on the way to the hospital. "Why are manhole covers round?" It took Ajay half the ride to admit that he did not know. He was having difficulty talking. He didn't know why. The only time he could talk easily was when he was with God. The explanation he gave himself for this was that just as he couldn't chew when there was too much in his mouth, he couldn't talk when there were too many thoughts in his head.

When Ajay got to Aman's room, he greeted him as if he were all right. "Hello, lazy. How much longer are you going to sleep?" His mother was always there. She got up and hugged Ajay. She asked how school had been, and he didn't know what to say. In music class, the teacher sang a song about a sailor who had bared his breast before jumping into the sea. This had caused the other students to giggle. But Ajay could not say the word *breast* to his mother without blushing. He had also cried. He'd been thinking of how Aman's accident had made his own life mysterious and confused. What would happen next? Would Aman die or would he go on as he was? Where would they live? Usually when Ajay cried in school, he was told to go outside. But it had been raining, and the teacher had sent him into the hallway. He sat on the floor and wept. Any mention of this would upset his mother. And so he said nothing had happened that day.

Sometimes when Ajay arrived his mother was on the phone, telling his father that she missed him and was expecting to see him on Friday. His father took a Greyhound bus most Fridays from Queens to Arlington, returning on Sunday night in time to work the next day. He was a bookkeeper for a department store. Before the accident, Ajay had thought of his parents as the same person: MummyDaddy. Now, when he saw his father praying stiffly or when his father failed to say hello to Aman in his hospital bed, Ajay sensed that his mother and father were quite different people. After his mother got off the phone, she always went to the cafeteria to get coffee for herself and Jell-O or cookies for him. He knew that if she took her coat with her, it meant that she was especially sad. Instead of going directly to the cafeteria, she was going to go outside and walk around the hospital parking lot.

That day, while she was gone, Ajay stood beside the hospital bed and balanced a comic book on Aman's chest. He read to him very slowly. Before turning each page, he said, "Okay, Aman?"

Aman was fourteen. He was thin and had curly hair. Immediately after the accident, there had been so many machines around his bed that only one person could stand beside him at a time. Now there was just a single waxy yellow tube. One end of this went into his abdomen; the other, blocked by a green bullet-shaped plug, was what his Isocal milk was poured through. When not being used, the tube was rolled up and bound by a rubber band and tucked beneath Aman's hospital gown. But even with the tube hidden, it was obvious that there was something wrong with Aman. It was in his stillness and his open eyes. Once, in their house in Queens, Ajay had left a plastic bowl on a radiator overnight and the sides had drooped and sagged so that the bowl looked a little like an eye. Aman reminded Ajay of that bowl.

Ajay had not gone with his brother to the swimming pool on the day of the accident, because he had been reading a book and wanted to finish it. But he heard the ambulance siren from his aunt and uncle's house. The pool was only a few minutes away, and when he got there a crowd had gathered around the ambulance. Ajay saw his uncle first, in shorts and an undershirt, talking to a man inside the ambulance. His aunt was standing beside him. Then Ajay saw Aman on a stretcher, in blue shorts with a plastic mask over his nose and mouth. His aunt hurried over to take Ajay home. He cried as they walked, although he had been certain that Aman would be fine in a few days: in a Spider-Man comic he had just read, Aunt May had fallen into a coma and she had woken up perfectly fine. Ajay had cried simply because he felt crying was called for by the seriousness of the occasion. Perhaps this moment would mark the beginning of his future greatness. From that day on, Ajay found it hard to cry in front of his family. Whenever tears started coming, he felt like a liar. If he loved his brother, he knew, he would not have thought about himself as the ambulance had pulled away, nor would he talk with God at night about becoming famous.

When Ajay's mother returned to Aman's room with coffee and cookies, she sometimes talked to Ajay about Aman. She told him that when Aman was six he had seen a children's television show that had a character named Chunu, which was Aman's nickname, and he had thought the show was based on his own life. But most days Ajay went into the lounge to read. There was a TV in the corner and a lamp near a window that looked out over a parking lot. It was the perfect place to read. Ajay liked fantasy novels where the hero, who was preferably under the age of twenty-five, had an undiscovered talent that made him famous when it was revealed. He could read for hours without interruption, and sometimes when Vinod came to drive Ajay and his mother home from the hospital it was hard for him to remember the details of the real day that had passed.

One evening when he was in the lounge, he saw a rock star being interviewed on *Entertainment Tonight*. The musician, dressed in a sleeveless undershirt that revealed a swarm of tattoos on his arms and shoulders, had begun to shout at the audience, over his interviewer, "Don't watch me! Live your life! I'm not you!" Filled with a sudden desire to do something, Ajay hurried out of the television lounge and stood on the sidewalk in front of the hospital entrance. But he did not know what to do. It was cold and dark and there was an enormous moon. Cars leaving the parking lot stopped one by one at the edge of the road. Ajay watched as they waited for an opening in the traffic, their brake lights glowing.

"Are things getting worse?" Ajay asked God. The weekend before had been Thanksgiving. Christmas soon would come, and a new year would start, a year during which Aman would not have talked or walked. Suddenly Ajay understood hopelessness. Hopelessness felt very much like fear. It involved a clutching in the stomach and a numbness in the arms and legs.

"What do you think?" God answered.

"They seem to be."

"At least Aman's hospital hasn't forced him out."

"At least Aman isn't dead. At least Daddy's Greyhound bus has never skidded off a bridge." Lately Ajay had begun talking much more quickly to God than he used to. Before, when he had talked to God, Ajay would think of what God would say in response before he said anything. Now Ajay spoke without knowing how God might respond.

"You shouldn't be angry at me." God sighed. God was wearing his usual cardigan. "You can't understand why I do what I do."

"You should explain better, then."

"Christ was my son. I loved Job. How long did Ram have to live in a forest?"

"What does that have to do with me?" This was usually the cue for discussing Ajay's prospects. But hopelessness made the future feel even more frightening than the present.

"I can't tell you what the connection is, but you'll be proud of yourself."

They were silent for a while.

"Do you love me truly?" Ajay asked.

"Yes."

"Will you make Aman normal?" As soon as Ajay asked the question, God ceased to be real. Ajay knew then that he was alone, lying under his blankets, his face exposed to the cold dark.

"I can't tell you the future," God said softly. These were words that Ajay already knew.

"Just get rid of the minutes when Aman lay on the bottom of the pool. What are three minutes to you?"

"Presidents die in less time than that. Planes crash in less time than that."

Ajay opened his eyes. His mother was on her side and she had a blanket pulled up to her neck. She looked like an ordinary woman. It surprised him that you couldn't tell, looking at her, that she had a son who was brain-dead.

In fact, things were getting worse. Putting away his mother's mattress and his own in a closet in the morning, getting up very early so he could use the bathroom before his aunt or uncle did, spending so many hours in the hospital—all this had given Ajay the reassuring sense that real life was in abeyance, and that what was happening was unreal. He and his mother and brother were just waiting to make a long-delayed bus trip. The bus would come eventually to carry them to Queens, where he would return to school at P.S. 20 and to Sunday afternoons spent at the Hindi movie theater under the trestle for the 7 train. But now Ajay was starting to understand that the world was always real, whether you were reading a book or sleeping, and that it eroded you every day.

He saw the evidence of this erosion in his mother, who had grown severe and unforgiving. Usually when Vinod brought her and Ajay home from the hospital, she had dinner with the rest of the family. After his mother helped his aunt wash the dishes, the two women watched theological action movies. One night, in spite of a headache that had made her sit with her eyes closed all afternoon, she ate dinner, washed dishes, sat down in front of the TV. As soon as the movie was over, she went upstairs, vomited, and lay on her mattress with a wet towel over her forehead. She asked Ajay to massage her neck and shoulders. As he did so, Ajay noticed that she was crying. The tears frightened Ajay and made him angry. "You shouldn't have watched TV," he said accusingly.

"I have to," she said. "People will cry with you once, and they will cry with you a second time. But if you cry a third time, people will say you are boring and always crying."

Ajay did not want to believe what she had said, but her cynicism made him think that she must have had conversations with his aunt and uncle that he did not know about. "That's not true," he told her, massaging her scalp. "Uncle is kind. Auntie Aruna is always kind."

"What do you know?" She shook her head, freeing herself from Ajay's fingers. She stared at him. Upside down, her face looked unfamiliar and terrifying. "If God lets Aman live long enough, you will become a stranger too. You will say, 'I have been unhappy for so long because of Aman, now I don't want to talk about him or look at him.' Don't think I don't know you," she said.

Suddenly Ajay hated himself. To hate himself was to see himself as the opposite of everything he wanted to be: short instead of tall, fat instead of thin. When he brushed his teeth that night, he looked at his face: his chin was round and fat as a heel. His nose was so broad that he had once been able to fit a small rock in one nostril.

His father was also being eroded. Before the accident, Ajay's father loved jokes—he could do perfect imitations—and Ajay had felt lucky to have him as a father. (Once, Ajay's father had convinced his own mother that he was possessed by the ghost of a British man.) And even after the accident, his father had impressed Ajay with the patient loyalty of his weekly bus journeys. But now his father was different.

One Saturday afternoon, as Ajay and his father were returning from the hospital, his father slowed the car without warning and turned into the dirt parking lot of a bar that looked as though it had originally been a small house. It had a pitched roof with a black tarp. At the edge of the lot stood a tall neon sign of an orange hand lifting a mug of sudsy golden beer. Ajay had never seen anybody drink except in the movies. He wondered whether his father was going to ask for directions to somewhere, and if so, to where.

His father said, "One minute," and they climbed out of the car.

They went up wooden steps into the bar. Inside, it was dark and smelled of cigarette smoke and something stale and sweet. The floor was linoleum like the kitchen at his aunt and uncle's. There was a bar with stools around it, and a basketball game played on a television bolted against the ceiling, like the one in Aman's hospital room.

His father stood by the bar waiting for the bartender to notice him. His father had a round face and was wearing a white shirt and dark dress pants, as he often did on the weekend, since it was more economical to have the same clothes for the office and home.

The bartender came over. "How much for a Budweiser?" his father asked.

It was a dollar fifty. "Can I buy a single cigarette?" He did not have to buy; the bartender would just give him one. His father helped Ajay up onto a stool and sat down himself. Ajay looked around and wondered what would happen if somebody started a knife fight. When his father had drunk half his beer, he carefully lit the cigarette. The bartender was standing at the end of the bar. There were only two other men in the place. Ajay was disappointed that there were no women wearing dresses slit all the way up their thighs. Perhaps they came in the evenings.

His father asked him if he had ever watched a basketball game all the way through.

"I've seen the Harlem Globetrotters."

His father smiled and took a sip. "I've heard they don't play other teams, because they can defeat everyone else so easily."

"They only play against each other, unless there is an emergency—like in the cartoon, when they play against the aliens to save the Earth," Ajay said.

"Aliens?"

Ajay blushed as he realized his father was teasing him.

When they left, the light outside felt too bright. As his father opened the car door for Ajay, he said, "I'm sorry." That's when Ajay first felt that his father might have done something wrong. The thought made him worry. Once they were on the road, his father said gently, "Don't tell your mother."

Fear made Ajay feel cruel. He asked his father, "What do you think about when you think of Aman?"

Instead of becoming sad, Ajay's father smiled. "I am surprised by how strong he is. It's not easy for him to keep living. But even before, he was strong. When he was interviewing for high school scholarships, one interviewer asked him, 'Are you a thinker or a doer?' He laughed and said, 'That's like asking, "Are you an idiot or a moron?"'"

From then on they often stopped at the bar on the way back from the hospital. Ajay's father always asked the bartender for a cigarette before he sat down, and during the ride home he always reminded Ajay not to tell his mother.

Ajay found that he himself was changing. His superstitions were becoming extreme. Now when he walked around the good-luck tree he punched it, every other time, hard, so that his knuckles hurt. Afterward, he would hold his breath for a moment longer than he thought he could bear, and ask God to give the unused breaths to Aman.

In December, a place opened in one of the good long-term care facilities. It was in New Jersey. This meant that Ajay and his mother could move back to New York and live with his father again. This was the news Ajay's father brought when he arrived for a two-week holiday at Christmas.

Ajay felt the clarity of panic. Life would be the same as before the accident but also unimaginably different. He would return to P.S. 20, while Aman continued to be fed through a tube in his abdomen. Life would be Aman's getting older and growing taller than their parents but having less consciousness than even a dog, which can become excited or afraid.

Ajay decided to use his devotion to shame God into fixing Aman. The fact that two religions regarded the coming December days as holy ones suggested to Ajay that prayers during this time would be especially potent. So he prayed whenever he thought of it—at his locker, even in the middle of a quiz. His mother wouldn't let him fast, but he started throwing away the lunch he took to school. And when his mother prayed in the morning, Ajay watched to make sure that she bowed at least once toward each of the postcards of deities. If she did not, he bowed three times to the possibly offended god on the postcard. He had noticed that his father finished his prayers in less time than it took to brush his teeth. And so now, when his father began praying in the morning, Ajay immediately crouched down beside him, because he knew his father would be embarrassed to get up first. But Ajay found it harder and harder to drift in the rhythm of sung prayers or into his nightly conversations with God. How could chanting and burning incense undo three minutes of a sunny August afternoon? It was like trying to move a sheet of blank paper from one end of a table to the other by blinking so fast that you started a breeze.

On Christmas Eve his mother asked the hospital chaplain to come to Aman's room and pray with them. The family knelt together beside Aman's bed. Afterward the chaplain asked her whether she would be attending Christmas services. "Of course, Father," she said.

"I'm also coming," Ajay said.

The chaplain turned toward Ajay's father, who was sitting in a wheelchair because there was nowhere else to sit.

"I'll wait for God at home," he said.

That night, Ajay watched *It's a Wonderful Life* on television. To him, the movie meant that happiness arrived late, if ever. Later, when he got in bed and closed his eyes, God appeared. There was little to say.

"Will Aman be better in the morning?"

"No."

"Why not?"

"When you prayed for the math exam, you could have asked for Aman to get better, and instead of your getting an A, Aman would have woken."

This was so ridiculous that Ajay opened his eyes. His father was sleeping nearby on folded-up blankets. Ajay felt disappointed at not feeling guilt. Guilt might have contained some hope that God existed.

When Ajay arrived at the hospital with his father and mother the next morning, Aman was asleep, breathing through his mouth while a nurse poured a can of Isocal into his stomach through the yellow tube. Ajay had not expected that Aman would have recovered; nevertheless, seeing him that way put a weight in Ajay's chest.

The Christmas prayers were held in a large, mostly empty room: people in chairs sat next to people in wheelchairs. His father walked out in the middle of the service.

Later, Ajay sat in a corner of Aman's room and watched his parents. His mother was reading a Hindi women's magazine to Aman while she shelled peanuts into her lap. His father was reading a thick red book in preparation for a civil service exam. The day wore on. The sky outside grew dark. At some point Ajay began to cry. He tried to be quiet. He did not want his parents to notice his tears and think that he was crying for Aman, because in reality he was crying for how difficult his own life was.

His father noticed first. "What's the matter, hero?"

His mother shouted, "What happened?" and she sounded so alarmed it was as if Ajay were bleeding.

"I didn't get any Christmas presents. I need a Christmas present," Ajay shouted. "You didn't buy me a Christmas present." And then, because he had revealed his own selfishness, Ajay let himself sob. "You have to give me something. I should get something for all this." Ajay clenched his hands and wiped his face with his fists. "Each time I come here I should get something."

His mother pulled him up and pressed him into her stomach. His father came and stood beside them. "What do you want?" his father asked.

Ajay had no prepared answer for this.

"What do you want?" his mother repeated.

The only thing he could think was, "I want to eat pizza and I want candy."

His mother stroked his hair and called him her little baby. She kept wiping his face with a fold of her sari. When at last he stopped crying, they decided that Ajay's father should take him back to his aunt and uncle's. On the way, they stopped at a mini-mall. It was a little after five, and the streetlights were on. Ajay and his father did not take off their winter coats as they ate, in a pizzeria staffed by Chinese people. While he chewed, Ajay closed his eyes and tried to imagine God looking like Clark Kent, wearing a cardigan and eyeglasses, but he could not. Afterward, Ajay and his father went next door to a magazine shop and Ajay got a bag of Three Musketeers bars and a bag of Reese's peanut butter cups, and then he was tired and ready for home.

He held the candy in his lap while his father drove in silence. Even through the plastic, he could smell the sugar and chocolate. Some of the houses outside were dark, and others were outlined in Christmas lights.

After a while Ajay rolled down the window slightly. The car filled with wind. They passed the building where Aman's accident had occurred. Ajay had not walked past it since the accident. When they drove by, he usually looked away. Now he tried to spot the fenced swimming pool at the building's side. He wondered whether the pool that had pressed itself into Aman's mouth and lungs and stomach had been drained, so that nobody would be touched by its unlucky waters. Probably it had not been emptied until fall. All summer long, people must have swum in the pool and sat on its sides, splashing their feet in the water, and not known that his brother had lain for three minutes on its concrete bottom one August afternoon.

CHAPTER FIVE

ENERGY

Are you creating work readers are excited about reading? Or are you writing stuff people read only because they feel they have to: It's for class, or they're polite, or they're your friend, or maybe they're in love with you.

As readers, we get bored easily. Competing for our attention are pages and pages of great writing, social media, and many responsibilities, distractions, and endeavors. As writers, we have to be creative to capture and keep our readers. You can make *everything* you write more interesting and attractive to readers by paying attention to a single concept: **energy**.

> *Think of the fierce energy concentrated in an acorn! You bury it in the ground, and it explodes into an oak! Bury a sheep and nothing happens but decay.*
> — GEORGE BERNARD SHAW

THE PRINCIPLES OF ENERGY

Writers work with three principles in order to increase the energy and interest level in all types of creative writing.

1. **Subjects.** A good writer can make any topic interesting. Subjects that will lead to energetic writing are those (a) that you experience firsthand, (b) that you wonder about passionately, and (c) about which you are the sole expert. If you are into it, your reader will follow.
2. **Leaps.** Writers leave gaps on purpose so that the reader has the pleasure of filling in pieces of the picture on his or her own. Leaping is one of the most effective energizing techniques available, and one of the simplest to master. Visual artists use negative space to add drama to their work, and so do writers. If you are explaining everything, your reader will lose interest. You have to stay one step ahead of your reader.

3. **Words.** Some words spark and sizzle and pop (like the words *spark, sizzle,* and *pop*). Words in unexpected places create energy, too. The words in some documents (think of a legal brief, a handbook, or anything boring you have read lately) make the reader's eyes glaze over ("Faculty research abstract platform decisions will be considered . . .").

PRACTICE

Locate a piece of writing (yours, someone else's) that you find exceptionally boring: directions for assembling a desk, a tedious textbook, a poorly written travel blog. Also locate a piece of writing you find extremely interesting, lively, a joy to read and reread: the first page of your favorite novel, love letters, juicy texts or song lyrics, your favorite piece from this textbook or this course so far. Contrast the two pieces. Can you find in each an example (good or bad) of each of the three qualities of energy? Compare your findings in class.

Subject: Focus on What's Fascinating

As humans, as readers, we're automatically drawn to the new. If you write about something you alone on the planet can write about, your writing is going to be interesting and energized.

> *I merely took the energy it takes to pout and wrote some blues.*
> — DUKE ELLINGTON

What to choose for a subject? What only you know about, and no one else. Everyone knows what it is like to grow up, turn seven years old, struggle with your mother's rules. But no one knows what it was like to turn seven inside Apartment 8R on Prospect Avenue, where a kid sat on a cake, and the mother drank three martinis, and all this happened before noon. And your Superman underwear was really, really itchy.

Most people know high school graduation, loneliness, flat tires. But no one knows *your* specific experience. It doesn't matter if you are writing poetry, fantasy fiction, love letters, short stories, or screenplays. And you do not need to write autobiography. It's your specific repertoire of emotions and details that makes good writing good. The American playwright Edward Albee is gay, but he writes male-female marital discord better than anyone else. Writers use their own firsthand experience—with their parents, friends, coworkers—to create an energetic backdrop, landscape, and engine for original creative writing.

If you can *put* yourself there, using only the power of your mind, you can write it. You can tell you have chosen a good, alive subject if it gives you energy to work on it. A good creative writing topic unnerves you a little. When a subject in this class is alive, it's going to shift as you work, too. You'll start out writing about your relationship with a lover, and realize you are also writing about your parents! You'll start out writing about how ridiculous your relationship was, and realize, by the end of your piece, how complex two people really are. Some students feel uncomfortable with that fact—subjects shift and drift. But good subjects *are* alive. Good subjects aren't static (if they are, they are B-O-R-I-N-G). If you already know what you are going to say about your subject, you're going to struggle to keep the writing energized.

> *There is a vitality, a life force, an energy, a quickening, that is translated through you into action, and because there is only one of you in all time, this expression is unique.*
> — MARTHA GRAHAM

Good writers choose a topic they know a lot about—relationships, travel, growing up, bedrooms, hotels, restaurants, the mosque on 42nd Street—and they trust (this is the hard part) that they will discover things about the topic as they work.

You also create energy and grip your readers by engaging with powerful subject matter that may be quite far from your own everyday experience—but you still have to be up close to your subject, able to write what you see before you, and from firsthand knowledge. It's very hard to write about war, death, torture, or apocalypse if your sole source of information is media and not witnesses. In fact, poet Carolyn Forché terms her work "poetry of witness." When she traveled with Amnesty International to El Salvador, she found the country in crisis: in the midst of a civil war. She witnessed hospitals and clinics in shambles. She learned, from parents, about the sexual mutilation of girls. She learned, firsthand from talking to people there, about torture and brutality going unreported in the news. When she set pen to paper, she wrote about her experience, powerfully. When you read her famous prose poem "The Colonel," notice where the energy comes from. This piece also provides a terrific example of "Going Cold," a technique discussed on page 322.

Carolyn Forché
The Colonel

What you have heard is true. I was in his house. His wife carried a tray of coffee and sugar. His daughter filed her nails, his son went out for the night. There were daily papers, pet dogs, a pistol on the cushion beside him. The moon swung bare on its black cord over the house. On the television was a cop show. It was in English. Broken bottles were embedded in the walls around the house to scoop the kneecaps from a man's legs or cut his hands to lace. On the windows there were gratings like those in liquor stores. We had dinner, rack of lamb, good wine, a gold bell was on the table for calling the maid. The maid brought green mangoes, salt, a type of bread. I was asked how I enjoyed the country. There was a brief commercial in Spanish. His wife took everything away. There was some talk then of how difficult it had become to govern. The parrot said hello on the terrace. The colonel told it to shut up, and pushed himself from the table. My friend said to me with his eyes: say nothing. The colonel returned with a sack used to bring groceries home. He spilled many human ears on the table. They were like dried peach halves. There is no other way to say this. He took one of them in his hands, shook it in our faces, dropped it into a water glass. It came alive there. I am tired of fooling around he said. As for the rights of anyone, tell your people they can go fuck themselves. He swept the ears to the floor with his arm and held the last of his wine in the air. Something for your poetry, no? he said. Some of the ears on the floor caught this scrap of his voice. Some of the ears on the floor were pressed to the ground.

Read the prose poem aloud. Read it two more times—a lot of energy is packed into these few lines. Notice the simple title, shining like a flashlight down the spine of the prose poem. This is a portrait poem, and it's a terrifying portrait of a brutal military leader. The speaker, a writer, probably the poet herself, writes very plainly, addressing the poem to "you." Instead of talking in general, which causes energy to dissipate, she confines the energy in the form of an intimate letter-like address: "What you have heard is true." Contrast her opening with a typical report, devoid of energy, which might begin something like this: "In today's society, there are many examples of brutality."

Forché's use of energy entices us to keep reading—we feel we are being let in on a secret or a private confession between two people. As the piece progresses, she shows in each line what she sees. She doesn't write emotions or feelings: We watch as she watches the details of a domestic evening unfolding—nail filing, son going out. Moon on cord. There's energy in the descriptions because they are active, precise, and unusual, too. Moon on cord? In line 6, there's a turn. This place is not a safe place; this is the home of a dangerous and brutal man, where instruments of torture are also items of decoration. Forché doesn't put in her emotions: She wants the energy to leap off the page of the poem and into the reader without her own intervention to soften the blows. She builds the energy by juxtaposing horror (scooped kneecaps) with beauty, pleasure, and sustenance (mangoes, parrots, bread).

She writes in short sentences, not quite breathless, but with one action or observation per sentence, the piece reads very quickly: boom, boom, boom. "It came alive there. I am tired of fooling around he said." These leaps from observation to dialogue create energy, too.

PRACTICE

Discuss the energy in Forché's "The Colonel." What do you make of the ending? Does it increase the energy? Where do you find subtext in the piece? How might subtext also add to the energy?

Energy is an essential requirement of any piece of creative writing. To hone energy skills, it can be helpful for writers in any genre to study plays and screenplays. Screenwriters, along with playwrights and graphic/comic writers, have to focus very carefully on energy when they create a new piece. In these genres, there is simply nowhere to hide, no room for a long descriptive passage or a foray into theme. Every single syllable has to crackle. Screenwriters know to choose settings and characters that spark and bristle with aliveness. They begin their pieces with action. Above all, they make sure to put enormous energy in the dialogue—each line spoken aloud in a screenplay or a play must sizzle with energy. Think about energy in dialogue this way: Let's say you speak about three thousand sentences in a day. Of these sentences, how many would be energized enough to make it onto the page, lively enough to create a spark for a reader? Twenty? Ten? One? (Many writers carry around a writer's notebook in order to catch energized details, actions, and lines overheard, and these observations and quotes feed life into their works.)

PRACTICE

Read the excerpt from Charlotte Glynn's "Duct Tape Twins" (p. 218), written when she was a student, and make a list of all the places you find energy. Does the screenplay have any subtext—information for the reader that isn't spelled out on the page?

Guidelines for Increasing Energy

Provide Interesting Information. Deliver information-rich writing, using specific insider details and expert vocabulary. Be generous with details. This is a valuable way to keep your reader interested in your work. We read for many reasons, but one is to learn. Smart writers include interesting facts and weave in startling, unusual, and specific details.

Read the poem "What Every Soldier Should Know" by Brian Turner (p. 217). Notice how Turner provides *images* from the war, and notice how lively the poem is. The Arabic words he utilizes teach the reader something of the language, the culture, the danger, and the complexity. RPGs, parachute bombs, how much it costs to kill a man— this poem is jam-packed with *interesting information*.

Avoid the General, which always lacks energy: Strive for specifics in your subject. Good writers always get the real name, the actual address, the specific phrase, the right translation, because the power in writing lies in that exactness.

Write about Lively, Particular Subjects You Know Intimately. Some topics are hard to make interesting, though clever writers always find a way. Homeless people you know nothing about, historical figures you're mildly familiar with, general types, indistinct locations—these are all energy black holes. Subjects that force you to write about passive conditions—dreaming, falling asleep, driving—are all hard to infuse with energy. Conversely, you can write energetically when your focus is last night's brawl at the Dirty Parrot. Your rich aunt's summer visit to your trailer park. A pack of high school punks wreaking havoc, Robin Hood–style, in the Sunset Heights subdivision at the edge of Detroit—that's the kind of subject that is already infused with energy.

In sum, you don't need to reveal your deepest, darkest secrets, but you do need to make readers feel you are giving them your best stuff. What's juicy? What do you know about that is strange, interesting, unusual? What kinds of things have you seen that are outside normal day-to-day experience? Use a microscope to view your life, the lives of people you know, your past. If you haven't been to a war zone, it may be very difficult for you to create energy in your piece of writing; if all your images come from what you have learned from television, video games, and movies, your writing is likely to be flat and not energized with interesting, closely observed specifics. However, if you observe normal day-to-day experience closely enough, you will create energy.

PRACTICE

Make two two-column lists. First, list all the places you have lived (include summer camps, extended vacations, weekend stayovers). In the second column, list the most dramatic thing that occurred at each location. Next, make another list, of the outdoor settings of your life from ages five to eighteen. Start with your backyard on Jenson Street. Pan your mind's movie camera (you have to "flash" or see the location in order to put it on your list) across the kindergarten playground, the big plastic slide. Then, slowly panning the exterior shots of your life, to the grocery store parking lot, then the sandlot where you played baseball, then the creek where you went every day in fifth grade. Your secret woods spot in middle school. The train tracks where you kissed. In the second column for this list, write down the name of one or two other people who were also there.

You now have subjects. Mine these lists for the rest of the semester, for fiction, poetry, nonfiction, or plays. You can invent situations, but they will always be based in a real, energized scene. That's the secret of subject: grounding in the real.

Leaps: The Power of Gaps

Remember Amy Fusselman's memoir (p. 76) of her father, her pregnancy, and her daily life as an itinerant musician? In those short sections, Fusselman *leapt* from topic to topic. She kept cycling through key moments in the three braids, those three stories. The short sections create energy. When you look at the page, your eye leaps around, as with a poem. The interplay among the white space, the numbered sections, and the tinier sections within the numbered parts invites the reader to leap.

Readers like short sections.

Readers are attracted to *movement*. Fiction writers, essayists, and poets employ the method of leaping in order to leave plenty of room for the reader to engage with the material.

Spelling everything out, providing detailed transitions, explaining and reviewing and going over it again: That may be effective for your chemistry textbook, but it's death to art. Art is more like a game, a pleasing game, one that's got a bit of a challenge in it.

> *The artist never entirely knows. We guess. We may be wrong, but we take leap after leap in the dark.*
> — AGNES DE MILLE

The reader *wants* to figure things out. The reader wants to play. So creative writers leap because leaping creates energy. Notice in "What Every Soldier Should Know" on page 217 that the couplets (two-line stanzas) force the reader to make leaps from section to section—fourteen leaps! The poet, Brian Turner, didn't want the lulling calm of a prose poem or the warmth of long stanzas. Rapid-fire couplets keep the reader hopping, on the move, an effect that suits Turner's subject extremely well. Leaps create a lot of energy.

PRACTICE

Read Brian Arundel's "The Things I've Lost" (p. 216). Make a list of the leaps, and analyze how leaps energize this piece.

When you employ leaps in your work, you are comprehensible and interesting on the first reading, but the aware reader knows there's more there. The reader gets a full, confusion-free experience the first read. On a second and third reading, the piece reveals more information, more connections. Leaps leave room for that dynamic between a reader and a work.

Read the following excerpt, from Jessica Shattuck's story "Bodies" (p. 263).

> *When in doubt, make a fool of yourself. There is a microscopically thin line between being brilliantly creative and acting like the most gigantic idiot on earth. So what the hell, leap.*
> — CYNTHIA HEIMEL

In the fluorescent light of the refrigerator, the halved parsnips look naked—pale and fleshy as limbs. Annie pauses before pulling them out. A refrigerator is like a hospital, a bright place that is not cheerful. A protective but uncertain place to wait.

Compare the writing above to this prose excerpt from another writer.

When the alarm clock went off, I woke up and I reached over and turned it off and got out of bed. I walked across the room and I went to the bathroom which was close by and when I went in, I turned on the light so I could see. I was wondering what I was going to do today. I was just waking up.

Which piece has more energy? Why?

In the second excerpt, we find a blow-by-blow description of a fairly typical morning. This example shows the opposite of leaping. Here, things are filled in completely, with no surprises. Everything is predictable and explained. The reader may read along, but what is the point of this piece? Would you read it again? Does it have any energy?

Don't explain. Leap—from bathroom to office, from something interesting to the next interesting thing. Leaps are the places where the writer purposely leaves something out, skips ahead, or changes topic. Leaps, like dotted lines, trace complete thoughts, but *gaps* allow the reader to actively participate in creating the image, thought, or meaning.

We readers like to be set up for success. We want to feel smart when we read, not clueless, and we want to make sure you the author know what you are doing. We don't want to be set up for a fall (there's no pattern, there's no point, or you don't really let us see). To follow the random associations of someone thinking out loud can be confusing, boring, or pointless. To be provided with planned surprises—that's energy.

Adjust your focus: Write what you see; leap, leave out filler sections (or simply take them out before sharing your work with others). Once you start using the leaping technique, you will be amazed at how much explanation you can leave out. Readers are pretty savvy—they figure out a lot from just a few hints.

By writing what you see, you allow the reader to form an image and *draw his or her own conclusions.*

One of the most important places this principle occurs is in dialogue. Good dialogue leaps. Nothing is deadlier to creative writing energy than dialogue that explains and tells.

JOEY: What's wrong, Emily? You look really sad. Are you blue because you got a D– on your history test this morning in first period? It seemed like you were really struggling with that test.

EMILY: Thanks for noticing, Joey. That test was so hard. I'm really feeling
    bad about this.
JOEY: This is terrible. Is it going to kill your average?
EMILY: It may cause me to fail the class.
JOEY: What can you do?
EMILY: I don't know.

Here, the author is using one character to get information out of the other
character. In good creative writing, dialogue bristles with energy when each
character has his or her own agenda, and the agendas conflict, causing gaps,
leaps. Good dialogue (as you know from being in great conversations) is like a
tennis match. The energy moves back and forth, with equal force on both
sides. Each person is trying to win. Here, no one is even in the game. Emily
did poorly on a test. Okay. Why should I care? Unless she cares passionately,
I'm not going to. And what's Joey's angle? Does he want to sell her an answer
key? Drugs? Get a date? Unless he wants something that directly conflicts with
what Emily wants, there's no energy. There are no leaps. Both characters are
on the same topic, plodding along. Explaining. Carefully, slowly, boringly, filling in all the gaps.

In dialogue, you'll be able to leap if your characters are at cross purposes.
They'll each be going in a different direction. Your reader will have to move
quickly to keep up—that's what you want.

Compare this example of crisp, energetic dialogue from *The Sopranos* by
James Manos Jr. and David Chase. Tony and his daughter Meadow are visiting
colleges. Meadow comes out of the admissions office, and her father asks her
how it went.

MEADOW: They've got a 48 to 52 male-female ratio which is great—strong
    liberal arts program, and this cool Olin Arts Center for music. Usual
    programs abroad—China, India—
TONY: You're just applying here and you're already leaving?

Notice the energy. Meadow is specific. She broad-
casts her agenda. She leaps from social benefits to
infrastructure to study abroad. Tony's agenda probably isn't for his daughter to enjoy the benefits of
an equal male-female ratio. When he asks her for
more information, the reader *leaps*: We know he
doesn't care how she answers the question. He is

> *We must walk consciously
> only part way toward our
> goal, and then leap in the
> dark to our success.*
> — HENRY DAVID THOREAU

not asking her *for more information*. There's a gap in what he says—on the
surface—and in what he intends. Meadow lists what she likes about the college. She doesn't really care what her father thinks at this point. Tony doesn't

want her to go away, to be too far out of his control. No filler. No explanation. The leaps and gaps leave plenty of room for the reader to figure things
out—that's the pleasure of energy. We readers are set up by the author to
know *more* than the characters themselves. The dialogue leaps, and we scoot
along to keep up.

The Tony-Meadow conversation continues like this as they stroll across
campus:

> MEADOW: It's an option, Dad. Junior year.
> TONY: What do you study in India? How to avoid diarrhea?
> MEADOW: They don't require SAT scores but mine'll help 'cause they're
>   high. Socially—I don't know. This one girl told me there's this saying,
>   "Bates is the world's most expensive form of contraception."
> TONY: What the hell kind of talk is that? You mean the girls at the other
>   colleges we been to just put out?
> MEADOW: Oh, my God.
> TONY: And another thing—every school we visit there's the gay/lesbian this
>   and that—the teachers know this is going on?
> MEADOW: Oh, my God. (*Stops, admires campus.*) Pretty, huh?
> TONY: (*Agrees, then—*) Two to go. Colby up. (*They walk through the
>   leafiness.*)
> MEADOW: Dad . . . how come you didn't finish college?
> TONY: I had that semester and a half at Seton Hall.
> MEADOW: Yeah? And?

This dialogue emits a high level of energy because the characters leap just as we
do in real-life conversations. Meadow is simultaneously thinking out loud, sig-
naling her father to stop being an idiot, and admiring the college. Tony leaps
from social criticism, to fatherly overprotectiveness, to homophobia, to the next
college on the list.

Notice what isn't here, what isn't explained. By leaping, a writer generates
reader involvement. Information about conflict, values, and character comes out
between the lines. We readers (or viewers) know, without it being said—this
information comes through in the gaps, called the **subtext**—that Tony wants
his daughter to have a good education and a conventional life. We know he is
embarrassed by his lack of formal education. We know he is afraid of her leaving
home. We know Meadow isn't afraid of her father. She's curious about him, and
she doesn't know a lot about his history. She's mostly concerned with her ability
to enjoy the social benefits of her educational experience. Is Meadow in some
ways more worldly than her father? Is she embarrassed by him? Does Tony feel
in over his head? Is he giving up fighting with her when he says, "Two to go.
Colby up"?

Just when the reader has gotten the pace, the thread, the track, the good writer switches up again. Tony landed someplace different in that line, didn't he? Not where we expected (Meadow's interrogative). The leaps vary in length and pace.

Consider again Joey and Emily: We know so very little about their values, backgrounds, and conflicts. Their dialogue lacks energy—of subject, of gap (they mean exactly what they say). The dialogue is used to interview one character for one reason alone: to give information to the reader. There's not enough energy in that purpose.

Which brings us back to words. Contrast the word choices in the Joey-Emily and Tony-Meadow examples. As you read in Chapter Three, words are a powerful way to energize your work.

Words

Words are what creative writers use to make their art forms. It's worth taking a closer look at these building blocks.

All the words in everything you write are important. You might have a great subject and leap like Stephen King, but if the words you are using are dead, flat, or abstract, energy will leak out of your piece with a slow, steady *woosh*.

Writers are people for whom words are *interesting*. Writers like messing around with words, adjusting, fussing, trying out different ones. Use language like painters use their tools. Make a mess. Play around. See what combinations flicker with energy, see which ones beam.

Most creative writers find it easier to fine-tune, adjust, mess with writing as they are doing it. Few writers feel their first drafts are ready to share. Experimenting with different words—*word by word*—is part of the pleasure, and the challenge, of creative writing. Notice how you work best. Do you fiddle around with sentences, lines, and dialogue, testing different word choices as you go? Or do you work better when you write a whole draft and then go back and look for flat, ineffective, vague word choices?

Specificity. Words that generate energy create a spark in the reader's brain. These are fresh, lively, simple, clear, or unexpected words that capture our attention while aiding our apprehension of the image. **Word packages** are overly familiar phrases in which perfectly fine words lose energy because they are constantly yoked together: *beautiful blue eyes, red rose, gaping hole, awkward moment.* Good writers enjoy busting up word packages and recombining their elements to create original effects: *gaping moment, awkward rose.* See the difference? Avoid your thesaurus, and focus on moving words around into interesting, unusual combinations, and you will instantly energize your work.

Rank the following words, using a scale of 0 to 10. A 10 is high octane, a 0 is very low pulse rate. Do you notice anything about what the 5+ words have in common?

Frizzed	Blue
Surge	Beautiful
Important	Wondering
Understanding	Apartment
Very	Flapjack

Abstract words (think SAT vocab words) clot your writing with low-energy spots. When the reader has to *think*, she's not in your piece of writing. She's working. Readers want to enjoy the reading experience, and you, the writer, need to do the work to make that happen. Fiddle around, don't write from habit: Choose words that are surprising, fresh, unexpected, and different (but not distracting). Simple one-syllable words are going to make your writing pulse.

Consider the differences between the two words in each of the following pairs:

road	avenue
jerk	unpleasant person
party	reception
fun	enjoyable
tunes	aural interlude

Many writers, when they are starting out, feel obligated to sound "writerly." They choose words that sound bookish and important. Their poor readers. Some overly writerly words include many adverbs (*suddenly, finally, interestingly, absolutely*) and clichéd shortcuts to rendering emotions: *she furrowed her brow, he raised an eyebrow, tears streamed from her face, his jaw dropped.* Use what you learned in Part One, and write what you see. What does your character *really* do when he or she is frustrated, skeptical, or shocked? Use the words that describe your actual scene, not the general population's explanatory shorthand.

Every word counts.

Good writers choose a straightforward, fresh, simple, lively vocabulary. Crisp nouns and simple adjectives, used sparingly, are energetic and produce a picture, like a movie or a dream, in the reader's mind. One of the following examples uses words that are trying too hard to sound "literary" and abstractions that short-circuit energy instead of creating it.

Consider the following paragraph by Rick Moody, from his energy-rich short story "Boys" (p. 212).

Boys enter the house, boys enter the house. Boys, and with them the ideas of boys (ideas leaden, reductive, inflexible), enter the house. Boys, two of them, wound into hospital packaging, boys with infant pattern baldness, slung in the arms of parents, boys dreaming of breasts, enter the house. Twin boys, kettles on the boil, boys in hideous vinyl knapsacks that young couples from Edison, NJ, wear on their shirt fronts, knapsacks coated with baby saliva and staphylococcus and milk vomit, enter the house.

Compare this to the following paragraph. What do you notice about the differences in language choices?

They were just typical kids. You know kids. The normal American kind. The boy was thinking about how he just wanted the day to end so he could get out of school and get to the project. He had been dreaming about this project for years. It was so great to finally be so close. So close. And yet so far, too. It seemed as though he and his buddy would never be able to really get there. Those afternoons were slow.

PRACTICE

For the examples above, underline each word that has some spark, some specificity — some energy. Which words are vivid, energetic? Circle all the words in each passage that are deadweight, predictable, blocking energy rather than creating it. Which passage has higher octane? Reflect on where you "see" the writing, intuitively, versus where you use your intellect to make a picture. Does the higher-energy passage "pop" images into your mind's eye?

PRACTICE

Reread the excerpt from Amy Fusselman's memoir *The Pharmacist's Mate* (p. 76), and read Rick Moody's story "Boys," which appears in full on page 212. In each piece, locate at least six phrases that do not usually occur in that combination. *Wild horses* and *thin man* are word packages. You are looking for fresh, unusual combinations (and energy), such as *elephant pants, Sleeping Tubby and Snow Weight, shirtsleeves aglow with torchlight.* You will end up with a list of twelve phrases. Number your pairs, with 1 being the most energetic, high-wattage combination, and 12 being sparkly, but not as much as the others.

Verbs. The most energetic word — the pulse point in any sentence — is the verb. Verbs must be strong, vivid, clear, and simple so that the reader stays interested in your writing. When you describe actions, the verbs, crisp action verbs — *run, fling, pour, pinch* — are the muscles of your sentences. Readers move through your

> *Drama is life with the dull parts left out.*
> — ALFRED HITCHCOCK

sentence or line hungry for action, for movement, and when they get to the verb, something needs to happen.

When you describe *thinking* (*I wondered, I reflected, I worried, I thought, He reminded me of, He was brooding, I concluded*), the energy decreases, sharply. These **filters**—words that refer to mental activity—are flabby and can be deadly to strong, energetic writing.

Muscles. Let's say you are writing a story about a college freshman's visit to his physics professor's office. The purpose of the visit is to go over a flunked test. As he waits for his prof to call him into the office, the student thinks to himself, "I don't like this guy, I don't like the way he lectures, the textbook is confusing, and my roommate, who put the exact same thing for the essay question as I did, got a B–."

No action. No muscle. A guy, in a chair, *thinking*. There aren't any action verbs—any muscles—any vehicles for energy. It's all taking place in a human head. Good writers don't do this. They find ways to set up situations where they can show off their facility with *verbs*.

PRACTICE

Go through Rick Moody's "Boys" (p. 212) with a highlighter (or make a list). Locate every single verb: *enter, wound, slung, wear, coated, dreaming, striking, speaking*, etc. What *kinds* of verbs does Moody choose? What verbs does he avoid using? Of his verb choices on your list, which are the most energetic, the strongest? Would you like to incorporate a few of these verbs into your own writing?

As you scan back over the work you have read so far this semester, you may notice that the published writers choose their verbs very carefully. Authors like verbs that pack a punch, avoiding the forms of the verb *to be* and reflective, passive verbs.

In our student-professor tale, if we apply muscles to our sentences, as Moody does, what happens? What if instead of having him *think* this in the department foyer, you had him *say* this to the department secretary, another student, or the professor himself? Could your student boil over, cross, shimmy, shoot? What would be interesting? Notice that all the aspects of energy—subject, leaps, and words—interrelate and overlap.

PRACTICE

List three activities you are *very* familiar with: soccer, cooking, sailing, tae kwon do, sewing, babysitting. Make three columns, with your topics at the top. Fill each column with the verbs associated with that activity: flying could lead to *fuel, pitch, roll, yaw, soar, dive, crash, loft, jet*. Running might give you *sprint, pace, bolt, trudge, fly, race*. Return to your lists often, to replace the verbs you circle as weak in your writing with these more energetic words. Add to your lists when you think of new verbs; when you are reading, note verbs that are interesting, ones you could use yourself, such as *remove, leap, drop, cover, smell, swoop, fry, angle*.

Filters. We call thought words like *seemed, felt, wondered,* and *realized* filters. They describe mental activity and weaken your writing by drawing attention to the writer's thought process instead of the scene at hand.

In first-year composition, where students are taught to write expository essays, a list of commonly used verbs is often distributed.

acknowledges	*claims*
advises	*concludes*
agrees	*declares*
allows	*disputes*
answers	*feels*
asserts	*remarks*
believes	*thinks*

These words, while useful for writing essays for academic classes, are the *opposite* of the words creative writers use. Expository essays appeal to the intellect. Creative writing and all the other arts — dance, painting, sculpture, music, drama — appeal to the senses, to the feelings and emotions, the eyes, the heart. Our words must be, therefore, visual and anchored in human *physical* responses. Art gets to the brain through the body. The brain filters information. It's like a police officer deciding who can get through. Avoid the filtering agent. Let your creative writing appeal, unfettered, to the heart and the eyes of your reader. You are trying to create a movie in the mind of your reader. Imagine how irritating it would be to have an official at the front of the local Star Theatre movie screen, explaining the import and meaning of each scene. "Here, Tom Cruise believes . . . ," "We can now conclude Natalie Portman realizes . . . ." The reader can figure out what's going on, as long as your images are clear. Don't explain.

The best way to avoid filters is to avoid writing about trite situations where the character will be left alone with his thoughts, prone to brooding: solo car trips, waking up, airplane travel, staring out windows. In poetry, start somewhere specific. Orient us in time and place — make those images captivating by using strong verbs, and you buy yourself a little platform of time to talk, muse, or think aloud. When writing prose, you can avoid much filtering by simply always having two or three characters onstage at once, never one character *alone with his or her thoughts.*

Remember: We read in order to be *transported*, to experience, as you learned in the first two chapters of this book, a world for ourselves. We don't read to get the writer's feelings and opinions; we read in order to form and extend and see our own feelings and opinions. We read to *have* an experience, not hear about one. The stronger your verbs, the more clear your images, and the less you are proselytizing, sermonizing, musing, or rambling around, the more we see.

PRACTICE

Divide a sheet of paper into two columns. Label the columns Forché and Self. Reread Carolyn Forché's prose poem "The Colonel" (p. 185). List the words in her piece that give off the most energy. Next, choose a poem or very short prose piece of your own, and make a list of the words that generate energy. Now go over the two pieces one more time. Do you find any filters? Skip down a few lines in each column, and label this part of the list Filters, making note of each filtering word you find.

One of the most common mistakes writers make is to unintentionally distance the reader. Because writers tend to be fairly observant, thoughtful, introspective people, it's natural for them to record the fact that they are thinking, observing, watching, musing. This is a mistake. Readers don't want a filter, a block, an *entity* processing information for them. It's like pre-chewed food. We want to chew for ourselves. We want it to feel like *we are seeing* this, that it's happening before our eyes.

Passive verbs like *was* and *were* drain energy. Watch out for *-ing* words in both prose and poetry. Check for passive constructions that use *should, could, would, might,* and *may.* Helping verbs like *had* (as in *had seen*) and *had been* reveal a sloppy relationship to time, resulting in the fizzling out of energy.

PRACTICE

Experienced writers use this energy-increasing exercise, checking everything they write. Trade one of your recent pieces of writing with a partner. Circle all the verbs. Now, working from your lists created earlier in this chapter, substitute new verbs for every single verb in your partner's piece. Don't worry about making sense or messing up the piece. This is just an exercise. You want to spark surprising combinations, new energy.

Read the new pieces aloud. Now, looking over your piece, which has been revised by your partner, decide which substitutions you will keep. Can you find at least one place where a verb that seemingly does not fit actually ends up making *more* sense than the expected verb?

MANIPULATING ENERGY

Choosing energetic subjects, setting up your writing so that it invites the reader to make his or her own connections (to leap), and paying close attention to every single word: Whether you are a minimalist poet or a lush, expansive novelist, these are the basic principles that form the foundation for everything creative writers do.

As you practice these principles, notice two other tools for increasing and intentionally modulating energy in your work: pace and point of view.

Pace

By increasing the pace, you increase the energy, of course. However, once your reader adjusts to the speed, the energy flattens out again. Varying pace is a key to sustaining energy. After about three beats, three "points," the reader is adjusted. It's time to change things up again. That's one reason the waking-up paragraph example earlier in this chapter falls flat. Everything is at the same pitch, the same pace.

Pacing means being attentive to how much time passes through your paragraphs or stanzas. In Rick Moody's story "Boys," the author presents the intense, fast coming-of-age arc of boys' lives. Moody speeds time up and then slows it down, varying the pace. As the writer, use pace to create the effect you want on your reader. What you don't want to do is *just write*, laying down sentences or lines of poetry block by block like so much cord wood, oblivious to pace.

Good writers, the ones we read again and again, use the full continuum of pace, the full range, just like good musicians do. Practice moving from slow to fast, and to medium. Change how far, how close you are when you are looking at the scene before you. Take a step back. What do you see now? Move closer than is polite. What senses are engaged now? Practice getting fluid with your camera, and watch what happens to the pace of your writing.

> *Vary the pace — one of the foundations of all good acting.*
>
> ELLEN TERRY

As the writer, you calibrate pace based on the effects you want to achieve. Ignore pace, and you risk letting all the excitement evaporate. Most writers intuitively know that when you want to increase the energy of your writing, you use short sentences to describe a lot of action:

> The man took the knife. He held it over her throat. There was a loud noise. Her eyes flashed in terror. Suddenly . . .

But what truly effective writers do is more subtle and more interesting. First of all, if you are moving fast — lots of action, lots of images per second — you have to be headed somewhere slow; the pace has to change if you want the effect to work. Writing everything at breakneck speed is just as boring as slow writing that drags on and on. It's *variety* of pace — slowing down, speeding up, slowing way down — that keeps the human mind intrigued, on point. Think about how a roller coaster works. It's not all whooshing downhill at 150 miles an hour. There's the slow climb. A short fast dip. A quicker climb. A pause at the top — then the giant fall. Think about driving at exactly seventy-five miles an hour on the highway, your engine set on cruise. After a while, have you noticed how that speed feels almost slow? Compare the experience of idling along at six miles an hour, and then suddenly peeling out, getting to sixty in six seconds. You're going slower than seventy-five, but which feels faster? Which is more exciting? The energy is in acceleration, not in top speed.

Rick Moody is a master of pace. Watch how he speeds up time in this passage from the story "Boys." (Moody is also a musician.)

> Boys enter the house carrying their father, slumped. Happens so fast. Boys rush into the house leading EMTs to the couch in the living room where the body lies, boys enter the house, boys enter the house, boys enter the house.

Moody puts single-word phrases at the ends of his sentences ("slumped") and uses sentences with missing pieces ("Happens so fast"). Those techniques add speed to the story, which is one long paragraph, isn't it? He repeats the word *boys* — a lot — and lists make his sentences jolt, surge, and compress. In his paragraph, he covers a whole childhood, which ends with the death of a father. That's a large scope for a short-short story! Moody packs in the detail. He uses pace to force the reader through the story, headlong.

Notice how much detail he includes: Edison, NJ; balsamic vinegar; the Elys' yard. Pump action BB gun, Stilton cheese, mismatched tube socks. When you cover a lot of time in a short space, you create energy. Bind the reader to your words by making every single one bristle with specificity. In fast-paced writing, you can't afford to be general. We have to grasp, fully, each thing you name, completely, before you rush us on to the next thing. A common mistake, easy to avoid and easy to fix, is to write fast and without detail. Your first year as a writer, overwrite the detail. You can pull back on it later, if you need to.

| PRACTICE |

Find three other examples of fast pace followed by a close-up, a slowing down, in Moody's story "Boys" (p. 212).

Slow Down to Increase Energy. There's a whole movement afoot in the world—you may have heard of it, the Slow Movement. It started with slow food, in Italy, to counter the encroachment of fast food. It has spread to involve conferences and books devoted to slow workouts, slow driving, slow living, even whole Slow Cities.

There is power in Slow. You notice a lot more. You remember a lot more.

Remember: Pace doesn't have to be breakneck to be classified as energetic. Pace doesn't mean *fast*. It means paying attention to the flow, the *intensity*. Pace means focusing on what's most interesting—and the easiest way to make things more interesting for your reader is to give the reader more information. Information, by its very nature, is definition. Taking giant steps closer to your subjects so that you can see their pores, smell their breath, feel their heartbeats—that's a powerful place to write from. Many beginning writers work in the same way amateur videographers do. They film everything from the same distance, move the camera around at the same rate (if at all), never getting close enough to the interesting thing going on in the corner. Slowing down, moving in for a super-close-up, and spending a lot of time on one interaction provide writing with an energy boost.

Practice increasing the energy of your writing by slowing time down.

| PRACTICE |

Choose as your subject something fast that you are very familiar with. Your sister's driving. Shivering Timbers Roller Coaster rides. NASCAR. Flying down Suicide Hill on your Trek. Use the slow-motion techniques to cover a few minutes of time in several pages of writing.

Something very simple and plain can be made riotously funny by slowing down and spending a great deal of time on the topic. Think of the *Seinfeld* episodes where George deliberates over taking the éclair out of the wastebasket, or where the entire cast is lost in a parking garage. Take a little thing—a common misunderstanding—and make a big deal out of it. That's using pace to increase energy.

Writing that flies—short sentences, quick winks, strong verbs, lists, breaks, dashes—can be so purely pleasurable to read that it's as much fun as roaring down a waterslide.

PRACTICE

Make a sketch of the room you woke up in this morning. Who/what is there? Notice the little things around you. When you have completed your sketch, fill three pages with a blow-by-blow description of five minutes—only five!—from your early-morning waking routine. Include what you said, what you did, what you saw. While you are working, select verbs that have energy and avoid filters. Read your piece to a partner or a group. Where does slowing down increase the energy? Where does slowing down deaden, kill the energy? What's interesting slow and close up? What's more interesting told at breakneck speed? Discuss.

Vary Pace to Sustain Energy. The quality of pace that is most important to practice is this: variety.

Some writers rush the reader pell-mell through a poem or story—gobs of action, flying snakes, car wrecks, superheroes, mayhem, and then alligators! They believe they have created something with a lot of energy. Actually, because of the way the human brain is wired—we quickly adjust to whatever the pace—it's *change* that fuels our interest. If you *unexpectedly change pace*—fast, slow, slow, fast, slow, fast—we'll stay interested. Good writers keep their writing energized by varying the pace. They know we adjust quickly and use as our new default setting whatever you put in front of us.

Camera Work

As a writer, you are always looking at something interesting—your subject—through a kind of lens: your mind's eye. Often, creative writers take on viewing the subject through *someone else's eyes*: a character or a speaker does the seeing, recording, remembering; it's a specific person, not the writer, to whom everything interesting in the piece happens. The location of the writer's camera—in the brain/mind/eye of Joey, or on the ceiling, or in the collective head of the Student Body at Poindexter U —is called the **point of view**. Point of view simply refers to where you set your camera in order to transmit the scene being viewed by your reader. Paying attention to point of view—camera work, like human activity, rarely stays fixed or static—is an important way to increase and control the energy in your work.

Already you can probably see that if point of view deals with the vantage point of the writer, in whatever guise he or she has taken on for the particular story or poem, it's going to also deal with the relationships that speaker/character has with the other people in the piece. Usually, writers pick one head to be inside of, and they look out at the world with that person's eyes. But you don't have to limit yourself in that way. Pay attention to the camera work when you read. Where is the camera? What is being recorded? Where is the author? What is the reader directed to focus on? Does the camera move? Does the viewer of the scene change?

As always with creative writing, your job as writer is to pay attention to the experience your reader will have when he or she reads your work. If you jerk the camera around a lot, it's probably going to be kind of interesting at first, and then maybe mostly annoying, like amateur video or a movie filmed by a clueless three-year-old.

There are endless variables to point of view. For now, we will consider two aspects to point of view—two settings on your camera—as you play with various energy effects.

PROXIMITY   What are we looking out at? How close are we?

INTIMACY   Whose head are we in? How deep inside that head are we?

The more proximity and the more intimacy, the more energy you create. As with pace, movement and change support energy. Control is key. Think of a child with a video camera, wildly flailing the lens around—not very interesting film-making. Think of the great film directors you love: Tarantino, Scott, Scorsese. A shot of the party, from overhead. A close-up on the heroine. A middle-distance shot of the villain and his evil henchman. A carefully planned-out pace. A sequence, with variety. Writers use their knowledge of movies to enhance their ability to play with point of view. Watching film with the sound off or the commentary on is great practice for writers studying energy and the effects artists use to increase energy in their work.

You can do whatever you want with point of view, but traditionally, creative writing uses three categories for "viewing."

FIRST PERSON   "I sent for the chief of staff." (Camera planted in the brain of "I.")

SECOND PERSON   "You send for the chief of staff." (Camera planted in the brain of "you.")

THIRD PERSON   "The man sent for the chief of staff."

In general, it's best to limit your point of view to one consciousness, one person's viewpoint. You increase energy by going deep into that one consciousness (be aware that withholding vital information—he really is the murderer!—can be considered cheating at worst, manipulative at best).

In each example, the author chooses how much information to reveal. We readers can be told everything by "I," or nothing at all. "I" can be lying about the whole chief-of-staff-sending issue, and the author can indicate to us, or not indicate, the real truth. Point of view is all about intimacy—how far in do we go?

In second person, the "you" can function as an "I" or a "he," depending on how much information the author gives us about the interior life—the thoughts, dreams, fears, insights—of the "you." In third person, we can be really far back as viewers, seeing the "man" from across the city, from an airplane, or from a camera implanted in his brain. If we learn that "the man felt terrible that he had just taken a sip of the chief's coffee," it's as if we are *inside* him.

Instead of worrying too much about point of view, writers are well served by consistently asking one question: What point of view supports the energy of this piece of writing?

Poetry tends to use the term *speaker* to identify who talks in a poem (the speaker may or may not be the poet). In screenplays and drama, the characters talk and we experience the play from their points of view in a general way—they may tell us what they are thinking deep inside, but we don't see things through their eyes. In graphic novels and comics, examine point of view by looking at where the "camera" is positioned. The close-up, the long shot, the dream sequence, the cityscape are all different points of view. Changing point of view in graphic forms adds energy.

Unlike in film and cartoons, however, in forms purely using words—novels, stories, memoir, creative nonfiction—sudden movements of the camera angle tend to suck energy out of a piece. The reader has to scramble to reorient; the movie in the reader's mind is fractured whenever he or she has to *think*. We read to get lost in a world, not see the hand of the writer.

As you study and practice creative writing, you may hear terminology familiar to you from your literature courses. To review:

First person means you are writing "I," as in, "I came in and sat down."

Second person means you are writing "you," as in, "You came in. You sat. You wondered where the heck Judy was."

Third person means you are writing "she" or "he" or "they," as in, "Judy left the apartment and went to the store. She was exhausted."

Omniscience means that the point of view knows all—he or she can go inside any head, any time, as superficially or deeply as he or she chooses.

Objective describes an approach in which the point of view reports everything that happens as though we readers are perched on the shoulders of the characters—not inside their heads, but very close. We readers can smell them. We can guess at their interior lives.

There is another way to approach point of view: As the writer, you can choose to present the point of view of a group. Instead of using "I" to focus your camera, you use a plural point of view, "we." Kate Walbert, in her award-winning book of linked short stories, *Our Kind*, uses the "we" camera, or point of view. She focuses on a group of women in the 1970s who all live in the same neighborhood. Their kids are grown, their husbands work long hours or have traded in for younger spouses. The women go to the same church, same country club, same grocery store. They get a crush on the same tennis instructor and decide to conduct an "intervention" on a local man.

> Know that we are a close-knit community. We've lived here for years, which is not to say that our ancestors are buried here; simply, this is the place we have all ended up. We were married in 1953. Divorced in 1976. Our grown daughters pity us; our grown sons forget us. We have grandchildren we visit from time to time, but their manners agitate, so we return, nervous, thankful to view them at a distance.
>
> Most of us excel at racquet sports.
>
> It is not in our makeup to intervene. This goes against the grain, is entirely out of our character. We allow for differences, but strive not to show them. Ours are calm waters, smooth sailing. Yes, some among us visit therapists, but, quite frankly, we believe this is a passing phase, like our former passion for fondue, or our semester learning decoupage.
>
> We've seen a lot. We've seen the murder-suicide of the Clifford Jacksons, Tate Kieley jailed for embezzlement, Dorothy Schoenbacher in nothing but a mink coat in August dive from the roof of the Cooke's Inn. We've seen Dick Morehead arrested in the ladies' dressing room at Lord & Taylor, attempting to squeeze into a petite teddy. We've seen Francis Stoney gone mad, Brenda Nelson take to cocaine. We've seen the blackballing of the Stewart Collisters. We've seen more than our share of liars and cheats, thieves. Drunks? We couldn't count.

PRACTICE

Determine the point of view in Carolyn Forché's "The Colonel" (p. 185). What about Moody's "Boys" (p. 212)? Jarod Roselló's "The Neighbor" (p. 27)? Pamela Painter's "The New Year" (p. 69)? To figure out the point of view, answer the following questions for each story: Who talks? And to what or whom? Are we, as readers, living inside that person, or being shown that person from the outside? Do we have access to everything the point-of-view character thinks and feels, or is our access as readers limited? Does the author talk? Write out the answers to these questions for each of the four stories. Which point of view allows the author to generate the most energy?

You've watched amateur video—maybe your dad's proud footage of all your dance recitals. Amateur videographers tend to stand in one place, without moving the camera. They are too far back from the action. Avoid those mistakes in your writing: Pan slowly (you won't run into a pillar or a ballet teacher—you're in your chair), vary your distance, and shoot much, much closer than you think you need to be.

Pay attention to where your camera is, who is operating it, and move closer—most beginning writers "film" from too far back. By moving your camera closer to your subject and limiting shifts in point of view, you increase and sustain energy in creative writing. To act as though you are deep inside someone's head, seeing the world from behind their eyes, means you must stay limited to just what they could know, see, feel, understand. Whatever your character/speaker knows, the reader knows; they are sharing a brain. Looking through someone else's eyes—that's part of the power and drama of literature, and the reading experience.

Point-of-view changes come at an energy cost. If Amy Fusselman had told her memoir from the points of view of her husband, unborn child, mother, brother, *and* herself, we would learn interesting perspectives, but we would miss out on the development and depth of her own perspective. Usually, shorter works (poems, short-short stories, songs) are from a single person's (or sometimes an animal's or a piece of furniture's) point of view—one brain, one set of eyes, one recording consciousness that we readers adopt for the duration of the reading. Longer works (novels, sagas, ballads, television series) may allow us to live through multiple characters. Usually, the writer focuses on a few "leads"—heads we go into. Minor characters add energy in other ways: comic relief, plot information, setting, or thematic detail.

How do movies and plays address point of view? As you watch these forms this semester, pay attention to the role of energy and point of view. Whose mind—whose deepest thoughts, desires, reactions, dreams—do we audience members have the most access to? When the camera pans across the town or over New York City from a bird's-eye view, what's the effect on point of view? Are there equivalents in novels and poems and plays?

Some authors like to play with point of view. You may write a story or a poem from a collective point of view—the "we" that comprises a group of waiters or office workers or moms. If part of the premise of your piece is that these souls have so much in common that their perspective is "one," your point of view will have energy; just be consistent.

Point of view is a continuum. Choosing one point on the continuum and staying there with intense focus is an important way to keep your creative writing on track.

Too Much Energy?

Energy is about focus, and it's about control. It's about paying super-close attention to what will happen in your reader's brain when you use a technique, turn up the volume, withhold information, leap ahead.

Think about some of the ways you use energy already. In a conversation, when things flag, get boring, or there's a long silence, you keep the energy going by asking more questions or introducing a more exciting topic. But if you keep all your conversations going all the time by just talking, yourself, nonstop, if you suck up all the air in the room, your interlocutors grow tired, disinterested.

Conversation, like good writing, is a kind of game. It's a passing back and forth. Too much revelation at the wrong time is misplaced energy. Yelling when whispering would be appropriate is too much energy.

It's the same in writing. Modulation is what calibrates the amount of electricity in your work. You want the sparks to fly, but only when you have your readers exactly where you want them. As a good writer, control the energy flow.

As you may have already noticed, there is such a thing as too much energy: too many words, too many images, too much information, too many full-throttle, high-pitched events, too much action, too many disturbing revelations. When readers get overwhelmed, they tune out. Manic, wild, out-of-control passages can be really fun to write, and a little fun to read—but probably not for hundreds of pages.

Some beginning writers mistakenly believe that good writing is dense, incomprehensible, and obscure. Other writers rely on adjectives and adverbs, the stimulants of writing, in order to pep up their paragraphs. It may be counterintuitive at first, but flowery language and extra words kill energy. Strong verbs and clearly visualized scenes will always do more to transport your reader than flash and verbiage.

Some writers resort to excessive embellishment—too many words per square inch. Writing in this hyperactive mode is like turning on all the lights in your house: It misses the point. Focus, highlight, and *modulate* the energy. Slowly dim the lights in the most special room in your house, and boom, you have our attention.

Sometimes, using all your energy tools at once, at full volume, is a way of avoiding the truth of what you have to say, a way of putting off real writing. It's sometimes more fun to show off than to show up, unadorned, saying what's true, small, tender, and difficult.

TROUBLESHOOTING ENERGY

The troubleshooting chart below will help you evaluate and control the level of energy in your creative writing as you work on various pieces in various genres. If you choose all the tools from the "Decreases Energy" column, you might still write a great piece, but it might be harder to make that piece realistic for your

	Increases Energy	Decreases Energy	Depletes Energy
Subjects	Subjects known intimately from real life.	Subjects known secondhand from friends, family members.	Subjects informed by television, movies, general assumptions and impressions.
Leaps	Leaps from one juicy piece of information to another.	Answers that fit the questions.	Explanation.
Word Choice	Specific, sharp, concrete nouns and action verbs.	General words, filler words. Adjectives, adverbs.	Abstract words, filtering verbs.
Conflict	Conflicting agendas.	Long answers. Agreement.	One person alone with thoughts.
Pace	Varied pace.	Even pace.	Lack of attention to pace.
Distance	Close-up camera work.	Long shots, pulling back, writing from far away.	Camera in one spot.
Point of View	Tiny details observed from a single point of view.	Multiple points of view.	Author talking, author reporting (point of view not a character or speaker).
Sentence Variation	Variety in sentence length, word choice.	Lack of variety in constructions.	Lack of attention to length and shape of sentences, sections.

reader. If you write about your sister's cancer, for example, write about your experience of living with someone very ill. If you focus on your sister's experiences, then you will want to choose from the "Increases Energy" column for your other tools so that you write from her point of view, close up, and with words only she uses, focusing on the tense, leaping scenes that reveal the most intimate aspects of her story. You won't be able to include much explanation and still sustain your readers' interest. If you are the main character in that story, though, there will instantly be more energy, so the reader will go with you to the doctor's office, learn with you as you comprehend the details of the illness—just as long as you leap!

WRITING PROJECTS

1. Write a prose poem, a short-short, or a very brief play (dialogue or monologue) using every word or phrase (in any order, any combination, repeating words as needed) from your practice with fresh word combinations on page 195. Use all the words from your list! Is the piece more energetic and lively than a typical piece of writing? Do you have a favorite line or combination?

2. Make a list of everything that kills energy. Then write a piece in which you commit every crime on your list. Read your new version aloud. Is there any remaining energy?

3. Pull out a piece of writing you did earlier in the term. Using your list from the practice on pages 196–97, in which you developed a list of strong verbs, replace every single verb in your piece of writing. It's okay if the meaning changes a little or a lot. Read the two pieces aloud, and notice which one has more energy.

4. Take any one of your pieces from this semester, and change the point of view. If it's a poem, have someone else speak. When you are finished, write a short paragraph about what the piece gained and what it lost with the new point of view. What's *different* now in terms of the energy level? Where in the piece has the energy increased with the new point of view? Are there places where the original has more energy?

5. Using your lists of topics, choose one and write a story, poem, or memoir— anything you like—in short sections. Pay special attention in this piece to filters. Watch for filters and avoid using verbs that relate to thought. Make

the sections fragments—leave out information. When you read the piece aloud, do your readers tell you they can fill in the gaps?

6. Write a piece with a very fast opening, a slow middle section, and a speedy end. Don't use the passive voice in any sections, or filters—check back over the piece before you turn it in and substitute filters with verbs from your lists.

7. Write a piece that imitates Rick Moody, using your own life experiences. Trade pieces with a partner from your class. Where does your piece have the most energy?

8. Write a very short piece about an incident that occurred at a secret place you favored as a child. Now rewrite the piece from another kid's point of view—choose a kid who was very different from you. Use the first person, or "I," for your first and second versions. In a third version, write in the third person ("she"), from the point of view of your mother, who stumbles upon the scene. Don't use filters.

9. Write a scene for a screenplay where the main character shares a piece of shocking news with two other characters. Include leaps and sparky word choices, and make sure the dialogue sounds fresh and accurate. Let your characters ignore the question, change the subject, introduce random material, rant, and misunderstand.

10. Write a prose poem that is a description of action, setting, and dialogue, in which you or your speaker are witness to something many people don't see.

11. Read some background information on "poetry of witness" and consider an issue in your community that needs witness: conditions at the bus station, elder care, the treatment of the dolphins at the aquarium, systemic segregation, hazing, or discrimination of any kind. Try writing a prose poem of witness.

ENERGY WORKSHOP

The prompts below will help you constructively discuss your classmates' work.

1. Identify an example of each of the principles of energy—subject, leaps, word choices—in the student piece you are reading. Highlight or underline at least one good example of each principle.

2. Identify a place in the student piece where the energy could be increased by moving the camera closer in on the people/place in the piece. Circle this moment and label it "close-up."

3. Identify a place in the student piece where the pace changes throughout a paragraph or stanza. Underline this section, this series of sentences, and label it "good pace."

4. Identify a passage in the student piece where the pace stays at about the same level for longer than it probably should. A passage where the writer has clearly established the emotional climate but hasn't provided any accelerations or decelerations. Circle it and label it "pace?"

READINGS

Rick Moody
Boys

Boys enter the house, boys enter the house. Boys, and with them the ideas of boys (ideas leaden, reductive, inflexible), enter the house. Boys, two of them, wound into hospital packaging, boys with infant pattern baldness, slung in the arms of parents, boys dreaming of breasts, enter the house. Twin boys, kettles on the boil, boys in hideous vinyl knapsacks that young couples from Edison, NJ, wear on their shirt fronts, knapsacks coated with baby saliva and staphylococcus and milk vomit, enter the house. Two boys, one striking the other with a rubberized hot dog, enter the house. Two boys, one of them striking the other with a willow switch about the head and shoulders, the other crying, enter the house. Boys enter the house, speaking nonsense. Boys enter the house, calling for Mother. On a Sunday, in May, a day one might nearly describe as *perfect*, an ice cream truck comes slowly down the lane, chimes inducing salivation, and children run after it, not long after which boys dig a hole in the backyard and bury their younger sister's dolls *two feet down*, so that she will never find these dolls and these dolls will *rot in hell*, after which boys enter the house. Boys, trailing after their father like he is the Second Goddamned Coming of Christ Goddamned Almighty, enter the house, repair to the basement to watch baseball. Boys enter the house, site of devastation, and repair immediately to the kitchen, where they mix lighter fluid, vanilla pudding, drain-opening lye, balsamic vinegar, blue food coloring, calamine lotion, cottage cheese, ants, a plastic lizard that one of them received in his Xmas stocking, tacks, leftover mashed potatoes, Spam, frozen lima beans, and chocolate syrup in a medium-sized saucepan and heat over a low flame until thick, afterwards transferring the contents of this saucepan into a Pyrex lasagna dish, baking the Pyrex lasagna dish in the oven for nineteen minutes before attempting to persuade their sister that she should *eat the mixture*; later they smash three family heirlooms (the last, a glass egg, *intentionally*) in a two-and-a-half hour stretch, whereupon they are sent to their bedroom, until freed, in each case thirteen minutes after. Boys enter the house, starchy in pressed shirts and flannel pants that *itch so bad*, fresh from Sunday School instruction, blond and brown locks (respectively) plastered down, but even so with a number of cowlicks protruding at odd angles, disconsolate and humbled, uncertain if boyish things—such as shooting at the neighbor's dog with a pump action bb gun and gagging the fat boy up the street with a bandanna and showing their shriveled boy-penises to their younger sister—are exempted from the commandment to *Love the Lord thy God with all thy heart and with all thy soul, and with all thy might, and thy neighbor as thyself.* Boys enter the house in baseball gear (only one of the boys can hit): in their spikes, in mismatched tube socks that smell like Stilton cheese. Boys enter the house in soccer gear. Boys enter the house carrying skates. Boys enter the house with lacrosse sticks, and, soon after, tossing a lacrosse ball lightly in the living room they destroy a lamp. One boy enters the house sporting basketball clothes, the other wearing jeans and a sweatshirt. One boy enters the house bleeding profusely and is taken out to get stitches, the other watches. Boys enter the house at the end of term carrying report cards, sneak around the house like spies of foreign nationality, looking for a place to hide the report cards for the time being (under the toaster? in a medicine cabinet?). One boy with a black eye enters the house, one boy without. Boys with acne enter the house and squeeze and prod large skin blemishes in front of their sister. Boys with acne treatment products hidden about their persons enter the house. Boys, standing just up the street, sneak cigarettes behind a willow in the Elys' yard, wave smoke away from their natural fibers, hack terribly, experience nausea, then enter the house. Boys call each other *retard, homo, geek,* and, later, *Neckless Thug, Theater Fag,* and enter the house exchanging further epithets. Boys enter the house with nose hair clippers, chase sister around the house threatening to depilate her eyebrows. She cries. Boys attempt to induce girls to whom they would not have spoken only six or eight months prior to enter the house with them. Boys enter the house with girls efflorescent and homely, and attempt to induce girls to sneak into their bedroom, as they still share a single bedroom; girls refuse. Boys enter the house, go to separate bedrooms. Boys, with their father (an arm around each of them), enter the house, but of the monologue preceding and succeeding this entrance, not a syllable is preserved. Boys enter the house having masturbated in a variety of locales. Boys enter the house having masturbated in train station bathrooms, in forests, in beach houses, in football bleachers at night under the stars, in cars (under a blanket), in the shower, backstage, on a plane, the boys masturbate constantly, identically, three times a day in some cases, desire like a madness upon them, at the mere sound of certain words, words that sound like other words, *interrogative* reminding them of *intercourse, beast* reminding them of *breast, sects* reminding them of *sex,* and so forth, the boys are not very smart yet, and, as they enter the house, they feel, as always, immense shame at the scale of this *self-abusive cogitation,* seeing a classmate, seeing a billboard, seeing a fire hydrant, seeing things that should not induce thoughts of masturbation (their sister, e.g.) and then thinking of masturbation anyway. Boys enter the house, go to their rooms, remove sexually explicit magazines from hidden stashes, put on loud music, feel despair. Boys enter the house worried; they argue. The boys are ugly, they are failures, they will never be loved, they enter the house. Boys enter the house and kiss their mother, who feels differently, now they have outgrown her. Boys enter the house, kiss their mother, she explains the seriousness of their sister's difficulty, *her diagnosis*. Boys enter the house, having attempted to locate the spot in their yard where the dolls were buried, eight or nine years prior, without success; they go to their sister's room, sit by her bed. Boys enter the house and tell their completely bald sister jokes about baldness. Boys hold either hand of their sister, laying aside differences, having trudged grimly into the house. Boys skip school, enter house, hold vigil. Boys enter the house after their parents have both gone off to work, sit with their sister and with their sister's nurse. Boys enter the house carrying cases of beer. Boys enter the house, very worried now, didn't know more worry was possible. Boys enter the house carrying controlled substances, neither having told the other that he is carrying a controlled substance, though an intoxicated posture seems appropriate under the circumstances. Boys enter the house *weeping* and hear weeping around them. Boys enter the house, embarrassed, silent, anguished, keening, afflicted, angry, woeful, *griefstricken*. Boys enter the house on vacation, each clasps the hand of the other with genuine warmth, the one wearing dark colors and having shaved a portion of his head, the other having grown his hair out longish and wearing, uncharacteristically, a tie-dyed shirt. Boys enter the house on vacation and argue bitterly about politics (other subjects are no longer discussed), one boy supporting the Maoist insurgency in a certain Southeast Asian country, one believing that *to change the system you need to work inside it*; one boy threatens to *beat the living shit out of the other*, refuses crème brûlée, though it is created by his mother in order to keep the peace. One boy writes home and thereby enters the house only through a mail slot: he argues that the other boy is *crypto-fascist*, believing that *the market can seek its own level on questions of ethics and morals*; boys enter the house on vacation and announce future professions; boys enter the house on vacation and change their minds about professions; boys enter the house on vacation and one boy brings home a *sweetheart*, but throws a tantrum when it is suggested that the *sweetheart* will have to retire on the folding bed in the basement; the other boy, having no *sweetheart*, is distant and withdrawn, preferring to talk late into the night about family members gone from this world. Boys enter the house several weeks apart. Boys enter the house on days of heavy rain. Boys enter the house, in different calendar years, and upon entering, the boys seem to do nothing but compose manifestos, for the benefit of parents; they follow their mother around the place, having fashioned their manifestos in celebration of brand-new independence: *Mom, I like to lie in bed late into the morning watching game shows*, or, *I'm never going to date anyone but artists from now on, mad girls, dreamers, practicers of black magic*, or *A man should eat bologna, sliced meats are important*, or, *An American should bowl at least once a year*, but these manifestos apply only for brief spells, after which they are reversed or discarded. Boys don't enter the house, at all, except as ghostly afterimages of younger selves, fleeting images of sneakers dashing up a staircase; soggy towels on the floor of the bathroom; blue jeans coiled like asps in the basin of the washing machine; boys as an absence of boys, blissful at first, you put a thing down on a spot, put this book down, come back later, *it's still there*; you buy a box of cookies, eat three, later three are missing. Nevertheless, when boys next enter the house, which they ultimately must do, it's a relief, even if it's only in preparation for weddings of acquaintances from boyhood, one boy has a beard, neatly trimmed, the other has rakish sideburns, one boy wears a hat, the other boy thinks hats are ridiculous, one boy wears khakis pleated at the waist, the other wears denim, but each changes into his suit (one suit fits well, one is a little tight), as though suits are *the* liminary marker of adulthood. Boys enter the house after the wedding and they are slapping each other on the back and yelling at anyone who will listen, *It's a party!* One boy enters the house, carried by friends, having been arrested (after the wedding) for driving while intoxicated, complexion ashen; the other boy tries to keep his mouth shut: the car is on its side in a ditch, the car has the top half of a tree broken over its bonnet, the car has struck another car which has in turn struck a third, *Everyone will have seen.* One boy misses his brother horribly, misses the past, misses a time worth being nostalgic over, *a time that never existed*, back when they set their sister's playhouse on fire; the other boy avoids all mention of that time; each of them is once the boy who enters the house alone, missing the other, each is devoted and each callous, and each plays his part on the telephone, over the course of months. Boys enter the house with fishing gear, according to pre-arranged date and time, arguing about whether to use *lures* or *live bait*, in order to meet their father for the *fishing adventure*, after which boys enter the house again, almost immediately, with live bait, having settled the question; boys boast of having caught fish in the past, though no fish has ever been caught: *Remember when the blues were biting?* Boys enter the house carrying their father, slumped. Happens so fast. Boys rush into the house leading EMTs to the couch in the living room where the body lies, boys enter the house, boys enter the house, boys enter the house. Boys hold open the threshold, awesome threshold that has welcomed them when they haven't even been able to welcome themselves, that threshold which welcomed them when they *had* to be taken in, here is its tarnished knocker, here is its euphonious bell, here's where the boys had to sand the door down because it never would hang right in the frame, here are the scuff-marks from when boys were on the wrong side of the door *demanding*, here's where there were once milk bottles for the milkman, here's where the newspaper always landed, here's the mail slot, here's the light on the front step, illuminated, here's where the boys are standing, as that beloved man is carried out. Boys, no longer boys, exit.

Brian Arundel

The Things I've Lost

Fleece hat and gloves: in the backseat of a Boston cab in 2002, before driving back to Maine. Round, purple sunglasses: in an Atlanta pool hall over drinks with Ashy, whose wife was determined to save their marriage by having a baby. A measurable dose of self-skepticism: at about 14, when I realized I was very good at both playing violin and baseball, while not necessarily everyone else was. A school-wide presidential election in sixth grade, after I was drafted to run by Mrs. Sticoiu, the most frightening teacher in the school, while I was out of town. A copy of *The Little Prince*, in Mrs. Sticoiu's class the previous year. A floppy disk that contained my paper on ideological subversion in Wendell Berry, the first essay I'd written after returning to graduate school following a four-year respite. A black scarf from Pigalle: somewhere in Maine before moving west.

The chance to kiss Leslie Wertmann, and, later, that redhead in seventh grade with a smile that could buckle steel — Kim, Christine, or Kathleen maybe — and the blonde at the freshman dance because I couldn't recognize flirtations, even when told that I looked like Bruce Springsteen. My virginity: in 1980, a couple weeks short of 16, in a ritual so brief, awkward and forgettable that I have, in fact, forgotten it. My heart, or so I thought, in 1985, when Susie dumped me; my naivete, three months later, when I learned that she'd slept with at least three other guys I knew while we'd been dating.

Belief that my mother was somehow more than human: in 1972, the first time I saw her fall down after getting drunk. Belief that my father was more than human: a few months beforehand, after learning that he'd had an affair and was being thrown out of the house. The belief that my sister was stable: 1976, when she began pointing at random objects and saying their names, a few months before getting arrested, the first of many times, for disturbing the peace by refusing to leave a Western Union office until they gave her a job. A ten-dollar bill on a DC subway in 1985, on my way home to my friend Tommy's, where I was staying after leaving my father's house — after he'd moved back in, once my mother remarried and moved south.

The chance, in 1986, to meet Raymond Carver: the only person invited to sit in on an interview, I instead drank all night with friends and overslept. A quarter-inch off the tip of my left thumb, in 1987, while slicing Muenster cheese on an electric Hobart slicer. My shit, figuratively, that same summer when Bob Weir sang "Looks Like Rain" just as my acid trip was peaking at a two-night Dead stand in Roanoke, Va. The Buick a friend had given me as a tax write-off in 1996, which I let someone take for a test drive without holding collateral.

The thought that officials were somehow more evolved than those who elect them: in 1972, listening to my father explain the Watergate burglary. Faith in politics — particularly a two-party system relegated to fundraising contests perpetuated by shallow sound bites, mudslinging and outright lies for the Mindless American Voter so that each party can pursue a majority with which to repress the other, with complete disregard for actually trying to improve the lives of citizens: gradually over time, culminating in 2000. Fundamental hope that Americans really would overcome their vacuity, fear and greed to evolve beyond sheep determined to re-elect George W. Bush: 2004.

The ability to drink until late at night and go to work the next day without feeling like I need to be zipped inside a body bag: sometime in my early thirties. General insecurity and inadequacy: during the past seven years, as I've tried to allow myself to be loved without guilt or judgment. Self-pity and -importance, at least most days, while striving to look beyond the borders of my own desires in a steady ascent that some might refer to as maturation. The desire to remain in this country: since 2004. A black beret: in a Minneapolis bar, just a few days before relocating to Georgia in 1993. A taste for soy sausage patties: inexplicably, sometime in the past six months, leading up to a Saturday brunch three weeks ago.

Brian Turner
What Every Soldier Should Know

> To yield to force is an act of necessity, not of will; it is at best an act of prudence.
>
> — JEAN-JACQUES ROUSSEAU

If you hear gunfire on a Thursday afternoon,
it could be for a wedding, or it could be for you.

Always enter a home with your right foot;
the left is for cemeteries and unclean places.

O-guf! Tera armeek is rarely useful.
It means *Stop! Or I'll shoot.*

Sabah el khair is effective.
It means *Good Morning.*

Inshallah means *Allah be willing.*
Listen well when it is spoken.

You will hear the RPG coming for you.
Not so the roadside bomb.

There are bombs under the overpasses,
in trashpiles, in bricks, in cars.

There are shopping carts with clothes soaked
in foogas, a sticky gel of homemade napalm.

Parachute bombs and artillery shells
sewn into the carcasses of dead farm animals.

Graffiti sprayed onto the overpasses:
I will kell you, American.

Men wearing vests rigged with explosives
walk up, raise their arms and say *Inshallah.*

There are men who earn eighty dollars
to attack you, five thousand to kill.

Small children who will play with you,
old men with their talk, women who offer chai—

　　　and any one of them
　　　may dance over your body tomorrow.

Charlotte Glynn

Excerpt from *Duct Tape Twins*

```
INT. BEDROOM—EARLY MORNING

Two young women, early 20s, sleep on their backs next to each
other. The sun rises into their room.

Each side of the room looks like it's from a different house.
One side of the room is neat, the bedstand has one book and a
picture frame with a collage of pictures of the two girls at
different ages. The other bedstand is full of crap: water
glasses, earrings, candles, magazines, books.

The alarm goes off on the clean side of the room. TWIN TWO
turns the alarm off and kicks the blankets off the two girls
revealing that they are duct taped together along the whole
side of their abdomens.

INT. BATHROOM—MOMENTS LATER

TWIN TWO showers and TWIN ONE stands out of the shower
brushing her teeth. Toothpaste drips onto the floor. She
notices it and does nothing.

Like perfect synchronized dancers, Two gets out of the shower,
quickly covering herself with a towel, and One steps in.

Two stands outside of the shower, drying off.
```

INT. KITCHEN—LATER

Two moves through the kitchen making herself breakfast and
coffee. One brushes her hair and moves with Two like a toddler
being dragged around by their mother.

INT. BEDROOM—MOMENTS LATER

One checks herself out in the mirror and puts on make-up. Two
flosses and turns on the radio. The sound of the BBC fills the
air. One rolls her eyes.

EXT. BUSY STREET—MORNING

Twin One and Two walk down the street in perfect step. They
are dressed differently—each sister expressing themselves
through their clothes, Twin One is stylish and colorful while
Twin Two is in typical Ann Taylor type business attire. One
drinks a cup of coffee. Two listens to headphones and smiles.

They walk into the revolving doors of a nice office building,
in perfect step.

INT. OFFICE BUILDING—CONTINUOUS

One and Two sit at the reception desk of a fancy office. Two
talks on the phone and types on a computer. One picks the
rubber bands out of the paperclip container. A BUSINESS GUY
walks up to Two with an envelope. Seeing that she's busy he
turns to One.

                    BUSINESS GUY
          One, can you see that Two mails
          this out for me?

One takes the envelope and carelessly drops it by Two.

Two gets off the phone and glares at One.

INT. THERAPIST OFFICE

Traditional shrink's office. One and Two sit on the couch side
by side. Two wears silencing headphones, listening to music and
reading a gossip magazine. Two faces away from the conversation
happening between One and the Therapist.

                    ONE
          I wanted to get on the front of the
          train and she wanted to get on the
          back. I hate the smell of bananas.
          I'm not sure I like boys anymore. I
          want to be able to get a . . . I don't
          know. I hate work and I wanted to
          call in sick today. I want to work
          in a bar. I think we'd be really
          good at that.

The therapist, older woman, 60s, conservative, and overly attentive in an analytic rather than nurturing way, looks at One and nods.

> ONE (CONT'D)
> I hate volunteering. I want to read
> more. I want to stay up until the
> sun rises and eat French Fries and
> take my clothes off in public and
> scare little kids on the street and
> get a massage. I want to start a
> band and write a book and then not
> do anything and be quiet for days
> on end and then scream really loud.

One's quiet for a moment, then scratches her stomach and right arm that's next to Two's.

> ONE (CONT'D)
> I feel itchy.

> THERAPIST
> I can imagine that. It's very hot
> today.

One nods in agreement.

> ONE
> I was watching these little kids at
> the park. They were playing on the
> jungle gym, like climbing around
> and stuff. We never did that. We
> weren't allowed to. I've never been
> on a slide.

One continues to look down at her feet. She wears sandals. Her toenails are painted and are chipping.

> ONE (CONT'D)
> I'm the oldest virgin in the world.

> THERAPIST
> I doubt that.

> ONE
> I've never been on a slide.

> THERAPIST
> You know there is nothing stopping
> you from doing these things.

> ONE
> I know.

One doesn't look up.

INT. DRUG STORE—NIGHT

Twin One and Two slowly move down the shampoo aisle, parallel to the merchandise. They walk in an almost exaggerated style, one foot over the other. Twin One's fingers run across the bottles of shampoo.

Two talks on the phone.

>   TWO
>   Oh my god, I love trivia.

Two picks some shampoo and drops it in the basket One is holding.

>   TWO (CONT'D)
>   Umm. Yeah. I'm free . . . Hold on . . .
>   (turning to One)
>   Are we free tomorrow night?

>   ONE
>   Why?

>   TWO
>   (into the phone)
>   Yeah she's free. Okay.
>   (aside to One)
>   Trivia with Jackie?

They turn the corner past a display of back to school supplies. One accidentally knocks over the scissor display. Colorful scissors spill onto the floor.

Twin Two rolls her eyes as they both crouch down and Twin One picks up the spilled scissors. Twin Two continues talking on the phone.

>   TWO (CONT'D)
>   It's going to be the best ever.
>   Think of a good team name.

In the middle of the clean up One stops and stares at the scissors. She looks at Two, who is oblivious, still talking on the phone. One looks at the scissors again and slides a red pair into her coat pocket. Two doesn't notice.

>   TWO
>   Ooo, that's a good one!

CHAPTER SIX

TENSION

Writers use tension to make their work more readable, and more meaningful, and more interesting. Writers hook a reader into a piece by paying attention to energy and images. To keep the reader engaged, delighted, and connected to your writing, manipulate the level of tension.

> *There are no dull subjects.*
> *There are only dull writers.*
> — H. L. MENCKEN

Tension is defined as trouble on the page. Tension is conflict; it's a technique a writer uses to keep readers a bit off balance, making them guess, forcing them to wait, allowing them to worry, or to wonder, or to hope.

There is a lot of beautiful writing that simply does not hold the reader's interest. Tension allows you to make sure *everything* you write has enough pull to keep your reader with you for the whole ride.

PRACTICE

Read "Where There's Smoke" by Jenifer Hixson (p. 162). This is a dramatic story. What techniques does Hixson use to increase the tension for the reader?

THE PRINCIPLES OF TENSION

Desire + Danger = Tension

To make sure your writing has enough tension to keep a reader engaged, focus on your character/speaker's main desire: Keep every sentence, line, or stanza in the piece *closely* focused on what this person wants, and what forces are keeping her from getting it. Usually, the writer presents the desire both externally and internally. The character or speaker wants a ride to the concert, drugs for her sick child, or quieter kids. She must keep a secret that can't be kept. Externally, we see her trying to get the thing she wants by her actions. Internally, her thoughts reveal the significance and the conflicts her desire holds. She hopes to meet her ex-boyfriend at the concert, she hopes her child will grow up to be a doctor, or she wants the children to spend more time with their father.

If there is no danger, if nothing *bad* will happen if she doesn't get what she wants, you have no tension. If the kid just has a mild case of the sniffles, the reader is going to wonder why you are making him read about this kid. If meeting the ex-boyfriend doesn't hold the promise of a life-altering interaction — she wants to go back to him and desert her husband (her desire + her danger) — why drag the reader along through a tedious explanation of who Ellen is, who Joey is, why set the scene in the restaurant, why bother at all?

When you combine desire (the thing a character or speaker wants — connection, money, to score points, to not be stupid) and danger (the potential harm that will come to the person — rejection, a scam, loss, shame), you automatically create tension.

Desire without danger is boring. Beautiful, perhaps. But boring.

Danger without an individual character's strong, focused, clear desire is perhaps exciting, but only for a short time.

Consider these situations.

1. It's the first day of the last semester of your college career. You are wait-listed for three classes: Math, Physics, and Biology. The registrar's office: inconveniently closed the entire break. You need all three of these classes in order to graduate. On your schedule, you have one class only, Tennis, and you do not need this elective, not at all. You can't afford a fifth year. When you arrive at the math and science building, there is a line of a hundred students, jamming the front doors, spilling out onto the lawn. Every single student has an add slip. Every student needs Math.

   Desire to Graduate + Horrendous Drop/Add = Drama
   Tension.

   A boy wakes up, wonders what he will do that day, eats a nice breakfast, strolls down the sidewalk to school. Gets there safely. Recess goes well.

   No Desire (mild wish to get to school) + Safe Arrival = Boring
   No tension.

2. You are dating two people. Both of them live in the same building, Joey on the floor above you, Carlo just underneath you. They don't know about each other. Both Joey and Carlo have declared themselves loyal to you, and you

have promised each, in the heat of the moment, that he is The One. Every time you walk into that building, you feel it: tension. Tonight both Carlo and Joey meet you at the mailboxes. It's clear they have been talking. Joey has a knife in his hand. Carlo is holding a letter, thwapping it against his flat palm.

> Desire for Joey + Desire for Carlo + Assurances That Are Lies ("You are the only one") + Human Propensity toward Jealousy, Violence = Drama
> *Tension.*

A man looks around his room, remembering all the pleasant moments of his life. The luxurious cars, the silk suits, the comfortable gardens. He realizes he has lived well. He has worked hard, and it has been worth it. He turns on the classical station, sits on a large leather sofa, stares out the window at a beautiful view. His nice wife brings him a gin and tonic. It tastes great.

> Happy Man + All Desires Fulfilled = Boring
> *No tension.*

3. You work twenty-nine hours a week. You despise this job, which a small child could do. You are behind in all your classes. You have nineteen cents in checking, and your Visa is maxed out and two payments behind — the account was frozen this morning. You are driving home — speeding — to spend Friday evening with your mother, who has a bad heart; your girlfriend is pissed you're missing her sorority social; you told her you bought her a corsage, and she can pick it up at the florists right about now, but your card was declined, of course — there is no corsage at Julie's Flowers for her. You race home to your mother worrying about your midterm grades; you need a *much* higher GPA to compete for a good job upon graduation. The cops pull you over. Seventy-five in a thirty.

> Desire to Be a Good Son and Boyfriend + No Money, Bad Grades, and Lack of Attention to Posted Speed Limits = Drama
> *Tension.*

It's hard to create tension without focusing your reader's attention on *both* a strong unmet desire *and* risk factors — the *problems* — that will affect you adversely.

Your obstacles — the risk factors — needn't be murders, car chases, or battlefields. Often it is the subtle, tiny annoyances that actually create the most tension. The low-level constant needs children present, climaxing when they get tired, hungry, bored. The kind of day where you lose your keys, get a flat, are served with a speeding ticket, and your boss says, "No, you can't

> *Art disturbs, science reassures.*
> — GEORGES BRAQUE

have that extension on the Miller file." It's not life-or-death drama that truly feeds the pulse of tension.

It's the little stuff.

In this chapter, you'll learn to practice paying attention to what *increases* tension. And you will learn a few tricks for avoiding the things that kill tension (explanation, clichés, generalizing, distance).

| PRACTICE |

Desire + Danger = Drama. Write five to ten tension "formulas," the essential conflicts for potential stories, poems, essays, or plays. Be radical, weird, wonderful, serious, or silly: You are just swinging your racket here, getting loose, getting a feel for the nature of tension. For example: Girl wants to be free of her mother and grow up and have fun + Mother is overbearing and whole town watches her every move = "Girl" — a mother-versus-daughter showdown: Will she rebel? Or obey?

Setting the Thermostat: The Four Elements of Tension

Read the following example, and rate the tension level on a scale of 1 to 5:

> I wake up when my alarm goes off and I get out of bed. It's 7:47 a.m. I can't believe I have to go to work. I get dressed, and drive— the traffic is terrible. I get out of my car and stand on the gravel. I see my aunt waiting for me. She is wearing tan clamdiggers and her black shirt complements her dark olive skin and her black hair. Her Teva-saddled feet are next to a white ball. Sneaky sees me, his stomach hanging down to his hind legs. When he reaches me I pick him up. Marilyn says hey I'm glad you made it. I'm just glad I am not too late.

> *Sanity is madness put to good uses.*
> — GEORGE SANTAYANA

The piece seems fine, in many ways. It's showing action, describing people, including setting, staying in one point of view. The characters are doing things. But somehow, the piece falls flat. Not a lot is happening. The narrator is late, but what are the consequences? Will anything *result* from these events? Is there any danger, really? A true problem?

A person wakes up, goes to work, finds her aunt, and collects a dog into her arms.

Readers say: So what? Why are you telling me this?

You don't ever want your reader saying "So what?" You always want your reader saying, "How is this going to turn out? What happens next?"

How do you move from "So what?" to "What's next?" Set the thermostat. One person wants something strongly *and is not able to get it*. Right away, and all through the piece. Then, immediately, you change the level of tension, increasing or decreasing it. You *change* the thermostat. And never let your reader go.

PRACTICE

Read the story "What I Saw from Where I Stood" by Marisa Silver (p. 251). Make a list of the three most tense scenes or sections in the story. Then write a short comparison/ contrast of the tension in the opening of this short story and the opening in Akhil Sharma's "Surrounded by Sleep" (p. 171). Which is the more tension-filled opening? Why?

Compare the passage on page 225, about the alarm clock going off, to the first paragraph from Marisa Silver's story "What I Saw from Where I Stood":

> Dulcie is afraid of freeways. She doesn't like not being able to get off when-
> ever she wants, and sometimes I catch her holding her breath between exits,
> as if she's driving past a graveyard. So, even though the party we went to last
> week was miles from our apartment in Silver Lake, we drove home on the
> surface streets.

This paragraph has more tension than does the first example. What contributes to the tension in this passage?

First of all, a woman named Dulcie (and just naming a character creates a little bit of tension — we will invest more in someone with a name than in "the girl" or "a man") is afraid. There is a *clear threat*. Weird, but clear: freeways.

Dulcie drives the other person in the story home the long way. She wants something. *To avoid something? To extend her time with the driver? To delay going home?*

The "I" (the narrator) catches Dulcie "holding her breath." Dulcie's tense. That makes us tense. Plus, we worry about the effect of all of Dulcie's desires on the narrator: the fear of freeways, the route demands, her anxiety. What is *up* with her?

Three simple sentences. Quite a bit of tension. How? The focus is on the character's desire, which is used to set the thermostat: to create heat. Start your piece with a problem.

To establish the tension temperature, we need: a person; the person wanting something rather strongly; and finally, something keeping that person from get- ting what she wants.

In chart form, it looks like this:

The Four Elements of Tension

Component	Considerations
1. PERSON: A person with a problem.	Be specific. Provide age, station in life, situation, location, cultural/social information.
2. DESIRE: The person wants something specific—has a strong desire.	What the person wants drives the entire passage. Ideally, the character/speaker has an external, physical desire that parallels or contrasts with an interior, psychological need.
3. STAKES: What the person wants is very important—it has to matter to her, greatly.	What is at stake for this person? What if she doesn't get what she wants? How bad will it be? Whatever she wants, she needs to want it *a lot*, even (especially) if it is a little thing. If your character doesn't care about what happens, the reader won't either.
4. OBSTACLES: The person has to be thwarted by obstacles that keep her from getting what she wants. Obstacles can be opponents (another person or people interfering with the goal) or forces (grief, fear, weather, etc.). Obstacles need to be realistic and meaningful and have consequences.	When the person gets what she wants, the piece is over, the tension is resolved. During the piece, don't let the character get what she wants and/or keep creating new needs, new wants. Your job as a writer is to move her closer to her need, and then either move her farther away or have the meeting of the need create a new desire.

PRACTICE

Find the four components of "setting the thermostat" in a section of Marisa Silver's story "What I Saw from Where I Stood" (p. 251). What tension(s) are set in the section of the story? Use the chart above to create an analysis of the four elements of tension.

In Silver's story, Dulcie wants to manage her fears. She wants to be happy again (interior psychological want). This is a high-value desire: She might ruin her relationships, asking too much of those who love her. She might never recover from grief. What she wants—the bad things to not have happened—is

> *One must still have chaos in*
> *oneself to be able to give birth*
> *to a dancing star.*
> — FRIEDRICH NIETZSCHE

completely and utterly not-gettable. The force of despair is as strong as her desire to change her life situation.

Notice that in this short story, as in most, things start bad—fear of freeways—and the writer keeps giving more information that *increases* the tension. Moving in closely again on that excerpted passage, notice that in addition to the freeway fear, Dulcie holds her breath. The party is far away (higher stakes). Notice how Silver, the writer, is dialing up the tension one notch at a time, one sentence at a time.

Narrative poetry (poetry that tells a story, as opposed to lyric poetry, which expresses a single feeling or emotion) also uses the components of tension in order to set the thermostat and keep reader interest high.

PRACTICE

Find Theodore Roethke's poem "The Waking" online and consider how he balances the forces of tension. Does he use all four components from the chart on page 227? Find words or phrases that support each component.

In Theodore Roethke's famous poem "The Waking," the battle is between the speaker and his question about his own life, his struggle to trust that his intuition, rather than his intellect, might take him where he needs to go. Life is a process, not a destination, he seems to say in this powerful poem. The speaker desires a meaningful life, and one that has room for questions and paradoxes; thus, "I wake to sleep" creates enormous tension. "I feel my fate in what I cannot fear" reveals high stakes—not much is more important to us than fate—and strong desire—I want to live a certain way. Obstacles abound. What might seem clear and certain to others—light, nature, the ground, God, truth—for this speaker creates an opportunity to question, to pause. He preserves, against great odds, a dream-like state. Sleep—not knowing—reveals connection to intuition. Intuition will guide him. It's slow living this way, worm-slow. But step-by-step, maintaining awareness in the face of tension—you get where you need to go.

MAINTAINING TENSION

Work with Two or Three Characters

Never work with one character who is alone. Always work with two or three characters so that you can have "sides." When you write just one person, you tend to rely on thoughts because there can be nothing at stake. It's hard to create tension with a character alone onstage, lost in thought. We don't see a lot there.

We don't have much to engage with as readers. Solo is boring. Two's a game. Three is always interesting—because there is so much more opportunity for *problems* to arise.

Match Your Opponents

When do you leave a game early, before the final score? When it's clear one side will win. Nothing is at stake in the fourth period when the score is 108–15. As a writer, the same rule applies. You will lose your reader unless you keep the stakes high.

The "sides," the power struggle—the thing the person wants and the thing keeping her from getting it—have to be equally matched.

Power shifts generate and sustain tension. Review our formula for creating tension:

> A person who wants something important badly, who is experiencing difficult obstacles that are keeping him/her from getting the things he/she wants.

Think of a sporting match. A good game. What do you notice? There are *two sides*. If your team goes out on the field to practice, the group doesn't pretend to have a game *against no one*. You divide up, shirts and skins. You *have to have sides*.

In a great game, a really tense match, the kind you stay into triple overtime in pouring rain to see finalized, the sides are evenly matched—it's not going to be a blowout.

Super close. Triple overtime. We in the stands are on the edges of our seats, worrying the whole time. *Who is going to win?* And, more important, *how are they going to get from where they are now to that win?* Each play is riveting. Every step, every pass, every glance matters.

If you are on the winning team, a blowout can be fun, but not for the spectators (i.e., the readers). For them, there is no tension. You don't want to be the writer having all the fun—the piece *has* to work for the readers.

> *Dimension means contradiction.*
> — ROBERT McKEE

In "What I Saw from Where I Stood," Grief is a worthy opponent. Charles uses his love for Dulcie to combat Grief. For Dulcie, Grief keeps taking form: first the hoodlums, then the pestilence. We don't know if she—and she and her partner—will make it or not. That's the tension in the story. Dulcie and Charles are good and young and strong. But they have been hit hard. Will they make It? That's the tension. To find out the answer to that question, we track the battle that is the story. Even the title indicates this is a report from the front lines, an eyewitness account.

Good poems always have tension, too. In Sebastian Matthews's "Buying Wine (p. 70), the children have a powerful hope that things will be okay in their family; but the adult has all the power and, in this case, is not safe. But he has young children. Opposing forces. In a play or memoir or comic, the tension lines dictate the story. The more tense a piece is, the more readers will be attracted to it.

| PRACTICE |

Read two pieces in this textbook, from two different genres. For each piece, find the four elements of tension. What are the opposing forces? Remember: The "battle" can be between two people or two forces. Are the opposing forces equally matched?

Stay Specific

Generalizations kill tension. Another habit writers accidentally fall into is writing *general* instead of writing *specific*. "They fought" sums up what happened; no tension there. The summary gives a general impression and will never be as tense and interesting as us getting to see the specifics of *how*. "Carlo sliced the letter across Joey's face, and the papercut beaded blood drops on Joey's pale cheek."

Compare "it was such a drag driving across town and always boring" to the paragraph detailing Dulcie's highway-avoidance rituals. Detail—getting very specific—is actually a method you use to create and sustain tension.

> *The business of the novelist is not to chronicle great events, but to make small ones interesting.*
> — ARTHUR SCHOPENHAUER

Robert Kurson, author of *Shadow Divers*, employs this principle. He avoids the general and always names the specifics, which increases the tension in his award-winning writing. Notice how the visual details, the images, increase the tension in this piece.

A good diver reveals himself in the way he gears up. He is at one with his equipment. He knows where every piece goes; every strap is the perfect length, every tool expertly placed, and everything fits. He moves instinctively, his hands and stuff in a swoop-tug-and-click ballet until he is transformed into sea creature. He rarely needs help. If another diver moves to assist him, he will usually decline, saying, "No, thank you" or, more likely, "Don't touch my shit." He favors ten-dollar knives over the hundred-dollar versions because when he loses the cheaper ones, he does not feel obligated, under the pressure of narcosis, to risk his life searching the bottom to rescue them. He cares nothing for the prettiness of his gear, and often tattoos it with patches, stickers, and graffiti that testify to past dive exploits. Neon colors do not exist for him; greenhorns who choose those hues don't have to wait long before hearing the boat's opinion on such loudness. When he is fully geared up, a good wreck diver looks like a German car engine; more ordinary divers resemble the interior of a child's toy chest.

Kurson could simply say that professional wreck divers relate to their equipment differently than amateur divers. The "versus" is implied: good divers versus newbies. However, there's not a lot of tension there. The fight isn't really equal; of course the better divers are *better*. To keep the tension in this passage high, Kurson uses specifics. We see that the quirks of the great divers all have a reason, an important reason. The better divers are smart. They're odd, they're messy, they're arrogant ("Don't touch my shit"). They have to be, in order to survive. The same specific qualities that aid them in getting dressed, on land, Kurson shows us, are the very ones that let them live while others may die.

PRACTICE

Turn back to the excerpt from Amy Fusselman's memoir *The Pharmacist's Mate* (p. 76). How many specifics do you find? List each specific word or phrase. Then write a brief response explaining how six of these specifics work to increase the tension. Lastly, identify places where tension would be lost or decreased without the specifics.

PRACTICE

Read Rod Kessler's "How to Touch a Bleeding Dog" (p. 250). Circle each specific image or word. In what ways do the specifics create and increase the tension?

Write from Close Up

He sat in the room for a long time.

What do you see in that sentence? What image appears in your mind's eye? What do you feel about the "he"? Anything at all?

The writer of this sentence has *generalized* time (it's a "long" time, but we have no idea *how* long and, more important, *when*). The writer has also generalized *space*. It's just generally a room. There's no situation. There's not actual space we can touch and move around in.

There is no tension because *there's nothing there*.

Write from close up. Be in the time — the exact moment — and the space — Apartment 4D, Sunset Heights, golden retriever and girlfriend on sofa — you are writing.

Distance kills tension. You want to avoid distance. Write from a close-up position, tight with your characters, the details, and the emotion; not from too far back. Your images training in Chapter Four has prepared you to write from *within* the experience, not hovering above, a reporter, or hiding behind the veil of time.

Many beginning writers write as though they are on a stage. The audience — the reader — is looking at the curtain, waiting for it to rise. But the beginning writer often reports to the audience — so that the play is going on behind the curtain. The writer sees it, and explains what is happening back there. This is not very pleasurable for the audience. We want the intermediary removed.

When you write, move closer, and you will increase the tension every time. Be in the room with the famous musician; be in the yard that is forbidden, looking for your lost baseball; be driving with your grieving girlfriend, clueless as to what to do next. Don't write *about* the experience, or you kill the tension. Don't look back, remember, think, or reflect: *Stay in the moment.* And stay close in. Write from a few inches away from your subject.

MANIPULATING TENSION

A lot of what you are doing when you work to create or increase the tension in a piece of creative writing is about *creating oppositions.* That is, you set qualities in the work against each other. A beautiful beach scene is the location for a woman telling her husband she wants a divorce. A boy tells a girl how much he hates his parents while carefully cleaning out the family garage, devoted to his task (his dialogue shows us he just wants to look cool in front of the girl).

In each of these cases, the setting and the action clash. Tension is created by working with exterior visual oppositions. But oppositions also must be created within characters.

The good guy has to have some weaknesses. Seinfeld is a neat-freak and germaphobe. The bad team has to have some good traits. Newman is a brilliant strategist and usually gets what he wants. Hamlet is kind and insightful but hesitates to make decisions. The Joker is evil, but very, very funny. Readers have to be able to connect with both "good" and "bad" characters for the piece to work on them.

Consider the power of juxtaposition. If the kittens are terribly cute, and you smile when you play with them, and their ribbons are pink, you are putting cuteness next to delight next to adorableness — there's not any surprise there. There's nothing for the reader to engage with. No tension.

You create tension when you put things that don't rest easily next to each other: adorable kittens, deep rejection, your angry mother. A broken barrette, a brother in trouble, a new car, the perfect pizza. A great date, a car accident.

Three useful strategies help you create and sustain tension in a piece of writing: the "thermostat" — the amount of tension in any given line or sentence; layers, which allow you to create and increase tension by moving your work from the simple to the complex (e.g., more than one thing is going on at once; you aren't stating the obvious); and, dialogue, used in special ways. All three strategies help create the oppositions and layers that make creative writing interesting to read.

Thermostat Control: Adjusting the Temperature

The secret to creating tension, in life and on the page, is to *vary the situation*. Ups and downs are much harder for us (and therefore much more successful in literature) than a steadily awful time. If things go from bad to worse, we can usually adapt. What drives us to the brink of madness is when the situation is bad (the line for Math Add is terrifically long), but it improves (Joe lets us cut ahead of him in line), and then gets worse (the Drop/Add people are leaving for lunch *just* when you get to the front of the line), and then much worse (your two boyfriends show up at the Drop/Add counter to confront you, loudly).

And then better.

Then worse.

In real life it's called "being jerked around."

Tension is ups and downs, back and forth, tension and the release of tension. This up-and-down is the rhythm of creative writing. Change appeals to our basic need for stimulation. Don't let your reader adapt. Once he gets the emotional tenor of one line, you have to change it up again. Be thoughtfully unpredictable. Don't let your piece remain at the same tension level for long.

Reread the poem "Buying Wine" by Sebastian Matthews (p. 70). Notice the tension level in the first stanza. A choice is always imbued with some tension; here the choice is backseat or Wine Mart. Each one has pluses and minuses. Somewhat arbitrarily, we could assign a number to that level of tension, on a scale of 1 to 5. Let's say it's a 2. Because the speaker in the poem is a child, either choice is at least a little scary.

In the second stanza, the tension goes down—the boy is in the store, trailing Dad, and things look good, orderly, even familiar, "like bat racks." The tension is perhaps a 1. But not for long. In stanza 3, the cart is "ever-filling"—and this is not good and it's getting worse because the father is "unkempt" and pretty much flinging liquor into the cart in the aisle. Tension in stanzas 3 through 5 could be said to dial up quickly; 2, 3, then 4. In stanza 5, Matthews ratchets the tension meter back down—the speaker, a child, sees his father shopping here as he shops at the meat store. Things are okay, aren't they? We're just shopping for food. It's good to match wines and food, put a pinot grigio with scallops . . . right? The tension dances down to near 1.

Notice the leap that occurs between stanzas 7 and 8. While the boy is adjusting to his father's wine-shopping ritual, he slips into a reverie, remembering other wine store trips where he made the other choice and stayed in the car. Whenever a writer switches locations, pops into a flashback, moving back in time and space, the reader experiences a tension shift. "Often, we'd stay in the car" moves the tension from 1 back up to 2 or 3, and then in the second line of stanza 8—notice the tension shift in that "dwindling capacity to believe our father" comment. Boom. This isn't a kid who still worships his dad. This is a kid who has been disappointed by this dad many, many times. That statement charges the poem with energy, intensity.

That intensity is increased—to a 5, perhaps, on the tension meter—in the next stanza, where the kids in the backseat are imagined as free from the car, roaming. Unsupervised offspring of an alcoholic father, "like horses" for a moment, and anything could happen. Lots of tension here. Which drops back down when the boys are, sadly, drawn to the liquor store window, to peek in, glimpse "snippets of [the] father's profile." They want to be like him. They want to be with him. They want to be free. The tensions in the poem are further dialed up a notch in the line when he disappears "behind the tall cardboard stacks" as if he's being swallowed up by liquor, which, in fact, he is.

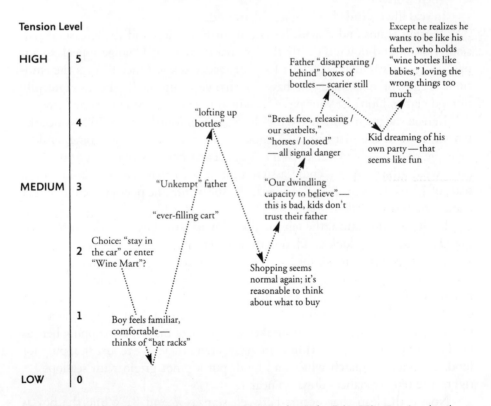

Map of tension in Sebastian Matthews's poem "Buying Wine" (p. 70). Tension level ranges from 1 to 5. The arrows represent the direction of the tension; the length of the arrows indicates how much the tension increases or decreases.

When the kid loads up his own cart in stanza 12, do you see that as more or less drastic than the preceding stanza? Some readers will say it's just as tense: a 4 or a 5. Because the boy is hurt so deeply in the preceding stanza, seeing his dad disappear, other readers will see this stanza as less tense—a kid acting like a kid. Readers will react differently; what's important for you as the writer is to keep *changing* the intensity.

When the speaker is dreaming of parties, some readers may feel this is the most tense part of the poem because it's so easy to imagine the speaker going down a bad path. Others will believe that the final image, of the father holding "wine bottles like babies in his hands," creates the deepest emotional impact of the entire poem, as we see the father being more careful with the wine than with his real children.

Remember: If everything is at the same high level of excitement, your reader will grow just as bored as if there were no tension at all. Scientists and psychologists have shown definitively that the human mind adjusts quickly; it is designed to *adapt*. It's part of the human genius. We get used to things very, very quickly—loud background noise disappears, our surroundings homogenize, we don't notice changes in family members we see every day. Give us a bad situation, and it's human nature to adapt. Just when the room is getting too hot, turn down the thermostat; make the reader cool off. Then, just as the reader is cooling, crank the heat back up. That's the oppositional nature of this strategy: When things get bad, they have to get worse. When they get worse, they then have to get better.

As you practice, you will find more ways to intensify and manipulate the temperature. The chart on page 236 lists various elements of a piece of writing, presenting ways for adjusting the thermostat and modulating tension.

Read the poem "Hustle" by Jericho Brown (p. 112), written in a form called ghazal. Read the poem aloud and again silently. The title offers a key to understanding how the seemingly unrelated couplets connect: "Hustle" has several meanings; one is to treat someone roughly. In a ghazal, each couplet introduces a different aspect of the main topic. In the first couplet (a couplet is a two-line stanza), we read a mysterious set of lines about being in prison. We may need to look up the reference to Dwayne Betts. (At sixteen, Betts, a stellar student, made some very poor decisions, committed a crime, was tried as an adult, and spent eight years in prison. He's now a professor, poet, and memoirist.) Brown's poem continues to ask us to look up things we do not know, to read on for more information. In this way, he creates tension for the reader—an insistent need to know more. Who are these people? How do these things relate to each other? Alice Walker's famous novel is referenced, as are other accounts of violence and injustice. Brown insists the reader put the story together on his or her own. He wants the reader to feel tension: That's part of his point.

In a ghazal, the couplets aren't supposed to connect directly. The poem is actually thirteen two-line minipoems. For some readers, this is simply too much tension. But for patient readers, the rewards are great. The point here is this: Practice adjusting the thermostat, moving from high-tension moments to simple moments, intense heat to calm peace. Thermostat control gives you power over your reader.

Adjusting the Temperature: Ways to Decrease and Increase Tension

Decreases Tension	Increases Tension
Agreement	Disagreement
Safety	Danger
Things are okay	Things are not okay
Generalization	Specific information; intimate details
One thing is going on	Two or three things happening at once
Linear, chronological exposition	Leaps
Moving ahead as expected	Reversals
Having all needs met, ease, simplicity	Wanting something badly, needing, yearning
Overcoming obstacles easily	Thwarted again and again
Solution = resolution	Solution to problem creates ew problem
Explanation, telling	Mystery, withholding
Static character, doing nothing	Character in action
Character alone with thoughts	Character in a triangle with two other characters
Speeches, interior dialogues	Crisp dialogue based on an argument
One technique used at length (all description, all dialogue, all interior thoughts . . .)	Variety of techniques (dialogue first, then description, then interior thoughts, then more dialogue . . .)
All long or all short sentences or lines	Short sentences or lines mixed up with longer ones
Seeing the big picture; long shots	Seeing things from *very* close up

Poetry and drama, including graphic novels and comics, thrive on these increases and decreases in tension. As you studied in the Building Blocks chapter (Chapter Three), narrative forms are composed of scenes, which contain the ups and downs — conflicts — between characters.

Layers: Adding Dimension

A stack of halved parsnips, looking like naked human limbs, maybe dead, in the fluorescent light of a refrigerator — not very interesting. Slightly creepy, perhaps, but what's the point? You have a pile of scary vegetables. So what? The image is two-dimensional.

Add a young woman with cancer, who has to cook these parsnips for a wealthy family, where there may be adultery, deceit, neglect — a family with emotional cancers — and you've got something. Layers infuse your images with meaning, interest, and excitement. Jessica Shattuck's "Bodies" is rich with layers.

PRACTICE

Read the short story "Bodies" by Jessica Shattuck (p. 263), and as you read, see if you can notice the layers in the piece. When does one action or element of the story indicate or inform another action, character, or element?

Writers don't always plan and control the layers in the poems, plays, memoirs, and stories they craft. Often, getting two tracks going — a needy kid watching *The Lion King* in the other room, a babysitter with cancer dabbing the parsnips with butter — results in the images talking to each other and creating more than the sum of their parts. When Shattuck describes Annie's view of little Anthony, her charge, Annie sees the old man in the tiny five-year-old. "He is five years old, blond, and freckled, with close-set blue eyes. Something about his mouth and his stubby but prominent little nose hints already at the old man he will be — stubborn, soft-spoken, a little unforgiving." Annie is aware of death, even in a little kid. The themes of the story — who talks, who forgives, what gets passed on — are embedded in the description of a five-year-old. Images are layered, and themes come out for the reader. The writer stays close up — close enough to see the mouth, the exact nature of the nose, close enough to count the freckles on a cheek — and writes what she sees. As she works on her story, she becomes aware of patterns, images that keep coming up, calling for attention.

Bottom line: If you provide only one layer in your writing, readers will not find the tension in your

> *Nothing is more odious than music without hidden meanings.*
>
> — FRÉDÉRIC CHOPIN

piece, and will grow bored at best, and stop reading at worst. Girl goes to party, has fun, meets great guy, parties all night, has to dash to work late the next day—that's one layer. You need more layers in order to transform this series of events into creative writing.

Layering Images. Earlier, we noted the energy a writer gains by juxtaposing images, layering a series of "health" images over a series of "illness" images. Look at how Jay's devotion to buffing his body contrasts with Annie's illness. She imagines Jay doing handsprings; she herself pretends to be woozy when she isn't. He gets more muscular; she gets sicker. "Bodies" is a good title for this story, which is about death, sex, passion, children—all the things that tie us irrevocably to the body.

One way to layer images in a poem or a narrative is to locate, in a draft already in progress, some oppositions or potential oppositions. Notice that when you are following images where they are alive—in a state of flux, moving, action-oriented, when things are changing—it will be easier to layer.

A moving image has traction—other images will stick to it. Layer the important stuff, not the background stuff. Layers not only create and increase tension, but tell the reader to pay attention—*this is important!* Layers make meaning.

PRACTICE

Find at least four examples of image layers in Marisa Silver's story "What I Saw from Where I Stood" (p. 251). List the layers and write a brief explanation.

Layering with Triangles. Triangles are a simple strategy for creating complex tensions. Think about triangles when looking for ways to layer your work to increase complexity. "Bodies" and "What I Saw from Where I Stood" both use triangles in order to make the work tension-filled and interesting. Unlike a beginning painter, who might stick a tree in the middle of the canvas and call it good, a skilled artist employs many triangles, laid over each other. In the popular sitcom *Friends*, as in most film and television, triangles form the architecture of the series and create almost all the opportunities the writers have to use tension. Consider the two triangles that every episode uses: Joey-Chandler-Ross and Monica-Phoebe-Rachel. The setting is also a triangle: two apartments and the coffee shop. Can you think of others?

PRACTICE

Poems often use triangles to generate tension. Read Natalie Diaz's "My Brother at 3 a.m." (p. 159) and locate triangles. Nonfiction also relies on the triangle strategy to keep the tension high and complex. List the triangles—as many as you can find—in the creative nonfiction piece "Son of Mr. Green Jeans" by Dinty W. Moore (p. 305). The monologue "Where There's Smoke" by Jenifer Hixson (p. 162) uses the triangle technique, too. List the triangles you find when you read or listen to her monologue.

Triangles form the basic tensions in "Bodies." There's a Cleo-Annie-Jay triangle. Annie is drawn to Jay. Cleo is married to Jay. Jay is attracted to and repelled by Annie—she scares him, her illness scares him, she lives in his house, cares for his children (more attentively than Cleo, the mother of his children). Cleo loves Jay, relies on Annie. This is a love triangle, but it's also a triangle created by *complex* human relationships. Good creative writing relies on relationship triangles. Pieces with just one character, or two characters in a simple relationship, aren't going to hold reader interest as readily as triangle pieces.

Shattuck is a very skilled writer. She uses triangles to create friction in her main characters and amplifies those tensions with yet another triangle, the Michele-Cleo-Jay triangle. The Michele-Cleo-Jay triangle provides the subplot, the undercurrent, and this triangle operates as the catalyst for the story. Michele, Cleo's niece, is in love with Jay, who maintains a secret relationship with the girl. Annie is stunned, as we are, by this secret triangle. Anthony is quite literally stuck in the middle of these adult relationships, which make a complex web around him. Good writers, just like visual artists, think in terms of threes because groups of three add dimension, excitement, possibility, and interest. Threes always work.

Creative writers always avoid having one character alone with her thoughts. Basic tension is achieved when two people are in conflict with each other, presenting desires that are at odds. Better yet is creative writing that involves three points of conflict, three forces. In a sophisticated or longer piece, writers layer

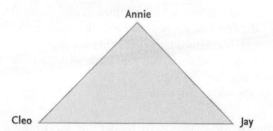

Tension triangle in Jessica Shattuck's story "Bodies." Annie, Jay, and Cleo form a triangle. There will always be tension whenever these three are together at the same time.

one triangle over another in order to create dimensions. This is how tension works in creative writing.

With triangles, you create a space for the reader to form conclusions and insights. As a writer, you can use triangles to guide and deepen your images, to keep you on track. You have a triangle whenever three people are involved, each of whom represents a different agenda.

Recall the scene where Jay enters the kitchen (Cleo's abandoned space) to pour vitamins "fat as roaches into his palm." Notice the specificity—all the vitamins are named, described. Annie thinks about Cleo—so Cleo is present, although not physically. Notice the triangulation. Jay asks Annie to touch him. The images are intensified because they come at an intersection—sickness, the mad pursuit of perfect strength, milk/mother/Cleo/kitchen. Shattuck stays a long time, makes a big deal out of Annie's fingers on Jay's "warm wrist." Notice how much more time—five paragraphs, a dialogue conversation—is spent here. We stay on these images because they are dramatic, intense, uncomfortable—skin on skin. The kitchen scene's images link up with the roof scene later—when Annie gets her strength back, Shattuck doesn't have to explain it to us—Annie feels "her own blood finally—she is aware of its quick rhythm in the channels of her veins." And "It is as if some door had opened inside her and she could hear everything."

Layering Dialogue and Action. Some beginning writers fill whole pages with direct dialogue, including long conversations that often don't create images in the reader's mind. No images: no tension. People yakking away mindlessly, or people stating the obvious in direct dialogue, is not good creative writing. Long speeches, monologues, and he said/she said predictable dialogues weaken good creative writing. Writer and teacher Robert Boswell explains that while we probably say three thousand lines of dialogue out loud every day in our regular lives, perhaps twenty of those lines are worthy of including in a piece of literature. Like everything else in your poem, story, or play, dialogue has to have layers.

Here's an example of unlayered dialogue and action:

> "I love you," he said. He handed her the flowers and the card.
> "Thank you," she said. She opened the card. "It's so beautiful!"
> "Thanks," he said, and leaned over to give her a kiss.
> "I love you," she said, and she kissed him back, with pleasure.
> "We're so great together," he said.
> She said, "I totally and utterly agree."

There's no reason to use dialogue to render the happy moment. The skilled writer covers this scene in two words, *They kissed*, and moves on to the next moment of tension. Save dialogue for the places in your story or poem or essay where the emotions are mixed, and tease out the tension by layering the dialogue and action.

Other beginning writers avoid dialogue altogether, relying too heavily on description and reflection.

Notice the poems in this book that you have read so far that use dialogue. How often do people speak? How often is their speech summarized for us so that we have a sense of exactly what is spoken? In the fiction we have been studying, how much dialogue is used? When? How do you blend the dialogue into a piece of creative writing so it doesn't stick out, so it flows?

Dialogue is always going to attract a lot of attention from your reader. It's close up (someone is actually talking, the author is far back, summarizing a conversation). It's specific, by definition, and usually at least two characters are present, since it's a conversation.

| PRACTICE |

Read aloud just the dialogue—nothing else—from the short story "Bodies" by Jessica Shattuck (p. 263). What do you notice about the dialogue? Now go back through and highlight the actions that attend each spoken bit. How do the actions create oppositions? Tension? What is lost if we hear just the spoken parts? Which dialogue-action bits have the most tension? Rank them in order of most tense to least tense.

To sustain tension in dialogue, it's useful to remember that dialogue never occurs outside human action. When we speak, we use our full body, our face moves around, and our arms and gestures and habits punctuate our phrases. We interrupt, we slam the book on the table, we cross our arms, we roll our eyes, scoot our chair back, stroke the arm of our partner—all that is part of the conversation. Dialogue can't be separated from action, and so action is automatically a crucial part of *what is said*.

Recall this scene from the short story "Bodies." A man walks into the kitchen; the image starts. A woman pours a glass of milk, asks about his resting pulse, feels his wrist, and he talks to her, revealing his fear. Everything that happens in those five minutes, in that little micro-movie, is the image, and dialogue is part of the sound track. As a writer, you want to vary the way you represent direct speech—sometimes you start with an action, then use a direct quote. Then you have someone look away—no direct speech. Next time, you have one person look, move, try to speak, but they can't. Person B starts to talk, Person A interrupts. You want to vary the position of your camera eye, the closeness, the angle, the length of time spent on a conversation.

Dialogue needs to be written so that the reader feels somehow present as a witness or eavesdropper.

Work with dialogue and action as units, as a single thing with two layers: the speech *and* the motions. Try to avoid disembodied dialogue, which loses energy fast.

When writing dialogue, it's vital that you use your training with the image. Often, new writers can sound like television programs because so much of the dialogue we hear comes from that source. Focus on what your characters truly say, even—especially—if it surprises you. Don't make it up. Take dictation. Let them surprise you. Never force characters in your work to say things just for the sake of the piece you are writing.

Avoid using clichés—overly familiar dialogue expressions, things people never *really* say. And avoid not just spoken clichés but also action clichés, called emotional shorthand: raised eyebrows, grimaces, smiles, winks, pounding fists. Those are all shortcuts, cartoon gestures for real emotions, and a sign of lazy writing. Stay focused on the image, and write what you truly see there. Action-dialogue units need to have freshness and truth in them. Stay very real, very focused.

Write exactly the tiny things you see in the conversation. Does she stick her pen in her mouth after each sentence? Shift her weight so that her pant leg hikes up? Shoot her fingers at you like she thinks she is so cool? Click her tongue and spit with each sentence? The tiny things that give an individual away—the things Carlo does when he talks that Joey *never* does—let those movements become part of the dialogue itself.

Practice listening to your friends and coworkers. What lines do they say that are worthy of putting in a piece of creative writing? "Hey, how you doing?" probably isn't going to make it. As mentioned before, *most* of what we say day-to-day isn't going to make the cut for a piece of writing. "Ya gotta beat the best to be the best." That might make it. "Do you miss the fish?"

Now we're talking *tension*.

Façade

As you are well aware, people don't always say exactly what they mean. Much of the pleasure in reading dialogue is knowing more than a character or speaker knows about him- or herself. Now that you have had practice layering dialogue and action to build tension, you want to *increase* the tension between what is said, thought, and done, between interior and exterior. There's a triangle here, an opportunity for opposition. In fact, in good creative writing, controlling tension in dialogue is not optional—it's required. And this technique, named by writer and teacher Jerome Stern, is called **façade**.

"Hey, how's it going," your friend says, but we can tell by her tone, how she is hanging her shoulders and dragging her toe around, making a bored circle, that she doesn't care how we are doing at all. She just wants us to ask her how *she's* doing.

That gap—the "false front" she is putting up—between what she presents to the outside and what is really going on inside her is a façade. We say "I hate you" when we mean "I love you."

PRACTICE

Read Peter Morris's short play "Pancakes" (p. 274). When do the characters say what they do not mean? How do you know this?

Dialogue in creative writing works best when it is used *not* to announce a character's thoughts or direct desires, *but to contradict them and create a gap, a false front*. Dialogue-action units let you juxtapose what's said with what's done; façade helps you broadcast the gap between what someone says and what he or she really thinks or feels or wants.

In architecture, a façade is the front of a building. Think of a cheap building that has a fake brick front but really is just a metal pole barn. That image has tension. That building is pretending to be something it is not. Think of a house with an imposing façade—a grand entry, three stories of glass. But really, the house is just a three-bedroom tract house with a tiny kitchen, cheap carpet, and vinyl siding. A façade is a false front, and it's your most important dialogue tool. Without façade, most dialogue falls flat, and your readers will skip and skim.

When people talk to us in real life, they hint at things and focus on side issues, they beat around the bush. Usually, every conversation that is interesting has several levels. People have agendas.

Façade, layered on top of dialogue-action units, is the technique writers use to keep the tension levels high.

> "I just can't do it," Valerie cried. "It's all those thirty-second notes. My fingers just won't let me do it!"
> "Yes they will. You just have to trust them," her instructor replied patiently.
> "But my concert is in five weeks! I'm never going to be ready by then!"
> "Well, with that attitude, you won't be. But I'll help you."
> "Okay," Valerie said.

What do you notice about this passage? There's an awful lot of time to get ready—five weeks. Not very tense. There's a helpful teacher who is kind and patient. Not a very good opponent! But also notice the dialogue, how it works against tension, not toward it. Valerie explains exactly what her problem is and tells us everything we need to know. Dialogue has to reveal new emotional nuances; it can't simply deliver information to the reader about character, situation, station in life.

She wants to play faster. Her talent isn't up to the demands of the piece at this moment. She lodges two complaints, *I can't* and *I won't be ready*, and then she says, "Okay!" This is the opposite of what you want to do.

It's much more interesting for your reader if the character is revealing more than she thinks she is. Gaps and misinterpretations give the reader a place to worm into your writing.

Some of your dialogue can use the dialogue-action technique to keep tension modulated. But not all your dialogue can be a direct statement. You need some false fronts in order to make your piece complex and tense.

Examine this dialogue exchange from Marisa Silver's "What I Saw from Where I Stood."

> "We saw them," she said. "We know what they look like."
> "They weren't killers. They were thieves. There's a difference, I guess," I said.
> "No," she said, twisting her straight brown hair around her finger so tightly the tip turned white. "It doesn't make sense."
> Dulcie needs things to be exact.

In the passage above, Dulcie's dialogue lines are interesting because we have to pay attention to understand what they are about. She hides as much as she reveals when she talks. The reader is *drawn in*. These are not talking heads, making a point to serve the writer's goal. These are stressed-out people, in pain, trying to communicate. They say the wrong thing, or try to impress the cops, or come off as serious and devoted, when really they are terrified inside.

Dulcie is real to the reader. She is saying things that do make sense and that don't make sense, all at the same time. She is experiencing a great deal of tension inside herself. We feel for her.

Read the dialogue farther on:

> "I should have noticed them tailing me," Dulcie said now. "How could I not notice a car that close?"
> "Don't do that," I told her. "Don't think about what could have happened."
> "I have to think about it," she said. "How can you not think about it? We were this close," she said, holding her fingers out like a gun and aiming at my chest.

What makes this dialogue passage tense? The use of façade. Dulcie has changed direction again: Earlier she said she noticed everything; now she is kicking herself for not noticing things right in front of her face. Usually, when people beat themselves up for something, something else is bothering them, too. What's on Dulcie's mind, besides the thieves? Then her companion tells her not to worry about "what could have happened." But that isn't what she is worried about. When people are tense, they misunderstand. They hear what they need to hear. Their own motives and concerns come out in the dialogue. He's trying to help. But is he barking up the wrong tree? What's his agenda in that line?

To write façade, know what your character wants, and have him speak to it a little sideways. Have him talk about one thing *by way of* talking about what really bothers him, a whole other thing. In the passage above, Silver heats up the exchanges beat by beat—each exchange a little more tense, a little edgier, than the one before. She saves her most dramatic part of the dialogue, which is Dulcie communicating with her fingers, for last. By "We were this close," do you think she means in more ways than one?

Usually, we reveal a lot more than we think we do when we talk to other people. When we are stressed and tense (those are the moments worthy of dramatizing through creative writing, remember!), our internal censors are less able to protect us. We say too much, or not enough. We don't mean to, but we reveal our deepest feelings and desires. That is probably the highest form of tension in literature.

This is a lot to practice.

What we are striving toward are dialogue action units with internal tensions (what's said works against what the character is doing) working against the façade (what's said isn't what the character *really* means). That triangle is the essential heartbeat of tension.

In addition, the character's conversation and action lines work against the setting (you are close up as you write all this), and her obstacles are *exactly* what she doesn't want. Set the thermostat, match your opponents, stay specific. Layer images, dialogue, and work toward false fronts—you'll be a tension-generating machine.

PRACTICE

Evaluate the changing levels of tension in Peter Morris's short play "Pancakes" (p. 274) by jotting a number in the margin to represent the tension level. When the level changes, write down a new number.

PRACTICE

Read Rod Kessler's "How to Touch a Bleeding Dog" (p. 250). What are the elements of tension you find in this piece of writing? Try to locate four to six concepts from this chapter in the "story."

WRITING PROJECTS

1. Write a passage or poem utterly lacking in tension, interest, or excitement: Be boring. Or bring in the most boring piece of writing you can find. Read the boring passages aloud. Discuss: What are the most numbing, tension-killing things a writer can do? Long passages of description. Many difficult, look-it-up-in-a-dictionary word choices. What makes *boring* boring? Create a "what kills tension and reader interest" checklist. Avoid these pitfalls.

2. Write a narrative or poem detailing the actions and images that you experience on your route to work or school. Describe the images. Focus on what you do. Choose a day when things go fairly smoothly. Set the tension in this short passage at 1 or 2, on a scale of 1 to 5. Then draft a second short passage, same route, but this time introduce three subtle annoyances hindering your progress, and include another person, a passenger or another figure. Give one of the two of you some psychological quirk that makes your journey subtly more difficult. Try to make the tension somewhat higher than in your first passage; set the thermostat at 3 and try to take it to 5.

3. Write an argument between equals. Using only dialogue and letting the conversation take up about two pages, write a dialogue in which two equally strong characters fight.

4. Write a poem or short-short in five lines or sentences. Use this recipe to adjust the tension of each line or sentence: 3, 2, 1, 4, 5. You may wish to write the parts in a different order and then assemble them so that the tension meter reading fits the pattern. Title it using a word from the piece.

5. Write a piece of fiction or creative nonfiction that uses the tensions of a close game. The only subject you can't use is that of an actual sporting event. Write about a bad date, shopping with your father, babysitting a brood of nightmare children; let the ups and downs—the tension—be inspired by the forward/backward rhythm of a fantastically close game, one that goes into triple overtime. It's that exciting. Use the chart on page 236 to guide your thermostat changes. Surprise your reader by letting the apparently weaker person win.

6. Layer your earlier work. Take a piece in progress from earlier this semester. With a writing partner, identify some of the images in the piece. Discuss oppositions you could make more out of, or add, in order to create at least three image layers. Rewrite the piece, working on layering images as a way of increasing the tension and power.

7. Write a story, poem, or creative nonfiction piece that uses four to six people. Present scenes or sections of three people, each of whom wants something different from the others. Cycle through at least three different combinations of your ensemble. Focus on images—don't explain what the people want. Simply show us.

8. Try layering dialogue and action. Using the following template, create a piece that alternates a line of speech and an action between two characters. Time yourself—keep your hand moving for thirty minutes. Briefly write a few sentences to set the scene, as in a play: Who is onstage, where are we, what's the weather / atmosphere / time of day / quality of the light? Then divide your paper into two columns, as shown here.

Character 1	Character 2
Write a few sentences about Character 1: what he is wearing, how he is sitting, what he's fiddling with, his emotional state, desire.	Write a few sentences about Character 2, as you did for Character 1.
Write a line of dialogue for Character 1.	What is Character 2's response (first, in a line of dialogue)?
	What exact gesture or tiny action do you see Character 2 do? (Be sure you are *in* the image.)
What is Character 1's response to the comment/gesture by Character 2? Write the physical action, the tiny gesture you see. Your characters can get up, move around; the image is alive.	Character 2 responds, first with dialogue, then with a gesture. Repeat, following the pattern until the end of the time.
What does Character 1 say to Character 2? (Use your ears; don't make it up.)	

9. Try writing a short play using façade. Recall a conversation you had recently that was extremely personal and tense for you. You might begin with a quick list of ten tense conversations from the past month. Choose one and do a little sketch first, using your diagram to answer the questions from the table above. Then focus on the speech and tiny actions that make up the

dialogue—however, the characters must be talking about something else (buying a house, picking out a puppy) besides the topic of the argument (one character wants to get married, the other doesn't, or one wants to have a baby, the other doesn't). Let the real fight come through in both dialogue and actions. But never mention the real fight directly.

10. Write a poem using only dialogue, using the principles of façade. Limit your poem to two speakers.

TENSION WORKSHOP

The prompts below will help you constructively discuss your classmates' work.

1. Write the tension formula—desire + danger = drama—for this piece. Describe the central *desire* in the main character/speaker. Is this danger presented clearly enough? How could the stakes or danger be increased? Could the desire part of the equation be intensified? How?

2. Create a tension map for the piece, assigning a number to represent the amount of tension in each paragraph (for prose) or line (for poetry). Does the piece "flatline" (the same number repeats) in certain places? How could the numbers vary more? In which one place do you suggest the author work hardest to increase the tension?

3. Are there two or more characters to care about? Are they equally matched? How so?

4. What specific details and images function to *increase* the tension in this piece?

5. What's the central tension? Does the central tension have an internal as well as an external manifestation in this piece?

6. Identify one example of tension from the writer's use of close-ups. Highlight or underline the passage where the writer employs this technique. Next, find a passage where the tension would increase if more close-ups were used.

7. Identify three places in the piece where there could be more tension, and write in the margin one suggestion for a technique the writer could try from the following: triangles, layers, opposition. Try to suggest each technique if appropriate.

8. List at least two uses of triangles or potential triangles that could be developed. Are these passages also the places where the tension numbers are highest (from your mapping of the thermostat changes, above)?

9. Read just the dialogue aloud. Does it sound natural? Do you find layers in what is said and what is really meant? Do you find oppositions? Is the dialogue tension-filled or predictable? Note the best use of dialogue and say why. Note the weakest passage of dialogue and say why.

10. Has the writer used the façade technique? Where might the writer try to use façade more fully or boldly?

READINGS

Rod Kessler
How to Touch a Bleeding Dog

It begins as nothing, as a blank. A rose light is filtering through the curtains. Rosy and cozy. My blanket is green. My blanket is warm. I am inside. Inside is warm. Outside is the dawn. Outside is cold. Cold day. My arm reaches for a wife who is no longer there.

The stillness is broken by the voice of a neighbor, yelling from the road outside. "The dog! Your dog's been hit!" It's the farmer down the road, keeping farmer's hours. "The dog!"

It's not my dog, but it's my responsibility. It is Beth's dog. I don't even like him, with his nervous habit of soiling the kitchen floor at night. I used to clean up after the dog before Beth came yawning out of our bed, and that was an act of love, but not of the dog. Now it doesn't matter why I clean up. Or whether.

Beth's dog is old and worn. He smells like a man given to thin cigars. Beth found him at the animal shelter, the oldest dog there.

I find the dog quivering on his side where he limped from the road. He has come to the garden gate, where the rose bushes bloom. A wound on his leg goes cleanly to the bone, and red stains appear here and there on the dull rug of his coat. He will not stand or budge when I coax him. A thick brown soup flows out of his mouth onto the dirt.

On the telephone, the veterinarian asks me what he looks like, and I say, stupidly, like an old Airedale. He means his wounds. After I describe them, he instructs me to wrap the dog in something warm and rush him over.

I make a mitten of the green blanket and scoop weeds and clods as well as the dog. The dew on the grass looks cool, but the blood that blossoms on the blanket is warm and sick. He is heavy in my arms and settles without resistance in my car. He is now gravity's dog.

Driving past the unplowed fields toward town, I wonder if my clumsiness hurt the dog. Would Beth have touched him? The oldest dog in the shelter! It's a wonder that she thought having a dog would help.

The veterinarian helps me bring the dog from the car to the office. We make a sling of the blanket, I at the head. We lay him out on a steel-topped table. I pick weeds and grass from the blanket and don't know what to say.

The veterinarian clears his throat but then says nothing.

"He's my wife's dog," I say. "Actually, he came from the shelter over on High Street. He wasn't working out, really. I was thinking of returning him."

The veterinarian touches a spot below the dog's ear.

"Maybe," I continue, "maybe if it's going to cost a lot . . ."

"I don't think you have to make that decision," says the veterinarian, who points out that some papillary response is missing. "He's dying," he says. "It's good you weren't attached to him."

Beth, I remembered, enjoyed taking the dog for rides in the car.

"These breaths," the veterinarian is saying, "are probably his last."

He seems relieved that he needn't bother to act appropriately for the sake of any grief on my part. He asks, "Did he run in the road a lot?"

"Never," I say. "He never ran at all."

"What do you make of that?"

"Beats me," I say, lying. I watch the dog's chest rise and fall. He's already far away and alone. I picture myself running out into the road.

I watch my hand volunteer itself and run its finger through the nap of his head, which is surprisingly soft. And, with my touch on him, he is suddenly dead.

I walk back to the car and am surprised by how early in the day it still is. Blood is drying on the green blanket in my hand, but it will come off in the wash. The blood on the carpet of the car is out of sight, and I will pretend it isn't there. And then there's the touch. But soon the touch, too, will be gone.

Marisa Silver

What I Saw from Where I Stood

Dulcie is afraid of freeways. She doesn't like not being able to get off whenever she wants, and sometimes I catch her holding her breath between exits, as if she's driving past a graveyard. So, even though the party we went to last week was miles from our apartment in Silver Lake, we drove home on the surface streets.

I was drunk, and Dulcie was driving my car. She'd taken one look at me as we left the party, then dug her fingers into my pants pocket and pulled out my keys. I liked the feel of her hand rubbing against me through my jeans; she hadn't been touching me much lately.

I cranked open the window to clear my head as we drove through Santa Monica. Nice houses. Pretty flowers. Volvos. Dulcie and I always say we'd never want to live out here in suburbia, but the truth is, we can't afford to, not on our salaries. Dulcie's a second-grade teacher in Glendale, and I'm a repairman for the telephone company.

When we reached Hollywood, things got livelier. There were skinny guitar punks patrolling the clubs on the strip with their pudgy girlfriends in midriff tops and thigh-high black skirts. A lot of big hair, big breasts, boredom. Farther east, there were boys strutting the boulevard, waiting to slip into someone's silver Mercedes and make a buck. One leaned against a fire hydrant and picked at his sallow face, looking cold in a muscle T-shirt.

We hit a red light at Vermont, right next to the hospital where Dulcie lost the baby, a year ago. She'd started cramping badly one night. She was only six months pregnant. I called the emergency room, and the attendant said to come right over. By the time we got there, the doctors couldn't pick up a heartbeat. They gave Dulcie drugs to induce labor and the baby was born. He was blue. He was no bigger than a football.

Dulcie looked up at the hospital and then back at the road. She's a small girl and she sank behind the wheel, getting even smaller. I didn't say anything. The light turned green. She drove across Vermont and I nodded off.

I woke up when a car plowed into us from behind. My body flew towards the windshield, then ricocheted back against my seat. Dulcie gripped the wheel, staring straight ahead out the windshield.

"Something happened," she said.

"Yeah," I heard myself answer, although my voice sounded hollow. "We had an accident."

We got out to check the damage and met at the back of the car. "It's nothing," Dulcie said, as we studied the medium-sized dent on the fender. It was nothing to us, anyway; the car was too old and beat-up for us to feel protective of it.

Behind me, I heard the door of a van slide open. I hadn't thought about the people who'd hit us, hadn't even noticed if they bothered to stop. I started to wave them off. They didn't need to get out, apologize, dig around for the insurance information they probably didn't have. But when I turned around, there were four or five men in front of me. They were standing very close. They were young. I was beginning to think that Dulcie and I should just get back into our car and drive away, when the van's engine cut out and a tall guy wearing a hooded sweatshirt called back towards it. "Yo, Darren! Turn it on, you motherfucker!"

His cursing seemed to make his friends nervous. Two of them looked at their feet. One hopped up and down like a fighter getting ready for a bout. Someone was saying "Shit, shit, shit" over and over again. Then I heard "Do it, do it!" and a short, wide kid with a shaved head and glow-in-the-dark stripes on his sneakers pulled out a gun and pointed it at my face. It didn't look like the guns in movies. Dulcie screamed.

"Don't shoot. Please don't shoot us!" Her voice was so high it sounded painful, as if it were scraping her throat.

"Your keys!" the tall one shouted. "Give us your motherfucking keys!"

Dulcie threw the keys on the ground at their feet. "Please! I don't have any money!"

"I'll get it," I heard myself say, as if I were picking up the tab at a bar. I was calm. I felt like I was underwater. Everything seemed slow and all I could hear was my own breathing. I reached into my back pocket and pulled out my wallet. I took out the bills and handed them over. The tall guy grabbed the money and ran back to the van, which made me feel better until I noticed that the kid with the shaved head was still pointing the gun at me.

That's when I got scared. As though someone had thrown a switch, all the sound returned, loud and close. I heard the cars roaring past on Sunset. I heard Dulcie screaming "No! No! No!" I heard an argument erupt between two of the guys. "Get in their car! Get in their fucking car or I'll do you too!" I grabbed Dulcie's hand, and I pulled her around the front of our car, crouching low. I could feel the heat of the engine under the hood. The van revved up. I stood, bringing Dulcie up with me, and there, on the driver's side, no more than three feet away, was the kid with the shaved head. He had the gun in one hand and Dulcie's keys in the other. I could see sweat glistening over the pimples on his face.

"Hey!" he said, looking confused. "What the fuck?"

Then it was as if I skipped a few minutes of my life, because the next thing I knew, Dulcie and I were racing down a side street toward the porch lights of some bungalows. We didn't look back to see if we were being followed. Sometimes Dulcie held my hand, sometimes we were separated by the row of parked cars. We had no idea where we were going.

After the police and their questions, and their heartfelt assurance that there was nothing at all they could do for us, we took a cab back to our apartment in Silver Lake. Dulcie was worried because the crack heads — that's what the police called them — had our keys, and our address was on the car registration. But the police had told us that the carjackers wouldn't come after us — that kind of thing almost never happened.

Still, Dulcie couldn't sleep, so we sat up all night while she went over what had happened. She'd seen the van on the street earlier, but hadn't it been in front of us, not behind? Why had they chosen our car, our sorry, broken-down mutt of a car? How close had we come to being shot?

"We saw them," she said. "We know what they look like."

"They weren't killers. They were thieves. There's a difference, I guess," I said.

"No," she said, twisting her straight brown hair around her finger so tightly the tip turned white. "It doesn't make sense."

Dulcie needs things to be exact. You have to explain yourself clearly when you're around her, so she's probably a good teacher. For a minute I wondered whether she wished we had been shot, just for the sake of logic.

She'd done this after losing the baby, too, going over and over what she might have done to kill it. Had she exercised too much? Not enough? Had she eaten something bad? She wanted an answer, and she needed to blame someone; if that person turned out to be her, that would still be better than having no one to blame at all. A few days after the delivery, a hospital social worker called to check on her. She reassured Dulcie that what had happened hadn't been her fault. It was a fluke thing, the woman said. She used the word *flukish*.

"I should have noticed them tailing me," Dulcie said now. "How could I not notice a car that close?"

"Don't do that," I told her. "Don't think about what could have happened."

"I have to think about it," she said. "How can you not think about it? We were this close," she said, holding her fingers out like a gun and aiming at my chest.

I drove Dulcie's car to work the next day. When I got home that night, Dulcie had moved our mattress from our bed into the living room, where it lay in the middle of the floor, the sheets spilling over onto the carpet. She'd taken a personal day to recover from the holdup. Her eyes were red, and she looked as though she'd been crying all afternoon.

"It's the rat," she said. "He's back."

A month earlier, a rat had burrowed and nested in the wall behind our bed. Every night, it scratched a weird, personal jazz into our ears. We told the landlord and he said he would get on it right away, which meant: You'll be living with that rat forever, and if you don't like it there're ten other people in line for your apartment. I checked around the house to make sure the rat couldn't find a way inside. I patched up a hole underneath the sink with plywood and barricaded the space between the dishwasher and the wall with old towels. After Dulcie was sure that there would be no midnight visitor eating our bananas, she was okay with the rat. We even named him—Mingus.

She wasn't okay with it anymore.

"He's getting louder. Closer. Like he's going to get in this time," she said.

"He can't get in. There's no way."

"Well, I can't sleep in that room."

"It's a small apartment, Dulcie." The living room was smaller than the bedroom, and the mattress nearly filled it.

"I can't do it, Charles. I can't."

"All right. We can sleep anywhere you want," I said.

"I want to sleep in the living room. And I want you to change the message on the answering machine," she said. "It has my voice on it. It should have a man's voice."

"You're worried about the rat hearing your voice on the machine?"

"Don't make fun of me, okay? Those guys know where we live."

Later that night, I discovered that she wanted to sleep with all the lights on.

"I want people to know we're home," she said. "People don't break in if they think you're there."

We were lying on the floor on our mattress. She felt tiny, so delicate that I would crush her if I squeezed too hard or rolled the wrong way.

"You don't mind, do you?" she said. "About the light. Is it too bright?"

She'd let me throw one of my shirts, an orange one, over the fixture hanging from the ceiling. It gave the room a muffled, glowy feel.

"No," I said. I kissed her forehead. She didn't turn to me. Since the baby, we've had a hard time getting together.

Dulcie sat up again. "Maybe it's a bad idea," she said. "Maybe a thief will see the light on at four a.m. and think that we're actually out of town. I mean, who leaves their light on all night when they're home?"

"No one."

"You know," she said, "I saw in a catalogue once that you could buy an inflatable man to put in a chair by your window. Or in your car. You could put him in the passenger seat if you were driving alone."

She looked at me, but I didn't know what to say. To me, driving with a plastic blow-up doll in the seat next to you seemed very peculiar.

"Lie down," I said, stroking her back beneath her T-shirt. Her skin was smooth and warm.

She lay down next to me. I turned over on my stomach and laid my hand across her chest. I liked the feel of the small rises of her breasts, the give of them.

Dulcie's milk had come in two days after the delivery. The doctor had warned her that this would happen and had prescribed Valium in advance. I came home from work and found Dulcie, stoned, staring at her engorged breasts in the bathroom mirror. I'd never seen anything like it. Her breasts were like boulders, and her veins spread out across them like waterways on a map. Dulcie squeezed one nipple, and a little pearl of yellowish milk appeared. She tasted it.

"It's sweet," she said. "What a waste."

For the next two days, she lay on the couch holding packs of frozen vegetables against each breast. Sometimes we laughed about it, and she posed for a few sexpot pictures, with the packs of peas pressed against her chest like pasties. Other times, she just stared at the living room wall, adjusting a pack when it slipped. I asked her if her breasts hurt, and she said yes, but not in the way you'd think.

I slid my hand off Dulcie's chest, turned back over, and stared at the T-shirt on the light fixture.

"Did you know," she said, "that when you're at a red light the person next to you probably has a gun in his glove compartment?"

"Defensive driving," I said, trying for a joke.

"Statistically speaking, it's true. Until yesterday, I never thought about how many people have guns," Dulcie said. "Guns in their cars, guns in their pocketbooks when they're going to the market, guns . . ."

A fly was caught between the light and my T-shirt. I could see its shadow darting frantically back and forth until, suddenly, it was gone.

The next evening as I was driving home from work, someone threw an egg at my car. I thought it was another holdup. I sucked in so much air that I started to choke and almost lost control. Two kids then ran by my window. One was wearing a Dracula mask and a cape. The other one had on a rubber monster head and green tights. I'd forgotten it was Halloween.

Dulcie takes holidays pretty seriously, and when I got home I expected to see a cardboard skeleton on the door, and maybe a carved pumpkin or two. Usually she greets the trick-or-treaters wearing a tall black witch hat that she keeps stashed in a closet the rest of the year. When she opens the door, she makes this funny cackling laugh, which is kind of embarrassing but also sweet. She's so waifish, there's not much about her that could scare anybody. But when I got home and climbed the outside stairs to our second-floor apartment, there was nothing on our door and the apartment was dark.

"What are you doing with all the lights off?" I asked when I got inside. She was sitting at the kitchen table, her hands folded in front of her as if she were praying.

"Shut the door," she said. "A whole pack of them just came. They must have rung the bell five times."

"They want their candy."

"We don't have any."

"Really? You didn't buy any?"

"Charles, we don't know who any of these people are," she said slowly, as if I were six years old. "I'm not going to open my door to perfect strangers."

"They're kids."

"What about the ones who come really late?" she asked. "All those teenagers. They're looking for trouble."

I sat down and reached across the table for her hands. "It's Halloween, Dulcie. It's just kids having fun."

"Plenty of people aren't home on Halloween. This is just going to be one of those places where nobody's home."

The doorbell rang.

"Dulcie—"

"Sh-h-h!" She hissed at me like a cat.

"This is ridiculous." I got up.

"Please, Charles!"

The bell rang again. I grabbed a box of cookies from the shelf and went to the door. A little kid was walking away, but he turned back when he heard the door open. He was six, eight years old. An old man I recognized from the neighborhood, maybe his grandfather, stood a few steps behind him.

The boy wore a cowboy outfit—a fringed orange vest over a T-shirt with a picture of Darth Vader on it, jeans mashed down into plastic cowboy boots, and a holster sliding down over his narrow hips. He took a gun out of the holster and waved it around in the air.

"Bang," he said, without enthusiasm.

"You got me," I answered, putting my hands to my chest and pretending to die.

"It's a fake gun," the boy said. "No real bullets."

"You mean I'm not dead?" I tried to sound amazed, and I got a smile out of the kid.

The grandfather said something impatiently in another language, Russian or maybe Armenian.

"Trick or treat," the boy said quietly. He held out a plastic grocery sack with his free hand.

I looked into the bag. There were only a few pieces of candy inside. Suddenly the whole thing made me sad. I offered my box of mint cookies.

The boy looked back at his grandfather, who shook his head. "I'm only allowed to have it if it's wrapped," the boy said to me.

I felt like a criminal. "We didn't have a chance to get to the store," I said, as the boy holstered his gun and moved off with his grandfather.

When I went back inside, Dulcie was standing in the middle of the dark living room, staring at me. Three months after the baby died, I came home from work and found her standing in that same place. Her belly underneath her T-shirt was huge, much bigger than when she'd actually been pregnant. For one crazy second, I thought that the whole thing had been a mistake, and that she was still pregnant. I felt a kind of relief I had never felt before. Then she lifted her shirt and took out a watermelon from underneath it.

A group of kids yelled "Trick or treat!" below us. They giggled. Someone said "Boo!" then there was a chorus of dutiful thank-you's. I heard small feet pound up the rickety wooden stairway to the second floor apartments. I walked over to Dulcie and put my arms around her.

"We can't live like this," I said.

"I can," she said.

Dulcie went back to work three days after the carjacking. I dropped her off at school in my car, and she arranged for one of her teacher friends to give her a lift home. I took it as a good sign, her returning to work. She complains about the public school system, all the idiotic bureaucracy she has to deal with, but she loves the kids. She's always coming home with stories about cute things they did, or about how quickly they picked up something she didn't think they'd understand the first time. She was named Teacher of the Year last spring, and a couple of parents got together and gave her this little gold necklace. Her school's in a rough part of Glendale. The necklace was a big deal.

She was home when I got off work, sitting on the couch. She waved a piece of pink paper in the air.

"What's that?" I said.

"We're not allowed to touch the children anymore," she said.

"What are you talking about?"

She told me that a parent had accused a teacher of touching his daughter in the wrong way. Social Services came in, the works. When they finally got around to questioning the girl, she told them the teacher had just patted her on the back because she answered a question right.

"Now the district's in a panic—they don't want a lawsuit every time some kid exaggerates. So, no touching the students."

"That's nuts," I said. "Those kids need to be hugged every once in a while. They probably don't get enough affection at home."

"That's a racist generalization, Charles," she said. "Most of the parents try hard. They love their kids just as much as you and I would."

Neither of us said anything. Dulcie hadn't brought up the idea of our having kids since we'd lost the baby. She had just stepped on a grenade, and I was waiting through those awful seconds before it explodes.

"This is a fucked-up town," she said finally.

I wasn't sure what had made her say this. The school thing? The carjacking?

"Maybe if we turn on the TV we'll catch a freeway chase," I said.

"Or a riot."

"Or a celebrity bio."

She started laughing. "That's the real tragedy," she said. "The celebrity bio."

We laughed some more. When we stopped, neither of us knew what to say.

"I'm not racist," I said at last.

"I know. I didn't mean that."

"I may be prejudiced against celebrities, though."

She squeezed out a smile. It was worth the stupid joke.

The next Saturday, Dulcie called an exterminator. She'd decided that we should pay for one out of our own pocket, because she'd read that some rats carry airborne viruses.

"People died in New Mexico," she said. "Children too."

It turns out that the exterminator you call to get rid of bugs is not the kind you call to get rid of a rat. There's a subspecialty—Rodent Removal. Our rodent remover was named Rod. Rod the Rodent Remover. I was scared of him already.

When he came to the door, he was wearing a clean, pressed uniform with his name on it. "Rod," I said, "thanks for coming."

"It's really Ricardo, but I get more jobs as Rod. Ricardo is too hard for most people to remember. You have a problem with rats?" he said helpfully.

"Yeah. In here." I opened the door wider and led him into the apartment. "It's not really *in* the apartment, but we hear it from in here."

If Ricardo thought it was strange that the mattress was on the living room floor, he didn't say anything. Dulcie was waiting for us in the bedroom.

"It's there," Dulcie said, pointing to a gray smudge where the head of our bed frame met the wall. "He's in there."

Ricardo went over and tapped the wall with his knuckle. Dulcie held her breath. There was no sound from the rat.

"They usually leave the house during the day," Ricardo said.

"How does he get in?" Dulcie said.

Ricardo raised his finger toward the ceiling. "Spanish tile roof. Very pretty, but bad for the rat problem," he said. "They come in through the holes between the tiles."

"So there's nothing we can do?" Dulcie asked, alarmed.

"We can set a trap in the wall through the heating vent there," Ricardo said, pointing to the one vent in our entire apartment, which was, unhelpfully, in the hallway outside our bedroom.

"Then he'll die in the wall?"

"It's a bad smell for a few days, but then it goes away," Ricardo said.

I could see that none of this was making Dulcie feel any better.

"Or I can put a trap on the roof," Ricardo said.

"Do that," Dulcie said quickly.

"Okay," he said. "Now we have a plan."

He reached into his pockets and took out two yellow surgical gloves. Dulcie was horrified, the gloves confirming her suspicions about disease. But Ricardo smiled pleasantly. This was a guy who dealt with rats every day of his life, and it didn't seem to faze him.

"Why do they come inside?" Dulcie said, as we followed Ricardo towards the door. "The rats. Why do they live in the walls? There's no food there."

"To keep warm," Ricardo said. "Sometimes to have their babies."

He smiled and gave us a courtly nod as I let him out. When I turned back, Dulcie was still staring at the closed door, her hand over her mouth.

"It's just a rat," I said. I touched her shoulder. She was shaking.

A month after the baby died, the mailman delivered a package that I had to sign for. We don't get a lot of packages, so it was an event. The box was from a company called La Tierra. The name sounded familiar, but I couldn't place it; I was about to call back into the apartment for Dulcie when I remembered. La Tierra was the name of the company that cremated the baby.

"What is it?" Dulcie said from behind me. "Who was at the door?"

I turned around. This will kill her, I thought.

"What is it?" she said again, holding out her hand.

I had no choice but to hand it to her. She looked at it. Her face crumpled. "It's so light," she said finally.

I went to put my arms around her, but she stepped back. Then she started laughing. Her laughter became the kind of giggling you can't turn off. She bit her lips and clenched her teeth, but the giggles kept coming, as if they were tickling her insides in order to get out.

"You probably thought it was something from your mom," she said through her laughter. "Or some freebie from a computer company. Oh, my God," she said. "Can you believe this is our life?" I smiled, but it was that weird, embarrassed smile you offer when you feel left out of a joke.

We decided to take the ashes to the beach and scatter them on the water. We drove out to the Ventura County line, to a beach called El Pescador. You have to climb down a steep hillside to get to it, and there's usually no one there, especially in the off season. We parked and scrambled unsteadily down the trail. We were so busy concentrating on not falling that we didn't see the ocean until we were at its level. We both got quiet for a moment. The water was slate gray, pocked by the few white gulls that every so often swooped down to the surface and then rose up again. There were no boats in the ocean, only a couple of prehistoric oil derricks in the distance. "I think we should do it now," Dulcie said.

We opened the box. Inside was some Styrofoam with a hole gouged out. Nestled inside that hole, like a tiny bird, was a plastic bag filled with brown dust. There could not have been more than a tablespoonful. I took the bag and handed the box to Dulcie. Then I kicked off my shoes, rolled up my jeans, and walked out into the water. When I was calf deep, I opened up the bag. I waited for something to happen, for some gust of wind to kick up and take the ashes out to sea. But the day was calm, so I finally dumped the ashes into the water at my feet. A tiny wave moved them towards the shore. I worried that the ashes would end up in the sand, where somebody could step all over them, but then I felt the undertow dragging the water back towards the sea.

"I think that's the bravest thing I've ever seen a person do," Dulcie said as I came out of the water.

As we headed back to the trail, she picked up a smooth stone and slipped it into her pocket. Halfway up the path, she took the stone out and let it drop to the ground.

A week after the holdup, the police called. They had found our stolen car. Once the kids run out of gas, the officer explained, they usually abandon the car rather than pay for more. He gave us the address of the car lot, somewhere in South Central.

"Go early in the morning," the officer warned. "Before they get up."

"'They'?" I asked.

"You a white guy?" the policeman asked.

"Yeah."

"You want to be down there before wake-up time. Trust me."

Dulcie said it was a self-fulfilling prophecy. Everybody expected things to be bad, so people made them bad. She saw it at her school. The kids who were expected to fail, well, they blew it every time out, even if they knew the work cold.

Still, we took the officer's advice and went down to the lot at seven in the morning. I admit I was nervous, driving through those streets. You like to think you're more open-minded than that, but I guess I'm not. I kept thinking about drive-by shootings and gangs and riots and all the things you read about, thinking, Those things don't happen near where I live, so I'm okay.

We found our car. It was a mess. It had been stripped; even the steering wheel was gone. There was every kind of fast-food wrapper scattered on the back seat, and French fries and old hamburger buns on the floor. You get hungry when you're high. It wasn't worth the price of towing, so we signed it over to the pound and left it there.

As I drove Dulcie to work, I told her the police had asked us to come identify the suspects in a lineup.

"But they'll know it was us who identified them," she said. "They know where we live."

"They were busy getting high. I don't think they were memorizing our address."

"I don't even remember what they looked like. It was dark."

"Once you see some faces, it might come back."

"Charles, don't make me do this. Don't make me!" she cried.

"I'm not going to make you do anything. Jesus. What do you think I am?"

She didn't answer me. I dropped her off at the school. She got out and walked towards the front door, then turned to wave at me, as if it were any regular day, as if we weren't living like some rat trapped in our own wall.

I took the day off. I'd already used up my sick days, and I knew we couldn't throw away the money, but I thought I'd go crazy if I had to be nice to a customer or listen to some technician talk about his bodacious girlfriend or his kid's troubles in school.

I didn't have a plan. I picked up a paper and got breakfast at a hipster coffee shop on Silver Lake Boulevard. There were a lot of tattooed and pierced people eating eggs and bacon; they looked as though they were ending a night, not beginning a day. I tried to concentrate on my paper, but nothing sank in. Then I got back into my car. I ended up driving along Vermont into Griffith Park, past the roads where guys stop to cruise, all the way up to the Observatory. I parked in the empty lot and got out.

The Observatory was closed; it was still early. I was trying to think of something to do with myself when I saw a trail heading up into the hills. The path was well worn; on the weekends, it was usually packed with tourists and families making a cheap day of it. But that morning I had it to myself. I wanted to walk. I walked for hours. I felt the sun rise up, and I saw the darkness that covered the canyons lift, as if someone were sliding a blanket off the ground.

By the time I stopped, others were on the trail — runners, or people walking their dogs, some kids who were probably playing hooky. I looked out over the canyon and thought about how I could go either way: I could stay with Dulcie and be as far away from life as a person could be, or I could leave.

I had been looking forward to the baby. I didn't mind talking to Dulcie about whether or not the kid should sleep in bed with us, or use a pacifier, or how long she would nurse him, or any of the things she could think about happily for days. I got excited about it, too. But I had no idea what it meant. What was real to me was watching Dulcie's body grow bigger and bigger, watching that stripe appear on her belly, watching as her breasts got fuller and that part around her nipples got as wide and dark as pancakes. When the doctors took the baby out of her, they handed him to me without bothering to clean him up; I guess there was no point to it. Every inch of him was perfectly formed. For a second, I thought he would open his eyes and be a baby. It didn't look like anything was wrong with him, like there was any reason for him not to be breathing and crying and getting on with the business of being in the world. I kept saying to myself, This is my baby, this is my baby. But I had no idea what I was saying. The only thing I truly felt was that I would die if something happened to Dulcie.

A runner came towards me on the trail. His face was red, and sweat had made his T-shirt transparent. He gave me a pained smile as he ran past. He kicked a small rock with his shoe, and it flew over the side of the canyon. For some reason, I looked over the edge for the rock. What I saw from where I stood was amazing to me. I saw all kinds of strange cactus plants — tall ones like baseball bats, others like spiky fans. There were dry green eucalyptus trees and a hundred different kinds of bushes I couldn't name. I heard the rustle of animals, skunks or coyotes, maybe even deer. There was garbage on the ground and in the bushes—soda cans, fast-food drink cups, napkins with restaurant logos on them. I saw a condom hanging off a branch, like a burst balloon. For some reason, the garbage didn't bother me. For all I knew, this was one of those mountains that was made of trash, and it was nature that didn't belong. Maybe the trash, the dirt, the plants, bugs, condoms—maybe they were all just fighting for a little space.

I got home before Dulcie. I dragged the mattress back into the bedroom. I took my shirt off the light fixture in the living room and put it in the dresser. When Dulcie came back, she saw what I had done, but she didn't say anything. We ate dinner early. I watched a soccer game while she corrected papers. Then I turned off the lights in the living room, and we went into the bedroom. She knew my mind was made up, and she climbed into bed like a soldier following orders. When I snapped off the bedside lamp, she gave a little gasp.

We lay quietly for a while, getting used to the dark. We listened for the rat, but he wasn't there.

"You think the traps worked?" she said.

"Maybe."

I reached for her. At first it was awkward, as though we were two people who had never had sex with each other. Truthfully, I was half ready for her to push me away. But she didn't, and, after a while, things became familiar again. When I rolled on top of her, though, I felt her tense up underneath me. She started to speak. "I should go and get—"

I put my fingers on her mouth to stop her. "It's okay," I said.

She looked up at me with her big watery eyes. She was terrified. She started again to say something about her diaphragm. I stopped her once more.

"It's okay," I repeated.

I could feel her heart beating on my skin. I could feel my own heart beating even harder. We were scared, but we kept going.

Jessica Shattuck
Bodies

In the fluorescent light of the refrigerator, the halved parsnips look naked—pale and fleshy as limbs. Annie pauses before pulling them out. A refrigerator is like a hospital, a bright place that is not cheerful. A protective but uncertain place to wait.

"What are you doing?" Anthony says. He's standing in the doorway.

"Starting dinner," Annie says, flicking on the lights. They both blink in the sudden brilliance.

Anthony climbs up onto one of the tall stools on the other side of the kitchen island. He is five years old, blond, and freckled, with close-set blue eyes. Something about his mouth and his stubby but prominent little nose hints already at the old man he will be — stubborn, soft-spoken, a little unforgiving.

The music of *The Lion King* drifts toward them from the playroom.

"Not in the mood for the movie?" Annie asks.

Anthony shrugs and lays his head down on his outstretched arm.

Annie dabs small pieces of butter on the parsnips, draining water from the dish. Outside the window, twenty stories below, there is a bright stream of traffic on Fifth Avenue. Beyond that, Central Park is black — lit paths twist through it like constellations. She rinses beans, wraps bread in aluminum foil, rubs garlic and pepper on steaks, washes the pretty purple-and-white salad leaves whose name she can never remember. She and Anthony are comfortable with silence. When she first moved in with his family, he made her nervous. He is an intense child, with a sharp, scrutinizing gaze, and his frankness can be almost cruel. Annie tried to protect herself with chatter, elaborately inventive games, even bribes. But they are friends now. She feels more at home around Anthony than around anyone else she knows.

"Will you read to me?" Anthony asks after the steaks are in the broiler and the beans are steaming on the stove.

Annie looks at the clock. "For five minutes," she says.

"Yes, yes, yes," he chants, sitting up straight now.

Annie is in what her doctor refers to as the "hunker down and wait" period of treatment for Stage III Hodgkin's lymphoma. For the most part, she has been lucky. She has gone through ten remarkably smooth cycles of chemotherapy; the success has yet to be determined, but the side effects have been mild. Her straight, pale-brown hair is thinner, but she still has it. Though she needs at least twelve hours of sleep a day, she is not constantly exhausted. She takes her pills every morning — vitamins, herbs a Chinese doctor prescribed, green algae. She eats kale and radishes and drinks a full gallon and a half of water a day. She lives like someone who has built a home on the San Andreas Fault: She takes what small, possibly ridiculous precautions she can, and then chooses not to think about it.

Until November, Annie worked as a secretary for Anthony's mother, Cleo. Cleo is the creative director of a large international advertising agency — the first woman in the company's history to have this role. She is tall and levelheaded and big-boned, but glamorous. She works fifteen hours a day, and most weekends as well. She is an adept psychoanalyst of the public mind. "That'll make people think of getting old. People don't want to think of getting old," she'll say about a mockup of an ad for a real-estate Web site. Suddenly everyone will realize that the little boy bouncing his ball down the walk into his grandmother's garden reminds them of their lost childhoods—of time passing, of old dreams, and of dying. Cleo will substitute a girl for the boy, an older brother for the grandmother, and it will become an entirely different story. Annie would like to crawl into Cleo's confidence and curl up in her powerful vision of the world as an infinitely malleable, manageable place.

Annie's own days at the agency have been put on indefinite hold, and she misses them—the feeling of purpose and efficiency. Now she lives with Cleo and her family in their penthouse on Fifth Avenue, which has lots of extra room. It is a perfect arrangement, really; Annie did not have many people she could move in with when she got sick. There was her high-school sweetheart, who is now her ex-husband, in San Diego, and her brother, Todd, in Long Beach. But the last time she saw Todd he locked her in the closet and broke a bottle against the door. And her ex-husband has found God.

Besides, Cleo and her husband, Jay, need someone in addition to their baby-sitter to look after their two children. Mrs. Tibbs, they worry, will teach the children bad grammar and imperfect diction. Now Annie reads them stories and plays interesting, educational games, and is careful to choose her words exactly, hold on to silent "g"'s, never say "gonna" or use "real" as an adjective. She is used to this from the office—the only difference is that it is no longer a work-related necessity but something she has to do at home, because that is what Cleo and Jay's apartment has become.

Annie has made it to page 5 of *Goodnight Moon*, Anthony's favorite book, when the doorbell rings. "No," Anthony says, putting his hand on her hip as she starts to get up. "No." He is clingy and uncertain in the evenings.

"I have to get the door," Annie says gently. "It might be important."

But it is Cleo's niece Michele, who lives with her mother, Cleo's sister, two buildings down.

"Hi," Michele says with a bright, insincere smile. "Is Cleo home yet?" She peers over Annie's shoulder into the apartment as if Annie might not be trusted to tell the truth. Michele's mother drifts in and out of rehab programs, and Cleo worries about her niece. She is a beautiful girl: blond, long-legged, with perfectly straight, well-proportioned features. Tonight she is wearing a short, hot-pink skirt and impossibly high platform heels. Around Michele, Annie feels dumpy, prudish, and overwhelmingly average—average height (five feet five), average prettiness (small nose, brown eyes, and pale skin), average age (thirty-two), and average-sized breasts (34B). She remembers that she has not showered in two days, that her sweater is pilly, that her jeans are baggy at the knees.

"Not yet," she says. "Would you like to come in and wait for her?"

"Story!" Anthony demands from the couch.

Annie hopes Michele will say no.

"I can't," Michele says. "I'm on my way downtown, but I wanted to give her this." She holds out a thick silver-paper envelope with writing in metallic gold. "My sweet-sixteen party. At Au Bar," she adds, unable to restrain herself.

"Ooh," Annie says, "that'll be nice," hoping this is an appropriate response. But it sounds fraudulent, schoolteacherish. "I'll give it to her."

"Thanks," Michele breathes, and flashes another studied smile. "Say hi to Jay."

Annie closes the door behind her and walks back over to Anthony.

"O.K.," she says, settling onto the sofa. "Where were we?"

"Here," Anthony says, squirming closer, collapsing against her as soon as she leans back. She is thankful for his helplessness.

Since it is Thursday night, they are all eating together. This is Cleo's rule. Sundays and Thursdays, they dine at seven so that Anthony and his baby sister, Eden, can join them and afterward Cleo can put them to bed. On other nights, Cleo and Jay eat late, or have dinner engagements, or, often, Cleo is out of town. Tonight, Cleo has brought pink and orange dahlias home from the florist on Madison, which Annie has arranged in the center of the table. In the candlelight, they project pointed orange shadows onto the walls.

"What did you do, invite Alain Ducasse over to cook?" Jay says, surveying the food. "This looks fantastic." Jay is tall and in his early forties. He is technically good-looking, but there is something about him that seems still unformed, as if he had never, for even a moment, experienced pain.

"Abble, abble, abble, abble," Eden chants from her high chair. Saliva runs down her lower lip.

"Did you work out with Mel today?" Cleo asks Jay, wiping Eden's chin with her napkin. Mel is Jay's trainer. "I thought that was Monday, Wednesday, Friday."

"Bumped it up — Thursdays, too," Jay says, helping himself to a steak. Jay sold his Internet company for "a bundle," as he likes to say, before the market went bust, and since then he has devoted himself to "independent projects," which originally consisted of learning to play the guitar, writing a how-to (in his case, how to sell your startup company for millions) book, and getting in shape. Now his projects consist entirely of getting in shape — kick-boxing class, weight lifting, training for the New York marathon. In the four months since Annie moved in with them, he has gone way past "in shape." His muscles, which are by nature invisible, have become hard and round and move like an animal's beneath his skin. He can bench-press two hundred and thirty pounds and run to the tip of Manhattan and back in an hour and twenty minutes.

"Four times a week?" Cleo asks, her eyebrows raised.

"What's that supposed to mean?" Jay demands.

"Nothing," Cleo says. "Did you have a chance to call the Hornbys?"

Cleo is so smooth. Jay will have to run after this question now. He is volatile, but easily distracted. Annie has seen him agitated, cranky, even nasty a few times, but she has never seen Cleo so much as ruffled.

"They're coming on Saturday." Jay turns to Anthony and tousles his hair. "With Davey-boy, so you'll have a friend, too."

"I don't like him," Anthony says, slumping back in his chair.

"But he's your buddy," Jay says with a mixture of surprise and disappointment. "He's a good guy."

"Why not?" Cleo asks at the same time.

Anthony grunts and kicks the table leg. Annie has begun to notice that he is different with Cleo. Less communicative. More petulant. Gently, Annie stills his leg under the table.

"Na, na, na, na," Eden begins chanting. She has been released from her high chair and is crawling around under the table. Then she sits down and begins sucking on the remote control of Jay's new stereo.

"She loves to put things in her mouth," Annie says, removing the remote control gently from Eden's grasp.

"Well!" Jay says, standing up. "Just like your mother, aren't you?" He laughs and wiggles one of Eden's fat toes.

"Could you get the salt while you're up?" Cleo asks, with no hint that she has heard.

Annie suspects that Cleo and Jay have a wild and theatrical sex life. There is all of Jay's working out. There are his crass jokes. There is the way he smells when he comes into the kitchen for breakfast before showering. But these are merely complements of something Annie sees in Cleo. She is too confident, too invulnerable to be seductive. But when she is relaxed, when she and Jay come in from an evening out at a benefit, or a day of sailing on the Sound, there is something raw about her—a loose, substantial physicality that reminds Annie of a high-school athlete. It is slightly masculine. Unabashedly sexual.

The first time Annie thought about this, an image of Cleo, bent over, her brown hair trailing on the floor, popped into her mind. She was being fucked from behind. She was wearing a bustier and garters, and her wide pale feet with their unpainted toenails looked inanimate. The image was so vivid that Annie almost can't remember whether she has actually seen it. She imagines that Cleo likes frilly nighties in little-girl colors. That Jay, with his newly built body, comes out of the bathroom shirtless, in black briefs. That Cleo is coy, that Jay will do anything to get a blow job—David Hasselhoff impersonations, handsprings, a wrestling move in which he pins Cleo roughly against the headboard. It is both comical and dangerous. And Annie is shocked at how readily it springs into her imagination.

"Stop doing dishes," Cleo says, coming into the kitchen from the children's room. "Mrs. Tibbs will do those in the morning. You have better things to do."

"I like doing dishes," Annie says.

"Anthony would like you to go in and give him a kiss goodnight."

Annie tries to interpret Cleo's voice. Lately, when Cleo wants to read Anthony a story, he says no, he'd rather have Annie. Cleo turns it into a joke—you're a more fun mommy than I am, she says. But here, alone in the kitchen, Annie feels tension spring up between them like a wire. It makes Annie nervous; beneath Cleo's unflappable exterior, Annie has noticed lately, she has a capacity for cruelty.

"O.K." Annie wipes her hand on the dish towel and adds, "I feel a little woozy," which she does not, as if somehow this could make things equal.

Anthony's bedroom is at the far end of the apartment, across the darkened living room with its glass doors that lead out to a roof garden and the hollow rush of the city. Anthony is lying on his back, staring at the glow-in-the-dark stars Jay arranged on the ceiling in the shape of a baseball. "I knew you'd come," he says, turning onto his side as soon as she opens the door.

"Well, you asked for me, right?" Annie says gently. She sits down on the edge of his bed and can feel his legs, warm under the covers, pushing against her back.

"It's too dark," he says. "I want to sleep with the light on."

"Why?" Annie says. "Darkness is good. It's nothing to be afraid of."

"I'm not afraid," he says rolling onto his back. His voice has an anxious hitch to it, though.

"That's good."

"What is 'afraid'?" Anthony asks.

All around her the room is full of indistinguishable objects and flickering shadows from the roof garden—living things blowing, husk-like, in the March wind. A siren howls from below, muffled by the distance it has to travel.

"Annie?" Anthony is looking at her, his eyes demanding.

"It's a feeling," she says. "It's a way you feel." The words come out sounding thick and automatic. She concentrates on the pressure of his knee, bony and hard against the small of her back. "I think you know," she adds softly, when her voice seems more like her own again.

When she leans over to kiss him, he clasps her cheeks in his small damp hands. "Sleep tight," she whispers. Anthony doesn't let go. "Sleep tight," she repeats, gently peeling off his fingers.

In the front hall, Cleo has on the long tailored coat, gray slacks, and platform sneakers she refers to as her plane PJs. "Asleep?" she asks cheerfully. She already has more important things to think about.

"Almost," Annie says.

"I'm catching the red-eye. Be back Saturday at noon." She puts on a gray felt hat.

"You leaving, babe?" Jay comes in from the living room holding the *Wall Street Journal* in one hand.

"Mm-hmm," Cleo smiles, adjusting the hat just in time for Jay to knock it askew by enveloping her in his arms for a newspaper-crumpling bear hug and a kiss.

Cleo laughs and kisses him back. A firm but restrictive press of the lips.

"Call when you get there?" Jay says over his shoulder, already walking away across the hall.

"I will." Cleo makes a what-can-you-do face at Annie as she tucks her hair behind her ears and pulls the hat back into place. "Oh, will you make sure Mrs. Tibbs gets the envelope I put on the counter?"

Annie nods.

"You O.K.?" Cleo fixes Annie with her gaze, but there is something prohibitive about it, just as there was in her kiss.

"Yes," Annie says. "Have a safe trip."

"Be strong, kiddo." Cleo gives Annie a cool, dry kiss on the cheek.

Annie forces a smile and then closes the door after her.

In the kitchen she has the desire—the first in a long time—for a drink. She has not touched alcohol since she was diagnosed. In high school, there were two or three times she got really drunk—an exhilarating, freeing drunk where she became loud, sexy, and silly, the kind of girl who took drama instead of typing. This was a long time ago, when she was a Californian. When she was still living in Long Beach, answering phones at the tattoo parlor her brother worked at, and imagining she would go to design school, marry someone famous, live in a mansion. It was before junior college, before Todd really lost it, certainly before New York.

Annie opens Cleo and Jay's liquor cabinet, pulls out the Johnnie Walker, pours herself a glass. It tastes sharp and pure as medicine. Then she turns on the tap to finish the dishes. With her hands immersed in the warm water, the whiskey hot inside her, she tries to listen to her body—tries to feel the movement of her blood, the labored breathing of her cells. But she feels nothing—not even the beating of her heart.

"Hey, why don't you turn a light on?" Jay is standing in the doorway, where Anthony stood before.

"Oh," Annie says. "I forgot." But this isn't true. She has chosen the darkness. Seeing clearly seems like a distraction; she is surrounded by other people's clutter.

Jay flips the switch from the doorway but he hesitates before entering. Annie has the feeling he is afraid she is crying.

"Vitamins," he says. "Forgot my vitamins."

Annie wipes her face with her sleeve. She takes another sip of whiskey.

"Should you be drinking that—with—you know, your treatment and all?" Jays says the word "treatment" as if it were a euphemism for something sordid.

He pours four pills as fat as roaches into his palm. In the refrigerator, bottles of zinc, vitamins C, A, and B, iron, protein powder, and Strong Body Multitabs occupy an entire shelf of the door.

She and Jay have never addressed her illness, a reticence that is not exactly strange but tiring. Cleo, with her strong sense of calm, her reliance on order and the ability to manipulate, has always been the arbiter of conversations about Annie's health. Jay usually pretends not to be listening, as if it were some other intimate, distinctly feminine problem they were discussing. "He doesn't get it," Cleo told Annie once. The comment was slightly unnerving—what was it, exactly, according to Cleo, that Jay didn't get?

Now, instead of looking at her, he occupies himself with a carton of skim milk.

"Here," Annie says, handing him a glass. When he pours the milk, the muscles under his taut, sallow skin rise and subside. Annie feels a corresponding rise of something unidentifiable in her gut.

"Your heart rate must be low," she says unsteadily.

"Forty-nine at rest." Jay brightens. "Last year it was seventy-two. Count it," he says, extending his arm.

Annie wraps her fingers around his warm wrist. His pulse crawls as sluggishly as ink through water. Annie counts forty-nine but doesn't let go. "Fifty, fifty-one, fifty-two, fifty-three," she recites out loud and tightens her grip. She concentrates on the flawless rhythm of his blood working its way through his body, nourishing his bones and muscles—she would like to absorb it, gobble it up, make it her own. Jay looks at her quizzically but doesn't pull away. She raises his wrist to his chest, bending his arm at the elbow, and watches his biceps swell. Suddenly, she can imagine it, pressed against her collarbone—his arm wrapped heavily around her neck and her teeth grazing the pale, damp, almost womanly skin at the crook of his elbow. Her own low breathing, she realizes when the hum of the refrigerator switches off, is the loudest sound in the room.

"Annie," Jay says, peeling her fingers from his wrist. "I think you need to get some sleep."

Annie removes her hand. "Maybe." She is surprisingly unembarrassed, even when she sways slightly against the door frame. She can feel Jay's eyes following her across the floor.

In the morning, Annie fixes herself breakfast. Early buds have appeared overnight on the trees in the Park, and the ground looks black and wet with spring. Friday mornings are when she usually goes in to see Dr. Tatel, but this week she is going in on Monday because Dr. Tatel is going out of town. This small irregularity feels exciting—evidence that she is well enough to be rescheduled.

In the last few months, she has learned how to turn her body over to medical science as if it were a sick pet. She can be poked and prodded now without feeling judged by the hands examining for error, can watch her blood coil up out of her arm without getting nauseated, can take the cold metallic sting of the stethoscope without feeling light-headed at the idea of her own beating heart. She has had practice, after all. She went to the emergency room at least four times with her brother before he took off. "Annie," he would joke afterward, "you watch those doctors like you're in training."

From the kitchen, Annie can hear Jay grunting on his chin-up bar. In about an hour, he will come out of the study and walk around the apartment, stretching his elbows behind his head, picking up newspapers and magazines, tossing them back down. At about eleven, he will try to sit at the computer and "organize his notes" before he goes to the gym at two o'clock, but will end up online playing a pro-sports betting game based on the stock market instead.

Annie puts on her sneakers and jacket to go for a walk. She has not left the apartment for four days. On Fifth Avenue, she is quickly swept up in the rush of taxis, buses, tourists, shoppers, and can collectors rattling their metal carts over the uneven sidewalk. At the corner of Park and Sixty-fifth Street, there is a Japanese man with thick glasses trying to feed a chocolate popsicle to a pigeon with a stump instead of a foot. Almost half the pigeons collecting tentatively around him have mutant feet—grotesque, fleshy bulbs or string-tangled toes. Annie can barely look at them, but at the same time cannot look away. She watches them hop around the cracked concrete eating invisible morsels, pecking at each other, and clumsily, violently, trying to mate. Why have they chosen this meagre, earthbound existence when they could be airborne, soaring up above the garbage and pollution—beyond the need to fight over an old man's crumbs?

It is almost noon by the time Annie realizes she is too cold to stay out any longer. The sun is flat and white and the budding trees cast a blurry shade on the path. Annie heads uptown, suddenly worried that she has exhausted herself, although she feels quite all right. Nannies and baby carriages and strollers have taken over the sidewalk. Nursery schools and half-day programs are getting out—it is the hour of the under-five-year-old. In the apartment, Jay will be fixing lunch—a protein shake, a bowl of cottage cheese, a chicken breast, and iceberg lettuce. The image of his biceps gathering into a round knot and then releasing under her hand appears in her mind. The thick skin, the light hairs, the full, invincible blue-green veins. Mrs. Tibbs will not bring Anthony home for another half hour.

Annie greets Philipe, the doorman. She suspects he sees her as some sort of charity case of Jay and Cleo's, or, worse yet, as a freeloader. But today her self-consciousness has vanished. Crossing the black and white marble tiles she feels transparent, like one of those tiny clear fish whose slippery bodies filter and refract light, break it into dancing pieces. A clammy layer of perspiration has built up on her lower lip and under her shirt, where the raggedy, nylon-covered underwire of her bra sits against her rib cage. Anticipation—Annie recognizes the same fluttering feeling that rose in her last night.

The elevator opens directly into the apartment, which takes up half the building's twentieth floor. It is bright inside, full of sunlight, dust particles hovering, visible in the air. She has started to shrug her coat off before she realizes there is a hysterical voice coming from the living room. Annie freezes with the coat around her elbows.

"Michele, you can't—" Jay's voice interrupts the higher sound of the girl's voice.

"I can't? Oh, really, I can't? You don't know anything about what I can do, Jay. You don't know shit about me." There is the sucking sound of the sliding door to the roof deck being opened.

The hazy bubble of expectation that has carried Annie upstairs bursts in an instant. Of course Jay has been sleeping with Michele. Hasn't she known this all along? It is her first thought, followed immediately by the urge to back up and away—to get into the elevator, go down to the lobby, out onto the cold street.

"Jesus Christ," Jay says. "What are you? Don't—"

But Annie is no longer listening to the words, just to the tense, terrified sound of his voice, which propels her forward, silently, across the sun-bright floorboards. When she gets to the entrance of the living room, she can see Jay standing in the open expanse of the sliding door and beyond him Michele, looking as though she's about to climb up onto the chest-high brick wall that marks the edge of the terrace. Her hair is pulled back in a severe ponytail that the wind is blowing up in all directions. She looks frightened, a little haggard. And she is high. Annie recognizes the signs from when she lived with Todd.

Both Jay and Michele turn at the same time to look at Annie, although she is not aware of having said anything. "Annie—" Jay says. It is possible that he is crying; his face has an ashen, uncomposed look to it. Annie averts her eyes. He is cowering in the doorway of his own living room, sucked dry by his own fear. The wall Michele is standing at is not even at the edge of the roof—beyond it there are several yards of tar and loose gravel.

Michele says nothing to Annie, but turns to Jay, wide-eyed with a new burst of rage. "You're probably sleeping with her, too. Aren't you? You're probably fucking her right under Cleo's nose. That's convenient. You don't even have to worry about the future, you sick asshole."

"No, no, no," Jay protests, and Annie stands absolutely still, bracing herself against the blow implicit in Michele's words. But they seem to float above her.

The girl looks almost shocked herself, still breathing too fast, but quiet now.

"I'm not dying," Annie says calmly. "I'm waiting."

She is aware of a new edge in her voice. A light, powerful feeling begins to course through her. She can feel her own blood finally—she is aware of its quick rhythm in the channels of her veins. She is aware of its feeding her bones and tissues, rushing from one region of her body to another, fuelled by something bright and strong and weightless, impervious to treatment or disease. It is as if some door had opened inside her and she could hear everything—not just her own heartbeat but the hollow, coddled ticking of Jay's body, the more chaotic, unformed racing of Michele's, and the troubled cacophony all three of them are making. The sound is real and essential and utterly irrelevant. It makes her think of the time her brother gave her a tattoo—a spindly leaf and its shadow curving along the jutting bone of her ankle. It had hurt like nothing she'd known before, and she'd squirmed and bit her lip until it was bloody, feeling nothing but the prick of the needle against delicate nerve endings, the burn of the ink under her skin. That's not you, Todd had said, pointing at her ankle. That's your body— leave it for a minute and come back.

"In fifteen minutes, Anthony will be coming home," Annie says to Michele. "And then Eden. You'd better go home before that."

From his place at the glass door, Jay is watching her.

"What makes you such an expert at what I should do?" Michele says. "You just live here. This isn't even really your home." But her voice is losing its conviction.

"No, it's not," Annie replies. "But I know you should leave now. You should go home and get some rest."

Michele heaves a deep sigh and runs her hand over her hair in a habitual gesture. "If I leave, it's for her sake, not yours, Jay," she says, in a voice that trembles, straining to be haughty. "And for poor Anthony. I'm sorry he has a twisted fuck of a father like you." Then she takes a few steps across the terrace and past Jay into the living room—stiff, careful steps shaped by some combination of pride and restraint. She plucks her leather jacket up off the sofa and walks across the beige-and-white Chinese carpet, leaving faint gray footprints on the plush surface which Carolita, the cleaning lady, will have to spend hours on her hands and knees scrubbing to remove. The thought flits through Annie's mind involuntarily.

When Michele gets to Annie, she pauses, close enough for Annie to smell the acrid, strung-out scent of her sweat. "Don't let him touch you," she says fiercely. There are little bubbles of saliva in the corners of her mouth. In a moment, she is gone, and the heavy oak door to the elevator vestibule clicks shut.

When Annie turns back toward Jay, he has sunk down onto the sofa with his knees wedged in against the coffee table and his head in his hands. He looks too big and ungainly for the spot he has climbed into. The curve of his back has the slump of defeat. What could she ever have thought his body had to offer?

"It's not what you think," Jay begins. "Michele is on something. She's upset—" He breaks off under Annie's gaze.

"It's not my business," she says. "It isn't my home."

"Of course it is. You live here. You take care of Anthony."

Jay shifts his gaze out toward the terrace in a self-conscious, nearsighted way. Looking at him, Annie is filled with the knowledge of things outside this room, of hospital waiting rooms and of the bowels of complicated machines that can see through flesh to what lies beneath it, of wet sidewalks and empty hallways, of the smell of new leaves and spring earth and grease coming out of coffee-shop air vents, of babies in the Park and the serious yellow of taxis and how simple it all looks from above. She is filled with the knowledge of loneliness and suspense and courage. Unlike this man protected by the mantle of good health and good fortune, she knows what is required not to be afraid.

Jay ventures a nervous glance up at her. His face is still pale and covered with a thin sheen of sweat. "I'm sorry—" he begins. "I'm sorry about what Michele—"

"It's all right," Annie interrupts. "It doesn't matter." And she means it.

From the hall, there is the whirr of the elevator door opening and the sound of Anthony's high, excited voice, then Mrs. Tibbs's lower, wearier murmur of response. In a moment, Anthony is rushing toward Annie, flushed with fresh air and emotion. He is waving a sheet of paint-stiffened paper so that colored chips fall from it to the floor. "For you—" He is panting. "I made this. I didn't know if you'd be here."

Peter Morris

Pancakes

CHARACTERS

SAM, a businessman, late 20s–early 30s.
BUDDY, an unemployed man, late 20s–early 30s.

SETTING

An apartment.

TIME

The present.

Lights up on the table and two chairs. On the table are a butter dish, a knife and fork, a bottle of syrup, a glass of milk and a plate with an enormous stack of pancakes—four dozen at least. Sam sits at the table eating. He wears a blue business suit with a white shirt and red tie. Buddy enters, running in and sliding to a stop. He wears boxer shorts and a tee shirt and has a severe case of "bed head." He takes a deep breath, inhaling the pancake aroma, then crosses to the table and sits. He stares at Sam. There are several moments of silence with nothing being heard but the sound of Sam eating.

BUDDY: Good?

SAM: Uh huh.

BUDDY: They look good.

SAM: *(His mouth full.)* They are good.
    (Silence.)

BUDDY: Make 'em from scratch?

SAM: *(Mouth still full.)* Bisquick.

BUDDY: Bisquick is good.

SAM: I like Bisquick.

BUDDY: Makes a lotta pancakes.

SAM: I guess.

BUDDY: That's a lotta pancakes.

SAM: I like pancakes.
    (Silence. Buddy watches Sam pour more syrup on his pancakes. Buddy stands and exits. Sam continues to eat.)

BUDDY: *(Offstage.)* There's no more Bisquick.
    (No response. Sam just smiles.)

BUDDY: I said, there's no more Bisquick.

SAM: *(His mouth full.)* So?
    (Buddy re-enters with empty Bisquick box.)

BUDDY: You used it all up.

SAM: I know.

BUDDY: You could've left me some.

SAM: Well, I didn't.

BUDDY: That sucks. I live here too, you know.

SAM: Just barely.

BUDDY: You gonna bring that up again?

SAM: Just reminding you.

BUDDY: I don't need to be reminded. *(Silence. Buddy sits at the table opposite Sam.)*

BUDDY: Why won't you give me some of those pancakes?

SAM: Because they're mine.

BUDDY: You can't possibly eat them all.

SAM: Just watch me. *(He shoves an entire pancake in his mouth.)*

BUDDY: It's not fair.

SAM: Says you.

BUDDY: You have to give me some.

SAM: I do not. Who said I do? It's not a law. It's not in the Declaration of Independence or the Constitution. Nowhere do they say I have to give you some of my pancakes. What they *do* say is that everyone — *everyone* — is entitled to his own pancakes. This is a land of opportunity. Anyone is free to go out and get all the pancakes he can get his hands on.

BUDDY: What about the Bible?

SAM: What about it?

BUDDY: "Love thy neighbor"?

SAM: That only means you have to love him, not feed him.

BUDDY: You're taking it too literal. You're missing the spirit of the thing.

SAM: Spirit, schmirit, it doesn't say a fucking thing about pancakes.

BUDDY: I can't believe you're not going to give me any.

SAM: Make your own.

BUDDY: There's no more Bisquick.

SAM: Then eat something else.

BUDDY: There *is* nothing. Nothing but some pickle relish and a box of baking soda. I can't make anything out of that.

SAM: Not my problem.

BUDDY: Is that your attitude? "Not my problem"? You're satisfied so to hell with everybody else?

SAM: Not everybody else — just you. *(He resumes eating.)*

BUDDY: Look at you, stuffing your face. You should be ashamed.

SAM: Leave me alone. I'm trying to eat.

BUDDY: So am I! Only I have no food!

SAM: *(Stands and confronts Buddy.)* Then do something about it. Don't stand around begging. That's all you ever do and I'm sick of it. You want some food? Go get it.

BUDDY: Fine! I will! *(Buddy storms out. Beat. Sam sits back down and resumes eating. Buddy storms back in.)* Do you have ten bucks?

SAM: What?

BUDDY: Can you loan me ten bucks?

SAM: On top of the back rent you already owe me?

BUDDY: I said I'd pay you.

SAM: How? You have no job.

BUDDY: I'm looking.

SAM: Look harder.

BUDDY: I just need a little loan.

SAM: What about the big one I've already given you? I've been carrying you for months now but I'm through with it. Do you hear me? I work hard for my money, Buddy.

BUDDY: I'd be happy to work for mine too if someone would just let me. But I can't find a job, OK? I've looked and I've looked and I can't find a job. There's just not a big market these days for philosophers.

SAM: Then do something else.

BUDDY: But I was a philosophy major in college.

SAM: People don't need philosophers.

BUDDY: Yes, they do. They just don't know it. But they will. One day they'll wake up with a spiritual malaise, then they'll need me.

SAM: What the hell is a spiritual mayonnaise?

BUDDY: Malaise! Not mayonnaise! Spiritual malaise! And people like you are gonna get it bad! Trust me! Then I'll be in big demand! You wait and see! (*Pause. Buddy, realizing he is becoming unhinged, pulls himself together. He sits on the floor and begins meditating in the lotus position. Sam just looks at him.*)

SAM: You don't wanna work, do you?

BUDDY: (*In the same rhythm as his chanting.*) Yes, I do.

SAM: You don't. If you did, you wouldn't be sitting around unwashed, unshaved and undressed on a weekday.

BUDDY: It's eight o'clock in the morning.

SAM: Early bird catches the worm.

BUDDY: I don't want worms. I want pancakes.

SAM: Then earn them.

BUDDY: How?

SAM: You can do a little job for me.

BUDDY: What kind of little job?

SAM: You can shine my shoes.

BUDDY: You want me to shine your shoes?

SAM: I'll give you a pancake for each shoe.

BUDDY: One pancake for each shoe.

SAM: That's the offer.

BUDDY: Is that what you want, to humiliate me? Demean me? Well, forget it! I won't do it! I won't! I want at least two pancakes per shoe!

SAM: Deal.

BUDDY: Deal.

    (*They shake hands.*)

BUDDY: Take off your shoes.

SAM: No.

BUDDY: Then how am I supposed to shine them?

SAM: Get down on your knees.

BUDDY: What?

SAM: Get down on your knees and shine my shoes.

BUDDY: Are you serious?

SAM: You want some pancakes, don't you?

BUDDY: You know I do.

SAM: Then get down on your knees.

BUDDY: Sam, please.

SAM: Down!

> *(Silence. Buddy gets down on his knees.)*

BUDDY: What do I use to shine them with?

SAM: *(Deliberately, biting each word.)* Your tongue.

BUDDY: No.

SAM: *(Dangling a pancake in Buddy's face.)* Mmmmm, these are so good.

BUDDY: I won't do it.

SAM: They're so light and fluffy, sweet and delicious. Mmmm-mmmm-mmmm.

BUDDY: You're a pig.

> *(Sam pushes Buddy over with his foot.)*

SAM: *(Seething.)* Watch your mouth, Buddy. You're only here thanks to my good graces. I could've thrown you out months ago. I could throw you out right now. But I won't. Because I pity you. Do you hear me? You're pathetic. Look at you, about to kiss my feet for some lousy pancakes.

BUDDY: I'm hungry. All I've eaten in the last week were some stale Saltines.

SAM: Those were *my* stale Saltines. Bought and paid for with my money. And you didn't even say thank you, did you?

BUDDY: *(Weakly.)* Thank you.

SAM: What was that?

BUDDY: Thank you. I said thank you.

SAM: That's better. *(Sam sits. Buddy slowly gets up off the floor.)* What is it with guys like you? You've always got your hand out. Soft, fleshy hands that haven't seen a day of work.

BUDDY: I need help.

SAM: "The Lord helps those who help themselves." Now *there's* a Bible quote for you.

BUDDY: That's not from the Bible.

SAM: Well, it should be. Now stop bothering me.

BUDDY: How can you be so heartless when you have so much? Look at you, you have all the pancakes.

SAM: That's right. They're all mine. And what, I should just give them to you?

BUDDY: You could share them.

SAM: Why in hell would I want to do that?

BUDDY: It might make you feel good.

> *(Sam bursts out laughing. Buddy watches in silence.)*

SAM: That's the stupidest thing I ever heard.

BUDDY: Some people find great solace in charity.

SAM: What they find, Buddy boy, is a tax deduction. No one does anything without getting something in return. Now, can all the philosophical mumbo jumbo. I have to finish eating. I have a morning conference. They're putting me in charge of the national ad campaign for Good Will. *(He resumes eating.)*

BUDDY: Good Will. They're putting you in charge of "good will." Well, that's just perfect. It's like putting a fox in charge of the hen house.

SAM: *(His mouth full.)* Very funny.

BUDDY: It is. It's hilarious. But I just can't bring myself to laugh. It's a very amusing paradox but I just can't laugh. I'm too weak. I'm hungry and light-headed and I just don't have the strength to laugh. But it is funny. Not slap-your-thigh funny but wry and ironic. Only God could make a joke like that. The same God that gets a kick out of holocausts and plagues and famines. What a sense of humor that guy's got. He gave you all the pancakes and he gave me none.

SAM: That's life. Some of us have pancakes and some of us have not.

BUDDY: Yup, and you have them. You're the pancake king.

SAM: That's me.

BUDDY: Here, your majesty, why don't I give you some more syrup?

SAM: I don't want any more syrup.

BUDDY: Sure you do. Everybody wants more syrup. *(He picks up the bottle of syrup and begins pouring it on Sam's head.)*

SAM: What the fuck!

BUDDY: And butter? What about some more butter? *(Buddy picks up the butter knife and plunges it in Sam's gut—one, two, three times. Sam falls to the floor.)* You want pancakes? Here, eat some pancakes! *(Buddy begins shoving pancakes into Sam's mouth. He coughs and hacks and begins choking.)* Have another! And another! And another!

(Suddenly, Sam's body goes limp. Buddy sits in his chair and begins ravenously eating pancakes.)

BUDDY: Hungry. So hungry. *(After a moment he looks down at Sam's body.)* You were right, the Lord does help those who help themselves. *(He kicks the lifeless body then resumes eating the pancakes.)*

(Fade to black.)

CHAPTER SEVEN

PATTERN

Pattern—artful, intentional repetition—has a number of important functions in creative writing. First, pattern is a system of road signs or signals for your readers, designed to move them through your piece smoothly while guiding their attention to the most important parts of the work.

Pattern is also one of the ways writers *make* meaning. A minister or an essay or a traffic light may *tell* you the meaning. Creative writers *create meaning*. Pattern makes any piece of art—dance, painting, sculpture—more complex, layered, and interesting.

Pattern is partly why art is different from real life. Real life rambles. Pattern contains a piece, helps give it a shape, a design.

When you were in secondary school, it's likely you were taught to write in three stages: generate, write, rewrite. You were supposed to brainstorm ideas, then write them all out, and then revise. Few creative writers work this way, however. The writing process is a lot messier than teachers told us in school, and it can be a lot more fun than slogging through those three stages. One of the ways you can enjoy the writing process more is to keep an eye on pattern as you work. Attending to patterns—intentionally creating repetitions of sound, image, and rhythm—provides an alternate way of working, one that's much more fun than the old write-and-revise model.

> *Art is pattern informed by sensibility.*
> — SIR HERBERT READ

Usually, as they create a piece of writing, writers enhance the patterns already organically showing up in the writing, focusing on various potentials for repeating sounds, images, and rhythms.

Working with pattern may not come easily to you, especially at first. Try to be patient with yourself as you learn this new strategy. Many of us have been taught that repetition, like imitation, is a fault and a flaw. You may have an unconscious bias against or some preconceptions about repetition. "It's a pattern of behavior." "You're stuck in a pattern." But pattern is repetition with a purpose. When we accuse someone of repetition, we imply that he or she is using a pattern without purpose, repeating design elements that either are not worthy of repetition (recall the classic all-pattern song "100 Bottles of Beer on the Wall") or are repeated mindlessly, without a larger goal.

Intentionally repeating yourself is brave. Repeating yourself calls attention to what you are saying. It takes some confidence to believe that your sounds, images, gestures, and ideas are worth repeating, deserving to be underscored. The artful use of pattern is how you make a great poem out of a good poem; it's how you make fiction out of a stack of anecdotes, how you shape a play from snatches of dialogue. When you make patterns, you make art.

> *Art is the imposing of a pattern on experience, and our aesthetic enjoyment is recognition of the pattern.*
> — ALFRED NORTH WHITEHEAD

In Part Three, Genres, you will find a series of writing projects that offer good practice in pattern, including anaphora and list. No matter what genre you are most interested in working on — novels, screenplays, comics, nonfiction — you'll be well served if you train in the principles of pattern. Just as football players practice ballet in order to strengthen precision and control, as a writer you want experience writing in tight, pattern-rich forms such as the ghazal, pantoum, sonnet, sestina, and villanelle. These recipes are essentially short courses in all of the techniques presented in this chapter. Some students find the recipes for these pattern-intensive pieces daunting at first, but with just a little practice, you will find in these pieces a fantastic set of tools that will really pay off as you work on depth, meaning, voice, flow, and power in any other genre. Patterns deepen and enrich all genres, so refuse to be anxious about poetry, knowing that the skills you learn by studying and writing poems will feed all of your other writing.

PATTERN BY EAR

Rhyme and Echoes

Perhaps the first pattern we encounter as young readers is rhyme. As small children, we were drawn to pattern, and we found things that repeated and rhymed especially pleasing: "red fish, blue fish, old fish, new fish" is more intriguing to the ear than "miscellaneous finned creatures varying in color." Rhyme gives us pleasure. Rhyme provides a pattern so that we can memorize a piece of writing, carrying it with us always.

Yet rhyming for the sake of rhyming can be annoying:

You are the one I love.
More than the stars above.

The verse seems clunky, forced, amateur, because the word *above* is being used only to rhyme with *love*. It sounds goofy to describe stars and love this way when there are so many more interesting ways to talk about one's lover. This writer is not concerned with the image, and nothing pops into the reader's head. You can't see *above*—the word is the opposite of a specific, forcing the reader to think rather than see. The ear may be satisfied, but that is never enough in creative writing. Eyes, ears, mind's eye, touch—the whole system has to be activated. Rhyming is the most overt sound pattern, and if it is to be effective, the rhyming words need to be fresh, natural, surprising, clear, and interesting.

> *For constructing any work of art you need some principle of repetition or recurrence; that's what gives you rhythm in music and pattern in painting.*
> — NORTHROP FRYE

In contrast to the *love-above* rhyme, consider the rhymes from the first six lines of Gregory Orr's poem "The River," which appears in full on page 302.

I felt both pleasure and a shiver
as we undressed on the slippery bank
and then plunged into the wild river.

I waded in; she entered as a diver.
Watching her pale flanks slice the dark
I felt both pleasure and a shiver.

Shiver and river rhyme, but not in a predictable way. Both words belong in the poem and add to the story in the poem. Both words create an image for the reader. And, importantly, Orr doesn't limit himself just to words that rhyme. In the poem, he creates a matrix of repeating sounds so that the rhyming words don't stick out weirdly. The words *pleasure* and *shiver* echo, as do the "s" sounds in *undressed* and *slippery*. *Pleasure, plunged,* and *pale* create a sound pattern (alliteration), echoing through the poem, and *pleasure, shiver,* and *diver* connect, nearly rhyming, adding more richness to the subtle, beautiful, sensual texture of sound patterns in the poem. Orr orchestrates exact rhymes (*shiver* and *river*) along with near rhymes and echoes (*bank, dark / diver, shiver*) to create sophisticated, surprising sounds that aren't singsong, predictable, pointless, or clichéd.

Here each word that rhymes also fits the poem, contributes to the visual image the poet wants to create. The rhymes and near rhymes aren't random. They serve the image, and the words are interesting and specific.

Rhyme isn't just for poets. Attention to the pattern of language is one of the most important features that distinguish creative writing from writing that informs, instructs, records, or explains.

Consider this line of fiction from short story writer Aimee Bender:

> The walk home from school was a straight line and the boy was not the wandering kind.

Notice the rhyme. Bender's rhyme makes the sentence showy, interesting, fresh, and intriguing—good for a first sentence.

PRACTICE

Read Gregory Orr's "The River" (p. 302) aloud in its entirety, and discuss the pattern of rhymes and other sound repetitions.

PRACTICE

Read the first paragraph of Raymond Carver's short story "Cathedral" (p. 119). Make a list of all the words that have sounds that appear in other words in the paragraph. Do you notice a pattern? Do you think this is intentional on Carver's part? Practice substituting other words for some of his choices, ones that do not echo existing words in the passage. What changes?

Once creative writers discover the intricate nuances of sound, they use sound repetition to underline or highlight or even evoke, literally, specific moods and feelings in their readers. Orr repeats "river" and "shiver"—the poem is about skinny-dipping, and it's also about taking another kind of dive: the leap into a new relationship. The words *river* and *shiver* amplify Orr's meaning and serve to create, through pattern, subtext for the poem. If he had repeated words like *lump*, *thump*, and *clump*, we would experience a completely different set of meanings. The words you repeat are like flashlights, shining light where you want your reader to focus attention. Pattern isn't random.

Consonants and Vowels

To use the flashlight technique, writers often use echoes: sounds or images (instead of direct rhymes) that are repeated throughout a piece. Orr keeps repeating *river* and *shiver*, but he also creates a carefully controlled soundscape for his poem, using sound echoes. Notice how much power writing can generate just through the use of sound echoes. Instead of directly rhyming and getting trapped into using simplistic or nonimagistic word choices, you can use echoes.

PRACTICE

Read Randall Mann's "Pantoum" (p. 302). How many repeating sounds do you find in the poem? Pay attention to the sounds Mann uses to end each line. Do you see or hear sound patterns that help the poem convey its meaning?

PRACTICE

Read aloud Laure-Anne Bosselaar's "Stillbirth" (p. 303). Read the poem several more times, and carefully consider how the title explains the situation. Trace at least two sound patterns — sounds that echo or nearly rhyme / directly rhyme — throughout the poem. What is the effect of these sounds on the mood or feeling of this poem?

Using patterns of sound — not only rhyme, but also assonance (the repetition of vowels), consonance (the repetition of consonants), and alliteration (the repetition of the first letters of words) — isn't just a technique poets use. Prose writers attend just as carefully to sound patterns.

PRACTICE

Read the short story "Sticks" by George Saunders (p. 304). What sounds are repeated? What whole words are repeated? Do you find examples of images or themes that are repeated as well?

Instead of thinking about sound simply as rhyme, zoom in. Pay attention to the vowels and consonants in your sentences. For practice, track the sound patterns — the repeated consonants and vowels — in this paragraph from Nick Flynn's memoir *Another Bullshit Night in Suck City*. What sounds are repeated, and what are the effects of these sounds?

> *When I write poetry, what I really get first is one or two phrases with a very insistent rhythm. The phrases keep insisting and the poem builds up by a process of accretion.*
>
> — KENNETH REXROTH

In Boston the bars close at one. The next wave of revelers, more gregarious than the earlier crowd, bleary and headed home, push their way inside. Sometimes they give you a hassle, sometimes they flip you a few bucks. A little lit, sometimes they try to start up a conversation, sit on the floor next to you, offer you a drink, want to know your name.

The emphatic "b's" in the first sentence give way, just as the night does, to looser, more open sounds. Notice the "eh," "ay," "eh," "ay" pattern of vowel sounds in the second sentence. Flynn's writing sounds good. We often take sound for granted when we read; sound can be very subtle.

You might be thinking to yourself, "Do I really have to look at every single vowel, every single letter?" Yes. You do. Sound is going to come out of your piece, whether you want it to or not. You have a chance to shape the way your reader feels. Few writers are willing to leave that to chance.

What if Flynn had written without attention to sound and instead started his paragraph this way:

In my town, stuff closes early.

And then:

More people come into the bar after the first set goes home.

See the difference? The first passage sounds better. Why? The sound patterns aren't screaming for attention; Flynn pays attention to how he can connect words and sentences by using similar sounds. When this attention to sound is absent, we might say the writing "doesn't flow."

Some writers feel tempted to go crazy with sounds:

Hilary heaped hundreds of hippos on the hydrodam.

Uh-oh. Now we are back to nursery-speak, hitting one sound *too* hard, way too hard. Fun to write, this kind of sound is unlikely to capture the attention of a serious audience. It's really fun to speak this way, and you'll evoke laughter in your reader unless your sound pattern is blended in, serves the purpose of the passage, and, like all good patterns, supports the rest of the piece instead of taking center stage. When a pattern of similar sounds evolves, the piece of writing feels more unified. It flows. Often, the consonant and vowel patterns are subtle. You would notice them only if they weren't there.

> *Refrain is one of the most valuable of all form methods. Refrain is a return to the known before one flies again upwards. It is a consolation to the reader, a reassurance that the book has not left his understanding.*
> — JOHN STEINBECK

> *Writing is the science of the various blisses of language.*
> — ROLAND BARTHES

Word Order

Compare:

He came. He saw. He conquered.

To:

He woke up when his alarm clock went off. It looked to be a great day. He thought about what to wear. Maybe he would get up and brush his teeth and wash his face and then get into his clothes or something.

Syntax is the order of the parts of the sentence. In the first example, notice how the syntax echoes—it makes a pattern. Each sentence is two words, the parts of speech echoing. The second example doesn't pay attention to syntax. The writer hasn't thought about how to make a pattern with the sentences themselves. He is missing an opportunity to make his writing reader-friendly, powerful, and effective.

Syntax matters to writers in the same way that reading music matters to composers, and the way strategy matters to military generals. The word *syntax* comes from the Greek word *tassein*, meaning "to arrange" (the word *tactics* is closely related). To write "with syntax" means to write "with tactics." The order of the words matters. Writers *choose* the order, instead of leaving it to chance.

Let's look at Aimee Bender's sentence again:

The walk home from school was a straight line and the boy was not the wandering kind.

Notice how she repeats the same verb, *was*, and sets up the syntax of the sentence so that its two parts mirror each other. How differently we would feel about this sentence if she wrote, "The boy walked home. He really didn't get lost much."

Many new writers rely on one basic sentence structure, learned early on. Their basic dance step uses the subject-verb-object or subject-verb-modifier syntax. Like this:

She left the building.

He woke the dog.

Janet sang loudly.

There is nothing inherently wrong with this syntax pattern. But when a writer uses only that one pattern, the writing falls flat.

In the following example from Tobias Wolff's memoir *This Boy's Life*, notice how the author uses the basic pattern, inserts a variation, and returns to the basic pattern.

So I passed the hours after school. Sometimes, not very often, I felt lonely.
Then I would go home to Roy.

The speaker is struggling with an abusive stepfather. He tries to have regular hours after school, messing around outside, hanging out by himself, avoiding his own house. When he feels lonely (the variation, not normal, not desired, not expected), Wolff uses an atypical sentence pattern to emphasize the unusual, the not-okay-ness—"sometimes, not very often,"—the sentence begins with a stutter-step, pauses—we breathe differently when we read it. It's a little jolt, a little break. The return to subject-verb-object/modifier matches the sense of inevitability—Tobias has nowhere else to go. He has to go home. Messing around with the basic sentence pattern creates energy and power.

It's a little jolt, a little break. The author carefully uses sentence variety to underscore the difficulties in the narrator's life. Tobias has to go home. But it's not just home home—it's home *to Roy*. Ending the sentence with those two words—*to Roy*—avoids the predictable pattern ("I went home") and makes a strong and chilling point. Varying sentence patterns creates energy and power and increases tension. Notice the difference between "Good is what I am" and "I am good." Reread each sentence aloud. Do they sound the same? Do they even mean the same thing? Does the first version have implications that the second one doesn't?

PRACTICE

Write a short analysis of the word order and repetition Brenda Miller uses in her memoir "Swerve" (p. 118).

The poet E. E. Cummings inverts word order so frequently that it becomes his signature move. Here is Cummings's poem about a mouse, poisoned by someone who doesn't want mice in the house.

E. E. Cummings
(Me up at does)

Me up at does

out of the floor
quietly Stare

a poisoned mouse

still who alive

is asking What
have i done that

You wouldn't have

What's important to remember is that our point of view is inverted in this poem—we are the mouse, looking up at the human. The words are reversed, and so is our usual perspective—we don't typically identify with rodents. The syntax is jerky; words seem to be missing. Do you almost hold your breath—choke?—as you read the poem? (Another pattern to notice: Why are some words capitalized? Do the capitalized words make a pattern you can make sense of? That's a visual pattern; more on that on p. 296.)

Readers appreciate "figuring out" the puzzle that is pattern, but the harder the puzzle is, the more payoff there needs to be. The mouse poem above is, like the mouse's life, quite brief. (Would you be likely to read a novel written in this style?)

Rap lyrics offer an excellent model for improving your use of word order. Listen to an excerpt of *Hamilton* online, and consider how the order of the words both creates music and adds to the meaning and pleasure we gain from the song.

PRACTICE

Read the story "Sticks" by George Saunders (p. 304) or the monologue by Jenifer Hixson (p. 162). Track sound and syntax patterns, noting each example. In what ways is the author "rhyming" sentences, sections, or paragraphs?

Rhythm

Notice the differences in rhythm in the following two samples, one from a text-book, the other from the novel *Risk Pool* by Richard Russo:

> The preceding section illustrates the relationships between numerous cohesive devices.

> My father, unlike so many of the men he served with, knew just what he wanted to do when the war was over. He wanted to drink and whore and play the horses.

The rhythm in these two sentences is *very* different. The first is very monochromatic in tone, in part because the rhythm is flat. The second sentence bounces, moves, pulses. It has an interesting beat to it.

A beginning writer may write:

> My father was a party animal.

Russo, an experienced novelist, writes:

> He was celebrating life. His.

In the second example, Russo uses the typical S-V-O/M construction, but he slams on the brakes; instead of writing two S-V-O/M sentences in a row, he slaps down a one-word sentence. Both sentences begin with the sound of the letter "h," creating a sound pattern that is counterpointed by the rhythms in the opposing sentences. Four words juxtaposed with one word: *his*. Russo creates humor and energy with syntax.

> *Meter is like the abstract idea of a dance as a choreographer might plan it with no particular performers in mind; rhythm is like a dancer interpreting the dance in a personal way.*
>
> — JOHN FREDERICK NIMS

The creative writer uses rhythm to punctuate, highlight, and emphasize content and to keep the reader engaged in the piece. Rhythmless writing = boring writing.

Law briefs lack rhythm. Memos from your boss lack rhythm. Bureaucratic writing is trying to be neutral, and creative writing is trying to be interesting, lively, memorable, and enjoyable to read. Rhythm is a pattern that lets you do that.

Meter

In creative writing, the pattern of rhythms is called **meter**. Just like a speedometer, meter measures how fast you are going, and it gives you information on what syllables or beats are stressed (emphasized) and which ones aren't. That's good information to have. Many new writers resist learning meter—it is complex, and they have to memorize a lot of impressive words—*spondee* and *trochee* and *pentameter*. But if your class decides to spend some time on meter, try to remember this: Meter isn't a strict set of rules. Poets and writers make up their rules, use exceptions, reinvent the rules. Meter is feedback. It's information you get about how your poem is going to play out for the reader. Meter is a tool, a fine one. It's not a prison. Your teacher (especially if she or he is a poet) may decide to pursue an in-depth unit on meter. For now, if you choose to learn just one thing about meter, focus on iambic pentameter. You already know a lot about it, and you probably write in it even though you may not be aware that you do. Read on.

Iambic Pentameter. Many poems are written in iambic pentameter. The term sounds fancy, but it isn't highbrow or obscure. It's our daily rhythm. It's a very natural way for speakers of English to put words together. Like the two-step in dance, or 4/4 time in music, it's a pattern of beats, or emphases on syllables, that is quite simple and direct. Chaucer, Shakespeare, Milton, Frost, and Stephen Crane wrote in iambic pentameter.

> *I would sooner write free verse as play tennis with the net down.*
>
> — ROBERT FROST

An iamb is a *da-DUM* sound; two syllables together, with the stress (the stress is the weight or the emphasis) on the second one, as in the word *adore*. The names Heather and Karen are *not* iambs. "Heh-THER" sounds wrong. "Ka-REN" sounds funny.

In English we usually begin sentences with an article — *the, an, a* — so the natural rhythm follows: the house, an egg, a boy. *Da-DUM, da-DUM, da-DUM.*

Set next to each other in a row, in a sentence, iambs always make a pattern:

i-AM-bic ME-ter GOES like THIS.

Some people say that iambic pentameter echoes the pattern of a heartbeat (*da-DUM da-DUM*) or footfalls when people walk. It's a powerful pattern.

Pentameter means five units, so iambic pentameter means five *da-DUMs* per line, which is ten syllables per line, as in:

My mistress' eyes are nothing like the sun;

Why five? Humans like fives. We count in fives for a good reason (check your hand). There might be another reason: Take a deep breath. A very deep breath. Now take a deep breath again, and this time, count how many times your heart beats. The poet John Frederick Nims calls iambic pentameter "a breathful of heartbeats." Have you taken CPR? What is the ratio of breaths to chest compressions, the substitute heartbeats?

If one purpose of poetry is to resuscitate the human soul, to give us back ourselves, it's no surprise that iambic pentameter has become our most common rhythm.

PRACTICE

Compose five lines of poetry in iambic pentameter. Then rewrite them, trying to pay no attention to the beat at all. Do you feel as though you have a good internal sense of rhythm? When you read the two versions out loud, does one sound better than the other?

Look back at some of your poetry. Are you writing in iambic pentameter without even knowing it? If you are writing in English, you are probably using this meter — at least some of the time — unconsciously. Studying creative writing is all about becoming more aware of what you do and learning how to direct your attention and your power to greater effect. Readers like iambic pentameter. It's reassuring, predictable, steady, controlled, and clear.

PRACTICE

Read the Sonnet section (p. 453), and try writing a sonnet in iambic pentameter.

Free Verse. You may not want to write in iambic pentameter all the time. After experimenting with that rhythm, you may reject it as a pattern for your work. That's fine. Free verse is just as popular as iambic pentameter. When you write poetry with no rules about syllables or stresses or line length, when you are not following a pre-existing pattern, you are writing **free verse**. In this case, the reader instead of the writer supplies the verbal emphases and controls the rate of speed, the cadences.

Look at the following example, which does not follow the most common meter, iambic pentameter. Instead, it starts with two stresses together.

One, two
Buckle my shoe
Three, four
Shut the door

The pattern created by these short lines is brisk, curt, peppy, and bossy. Nursery rhymes are not written in long lines, and you probably won't write a poem about the death of someone very important in two-syllable lines; the pattern is too curt. Consider Walt Whitman's poetry and rap lyrics: Both use long lines to talk about the dead and dying. Long lines create soothing, reflective patterns and are well suited to political or philosophical musings.

Think about the difference between saying "Please consider allowing others to speak" and "Shut the hell up!" Emphasis matters. Line length matters. Rhythm matters.

Notice how you have been working this semester. Experiment. Don't be stuck in a rut, writing all medium-length lines, medium paragraphs, medium sentences. What happens when you lengthen the line, the sentence? Does the meaning start to shift, too? What about the tone? What happens when you shorten and tighten, make lines, sentences, stanzas, paragraphs staccato, short? Does the meaning shift? Do you see the piece going in a new direction entirely? This is how writers work. Pattern isn't decoration or afterthought. It's the engine that drives a piece, the heartbeat. It can be used as a tool for discovery, a way of giving new energy to an old piece.

PRACTICE

Memorize a short poem in iambic pentameter (you may use one from this book or find one on your own). Does the meter help you internalize the word patterns? Recite this poem aloud. When you say it aloud, do you keep to the meter, or do you vary it to add your own emphases?

PRACTICE

Reread the short story "Bodies" by Jessica Shattuck (p. 263). Look (and listen!) for sound patterns. First, locate two or three interesting syntax patterns, and copy these over. Then find three dialogue passages, and copy these out. Lastly, find a passage where iambs are repeated in a sequence. Noticing where she breaks the pattern each time, what can you say about how Shattuck uses sound to amplify the meaning and richness of the story?

PATTERN BY EYE

Objects

Writers also create patterns out of objects or images to make a piece of writing more meaningful and cohesive. This is called a unified pattern of imagery.

Take an inventory of the specific details, the objects, the "stuff" in your piece. Do you need to have a garage sale? Or do you need a personal shopper, and more carefully chosen objects to layer meaning into your piece?

> *Usually I begin with an image or a phrase; if you follow trustfully, it's surprising how far an image can lead.*
> — JAMES MERRILL

Many beginning writers need *more* stuff in their stories, poems, and plays. They refer to general worlds, but they don't populate these worlds with the details of real life, thereby missing an opportunity not just to be energetic but to create a complex, interesting, layered pattern of imagery. Don't just stick in random stuff. Choose objects that go with or work against the "stuff" in your piece, making interesting visual patterns. Some paper, an idea, blank walls. Hmm. What's the pattern? Vague emptiness? A cigarette, a broken baby stroller with a baby in it, a half-empty warm beer can — that's interesting. Those things make a pattern that affects the reader. There's a pattern of danger, neglect. The images make a pattern all on their own, and that pattern starts to tell a story.

The easiest way to learn more about creating a pattern of objects or images is to read as a writer. First, divide a sheet of paper into two columns, one labeled "Animate Objects" and the other "Inanimate Objects." Review the story "Bodies" by Jessica Shattuck (p. 263). As you come to each object in the story, record it in the appropriate column. Listing all these objects, fill up your columns like this:

Object Patterns in Jessica Shattuck's "Bodies"

Animate Objects	Inanimate Objects
Long-legged, blond, shiny Michele	Halved parsnips like limbs
Glamorous, big-boned, cool Cleo, creative director for a giant ad agency	Refrigerator like a hospital
Intense, frank Anthony, the kid	Gallon and a half of water a day
Drooling Eden, the baby	Pilly sweater, baggy jeans, pills, vitamins
Animal-like Jay	Black Central Park
Annie, her body like a sick pet, sneakers, jacket	Pink and orange dahlias projecting pointy orange shadows on the walls

The pattern of objects tells us a lot about the deeper layers of the story. The objects are signals, creating a kind of lighted pathway for the reader. The objects, when strung together, make meaning. That's the power of pattern.

Review your object patterns worksheet, and notice the pairs that emerge. Michele, looking at the vegetables and seeing limbs. Cleo, hospital. Anthony, too much water. The people in this story—animate objects who have health, sexuality, and beauty—are accompanied by objects that evoke artifice, insensitivity, greed. The weaker characters—young Anthony, sick Annie—are trying, but drowning, turning limp. We know this partly because they are associated with objects that are losing strength or suffocating.

The pattern makes meaning.

Look at the inanimate objects. Do they create a visual pattern? Do you hear echoes? Yes.

When pulled out and strung together, these objects spell out decay, loss, and fear, among other things.

By naming creepy inanimate things at regular intervals throughout her story, Shattuck creates a background sound track that is thrumming, unnerving, slightly menacing, unpleasant. The reader has an uneasy feeling. That feeling is underscored by the pattern, and the breaks in the pattern. Shattuck includes *Goodnight Moon* and the sound track to *The Lion King*: moving, heartfelt pieces.

The wholesome sweetness of these objects breaks the image pattern, breaks the sirens and the low-level fighting, underscoring the betrayal, sadness, and decay. To use heavy, dark, sad music in this story could have tipped the whole thing into melodrama.

If Shattuck had chosen to call our attention to the nice, brilliant nephew, the cute white doves in Central Park, the cheerful children in strollers, the helpful doorman in his pressed red suit, the fresh bread from the bakery on 107th Street, the crisp white paper it comes in—and all those things exist in this world, too—the tone of the piece, our feelings when we read, would be *quite* different.

A meaningful pattern of objects is key to a successful piece of creative writing.

When writing a piece set in a house, you don't describe every single room or list everything in the fridge. You choose the items that go with the other items, items that underline or highlight the feeling you want to evoke in the reader. You are a set designer. You can bring in only *a few specific objects*. What do you select to best amplify the drama, your themes? The objects are going to create a pattern—you want to control that pattern. When you bring in flowers, you bring in clashing colors, to echo Michele and Cleo. Instead of providing beauty, these flowers make scary Halloween shadows, like weapons, on the walls. Everything you bring onto your set, you use. The gift of the flowers contrasts with and bounces off Anthony's gift in the final sentence of the story, the painting, so thick with color that pieces of it are falling off as he gives it to Annie. Notice the patterns: Saliva on Eden's face at the beginning of the story pairs with Michele's "little bubbles of saliva in the corners of her mouth" at the end of the story; Michele is a baby, a dangerous baby. Anthony is curved in a sofa at the beginning of the story; Jay is "sunk down into the sofa with his knees wedged against the coffee table and his head in his hands." This pattern of imagery sharply underlines the differences in our desire to be comforted and our ability to give and receive love.

So you do what good set designers do. You have a storehouse of stuff, and you pull out different items until you find a pattern.

PRACTICE

Go through a story or creative nonfiction piece you have written recently, and do the animate/inanimate inventory. Consider the implications of the pattern, and name the unified images. Are these pointing the reader in the emotional direction you want? What adjustments would you make to create a darker, more intense piece? What different inventory would you collect in order to emphasize the more comic, lighthearted aspects of the piece? Can you add some contrasting items (*The Lion King* sound track playing while a family falls apart) to enhance the patterns?

You can also think of pattern as a way to generate topics for writing. Writers are often well served by choosing a single topic and staying with it, creating a pattern on the macro level, a sequence of objects, moves, images, or shapes that repeats. For example, Lynda Barry creates whole books featuring her character Marlys in various daily situations, or images. A. Van Jordan keeps circling back to his invented dictionary definitions throughout his award-winning book *M-A-C-N-O-L-I-A*. Betsy Sholl uses pattern as a topic in her poem "Genealogy" (p. 66) so that each stanza repeats the subject at hand, in a slightly different way.

Gestures

One of the most intriguing patterns to work with is that of movement — human physical movement or gestures — throughout your piece. Consider the story of Cinderella, as told in Disney's movie version for children. The first gestures are Cinderella's, dancing around the house getting her chores done. Imagine the footwork of the tale — that's the pattern we are tracking now. The next movement pattern is the festive dance of birds and the fairy godmother, getting her ready for the ball. Another dance, with a different shape or pattern to it. It relates to the grand ball, where Cinderella *dances* again, for real this time, with the Prince. The final dance: It's the community's turn, as everyone is thrown into a tizzy while the Prince fits the slipper, whirling through the town with his entourage until he finds his match. Tracking and working to align and intensify the patterns of movement in your creative writing allows you to cleverly connect the parts of your piece. Movement attracts the reader. Pattern reinforces theme and meaning.

When the pattern changes, we have the same reaction as when a poet using iambic pentameter inserts "Hark! Hark!" into a line. We pay attention.

Consider the patterns of gestures in Rick Moody's story "Boys" (p. 212). Throughout the whole story, the boys are running and swooping and diving and dashing, tossing and digging, scratching and hollering. So when they stop, stand still, and whisper, that break in the pattern is going to heighten tension and gather our attention, and the writer will be able to make a major point. Pattern is a powerful tool; gestures are the way writers choreograph their pieces.

Notice the opening pattern of gestures in "Bodies" (look back at the opening paragraph on p. 263). Annie makes dinner, turns on lights, a child lays his head down on his arm. Annie moves quietly through the kitchen, promises him attention; the boy sits up straight. Summary flashback: Annie moves carefully through her days at Cleo's, dancing with her illness. Notice the pattern: In the first section (before the space break), we see up close Annie's moves through her life — they are tender, evenly paced, smooth. In the second section, the patterns her feet make on the floor of her life are the same. They have been static for a long time—since she got sick—and we see the dance from above, from farther back. Pattern. Pattern. Then, in the third section, the pattern changes, yes? The doorbell rings. Anthony puts his hand on his hip—two staccato gestures, boom, boom. It's like a time change in music, a couple of quick leaps in dance. Enter Michele. She *peers, breathes, flashes,* and Anthony is *demanding, shouting, squirming, collapsing.* This is a new sequence, a new pattern. Notice the contrast, and how energy is created by establishing a pattern firmly and then changing it dramatically.

PRACTICE

In Rick Moody's story "Boys" (p. 212), the movements and gestures are easy to track. Make a list of the gestures you find in the story. These will be different from the verbs you collected earlier; *gestures* refers to actions made by human bodies. What patterns do the gestures create?

Pattern on the Page

Another important aspect of pattern is the way the elements of your writing play out on the page. What's the pattern created by your paragraphs, your stanzas?

Consider the visual patterns your work creates: How does your piece look on the page to the reader's eye? How does your writing cover—literally—the white page? If your paragraphs are taking up whole pages, can you initiate a more pleasing pattern of white space, indents, and breaks? Do your stanzas create a pattern—the same number of lines, lines about the same length? Are you deliberately changing the pattern, or is your creative writing sprawling across the page? Are your lines ragged on purpose? Or just because you haven't attended to that pattern yet?

> *Form is like asbestos gloves that allow you to pick up material too hot to handle otherwise.*
> — ADRIENNE RICH

White space matters. White space acts as a rest does in music; the reader gets to pause, to breathe. White space alternating with short blocks of text speeds the pace (a staccato effect). Repeating visual elements—big blocks of text (paragraphs, stanzas, speech) with white space—create a polished, professional look and invite the reader in. The piece feels crafted, not dashed off. Long sections of text with no white space breaks are more difficult, and the reader may become lost. Most writers employ *other patterns*— sound, syntax, rhythm—to help the reader stay on track through a long section.

The visual outline, or pattern, involves blocks of text and blocks of white space. Because as writers we are so limited by these two tools, it's absolutely essential that we attend to the nuances of shape—the way the piece looks on the page.

Take a look at the essay "Son of Mr. Green Jeans: An Essay on Fatherhood, Alphabetically Arranged" by Dinty W. Moore (p. 305). The pattern created on the page is quite noticeable. The pattern the author uses is inspired by dictionary definitions, similar to the pattern that A. Van Jordan employs in "af•ter•glow" (p. 67). But here, words or phrases, arranged alphabetically, provide the jumping-off point for the author's reflections on fatherhood. He writes about many disparate aspects of fatherhood, including random facts from bizarre nature programming, strange facts from the annals of television shows where fatherhood is a key theme, and autobiographical material about his own history of fathers, Irish men who've passed on to the author a mix of good and, in his opinion, not-so-good traits.

Dinty Moore uses pattern—visual pattern—on the page to create an inviting format to hold his wild leaps and jumps from one fatherhood insight to another. What would be lost if Moore wrote in traditional paragraphs? Much of the fun of the juxtapositions, such as "Jaws" next to "Kitten," "Quiz" next to "Religion." Part of Moore's thesis is that fatherhood forces a man to confront enormous uncertainty and that there is often violence and strangeness in the natural world and in growing up male. The pattern, created by key words in alphabetical order, inspires the author to go places he couldn't have gone without the conceit; and the visual placement of the text on the page is original, evocative, and fresh.

PRACTICE

Thumb through this textbook. Which pieces are most inviting to read, in terms of pattern on the page? Least inviting? How does noticing what invites you as a reader inform how you think about pattern in your own works?

PRACTICE

Type out Naomi Shihab Nye's poem "Wedding Cake" (p. 336) as though it's prose, using paragraphs and allowing the lines to go all the way to the right-hand side of the page. Then take the first twelve lines or so of George Saunders's "Sticks" (p. 304), and create shorter lines, breaking the lines so that you have about two to twelve words on each line. Print out hard copies of the two pieces, and compare them to the originals. How does the new visual pattern affect your reading of the piece?

PRACTICE

Consider the following pattern decisions. What if Rick Moody's "Boys" (p. 212) was presented in stanzas, or sometimes in long paragraphs, sometimes in short? How would those pattern changes affect the meaning of the piece? Why do you think George Saunders uses only two paragraphs total in "Sticks" (p. 304)? How does this affect your reading of the piece, if at all?

Where a piece begins on the page, where the title is placed, where a piece ends on the page—all of these things affect the pattern, the way the words are presented. Experiment to find the best pattern for your piece. Question why you indent where you do, and be flexible when testing options. Don't settle for your first instinct. Play a little. We have text, and we have white space. How much pattern can you eke out of those two options without distracting or alarming your reader? As always, pattern supports, complements, and underscores the theme and purpose of the piece; pattern shouldn't try to take over. Good patterns enhance and support the meaning of creative writing.

LAYERING PATTERNS

Musicians like Jack White can write a song that repeats simple, everyday words.

> No one never
> No one never
> No one never
> Going to let you down now

> *It started as a lark and then became something beautiful.*
> — JACK WHITE

However, White also employs drums, marimba, and live sounds to create other intersecting and overlapping patterns. Super-simple lyrics repeat effectively in music, but less successfully as stand-alone poems on the page. Often, song lyrics have to be sharp, hard, clear, simple, and straightforward in order to show up against all the other patterns in music. On the page, on their own, the words lack energy. What makes a beautiful wild paisley in the ear is a thin gray line on the page.

Creative writers, not supported by a three-piece band, have to write the bass line, the percussion, the melody, *and* the lyrics. Paged words *need* a higher volume—more intricacy, subtle sounds, rhythms, visuals—than do sung words. To give our work proper backup, we writers layer patterns, using more than one at a time. Just like a musician does.

After you have recorded the vocals, you're back in the studio, mixing, laying down new tracks, focusing each time on certain elements—the bass line, the percussion—and that's very much like the work we will do with pattern. While playing with pattern, think of yourself as the "mix master" and look for echoes. If you have something you like in your piece, repeat it.

PRACTICE

Rick Moody, in "Boys" (p. 212), and Brian Doyle, in "Two Hearts" (p. 340), are examples of prose writers using sound, rhythm, and rhyme—patterns of language—in addition to physical pattern. Make a list for each piece, in which you list every element that is used as part of a pattern.

Notice how writers use the principles of tension to make their patterns work harder. In Rick Moody's "Boys," the author uses a list pattern, like a grocery list, to name the kind of grief—sibling loss—that can hardly be spoken of coherently, the kind of pain that is with you every day, that never goes away, but is as unlike a typical list item as you can get. We were running along, through our lives, the story suggests, and then the world broke into two pieces, and we were never the same again. Instead of using a matching pattern, Moody chooses a syntax pattern that works *against* the other patterns of the piece.

Using clashing patterns on purpose creates energy and intensity and can even allow you to discover insight into your own work. In the excerpt from *The Pharmacist's Mate* (p. 76), Amy Fusselman uses the journal entries of her dad to write the history of his life. When she puts snapshots of her own life next to his pieces, she doesn't get a history of his life, as we might expect; she gets glimpses into the future—hers.

It's *how* you say what you say that marks you as a successful writer. In creative writing, originality lies not in subject matter—it's unlikely you will be able to come up with a new subject—but rather in your prowess with pattern.

WRITING PROJECTS

1. Make a list of stuff in your favorite childhood store, or in a current location—a coffee shop, club, or dorm lounge—where you spend a lot of time. Write a piece of creative nonfiction in which you use the list of objects as a pattern to organize the piece.

2. Make a list of *kinds* of writing with which you are quite familiar: the strategy guide for *Zelda*; the Chilton's manual for your Subaru; a field guide to mushrooms; your chemistry textbook. Choose one, and write a piece *about something very different.* In other words, use the syntax and rhythm and patterns from one kind of writing, but write about something that has nothing

to do with the original subject matter. Your piece may be poetry, creative nonfiction, a play, or fiction.

3. Construct a story from gesture patterns. Write a story that uses the same gesture pattern (simplify as needed so that the first two sections would be "slow," "slow," and then "fast" for the third, etc.) as in "Bodies" (or another story of your or your instructor's choosing).

4. Take any poem or prose piece you have been working on this semester, and tune the sounds. Work in some near rhymes, echo words and sounds, and line up vowels and consonants. Read the new version aloud. What do your listeners think are the best parts of the piece?

5. Reread "af•ter•glow" by A. Van Jordan (p. 67). List all the patterns you can find in this piece. Then try a prose poem of your own, using a dictionary definition format, employing as many patterns as Jordan does.

6. Write a short piece (a poem, story, memoir, or prose poem) in which you use a lot of inverted syntax. Make your piece about a situation that is upside down, or tell it from a perspective that is the opposite of what we expect.

7. Write a dictionary on mother-daughterhood or father-sonhood, or sister- or brotherhood. Choose twenty-six words corresponding to the letters of the alphabet, just as Dinty Moore does in his essay on page 305, and blend personal reflection with research on your topic. You may choose to incorporate research from popular culture as well as Weird Science, or you may have other subjects you would like to pursue as you explore the full range of human experience in this area.

8. Write a pantoum, a villanelle, and a sonnet. Which pre-cut pattern do you like the best?

PATTERN WORKSHOP

The prompts below will help you constructively discuss your classmates' work.

1. Read your peer's work, and highlight or underline patterns of rhyme and echo in this piece.

2. Locate at least three repeated consonant patterns and three repeated vowel patterns that serve to unify the piece or emphasize words in a special way.

3. Comment on the rhythm in the piece. If the piece is poetry, does the poet use iambic pentameter? If the poet does not, rewrite one of the poem's lines,

    transforming it into iambic pentameter, making any changes you must in order to make the rhythm follow the pattern.

4. When you look at the work on the page, do you notice any interesting visual patterns? Any awkward widows or orphans, lines left stranded at the bottom or top of a page, or space breaks? Can you find places or ways the writer could rework the piece in order to make it more visually interesting?

5. List the objects referred to in the writing. Can you think of a way—either by substituting objects or by naming more specific, more specialized versions of the objects already named—to create a pattern? Do the same for the gestures (human movements). Is there a pattern? Is the work choreographed?

6. End by giving the writer whose work you are examining four concluding comments: Name two aspects of pattern in the piece that are well done, and name the two techniques from this chapter that the author should focus on in revision.

Gregory Orr

The River

I felt both pleasure and a shiver
as we undressed on the slippery bank
and then plunged into the wild river.

I waded in; she entered as a diver.
Watching her pale flanks slice the dark
I felt both pleasure and a shiver.

Was this a source of the lake we sought, giver
of itself to that vast, blue expanse?
We'd learn by plunging into the wild river

and letting the current take us wherever
it willed. I had that yielding to thank
for how I felt both pleasure and a shiver.

But what she felt and saw I'll never
know: separate bodies taking the same risk
by plunging together into the wild river.

Later, past the rapids, we paused to consider
if chance or destiny had brought us here;
whether it was more than pleasure and a shiver
we'd found by plunging into the wild river.

Randall Mann

Pantoum

If there is a word in the lexicon of love,
it will not declare itself.
The nature of words is to fail
men who fall in love with men.

It will not declare itself,
the perfect word. *Boyfriend* seems ridiculous:
men who fall in love with men
deserve something a bit more formal.

The perfect word? Boyfriend? Ridiculous.
But *partner* is . . . businesslike—
we deserve something a bit less formal,
much more in love with love.

But if partner is businesslike,
then *lover* suggests only sex,
is too much in love with love.
There is life outside of the bedroom,

and lover suggests only sex.
We are left with *roommate*, or *friend*.
There is life, but outside the bedroom.
My *friend* and I rarely speak of one another.

To my left is my roommate, my friend.
If there is a word in the lexicon of love,
my friend and I rarely speak it of one another.
The nature of words is to fail.

Laure-Anne Bosselaar
Stillbirth

On a platform, I heard someone call out your name:
No, Laetitia, no.
It wasn't my train—the doors were closing,
but I rushed in, searching for your face.

But no Laetitia. No.
No one in that car could have been you,
but I rushed in, searching for your face:
no longer an infant. A woman now, blond, thirty-two.

No one in that car could have been you.
Laetitia-Marie was the name I had chosen.
No longer an infant. A woman now, blond, thirty-two:
I sometimes go months without remembering you.

Laetitia-Marie was the name I had chosen:
I was told not to look. Not to get attached —
I sometimes go months without remembering you.
Some griefs bless us that way, not asking much space.

I was told not to look. Not to get attached.
It wasn't my train — the doors were closing.
Some griefs bless us that way, not asking much space.
On a platform, I heard someone calling your name.

George Saunders
Sticks

Every year Thanksgiving night we flocked out behind Dad as he dragged the Santa suit to the road and draped it over a kind of crucifix he'd built out of metal pole in the yard. Super Bowl week the pole was dressed in a jersey and Rod's helmet and Rod had to clear it with Dad if he wanted to take the helmet off. On Fourth of July the pole was Uncle Sam, on Veterans Day a soldier, on Halloween a ghost. The pole was Dad's one concession to glee. We were allowed a single Crayola from the box at a time. One Christmas Eve he shrieked at Kimmie for wasting an apple slice. He hovered over us as we poured ketchup, saying, Good enough good enough good enough. Birthday parties consisted of cupcakes, no ice cream. The first time I brought a date over she said, What's with your dad and that pole? and I sat there blinking.

We left home, married, had children of our own, found the seeds of meanness blooming also within us. Dad began dressing the pole with more complexity and less discernible logic. He draped some kind of fur over it on Groundhog Day and lugged out a floodlight to ensure a shadow. When an earthquake struck Chile he laid the pole on its side and spray-painted a rift in the earth. Mom died and he dressed the pole as Death and hung from the crossbar photos of Mom as a baby. We'd stop by and find odd talismans from his youth arranged around the base: army medals, theater tickets, old sweatshirts, tubes of Mom's makeup. One autumn he painted the pole bright yellow. He covered it with cotton swabs that winter for warmth and provided offspring by hammering in six crossed sticks around the yard. He ran lengths of string between the pole and the sticks, and taped to the string letters of apology, admissions of error, pleas for understanding, all written in a frantic hand on index cards. He painted a sign saying LOVE and hung it from the pole and another that said FORGIVE? and then he died in the hall with the radio on and we sold the house to a young couple who yanked out the pole and left it by the road on garbage day.

Dinty W. Moore

Son of Mr. Green Jeans:
An Essay on Fatherhood, Alphabetically Arranged

ALLEN, TIM

Best known as the father on ABC's *Home Improvement* (1991–99), the popular comedian was born Timothy Allen Dick on June 13, 1953. When Allen was eleven years old, his father, Gerald Dick, was killed by a drunk driver while driving home from a University of Colorado football game.

BEES

"A man, after impregnating the woman, could drop dead," critic Camille Paglia suggested to Tim Allen in a 1995 *Esquire* interview. "That is how peripheral he is to the whole thing."

"I'm a drone," Allen responded. "Like those bees."

"You are a drone," Paglia agreed. "That's exactly right."

CARP

After the female Japanese carp gives birth to hundreds of tiny babies, the father carp remains nearby. When he senses approaching danger, he sucks the helpless babies into his mouth, and holds them there until the coast is clear.

DIVORCE

University of Arizona psychologist Sanford Braver tells the story of a woman who felt threatened by her husband's close bond with their young son. The husband had a flexible work schedule but the wife did not, so the boy spent the bulk of his time with the father. The mother became so jealous of the tight father-son relationship that she filed for divorce, and successfully fought for sole custody. The result was that instead of being in the care of his father while the mother worked, the boy was now left in daycare.

EMPEROR PENGUINS

Once a male emperor penguin has completed mating, he remains by the female's side for the next month to determine if the act has been successful. When he sees a single greenish-white egg emerge from his mate's egg pouch, he begins to sing. Scientists have characterized his song as "ecstatic."

FATHER KNOWS BEST

In 1949, Robert Young began *Father Knows Best* as a radio show. Young played Jim Anderson, an average father in an average family. The show later moved to television, where it was a major hit, but Young's successful life was troubled by alcohol and depression.

In January 1991, at age 83, Young attempted suicide by running a hose from his car's exhaust pipe to the interior of the vehicle. The attempt failed because the battery was dead and the car wouldn't start.

GREEN GENES

In Dublin, Ireland, a team of geneticists is conducting a study to determine the origins of the Irish people. By analyzing segments of DNA from residents across different parts of the Irish countryside, then comparing this DNA with corresponding DNA segments from people elsewhere in Europe, the investigators hope to determine the derivation of Ireland's true forefathers.

HUGH BEAUMONT

The actor who portrayed the benevolent father on the popular TV show *Leave It to Beaver* was a Methodist minister. Tony Dow, who played older brother Wally, reports that Beaumont actually hated kids. "Hugh wanted out of the show after the second season," Dow told the *Toronto Sun*. "He thought he should be doing films and things."

INHERITANCE

My own Irish forefather was a newspaperman, owned a nightclub, ran for mayor, and smuggled rum in a speedboat during Prohibition. He smoked, drank, ate nothing but red meat, and died of a heart attack in 1938.

His one son, my father, was a teenager when my grandfather died. I never learned more than the barest details about my grandfather from my father, despite my persistent questions. Other relatives tell me that the relationship had been strained.

My father was a skinny, asthmatic, and eager-to-please little boy, not the tough guy his father had wanted. My dad lost his mother at age three, and later developed a severe stuttering problem, perhaps as a result of his father's disapproval. My father's adult vocabulary was outstanding, due to his need for alternate words when faltering over hard consonants like B or D.

The stuttering grew worse over the years, with one exception: after downing a few whiskeys, my father could sing like an angel. His Irish tenor became legend in local taverns, and by the time I entered the scene my father was spending every evening visiting the bars. Most nights he would stumble back drunk around midnight; some nights he was so drunk he would stumble through a neighbor's back door, thinking he was home.

As a boy, I coped with the family's embarrassment by staying glued to the television—shows like *Father Knows Best* and *Leave It to Beaver* were my favorites. I desperately wanted someone like Hugh Beaumont to be my father, or maybe Robert Young.

Hugh Brannum, though, would have been my first choice. Brannum played Mr. Green Jeans on *Captain Kangaroo*, and I remember him as being kind, funny, and extremely reliable.

JAWS

My other hobby, besides television, was an aquarium. I loved watching the tropical fish give birth. Unfortunately, guppy fathers, if not moved to a separate tank, will sometimes come along and eat their young.

KITTEN

Kitten, the youngest daughter on *Father Knows Best*, was played by Lauren Chapin.

LAUREN CHAPIN

Chapin's father molested her and her mother was a severe alcoholic. After *Father Knows Best* ended in 1960, Chapin's life came apart. At age sixteen, she married an auto mechanic. At age eighteen, she became addicted to heroin and began working as a prostitute.

MALE BREADWINNERS

Wolf fathers spend the daylight hours away from the home—hunting—but return every evening. The wolf cubs, five or six to a litter, rush out of the den when they hear their father approaching and fling themselves at their dad, leaping up to his face. The father backs up a few feet and disgorges food for them, in small, separate piles.

NATURAL SELECTION

When my wife Renita confessed to me her ambition to have children, the very first words out of my mouth were, "You must be crazy." Convinced that she had just proposed the worst imaginable idea, I stood from my chair, looked straight ahead, then marched out of the room.

OZZIE

Oswald Nelson, at thirteen, was the youngest person ever to become an Eagle Scout. Oswald went on to become Ozzie Nelson, the father in *Ozzie and*

Harriet. Though the show aired years before the advent of reality television, Harriet was Ozzie's real wife, Ricky and David were his real sons, and eventually Ricky and David's wives were played by their actual spouses. The current requirements for Eagle Scout make it impossible for anyone to ever beat Ozzie's record.

PENGUINS, AGAIN

The female emperor penguin "catches the egg with her wings before it touches the ice," Jeffrey Moussaieff Masson writes in his book *The Emperor's Embrace.* She then places it on her feet, to keep it from contact with the frozen ground.

At this point, both penguins will sing in unison, staring at the egg. Eventually, the male penguin will use his beak to lift the egg onto the surface of his own feet, where it remains until hatching.

Not only does the male penguin endure the inconvenience of walking around with an egg balanced on his feet for months, but he also will not eat for the duration.

QUIZ

1. What is Camille Paglia's view on the need for fathers?
2. Why did Hugh Beaumont hate kids?
3. Who played Mr. Green Jeans on *Captain Kangaroo*?
4. Who would you rather have as your father: Hugh Beaumont, Hugh Brannum, a wolf, or an emperor penguin?

RELIGION

In 1979, Lauren Chapin, the troubled actress who played Kitty, had a religious conversion. She credits her belief in Jesus with saving her life. After *his* television career ended, Methodist Minister Hugh Beaumont became a Christmas tree farmer.

SPUTNIK

On October 4, 1957, *Leave It to Beaver* first aired. On that same day, the Soviet Union launched Sputnik I, the world's first artificial satellite. Sputnik I was about the size of a basketball, took roughly 98 minutes to orbit the Earth, and is credited with starting the US-Soviet space race.

Later, long after *Leave It to Beaver* ended its network run, a rumor that Jerry Mathers, the actor who played Beaver, had died at the hands of the communists in Vietnam, persisted for years. The rumor was false.

TOILETS

Leave It to Beaver was the first television program to show a toilet.

USE OF DRUGS

The National Center on Addiction and Substance Abuse at Columbia University claims that the presence of a supportive father is irreplaceable in helping children stay drug-free.

Lauren Chapin may be a prime example here, as would Tim Allen, who was arrested for dealing drugs in 1978 and spent two years in prison.

The author of this essay, though he avoided his father's drinking problems, battled his own drug habit as a young man. Happily, he was never jailed.

VASECTOMIES

I had a vasectomy in 1994.

WARD'S FATHER

In an episode titled "Beaver's Freckles," the Beaver says that Ward had "a hittin' father," but little else is ever revealed about Ward's fictional family. Despite Wally's constant warning—"Boy, Beav, when Dad finds out, he's gonna clobber ya!"—Ward does not follow his own father's example, and never hits his sons on the show. This is an excellent example of xenogenesis.

XENOGENESIS

(zen'*u*-jen'*u*-sis), n. *Biol.* 1. heterogenesis 2. the supposed generation of offspring completely and permanently different from the parent.

Believing in xenogenesis—though at the time I couldn't define it, spell it, *or* pronounce it—I changed my mind about having children about four years after my wife's first suggestion of the idea. Luckily, this was five years before my vasectomy.

Y-CHROMOSOMES

The Y-chromosome of the father determines a child's gender, and is unique, because its genetic code remains relatively unchanged as it passes from father to son. The DNA in other chromosomes, however, is more likely to get mixed between generations, in a process called recombination. What this means, apparently, is that boys have a higher likelihood of inheriting their ancestral traits.

My Y-chromosomes were looking the other way, so my only child is a daughter. So far Maria has inherited many of what people say are the Moore family's better traits—humor, a facility with words, a stubborn determination. It is yet to be seen what she will do with the many negative ones.

ZAPPA

Similar to the "Beaver died in Vietnam" rumor of the 1960s and '70s, during the late 1990s, Internet chatrooms and discussion lists repeatedly recycled the news that the actor who played Mr. Green Jeans was the father of musician Frank Zappa. But in fact, Hugh Brannum had only one son, and he was neither Frank Zappa nor this author.

Sometimes, though, he still wonders what it might have been like.

CHAPTER EIGHT

INSIGHT

Literature is devoted to exploring the human experience, and as creative writers, we're constantly attempting to show our readers, with words, the subtle and complex drama of being human. We want to entertain our readers, yes, but we also want readers to learn and understand more about who we are as humans. This kind of work is an important aspect of the craft of writing, one often overlooked in manuals and craft books: insight. We read and write in order to *see into* the human condition.

A writer looks closely at his or her subjects, and in rendering people and topics with action and dialogue, pattern and image, the writer brings to light some of the more interesting features of human nature—why we do the things we do, why we avoid certain situations, why we repeat behaviors that are clearly counterproductive. Thus insight results not from "deep thoughts" or isolated genius but rather from a writer simply paying close attention to the world and to people. Insight essentially boils down to looking at people and situations and nature up close and in depth and then questioning what it is one sees. Things other people might pass right by are the source for writers' insights. Most people hurtle so quickly through life that they risk missing some of the more interesting aspects and conclusions one can draw. Writing slows us down, asks us to pay attention. Literature captures what is missed when we're rushing through.

Of course you can't take a piece in progress and just decide to make it more insightful. Wisdom doesn't work that way. In fact, if you try to "put in" insight, you might end up writing clichés, or oversimplifying what's complex and interesting in your work. But you can use some principles and techniques that will help you generate work that is complex, layered, thoughtful, and meaningful.

Remember that having survived childhood, you know a lot more about human nature than you might think. And a core part of your lifelong work as a writer is knowing how to bring the insights—your inner wisdom—up from within your soul and out onto the page, reflected in the images you present to your reader. As you work on the strategy of insight, you'll find your previous work with energy, tension, images, and pattern has already prepared you to look and listen and shape raw material into subtle, complex, meaningful writing that is necessary and long-lasting.

| PRACTICE |

Identify one of your favorite pieces included in this textbook. Write a short paragraph about the insight into human nature that this piece offers. Can you put into words the wisdom in the piece?

Another way to think about insight in creative writing is to recall what you've learned about reading in your literature courses. In creative writing, insight—depth—is what is most meaningful in a piece, and often it's what's most memorable. In literature courses, you may have reduced pieces to a "theme" or message—that's one approach to talking about insight, but not always the most helpful approach for writers. The matrix of insights in a single piece of literature is often complex and varied, and most writers find their way *to* insight, or theme, from working with images and characters. The idea that writers take a Big Concept and then illustrate it, using their characters to play out an idea, is something of a myth. "No ideas but in things," the poet and physician William Carlos Williams famously said, meaning that writers, like scientists, must look at what is before them and accurately lay down what they see, and that very process will be the idea, or meaning.

For example, Raymond Carver's short story "Cathedral" (p. 119) contains numerous insights, small and large, into how sighted people behave around the blind and how married people behave in general, resulting in wisdom about human growth and the potential for people to change their vision of the world. But this wisdom is always embedded in the characters, their action and dialogue, and the setting itself. *The Pharmacist's Mate* (excerpted on p. 76), Amy Fusselman's memoir, contains wisdom about asking profound and unanswerable questions about death, music, and fertility. She offers valuable, rarely heard observations about the wisdom of changing your mind, taking risks, and following your passions and inner wisdom. But these ideas came to her *during* her writing process, not in advance. Insight is created less by Thinking Deep Thoughts and more by writing. Paying attention + writing = insight.

In presenting her portrait of truants in "We Real Cool" (p. 101), the poet Gwendolyn Brooks presents insight into the romanticized attitudes toward death held by members of a gang. She doesn't talk about her subject; she has the subject itself speak. "No ideas but in things" or, in this case, people. And Marisa Silver's short story "What I Saw from Where I Stood" (p. 251) plays out hard-won insights into just how complex it is to be young, in love, living in a large city, and up against some of life's toughest questions—the action of the story illustrates her ideas. Gregory Orr focuses his poem "The River" (p. 302) around insights into the exact nature of desire, and the risk we take when we fall—or in this case leap—into love. Many people might not think there's much to learn from listening to truants or quirky, struggling English majors or skinny-dipping couples on the brink. Creative writers, however, believe that examining everyday human situations—no matter how superficial or weird or sensual or sad or hilarious they might appear to someone else—is of great value.

Good writers learn how to reenter the scenes and moments in their writing that might yield an insight, and they let the speakers and the characters in their work discover insights. Working with the strategy of insight is really just a matter of *practicing* noticing and recording in this new way: Creative writers are explorer-discoverers, finding insights as they work rather than working from conclusions and then using the work to illustrate canned or packaged ideas. Good writers don't sit down and come up with brilliant insights, sticking in bits of wisdom here and there throughout a piece of writing as though mixing gelled fruit into a fruitcake batter. For example, if you take six photographs of your mother, study them closely, work hard to render these images of her into language, and re-create scenes that reveal specific aspects of her, you will likely discover more than one or two insights about your mother. Parts of her personality will come into focus. The reasons that she does things the way she does might suddenly become clear. This is much more interesting for your reader than your deciding, in advance, "I will write an essay about my mother the control freak," and then proceeding to marshal evidence you have already decided will fit your thesis.

> *There is only one trait that marks the writer. He is always watching. It's a kind of trick of mind and he is born with it.*
> — MORLEY CALLAGHAN

Writing makes us wiser, and insight is a kind of dance between knowing what you want to say and letting the writing take you to a new place of discovery. As William Stafford writes in *Writing the Australian Crawl*:

A writer is not so much someone who has something to say as he is someone who has found a process that will bring about new things he would not have thought of if he had not started to say them. That is, he does not draw on a reservoir; instead he engages in an activity that brings to him a whole succession of unforeseen stories, poems, essays, plays.

PRACTICE

Examine the short story "White Angel" by Michael Cunningham (p. 341). What wisdom is directly stated in the piece? What insights are implied? Can you find wisdom in any of the dialogue? Do any lines in the story that are in the thoughts of the main character strike you as wise? Does the author include insights about how people behaved in this time and place? Try to come up with a list of ten insights from the story.

PRINCIPLES OF INSIGHT

When it comes to reading and writing for insight, writers rely on two principles: accuracy and generosity.

Accuracy

To employ the strategy of insight in your writing, you'll practice a kind of laser-like, dead-on accuracy in your observations and details. Comedian Jerry Seinfeld's television show *Seinfeld* was popular partly because Seinfeld and his friends on the show spent an enormous amount of time simply observing and then naming, with great precision, everyday things we experience all the time but never notice: the low talker, the close talker. That's in large part what "smart" is: accurate. Noticing tiny true things that everyone else glides by. Seeing closely. You don't have to be "deep." You just have to get it *exactly* right.

> *A writer's mind seems to be situated partly in the solar plexus and partly in the head.*
> — ETHEL WILSON

How? By paying close attention to your subject.

In your writing, strive for a kind of scientific accuracy (describing things exactly as they are) and psychological accuracy (presenting human behavior exactly as you see it, not slanting actions one way or the other to make a particular point). What you discover *by writing* will always be more revealing, more likely to produce insight than what you *think of ahead of time*. The image work you did in Chapter Four is the best way to practice insight. To allow the deeper insights to come to the surface, practice looking closely at scenes and settings, and pay particular attention to what you see. Simply listing what you see when you look at a place can result in a piece chock-full of insight, as in Bob Hicok's poem "A Primer" (p. 74), about exactly what it's like to experience spring after a long Michigan winter.

When you focus on accurately rendering just what you see, pay special attention to each of these areas: gestures and dialogue. Often, these are the places wisdom comes shining through.

Gestures. Actions speak louder than words. When you write about people, write from close up, and focus tightly on their gestures—how they move their bodies and what those gestures imply about what they want and how they are feeling. You want to focus on action—it's our behavior that reveals our character. What kind of things, large and small, do the people you are writing about do? How exactly do they do it, and what tiny distinctions do you notice between one person's little actions and another's way of doing the exact same thing? Focus less on facial expressions—wrinkled brows, crinkly smiles, and raised eyebrows—which almost everyone does roughly the same way to demonstrate feelings of worry, happiness, and disapproval. Focus on the way a father walks wildly down the aisle in the liquor store; the way a lonely, newly married woman calls to a small cat, using a high, silly voice; the way a baby—who will, the speaker imagines, someday be a bride—grabs and pulls the laminated safety card in the airplane seat back pocket. Gestures are the things we do that make up the fascinating texture of our individual lives; if you look closely and record, you'll likely create a layer of revelatory insight.

PRACTICE

Examine Mary Robison's "Pretty Ice" (p. 166). For the mother, the daughter, and her fiancé, make a list of two or three gestures—the physical behaviors of the characters—and how each reveals an insight into that person's psychology. For example, the mother honks the horn repeatedly. What insight into that kind of person does this gesture show? Will smokes the mother's cigarettes. What does that gesture perhaps reveal about his nature?

Dialogue. In addition to the insights that come from watching human behavior as closely and carefully as a scientist, you also find insight by listening to exactly how people talk. There's a kind of shorthand, faked dialogue that marks amateur creative writing: Avoid writing down what you *think* people sound like; instead, be like a reporter and capture the exact things people say. Rather than giving your characters lines, let them surprise you. Interview them. Your characters may or may not speak wisdom. But your reader will find your insights into human behavior compelling if you record the ways in which people say and misstate what they mean, often hiding what they really think. In Raymond Carver's "Cathedral" (p. 119), the wife says to the blind man, "I want you to feel comfortable." He replies that he is comfortable. That dialogue has wisdom in it. The author is using the dialogue to say something deeper about the blind man's character, our definitions of comfort, and surface social interactions. The blind man doesn't need anyone's help to feel at ease. He is deeply at ease in who he is. He is, truly, comfortable. It's the others who aren't, but they don't know it.

The reader gleans insight.

PRACTICE

Read Ernest Hemingway's "Cat in the Rain" (p. 337) several times. What do you notice the characters saying? In what ways does their dialogue provide insight into their character? Or choose any short story or essay and read it, focusing tightly on the dialogue. Do any spoken words mean more than what they say on the surface? Write a brief analysis of the dialogue lines that seem to you to contain a deeper wisdom, or resonance.

Generosity

Perhaps you used to write for yourself, and maybe you still do. But now you are doing something different: You now write for readers. Good writers are generous to their readers, creating work that flows and is clear and enjoyable to read, filled with surprises, careful observation, and precise word choices. But writers are generous to their characters and subjects as well. Good writers make sure they include compassion and complexity in each piece of writing. If a character is all good or all bad, the reader will probably rebel and perhaps even start to side with your villain, or turn against your shining angel girlfriend character because, frankly, no one is that perfect and she makes us sick. Give your villains some good qualities. Give your heroes a few small flaws, and at least one large one. We are all flawed.

If you write from "on high," hypercritical of everyone and everything you write about, showing humans only at their most petty, most violent, most unaware, you will likely not be writing lasting, insightful work. Recall Raymond Carver's story "Cathedral" (p. 119). Carver is generous in his insights. He shows Robert's annoying qualities as well as his good ones. He does the same for the wife and, most importantly, for the narrator. The narrator has a lot of limitations. But he has some good points, too. Carver explores all these angles. He's a master of tension, and he uses these tensions to draw conclusions—insights—about how human psychology works. We don't always act in ways that get us what we want. Sometimes, we can't see what's right in front of us. We put on acts, try to impress others, when really we are insecure, afraid. Carver, like any highly evolved human, is generous to the narrator. He sees the man's limitations as well as the context for those limitations. He shows the reader what the narrator is trying to do. When the narrator fails, Carver shows us his pain. He shows his humanity.

Smart writers seek to understand human flaws, see weakness and strength, and balance their description by looking at a moment from many sides. Even artists famous for a dark or despairing view of the world, such as Franz Kafka or Quentin Tarantino or Sylvia Plath, thread humor or compassion or earnest attempts at human connection into their work. They are generous with compassion and empathy. "If it could happen to you, it could happen to me." That's the basic premise of *generosity* in art, and that's why art connects us.

PRACTICE

Reread "Boys" by Rick Moody (p. 212). What are his insights into boys and families? Which insights are stated directly? What wisdom does he have about boys and maleness that is stated indirectly, that is found between the lines? Is Moody generous in his insights? That is, does he say, "Here are the flaws, but look at how, and why, and see the good, the complexity"?

PRACTICE

Reread "Buying Wine" by Sebastian Matthews (p. 69). Is he generous to the people in this poem? Not generous? What lines in the poem give the most insight into who these people are and what's important to them? Does Matthews try to understand human weakness and create insight into it, or does he judge? Something else altogether?

CULTIVATING INSIGHT

What follows are eight practical avenues to insight. You can use these insight techniques to improve pieces in progress, to start new pieces in any genre, to get unstuck, or just to build observational skills. You can mix and match the techniques, but it will be most helpful to try each one on its own, at least once. You can also use these techniques when you read in order to see how authors layer insight into their works. You can use these techniques to practice a writerly habit of mind — noticing tiny details, focusing on images, staying open to questions, toying with reversals — all conducive to building the muscles of close observation, strengthening your ability to uncover inner wisdom. The goal is to develop works of creative writing, works that are rich, innovative, observant, fresh, and smart. Experiment out of your comfort zone. You know a lot more than you think you do! The trick is finding ways to get your depth and your inner wisdom out onto the page.

Use Experience

Most writers, when they are starting out, feel they don't *know* enough to be considered Wise and Writerly. Even experienced writers doubt they have enough to say or important things to say. For most writers, the feeling of having something to say varies daily, even hourly. Often, on any day we feel empowered to write, when we sit down to create a scene, we feel dumb, blocked, empty. Pointless.

The most important thing a writer can do to develop wisdom and insight is to trust that if she pays attention to her own experience in the world, if she looks long enough at the very things in front of her and closely enough at her own life and the lives of those she knows, then she will have a fairly good chance of writing some interesting stuff. This method for cultivating insight doesn't mean you are stuck writing only from personal experience. It means you work from life, starting close to home, writing what you know intuitively and emotionally, and working out from there. An important caveat: Use your actual experience in your lived life. If you write about firefighters, based on watching shows about firefighters, the reader will probably be able to tell that this is not your firsthand experience. Unless you work from your experience or very detailed, in-depth research—which requires you to actually talk to firefighters and experience the emotions they do when actively involved in a crisis—chances are the work will be thin, clichéd, false, or all three. Viewing actors portraying characters is not the same as having your own experience.

Remember: You have been in relationships with all kinds of people—brilliant, limited, powerful, mean, beautiful, spiritual, petty, stupid. As a writer, you combine and recombine details and experiences from your life.

In fiction, you create composite characters, using a bit of Brenda's cocky attitude and mixing it with Sarah's prim bossiness, blending character traits to create a convincing person of your own invention on the page. Even as a child, you knew a great deal about how complicated human situations are, and as a writer you draw on all your experiences with death in order to write a story about loss and grief. Your characters aren't foreign to you; they're combinations of people you've known intimately over the years.

Maybe your life has been straightforward—nothing too terrible. Or maybe you have struggled mightily for years because of all kinds of circumstances beyond your control. Regardless, you know a lot about the depths of the human psyche because you have owned and operated one for some time now. From your lifelong study of humans in the world—your humans, on your street, in your circumstances—you *do* have something to say. Maybe you haven't read *Moby-Dick* or traveled to South America. Maybe you don't speak two, three, four languages or study ancient cultures. Maybe you have no idea what you want to be when you grow up. You don't need to know more than you know right now in order to get started on insight. The great writers of the world have simply focused very tightly on the insights they can glean from what is right before them: Zora Neale Hurston's African American Floridians north of Orlando, living their lives. Ernest Hemingway's kid up north in Michigan, fishing, hunting, falling in love. Jay McInerney's superficial, greedy New York City partiers. Amy Tan's mother-daughter struggles in a tightly knit Chinese American family. Great writers look at what's in front of them, instead of thinking that wisdom is out of reach.

Whether you are writing fiction, nonfiction, poems, plays, or essays, tell the truth of what you know the most about — minigolf employee subculture; surfer slackers on the Great Lakes where there are no real big waves, literally and metaphorically; dorm life in the midst of a massive *World of Warcraft* addiction. Tell, as close and finely as you possibly can, everything about the behind-the-scenes subcultures you know. Tell the secrets of the inner lives. Notice every tiny detail. Tell it all.

We are each called to speak the truth — share the wisdom — from our little corner of the world, saying *this is how people are here, this is what they do, this is how they react to this, here is how they're going to respond to that, and here's why.*

> *A writer's duty is to register what it is like for him or her to be in the world.*
>
> — ZADIE SMITH

You don't have to write from personal experience. But you probably do need to consider writing about what keeps you up at night. What to understand about what you don't know about what you do know.

PRACTICE

Examine Jessica Greenbaum's "A Poem for S." (p. 335). It's a complex poem, and you'll want to read it aloud and to read it several times. The poem was written to offer solace to the poet's friend, S., whose wife is very ill. What is the wisdom in this poem? How does Greenbaum try to get her own personal insights on suffering, religion, death, and hope across to the reader? If Greenbaum didn't have a specific friend in pain, could she have written a convincing poem on the topic? Do you think S. received solace from her poem?

PRACTICE

Revisit the list of topics you made in the second Practice on page 17 (or try this Practice now). Choose one you haven't tackled this semester, one that would be hard to write about because it would ask you to reveal quite a lot. Write for ten minutes, listing all the human actions and reactions you can "see" in your mind's eye on this topic.

Trust Images

Creative writing is all about providing readers with a sensory experience. When working on insight, go back to the core strategy that informs creative writing: creating images that work like moving pictures—little movies—in the reader's mind. Creative writing works through the five senses. We don't write in order to hit the reader over the head with The Deep Meaning; in fact, in this particular art form, we actually avoid writing about ideas. In creative writing, wisdom is lodged inside images, layered between experiences; it's seen and felt and touched. The most powerful way to cue the sensory world in your reader is to provide "moving pictures"—images, as you learned in Chapter Four—that will play out in the reader's mind and evoke insight.

When writing about an abstract situation, such as love or injustice or doubt, creative writers often use techniques such as personification to ground their message in concrete images. Take a close look at the poem "Another Lullaby for Insomniacs" by A. E. Stallings (p. 335). Read the poem out loud several times, and notice how sleep is portrayed here as a fickle lover—an actual person—who refuses to visit the speaker of the poem, leaving the poor person tossing and turning and filled with jealousy because elsewhere people *are* sleeping.

PRACTICE

Read "The Colonel" by Carolyn Forché (p. 185) aloud several times. In what ways does Forché use images—action and dialogue—to make arresting political observations in this prose poem? If she had spelled out her ideas about brutality and power, what would be gained? Lost?

PRACTICE

Write a short piece in which you take an abstract situation or a feeling or an emotion such as insomnia, jealousy, fear, or boredom. Turn the concept into a person, and set the two of you in a scenario where you struggle. The more specific you can make the person and the more detail you can offer on your fight, the better.

Ask Questions

Instead of *answering* big questions on the page, insightful creative writing often *poses* questions. Artists, like children, ask many questions—huge, ridiculous, sacred, amazing, inappropriate, tiny, potent, unanswerable questions. Creative writing often points to conclusions even as it resists coming up with pat answers.

Creative writing isn't afraid of a little mystery. Why your ex behaved that way isn't ever going to be revealed. It's just not. But looking closely at the how and why of the tension between the two of you may well generate something more useful and interesting for both you and your readers. Questions usually lead us closer to the truth, toward deeper insights, and into the realm of wisdom. Asking the right question—

You never know what you will learn 'til you start writing. Then you discover truths you never knew existed.
— ANITA BROOKNER

specific, targeted, precise—*is* wisdom. When writing pretends to have all the answers, readers often keep the work at arm's length. Certainty can close things down, end things too quickly, cut off the very curiosity that keeps us learning, moving us toward insight. In fact, asking the right questions is often wiser—and more difficult, truth be told—than coming up with answers.

Getting in the habit of questioning—staying open to not knowing longer and longer—gives you a direct line to your innate wisdom. Practice letting your work pose small pointed questions, as well as giant life-mystery questions, so the reader remains engaged, active, surprised, and wondering right along with you. The secret here is to make sure your questions take place from within images—in scenes, in real places at real points of time.

Instead of having "great ideas" or answers for writing projects, get in the habit of asking questions about human behavior and motivation.

Asking good questions requires you to develop a habit of paying close attention to exactly what you were wondering at an exact moment. This takes time and practice, but you can do it just as well as anyone else—just ignore the uncomfortable feelings that will come when you first give it a try.

Good questions are usually not the first ones you think of. Use listing as your technique—before, during, and after writing—in order to generate insight-bearing questions. Wise questions often come in clusters—not freewriting, not thinking out loud, but a calculated, forceful deepening of the narrator's hopes and considerations.

The role of the writer is not to say what we can all say, but what we are unable to say.
— ANAÏS NIN

Instead of recording your feelings in your journal, get in the habit of keeping a writer's notebook in which you ask questions. You can use this notebook to explore the questions that keep you up at night. What is the nature of your father's essential personality, and what of that—good and bad—have you inherited? Why do we drive too fast, drink too much, act irresponsibly? What motivates us? Why do we keep dating *the same wrong person*? Why is doing the wrong thing sometimes *pleasurable*? Asking questions that don't have easy answers—or possibly any answers at all—is a great reason to start a piece of writing.

Writers spend time asking questions. We're the ones who pause on the street and say, "Wait. Stop. Did you notice that? Do you wonder why?"

PRACTICE

Read Brian Doyle's memoir "Two Hearts" (p. 340). The author asks a question in the piece, but many other questions are implied. Make two lists—one of overt questions and one of implied questions. In what ways do the questions the piece raises generate insight?

PRACTICE

Set your timer for ten minutes. By hand, quickly write a list of every single question that has crossed your mind in the past twenty-four hours. Leap from big questions (*Is there a God?*) to mundane ones (*Will I eat pizza for dinner?*) to ultra-personal to ultra-serious to wildly crazy questions. Type up your list, and if you share lists with a classmate, discuss the questions on the lists. Are any insights or wisdom implied in this list?

Go Cold

To allow the insight in your work to emerge, trying pulling back on writing about emotion directly.

In an essay she wrote for Brevitymag.com on the writer's craft, author Dylan Landis notes: "Early drafts (at least mine) and student writing are often marked by descriptions of strong feeling. Characters gaze at each other with overt love. They feel proud, ashamed, joyous and heartbroken, and the writers come out and say so. What could be wrong with that?" She goes on to describe how the great short story writer and playwright Anton Chekhov critiqued another author, telling her not to overwrite the emotions and feelings in her work. Chekhov said, "When you describe the miserable and unfortunate, and want to make the reader feel pity, try to be somewhat colder—that seems to give a kind of background to another's grief, against which it stands out more clearly. Whereas in your story the characters cry and you sigh. Yes, be more cold."

You've heard this before because it's another way of understanding *show, don't tell*. "Going cold" means that the more intense the emotion is, the less intense the writing should be. Going cold means that at moments of high emotional intensity the author actually pulls back on the writing itself so that the reader has more room to feel.

Landis explains: "The writer Tony Earley offers his writing students a numerical scale that illustrates the be-more-cold principle. He actually draws it on the blackboard: two vertical lines, each scored with markings from one to ten. One scale represents the character's expression of emotion, and the other, the reader's depth of feeling. It works like this: The total of the two scales must equal not twenty, but ten — always ten. This means only one person gets to do all the emoting: the character or the reader. The writer can't have it both ways."

Here's the scale with which you can measure the level of emotional intensity in your writing.

Intensity of Emotion Felt by Characters	Amount of Emotion Described by the Author
1	1
2	2
3	3
4	4
5	5
6	6
7	7
8	8
9	9
10	10

Remember: The total of any one piece of writing should equal ten — no more. So if you are writing about your adoration of potato chips and how fantastic your life is because of this invention of fried bits of spud, your language can go over the top and be filled with heat and energy — we'll laugh and have strong feelings of delight; that's your purpose.

But if you are writing about something very intense — falling in love or the death of your grandmother, probably an eight, nine, or ten on the scale — you can't have much emotional writing, if any at all — no sighing, no hugging, no crying, no sobbing, no lament. When you are writing about deeply emotional experiences, it's helpful to refer back to the lessons in Chapter Four, Images, where you learned how to write from your body, using real space and real time. When you write a highly charged emotional moment, you want to hew closely to what it was like to live the moments, how it looked from the outside. You write about how the streets looked on your way to the wake that afternoon, the broken mailboxes, the little kids on scooters in front of her house, how one had no shirt on and another one was poking a stick into the ground. You write about a mourner's wrinkled shirt at the service. You write about your fingernails — what bad shape they were in that day — and how the cheese on the casseroles had dried into a crust and seemed impenetrable. No tears. Nothing predictable. Nothing overtly emotional. When you go cold, you can trust your reader to get it, to get the power of all the emotion. At a funeral, we aren't only thinking, "Gosh, I am so very, very sad and miserable." We are actually noticing the details of the day, and strange little things capture our attention and stick with us. Going cold actually gives a better window into what a character actually experienced, and those experiences are what provoke emotion in your reader.

Let your reader, not your pages, have the emotions.

| PRACTICE |

Focus on an emotionally intense event: a car accident or a wedding, a distraught friend or a particularly fantastic time with your friends. List as many physical and sensory details from the event as you can remember. Now pick the ones you might use when "going cold" in writing about the event.

Some telltale signs indicate that you might be overwriting the emotion (going hot) and not trusting your reader to feel her own feelings as she reads your work. If you write about people sighing, crying, frowning, shrugging, or if you use flowery abstractions or heated, florid language — words like *devastated, sobbed, confused, upset, abandoned, inflamed, ravaged, exhausted, pulsating* or emotional language such as *crying, weeping, sighing, pissed* — try going cold. Using simple words, describe the place where this is happening. Write down exactly what the doctor said, and how he looked and what he wore. Compare your two efforts. Is one stronger?

If you are using clichés to describe heavy emotions — *she shuddered with fear, tears streamed down his cheeks, he fell to his knees* — you are probably ready to try going cold.

| PRACTICE |

Read "How to Touch a Bleeding Dog" by Rod Kessler (p. 250). Circle the words that refer to emotions. Apply the "going cold" scale: On a scale of one to ten, how much emotion is on the page in this piece? Then determine how much emotion is in the reader *because* the language is so pulled back and controlled. Is the total of the two numbers ten or less?

PRACTICE

Apply the "going cold" scale to Carolyn Forché's "The Colonel" (p. 185) and Brian Doyle's "Two Hearts" (p. 340). Assign a number to the quality of the language and to the intensity of emotion evoked by the piece. Now use the scale on some of your own pieces of writing. Do you think you need to write more emotion or less?

Reverse Course

Writing that lacks insight is usually flat and predictable writing. A simple strategy for adding a shot of insight to your writing is to be purposefully and boldly counterintuitive: Reverse yourself. Take what you wrote, and say the opposite. Let's say your poem opened this way:

> I struggle to say
> How I feel each morning
> When you awake next to me

Using the reversal technique, you'd write something like this:

> I don't struggle to say
> What I didn't feel last night
> When I slept away from myself

Which version is fresher and more surprising? Which version is more engaging? Often, the reverse version is more fun, livelier, more unexpected, and perhaps wiser. There is something intriguing about that notion of "sleeping away from oneself." The writer can ask herself, "What does that mean?" Perhaps it means that the relationship she is writing about takes her too far away from her core self, who she really is. Maybe she likes who she is when she spends the night with this person, but maybe she doesn't. Or maybe she's talking about the profound loneliness she feels when she is alone or, even worse, with someone but still feeling really alone. The reverse opens up possibilities. And in possibility, there is almost always an arrow pointing toward insight.

PRACTICE

Online, find Stefanie Wortman's poem "Mortuary Art." Highlight each of the reversals. In what ways does she "go cold"?

PRACTICE

Take a piece you wrote earlier in the semester. Copy over each line, but this time, say the opposite. Bring both versions to your writing group. Is one more successful? Can you use some lines in the reverse version to strengthen the original?

Go Big

Above, you experimented with reversing your field. Now try making your canvas enormous, epic. Go Big. Super-Big. Grounding your work in the great continuum of history can help you discover the fresh, deep wisdom that is in you, even though you are just a simple lad from Coldwater, Michigan, and your childhood wasn't bad. To snag a riveting insight, you may have to exaggerate your position, or change your stance, so that you aren't standing where everyone stands—at eye level, at a safe distance—seeing what everyone can plainly see. Going big means that you pull the camera lens back, way back, in space and in time, and you consider the decades and centuries of history that are behind your piece of writing. You consider the location of your piece, and you see the big picture that frames the events you're looking at.

Your creative writing is situated in a context. No matter how small, how sleepy, how "regular" your place may seem, events there take place against a backdrop that has historical, political, and cultural implications. Setting your memoir or story or poetry in the context where you live is a powerful and perhaps necessary task for every writer. Don't be fooled into thinking your place doesn't have historical significance. Every place has a past, and that past, when rendered with detail and insight and passion, is potentially fascinating. Don't be intimidated by what you don't know: Few people take the time to look into their own history or the history of the place where they now live. To bring insight into your work, go epic. Consider how the current story you're focused on interacts with (contradicts or mirrors) the history of the people in this place where you are situated.

"White Angel" by Michael Cunningham (p. 341) provides a great example of how authors use cultural context to deepen and enrich the insight readers can find in their works. Here the author uses the cultural backdrop of the 1960s to provide a metaphor for the chaos and breakdown and loss and heartbreak in the family in his story, as well as in the individual character of the younger brother.

PRACTICE

Reread "White Angel" (p. 341). List the "big" parts of the story. How are the larger references to history and culture metaphors for the individual experiences in the story?

Surprise Yourself

Your wisdom is in you, deep inside, often lurking just under the busy thoughts you walk around with all day. Since insight is in you, actively "looking inside" to let that quieter wisdom emerge usually works. Sometimes writers find that when they try to be "wise," they get lucky; more often, however, they end up sounding hollow, shallow, or pat. You need to have some strategies for sneaking up on the vault inside you where your wisdom rests, protected. Often, it's when you don't know what you are about to say that the deeper, more arresting truth comes out on the page. You can use several techniques to sneak up on your own insight, to spring a trap to release the gold that is in you.

Write by hand using the hand you don't normally write with. This is a great way to surprise yourself with what you know, deeply. Take an image you'd like to pursue or revise a piece that isn't working by writing it, slowly, with your non-dominant hand. Some students have had great luck by having one character (or part of self) ask a question in writing, using the dominant hand; then another character answers the questions, using the nondominant hand. It's important to keep your hand moving, to not stop and think.

Reversals and questions, discussed above, are both excellent techniques for forcing yourself to go to unexpected places in your writing. It sounds counter-intuitive: saying the opposite of what you think you want to say and using questions instead of answers. But your writing can become much more interesting and fresh by playing with these two techniques. Your task is to develop a variety of methods for letting the front mind wander off so that the deeper mind can come forward and surprise you. No surprise for the writer, no surprise for the reader, Robert Frost famously said.

Similarly, fill-in-the blank activities (like the one you did in Chapter Two with "Genealogy") let you move fast so you have less control over what you want to say. This exercise often works best if your teacher reads the prompts and you have only about one minute to write—no time to think, just let your pencil do what it wants to do. If you are forced to write quickly by hand, you'll surprise yourself.

This is a good time to try Writing Project 13 on page 332. Don't read the prompts ahead of time—you want to sneak up on yourself. Have your teacher or a writing partner read the prompts. Be sure to write fast—don't worry if you get behind or miss a few. The point is to rush, to keep your hand moving.

Create Subtext

The text is what's on the surface in a piece of writing. The subtext is what is beneath the surface. In good writing, the writer works hard to choose words that can be interpreted more than one way, words that come with a weight and depth, with a lot of substance beneath the top layer. Imagine an iceberg, part of it poking above the surface of the sea but most of it submerged. An insightful piece of writing almost always has subtext. All genres of creative writing use subtext, as do songs, dinner conversations, and political negotiations. You're well served, as a writer but also as a human, to hone your ability to pay attention to what's being said and also to what's *really* being said.

If a writer knows enough about what he is writing about, he may omit things that he knows. The dignity of movement of an iceberg is due to only one-ninth of it being above water.
— ERNEST HEMINGWAY

The opening of Mary Robison's short story "Pretty Ice" (p. 166) provides a compelling example of subtext.

I was up the whole night before my fiancé was due to arrive from the East—drinking coffee, restless and pacing, my ears ringing. When the television signed off, I sat down with a packet of the month's bills and figured amounts on a lined tally sheet in my checkbook. Under the spray of a high-intensity lamp, my left hand moved rapidly over the touch tablets of my calculator.

Belle, the narrator, is waiting for her fiancé's visit. She doesn't seem romantic, relaxed, or happy. She's anxious. She's doing her bills. She's *taking account*. Subtext means that whatever your characters are doing, there's an implied metaphor. What they're doing is interesting on the surface. But it's also interesting beneath the surface. What isn't Belle doing? Sleeping. Shaving her legs. Getting the apartment ready so it's nice for her fiancé. Because there is a gap between her behavior and what we expect her behavior to be, we wonder about the subtext. *Why is she restless and pacing? Does she have money worries? Does she love this guy for the right reasons? Maybe she's just anxious. But why?*

Providing subtext is one powerful way authors illuminate their writing with insight. In the next paragraph of "Pretty Ice," Belle's mother arrives. There's been an ice storm. Her mother honks. (Subtext: The mother is impatient, thoughtless, and oblivious—it's 6:15 in the morning. What does that say about her daughter? About their relationship? Why isn't the daughter—a grown woman—driving herself to pick up her fiancé?) We see that Belle has a very expensive ivory Mont Blanc pen. Money worries. Expensive pen. We learn that she hasn't gotten ready for her fiancé's arrival—she hasn't slept, she doesn't shower. Strange. Kind of awful. The story unfolds, and nine-tenths of the story is subtext. We are able to gather a lot of information and insight by paying careful attention to what's beneath the surface, all of which the author has carefully placed there, palpable though just out of view.

PRACTICE

Study "Magnolia" by Ely Shipley (p. 160). Do you find any examples of subtext in the poem?

PRACTICE

Read the excerpt from Charlotte Glynn's "Duct Tape Twins" (p. 218). Find three to five examples of subtext in the dialogue. How does the writing reveal a surface level and a deeper level?

THREE TIPS

When you are working with insight as a strategy for your creative writing, try to avoid a few common pitfalls. Literature isn't a code; it isn't designed to hold hidden meanings that torture readers. And poems aren't soapboxes; essays aren't sermons; short stories aren't propaganda pieces. Close observation generates meaning. If you follow your images, hew closely to accuracy, and steer toward empathy, your work will be insightful and rich. Sometimes, however, without even realizing it, we preach, overwrite, or neglect to respect our readers' intelligence. Here are the three most common ways writers fail to serve their readers, and what to do instead.

1. **Avoid preaching.** If you center your story, poem, or play on a single idea, from a single vantage point (abortion should be legal, homelessness is bad), you are likely writing a sermon or a position paper. Didactic writing—writing that instructs the reader—is not creative writing. Pontificating is the opposite of what art intends to do. Creative writing teaches by showing people involved in actions, from very close up, so that the reader sees things about her or his own life simply by watching these moments and overhearing the dialogue. The less the writer states directly, the more powerful the creative writing. It's not effective to have a character in a play or a speaker in a poem expound an idea you love or dislike—there's not enough tension to hold the reader's interest for long, unless perhaps she agrees with you, and then what's the point?

   UNWISE   Your personal diatribe on the conflict in Syria (You've never been there, but you read a lot online.)

   WISE   A poem from the point of view of a soldier-friend of yours, who is struggling with how to act back here at home. The scene takes place while the two of you are shooting pool at the local pub, and you capture her actual dialogue and the reactions of others who were there that night.

2. **Avoid overwriting.** Do not use overly poetic or writerly diction. If you are writing in order to sound smart or be "poetic" by using lots of words you don't normally use in conversation, trying to sound lofty, trying too hard to be difficult and complex, you will sound amateurish, not wise.

If you are writing in a flowery or fancy way, readers may conclude that you are trying to be ironic or funny. If they read you at all. Pretentious is the opposite of wise.

UNWISE   "It's been a long and winding road, this life I've lived, with ups and downs and ins and outs, terrible troubles, and truly amazing, wildly stupendous, drug-induced, God-seeing mind benders. I'm a seeker, a lover, a poet, and a cluster of consciousness the likes of which no one has ever seen!"

WISE   "We lived then in Cleveland, in the middle of everything. It was the sixties—our radios sang out love all day long." (Michael Cunningham, "White Angel," p. 341)

PRACTICE

Make a list of the words or phrases you see only in poems, never anywhere else. You might include words such as *azure*, *crimson*, *quavering*, *morn*, *tear-stained*, *emoting*, *wanderlust*, and *yearning*. Make it a habit to avoid these words in your writing.

---

3. **Avoid stating the obvious.** Treat your reader as a smart, informed, savvy person. Readers want to figure things out. They want to come up with multiple interpretations of events—just as we do in real life.

UNWISE   A poem about life written in general statements, so obvious as to be almost meaningless:

> Life is a mystery
> We do not know why
> We struggle so much
> And then we die.

WISE   Jessica Greenbaum's poem "A Poem for S." or A. E. Stallings's poem "Another Lullaby for Insomniacs." Each time you read one of these poems, you consider the questions a little more, a little differently; every reader has a unique reaction to the poem, different "answers." There's more than one meaning.

> *The most important thing in a work of art is that it should have a kind of focus, i.e., there should be some place where all the rays meet or from which they issue. And this focus must not be able to be completely explained by words.*
> — LEO TOLSTOY

Whether you are young, old, book smart, street smart, or none of these, you know a lot about how art and literature operate, and you know a lot about people, situations, how they change, what's important. Don't think too much—you'll likely end up in a rut. Write, focusing your energy and attention wholly on the action and the dialogue, the details of the setting, what people do and what they say, and where they are. Most published writers actually claim that their writing is smarter than they are. If you focus on images, you will find your wisdom. Trust that you have a reservoir of untapped genius in you—because you do.

WRITING PROJECTS

1. Write a scene from your life where you made a mistake—small or large. Show no mercy. Show yourself completely wrecking things, behaving badly; it's all your fault. Present other people in the scene in their best light—show them as helpful, concerned versions of themselves, while sticking to the truth. Highlight the bad in you and the good in those around you. Next, reverse. Write a completely opposite version of the scene. Write about the same screwup, which was in fact your fault, but present the details, setting, action, and dialogue (stick to the truth) that explains why you did this thing. Present yourself as a hero who made a small mistake in service of the greater good, or who was tricked, or trapped, or victimized by circumstances, a bad childhood—whatever the case may be. In this second version, present all the negative gestures, speech, action, stuff, and habits of the other people in this scene. Share both. Which one is closer to the real truth? Which one is more popular with your readers or listeners? Is the truth somewhere in the middle?

2. Write a poem that is a list of questions. Make sure each of your questions is surprising, fresh, unexpected. Try to include images—specifics, concrete words—in as many of the questions as you can. If you use images, you will likely find that your questions are smarter than you are. Try to steer toward the questions that are in front of us every day, but that few people slow down enough to really notice or articulate. If you know small kids, incorporate into your poem some of the questions you overhear them posing; listen closely and get the quotes exactly. Let your poem be at least twenty lines long.

3. Write a piece, set at dinner, in which a couple is breaking up. Never mention the breakup. Weight each action and detail and the dialogue so that even though the couple appears to be talking about the soup or salt or whatever, nearly every line has subtext. Though it's never stated, just like in Mary Robison's "Pretty Ice" (p. 166), we know they'll never see each other again.

4. Write a poem, a story, or an essay in which someone's question to you or the speaker changes everything you think. One caveat: You can't tell us how your thinking changed—you can show us only your interaction with the person before, during, and after The Question. Leave it to the reader to figure out what changed.

5. Write a prose poem, in the vein of Carolyn Forché's "The Colonel" (p. 185), in which the way someone behaves at a meal shows us surprising things about his or her life and true nature.

6. Using a piece you have worked on in this class, move in closer in every line, every sentence, using your image-creating skills to see more closely, to present more tiny details with greater accuracy.

7. Write a piece about something very emotionally intense—a death, a breakup—but use absolutely no emotion. In plain, almost flat language, describe the events and the setting. Go completely cold.

8. Write a poem called "I Don't Love You, ____," and fill in the person's name. List everything that annoys you about this person. All of his or her quirks. Or choose someone very annoying from your childhood, and title it "I Don't Hate You, ____." List everything annoying about the person, focusing on the tiniest aspects and nothing large.

9. Write a list poem of questions, reversing all the common questions people ask about love. Or choose any topic that lends itself readily to cliché— relationships, God, sunsets—and write a piece about twenty lines or sentences long, all in questions, with no clichés.

10. Write a poem or micro-memoir, like Naomi Shihab Nye's "Wedding Cake" (p. 336), in which you encounter a stranger and have an interaction. Focus on the tiny details and actions in that encounter, and ask at least four questions, musing perhaps on the truth of what you do wonder about regarding this person who has momentarily crossed your path. Consider an encounter on an airplane or a train.

11. Create two characters, completely invented, based on no one you have ever known and as far from your own personal self as you can get. Create a scene set in a place that you've actually never been—a battlefield, a hospital, a ship—and that you know very little about firsthand. Then write a scene based on what happened to you, exactly, the last time you ate with friends. Compare the two.

12. Take a truism ("Look before you leap" or "Power tends to corrupt, and absolute power corrupts absolutely") and write a piece, using concrete details, dialogue, and images/scenes, that proves the truism false.

13. The following prompts are based on an exercise created by Jim Simmerman that appears in *The Practice of Poetry* by Robin Behn and Chase Twichell.

Don't read the prompts ahead of time—have someone read them aloud to you as you write, without stopping writing. Work quickly. The prompt reader should allow only one minute before going on to the next prompt. If you get behind, don't worry. It's fine to skip. Just catch up when you can. It's important that you go fast and not think about what you are going to say. Planning out your answers is *wrong* in this activity. Leaping randomly, inviting silliness, going all over the place—that is what you are trying to do! You are writing twenty-two miniature individual poems. Don't try to connect them. Just write. When you are finished, read your entire poem aloud (this works well as a class activity). What do you notice?

1. Start the poem by begging for something tiny that you really, really, really want. Something you will probably never get.

2. Write "With one eye closed, I see _____. With the other eye closed, I see _____, _____, and wild _____."

3. Ask God (or the Creator or Earth) two questions.

4. Ask a question about your dinner this evening.

5. Tell an outrageous lie about yourself.

6. Tell an outrageous lie about your family.

7. Tell something tiny, weird, and true about yourself, something no one knows.

8. Directly apologize to someone, using the person's name, for something you have never apologized for, ever. But you did this thing.

9. Write "I love you, _____, and you are not even _____, _____, or _____."

10. Say something about your relationship with the person you are most in love with right now, something that makes absolutely no sense at all.

11. Mangle a proverb. (For example: *A rolling stone gathers no moss* becomes *A gallivanting raindrop loses kangaroo pouches.*)

12. Write the opposite of any one of the eleven lines above.

13. Speaking as your writing instructor, lavish praise on yourself. Use your name or the nickname he or she has for you.

14. Standing on the roof of your elementary school, speak the truth to someone you always wanted to confront. Yell your truth to this person, who can't see you. Yell it all, and use his or her name.

15. Include a snippet of song lyrics that always get stuck in your head.

16. Talk baby talk to yourself.

17. Include another snippet of song lyrics that always get stuck in your head. This can be from the same song as in number 15.

18. Confess a crush you have had or now have. Use a nickname or code name for this person. Tell this crush what you secretly love so much.

19. Proclaim, loudly, two things you will never do. One is a lie.

20. Answer with your *nondominant* hand the questions you asked in number 3.

21. Repeat any line in the poem.

22. Answer with your *dominant* hand the questions you asked in number 3.

INSIGHT WORKSHOP

The prompts below will help you read and discuss your classmates' work.

1. In the student piece you are reading, try to highlight two examples of accuracy, places where the writer names something small that we take for granted or just don't notice because we don't pay close enough attention.

2. Try to find two examples of generosity, where the writer shows both the good and the bad, or at least two different sides, in a character, speaker, or situation.

3. Underline passages where the writer asks questions that are then left unanswered. Or suggest places where questions could be used to provoke insight.

4. Identify a passage where the writer uses, or could use, the "going cold" technique.

5. Identify a place where the author uses subtext or could try using more subtext.

6. Identify any passages in the student's work that preach, overexplain, state the obvious, or sound grandiose or forced, as though the writer is trying too hard and not trusting his or her own voice and inner wisdom.

7. Identify your favorite piece of insight in this piece.

READINGS

Jessica Greenbaum
A Poem for S.

Because you used to leaf through the dictionary,
Casually, as someone might in a barber shop, and
Devotedly, as someone might in a sanctuary,
Each letter would still have your attention if not
For the responsibilities life has tightly fit, like
Gears around the cog of you, like so many petals
Hinged on a daisy. That's why I'll just use your
Initial. Do you know that in one treasured story, a
Jewish ancestor, horseback in the woods at Yom
Kippur, and stranded without a prayer book,
Looked into the darkness and realized he had
Merely to name the alphabet to ask forgiveness —
No congregations of figures needed, he could speak
One letter at a time because all of creation
Proceeded from those. He fed his horse, and then
Quietly, because it was from his heart, he
Recited them slowly, from *aleph* to *tav*. Within those
Sounds, all others were born, all manners of
Trials, actions, emotions, everything needed to
Understand who he was, had been, how flaws
Venerate the human being, how aspirations return
Without spite. Now for you, may your wife's
X-ray return with good news, may we raise our
Zarfs to both your names in the Great Book of Life.

A. E. Stallings
Another Lullaby for Insomniacs

Sleep, she will not linger:
She turns her moon-cold shoulder.
With no ring on her finger,
You cannot hope to hold her.

She turns her moon-cold shoulder
And tosses off the cover.
You cannot hope to hold her:
She has another lover.

She tosses off the cover
And lays the darkness bare.
She has another lover.
Her heart is otherwhere.

She lays the darkness bare.
You slowly realize
Her heart is otherwhere.
There's distance in her eyes.

You slowly realize
That she will never linger,
With distance in her eyes
And no ring on her finger.

Naomi Shihab Nye
Wedding Cake

Once on a plane
a woman asked me to hold her baby
and disappeared.
I figured it was safe,
our being on a plane and all.
How far could she go?

She returned one hour later
having changed her clothes
and washed her hair.
I didn't recognize her.

By this time the baby
and I had examined
each other's necks.
We had cried a little.
I had a silver bracelet
and a watch.
Gold studs glittered
in the baby's ears.

She wore a tiny white dress
leafed with layers
like a wedding cake.

I did not want
to give her back.

The baby's curls coiled tightly
against her scalp,
another alphabet.
I read *new new new*.
My mother gets tired.
I'll chew your hand.

The baby left my skirt crumpled,
my lap aching.
Now I'm her secret guardian,
the little nub of dream
that rises slightly
but won't come clear.

As she grows,
as she feels ill at ease,
I'll bob my knee.

What will she forget?
Whom will she marry?
He'd better check with me.
I'll say once she flew
dressed like a cake
between two doilies of cloud.
She could slip the card into a pocket,
pull it out.
Already she knew the small finger
was funnier than the whole arm.

Ernest Hemingway

Cat in the Rain

There were only two Americans stopping at the hotel. They did not know any of the people they passed on the stairs on their way to and from their room. Their room was on the second floor facing the sea. It also faced the public garden and the war monument. There were big palms and green benches in the public garden.

In the good weather there was always an artist with his easel. Artists liked the way the palms grew and the bright colors of the hotels facing the gardens and the sea.

Italians came from a long way off to look up at the war monument. It was made of bronze and glistened in the rain. It was raining. The rain dripped from the palm trees. Water stood in pools on the gravel paths. The sea broke in a long line in the rain and slipped back down the beach to come up and break again in a long line in the rain. The motor cars were gone from the square by the war monument. Across the square in the doorway of the café a waiter stood looking out at the empty square.

The American wife stood at the window looking out. Outside right under their window a cat was crouched under one of the dripping green tables. The cat was trying to make herself so compact that she would not be dripped on.

"I'm going down and get that kitty," the American wife said.

"I'll do it," her husband offered from the bed.

"No, I'll get it. The poor kitty out trying to keep dry under a table."

The husband went on reading, lying propped up with the two pillows at the foot of the bed.

"Don't get wet," he said.

The wife went downstairs and the hotel owner stood up and bowed to her as she passed the office. His desk was at the far end of the office. He was an old man and very tall.

"Il piove," the wife said. She liked the hotel-keeper.

"Si, Si, Signora, brutto tempo. It is very bad weather."

He stood behind his desk in the far end of the dim room. The wife liked him. She liked the deadly serious way he received any complaints. She liked his dignity. She liked the way he wanted to serve her. She liked the way he felt about being a hotel-keeper. She liked his old, heavy face and big hands.

Liking him she opened the door and looked out. It was raining harder. A man in a rubber cape was crossing the empty square to the café. The cat would be around to the right. Perhaps she could go along under the eaves. As she stood in the doorway an umbrella opened behind her. It was the maid who looked after their room.

"You must not get wet," she smiled, speaking Italian. Of course, the hotel-keeper had sent her.

With the maid holding the umbrella over her, she walked along the gravel path until she was under their window. The table was there, washed bright green in the rain, but the cat was gone. She was suddenly disappointed. The maid looked up at her.

"Ha perduto qualque cosa, Signora?"

"There was a cat," said the American girl.

"A cat?"

"Si, il gatto,"

"A cat?" the maid laughed. "A cat in the rain?"

"Yes,—" she said, "under the table." Then, "Oh, I wanted it so much. I wanted a kitty."

When she talked English the maid's face tightened.

"Come, Signora," she said. "We must get back inside. You will be wet."

"I suppose so," said the American girl.

They went back along the gravel path and passed in the door. The maid stayed outside to close the umbrella. As the American girl passed the office, the padrone bowed from his desk. Something felt very small and tight inside the girl. The padrone made her feel very small and at the same time really important. She had a momentary feeling of being of supreme importance. She went on up the stairs. She opened the door of the room. George was on the bed, reading.

"Did you get the cat?" he asked, putting the book down.

"It was gone."

"Wonder where it went to," he said, resting his eyes from reading.

She sat down on the bed.

"I wanted it so much," she said. "I don't know why I wanted it so much. I wanted that poor kitty. It isn't any fun to be a poor kitty out in the rain."

George was reading again.

She went over and sat in front of the mirror of the dressing table looking at herself with the hand glass. She studied her profile, first one side and then the other. Then she studied the back of her head and her neck.

"Don't you think it would be a good idea if I let my hair grow out?" she asked, looking at her profile again.

George looked up and saw the back of her neck, clipped close like a boy's.

"I like it the way it is."

"I get so tired of it," she said. "I get so tired of looking like a boy."

George shifted his position in the bed. He hadn't looked away from her since she started to speak.

"You look pretty darn nice," he said.

She laid the mirror down on the dresser and went over to the window and looked out. It was getting dark.

"I want to pull my hair back tight and smooth and make a big knot at the back that I can feel," she said. "I want to have a kitty to sit on my lap and purr when I stroke her."

"Yeah?" George said from the bed.

"And I want to eat at a table with my own silver and I want candles. And I want it to be spring and I want to brush my hair out in front of a mirror and I want a kitty and I want some new clothes."

"Oh, shut up and get something to read," George said. He was reading again.

His wife was looking out of the window. It was quite dark now and still raining in the palm trees.

"Anyway, I want a cat," she said, "I want a cat. I want a cat now. If I can't have long hair or any fun, I can have a cat."

George was not listening. He was reading his book, His wife looked out of the window where the light had come on in the square.

Someone knocked at the door.

"Avanti," George said. He looked up from his book.

In the doorway stood the maid. She held a big tortoiseshell cat pressed tight against her and swung down against her body,

"Excuse me," she said, "the padrone asked me to bring this for the Signora."

Brian Doyle

Two Hearts

Some months ago my wife delivered twin sons one minute apart. The older is Joseph and the younger is Liam. Joseph is dark and Liam is light. Joseph is healthy and Liam is not. Joseph has a whole heart and Liam has half. This means that Liam will have two major surgeries before he is three years old.

I have read many pamphlets about Liam's problem. I have watched many doctors' hands drawing red and blue lines on pieces of white paper. They are trying to show me why Liam's heart doesn't work properly. I watch the markers in the doctors' hands. Here comes red, there goes blue. The heart is a railroad station where the trains are switched to different tracks. A normal heart switches trains flawlessly two billion times in a life; in an abnormal heart, like Liam's, the trains crash and the station crumbles to dust.

So there are many nights now when I tuck Liam and his wheezing train station under my beard in the blue hours of night and think about his Maker. I would kill the god who sentences him to such awful pain, I would stab him in the heart like he stabbed my son, I would shove my fury in his face like a fist, but I know in my own broken heart that this same god made my magic boys, shaped their apple faces and coyote eyes, put joy in the eager suck of their mouths. So it is that my hands are not clenched in anger but clasped in confused and merry and bitter prayer.

I talk to God more than I admit. "Why did you break my boy?" I ask.

I gave you that boy, he says, and his lean brown brother, and the elfin daughter you love so.

"But you wrote death on his heart," I say.

I write death on all hearts, he says, just as I write life.

This is where the conversation always ends and I am left holding the extraordinary awful perfect prayer of my second son, who snores like a seal, who might die tomorrow, who did not die today.

Michael Cunningham
White Angel

We lived then in Cleveland, in the middle of everything. It was the sixties—our radios sang out love all day long. This of course is history. It happened before the city of Cleveland went broke, before its river caught fire. We were four. My mother and father, Carlton, and me. Carlton turned sixteen the year I turned nine. Between us were several brothers and sisters, weak flames quenched in our mother's womb. We are not a fruitful or many-branched line. Our family name is Morrow.

Our father was a high school music teacher. Our mother taught children called "exceptional," which meant that some could name the day Christmas would fall in the year 2000 but couldn't remember to drop their pants when they peed. We lived in a tract called Woodlawn—neat one- and two-story houses painted optimistic colors. Our tract bordered a cemetery. Behind our back yard was a gully choked with brush, and beyond that, the field of smooth, polished stones. I grew up with the cemetery, and didn't mind it. It could be beautiful. A single stone angel, small-breasted and determined, rose amid the more conservative markers close to our house. Farther away, in a richer section, miniature mosques and Parthenons spoke silently to Cleveland of man's enduring accomplishments. Carlton and I played in the cemetery as children and, with a little more age, smoked joints and drank Southern Comfort there. I was, thanks to Carlton, the most criminally advanced nine-year-old in my fourth-grade class. I was going places. I made no move without his counsel.

Here is Carlton several months before his death, in an hour so alive with snow that earth and sky are identically white. He labors among the markers and I run after, stung by snow, following the light of his red knitted cap. Carlton's hair is pulled back into a ponytail, neat and economical, a perfect pinecone of hair. He is thrifty, in his way.

We have taken hits of acid with our breakfast juice. Or rather, Carlton has taken a hit and I, considering my youth, have been allowed half. This acid is called windowpane. It is for clarity of vision, as Vicks is for decongestion of the nose. Our parents are at work, earning the daily bread. We have come out into the cold so that the house, when we reenter it, will shock us with its warmth and righteousness. Carlton believes in shocks.

"I think I'm coming on to it," I call out. Carlton has on his buckskin jacket, which is worn down to the shine. On the back, across his shoulder blades, his girlfriend has stitched an electric-blue eye. As we walk I speak into the eye. "I think I feel something," I say.

"Too soon," Carlton calls back. "Stay loose, Frisco. You'll know when the time comes."

I am excited and terrified. We are into serious stuff. Carlton has done acid half a dozen times before, but I am new at it. We slipped the tabs into our mouths at breakfast, while our mother paused over the bacon. Carlton likes taking risks.

Snow collects in the engraved letters on the headstones. I lean into the wind, trying to decide whether everything around me seems strange because of the drug, or just because everything truly is strange. Three weeks earlier, a family across town had been sitting at home, watching television, when a single-engine plane fell on them. Snow swirls around us, seeming to fall up as well as down.

Carlton leads the way to our spot, the pillared entrance to a society tomb. This tomb is a palace. Stone cupids cluster on the peaked roof, with stunted, frozen wings and matrons' faces. Under the roof is a veranda, backed by cast-iron doors that lead to the house of the dead proper. In summer this veranda is cool. In winter it blocks the wind. We keep a bottle of Southern Comfort there.

Carlton finds the bottle, unscrews the cap, and takes a good, long draw. He is studded with snowflakes. He hands me the bottle and I take a more conservative drink. Even in winter, the tomb smells mossy as a well. Dead leaves and a yellow M & M's wrapper, worried by the wind, scrape on the marble floor.

"Are you scared?" Carlton asks me.

I nod. I never think of lying to him.

"Don't be, man," he says. "Fear will screw you right up. Drugs can't hurt you if you feel no fear."

I nod. We stand sheltered, passing the bottle. I lean into Carlton's certainty as if it gave off heat.

"We can do acid all the time at Woodstock," I say.

"Right on. Woodstock Nation. Yow."

"Do people really *live* there?" I ask.

"Man, you've got to stop asking that. The concert's over, but people are still there. It's the new nation. Have faith."

I nod again, satisfied. There is a different country for us to live in. I am already a new person, renamed Frisco. My old name was Robert.

"We'll do acid all the time," I say.

"You better believe we will." Carlton's face, surrounded by snow and marble, is lit. His eyes are bright as neon. Something in them tells me he can see the future, a ghost that hovers over everybody's head. In Carlton's future we all get released from our jobs and schooling. Awaiting us all, and soon, is a bright, perfect simplicity. A life among the trees by the river.

"How are you feeling, man?" he asks me.

"Great," I tell him, and it is purely the truth. Doves clatter up out of a bare tree and turn at the same instant, transforming themselves from steel to silver in the snow-blown light. I know at that moment that the drug is working. Everything before me has become suddenly, radiantly itself. How could Carlton have known this was about to happen? "Oh," I whisper. His hand settles on my shoulder.

"Stay loose, Frisco," he says. "There's not a thing in this pretty world to be afraid of. I'm here."

I am not afraid. I am astonished. I had not realized until this moment how real everything is. A twig lies on the marble at my feet, bearing a cluster of hard brown berries. The broken-off end is raw, white, fleshly. Trees are alive.

"I'm here," Carlton says again, and he is.

Hours later, we are sprawled on the sofa in front of the television, ordinary as Wally and the Beav. Our mother makes dinner in the kitchen. A pot lid clangs. We are undercover agents. I am trying to conceal my amazement.

Our father is building a grandfather clock from a kit. He wants to have something to leave us, something for us to pass along. We can hear him in the basement, sawing and pounding. I know what is laid out on his sawhorses—a long raw wooden box, onto which he glues fancy moldings. A single pearl of sweat meanders down his forehead as he works. Tonight I have discovered my ability to see every room of the house at once, to know every single thing that goes on. A mouse nibbles inside the wall. Electrical wires curl behind the plaster, hidden and patient as snakes.

"Shhh," I say to Carlton, who has not said anything. He is watching television through his splayed fingers. Gunshots ping. Bullets raise chalk dust on a concrete wall. I have no idea what we are watching.

"Boys?" our mother calls from the kitchen. I can, with my new ears, hear her slap hamburger into patties. "Set the table like good citizens," she calls.

"Okay, Ma," Carlton replies, in a gorgeous imitation of normality. Our father hammers in the basement. I can feel Carlton's heart ticking. He pats my hand, to assure me that everything's perfect.

We set the table, spoon fork knife, paper napkins triangled to one side. We know the moves cold. After we are done I pause to notice the dining-room wallpaper: a golden farm, backed by mountains. Cows graze, autumn trees cast golden shade. This scene repeats itself three times, on three walls.

"Zap," Carlton whispers. "Zzzzzoom."

"Did we do it right?" I ask him.

"We did everything perfect, little son. How are you doing in there, anyway?" He raps lightly on my head.

"Perfect, I guess." I am staring at the wallpaper as if I were thinking of stepping into it.

"You guess. You guess? You and I are going to other planets, man. Come over here."

"Where?"

"Here. Come here." He leads me to the window. Outside the snow skitters, nervous and silver, under streetlamps. Ranch-style houses hoard their warmth, bleed light into the gathering snow. It is a street in Cleveland. It is our street.

"You and I are going to fly, man," Carlton whispers, close to my ear. He opens the window. Snow blows in, sparking on the carpet. "Fly," he says, and we do. For a moment we strain up and out, the black night wind blowing in our faces — we raise ourselves up off the cocoa-colored deep-pile wool-and-polyester carpet by a sliver of an inch. Sweet glory. The secret of flight is this — you have to do it immediately, before your body realizes it is defying the laws. I swear it to this day.

We both know we have taken momentary leave of the earth. It does not strike either of us as remarkable, any more than does the fact that airplanes sometimes fall from the sky, or that we have always lived in these rooms and will soon leave them. We settle back down. Carlton touches my shoulder.

"You wait, Frisco," he says. "Miracles are happening. Fucking miracles."

I nod. He pulls down the window, which reseals itself with a sucking sound. Our own faces look back at us from the cold, dark glass. Behind us, our mother drops the hamburgers sizzling into the skillet. Our father bends to his work under a hooded lightbulb, preparing the long box into which he will lay clockworks, pendulum, a face. A plane drones by overhead, invisible in the clouds. I glance nervously at Carlton. He smiles his assurance and squeezes the back of my neck.

March. After the thaw. I am walking through the cemetery, thinking about my endless life. One of the beauties of living in Cleveland is that any direction feels like progress. I've memorized the map. We are by my calculations three hundred and fifty miles shy of Woodstock, New York. On this raw new day I am walking east, to the place where Carlton and I keep our bottle. I am going to have an early nip, to celebrate my bright future.

When I get to our spot I hear low moans coming from behind the tomb. I freeze, considering my choices. The sound is a long-drawn-out agony with a whip at the end, a final high C, something like "ooooooOw." A wolf's cry run backward. What decides me on investigation rather than flight is the need to make a story. In the stories my brother likes best, people always do the foolish, risky thing. I find I can reach decisions this way, by thinking of myself as a character in a story told by Carlton.

I creep around the side of the monument, cautious as a badger, pressed up close to the marble. I peer over a cherub's girlish shoulder. What I find is Carlton on the ground with his girlfriend, in an uncertain jumble of clothes and bare flesh. Carlton's jacket, the one with the embroidered eye, is draped over the stone, keeping watch.

I hunch behind the statue. I can see the girl's naked arms, and the familiar bones of Carlton's spine. The two of them moan together in the dry winter grass. Though I can't make out the girl's expression, Carlton's face is twisted and grimacing, the cords of his neck pulled tight. I had never thought the experience might be painful. I watch, trying to learn. I hold on to the cherub's cold wings.

It isn't long before Carlton catches sight of me. His eyes rove briefly, ecstatically skyward, and what do they light on but his brother's small head, sticking up next to a cherub's. We lock eyes and spend a moment in mutual decision. The girl keeps on clutching at Carlton's skinny back. He decides to smile at me. He decides to wink.

I am out of there so fast I tear up divots. I dodge among the stones, jump the gully, clear the fence into the swing-set-and-picnic-table sanctity of the back yard. Something about that wink. My heart beats fast as a sparrow's.

I go into the kitchen and find our mother washing fruit. She asks what's going on. I tell her nothing is. Nothing at all.

She sighs over an apple's imperfection. The curtains sport blue teapots. Our mother works the apple with a scrub brush. She believes they come coated with poison.

"Where's Carlton?" she asks.

"Don't know," I tell her.

"Bobby?"

"Huh?"

"What exactly is going on?"

"Nothing," I say. My heart works itself up to a hummingbird's rate, more buzz than beat.

"I think something is. Will you answer a question?"

"Okay."

"Is your brother taking drugs?"

I relax a bit. It is only drugs. I know why she's asking. Lately police cars have been browsing our house like sharks. They pause, take note, glide on. Some neighborhood crackdown. Carlton is famous in these parts.

"No," I tell her.

She faces me with the brush in one hand, an apple in the other. "You wouldn't lie to me, would you?" She knows something is up. Her nerves run through this house. She can feel dust settling on the tabletops, milk starting to turn in the refrigerator.

"No," I say.

"Something's going on," she sighs. She is a small, efficient woman who looks at things as if they give off a painful light. She grew up on a farm in Wisconsin and spent her girlhood tying up bean rows, worrying over the sun and rain. She is still trying to overcome her habit of modest expectations.

I leave the kitchen, pretending sudden interest in the cat. Our mother follows, holding her brush. She means to scrub the truth out of me. I follow the cat, his erect black tail and pink anus.

"Don't walk away when I'm talking to you," our mother says.

I keep walking, to see how far I'll get, calling, "Kittykittykitty." In the front hall, our father's homemade clock chimes the half hour. I make for the clock. I get as far as the rubber plant before she collars me.

"I told you not to walk away," she says, and cuffs me a good one with the brush. She catches me on the ear and sets it ringing. The cat is out of there quick as a quarter note.

I stand for a minute, to let her know I've received the message. Then I resume walking. She hits me again, this time on the back of the head, hard enough to make me see colors. "Will you *stop*?" she screams. Still, I keep walking. Our house runs west to east. With every step I get closer to Yasgur's farm.

Carlton comes home whistling. Our mother treats him like a guest who's overstayed. He doesn't care. He is lost in optimism. He pats her cheek and calls her "Professor." He treats her as if she were harmless, and so she is.

She never hits Carlton. She suffers him the way farm girls suffer a thieving crow, with a grudge so old and endless it borders on reverence. She gives him a scrubbed apple, and tells him what she'll do if he tracks mud on the carpet.

I am waiting in our room. He brings the smell of the cemetery with him, its old snow and wet pine needles. He rolls his eyes at me, takes a crunch of his apple. "What's happening, Frisco?" he says.

I have arranged myself loosely on my bed, trying to pull a Dylan riff out of my harmonica. I have always figured I can bluff my way into wisdom. I offer Carlton a dignified nod.

He drops onto his own bed. I can see a crushed crocus, the first of the year, stuck to the black rubber sole of his boot.

"Well, Frisco," he says. "Today you are a man."

I nod again. Is that all there is to it?

"*Yow*," Carlton says. He laughs, pleased with himself and the world. "That was so perfect."

I pick out what I can of "Blowin' in the Wind."

Carlton says, "Man, when I saw you out there spying on us I thought to myself, *yes*. Now *I'm* really here. You know what I'm saying?" He waves his apple core.

"Uh-huh," I say.

"Frisco, that was the first time her and I ever did it. I mean, we'd talked. But when we finally got down to it, there you were. My brother. Like you *knew*."

I nod, and this time for real. What happened was an adventure we had together. All right. The story is beginning to make sense.

"Aw, Frisco," Carlton says. "I'm gonna find you a girl, too. You're nine. You been a virgin too long."

"Really?" I say.

"*Man*. We'll find you a woman from the sixth grade, somebody with a little experience. We'll get stoned and all make out under the trees in the boneyard. I want to be present at your deflowering, man. You're gonna need a brother there."

I am about to ask, as casually as I can manage, about the relationship between love and bodily pain, when our mother's voice cuts into the room. "You did it," she screams. "You tracked mud all over the rug."

A family entanglement follows. Our mother brings our father, who comes and stands in the doorway with her, taking in evidence. He is a formerly handsome man. His face has been worn down by too much patience. He has lately taken up some sporty touches—a goatee, a pair of calfskin boots.

Our mother points out the trail of muddy half-moons that lead from the door to Carlton's bed. Dangling over the foot of the bed are the culprits themselves, voluptuously muddy, with Carlton's criminal feet still in them.

"You see?" she says. "You see what he thinks of me?"

Our father, a reasonable man, suggests that Carlton clean it up. Our mother finds that too small a gesture. She wants Carlton not to have done it in the first place. "I don't ask for much," she says. "I don't ask where he goes. I don't ask why the police are suddenly so interested in our house. I ask that he not track mud all over the floor. That's all." She squints in the glare of her own outrage.

"Better clean it right up," our father says to Carlton.

"And that's it?" our mother says. "He cleans up the mess, and all's forgiven?"

"Well, what do you want him to do? Lick it up?"

"I want some consideration," she says, turning helplessly to me. "That's what I want."

I shrug, at a loss. I sympathize with our mother, but am not on her team.

"All right," she says. "I just won't bother cleaning the house anymore. I'll let you men handle it. I'll sit and watch television and throw my candy wrappers on the floor."

She starts out, cutting the air like a blade. On her way she picks up a jar of pencils, looks at it and tosses the pencils on the floor. They fall like fortune-telling sticks, in pairs and crisscrosses.

Our father goes after her, calling her name. Her name is Isabel. We can hear them making their way across the house, our father calling, "Isabel, Isabel, Isabel," while our mother, pleased with the way the pencils had looked, dumps more things onto the floor.

"I hope she doesn't break the TV," I say.

"She'll do what she needs to do," Carlton tells me.

"I hate her," I say. I am not certain about that. I want to test the sound of it, to see if it's true.

"She's got more balls than any of us, Frisco," he says. "Better watch what you say about her."

I keep quiet. Soon I get up and start gathering pencils, because I prefer that to lying around trying to follow the shifting lines of allegiance. Carlton goes for a sponge and starts in on the mud.

"You get shit on the carpet, you clean it up," he says. "Simple."

The time for all my questions about love has passed, and I am not so unhip as to force a subject. I know it will come up again. I make a neat bouquet of pencils. Our mother rages through the house.

Later, after she has thrown enough and we three have picked it all up, I lie on my bed thinking things over. Carlton is on the phone to his girlfriend, talking low. Our mother, becalmed but still dangerous, cooks dinner. She sings as she cooks, some slow forties number that must have been all over the jukes when her first husband's plane went down in the Pacific. Our father plays his clarinet in the basement. That is where he goes to practice, down among his woodworking tools, the neatly hung hammers and awls that throw oversized shadows in the light of the single bulb. If I put my ear to the floor I can hear him, pulling a long low tomcat moan out of that horn. There is some strange comfort in pressing my ear to the carpet and hearing our father's music leaking up through the floorboards. Lying down, with my ear to the floor, I join in on my harmonica.

That spring our parents have a party to celebrate the sun's return. It has been a long, bitter winter and now the first wild daisies are poking up on the lawns and among the graves.

Our parents' parties are mannerly affairs. Their friends, schoolteachers all, bring wine jugs and guitars. They are Ohio hip. Though they hold jobs and meet mortgages, they think of themselves as independent spirits on a spying mission. They have agreed to impersonate teachers until they write their novels, finish their dissertations, or just save up enough money to set themselves free.

Carlton and I are the lackeys. We take coats, fetch drinks. We have done this at every party since we were small, trading on our precocity, doing a brother act. We know the moves. A big, lipsticked woman who has devoted her maidenhood to ninth-grade math calls me Mr. Right. An assistant vice principal in a Russian fur hat asks us both whether we expect to vote Democratic or Socialist. By sneaking sips I manage to get myself semi-crocked.

The reliability of the evening is derailed halfway through, however, by a half dozen of Carlton's friends. They rap on the door and I go for it, anxious as a carnival sharp to see who will step up next and swallow the illusion that I'm a kindly, sober nine-year-old child. I'm expecting callow adults and who do I find but a pack of young outlaws, big-booted and wild-haired. Carlton's girlfriend stands in front, in an outfit made up almost entirely of fringe.

"Hi, Bobby," she says confidently. She comes from New York, and is more than just locally smart.

"Hi," I say. I let them all in despite a retrograde urge to lock the door and phone the police. Three are girls, four boys. They pass me in a cloud of dope smoke and sly-eyed greeting.

What they do is invade the party. Carlton is standing on the far side of the rumpus room, picking the next album, and his girl cuts straight through the crowd to his side. She has the bones and the loose, liquid moves some people consider beautiful. She walks through that room as if she'd been sent to teach the whole party a lesson.

Carlton's face tips me off that this was planned. Our mother demands to know what's going on here. She is wearing a long dark-red dress that doesn't interfere with her shoulders. When she dresses up you can see what it is about her, or what it was. She is responsible for Carlton's beauty. I have our father's face.

Carlton does some quick talking. Though it's against our mother's better judgment, the invaders are suffered to stay. One of them, an Eddie Haskell for all his leather and hair, tells her she is looking good. She is willing to hear it.

So the outlaws, house-sanctioned, start to mingle. I work my way over to Carlton's side, the side unoccupied by his girlfriend. I would like to say something ironic and wised-up, something that will band Carlton and me against every other person in the room. I can feel the shape of the comment I have in mind but, being a tipsy nine-year-old, can't get my mouth around it. What I say is, "Shit, man."

Carlton's girl laughs at me. She considers it amusing that a little boy says "shit." I would like to tell her what I have figured out about her, but I am nine, and three-quarters gone on Tom Collinses. Even sober, I can only imagine a sharp-tongued wit.

"Hang on, Frisco," Carlton tells me. "This could turn into a real party."

I can see by the light in his eyes what is going down. He has arranged a blind date between our parents' friends and his own. It's a Woodstock move — he is plotting a future in which young and old have business together. I agree to hang on, and go to the kitchen, hoping to sneak a few knocks of gin.

There I find our father leaning up against the refrigerator. A line of butterfly-shaped magnets hovers around his head. "Are you enjoying this party?" he asks, touching his goatee. He is still getting used to being a man with a beard.

"Uh-huh."

"I am, too," he says sadly. He never meant to be a high school music teacher. The money question caught up with him.

"What do you think of this music?" he asks. Carlton has put the Stones on the turntable. Mick Jagger sings "19th Nervous Breakdown." Our father gestures in an openhanded way that takes in the room, the party, the whole house—everything the music touches.

"I like it," I say.

"So do I." He stirs his drink with his finger, and sucks on the finger.

"I *love* it," I say, too loud. Something about our father leads me to raise my voice. I want to grab handfuls of music out of the air and stuff them into my mouth.

"I'm not sure I could say I love it," he says. "I'm not sure if I could say that, no. I would say I'm friendly to its intentions. I would say that if this is the direction music is going in, I won't stand in its way."

"Uh-huh," I say. I am already anxious to get back to the party, but don't want to hurt his feelings. If he senses he's being avoided he can fall into fits of apology more terrifying than our mother's rages.

"I think I may have been too rigid with my students," our father says. "Maybe over the summer you boys could teach me a few things about the music people are listening to these days."

"Sure," I say, loudly. We spend a minute waiting for the next thing to say.

"You boys are happy, aren't you?" he asks. "Are you enjoying this party?"

"We're having a great time," I say.

"I thought you were. I am, too."

I have by this time gotten myself to within jumping distance of the door. I call out, "Well, goodbye," and dive back into the party.

Something has happened in my small absence. The party has started to roll. Call it an accident of history and the weather. Carlton's friends are on decent behavior, and our parents' friends have decided to give up some of their wine-and-folk-song propriety to see what they can learn. Carlton is dancing with a vice principal's wife. Carlton's friend Frank, with his ancient-child face and IQ in the low sixties, dances with our mother. I see that our father has followed me out of the kitchen. He positions himself at the party's edge; I jump into its center. I invite the fuchsia-lipped math teacher to dance. She is only too happy. She is big and graceful as a parade float, and I steer her effortlessly out into the middle of everything. My mother, who is known around school for Sicilian discipline, dances freely, which is news to everybody. There is no getting around her beauty.

The night rises higher and higher. A wildness sets in. Carlton throws new music on the turntable—Janis Joplin, the Doors, the Dead. The future shines for everyone, rich with the possibility of more nights exactly like this. Even our father is pressed into dancing, which he does like a flightless bird, all flapping arms and potbelly. Still, he dances. Our mother has a kiss for him.

Finally I nod out on the sofa, blissful under the drinks. I am dreaming of flight when our mother comes and touches my shoulder. I smile up into her flushed, smiling face.

"It's hours past your bedtime," she says, all velvet motherliness. I nod. I can't dispute the fact.

She keeps on nudging my shoulder. I am a moment or two apprehending the fact that she actually wants me to leave the party and go to bed. "No," I tell her.

"Yes," she smiles.

"No," I say cordially, experimentally. This new mother can dance, and flirt. Who knows what else she might allow?

"Yes." The velvet motherliness leaves her voice. She means business, business of the usual kind. I get myself out of there and no excuses this time. I am exactly nine and running from my bedtime as I'd run from death.

I run to Carlton for protection. He is laughing with his girl, a sweaty question mark of hair plastered to his forehead. I plow into him so hard he nearly goes over.

"Whoa, Frisco," he says. He takes me up under the arms and swings me a half-turn. Our mother plucks me out of his hands and sets me down, with a good farm-style hold on the back of my neck.

"Say good night, Bobby," she says. She adds, for the benefit of Carlton's girl, "He should have been in bed before this party started."

"No," I holler. I try to twist loose, but our mother has a grip that could crack walnuts.

Carlton's girl tosses her hair and says, "Good night, baby." She smiles a victor's smile. She smooths the stray hair off Carlton's forehead.

"No," I scream again. Something about the way she touches his hair. Our mother calls our father, who comes and scoops me up and starts out of the room with me, holding me like the live bomb I am. Before I go I lock eyes with Carlton. He shrugs and says, "Night, man." Our father hustles me out. I do not take it bravely. I leave flailing, too furious to cry, dribbling a slimy thread of horrible-child's spittle.

Later I lie alone on my narrow bed, feeling the music hum in the coiled springs. Life is cracking open right there in our house. People are changing. By tomorrow, no one will be quite the same. How can they let me miss it? I dream up revenge against our parents, and worse for Carlton. He is the one who could have saved me. He could have banded with me against them. What I can't forgive is his shrug, his mild-eyed "Night, man." He has joined the adults. He has made himself bigger, and taken size from me. As the Doors thump "Strange Days," I hope something awful happens to him. I say so to myself.

Around midnight, dim-witted Frank announces he has seen a flying saucer hovering over the back yard. I can hear his deep, excited voice all the way in my room. He says it's like a blinking, luminous cloud. I hear half the party struggling out through the sliding glass door in a disorganized, whooping knot. By that time everyone is so delirious a flying saucer would be just what was expected. That much celebration would logically attract an answering happiness from across the stars.

I get out of bed and sneak down the hall. I will not miss alien visitors for anyone, not even at the cost of our mother's wrath or our father's disappointment. I stop at the end of the hallway, though, embarrassed to be in pajamas. If there really are aliens, they will think I'm the lowest member of the house. While I hesitate over whether to go back to my room to change, people start coming back inside, talking about a trick of the mist and an airplane. People resume their dancing.

Carlton must have jumped the back fence. He must have wanted to be there alone, singular, in case they decided to take somebody with them. A few nights later I will go out and stand where he would have been standing. On the far side of the gully, now a river swollen with melted snow, the cemetery will gleam like a lost city. The moon will be full. I will hang around just as Carlton must have, hypnotized by the silver light on the stones, the white angel raising her arms up across the river.

According to our parents the mystery is why he ran back to the house full tilt. Something in the graveyard may have scared him, he may have needed to break its spell, but I think it's more likely that when he came back to himself he just couldn't wait to get back to the music and the people, the noisy disorder of continuing life.

Somebody has shut the sliding glass door. Carlton's girlfriend looks lazily out, touching base with her own reflection. I look, too. Carlton is running toward the house. I hesitate. Then I figure he can bump his nose. It will be a good joke on him. I let him keep coming. His girlfriend sees him through her own reflection, starts to scream a warning just as Carlton hits the glass.

It is an explosion. Triangles of glass fly brightly through the room. I think for him it must be more surprising than painful, like hitting water from a great height. He stands blinking for a moment. The whole party stops, stares, getting its bearings. Bob Dylan sings "Just Like a Woman." Carlton reaches up curiously to take out the shard of glass that is stuck in his neck, and that is when the blood starts. It shoots out of him. Our mother screams. Carlton steps forward into his girlfriend's arms and the two of them fall together. Our mother throws herself down on top of him and the girl. People shout their accident wisdom. Don't lift him. Call an ambulance. I watch from the hallway. Carlton's blood spurts, soaking into the carpet, spattering people's clothes. Our mother and father both try to plug the wound with their hands, but the blood just shoots between their fingers. Carlton looks more puzzled than anything, as if he can't quite follow this turn of events. "It's all right," our father tells him, trying to stop the blood. "It's all right, just don't move, it's all right." Carlton nods, and holds our father's hand. His eyes take on an astonished light. Our mother screams, "Is anybody *doing* anything?" What comes out of Carlton grows darker, almost black. I watch. Our father tries to get a hold on Carlton's neck while Carlton keeps trying to take his hand. Our mother's hair is matted with blood. It runs down her face. Carlton's girl holds him to her breasts, touches his hair, whispers in his ear.

He is gone by the time the ambulance gets there. You can see the life drain out of him. When his face goes slack our mother wails. A part of her flies wailing through the house, where it will wail and rage forever. I feel our mother pass through me on her way out. She covers Carlton's body with her own.

He is buried in the cemetery out back. Years have passed—we are living in the future, and it's turned out differently from what we'd planned. Our mother has established her life of separateness behind the guest-room door. Our father mutters his greetings to the door as he passes.

One April night, almost a year to the day after Carlton's accident, I hear cautious footsteps shuffling across the living-room floor after midnight. I run out eagerly, thinking of ghosts, but find only our father in moth-colored pajamas. He looks unsteadily at the dark air in front of him.

"Hi, Dad," I say from the doorway.

He looks in my direction. "Yes?"

"It's me. Bobby."

"Oh, Bobby," he says. "What are you doing up, young man?"

"Nothing," I tell him. "Dad?"

"Yes, son."

"Maybe you better come back to bed. Okay?"

"Maybe I had," he says. "I just came out here for a drink of water, but I seem to have gotten turned around in the darkness. Yes, maybe I better had."

I take his hand and lead him down the hall to his room. The grandfather clock chimes the quarter hour.

"Sorry," our father says.

I get him into bed. "There," I say. "Okay?"

"Perfect. Could not be better."

"Okay. Good night."

"Good night. Bobby?"

"Uh-huh?"

"Why don't you stay a minute?" he says. "We could have ourselves a talk, you and me. How would that be?"

"Okay," I say. I sit on the edge of his mattress. His bedside clock ticks off the minutes.

I can hear the low rasp of his breathing. Around our house, the Ohio night chirps and buzzes. The small gray finger of Carlton's stone pokes up among the others, within sight of the angel's blank white eyes. Above us, airplanes and satellites sparkle. People are flying even now toward New York or California, to take up lives of risk and invention.

I stay until our father has worked his way into a muttering sleep.

Carlton's girlfriend moved to Denver with her family a month before. I never learned what it was she'd whispered to him. Though she'd kept her head admirably during the accident, she lost her head afterward. She cried so hard at the funeral that she had to be taken away by her mother—an older, redder-haired version of her. She started seeing a psychiatrist three times a week. Everyone, including my parents, talked about how hard it was for her, to have held a dying boy in her arms at that age. I'm grateful to her for holding my brother while he died, but I never once heard her mention the fact that though she had been through something terrible, at least she was still alive and going places. At least she had protected herself by trying to warn him. I can appreciate the intricacies of her pain. But as long as she was in Cleveland, I could never look her straight in the face. I couldn't talk about the wounds she suffered. I can't even write her name.

CHAPTER NINE

REVISION

Often, writers struggle to revise, spending hours getting nowhere fast. For many, revision goes something like this. The writer writes a sentence:

> She went down the stairs.

And then the writer checks email, texts a friend, goes for a run, comes back, and rereads the sentence. Something is off. So the writer deletes that sentence:

> ~~She went down the stairs.~~

She writes a new sentence, quite similar to the original, hoping it's better. Now the sentence has action and emotion. Right?

> She went down the stairs, quickly, sighing heavily.

Then she reads it. It's worse. And she deletes:

> ~~She went down the stairs, quickly, sighing heavily.~~

And she writes another new sentence, and another, and each one is *worse* — not better — than the previous ones:

> Downstairs. She decided: She had to get downstairs!
> ~~Downstairs. She decided: She had to get downstairs!~~
> "I'm coming down!" she announced. And so she descended the stairs.
> ~~"I'm coming down!" she announced. And so she descended the stairs.~~

Only to end up, an hour later, with her original sentence:

She went down the stairs.

This tortured writer concludes two things: Writing is hard, and revision is a waste of time.

But all this crossing out and fiddling with words—is this revision? No, moving words around and trying out versions of the same sentence over and over is not really revision at all. Changing one word, then another—that's editing. Editing, which is covered later in this chapter, is an entirely separate process from revision. Editing is comparable to cleaning up your room. Revision is deciding afresh which room you actually want to live in, and spending time hunting for the perfect furnishings for that space, and arranging them in a pleasing configuration. Revision isn't picking up or picking nits. *Revision is writing anew.* Slogging around on the sentence level, changing this word, moving that one—what many non-writers think we do all day—has very little to do with the reality of the revision process.

> *You don't find out you're an artist because you do something really well. You find out you're an artist because when you fail you have something within you—strength or belief or just craziness—that picks you back up again.*
> — JUNOT DÍAZ

To grow as a writer, it's crucial that you make a distinction between revision, editing, and proofreading and to work on these three separate tasks at the appropriate times in your writing process. You don't need to proofread an early draft. Editing at the sentence level too soon—before you really know what your piece means on a deeper level, before you have your basic images clear and stable—is probably a waste of time. Revision is defined as reseeing your work and applying

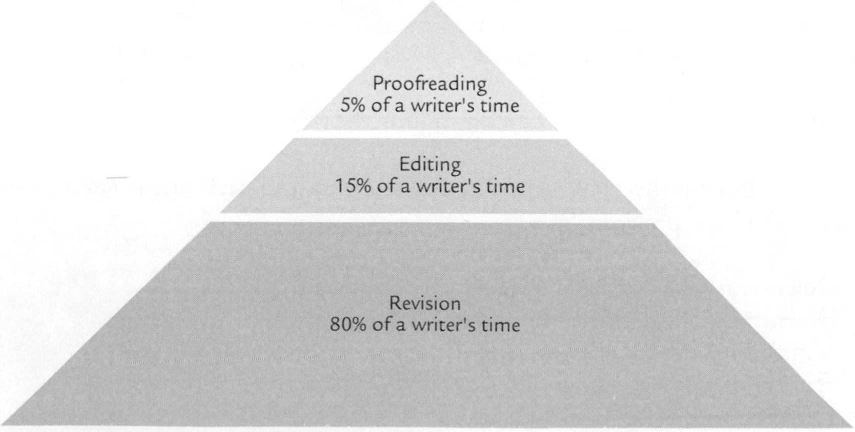

Pyramid diagram:

Proofreading
5% of a writer's time

Editing
15% of a writer's time

Revision
80% of a writer's time

Figure 9.1 Distinguishing between Revision, Editing, and Proofreading

the various strategies of creative writing to a work-in-progress. Editing involves tightening sentences, deleting unintentional repetitions, sharpening details, smoothing out sentences, and perfecting word choice. Proofreading is close reading for typos, grammatical errors, punctuation, and spelling. The three different processes use different parts of your brain and have very different purposes. Revision solidifies, editing strengthens, and proofreading perfects.

This chapter presents various student-tested methods for revision—try them out and take anything useful as you build your own personal revision process. Ultimately, you'll discover your own best practices for your personality as a writer. There are as many successful approaches to revision as there are writers.

REVISION IS SEEING AGAIN

Revision means "reseeing." Literally. In Latin, the word *revisere* means "to look again, to visit again." It comes from the word *videre*—"to see," as in *vision*. So revision actually means taking a new look at your whole piece, seeing it as a reader might see it. Picking over each word isn't reseeing. In revision, you try out options. You play with possibilities. You truly resee the whole piece, focusing as best you can on what readers will see in their mind's eye as they read your work.

Revision means you are like a painter walking to the far side of his loft. How does the piece look from twenty feet away? Fifty feet? One foot? Many writers take their pieces to a small group or a workshop and get feedback in order to help them see from different angles, to help them understand how the reader sees their work.

Look Closer

As you worked with each strategy in this book so far, you found ways to use the strategies of creative writing to create more adroitly. Reseeing and creating aren't separate—reseeing is writing, as you know: You've been reseeing all along. As you wrote, received comments from your instructor and other readers, and considered ways to improve, you were probably using the strategies of all good creative writing. These strategies are like a wheel the writer spins as he refines one aspect of a piece and then another. These tools help you focus the work of revision, in any order you choose.

> *There are only two or three human stories, and they go on repeating themselves as fiercely as if they had never happened before.*
>
> — WILLA CATHER

The goal of revision is to intensify the work so that it makes a moving picture inside the reader's mind. You are trying to make the reader forget she is reading at all—you want her to have an *experience*.

Most published works go through dozens and dozens of drafts. Novelist James Dickey says that it takes him fifty drafts to get the poem and then another

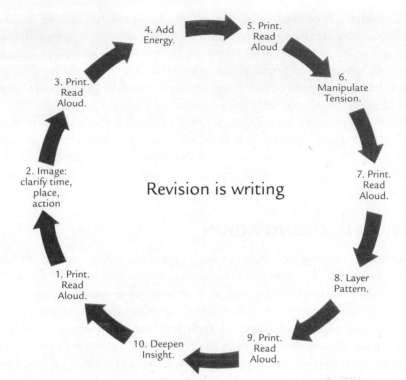

Figure 9.2 Revision Process Using the Strategies for Creative Writing

> *Life is a field of corn.*
> *Literature is the shot of*
> *whiskey it distills down into.*
> — LORRIE MOORE

150 to make it sound spontaneous. When you read something professional and polished, let yourself feel inspired by what is possible. Give yourself time to learn revision. Revision is actually a set of sequenced skills that require patience and practice.

PRACTICE

Reread the opening from any piece of writing you've created. Draw a quick sketch to locate the image: Where does this piece take place? Note the time of day, day of the week, and exact place where your piece opens. Sketch in the characters—stick figures are fine. And then list the sounds, smells, textures, and visual details. Take about five minutes to "resee" your opening. Do you see more? Looking over your lists and sketch, how might you start this piece in a more exciting, reader-friendly way?

The best way to improve your revision skills is to practice reseeing and notice what helps you improve your work. Try new forms. Try your writing projects in various genres. And along the way, learn what you can about your own revision process, what's effective for you and what isn't. While revision is essentially always some version of reseeing, there are as many good ways to revise as there are good ways to live.

PRACTICE

Write a short paragraph describing your revision process. Make a list of the three to five steps that are most useful to you — steps that really work for you when revising goes well.

Conquer Common Writing Blocks

What If in Revising I Make It Worse?   Oh you will. Often. But you don't have to see experiments that go awry as a problem. Bad writing is not a crisis. Author Greg Neri says he is successful because he is able to "tolerate my own suckedness for longer periods of time than most people." In revision, it's common and normal to make changes that confuse things, on the way to getting clearer about what you really want to show. Playing around with different options, and tolerating some bad writing, is all part of the process of producing good writing. Many successful writers explain their success this way: "My bad writing doesn't bother me that much, and it's a good thing because there is tons of it."

The solution is simple: Let yourself go a little bit. It's okay to make a mess. You have to have that freedom in order to grow as a writer. Then, before you rewrite, resee. Spend time trying to see what it is you want the reader to see in her mind's eye. To revise, use the same exact mind-set that you use when creating in the first place (here, you may want to review the section on "seeing" on p. 134 in Chapter Four). And give it your best shot. No one expects you to write crystal-clear, stellar, award-winning poetry and prose on the first try, or the second try, or the third, or even the twenty-second.

Your anxiety that you will make your writing worse is actually a good sign. If you aren't a little nervous about it, there's a good chance the work probably isn't alive to begin with. Karen Armstrong writes in her memoir *The Spiral Staircase* of becoming a writer in these very terms.

> [The writer] must fight his own monsters, not somebody else's, explore his own labyrinth, and endure his own ordeal before he can find what is missing in his life. Thus transfigured, he (or she) can bring something of value to the world that has been left behind. But if the knight finds himself riding along an already established track, he is simply following in somebody else's footsteps and will not have an adventure.

Once you have enough experience with it to gain a little confidence, revision is usually the writer's favorite part of writing. It's easier than beginning a new piece; it's more rewarding to shape and grow a thing that is already alive. But it is a lot more radical, a lot more scary, a lot more intense than many instructors admit. To revise a piece of writing requires that you take a large risk.

However, if you stay grounded in what's happening, to whom it's happening, and where the piece is taking place when you restart your poem or devise a new way to end your essay, if you can see the movie of what will happen more clearly, you probably won't make it worse. What's required is *letting go of your original ideas so new images can come forward.* Effective revision often means really reseeing the whole scene. It means not working on the sentence level, but rather working on the image level and starting with new sentences, new focus, new energy.

PRACTICE

Take a piece of writing from earlier in the semester. Intentionally make it worse. Use only abstractions. Avoid all images. Use words you never use in daily life, like *azure* and *emotive*. Use no dialogue and make sure nothing is happening, but whatever you do, do make sense. Turn your nice piece of writing into a horrible piece of writing. Share it with another person.

I Love My Piece/I Hate My Piece. Why Revise? It Seems Overwhelming. Loving your work too much or hating your work too much can be a writing block in disguise, a writing block that comes from an underlying fear of change. But too much love for your work or too much hate for your work can keep you from learning.

A kid beginning to ride a bike falls off the bike. He gets back on the bike, falls again, gets back on it again. Good writers know they have the tools and techniques to improve their writing; they know it's next to impossible to write a great first draft. Good writing is a matter of time and patience. It's a matter of getting back on the bike, over and over again. Okay, you wrote crap. Everyone does. So what? Really not a big deal. Let your mistakes go.

A beginner—in sports, in writing, in relationships—often feels like giving up too early. A successful writer (or football player, poet, parent, or spouse) is willing to let go of everything he or she has done so far in order to start afresh. This is hard to do, but it's the quickest way to improve. Just as *falling off the bike is part of the riding experience*—it's not wrong—*writing horrible pages is part of successful writing.* Let your first drafts be your teachers. Don't cling to them too tightly with love or punish them too harshly with hate. "Starting over" isn't punishment or going backward. It's actually moving the work—and your learning process—forward.

If you are overwhelmed, choose one strategy to focus on. To locate the part of the piece that most needs attention, read your piece aloud, or have someone read it to you. Did you hear a slightly lengthy, flat, boring description? Simply apply the strategy of Energy to that passage. Did you hear a confusing passage, where you aren't even sure what you meant? Apply the strategy of Image to that section. Did you hear a spot where nothing is really happening? Apply the strategy of Tension to that passage. Go slowly. Go one step at a time.

If that approach still feels too overwhelming, do what many published writers do: Start fresh. Instead of trying to salvage a mediocre piece, experienced writers just start anew. It's sometimes faster, easier, and more fun to just start an assignment over, from scratch. Set that first version to the side. Resee what you want to write, sketch it, focus on the sensory experiences you want your readers to create in their minds as they read, and begin in a new way. In fact, when you write this new version, your brain still remembers much of the first version. It's not wasted time — you aren't starting over with nothing. The first version still exists. Sometimes it's just easier not to be married to it. Starting a new version, based on the previous version, frees you up from your mistakes and allows room for new creativity to emerge.

Instead of liking or hating your work, see if you can shift your focus to building a revision practice that you can stick with, one that is a good fit for you personally.

What If I Don't Want to Change My Writing?

It can be painful to alter your words. Every writer feels this discomfort, at least some of the time. Good writers, like good athletes, get used to living with some pain. Revising is perhaps best defined as "learning how to continue to work on your writing." You develop this skill — the ability to see more to work on and how to work — as you write more pieces. You will learn how to feel less nervous about revision, and you will feel energized when you see things you know how to fix or adjust. A dialogue exchange is flat, and one day, you know why — you need three beats, not six. A passage of description, though you love it, has to go — and you're able to accept the cut.

> I've spent my life making blunders.
> — PIERRE-AUGUSTE RENOIR

Work to develop an openness to possibilities. That's the secret to being a successful artist, author, and, maybe, person. You are required to revise for this course, but you don't want to because you love your pieces just the way they are. You are also fairly confident you will make things worse if you start fiddling. Thus you resist revision, for some good reasons. But you won't grow as a writer until you play with what is possible. So save your first draft. Try the assignment another way. Choose one strategy to work on, and just try a different approach. You don't have to change a single word in your original. By all means, preserve that draft. Try a second draft, not to *improve your first draft*, but to see if anything else pops up. Cultivating a sense of play, taking a few risks, sneaking up on a new idea you didn't even know was there — that's in large part what keeps writers motivated.

> Getting to good writing means writing every day, just like playing the piano. To miss a day or two of piano requires three or four more of PRACTICE to get to where you were.
> — NICOLE LANTZ, STUDENT WRITER

PRACTICE

Take a piece of work from your pile of creative writing and write a different version, where you focus on the image, and the action, from a different angle. For example, you could take any short story from the semester and rewrite the opening from another character's point of view. You have the same scene, the same conflict, but you see the images — the movie that's playing out — from another angle, literally. Or take a poem, and instead of writing about the beach in summer, see it in winter. The idea is to practice reseeing, not "improving." Put the two versions next to each other, back to back, and ask a partner to comment on the strengths each one has.

REVISING EFFECTIVELY

Always dream and shoot higher than you know how to. Don't bother just to be better than your contemporaries or predecessors. Try to be better than yourself.
— WILLIAM FAULKNER

If revision is not your favorite part of the writing process, you can try some techniques that may help you see revision as part of what you have been doing all along: writing. Again and again you will hear (as you can see in the diagram on p. 358) that revising and writing are actually *the same thing*.

Many beginners start their revision process by reading the first sentence of their piece and feeling two powerfully contradictory emotions: "It's fine" and "It sucks." Which means "I haven't got a clue what to do with this sentence." It's confusing, even overwhelming, to feel two opposite emotions at once, so is it any wonder that doing laundry suddenly seems like a great idea? "I would much rather do laundry than try to figure out an impossible situation: A sentence is horrid and fine, both. Laundry makes sense. Horrid and fine together in one doesn't make sense."

What's up with this? Well, doing laundry is clear and it's fairly easy. You fill the washer with water, add soap, then put in clothes. The first steps in revision seem not to be clear at all. Feeling "great" and "awful" at the same time is confusing, but writers have to get used to that strange sensation. The truth is that your piece is fine, and yes, it could be better, too. That's kind of weird — that two opposite things are true at once. So you experience some friction, some tension — it can be a little challenging for the brain to process "It's good and it could be better." It's a little confusing! No wonder doing laundry is so appealing. Laundry is not confusing. It's dirty or it's clean.

Instead of starting with the first sentence, and then freezing up or freaking out, and redoing that opening sentence over and over and over, it may be helpful for you to come up with a set of directions, personalized just for you, for revising your work. Following are some clear steps — dos and don'ts — that form a checklist you can tailor to your needs. Try each of the strategies, and see how they work for you. Revision can be as clear and straightforward as doing laundry.

Here are the seven most useful strategies for revision that writers turn to again and again.

1. Limit Your Time

Use a timer, and keep your revision sessions short, regular, and defined—just like sports practice. It's much better to practice reseeing small parts of poems, plays, stories, and essays, a little bit each day. Spend just ten or twenty minutes, thirty at the most, per session. Work on the easiest parts first. Don't get bogged down with a "massive overhaul" of your entire oeuvre. Take one page at a time—draw it, resee it, choose a strategy, and work slowly, knowing you can always go back to your original if your strategy fails you. Staying up all night reworking an entire short story is akin to the track star who runs a marathon the night before the state meet. What will you really be able to accomplish the next day? Not much.

An amazing thing happens when you time your writing sessions and force yourself to stop when the timer goes off. Your mind will often come up with fresh solutions between sessions. Try it.

> *The main reason for rewriting is not to achieve a smooth surface, but to discover the inner truth of your characters.*
> —SAUL BELLOW

PRACTICE

Take a piece you are revising. Print a hard copy. Set your timer for ten minutes. Read your piece aloud. If you like, make marginal notes with your pencil as you read. If you finish reading before the timer goes off, take a moment to reflect. What is one thing that is not clear in your piece of writing? Turn the paper over. Visualize that unclear part, and on the back of the paper, write that part more clearly. Use your eyes. Write what you see. When the timer goes off, no matter how far you get, stop (even if you are still just reading).

2. Sketch, Then Write

Always quick-sketch your scene (no drawing talent is required—in your mind's eye, you just want to clearly visualize a "movie" of what you are writing), list the five senses that are present in this scene, and *then* begin writing. The key is to be very clear when and where your image is taking place before you start writing. You might want to sketch out various options until you find a scene that has tension and energy. Usually, the sentences aren't the problem: Weak

> *When the film is finished, it is never the film I said I wanted to make.*
> — FEDERICO FELLINI

writing is simply not well visualized. For example, one reason that Meghan, the writer at the outset of this chapter, is struggling so mightily to revise her sentence is that her character is going downstairs in the first place. Why is she telling us that she's going downstairs? Is it important? Visually interesting? Energetic? Potentially . . . if the character is being chased downstairs by an alien being or running to greet a movie star at her front door . . . but why not show *that*? Wouldn't most readers rather see the little green alien or someone famous and thrilling instead of the lone descending figure?

When Meghan decided to *see again,* instead of trying to fix her sentences, she started with a drawing of her scene. When she looked at her quick sketch—a girl walking down a staircase—she felt it was the most boring thing on planet Earth. When Meghan looked at the scene again, she realized that starting her short story with the stair descent was boring and pointless, visually and thematically. When she drew the scene again, she left out the staircase and instead drew the scene her character was headed to.

Figure 9.3 shows what Meghan drew during her first revision session.

Figure 9.3 Meghan's Sketch of Family Fighting in the Living Room

She drew what she could and noted other sensory details—the clock ticking at 8:00 p.m. on prom night; the stairs, couch, and front door forming a triangle—and her new opening is vibrant, funny, and visually rich. Just as filmmakers storyboard their scenes and graphic novelists picture the story frame by frame, get in the habit of seeing by sketching each part of your stories, poems, plays, and essays. It's a quick way to revise—you don't have to write lots and lots of stuff. You get to the meat, fast.

After looking and seeing again, Meghan quit trying to fix the stair sentence, and she started her story with the living room scene. The rest of the story? It pretty much wrote itself once she was on the right track.

For dramatic works—plays, monologues, screenplays, and comics / graphic novels—you can storyboard each scene, doing a quick sketch to locate the triangle of tension, and zoom in on the sensory images (sights, smells, sounds, textures, and tastes) for each scene, as in the example above. Then, after you have reseen your images and written them afresh, ask your friends, roommates, or classmates to read your piece aloud. You can tell which parts are flowing and which parts need to be reseen even more clearly by noticing where they pause, stumble, mess up, or laugh. If the flat parts aren't apparent to you, ask your readers. More than likely, they'll have plenty of useful ideas about what the character might really say or do.

3. Read to Get Unstuck

If you are feeling stuck when it comes to revision, and you are procrastinating or getting frustrated and unhappy, simply step away from the desk. Forget all about your troubled piece of writing. Set the timer for twenty minutes, and read. Read your favorite works—from this book or from your own collection or online. Reading excellent writing infuses you with the power to see your own work with new eyes. Uploading some writing you really love into your brain can have almost magical effects: Your work will often self-correct. At the very least, you'll be able to tap into the reasons you are writing in the first place. Some writers make a conscious effort to list what they love in their favorite pieces of writing. Others trust that spending time reading will automatically tune them to the right station. Some authors have a touchstone poem or a piece of sacred writing they reread at the outset of each writing session: Wendell Berry's "How to Be a Poet" or work by Rumi. Maybe reading a short chapter from Elizabeth Gilbert's book *Big Magic*. Others leaf through an anthology of contemporary writers, like the ones in this book, and just let pure chance decide what sentences they'll tune in to on any given day. Like a runner's wind sprints or a pianist's scales or a football player's stretches, reading is a great writer's warm-up. You may be in the habit of using music to get into the groove and stay in it; try using literature and see if it helps you restart your writing. When working on revision, allow reading—and rereading—to accompany you.

4. Work by Hand

Most writers tend to revise in a word-processing program; this is a dangerous practice. Word processing lets you erase everything. And it lets you spew out an enormous amount of verbiage in no time at all. So it feels really great: Blank screen! New hope! And then, a few sentences and three hours later: Oh, great, more crap. The great feeling doesn't last, and the frustration can easily kill a whole weekend. Instead of revising your first draft on the computer, print out what you have written and reread it kindly, as though it was written by a beloved, respected friend. Then set the hard copy aside. Draw your new image for this piece, and write that new section by hand, slowly, using your timer.

This way of working is actually much quicker than the "type–delete–type–delete–stare at blank screen" method most beginners use. Print out your current draft, and make your changes by hand on the hard copy. Try it a couple of times and see if you notice a change in the quality of your work.

5. Choose Where to Begin

You don't have to begin your revision process with the first sentence or first stanza or first line of dialogue. *You* get to choose, not the piece of writing. You are in charge. Start with the scene, stanza, or line that seems the easiest to resee. Start in the middle of your piece, if you like, or work on a stanza or paragraph toward the end. Highlight a few lines or paragraphs and read them aloud. What will the reader see, in her mind's eye, when she reads this section? Can you draw it? If you can, then keep reading, moving on to the next section of the piece. When you find a part that isn't easily pictured, stop. Set the piece down. Draw it, list the sensory images (see p. 363 for a quick-start guide to this method), and then resee your piece.

> I've found that every time I've made a radical change, it's helped me feel buoyant as an artist.
>
> — DAVID BOWIE

The opening is the hardest part of any piece. Save that for last. After you have reseen your ending and the exciting, tension-filled way your piece comes to a close, then return to your opening. Can you create any patterns that will link the ending to the beginning? Usually, the beginning is the last part you revise; it's best reseen in concert with the ending.

6. Delete It; Don't Fix It

You know how some parties just *don't work*? Sometimes, the wrong people are there. The feeling is off. There's no spark. It's not really anyone's fault—the party just doesn't come together. It's not fun. What do you do? Leave.

When something isn't working, here's a great strategy: Stop doing it.

The same is true for revision. You can simply abandon the pieces that just *don't work*. Maybe your junior high English teacher didn't tell you this. But it's true. If something is boring, it is really, truly okay to *say good-bye*. Life is short. Delete.

Choose to revise your best pieces, not your total failures. You have to be a little in love with your piece in order to give it the time, commitment, and respect it needs. You have probably written some pieces this semester that you truly loathe. You can let them go. You don't have to fix up terrible things. It's hard to improve as a writer by investing time in a piece you no longer care about. In fact, doing so can *impede* your growth as a writer. Choose to revise only the pieces you love, care about, feel invested in. Revising *good writing* is much more effective than laboring over duds.

The same thing is true on the micro level, in your individual pieces. Just let go of—delete—the suckiest parts. No need to revise boring passages or lines. Delete them. Find the energy in your subject, and spin the wheel of strategies there. Revision shouldn't feel as though you are punishing yourself and your piece. Revision is hard work, so save it for what you truly believe is *worthwhile*: the pieces you love and care about and the sections of those pieces that already have the potential to move and inspire and rock your reader's world.

7. Ask Your Writing Questions

Slowing down and seeing more clearly allows you to make your images, energy, and tension stronger and more focused. But how do you revise for insight? Revising for depth and insight is the hardest thing a writer does. "Okay, be smarter, more sensitive. Go! Now!" It usually doesn't work that way.

However, you can find ways to take a piece of creative writing and, as writer Jack Ridl says, let the piece itself be a kind of "Zen master all but whacking [you] behind the head." Weird as this sounds, when you want to revise for insight, try to listen to what the piece has to say. If you can get past any resistance and get into the playfulness of this technique, you might be able to find some interesting things to develop more deeply.

> *The secret of good writing is to strip every sentence to its cleanest components.*
>
> —WILLIAM ZINSSER

> *People often begin their best work when they think they are just playing.*
> — ABIGAIL THOMAS

A lot of the "juice" in creative writing comes not from our conscious waking thoughts but from a deeper part of the mind, one hidden from us much of the time.

To tap into that more mysterious part of the mind, some writers actually interview their own writing. It sounds strange, but this simple mental strategy can let you access parts of your mind you don't normally get to look into.

PRACTICE

Read Jack Ridl's poem "Repairing the House" (p. 395) and his conversation with the poem (p. 396). What do you learn about his revision process? What does he learn about his poem? Do you think this technique — asking questions of the piece and pretending the piece is "alive," with its own voice — will help him when he sits down to write his next poem?

You ask questions of a piece of writing in order to see what you have done and to see whether any obvious connections already exist in the work, ones you may want to develop further. Asking questions — instead of plunging into your word processor, hitting delete, and cranking out new lines — lets you work more slowly, more mindfully. Asking questions, having a conversation — it's a very *friendly* thing to do with your work. Think about it. When you wish that your friend would make a few changes — maybe stop hitting you up for money each time she sees you, or stop interrupting you all the time — is it better to just *revise* the person, telling her what to do? Or is it more effective to ask a question, a truly curious one, such as "You seem to need money frequently. What's going on in your life? Is your situation changing anytime soon? Tell me more about this because sometimes I worry. You're asking me a lot." If you say, "Do you notice you are interrupting people?" does your friend get defensive? Maybe. Maybe she actually considers the question, and maybe *that's* going to produce a behavior change, and less resistance, than the critical mode.

> *Writing, the activity itself, if you are faithful to it and don't cheat with it, allows you to transcend your own moral limitations — you become much more forbearing, much wiser, much more of a person than you ever are in daily living. When it's going as it should, you have all of the . . . intelligence and compassion of an angel.*
> — RICHARD BAUSCH

Interviewing writing isn't for everyone, and it doesn't work for every piece. You may feel very self-conscious and even a little bizarre. But try playing with questions before you reject it as a technique. You might be surprised at what comes forward.

Here are some of the questions you might ask a piece of writing:

What am I not telling my readers that I should be telling them?
What do you want to say more about?
Am I keeping any secrets?
Do you feel I'm being fair and telling the whole story?
Are any parts of the piece not really true? Am I just making them up?
Help me out. What's wrong with you?
Are you telling me to shut up?
What do you want?
This isn't what I mean. Am I confused about what you mean?

| PRACTICE |

Choose a piece of your own writing that you like but feel mixed about, a piece you'd like to work on further. If you could ask this piece of writing anything, and it could tell you the truth, what would you ask it? Take three to five minutes and jot down your dream questions.

| PRACTICE |

Choose a piece of writing that needs more insight and depth. Using your dominant hand, write out a question you have for the piece. Then, using your nondominant hand, write out the answer the piece might give if it could talk. Go slowly. Try to stay open. Create a dialogue between you and your piece, switching back and forth between hands—your dominant hand is you, and your nondominant hand speaks for the piece. Ask the piece ten questions. You can plan out some of the questions ahead of time, but you don't need to know all of them in advance. You're going to think of questions as the piece reveals itself to you.

Give it a try. *Anything* is better than the time-wasting, mind-numbing, going-nowhere-fast exercise of writing, crossing out, writing, crossing out. Take a chance, step outside your comfort zone, and play.

REVISION STEP-BY-STEP

Writers learn what they can about revision by practicing, by reading, and by getting feedback from instructors and other writers. But when it comes down to actually revising a piece of writing, each writer does it

> *The key for me . . . was to get back into my body. If I could figure out what my foot was doing, if I could feel how it was to sit in the blue chair, I could get back into the scene. . . . And that was how I got unstuck.*
>
> — CHARLIE WALTER,
> STUDENT WRITER

her or his own way. Examining how other student writers revise their works-in-progress may help you build your skills and confidence, as you come up with the methods that work best for your work ethic, your personality, and your writing style. Here, three students, with three very different approaches, revise their work.

Revising Fiction

Meghan Wilson, a student writer, first began her short story (untitled) this way:

> I closed my eyes to time. I succumbed to it. I let it creep along, and then be picked up by an accelerating wind. When I finally had the courage to open my eyes, time was gone. I let the years fly by, and I eternally scarred my parents in that process of growing up. There were countless arguments, and although I can't remember them, they always ended the same way: badly.
>
> Those treacherous adolescent years have long since passed, and I've actually become proud of who I developed into because of them. It was my parents who, as I found out, would simply not let it go.

Meghan chose this short story to work on for her portfolio because she really liked the subject—a teenage girl's super-hard high school experience, complete with sex, cocaine, and mean girls. Meghan used the Strategies method for revision (see her sketch on p. 364), going through her pieces one strategy at a time, in short, timed sessions.

She always starts with Energy as her first revision tool. She reviewed the concepts of energy (see Chapter Five), and she reread her short story, still untitled.

- Was the subject interesting? Superbly personal and important to her?
  Absolutely yes.
- Did she know the subject extremely well?
  Yes, since the character in the story was basically her, in high school.
- Were the words specific and the verbs grounded and muscular?
  She thought so, yes. At least in part.

"Succumbed, accelerating, scarred, developed—I thought this all sounded really momentous and dramatic and exciting." But when she reread her opening again, aloud, she cringed. "You can't even see who this is! It just sounds so overblown, and like, what are we even talking about? The winds of time? What even is that? It sounds like a bad college application essay! I don't know what I was thinking when I wrote this. I liked it a lot at the time. But what is the wind? This isn't really how I want to sound. Windy."

As Meghan looked at her short story opening with Energy in mind, she realized that the sentences had a lot of energy and power, but there was a lot of metaphor—stuff the readers couldn't really see, though they could probably relate. But what was treacherous? What was scarring? What was argued over? Meghan felt it would be more effective to show one of the battles, in real time. For the story to be truly effective, she thought that she needed to *show* the conflict, and not say, in the second paragraph, "I've actually become proud of who I developed into." First of all, it seemed kind of bogus, and second, Meghan thought if this was the story she was going to tell, that information should be on the last page.

So, with those goals in mind, she worked on the tool of Images next, setting her time. She decided to start with a sketch of an image of the most painful high school moment she could remember—and, surprisingly, it had nothing to do with her parents. It was waking up late. Figure 9.4 shows what she drew.

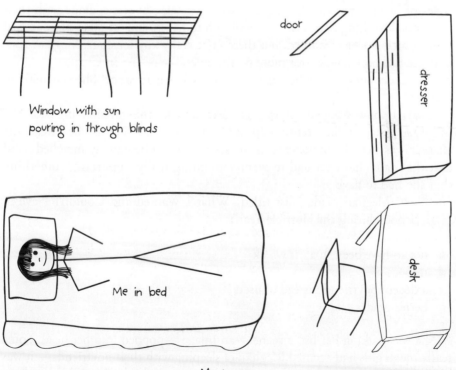

Figure 9.4 Meghan's Sketch of Herself Waking Up

And this is what she wrote, trying to shift from abstract, vague writing to something that was in action, in scene, making sure her piece took place in an actual space and at a specific time of day:

> The midday sunlight seeps through open spaces where the bedroom blinds aren't closed. A stream of light hits the center of my right eye, and I bury my face in the depths of my down pillow. I reach up with one hand, drawing the blinds completely closed. I'm not getting out of bed today. I'm not going to school. I turn over on my belly and pull my dirty hair into a tousled ponytail. I rest my thick dully throbbing head in my palm trying to talk myself out of getting sick. My eyelashes feel like I'm wearing lead mascara. How can I be this tired? I scan my bedroom. My thoughts are a muddled mess.

When she reread this piece the next day, she felt it was a lot better than the first draft. She took her revision to her writing group in class (the piece she took in was quite a bit longer than the excerpt above). The three members of the group felt the piece was in image, and that was good, but one group member said a character waking up was pretty much a cliché. Plus, it violated one of the principles of images: to avoid having characters onstage, in scene, alone with their thoughts. "Nothing happens," Meghan said to her group. "It takes place in real time, which is what I wanted, but there's not really any tension." Meghan realized she had no triangles (for more on triangles, see p. 238 in Chapter Six). She was in scene, but it was a boring scene. But she was in scene! She was making progress.

This is how Meghan chose her next step in the revision process: She skimmed Chapter Six, Tension (p. 222). What struck her as she reread the chapter was that the opponents in the scene have to be equally matched. And that the main character had to want something really important, something that she had to have.

Next, Meghan made a list titled "What I Wanted and Couldn't Have in High School during the Horrible Year":

- not to have been in a car wreck
- respect
- a decent boyfriend instead of users
- better grades

As she was making her list, a scene—an image—popped into her head. Some really mean girls had accused Meghan of sleeping with their boyfriends—it was like a bad teen movie. It made her face burn just to think of it now—and she hadn't thought of that day in a long time.

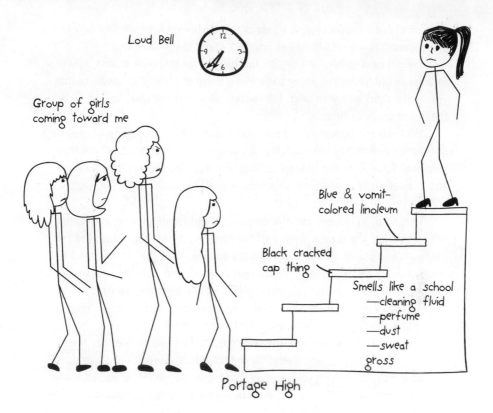

Figure 9.5 Meghan's Sketch of Herself at Portage High School

Meghan went back to her image-making revision tool and sketched a quick floor plan with notes.

> A truant high schooler, lurking by the stairwell, ditching class, freaking out when an army of powerful popular junior girls, dressed alike, barrel down the hall like they are the princesses of Portage High.

Meghan made a list of the sounds, sights, textures, and smells from that day at school, that single moment. And she started her third revision this way:

> At Portage Central
>
> Start by any given stairwell because after the tardy bell dings over the PA there usually aren't any educators around and the Hall Walkers are smoking the last cigarette down to the filter or crushing a Styrofoam cup into the trash receptacle, and they'll be out soon but not soon enough. So it's you, the walls

and stairs, and a couple of girls a year or two older round the corridor now like bloodhounds. One gnarls her lip at you, kick-starts the whole thing.

The girl next to her, let's say it's football season this time around, is wearing an old basketball jersey the athletic department sold to students that year, and a short torn jean skirt, tube socks, all yellow and blue, yes, she'll be the one to speak up first.

You know the caricature and now you've got to make a decision depending on whether or not they keep walking. Are you going to walk to class? Are they stopping? Sometimes they'll keep walking and brush into you as they walk by and in a voice so low you could've misheard she'll say, Meghan Wilson, yeah right.

They stop, in unison, and the dark haired girl (what sets her apart from the rest is that she claims she is half Russian/half Japanese), slants her body backward and places a hand on her jutted out hip, the other stands next to her, five or six inches shorter, mouth open, nose flared, the one who would be the bat boy on the baseball team, if this were a spectator sport. She forces some laughs it seems like, when the Japanese/Russian says, "Ohmygod Sara. She's wearing the same sweatshirt I wore yesterday."

The shorter one will echo, "The same one," before she bobbles her head in your direction and says, well, spits, "Burn that shit. We do not dress like sluts."

So you say something you've never said before but you've rehearsed it and you're nervous and don't quite get the catch-phrase spot-on but you say: Please shut the fuck up.

This is when you're late. This is how you're late. This is exactly the beginning of the whole thing.

PRACTICE

Compare Meghan Wilson's voice in her first, second, and third drafts. How would you describe the speaker in the first piece? In the second? In the third? How would you describe this kind of revising, starting over rather than reworking sentences one by one? Does Meghan's revision style seem harder than the one you typically employ? Easier? Do you think the second piece is better than the first? How? How not?

Instead of writing in general about something that happened long ago and far away, Meghan plunged herself into the heart of the conflict—a young high school girl, trapped by a gang of "mean girls." She eschewed all filters and generalities and wrote a single fast-paced scene, with specific word choices and close-up camera work. It took her multiple tries and four different revision sessions, but when Meghan began the final version, excerpted above, she didn't stop writing for three hours! She completed ten pages, by hand, and made very few changes when she entered her work into the computer. The piece ended up in her portfolio. She wrote in her artist's statement:

> I was, I realize now, all these months after making this portfolio, just really scared to tell the truth. I mean, I was calling it fiction, but all of this was so close to home from the beginning. Even in the story version, originally, her name is Meghan! Oh my god. I was scared to go for the heart of the scene, so I screwed around with the waking up crap. It was really, really, really hard to relive those moments with those girls. And face who I was then. I cried. But, I also knew, when I was writing—I know this sounds . . . whatever. I knew this—with the fuck you—this is what I wanted to write. The truth. But it was hard. It was. Worth it though. Yeah, it took me like seven tries. I'm not even showing you the really bad ones!

Revising asks you to move in between the strategies, trying one, then trying another, then going back, trying again. It asks you to be patient, honest, bold, and brave.

PRACTICE

Review the Energy troubleshooting table on page 208. Choose one of your pieces that you like a lot but that isn't as exciting as you want it to be. Using each of the energy sparkers, make changes in your piece. Don't just revise sentences—replace whole chunks with new writing.

PRACTICE

Pick any strategy—Images, Energy, Tension, Pattern, or Insight. Review that chapter, and revise your piece using the principles of writing you find in the chapter.

Instead of revising sentences, try revising the images themselves, choosing exciting visuals, changing camera lenses so you are using the telephoto, getting closer to your liveliest, most interesting subjects. Approaching revisions this way— with your senses, reconsidering what's really going on in the piece and why you are telling it—is hard work. But it's more efficient work, more rewarding, and ultimately more fun than crossing out a sentence and writing it over again, which just feels like punishment.

> *People ask for criticism, but they only want praise.*
> — W. SOMERSET MAUGHAM

Revising Poetry

A useful question to ask a writer is not "How many drafts did you do?" but instead "What did you do, as a writer, to make the poem better?" Student author

> *The hardest thing about this revision is seeing where it needs to go next. To me, the poem often feels done. But my peers push me to keep working.*
> — ANNALISE MABE, STUDENT WRITER

Alex Mouw can't count exactly how many drafts of "When I Was Sixteen, My Father and I Played Chess" he completed because he carried the sonnet with him for days, then weeks, working his way through the strategies.

Here's a quick tour of how Alex used the strategies to revise his poem. After his first draft was complete, he started with Images, working on the piece as a whole, going over and over it to make sure everything was "seeable." He also wanted to make sure he had a clear, cohesive story. When he moved to Energy, he quickly reviewed that chapter and then made marginal notes about pace and camera work. He tested words and changed the title. All his changes were made in pencil on hard copy, then entered into the computer, and printed out again. He moved on to Tension. Here, Alex focused on getting the best words in the best order. He wanted to have layers and depth, so he revisited the Insight chapter and in his journal asked himself questions. What was the point of having his girlfriend in the poem? What was the poem really about? What were the most important things he wanted to explore? Then, at the very end, he went to the Pattern chapter, using it to help him focus on the sounds of each word in his poem. He wanted all the sounds to create one effect. This is the part of the poem he is still working on.

In the first version of his sonnet, Alex simply laid out the scene in images: A father is in a chair, the speaker joins his dad, and there's a financial incentive for the son to win a game of chess.

As Alex wrote this first version, he focused almost solely on staying in the active image. He also wanted to write a perfect sonnet; he used Chapter Ten to review the sonnet rules (p. 453).

A Game of Chess

Dad sits up straight in a wood chair, repeats
the challenge of every game: *five dollars
the first time you beat me*. I take my seat,
move a knight two squares forward and one square
left. Dad takes his turn, his face turned down
for the bankrupt company he'll return
to Monday, his ninety employees doubting future mortgage payments. He is worn
by many. I ask for money to pay
for prom, he asks about my girl and a
chem test coming up. After our game he
paces the home office, phone in hand while

I clean off the table, asking if God
or he will find a way to provide.

Alex says of this first draft:

> It was messy, even in the nice neat sonnet container—there was a mess in
> there. I lingered without clear purpose over the movement of the chess
> pieces, and I used the weird diction of "my girl" even though romance is not
> an important thing in this scene. Money, work, and a son unable to help his
> father were the most critical images driving the poem. As I focused on the
> image, unnecessary description of the chess pieces gave way to the house for
> sale, which increased the tension: financial issues are at play. "My girl"
> (cringe) also fell away from the poem—there was just no reason to "see" her
> in this poem. A poem could be about a father and a girl, but as I took my
> notebook out each day, and focused on the heart of what was driving the
> piece, I saw *this* poem couldn't be about those two things.

Here's the second version of his poem:

When I Was Younger, My Father
and I Played Chess

Dad, spine straightened in a wood chair, repeats
the challenge of every game: *five dollars*
the first time you beat me. I take my seat
in the living room of our lakefront house,
two years up for sale. Dad plays knight, the game
a breath before Monday when he'll return
to his bankrupt spa company, his employees doubting future mortgage payments.
He is worn by many. Mom needs a check
for Grandpa's house-nurse but money is tight
and God may or may not provide. He makes
calls when the game is over, pacing lightly across the kitchen. I clean up, fill
a box with chess men and clutch my new bill.

When Alex got the poem back from his instructor, he was surprised.

> My professor suggested I let the rhyme scheme go. Forget the rhymes, she
> said, and really work out the clarity, action, and images. I tend to be a rule-
> follower and start sonnets as sonnets. But I tried a sonnet without rhyme. It
> helped me get some new images and eventually led me to this version:

When I Was Sixteen, My Father
and I Played Chess

Dad checks the clock then looks at me, repeats
the challenge of every game: *five dollars*
the first time you beat me. I take my seat
in the living room of our lakefront house,
two years up for sale. Dad plays knight, the game
a breath before Monday when he'll return
to his bankrupt spa company and the
fifty employees doubting their future
mortgage payments. We are all so needy:
Mom wants a check for grandpa's house-nurse, I
ruined the car meant to last at least three
more years. After our game ends he stands by
the stairs making calls. I clean up, hands filled
with chess men and my new five dollar bill.

I liked making changes to this poem. I could see it kept getting better. I guess my favorite change was to add tension with the clock: I think the clock adds a little urgency to the poem. We're on a schedule and everybody needs to get back to work.

A couple of important lessons in revision come to the fore when we look closely at Alex's revision process. He didn't try to write a perfect poem; instead, he used the poem in order to practice writing. Instead of trying to improve the poem as a whole, he broke his revision into steps, focusing in turn on image, energy, pattern, tension, and insight. When he was working on creating a clear image—a movie for the reader's mind—he let go of rhyming altogether. That was his first breakthrough.

His second breakthrough as a writer in this process was his realization that the poem couldn't have parts that were random, or lines or words that were written just to make the syllable count work or the rhyme scheme fit. Alex said that this was the most important turning point for him as a poet in the course. He realized that every single word really mattered. Each word had to be his choice, not "put in" to make the rhyme scheme work. And the poem had to be cohesive—everything had to fit together smoothly, like a well-designed engine or a professionally decorated room. He realized this was true for all poems, whether written in form or in free verse.

It's also important to notice that Alex didn't work alone. He had a class and a teacher, and he visited her during office hours. When he met with writing friends, the talk wasn't of frustration and despair, difficulty or drama. They talked about the work at hand and the best strategies for going back in and seeing more.

Alex says there was nothing painful about the writing process; it was partly work and partly play, and he enjoyed it. He says that even letting go of his original idea was freeing for him.

PRACTICE

What do you notice about the three versions of Alex Mouw's poem? What, if anything, do you think he did that made the poem better? Do you think he made too many changes? Not enough changes?

Revising Nonfiction

Nonfiction writers are truth tellers, not "prettifiers." They work as documentary filmmakers do, noting the truth of human experience in order to inform and enlighten. It's not always going to be pretty. Karissa Womack's essay began as many of her pieces do, as freewriting in her journal. "I need to come back and make this pretty," she wrote at the end of this particular entry. In fact, you will see as she works on the piece from its first inception to the final draft for her portfolio, what she ends up doing is the opposite of making the work "pretty."

> *The best writing comes not when you want to say something but when you want to find something.*
> — ANDRE DUBUS III

Here's an excerpt from the journal entry where the piece was first conceived:

> All of the men who make me uncomfortable every day. I think I have earned the right to be scared. . . .
>
> The man who owns the feed store is huge. He's dark haired. He is balding. Hair swarms on his arms and out the top of his white tees. He looks like a type of man. . . . He always carries the feed bags out to my truck. Usually two at a time.
>
> Today he didn't tell me to have a nice day and go back inside like usual. His wife and the kids weren't there today. And he lingered.
>
> He stood in the bed of my truck. "These old trucks are strong." He said that. Can hold all of him, he said. Not like all the new shit. "Be grateful," he said. "Every day you wake up alive be grateful. Some people fall asleep & that's it for them. They dead. Wake up dead. Be grateful for yourself."
>
> "Sure thing I am, yes sir."
>
> And he was leaning inside my truck . . . no one was nearby. I've got mace on my keychain I'm holding real tight. And would it just piss him off, like my

dad said. If someone wants to hurt you & they're out to it. They're gonna hurt you. Your little pink mace spray be damned.

How many days do women experience this? Oh hey, this guy made me uncomfortable because I didn't tell him, can you please stop leaning into my truck, you're making me nervous. Because I can't confront people like that. Why? Why can't I just say that? I think it's because the danger is real. But maybe that's what perpetuates. That's what makes us victims. Maybe next time just say & cut the whole thing short. & next time I need to buy feed, bring someone with me.

I think that's all I have to say on this.

I need to come back and make this pretty.

When Karissa first wrote this journal entry the afternoon after the feed store encounter, she wasn't thinking about writing an essay for a portfolio. "I just tried to get all of the details down. At the time I must have seen the story potential there, but I was too involved in the situation to write about it."

She forgot all about it.

Almost a year later, she had a project due in her creative writing class: a substantially revised new essay for a final portfolio, a piece that demonstrated the course concepts of Image, Energy, Tension, Pattern, and Insight. Using her journal as her source book, Karissa stumbled across the earlier entry. And from her journal entry, she typed up her first draft. She didn't do a drawing or list or freewrite; she just sat down and typed.

DRAFT ONE

Bent Creek

"Here's to the girls who regularly fish straw out of their bra."
— Bent Creek Feed, Facebook

Bent Creek Feed sits on 103rd street in Jacksonville, next door to the Blue Angel Gentleman's Club. The man who owns the store is huge and balding, with swarms of hair on his arms and falling out of his white tees. He is married to a blond, pony-tailed lady with a crooked smile. They have two young kids that hang around the store, a boy and a girl. They are very shy and never talk to me. Sometimes they have animals in boxes, like their prize fighting cocks. Sometimes the wife takes one out and holds him like a baby and tells me it's okay to pet him.

The man always carries the heavy bags of Seminole horse feed out to my truck, two at a time.

But one day they are all gone except the man. The sky looks like rain so I unlock the passenger side door of my truck for the feed bags. The man sets my bags on the floorboard. He doesn't tell me to have a nice day and go back inside like he did when the children were there.

I open my door. He stands on the running board of my truck, passenger door wide open. These old trucks are strong, he says, can hold all of me up. Not like all the new shit. I say, the rain is coming from out of nowhere. Be grateful, he says. Every day you wake up alive, be grateful. Some people fall asleep and that's it for them. They wake up dead. Be grateful. I say, I am, yes sir.

He looks at me. Tractor Supply hat too big for my head. Soffe shorts rolled high. Sports bra pink beneath a cream tank. I look young. I shake my head. I am grateful. The man sucks in air. He steps off of my running board and closes my passenger door.

Why didn't I just ask him to leave? Is it because real danger is a tenuous thing? If I say out loud, sir, why do you linger? Get out of my truck, he is exposed. He'll have to react, find out if I'm really like my old truck. But if I nod my head with my hands on the keychain and if he goes inside, then he's just a man offering advice.

When Karissa read it over, she had mixed feelings. Did she have enough on the page for a story? She wasn't sure. "I knew I had the Image. I knew the piece had Energy and I knew it had Tension. I knew the dialogue was right. But I left things out because I was afraid of making the piece too clunky. Really I was withholding the deeper truth and key aspects of my experience. But I didn't know that at the time. I wanted to write a piece I could turn in for a grade, and I wanted it also to be a piece I could show to my family."

Her professor praised the detail work, but, as Karissa remembers, "She asked prompting questions to keep me writing: 'Which day? Why are you there that day?' She told me to draw the scene so things would be more clear. I didn't take her advice."

Her professor encouraged her not to work on the sentence level yet, but to write more about what was hardest in that time of her life and to give more of the context for this moment, which didn't seem to be a whole story yet.

"Don't edit," Karissa recalls. "Resee, she kept saying. That's what I was trying to do." Karissa was frustrated. "My teacher said she really couldn't see the opening image. Where exactly was Bent Creek Feed in relation to the Blue Angel Gentleman's Club? What did the space look like? Where was this taking place?" If it was deserted, the reader needed to be able to see that. Most importantly, the professor wanted to know who this Karissa was, and what she was doing there, and what the piece was truly, deeply about for her.

I struggled with that opening line. I spent an hour on the phone with my boyfriend, completely trying to play around on the sentence level, to get the words right. He would offer suggestions and I would respond, "No, you don't see it. It doesn't look like THAT. I can't explain." In frustration, I *finally* tried what my professor had been suggesting all along and what we

> *What matters is the shape-making impulse.*
> — SEAMUS HEANEY

had learned in the first two weeks of class—I drew the scene. I snapped a photo of the drawing on my iPhone and sent it to my boyfriend. I called him back. We realized that what I'd been writing, and what the scene looked like drawn out, hadn't been connecting at all. I went back to a blank page and wrote the opening by hand. What came out after the drawing was so natural and connected with my body. The opening was complete!

Here is her new opening to the piece, after she drafted again and then revised by using the drawing technique:

DRAFT THREE

Bent Creek

Bent Creek Feed sits inside a concrete bunker off 103rd Street in Jacksonville, Florida. The Blue Angel Gentleman's Club is nestled into an otherwise deserted strip mall next door. A sign in the parking lot reads TOW AWAY ZONE, a warning. The man who runs Bent Creek is huge and balding, with swarms of hair on his arms and falling out of his white tee. He is married to a blond, ponytailed lady with a crooked smile. They have two young kids that hang around the store, a boy and a girl. They are very shy, looking down at their hands when I visit on Saturdays to buy Seminole Perform Safe pellets for my 15-year-old horse, Willow, who is crippled by abscesses. During the day I co-teach at Matthew Gilbert Middle School for AmeriCorps. Most evenings I visit Willow. I've never lived outside of Alabama before.

But one Saturday when I pull up in my dad's old Dodge truck, the parking lot is empty. U-Haul trailers line the edge of the lot, advertising to 103rd Street. There is pavement and the blue and yellow marquee for the gentleman's club. *Party with us*, the lettered sign invites.

At this stage in the revision process, Karissa knew the piece was missing something, but she didn't know what, and she was sick of working on "Bent Creek." She really wanted to be done.

When her professor again told her to keep working, she felt frustrated and daunted. She'd worked hard. She'd gotten a lot of praise from classmates, her boyfriend, and her best friend. Why continue to revise?

Karissa had worked hard in her draft to show why she was where she was. Some of the details were clearer. But questions remained for other readers, including her professor. What was her situation in life? Who was this person we were reading about on the page? We could see everything she saw, but we couldn't see *her*, arguably the most important person in the piece. That's always the great challenge in writing memoir: how to get your own self on the page in a way that's interesting, evocative, honest, compelling, and clear.

Her professor told her to keep revising — there was more to the story, and the images still weren't completely clear. Her writing partner told her: Listen to your professor, get over yourself, and work on the piece. Karissa then drove four hours to Jacksonville, Florida, went to the feed store, and photographed the parking lot. This technique — taking the time to physically immerse yourself in the location you are writing about — works extremely well for poets, fiction writers, playwrights, and of course graphic writers.

Once on-site, Karissa still struggled with capturing in words what she was seeing. Even when she looked at the feed store, trying to describe that location clearly was next to impossible. Having written and rewritten her opening paragraph in the feed lot many times, never able to get it right, she decided to try to come up with a whole new way of getting into the piece.

Here's the opening of her next version:

DRAFT FOUR

Bent Creek

I unroll my Soffe shorts. It's hot and I'll be glad I wore these later, but for now I need to make sure that my butt's not falling out. I race down the concrete steps of my second floor apartment and through the sandy courtyard filled with magnolia trees. I'm slathered in sunscreen, a bottle sticking out of my purse, pink print with blue horses running across the fabric. Frozen water bottles are slick and cold in my right hand. My Ariat boots aren't boutique; they're hard-toed, slick-bottomed cowgirl boots, pink stitching against brown leather.

Trimmed bushes and palms line my way to the parking lot. The Reserve at Waters Inlet really could be nice, like the pretty blue-skied pictures I'd seen online when I was apartment hunting.

It's morning and I'm hoping that everyone is still asleep. I'm hoping to jump inside my truck and click the lock before I run into Jack, or worse, Mike. Jack who swore I wouldn't make it down here three months before finding someone new. Mike, his shirtless body ripped and tattooed beneath flowing dreads, who kept a gun shoved into his waistband. "Don't be alone around him," Gary warned.

The prickly, green bushes scratch against my right shoulder. The parking lot is just ahead.

"Hey!"

I don't see anyone. The loiterers haven't arrived yet, backs pressed against the wooden apartment walls, joints dangling from their lips, pit bulls straining against their leashes.

"Hey teacher!"

It's my neighbor Gary on the second floor balcony of the adjoining building. I'd told myself I wouldn't stop. But I do, my boots catching a crack in the sidewalk. I'd feel better being caught in my work uniform; baggy khakis, red bomber jacket with the AmeriCorps logo, despite the Florida heat. Gary has only been a friend to me, helping my dad carry my bed into my apartment, reminding me to lock my glass patio door. But his eyes move slowly over my body—face, tits, hips. I've told him again and again that I work at the local middle school. I want him to remember that if he had custody of his two girls, if they didn't live away with their grandmother, that they could be in my class. I want him to think of his daughters when he looks at me.

Karissa set this new opening on top of the feed store part of the story and called it "done." She knew her professor would be impressed that she had tried a whole new approach in the opening. During her final conference, Karissa was surprised by the reaction she got.

Her professor said that it seemed the piece was about feeling vulnerable around men, living in a strange place you are really just passing through. "Stop revising the words on the page," her professor suggested, "and try something wildly different." For example, her professor said, make a list of all the men you interacted with that year. "Like all those faces at the opening of *Orange Is the New Black*." If Karissa used the list form, she might get outside the confines of the story she'd been telling herself, and the deeper meaning in the piece, and some surprises, might come forward. Karissa knew that she still didn't know how to show her own insights because she still didn't know what this piece was ultimately trying to say.

That night, Karissa reread the Insight chapter. But she didn't have any great insights. Not yet. She scanned the Forms chapter, and on page 436 she found the List form and decided to make a list of every man she had interacted with during that year.

When she reviewed her list, Karissa was anxious. The list of men contained a motley assortment—there were the apartment complex men and boys, her wild students, friends, men she had met at parties. Would there be enough of a story for the reader? Who cared about her dumb, embarrassing experiences during her gap year? And she had made mistakes with men. She would be embarrassed to show this new essay to her parents, even if she could find the courage to write it. Karissa was reading *The Empathy Exams* by Leslie Jamison during this time. And she noticed that when Jamison wrote about her own emotional anxieties, health issues, and issues with her boyfriend, Karissa was riveted as a reader. Karissa said: "It was exciting to live, while reading, inside the mind of another woman, her problems, her choices. It helps me understand my own life, my choices."

Karissa knew she was a perfectionist. She was frustrated and angry that revising was so difficult, but she knew she couldn't continue moving words around endlessly. The "Bent Creek" draft had become painful to look at. She had been adding and cutting words for months. She closed her laptop, stepped away from all her printouts, and started over, writing once again in the pink journal, by hand. "I could show the original Bent Creek piece to my family, my peers, without really giving up anything of myself. When my professor told me to try a list of men, I was immediately drawn to seeing Bent Creek in a whole new way. *Reseeing*. Oh my gosh. It finally hit me. This was what *reseeing* actually meant. Once I started over, the images kept jumping at me. I could see them all, these men. The essay came out in one clean handwritten draft. I didn't stop or start over or make a single change."

Here's the new opening:

DRAFT FIVE

Jacksonville, Florida, 2014: A List of Men

Paul

He was skinnier than he sounded on the phone, with a gun and holster strapped around his waist. He smoked cigarettes when we rolled 1,000-pound round bales of hay into the metal feeders for the horses. When I ran screaming about a snake in the grass, he cleaved it in half with a shovel. He kicked at the dead thing, "Damn, Karissa, it was only a rat snake."

Ethan

He didn't have a body for much of that year while he was still my boy-friend. I cried to him over the phone, which I held close to my mouth. Outside my apartment door, footsteps thudded across the walkway, then stopped. I heard tugging, metal clicking against wood. Lazy criminals checking doorknobs nightly. My deadbolt stayed locked.

I fell asleep breathing into the phone. Ethan said, "Let's start with curb appeal—will our home have shutters? How big is the front yard?"

A year later, we'll be sitting across a table in my new apartment

He'll say, "We had a good run," like I'm a horse put out to pasture.

He'll say, "This is really beautiful."

He'll say, "It's not your fault."

Jack

"Your boyfriend and you won't make it three months," he said. My other neighbors said that he wanted to date me. I saw his girlfriend once in my apartment complex's office, their newborn baby tucked into her arms. His father died that year and he left for Miami without telling anyone good-bye.

Gary

He was the only other white person in my apartment complex. He latched onto me early on.

"Hey teacher, I want to show you my cats."

Gary led me up concrete steps to his second floor apartment and closed the door. The lights were off, but the patio blinds were pulled back so the daylight shone in. The layout was the same as my apartment, except that there was a second bedroom for when his daughters visited. Gary reached behind his gray, fabric couch and pulled out a gun.

"Lock your back door."

He aimed the black gun at the glass patio.

"Next time, I'll be ready."

He wasn't home when someone scaled the wooden beams and slid through his unlocked patio door. There was nothing worth taking, but his furniture had been toppled, the fridge left gaping.

Gary shoved the gun into the waist of his jeans. His eyes moved slowly over my body—face, tits, hips. I hoped there really were cats.

I followed him to his daughters' bedroom. Plush Hello Kitties dotted the carpet. The twin bed was fitted with pink sheets, just like my own.

Gary had only been a friend to me, helping my dad carry my bed into my apartment. But I'd told him again and again that I worked at the local middle school. I wanted him to remember that if he had custody of his two girls, if they didn't live away with their grandmother, that they could be in my English class. I wanted him to think of his daughters when he looked at me.

Gary got down on his hands and knees, lifted the pink bed skirt.

"Meow, Bella, meow," he said.

Three small tuxedo kittens came mewing from under the girls' bed. I got down on the carpet to pet them. I watched fleas hop.

Deity

He's only a teenager. "I want her to suck my dick," he said about me too loudly when I escorted a line of middle school boys to their afterschool program, Team Up. His mom walked over from her job at R.L. Brown Elementary next door and hooked her fingers around his right ear.

"You're going to live with your father if you keep this up." He cried like a much younger boy, snot bubbling out of his nose.

The piece ended with the section about the owner of the feed store from the original "Bent Creek" draft—those original opening paragraphs.

Before turning the piece in for her final portfolio, Karissa showed it to her writing group. They said that the list was great but that it needed work. Ethan and perhaps the story about Angel, the owner of the feed store, needed to be threaded throughout. Some sections needed more detail; some needed less detail and more clarity.

At this point, Karissa was ready to give up. "I was frustrated and whiny. And I questioned everything. Not just the hard work but why was I writing this stuff? . . . Who cares what I have to say? What are people going to think about me, about the situations I wrote about in the essay?"

But something happened to Karissa at this point in the process. She had worked so hard on the piece. But she felt as though she was learning, at last, how to be a better writer—not just how to make this piece better, but how to listen to her readers. "Now, I could all of a sudden see how the braided stories of these men, these situations and conversations could leap to bring out a cohesive story. In my next draft, I set myself up to be working on Insight—Who am I? Why am I there? How is that different? Those deeper questions came from the braid. And, honestly, just working so long on it and getting to know the depth of it all better."

In her journal, she wrote, "I really don't know how to start this dang essay. The Jack section is sharp and short, but I need to first contextualize. Ew, I hate that word."

She visualized now as she wrote, focusing less on her feelings and more on what she could actually see. This time, when she got stuck and frustrated, she met with her writing partner and *talked through* what happened that first day, in order to get clearly grounded in space and time. To figure out how to make the opening setup clearer—where did Karissa live, and why did she live there?—her writing partner typed while Karissa talked.

> My dad was helping me move in . . . to that apartment in Jacksonville. I spent forever in the office signing papers and getting the key. I had saved up all this money working at the Red Lobster (which I despised!) to get my own apartment. I had to bring a money order and sign a billion papers. While I'm doing that, my dad's standing out by our pickups—they're packed with my stuff and wrapped up with tarps. I physically can't carry my real wood desk up the stairs, so we were hoping to run into someone who would help us. Jack saw my dad by the trucks and offered to help. We felt lucky.
>
> So after I get my key from the office, I go up to my new apartment (which is all shitty and broken and everything has been painted over, like really paper towels painted over in the cabinets). And I'm in this empty apartment looking around and the door opens and there is this guy and I'm like, WTF? And then my dad's right behind him and says, "Hey we got friends to help us move." This is Jack and he's like, "Let me get my boys; they'll help too." And I don't remember, but I know he was looking me up and down because he was always doing that.

Her writing partner asked what she really wanted to know: "What about the boyfriend? How does he know you have a boyfriend?"

Karissa explained while her partner wrote:

> The guys are all excited that I'm there. It's a pretty run-down place. A lot of the people are on food stamps and have a few kids. I'm this young, do-gooder girl. They start off asking if I want to hang out, I got a boyfriend? And I tell them about my boyfriend and it's all real serious — basically asking them to respect that and leave me alone.

"You need to show us *that*," her partner said. And Karissa began anew in her little pink notebook.

When she typed her next draft, she changed the opening to try to tell her reader who she was, what she was doing there, and what really mattered:

DRAFT SEVEN

I Remember All of You

Jack

> I'd never lived outside of Alabama before. I was twenty-three, working for AmeriCorps at a middle school in Jacksonville, Florida. Jack surprised me when he walked into my new apartment. My dad, at 6'2", seemed small, walking behind Jack's hulking frame. Jack was strong and did most of the lifting—a crew of his friends in tow. My dad bought them all ribs and beer as a thank-you. "That's my daughter," Dad said. "I'll be back to check on her."
>
> "Your boyfriend and you won't make it three months," Jack said when my dad left me. My other neighbors said that he wanted to date me. I saw his girlfriend once in my apartment complex's office, their newborn baby tucked into her arms. His father died that year and he left for Miami without telling anyone good-bye.

When Karissa submitted the piece again, her professor told her what she already knew. The opening *still* wasn't working. Karissa laid her head down on the professor's desk. *Are you kidding me?* "But I knew it wasn't right. I was still doing this bland expository thing. It just didn't go with the essay. I had to start with an image. Finally, I did it." (You can read the final version of Karissa's essay on p. 398.)

That night, Karissa read the final version to her sister. She remembers how she felt reading aloud:

> I was really nervous that my sister wouldn't like it, that she'd think I was a freak or self-indulgent. Anyway, by the end of the essay, when I got to the

Insight parts, my sister cried. She said she was so proud of my writing. Wow, that was so amazing. I love my sister dearly and to have her respect on such a personal piece renews my faith in writing nonfiction. . . .

It took me a long time to do what I know works. To write and revise in short timed sessions. To draw before I write. To use lists. To really get back in my body in space and time. Why did it take me so long? Fear. I was so scared to reveal myself and tell the truth. . . . The final list essay reveals a lot about me that I never intended to share. . . . It still feels weird to say, look I wrote this thing, but it's intensely personal and revealing, hope you still like it, and hope you still like me. I think this was my "welcome to nonfiction" moment.

Karissa describes what she learned from the revision process:

This essay taught me how to write. I learned how to sit down and write. I know that sounds crazy and basic, but it's not. I would get stuck in a draft and frustrated and think all day about the draft and how I can't write it good enough. That would take up a lot of my time, so it would feel like I'd been working, but really, nothing was progressing and I just felt terrible about it all. I learned to just start asking and answering questions to get myself writing. Obsessing and talking about your writing is not actually writing. Only the actual physical act of pen to paper, then fingers to keys will help me progress. And reading it aloud and being willing to do nineteen drafts. I now love revision even more than writing.

PRACTICE

Read Karissa Womack's first version of "Bent Creek" (p. 380). Reread her final version on page 398. What did she lose from her first version? How does the list form change the essay completely? Do you prefer one version over the other?

PRACTICE

Consider the steps Karissa Womack went through in revision. Using her steps, as you understand them, create a checklist, a quick-start guide to revision. Then, using the principles in this chapter and taking what you like from her model, design your own revision checklist: What would be most useful for you to do every time you revise?

EDITING AND PROOFREADING

Editing and proofreading are almost the opposite of revision. Editing and proofreading are late-stage activities—the very last things a writer does before showing the work. Revision is messy and wild, exactly like writing itself. Revision *is* writing.

> *Writing is about hypnotizing yourself into believing in yourself, getting some work done, then un-hypnotizing yourself and going over the material coldly.*
> — ANNE LAMOTT

But all three of these activities have one thing in common. In each case, the writer must have strategies for dealing with unhelpful judgmental thoughts. She has to concentrate when she is working, and to cultivate a *helpful* focused concentration, she must postpone judgmental thoughts.

Revision is reseeing and deep dreaming. Editing is making sure that the grammar and syntax are correct; that your verbs are in the appropriate tense; that your facts are accurate, sentences aren't clunky, line breaks are most effective. Editing is like giving your piece its annual physical examination. Are all the systems working properly? After you have reseen your work and chosen the best scenes and images, worked hard to tell your story or perfect your poem, honed the opening and closing, polished the dialogue, and deepened the significance—only then are you ready to edit. Revision works on the deep interior of the piece—the bones and the guts and the brain of the work. Editing checks to make sure that all the systems are hooked up to each other properly so we have a cohesive, smoothly running, healthy whole.

Proofreading is checking the skin. Proofreading is picking over the *surface* of your piece (as opposed to further illuminating the interior, as you do in writing and revising). Proofreading is the *opposite* of getting inside the piece

QUESTIONS TO ASK: Editing for Flow

Is your writing as strong as it can be? Consider the following questions.

1. Is your writing clear? Is it easy to understand who is talking, who is in the piece, where we are, and what is happening?
2. Do you rely on weak verbs such as *to be* verbs, *should, could, would, might,* and *may*? (See "Muscles," p. 196.)
3. Do you overuse filters, words that describe mental activity, such as *seemed, felt, realized,* and *thought*? (See "Filters," p. 197.)
4. Do you explain too much?
5. Do you include too much description?
6. Do you use unnecessary adverbs?

and reseeing all those alive moving images—it's the final check in the mirror before you go out the door. No awkward milk mustache. No bedhead. No bizarrely wrinkled pants, hanging threads, distracting mismatched socks. It's all surface stuff, but it's incredibly important. If you have a stain on your shirt during a job interview, it's going to distract the interviewer and define you as a sloppy person. Your words and experience won't be taken seriously. If you have typos, misspelled words, missing page numbers, or strange indents, your reader will be distracted. She wants to be transported by your play, engaged by your story, blown away by your poetry. Your writing must be proofread so that she can have a relaxing experience. You owe it to your reader. Proofread. Smooth. Polished. Professional. Tip: Proofread backward, starting at the end of the piece and looking for errors so that you are not caught up in the story or progression, but are more able to focus on the surface. Also, it's easier to find errors in other people's work than in your own. (Did you find any mistakes in this textbook?)

Clean with your eyes. Read the piece forward and backward. Literally, go from bottom to top at least twice so that you are more likely to find errors and less likely to be so caught in the "dream" you have worked so hard to create that you are blind to errors. And ask your writing group, or a partner, to look at your work, too. *Writers work with other writers.*

Your instructor probably will have specific guidelines for turning in work. Various assignments and magazines and editors also have specific guidelines and format requirements. Always follow them to the letter.

Ask your instructor and your readers what errors they see most often in your work, and concentrate on correcting those. Consult your grammar handbook and learn why you make those mistakes and how to fix them. To progress as a writer, now is the time to learn the rules of grammar and style. Neither editors, nor employers, nor publishers will take your work seriously if it is plagued with serious grammar problems.

QUESTIONS TO ASK: Proofreading for Common Grammar Errors

Use your grammar handbook to check for the following common mistakes.

1. Have you chosen the word you meant to use? Frequently confused word pairs include *lie* and *lay*, *less* and *fewer*, *it's* and *its*, *that* and *which*, and *they're* and *their*.
2. Do your subjects and verbs agree?
3. Do you have any misplaced modifiers?
4. Are there unintentional sentence fragments?

QUESTIONS TO ASK: Proofreading for Presentation

Sometimes you'll receive specific guidelines for preparing your work. Even if you don't, you should always address the following conventions.

1. Do you need a title page? If so, have you created one?

2. Are your pages numbered?

3. Are your margins at least one inch wide at the left, right, top, and bottom of every page?

4. Is the spacing between sentences, sections, and stanzas consistent?

5. Have you included any necessary headers and footers?

6. Have you followed punctuation conventions, especially for dialogue?

7. Have you checked your spelling?

8. Have you checked separately for typographical errors? For instance, you may have typed *from* instead of *form* or *then* instead of *than*. Spell checkers won't catch these errors since the words are spelled correctly. They just aren't the ones you intended to use.

WRITING PROJECTS

1. Select a piece of writing from this course that you are not happy with. Do the assignment over again, deliberately making the piece as terrible as you can. What do you notice about your original version?

2. Take a "failed" piece from the semester, one that you like but can't figure out how to improve. Draw a sketch or diagram of the opening scene—whether it's a poem, a play, a story, or an essay. Be clear on where the piece is taking place, who is "onstage," and what the weather, setting, and time of day are. Notice when the action begins. Using this point as your new starting place, rewrite your piece.

3. Choose any piece of writing from the semester, and generate a new piece using the last line of this piece as your starting point for the new version. Use nothing else from your first draft.

4. Take one of your poems from the course, and turn it into a short story. Or take a piece of nonfiction and fictionalize it. Or take an essay and turn it into one of the forms of poetry discussed in Chapter Ten. Notice how changing genres may let you improve a piece quickly and easily.

5. Using a hard copy of any piece, take scissors and cut the paragraphs or lines apart. Then reassemble the piece in a new order, taping the sections together in a way that produces leaps, clarity, and fresh collisions. What do you like better about the new piece? What do you feel is stronger in the original?

6. Choose one of the strategies chapters in Part Two, locate the workshop for that strategy, and answer the questions yourself, for your own piece of writing. Revise accordingly. Choose a second strategy, and apply the workshop questions to your work-in-progress. If possible, take the time to go through each strategy workshop. If you aren't sure which ones to start with, try Images, then Energy, and then Tension.

7. Choose one of your poems and write the opposite of each line. For example, if you wrote "My love is so strong," you might write in your new version, "My loathing is weak." What do you learn from this exercise?

8. Take a prose piece and go paragraph by paragraph, finding one thing you can render more clearly, more visually, in each paragraph. Make the changes.

9. Read aloud the titles of all the pieces of writing included in this book. Choose your favorites. Allow them to inspire better, more specific, more exciting titles for your pieces.

REVISION WORKSHOP

The prompts below will help you constructively discuss your classmates' work.

1. Read the piece aloud. Using a highlighter or underlining, indicate all the parts that are "in image": that is, where you can *see* what's on the page as an image in your mind's eye.

2. Circle any places where there are too many words or where the writer has trailed off into excess commentary or description. Often, revision involves simply cutting out extraneous material.

3. Reread the piece. Pretend it's a tiny movie. Make a list of the scenes — the visual, sensory moments — that the piece takes you through. Which are the most dramatic items on your list? Is the writer willing to cut the less dramatic sections, or replace them with new sections, or find a way to increase the depth and tension in these passages?

4. Review the Troubleshooting Energy checklist on page 208. In which places does the piece have good energy? In which places does the energy flag?

5. What patterns do you notice in this piece? Can you find visual patterns? Sound patterns? Where could the writer use pattern more actively?

6. Are questions raised in the piece? Would it be helpful if the writer inserted questions? Where?

7. Look back at Questions to Ask: Editing for Flow (p. 390). How does this piece of writing address the first three questions? How could it do so more overtly?

8. What is the single most memorable visual image from this piece of writing? What will you still be able to "see" in your mind's eye, long after this course has ended?

Jack Ridl

Repairing the House

We will learn the house can live
without our changes. We will

listen to its language. The cracks
along the stairway—they are sentences.

We will read what they say
when we go up, again when

we walk back down. When we
leave our sleep, our beds will hold

our place as the floor creaks under us.
If we fix the broken window, then

we will open it. The other windows
rise on their tracks; that's enough;

one staying shut, tight, will still bring
light for any day, the others the breeze.

And we will learn to be with the ivy
straying along the back brick walls,

twisting itself into the mortar, each spring
a chunk or two falling into the holly.

We will feel a draft under the porch door.
We could block the cold from sliding

toward our feet. Instead, we will wear
socks, ones you made, while we sit facing

each other, reading on the sofa, its stuffing shifting
under us, the pillows giving the way to what is left.

Jack Ridl and "Repairing the House"

The Poem and I Have a Little Conversation

This is a little conversation that attempts to reveal what happens most of the time when I try to write a poem. I start off, usually with some notion or twitch of an idea. That then becomes a title out from which I start writing. In this case the notion was the need to do some repairs on our house and the negative consequences of not attending to these needed reparations. I wrote a draft. It dealt with how not fixing the house could hurt a marriage. The following "conversation" came about as I listened to the poem trying to tell me what I had realized. The poem, any poem I try to compose, is invariably smarter than I am. But I'm stubborn; every time, I want to have my way. Then finally I start to listen. Here's the kind of thing I usually hear.

JACK: Ok. Done. Got down exactly what would happen if I don't make those needed repairs to the place.

POEM: It's all negative. The consequences are all negative.

JACK: Of course they are.

POEM: Of course they are?

JACK: Yes, of course they are.

POEM: You're sure?

(The poem is often like a Zen master all but whacking me behind the head.)

JACK: So what are you saying? You're telling me there are positives to not repairing the house?

POEM: Yes.

JACK: And I assume that you're implying that there are also negative consequences if I *do* repair the place.

POEM: I don't know about negatives, but there are certainly valuable things that won't happen if you make these repairs.

JACK: Help me out.

POEM: Oh, come on. Well, how about this: Can you two live without making those changes?

JACK: I guess we could.

POEM: No, I don't mean put up with not making them. I mean live.

JACK: Oh.

POEM: Look at me! What if the cracks are gone? What if you can no longer hear the creaks in the floor? What if you don't fix that one window; what will you notice? What if you don't fix the wall where the ivy is growing?

JACK: The place will go to hell!

POEM: Put me away. Go for a walk with the dog or rake some leaves or take a nap or read some poems or — just put me away.

PAUSE

POEM: You're back.
JACK: I am, and . . . . (*Jack starts writing again.*)
POEM: See?
JACK: Shut up.
POEM: Yes! That's it: don't fix the draft under the door. Yes, put on socks, those socks she made for you. Yes, see? She's putting on socks, too. Look at me! Sit on the sofa together. That's a good sound by the way, "sofa." I like what that sound feels like.
JACK: I like ending with those socks and sitting together on the sofa.
POEM: Well . . . I uh . . . .
JACK: You think it's cheesy.
POEM: Well . . . .
JACK: What do you want?
POEM: C'mon, can't you feel it? Comfort. I want to feel that.
JACK: And that's not cheesy?
POEM: That's not what I meant. Read me.
JACK: You want it more comforting. Ok, how about some pillows?
POEM: Well, sure, pillows are comforting but it's still —
JACK: Cheesy.
POEM: No, you got rid of that, but it's resolved.
JACK: So?
POEM: You know better.
JACK: Pillows give way. If they give way then . . . .
POEM: You got it. Now, finished?
JACK: A poem's never finished; it's —
POEM: Abandoned. Ready to abandon me?
JACK: Yep.
POEM: What did I end up being about?
JACK: A poem's always about a lot of things.
POEM: I say that it's about the socks.
JACK: The poem is about the socks?
POEM: Well, yes. And socks come in what?
JACK: All sizes.
POEM: No! These socks. These socks come in pairs.
JACK: So?
POEM: The socks.

JACK: The socks.

POEM: C'mon. You can't be this blind. What do you call two socks?

JACK: A pair.

POEM: Duh. And what does that have to do with me?

JACK: Oh my god! A pair of socks. Two pairs of socks. The couple is each wearing a pair of socks. The couple is on the sofa. Not fixing the house is to—

POEM: You got it!

JACK: To fix the couple. To re-couple!

POEM: You're kidding me? To re-couple?

JACK: Yeah.

POEM: To re-couple? What have you been talking about doing?

JACK: Repairing the house.

POEM: Uh huh. Repairing. Repair. To—

JACK: Pair! They are re-paired!

POEM: Genius. Now, what's wrong with the structure?

JACK: Nothing.

POEM: Well, ok. In one sense nothing. It's in one solid block.

JACK: Right. They are together, solid.

POEM: Think about *couple.*

JACK: Couple.

POEM: Couple.

JACK: Two.

POEM: Yes. Two. A pair is two, a couple is two, is a—

JACK: Couple, couples, oh my god, couplet! It can be in couplets.

POEM: Genius.

Karissa Womack

I Remember All of You

JACK

Jack wasn't really a middle school teacher, like he said. He was a janitor and he lived in the apartment below me. Muscular with a dragging stomach, he helped carry furniture into my new, empty apartment. I was a middle school teacher. Or at least I would be for that year with AmeriCorps.

Jack and his boys liked to stand outside my apartment steps, smoking joints and petting their bluenose pit bulls. Jack would stand right on the bottom step when I tried to walk down, his body filling the narrow stairwell.

"Your boyfriend and you won't make it three months," he said.

Neighbors told me *Jack wants you.*

Once, I saw Jack's girlfriend in the apartment complex's office, their new-born baby tucked into her arms. His father died that year and he left for Miami without telling anyone good-bye.

DEITY

He's only a teenager. "I want her to suck my dick," he said about me too loudly when I escorted a line of middle school boys to their afterschool program, Team Up. His mom walked over from her job at R.L. Brown Elementary next door and hooked her fingers around his right ear.

"You're going to live with your father if you keep this up." He cried like a much younger boy, snot bubbling out of his nose.

VERNON

He drew the curves and triangles of a hoof into the sandy dirt of the barn hallway. He knew I didn't have a lot of money and trimmed my horse Willow's hooves for free.

"I bet you don't have any trouble finding a boyfriend," he said. He admired my tattoo, wings peeking from the edges of a wife beater.

He showed me how to clean Willow's abscesses, to drop her hoof into a bag of Epsom salt and warm water, to duct tape it tight before she started thrashing.

He said, "If only I were your age."

ETHAN

He didn't have a body for much of that year while he was still my boyfriend. I cried to him over the phone, which I held close to my mouth. Outside my apartment door, footsteps thudded across the walkway, then stopped. I heard tugging, metal clicking against wood. Lazy criminals checking doorknobs nightly. My deadbolt stayed locked.

Ethan said, "Let's start with curb appeal—will our home have shutters? How big is the front yard?"

I fell asleep breathing into the phone.

GARY

He was the only other white person in my apartment complex. He latched onto me early on. He stopped me every afternoon when I came home from school.

One day he said, "Hey teacher, I want to show you my cats."

Gary led me up concrete steps to his second floor apartment and closed the door. The lights were off, but the patio blinds were pulled back so the daylight shone in. The layout was the same as my apartment, except that there was a second bedroom for when his daughters visited. Gary reached behind his gray, fabric couch and pulled out a gun.

"Lock your back door."

He aimed the black gun at the glass patio.

"Next time, I'll be ready."

He hadn't been home when someone scaled the wooden beams and slid through his unlocked patio door. There was nothing worth taking, but his furniture had been toppled, the fridge left gaping.

Gary shoved the gun into the waist of his jeans. His eyes moved slowly over my body—face, tits, hips. I hoped there really were cats.

I followed him to his daughters' bedroom. Plush Hello Kitties dotted the carpet. The twin bed was fitted with pink sheets, just like my own.

Gary had been a friend to me, helping my dad carry my bed into my apartment. I'd told him again and again that I worked at the local middle school. I wanted him to remember that if he had custody of his two girls, if they didn't live away with their grandmother, that they could be in my English class. I wanted him to think of his daughters when he looked at me.

Gary got down on his hands and knees, lifted the pink bed skirt.

"Meow, Bella, meow," he said.

Three small tuxedo kittens came mewing from under the girls' bed. I got down on the carpet to pet them. I watched fleas hop.

MIKE

He was always shirtless. His body ripped and tattooed beneath long dreads. A gun stayed tucked into his blue jeans. "Never be alone with him," my neighbor told me. I drank PBR on my patio and watched his toddler follow after him on a tipsy red tricycle.

ETHAN

He had begun building new dreams without me. A condo on the gulf with his brother.

He said, "You don't understand, I need the TV to sleep."

I needed quiet.

I needed his voice.

He said, "Are you drunk?" I was. I needed to be careful.

Outside my apartment walls were the footsteps of other men.

I fell asleep without ending the call.

ANGEL

I drove forty-five minutes away from downtown, toward the country to Bent Creek Feed, a concrete bunker off 103rd street. I went every other Saturday for Seminole horse feed. I bought my bags from Angel, the man who ran the store. He was huge and balding, with swarms of hair on his arms. His wife, a blond, pony-tailed lady with a crooked smile, held her favorite rooster like a baby. Their two children would look down at their hands when I greeted them.

But this Saturday, when I pulled up in my dad's old Dodge truck, the parking lot was missing the minivan, the trucks of other customers. Next door, the blue and yellow marquee flashed *Party with us,* above the Blue Angel Gentleman's Club.

I paid with a credit card. Angel slid the feed onto the floor of my cab. I slid in behind the wheel. He let the passenger door fall shut. But he didn't move. He didn't tell me to have a nice day and go back inside like he did when the roosters and children were there. I opened my door. He stepped onto the running board of my truck, and flung the passenger door wide open. We watched each other across my truck's open cab.

"Be grateful," he said. "Every day you wake up alive, be grateful."

His eyes were dark, deeper than brown.

"I am, yes sir."

Angel leaned into the truck, wide hands splayed across the passenger seat. I imagined there were women dancing behind the tightly shut door of the Blue Angel Gentleman's Club. Had Angel told any of them to be grateful? I wonder what they said?

JACOB

At a party, my friend Kasia walked in on us pulling Junot Díaz books from his shelf. "Baby, you say, baby, this is part of my novel." Another night we drank too much at Burrow Bar and rode home in the backseat of Kasia's car. His curly hair, wide nostrils, square frame glasses losing their shape. His hand was reaching inside my thigh. Kasia pulled the car to the side and I vomited out the window.

KYLE

Kasia's boyfriend went to the University of Alabama. He was the only man I'd met in Florida who'd been to Auburn, my alma mater and the home I dreamed about. I washed my clothes in their apartment and saw the black-strapped sex swing on their bedroom door, the bruises on Kasia's neck under a layer of base. They met on the sex meet-up app Tinder, but a year later they'll rent a house together near Bent Creek Feed, a house with a large front yard.

ETHAN

He said a lot of things to me:

> *You're my queen.*
> *You are beautiful.*
> *You cry too much.*
> *Send me a dirty picture.*
> *Please.*
> *I don't want children.*
> *I miss you.*
> *Where are we getting married?*
> *What kind of dress will you wear?*
> *I promise I'll visit.*
> *Where are you?*
> *Who are you with?*
> *I'm not coming.*

ANGEL

Willow ran out of feed again.

I said I wouldn't go back to Bent Creek, but by then I was used to compromising.

After he dropped the feed in my truck, Angel leaned his face down to mine. I could see the wide pores across his nose and the wispy hairs of an untrimmed mustache.

He asked, "Did I scare you?"

I never told him, any of them, that they were wrong. I never asked him to leave. Is that because real danger is a fragile thing? If I had said out loud to him, "Go away, get out of my truck," then he'd be exposed. He'd have to react. But if I nodded with my hands gripping the mace on my keychain and if he went back inside, then he was just a man offering advice.

GENRES

PART THREE

Act I, get your guy up a tree. Act II, throw rocks at him. Act III, get your guy outta the tree.

JULIUS EPSTEIN

The professional dedicates himself to mastering technique not because he believes technique is a substitute for inspiration but because he wants to be in possession of the full arsenal of skills when inspiration does come.

STEVEN PRESSFIELD

My role in society, or any artist's or poet's role, is to try and express what we all feel.

JOHN LENNON

CHAPTER TEN

FORMS

You're familiar with the four traditional genres used by writers in contemporary Western literature: poetry, drama, fiction, and creative nonfiction. This chapter seeks to extend and deepen your practice in the genres and also to invite experiment and invention as you define yourself as a writer. This chapter presents fourteen different forms, many of which can be deployed in more than one genre.

Specific subcategories in a genre are called **forms**. For example, a writer working in the genre of poetry may choose to create poems in the sonnet form or free verse form. A playwright may use various forms, including two-parters, ten-minute plays, or one-act plays, a common short form of play. Other writers push the boundaries of genre and work in between the traditional categories, writing in forms such as prose poems, spoken word, monologues in verse (rap is one example), or stories so short that on the page they're indistinguishable from poetry. Other forms of creative writing refuse to fit neatly into the four main genres: comics, graphic novels, vouvelles, and text-and-image experiments, to name a few. Practicing various forms across the genres—traditional and nontraditional—expands your skill and your vision as a writer. It's often been said that there's nothing new to say, only new ways to say it.

> *Twitter is the perfect form for poetry.*
> — AI WEIWEI

Some new writers come into creative writing with very fixed ideas about the genres they love most: *I am a poet*, or *I was born to craft plays*. Some students dread certain forms, perhaps the sonnet or the essay, because of a negative experience earlier in their education, or just a lack of familiarity with the breadth and range possible. However, cross-training in the genres is extrarodinarily helpful for writers' growth, development, and success, just as it is crucial for athletes to challenge themselves with various types of physical activity, helping them build endurance, strength, and flexibility. Football players study ballet. A fiction writer improves her ear when creating a scene for a screenplay. Poets learn necessary aspects of narrative structure by writing short stories. Creative nonfiction writers *must* practice the basics of scene and characterization in order to create vivid, compelling, character-rich essays; so for them, immersion in the craft of fiction is essential. And many writers quickly discover they are capable of much more than what lies within the bounds of an early genre choice. We often outgrow our early tastes as we read more widely and write more boldly; thus practicing in each genre is a requirement for creative writing students. Many would argue, though not all would agree, that pushing against genre constraints and placing a high value on experiments, mash-ups, creative collaborations, and genre-bending exercises is not only useful for a writer's growth; it's also rewarding and fun.

When you are first learning how to improve your craft as a creative writer, it's helpful to practice strategies for writing clearly, writing with energy and tension, enhancing the use of pattern, and increasing depth, putting the techniques first and postponing genre decisions. By the end of your course, you want to be able to create effective, fresh, cohesive work in any genre you choose.

You may try these genre-based projects throughout the course, choosing, say, one a week, in order to apply the techniques you are learning in Part Two, Strategies, as you progress. Or, at the end of the course, once you have practiced a wide range of creative writing activities, you might create a portfolio of pieces, choosing from the genre-specific projects in order to practice and demonstrate every strategy you've learned so far.

WRITING IN THE GENRES

Table of Forms

	Poetry	Fiction	Drama	Nonfiction
Abecedarius	X	X		X
Anaphora	X	X	X	X
Braid	X	X	X	X
Graphic		X		X
Flash		X		X
Ghazal	X			
Journey	X	X	X	X
List	X	X		X
Monologue	X	X	X	X
Play/Screenplay	X		X	
Pantoum	X			
Sestina	X			
Sonnet	X			
Villanelle	X			

Experiment

It's best to try each form at least twice. The first time you try a new form, attempt to conform to the guidelines carefully. The second time you try a new form, it's healthy to intentionally break the rules (once you know exactly how they work). Your reader will consider it poor "form" if you make a hash of the guidelines, breaking the rules willy-nilly. But artfully experimenting with form in order to create a fresh new form keeps creative writing *creative*. As you work, it's okay to make mistakes. Experiment. Start over. Make a mess. Play.

> *Passion, beauty, intensity—everything I care about in art—is made possible through the discipline of distance. Or, to say it another way: Powerful feeling in art takes place only through the particular kind of distance known as form.*
> — STEVEN MILLHAUSER

Interestingly, a recent study on perfectionism tested two groups of college students in their ability to read and then summarize a paragraph in a timed trial. The first group was made up of self-proclaimed perfectionists—hard-driving overachievers. The second group self-identified as "take it easy, like to have a good time" students. Professors who didn't know the groups' identities read the results of both groups. The self-proclaimed perfectionists *performed significantly worse than their counterparts!* They had trouble getting started. They kept starting over. They freaked out and often couldn't grasp the main point of the paragraph. The more easygoing students actually understood the deeper meaning of the reading and quickly wrote clear summaries.

When it comes to forms, *not* trying too hard actually turns out to be a good thing.

Finished Forms

The forms that follow are sequenced alphabetically. You might want to try each form, or perhaps you will focus on three or four genres: fiction, poetry, nonfiction, drama. Not only does each form require you to use all the strategies from the course—Images, Energy, Tension, Pattern, and Insight—but the forms, because they are complex shapes requiring several writing sessions and an ability to layer techniques, work well for revision practice, too. These more sophisticated projects ask you to read, then learn a form, and then work in steps as you build the form.

> *Play around. Dive into absurdity and write. Take chances. You will succeed if you are fearless of failure.*
> — NATALIE GOLDBERG

The forms are presented here like blueprints or recipes. Good cooks know that the secret to a great dish is high-quality ingredients. If you start with wonderful images and sparky words for spice, you will have a great stock to work from. Stir in tension and mix with energy; most of these forms generate pattern organically. Above all, have fun, taste as you go, and if it doesn't come out right, no worries! Just toss it and start again (that's what great chefs do). In art, as in cooking or love, we call failure *learning*.

A Note on Poetry

Many students, at first, find poetry to be the most challenging genre. Then, after learning and practicing a few times, they often produce such compelling work in the more demanding forms of verse that they change their minds, opening up to poems in a new way or even converting from another genre over to poetry. One student writer, Lakin Smith, said this about poetic form: "I'm not going to lie. At first I hated the sonnet. I hated the pantoum. I really hated villanelles. And then, at the end of the class, when I looked back over my work, those are my best pieces. I don't write that way—I'm not that confined all the time now—but what I learned about being compressed and imagery changed the way I write forever." Other students have observed that poems often come out more successfully because the forms require more time and effort. The forms are sometimes harder, but because they require concentration and effort, many students find that once they "crack the code," poetry is a rewarding genre.

ABECEDARIUS

An abecedarius is a piece of writing that is organized using the letters of the alphabet. For example, in a short story, the first sentence starts with the word "A" or a word beginning with "a," the first word of the second sentence begins with the letter "b," the first word of the third sentence begins with "c," and so on for twenty-six sentences; the first word of the final sentence begins with "z." In a poem, the first letter of each line is "a," "b," "c," "d," "e," and so on, and the poem is twenty-six lines long. The lines may be of any length, but poets often keep the lines about the same length.

Throughout history, people have used the alphabet to send coded messages and to communicate profound secrets, as well as to write trivial, superficial, goofy poems. The 119th Psalm is an abecedarius in Hebrew; Geoffrey Chaucer, Ezra Pound, and many other writers throughout the ages have used the form to great effect. The abecedarius can be silly or simplistic, but it can also be quite complex, beautiful, and intricate, with long lines or even paragraphs or chapters using the letters of the alphabet in sequence.

One tip: Avoid using words that correspond to the letters from your very first abecedarian book: "A is for Apple, B is for Boy." The hardest words are those starting with the letters "q," "x," and "z." What are the most predictable choices? *Queen, xylophone,* and *zebra.* Avoid. Those. Words. If your reader can predict your word, your choice probably isn't fresh enough; predictable choices can bore readers. And a successful abecedarius doesn't strain: If you don't use the word *zuegmas* in your daily life, then you probably won't be able to create a smooth, thoughtful abecedarius. The alphabetical words should blend in with the rest of the poem so the reader doesn't even notice the abecedarian form. Another helpful tip: Consider what's known as the "fifth exit on the highway" principle. Instead of going with your first choice, getting off at the first exit you see, try to stay on the highway of creative thinking until the fifth exit. If you go with your fifth choice, you can avoid what everyone else chooses, and your work will stand out as original. For example, for the letter "x," what are the first four words that come to mind? *Xylophone, X-ray, X-mas* . . . Now you're drawing a blank. No problem. It's legal to search online, using a word-finding tool. But it's just as helpful to keep working, from your own life, to get words that you actually use. *Xanthum gum.* On my desk right now is a snack wrapper with that word on it: *xanthum.* I see that word every day. So I look it up, and my abecedarius is about to have a topic: food allergies. But before I start writing, I make lists of words that start with the remaining tricky letters. And I want lists of five to ten words so that I have some freedom to make different choices, depending on how my poem is unfurling.

Ex-boyfriend. Does *ex* count as the letter "x"? It *sounds* as though it starts with an "x." Because the sound of words is as important as how they look on the page, I'm going to use *ex-boyfriend* and give *expat, ex-in-laws, exegesis,* and *examination* a whirl, too. Those later choices—not the first things that come to mind, but the fourth and fifth words you come up with—are the "exits" you want to take for this form, and for all forms.

Reading Abecedarii

Read Jessica Greenbaum's "A Poem for S." (p. 335). Now read the poem aloud, and again. It's a complex and richly textured poem. Did you notice the abecedarius form when you first read the poem? In a good abecedarius, the reader will be so caught up in the images and insights and pattern and sound work that she will not notice your form. Observe how the use of enjambment—ending lines in a poem mid-sentence, rather than ending lines with periods, at the end of a sentence—adds to the form: When we listen, when we read, we don't notice the letter scheme as much because of the enjambment.

In this abecedarius, the title begins with the letter "a." The poem is a kind of letter to the speaker's friend, S., whose wife is sick. And letters—and the words made from letters—are important in the poem's subject matter as well. Greenbaum takes a story, a religious story, that has to do with how God and letters and wisdom and beginnings and endings all interrelate. It's powerful, heady stuff. As you read the poem, try to simplify each line so that you can trace out the main action in the poem.

What letter is missing? Can you guess why? Some readers have posited that having to ask the "why" question is part of the power of the poem. That's what "S." is asking: "Where is the *why* in all this pain?" It seems like a solid theory and provides an interesting way into the subtext of the poem. But when Jessica Greenbaum was asked recently why the poem didn't have a line beginning with "y," she said, somewhat apologetically, "That was a mistake. I didn't actually even notice until after it was published."

In a successful abecedarius, the pattern won't be prominent—the goal is to have the reader *not* notice, right off, the actual rules of the form. Greenbaum's poem has so much energy and such strong imagery that the framework disappears into the background, as it should. Thus, the recipe serves the writer, helping her come up with images she wouldn't have thought of otherwise. That's the goal of this recipe, and every single recipe in this chapter: to push you out of familiar ways of thinking, to shake up your typical moves. The goal is surprise—surprise for you, the author, and surprise for the reader.

"Abecedarian Requiring Further Examination of Anglikan Seraphym Subjugation of a Wild Indian Rezervation" is the title of an abecedarius by poet Natalie Diaz that is easily found online. What do you notice about the title of this poem? Every letter of the alphabet is used in the title. In her title, Jessica Greenbaum writes a letter to her friend and uses his initial to cue that "this poem is about letters." The abecedarius is a form that allows you to play with language and letters in all their glory. It embraces puns, double meanings, hidden messages, acrostics, codes, and wordplay.

The first rule of intelligent tinkering is to save all the parts.

— PAUL EHRLICH

Lastly, the abecedarius is related to the acrostic, in which the first letters of the lines spell a word. In a double acrostic, the final letters of each line or sentence also render the alphabet (forward or backward) or spell a word that has special meaning once you've read the piece.

Creative writers can use the alphabet not only to generate and shape poems, but also to generate and organize prose pieces.

| PRACTICE |

Read Dinty W. Moore's memoir "Son of Mr. Green Jeans: An Essay on Fatherhood, Alphabetically Arranged" (p. 305). How does the alphabet help him structure his story of fatherhood? Why do you think Moore used the alphabet to structure a piece on parenting? If he hadn't used the alphabet and instead wrote the essay in randomly arranged paragraphs, how would your reading of the essay change?

Many writers find that using an artificial shape, such as the alphabet, prompts them to come up with images and insights they would not have otherwise been able to write. Go back through Greenbaum's poem and Moore's essay, and see if you can locate any examples of surprising images that surely were inspired by the use of the alphabet and may not have been possible without the abecedarius form.

In addition to the Natalie Diaz abecedarius mentioned above, you might also enjoy Edward Lear's "Alphabet" and Edgar Allan Poe's fascinating "A Valentine to ___ ___," an acrostic that uses the first letter of his beloved's name as the first letter of the first line, the second letter of her name as the second letter of the second line, and so on, so that her name is spelled out on the diagonal from the top left to the bottom right of the poem. Another type of alphabet poem makes every word in the line begin with the same letter ("Andrea ate aardvark and") and progresses through the alphabet line by line.

Writing an Abecedarius

1. Choose a friend or family member and write your piece to this person, someone you love or perhaps someone who is in need of comfort. Focus on the tensions and difficulties in the relationship (for example, a grieving friend who sometimes finds solace in faith, but not lately; a father-son relationship that is marked by neglect and misunderstanding, not fitting into the popular culture's definitions of fathering).

2. You don't have to write the first line first. If you have trouble thinking of a word beginning with "a," make a list of images that come to you when you think about this person (or your topic).

3. You can write your poem in paragraphs and then make the line breaks, fiddling with word choices. You don't have to write it line by line, in ABC order.

4. Remember to use enjambment. Don't end each line in the poem with a period — let your sentences wrap around to the next line.

5. Work to fit the images into the alphabet. Avoid strained word choices (words you wouldn't normally use in your daily conversations) and avoid inverted syntax (mixing up the natural order of the words to fit the pattern). And try to stay away from simplistic word choices: "A wonderful man was my father. / Boy, was that guy great." Whether you are writing a poem, an essay, or a story, you may want to do some research, as Dinty Moore did. (His piece is actually a braided essay in the form of an abecedarius. See p. 416 for more on braided essays.)

6. When you put your piece together, your first line or sentence begins with a word that starts with the letter "a," the next line or sentence begins with "b," then "c," and so on. Yes, you will have to work hard for "q" and "x" — that's part of the creativity that has made this form compelling over the centuries. (Note for poets: The abecedarius poem in this book doesn't rhyme, but yours can. You may want to keep all your lines about the same length.)

Further Reading

In This Book	Highly Recommended
• "A Poem for S." by Jessica Greenbaum (p. 335) • "Son of Mr. Green Jeans: An Essay on Fatherhood, Alphabetically Arranged" by Dinty W. Moore (p. 305)	• "Abecedarian Requiring Further Examination of Anglikan Seraphym Subjugation of a Wild Indian Rezervation" by Natalie Diaz • "Abecedarius" by Pia Aliperti

ANAPHORA

Anaphora is the repetition of the first words in each line or sentence. As a form based on repetition, it's one of the most powerful ways to structure a piece of writing. Writers in all genres use anaphora to increase the energy, tension, insight, and overall power of their work. You can use anaphora when you want to make a strong point and have your readers remember your words. One of the most famous examples of anaphora is from Martin Luther King Jr.'s "I Have a Dream" speech:

> **I have a dream** that one day this nation will rise up and live out the true meaning of its creed: "We hold these truths to be self-evident: that all men are created equal." **I have a dream** that one day on the red hills of Georgia the sons of former slaves and the sons of former slaveowners will be able to sit down together at a table of brotherhood. **I have a dream** that one day even the state of Mississippi, a state sweltering with the heat of injustice, sweltering with the heat of oppression, will be transformed into an oasis of freedom and justice. **I have a dream** that my four little children will one day live in a nation where they will not be judged by the color of their skin but by the content of their character. **I have a dream** today.

Essayists and speechwriters, poets and politicians, even parents all use the device when they want to make a point, a big point: "*You are not* leaving this house. *You are not* watching television. *You are not* texting. *You are not* playing FIFA. *You are not* leaving your room! *You are not!*"

Novelists use anaphora to establish authority, indicate profundity, and create energy. Perhaps the opening of Charles Dickens's *A Tale of Two Cities* is familiar to you:

> It was the best of times, **it was** the worst of times, **it was** the age of wisdom, **it was** the age of foolishness, **it was** the epoch of belief, **it was** the epoch of incredulity, **it was** the season of Light, **it was** the season of Darkness, **it was** the spring of hope, **it was** the winter of despair, **we had** everything before us, **we had** nothing before us, **we were all going direct** to Heaven, **we were all going direct** the other way. . . .

Reading Anaphora

Perhaps you have been told in a writing class, "Don't repeat yourself!" In grade school, you might have been mocked: "Stop repeating yourself. Stop repeating yourself. Stop repeating yourself." Anaphora requires you to repeat yourself. Notice the intentional use of repetition in the works you read and how the repetition affects you as a reader.

PRACTICE

Read A. Van Jordan's "af•ter•glow" (p. 67). Where do you see the anaphora form? The poem starts with anaphora: "The light," "the look," "the morning's afterglow," "the glow" give way, in line 4, to a variation of that repetition: "This balm, this bath of light / This cocktail of lust and sorrow, / This rumor of faithless love. . . ." How many times does the poet repeat "this ___"? What's the effect of all those repetitions?

PRACTICE

Read "I Go Back to Berryman's" by Vincent Scarpa (p. 65). This piece is written in the form of anaphora. Where do you see the form? What is the effect on the reader of the words that are repeated? Compare his use of anaphora to Michael Cunningham's in the opening of the short story "White Angel" (p. 341). Notice how Cunningham captures the tightness of the brothers by repeating the word *we*. Do you see anaphora elsewhere in "White Angel"?

In "White Angel," anaphora underlines how bound the younger brother is to his older brother. He thrives on the *we*. But by repeating *we*, Cunningham also indicates that the brothers' experiences are the experiences of a generation and a subculture: At this age, in these times, on these drugs, you aren't an *I*—you're a *we* and part of something larger, and nothing, nothing could be sweeter. Pulling out the sentences that use the first-person plural pronouns, the poetry of Cunningham's prose becomes clear:

> We lived in Cleveland
> Our radios sang out love all day long
> We were four
> Between us were several brothers and sisters
> We are not a fruitful or many-branched line
> Our father . . . , our mother . . .
> We lived in a tract
> We have taken hits of acid with our breakfast juice

Anaphora can be as radically repetitive or as subtle as you wish. (Think of the implied repetitions in Brian Arundel's "The Things I've Lost" on p. 216: The author doesn't keep saying "I lost"—but the reader gets it.) Author Michael Martone created a whole book of anaphora in his parody of contributor notes, titled *Michael Martone*, in which his own name, Michael Martone, appears over and over and over. Joe Brainard's book *I Remember* is an entire memoir in which each sentence begins with the words *I remember*. You may wish to explore the Poetry Foundation's section on anaphora at poetryfoundation.org.

With its focus on pattern, anaphora magically allows you to increase the depth and insight of your work, to stay with images longer to maximize their power, and to sustain energy and tension. It's a powerful technique for opening and closing a piece. It's loud, it's certain, and it's compelling. Anaphora makes it seem as though you know what you are talking about.

> *People like me write because we are pretty inarticulate. Our articulation is our writing.*
>
> — WILLIAM TREVOR

Writing an Anaphora

Anaphora is a form that amplifies whatever you are writing about. So for your anaphora, choose a topic you feel strongly about, something that is very personal to you. Here are some options.

1. Memoir anaphora: Think of a "we" you identified with strongly, a group you were very much a part of—a lifeguard crew in the summer of 2016; the high school "smoking behind the gym" girls; your rugby team; your basic training class. Write a memoir, letting the reader in on the very particular images that detail your exploits and passions, beginning each line with "We" and showing the group in action.

2. Write an anaphora poem that uses one of the following as the beginning for each line. In each case, write specific details, actions, and images. Name names. However old you are, that's how many lines your poem will have:

   - I used to _____ , but now _____ [1]
   - I am so sorry _____ (*List the things you are sorry for that no one even knows you did.*)
   - I am not sorry I _____ (*List all the things you've done that have caused fallout for others, but it was worth it.*)
   - Every night we _____
   - I wish I never _____

3. Use anaphora to revise a work-in-progress. Take one of your works-in-progress and apply anaphora to the opening and the closing by choosing a key sentence and repeating the first words in that sentence throughout. Read the new version of your piece aloud. Do you prefer the new version or the old one? What's lost? What's gained?

---

[1] This prompt is adapted from *Rose, Where Did You Get That Red?* by Kenneth Koch.

Further Reading

In This Book	Highly Recommended
• "Boys" by Rick Moody (p. 212) • "af•ter•glow" by A. Van Jordan (p. 67) • "I Go Back to Berryman's" by Vincent Scarpa (p. 65)	• "America" and "Howl" by Allen Ginsberg • "The Delight Song of Tsoai-talee" by N. Scott Momaday • "Song of Myself" by Walt Whitman

BRAID

A braided piece uses different strands — usually three separate story lines or topics — and alternates subjects sequentially among the three. Think of how hair is braided, or bread, or, if you grew up in the southern United States, pine needles. The three strands each have equal weight and are roughly the same length. A braided piece differs from a piece with a plot and a subplot. In the braided piece, each section matters as much as the other sections, and each of the narratives is fragmented — spliced among the two other strands in a neat pattern. Each topic is revealed to the reader slowly. As their third strand, writers often use someone else's voice — research, words from brochures or travel journals, and so on. This external voice is part of what gives the braid its depth and texture.

> *What I want from work front and center is the writer struggling with nothing less than how he or she has or hasn't solved the problem of being alive.*
> — DAVID SHIELDS

The simplest stories — the ones little kids love, and the ones they tell — are usually *not* braided. The baby duck is lost, the duck needs its mother, the duck is lonely, the mother duck appears with snacks. No braid — it's a one-shot deal. When kids relate their dreams, it's usually a sequence, with no braiding: The monster was big, he was purple, he ate the family, then we went to the moon, we found a lot of candy there, and it was good. No braids here. Not a lot of dimension. Very little is expected of the reader.

Braids — story lines interwoven to create the whole piece — add depth, energy, layers, tension, and insight to your writing. Braids allow you to establish and play with pattern. For most readers, a good piece of writing usually needs to have more than one thing going on. Braiding is an easy, effective way to keep your reader reading — he's always waiting for the next part of the story to unfold.

Reading Braids

Look back at Amy Fusselman's piece on page 76. This excerpt from her memoir very clearly is braided: It has three story lines, handled in an alternating pattern. The story lines include trying to get pregnant, coping with grief after her father dies, and excerpts from her father's journals. The three braids—pregnancy, grief, and diary entries—all go together in amazingly intricate, meaningful ways. Fusselman wants to create new life, there's been a terrible end of life, and intertwined with all this are her dead father's notes on healing, on life, on curing what ails us, as he moves through his daily life. Each braid comments on the others. Each moment in one story line is juxtaposed with moments in the others, both visually and emotionally. The reading experience is tension-filled. Braids keep your reader moving.

Here is the structure of Fusselman's piece:

STRAND A   Yearning for a family of her own

STRAND B   Grieving for her father

STRAND C   Journal entries from her father in the military

Fusselman sticks fairly closely to an ABC ABC ABC pattern for her whole book, alternating sections from each braid as she works through each of the three story lines.

When student writer Charlie Walter began an imitation of Fusselman's essay, he made three lists:

STRAND A   Dramatic scenes from his hearing loss / medical doctor saga

STRAND B   Dramatic scenes from trying out for a rock band

STRAND C   Dramatic scenes from his attempts to learn to play guitar

When Charlie was working on his braided essay, he told the three stories separately and then spliced them together in an ABC ABC ABC pattern; the final memoir had nine short sections. As he worked, he felt that his braids didn't really relate. But in his final piece, the sections interrelate in surprising and interesting ways. In a climactic scene about his ear surgery, the lights go out. That scene dovetails with Charlie's musical debut in front of five hundred people—the lights go on. But Charlie *can't* see his audience. He can't hear well. The auditorium is another kind of operating theater, and Charlie has a chance to look inside himself, perhaps to be "healed."

Braiding uses juxtaposition to ignite meaning and create depth and resonance. Braiding is subtle. You do not have to spell things out for the reader. You rely on pattern, withholding, and pace. Story guru Bill Kittredge is famous for his instruction: Readers do not want to put their feet in the same story twice. Braids keep your story moving forward. Braids are good for topics that are heavy: your mom's cancer, your profound anxiety disorder, the death of your high school girlfriend. Often those subjects grow ungainly and sentimental and feel overwhelming or too heavy; braids force leaps, and leaps keep your writing fresh and fascinating. Essentially, a braid is a mosaic of discrete, independent images that work together to form a cohesive whole.

PRACTICE

Read Dinty Moore's braided essay on fatherhood (p. 305), and notice how he braids procreation esoterica, pop culture notions of fatherhood, and personal thoughts on parenting (all while sticking to the abecedarius format). Three story lines in one essay—science, pop culture dads, and personal reflection—each one commenting on, casting light on, the other two. Discuss how the three different story lines in Moore's essay inform, contradict, and enrich one another. Is the author telling three separate stories in each of the braids, or is the essay more of a collage?

Writing a Braid

1. Make a list of twenty moments in your life that have been most difficult for you. They should be action-oriented, not thought-oriented—you need moments when you were doing something around other people. Dating, auditioning, getting engaged (a different kind of auditioning), buying a new car, dealing with a judge during a court case, moving out from your apartment and into a new place, your first day on the curling team, being the daughter of a bipolar mother at your sister's wedding, the time when your anger management class went horribly wrong—you want a list of lively and dramatic difficulties. Trying to choose a major, deciding to go to law school, thinking about how weird your family is—those are hard to braid because they are thoughts, not scenes and images. You need passions that take you out into the world. Things you don't do well but care about immensely (Moore's fatherhood experience, Charlie's guitar lessons) are good subjects for braiding because they inherently lend themselves to tension-filled scenes (see Desire + Danger = Tension, p. 222). Awkward arguments with your autistic brother. Your struggle to stay on the basketball team to please your father. Your ongoing failure to ask the woman you love to go out with you. These are dramatic. These are good threads for your braids. Food allergies. The death of your best friend. Your learning disability. The things on your list might not be important in the grand scheme of things, but they matter a great deal to you.

2. Discuss your twenty ideas with a writing partner and your instructor. They can tell you what's most interesting to them. Choose two topics.

3. For each topic you choose, make a list of all the dramatic images that make up this story line. For example, in the "Failed to Ask Emily Out Ever" story, the key images are the day you first saw her in Health Dynamics; the day you fell down the stairs and she was standing at the bottom and she didn't laugh; the week you spent preparing to ask her out, but each day you walked right past her and pretended you didn't know her; the day when you sat next to her in class and said, "Dude, hey." Using your mind's eye, cast over this story from day one, when it all started, which may be a few years back. Do this for both of your story lines. If you don't like your images or you want to change your mind, review your list of ideas and choose a different strand to work with. Once you decide on the two best topics, make a list of about five to ten action scenes for each topic.

4. For your third braid, use text someone else has written (citing your sources, of course). You can use family letters or someone's journal (as long as you have permission). One student wrote about the tragic death of her room-mate (braid A) and her own depression (braid B). For braid C, she inter-spersed quotes from brochures at the health center, which were inadvertently hilarious and added levity but also some political commentary: Not a single brochure was even remotely helpful. Another student writer, Christian Piers, used his great-great-uncle's journals, which told of the family's coming to America on a ship called *The Albatross*; while on this long sea journey, the uncle fell in love and got married. Christian braided short, lively excerpts from the journals with two personal stories: his (consistently disastrous) dat-ing quests and his experience with a historical college tug-of-war. When Christian showed the class his pieces, which he didn't think went together well, he was shocked at what his classmates noticed. First of all, he was a lot like his uncle. Second, the river over which the epic tug-of-war took place was the same river *The Albatross* had come up 150 years earlier! Christian had not made the connection. And that was just on page 1. Braids create surprise, meaning, pattern, and depth.

Brainstorm ideas for your braid C, drawing from science texts, found texts, magazines from the 1940s, vintage etiquette books for girls or boys, travel guides, or brochures from your campus health office. If you are writ-ing about a video game obsession, the online cheat codes and attendant commentary might be braid C. If you are writing about your shopping compulsion, the guidelines from Consumer Credit Counseling might create an ironic counterpart. If you are writing about your autistic brother and your own struggles to bring creativity into your life, your braid C might draw from recent neuroscience exploring how creativity and the autistic brain work. Bring a list of ten ideas to class and have others help you choose the most interesting one.

PRACTICE

Working from your lists of images, write the images from your three topics and alternate them ABC ABC ABC ABC ABC so that each braid has five sections. You can put the images in chronological order, or you can use a different format, as Dinty Moore and Amy Fusselman do.

Further Reading

In This Book	Highly Recommended
• Excerpt from *The Pharmacist's Mate* by Amy Fusselman (p. 76) • "Son of Mr. Green Jeans: An Essay on Fatherhood, Alphabetically Arranged" by Dinty W. Moore (p. 305)	• "Swimming" by Joel Peckham • "A Braided Heart" by Brenda Miller

GRAPHIC NARRATIVE AND COMICS

Cartooning is not really drawing at all, but a complicated pictographic language intended to be read, not really seen.
— CHRIS WARE

Graphic narratives and comics are stories using a combination of text and image. Drawing skill can vary widely in this form. Creative writers—even poor drawers—can learn a lot from practicing storytelling in this form, which has recently surged in popularity. As student writer Annalise Mabe explains: "Some writers collaborate with artists. Other writers learn how to draw or have always drawn. The styles range from very realistic to very cartoony and simplistic, so really, anyone can comic (yes, it's a verb too)."

Graphic and comic narratives can be humorous, fictional, serious, historical, ridiculous, memoir, instructional, fantastic. In some examples, the artwork is quite impressive and inventive; in others, stick figures and rough sketches contribute to the visual charm of the form. Some prefer the term "comics" to "graphic narrative" because they feel the form shouldn't be "dressed up" or falsely marketed. No apologies: It's comics. But the term "graphic narrative" is widely used.

Reading Comics and Graphic Narratives

From the comics in daily newspapers, to the longer, richer Sunday comics, to Marvel comic books, manga, *Peanuts* and Fantagraphics anthologies, and on to the prize-winning books by Art Spiegelman (*Maus*) and Marjane Satrapi (*Persepolis*), we find the house of graphics to be a rich and many-roomed mansion. Some people adore reading this form; others feel challenged trying to track both a visual and a verbal narrative.

Some graphic stories are designed specifically for electronic readers. And, of course, some video games are essentially interactive graphic novels, some of them wildly innovative and sophisticated in terms of not only the visual elements but also the story and philosophy behind the visuals.

This is an important form to study. Its power has saturated the publishing industry, with new textbooks in composition, physics, and speechmaking using the conventions of the graphic novel. Challenge yourself to read widely in this genre and branch out from your stable of beloved favorite authors. Authors who have broad crossover appeal include Lynda Barry, Roz Chast, Alison Bechdel, David Small, and Maira Kalman. You may be interested in GB Tran's *Vietnamerica: A Family's Journey*, the Hernandez Brothers' *Love and Rockets* series, Chester Brown's *I Never Liked You*, graphic short stories by Adrian Tomine, and Gabrielle Bell's "Book of" series (*Book of Sleep, Book of Insomnia, Book of Black*, and others). Bell is well known for creating a comic a day for a month and then making booklets of these works. The two most respected print publishers of graphic works are Drawn and Quarterly and Fantagraphics; you can examine their catalogs for new and classic examples. Online, look for comics at *Hobart* and *The Rumpus*. Each time you search, you may find that a new zine pops up, featuring artists from around the world.

The classic resource on how to develop work in this form is Scott McCloud's *Understanding Comics: The Invisible Art*, an outstanding textbook in comic form. The excerpt from the introduction on page 422 explains the premise of this seminal text. Lynda Barry's comic books on craft are also extremely helpful, especially *One! Hundred! Demons!*, *What It Is*, and *Syllabus*. Alan Moore's *Writing for Comics* and Jessica Abel and Matt Madden's *Mastering Comics* are two other widely used, information-packed resources.

PRACTICE

Read the comic "The Neighbor" by Jarod Roselló (p. 27). Is this comic most like fiction, nonfiction, poetry, or a play? Do you see the essential strategies of pattern, tension, and image in both the writing and the pictorial images? How do the words and pictures support each other? Frame by frame, what do the visuals accomplish, separately from the words? Does each frame contain conflict? Are there different *kinds* of frames? Take some time with others in your class to examine his work. Why do you think Roselló told this story in graphic form, rather than in traditional prose with words alone? What can the graphic work do that nongraphic forms simply can't accomplish? Do you think anything is lost by presenting the work graphically?

Scott McCloud. "Introduction" from Understanding Comics. Copyright © 1993, 1994 by Scott McCloud. Reprinted by permission of HarperCollins Publishers.

Writing a Comic or Graphic Narrative

This flexible form encompasses a wide range of possibility. You might create a single-panel comic, with your image and text in one frame. Common forms include the three-panel strip, the four-panel strip, and multiple strips stacked on top of each other or combined together to tell a story, as in Sunday newspaper comic sections. Then there are comic books (usually twenty-two-page booklets), anthologies of comics, webcomics, and long-form graphic novels and graphic memoirs.

In creating the form, you'll notice that it has a lot more in common with plays and screenplays than with other traditional genres. Screenplays and graphic works are both visual forms, driven by strong story-telling interlaced with powerful images: the perfect training ground for a new writer.

> *The humble art of cartooning, at its essence, amounts to no less than a geometry of the human soul.*
>
> — GIAMBATTISTA VICO

PRACTICE

To get started, practice the basic rhythm of the graphic form. Divide a sheet of paper into four squares. Using text and image in each square (and ignoring your limitations as a visual artist for now—just use stick figures if you like), answer these four questions, one in each panel:

1. What is your name?
2. Where are you from?
3. Who is your family?
4. What do you do?

Members of your class may choose to hang their drawings on a wall of the classroom to share them and get to know one another better.

Another assignment for those who would like to sample the power of this form: Divide a sheet of paper into nine frames (a giant tic-tac-toe grid). Using text and image in the frames (some panels might be just one or the other), take us through your day today, starting with breakfast and projecting on into the evening.

Creative writers also use graphic narrative as a tool for close reading, creating a visual outline of a story or poem in order to see its working parts cleanly and clearly.

PRACTICE

Working from an existing text, re-create the story using only dialogue and panels. You don't need drawing talent—stick figures are fine. You can use any of the works included in this textbook; for example, try creating a few frames from Jenifer Hixson's monologue "Where There's Smoke" (p. 162). What scenes would you choose to illustrate? Practice placing the dialogue in panels, using notes or quick sketches to designate what the reader would encounter visually in that panel.

Then try your skill with a short story, such as George Saunders's "Sticks" (p. 304), or a narrative poem, such as Adam Scheffler's "Woman and Dogs" (p. 67).

Share your comics with the class. Discuss. Does "reverse engineering" or storyboarding existing work help you better understand how to structure creative writing?

To write a longer or a full-length graphic novel, memoir, or short story, the first decision is straightforward: Will you use a story you've already written and convert it into the format required for a graphic novel? Or will you create a brand-new story? You will most likely choose to write a fast-moving, hard-hitting, character-driven tale with an exciting linear plot. You'll probably follow the journey form (p. 433) or the traditional three-part conflict-crisis-resolution structure (see p. 90). But you might choose a more meditative or poetic approach, using lists (see the Practices on p. 437), anaphora, or a more impressionistic structure.

1. Choose or create a story.
2. In a graphic narrative, you don't have the time or space to include descriptions of setting, interior thoughts, reactions, or detailed histories of the characters, their conflicts, or their world. Everything has to move — fast — and you will be using dialogue and action scenes to make things move.
   a. Read your story draft and imagine each interior or descriptive passage as one of these three options:
      - Create dialogue scenes. (Can one character ask another a question to get this information across?)
      - Cut the passage. (Can you delete most of the backstory and save only the sentences that are crucial for reader understanding?)
      - Simplify. (Can you pare the story down to its essential bones?)
   b. Cut dialogue scenes where conversation is filler. Conversations in which nothing is moving forward don't work in graphic novels any better than they do in prose. Shorten or eliminate as many conversations as you can — any talking that isn't significant should be deleted. Writing sparingly is excellent training

for any writer. (Maybe all novelists should have to try their projects as graphic novel scripts.)

   c. Translate dialogue into quick strokes. In a graphic novel, dialogue is a series of swift, short sentences. The dialogue bubbles are very small, and the art takes up most of the room in each frame, so there's no room for chitchat. As a general rule, budget yourself to forty words per panel. Try not to go over budget.

3. Storyboard your project. Once you have streamlined and pared down your story to basic speech and action, the fun begins. Think of your story's steps in terms of pages. Each page is its own micro-world. A graphic novel or memoir is often 96 physical pages, printed front and back, for a total of 192 content pages. Pages that face each other relate events in the reader's mind in a different way than do back-to-back pages. With physical books, when you turn the page, there's a beat, a pause. You'll want to practice setting story steps out on pages so you get a feel for the flow of your book. Even if you are practicing with a shorter graphic work, storyboard each page so that you know the shape of your project.

You don't necessarily need art talent to do this kind of work, though of course it helps. And the more you draw, the better you will get, just as with your writing craft. Meanwhile, your training as a poet (having to get a lot of information into a small space in a meaningful and interesting way) will serve you well. Your training as a story writer is your foundation. You can do sketches or simply use words to practice building pages. In fact, many successful graphic novelists and memoirists collaborate with artists; very few people are highly skilled in both *story structure* and *drawing*. But you can create evocative, interesting images by hand— you'll be surprised at how much you already know. Lastly, consider using graphic elements in poems and texts. Bruce Eric Kaplan's *I Was a Child* is a perfect example of how drawings can enhance a story.

Further Reading

In This Book	Highly Recommended
• "The Neighbor" by Jarod Roselló (p. 27) • Excerpt from *Understanding Comics* by Scott McCloud (p. 422)	• *Fun Home* by Alison Bechdel • *Sacred Heart* by Liz Suburbia • *Far Arden* by Kevin Cannon • *Nimona* by Noelle Stevenson

FLASH

Is it possible to write a novel in six words? Ernest Hemingway allegedly wrote what he called a novel in a sentence:

For sale, Baby shoes, Never worn.

Is this a novel? A short story? Based on the sentence, what do you know about the situation? Whether or not authorship can be attributed to Hemingway, these six words serve to illustrate just how much a writer can accomplish in a tiny amount of space. In the digital age, brevity is ever more relevant— Facebook, Tumblr, blogs, and Twitter all help flash and micro-forms flourish. But print magazines, too, feature high-quality, critically acclaimed flash and micro-forms, and these small tableaus create a growing canon in the field of creative writing.

Flash fiction is a short story that is 2,000 words or fewer. The stories are sharply focused, imagistic, and tightly wound pieces of prose, usually centered around intense moments of human experience. Some practitioners set the word limit at 750 words, others at 250 words. Nano-fiction is even shorter: 100 words or fewer. Flash fiction came into its own in the 1990s; some key anthologies of the genre include *Sudden Fiction*, *Flash Fiction*, and *Micro Fiction*.

Short nonfiction has long been a mainstay in periodicals and newspapers. As a form for creative writers, it began to flourish anew in the 1990s. *In Short*, *In Brief*, and *Short Takes* featured writers such as Naomi Shihab Nye, Michael Ondaatje, Terry Tempest Williams, Denis Johnson, and Russell Edson, many of whom published prose poems before the terms "brief essay," "flash nonfiction," and "micro-memoir" gained wide acceptance. Micro-memoir has this in common with prose poetry: It's short, with tightly packed language and concise imagery. Micro-memoir uses quick scenes; it turns on action. *The Rose Metal Press Field Guide to Writing Flash Nonfiction*, edited by Dinty Moore, lists journals that are well known and well respected for their focus on flash and micro: *DIAGRAM*, *Hippocampus*, and *Sweet: A Literary Confection*. *Creative Nonfiction* features an ongoing "#cnftweet" competition called "Tiny Truths," which requires that stories be no longer than 140 characters.

Flash pieces aren't excerpts from longer works. They stand on their own. They require urgency, intensity, and a high level of energy. Dinty Moore explains:

Imagine there is a fire burning deep in the forest. In an essay of a conventional length, the reader begins at the forest's edge, and is taken on a hike, perhaps a meandering stroll, into those woods, in search of that fire. The further in the reader goes, with each page that turns, the more the reader begins to sense smoke in the air, or maybe heat, or just an awareness that something ahead is smoldering.

In a very brief essay, however, the reader is not a hiker but a smoke jumper, one of those brave fire fighters who jump out of planes and land 30 yards from where the forest fire is burning. The writer starts the reader right at that spot, at the edge of the fire, or as close as one can get without touching the actual flame. There is no time to walk in.

Short pieces need to be highly compressed, filled with tension, and carefully observed. They're often filled with lyrical language. The author's intention is always to have the story linger in the reader's mind.

Reading Flash Fiction and Micro-Memoir

Flash fiction and micro-memoir, because they share some of the compression of poetry, will reward the reader who spends time going over the piece, reading more than once, reading aloud. In most of these pieces, as with poetry, you will find one or two hard "turns" — changes in direction. Because these are narratives, look for dialogue, conflict, and scene — just as in a full-length story or memoir.

PRACTICE

One of the most respected Web sites for micro-memoir is Brevitymag.com. The site features many examples of the form as well as craft essays, in which writers discuss strategies for succeeding with these jewel-like pieces. Find two pieces on the site that you really like, and write a brief commentary on what it is you enjoy about these works and what you might try to model in your own work.

PRACTICE

Read a flash fiction piece and a micro-memoir from this textbook: "The New Year" by Pamela Painter (p. 69) and "Swerve" by Brenda Miller (p. 118).

Read the pieces aloud. Take some time to annotate the pieces, noting in the margins where you see (1) the details that provide clues to the conflict, (2) the details that serve to deftly characterize, and (3) the places where the stories make hard turns, changing direction, giving up a large surprise, leaping in time, or changing location. Does each piece have two hard turns?

In creative writing, it's often said that the tighter the container, the more powerful the emotions the author can present to the reader. Because the flash form is compressed, writers are able to write about powerful, overwhelming subjects — betrayal, domestic abuse, lives imploding. In a longer work, the reader might be overwhelmed with unrelenting heaviness. In flash, hot bursts of intensity work extremely well.

Writing Flash Fiction

1. Work with a designated word limit: one sentence, or perhaps 250 words, 500 words, or 750 words.
2. For your subject, choose a moment of high intensity, and *do* think in scene: For inspiration, focus on the moment you quit your job, the moment you got busted for cheating, the last car ride you took with your wildest friend, the moment you realized he wasn't just wild, but actually dangerous. Choose something you know well.
3. Try sketching the scene that will anchor your flash.
4. Begin with the words "It's [time of day] on [day or holiday] at [specific place—house, restaurant, dock] when [person] [action] [at least four details]." Notice how that one action in Pamela Painter's "The New Year" creates the whole first paragraph and, essentially, the first act.
5. In your next paragraph, move to the next part of the story—your main character is in a new location and surprised, very surprised. In paragraph 3, you are allowed a sentence or two of backstory. In paragraph 5, you can use strong action lines and detail to dramatically move your character through space and time.
6. Then consider your turns. In the last sentence, will you leap forward in time? Painter uses a photograph, which serves to frame her short-short. Try to show your main character, still struggling, but in a different relationship to the issue than he was at the opening.

Of course, there are endless ways to construct flash. Read widely to find models you enjoy, and consider using them as inspiration for your own stories.

Writing Micro-Memoir

When writing micro-memoir, you can follow the same approach you use for writing flash fiction, with a very important caveat: You can't make anything up. If you use direct dialogue, in quotation marks, it should be exactly what was spoken. If you can't remember exactly what was said, you might use italics for the dialogue or adopt Brenda Miller's technique in "Swerve": "I would apologize for the eggs being overcooked, and for the price of light bulbs, and for the way the sun blared through our trailer windows and made everything too bright. . . ." She clearly indicates what was said, but she doesn't put it in direct dialogue.

She doesn't have the exact quotations. And what matters is the content, and the fact that she said these things many, many times.

Here are the keys to writing successful micro-memoir:

1. Use specific details set in a strong action line.
2. Pattern and repetition are your friends.
3. Strive for two turns.

In both flash fiction and micro-memoir, there are some important ground rules:

1. Surprise endings do not work. Some endings have been used so often that they are no longer effective: "And then he woke up." "And then her alarm went off." "And then she was dead." Moreover, lines like these don't work because the reader has just experienced a trick, not a meaningful exchange of emotion in image.
2. Don't go over the word count, adjust your font or margins, or bend the rules in any other way.
3. Don't write about thoughts and feelings (there are always exceptions). Flash fiction and micro-memoir are mini-movie forms. Use characters, scene, action, and dialogue, and stick with the presentational mode.

Further Reading

In This Book	Highly Recommended
• "The New Year" by Pamela Painter (p. 69)	• "The Rememberer" by Aimee Bender
• "I Go Back to Berryman's" by Vincent Scarpa (p. 65)	• "Lost" by Pamela Painter
• "How to Touch a Bleeding Dog" by Rod Kessler (p. 250)	• "The Deck" by Yusef Komunyakaa
• "Swerve" by Brenda Miller (p. 118)	• *Brevity* magazine
• "The Things I've Lost" by Brian Arundel (p. 216)	• *In Brief: Short Takes on the Personal* edited by Judith Kitchen and Mary Paumier Jones
• "The Colonel" by Carolyn Forché (p. 185)	• *Short: An International Anthology of Five Centuries of Short-Short Stories, Prose Poems, Brief Essays, and Other Short Prose Forms* edited by Alan Ziegler
• "Sticks" by George Saunders (p. 304)	
• "Two Hearts" by Brian Doyle (p. 340)	• World's Best Short Short Story Contest at *The Southeast Review*

GHAZAL

The ghazal is a nonlinear poem written in long-line couplets (two-line stanzas) in which the end word or end words in the second line of each stanza repeat or echo. The couplets are not written in a straightforward story format: In the ghazal, each couplet is a mini-poem, meant to stand on its own, almost like a proverb or a saying, only very loosely related to what has come before. So the idea is to leap around, covering many topics, always coming back to the key repeating words in line 2 of every stanza. Ghazals are always written in couplets, usually five to twelve stanzas (ten to twenty-four lines) in length, but they can be much longer.

The ghazal comes from Persian poetry; it flourished in the Middle East between 1100 and 1500. The form appears in Arabic, Urdu, and Turkish traditions. In Arabic, *ghazal* (pronounced "guzzle") means "the talk of boys and girls." In their earliest versions, ghazals focused on flirting, chatting up, seducing with song. Later poets used the ghazal for spiritual, philosophical, and religious purposes. There is a long tradition of ecstatic spiritual ghazal, focusing on the mystical aspects of devotion to one's God. The form became popular in the Western world in the 1960s.

> *God is really only another artist. He invented the giraffe, the elephant, and the cat. He has no real style. He just goes on trying other things.*
>
> — PABLO PICASSO

Often the poet will work his or her name into the last stanza of the poem, in effect "signing" the ghazal.

Reading Ghazals

The ghazal is associative (like a list). Instead of taking one idea and developing it as in a sonnet or a story, the poet takes disparate images and lays them next to each other, as you might on your coffee table — your personal arrangement of beautiful or intriguing objects. The two-line stanzas (couplets) sit in the reader's mind side by side, not to develop a linear argument, but to refract off each other.

PRACTICE

Read "Hustle" by Jericho Brown (p. 112). In this ghazal, what do you notice about the structure? The first stanza uses rhyme in a special way; the lines end "hears in prison" and "years in prison." Notice how the rhyme is just before the repeated last two words, "in prison." In the following stanzas, notice the sound patterns. The first lines don't have direct rhymes, but they have echoes: the "a" sound in "ball" and "race," and the near rhyme in "403" and "breathe." What other sound patterns do you find at play?

That specific sound pattern and word repetition — rhyming words before the end words, not at the end of the line, and the repeated end words in the second line of each couplet — are the hallmarks of the ghazal. In Jericho Brown's ghazal, the couplets are completely separate miniature poems. But in every stanza, though he isn't telling a direct story, he is illuminating a different image from his life, and all the images have to do with imprisonment of one kind or another. Dwayne Betts is a famous poet who served time. Brownfield is a central character, who spends time in prison, in Alice Walker's debut novel, *The Third Life of Grange Copeland*. Using the ghazal, with its thrumming repetitions, Brown creates an accruing sense of doom; prison is the backdrop in many aspects of life—literary, political, personal. Every move he makes, everything he loves, prison is there, in the shadows. In the final couplet, he uses his name and makes a powerful statement about breaking the pattern in his family.

In Brown's ghazal, all the couplets relate quite closely, but they do not have to. If you are an uber-linear-type person, this nonlinear, messy, wandering form might drive you crazy. If you hate writing sonnets or despise constructing five-paragraph essays on a specific theme, you will probably love ghazal writing; it might become your new passion.

PRACTICE

Read a few more ghazals online. Agha Shahid Ali is a renowned practitioner. You might enjoy "Hip-Hop Ghazal" by Patricia Smith, "Derecho Ghazal" by Luisa Igloria, and "Red Ghazal" by Aimee Nezhukumatathil. These along with many more excellent examples of the ghazal can be found at the Poetry Foundation Web site. Print out and annotate your favorites, noting in the margins what each couplet boils down to, and underlining the sound repetitions.

As always with form poems, you read the recipe, study a few examples, and sometimes may feel a bit daunted. It's in writing the poem that it all comes together, so be patient. Give yourself time to work through the instructions. Following the format for ghazal may be difficult to read about and easier just to write.

After you write a traditional ghazal, try one that breaks the rules. For example, for your rhyming word, your ghazal might use variations on the "a" word: *red, read, dread, bred, reddened,* and *unread* (as author Aimee Nezhukumatathil does). Or you can use ear rhyme, as poet Ellen Doré Watson does in her ghazal "Ghazal," rhyming the words *core* and *corps*, which is an interesting and creative way of "breaking the rules." Feel free to do the same, choosing words like *son* and *sun* or *be* and *bee*, words that sound alike but have different meanings. Heather McHugh has a complex ghazal titled "Ghazal of the Better-Unbegun" that is worthy of study.

Check out the examples on YouTube. This lively Middle Eastern poetic form has a long tradition of being sung; you can find many ghazals performed online. It is in fact an early form of spoken word.

Writing a Ghazal

1. Learn the format. Each stanza has one couplet (two lines). Each letter stands for the last word in the line. So "a" in lines 1 and 2 is the repeated word at the end of each of those lines. Line 3 ends with a new word, which should *not* rhyme with the "a" word. In poetry, the "a" word doesn't just rhyme; it's a repetition of the same word.

STANZA 1	STANZA 2	STANZA 3	STANZA 4	STANZA 5
a	b	c	d	e
a	a	a	a	a

2. Use the pattern above to construct your first five couplets—a ghazal should have at least five couplets, but you can write up to twelve couplets or more. Each couplet line in the poem is the same length. The lines are long, at least fourteen syllables. You don't have to link the couplets together; each couplet is a separate poem.

   To write a successful ghazal, here are some tips:

   ▪ Make your lines long and all about the same length.

   ▪ Write about your current important obsessions, faith, politics, siblings, or love.

   ▪ When you get stuck (and you will!), look around where you are right now and start with this moment. Write about what you see and what you feel right now. Write two long lines; then take a break. Come back. Notice this moment, again.

3. Optional: Put your name in the final couplet. (Historically, the last couplet is the "signature" couplet, in which the poet includes his or her own name.)

Further Reading

In This Book	Highly Recommended
• "Hustle" by Jericho Brown (p. 112)	• "Hip-Hop Ghazal" by Patricia Smith • "Red Ghazal" by Aimee Nezhukumatathil • "Where You Are Planted" by Evie Shockley • "Many" by Agha Shahid Ali • "Derecho Ghazal" by Luisa Igloria

JOURNEY

The journey is a basic structure often used by short story writers, storytellers, epic poets, screenwriters, and novelists. It describes a character (hero or antihero) who embarks on a quest and returns changed in significant ways. Journeys are portrayed in many genres, including short poems, epic novels, graphic novels, and movies.

The journey is the basic story recipe for much of the world's folklore, myths, and literatures; journey is also the foundational structure for many sacred texts. Joseph Campbell has written extensively on the journey story shape, and his book *The Hero with a Thousand Faces* is required reading in many film schools. Video games rely heavily on the journey structure, as do many popular and critically acclaimed television series and movies, such as *Breaking Bad*, *The Matrix*, and *Aladdin*. *Harry Potter*, *Lord of the Rings*, and the video games *Legend of Zelda* and *Final Fantasy* are all examples of journey, brought to artistic perfection. *The Wizard of Oz* is a fantastic example of the journey, and beginning writers can learn a great deal by analyzing the film using the journey's elements. Many famous musicians and performers study journey in order to bring depth and meaning to their creations, to give their work universal reach and staying power, and to appeal to a wide audience. It's to your advantage as a creative writer to practice the journey form.

Reading Journeys

The basic journey story requires you to start with a character who is called the hero. Traditionally, the hero has a strong character and is very likable. In most contemporary works, the hero is just as often an antihero, someone who is outside the norms of society. The high school teacher who runs a meth lab (in order to pay his medical bills and provide for his family) is a wonderful example of an antihero, as are the characters in *Glee*—outcast misfits—who journey toward competitions, learning life lessons along the way. The husband in Raymond Carver's "Cathedral" (p. 119) is an antihero—he is an unlikable person with biases and flaws, but he nonetheless embarks on a journey toward *seeing*, and at the end of the story, we see that he is transformed. Poems, too, can use the journey effectively as an organizational strategy. The hero in "Buying Wine" by Sebastian Matthews (p. 69) is a boy who loses his innocence but gains some insight as he journeys with his father through the liquor store. In "Swerve" (p. 118), Brenda Miller is on both a literal and a metaphorical journey. As the hero, she realizes that her journey has taken her into an underworld, and she emerges, she hopes, with wisdom.

In general, the journey breaks down into three stages. Notice the bones of the traditional conflict-crisis-resolution structure here, which is addressed at length in Chapter Three (p. 90). Here are the three stages:

I. SEPARATION	The hero leaves the world he or she knows, sometimes known as the "ordinary world."
II. INITIATION	The hero has adventures and victories and learns a secret knowledge.
III. RETURN	The hero comes back to the ordinary world with a gift.

PRACTICE

Read "What I Saw from Where I Stood" by Marisa Silver (p. 251) and "Cathedral" by Raymond Carver (p. 119), and track the stages of separation, initiation, and return. Or read the stories "How to Touch a Bleeding Dog" by Rod Kessler (p. 250), the excerpt from Amy Fusselman's memoir *The Pharmacist's Mate* (p. 76), and Dinty Moore's "Son of Mr. Green Jeans: An Essay on Fatherhood, Alphabetically Arranged" (p. 305). Can you find the basic steps of the journey in these stories?

You can also analyze your favorite movies — watch one and take notes. Can you find the scene that denotes the beginning of separation? The scene that acts as the climax of the initiation? The scene that holds the most important moment in the return? Try doing this same activity with your favorite video game. Is journey the province only of role-playing games, or is it used in other genres of video games as well?

> *I write because I want to have more than one life.*
> — ANNE TYLER

The visitation structure is a variation of journey — its opposite, or inverse. In this structure, the hero — the person who is going to experience the most significant change in the story — is *visited by someone or something that will allow him or her to experience a character transformation.* "Cathedral" can be read as a classic visitation because the husband's journey takes place in his own living room; the travel he does is interior and psychological. He ends up far different from the callous, shut-down man he was at the beginning of the story because of the catalyst: the blind man's *visit*. The classic movie *E.T.* is a visitation story, as are *Toy Story, Jurassic World, Avengers: Age of Ultron*, and *Avatar*. In this textbook, Jessica Shattuck's story "Bodies" (p. 263) is a visitation story, too. Think about these stories, and see if you can find the stages of the hero's journey.

Writing a Journey

Before you write, you may want to practice outlining a couple of journey stories, using the stages above. Then choose a journey of your own to write. The form works extremely well for graphic novels, screenplays, plays, longer short stories, and novels. But you can also create a poem or myth or folktale or children's book that follows the journey structure. (Try analyzing *Where the Wild Things Are* through the lens of journey.)

To write a journey, follow these steps:

1. First, choose a hero, someone who is likable but flawed. Imagine a world that will throw the hero into a series of complications for which he or she is completely unprepared.
2. Provide a quirky helper, and make a list of trickster figures who have motivation for blocking the hero's quest. What do they—the tricksters or villains—lose if the hero gains the gift?
3. Imagine the list of challenges carefully so that you can arrange them in a compelling order.

    a. Brainstorm various challenges that might confront your hero (use the sketching technique from p. 363).
    b. Consider interesting settings that will be visually and metaphorically rich as your characters embark on their quest. For example, if your hero is a bride and her quest is the wedding dress, you could visit all the bridal shops in your area and collect details for great scenes for the journey.
    c. Think about how bad things could get: At the bottom of the diagram is a near death, a crucifixion, or some kind of transformation that is violent and traumatic. The hero emerges from this powerful experience *changed*. How? What physical manifestation of the hero's new "gift" could you create? Take some time to plan out various options.
    d. When the hero returns to the ordinary world with his or her gift, it may take some time to restore the ordinary world to order. The hero still faces challenges. What are they?

Remember: You don't have to use all of the steps, but they give you a solid foundation of workable story steps.

Further Reading

In This Book	Highly Recommended
• "What I Saw from Where I Stood" by Marisa Silver (p. 251)	• Short stories by Kelly Link, Miranda July, Junot Díaz
• "Swerve" by Brenda Miller (p. 118)	• Films: *Star Wars, Easy Rider, Thelma and Louise, Little Miss Sunshine, Mad Max: Fury Road*
	• Television: *Breaking Bad*

LIST

Lists direct, even dominate, our daily lives: lists of contacts, grocery lists, the college graduation requirements checklist, the bucket list. Using a list is a simple, straightforward way to structure a piece of creative writing, equally useful for both prose and poetry. Lists of questions, lists of wants, lists of fears, lists of tiny details, lists of gestures, lists of overheard dialogue on the subway, lists of regrets, lists of apologies, lists of images—anything that forces you to stay focused on a single subject will potentially generate a powerful piece of writing. Listing is an ancient form, used in the Bible, for example, in Song of Solomon, in which a lover lists everything he loves about his partner, and in those lineages tracing family origins. Parts of the *Iliad* are a list.

Today, listing is relevant for a wide range of authors. On television, there are Top Ten lists. The movie *Thirty Two Short Films about Glenn Gould* is structured as a list of images. Some of the forms you've already studied, such as abecedarius and anaphora, are essentially lists, too. Lists can be used to structure lectures, formal essays, educational materials, and text-and-image experiments based on the quirkiest of passions. For example, take a look at "Why the Mantis Shrimp Is My New Favorite Animal" at The Oatmeal. It's a list.

Lists can be of any length, and in poetry, they can be rhymed or unrhymed. In the famous list poem "Jubilate Agno" by Christopher Smart (1722–1771) about his cat, Jeoffry, the author lists everything his cat does.

> For first he looks upon his fore-paws to see if they are clean.
> For secondly he kicks up behind to clear away there.
> For thirdly he works it upon a stretch with the fore-paws extended.
> For fourthly he sharpens his paws by wood.

The list of cat behaviors goes on for several pages, and the energy comes from the author's ability to notice, with such fine observational skills, just what his cat does and exactly how he does it.

The keys to success with the list are threefold: superbly close observation, generous detail, and a subject matter on which you are the primary expert.

Reading Lists

Lists are usually easy and enjoyable to read because the form is so simple, direct, and pure. The form can be used for prose or poetry. The title is extremely important; not only does the title give a clue to the topic of the list, but it often points to the subtext of the list. In creative writing, a good list is greater than the sum of its parts.

You might be interested in reading list poems by Walt Whitman and Allen Ginsberg. If you like surreal poetry, you might enjoy list poems by James Tate, such as "The List of Famous Hats."

Memoirist Marion Winik wrote an entire book titled *The Glen Rock Book of the Dead* using the list form. In the table of contents, she lists everyone she knows who has died: The Neighbor, The Eye Doctor, The Driving Instructor, The Realtor, The Virgin. Each chapter is a page or two long, and the entire memoir works as a wonderfully moving, even funny (not depressing) exploration of life. Fiction writer Lorrie Moore uses lists in her short stories "How to Talk to Your Mother (Notes)" and the "Kid's Guide to Divorce."

The list is one of the most flexible and welcoming forms. When you are stuck as a writer, try listing. The form comes with one simple caveat: In every sentence, use skillful observation (or the list quickly becomes boring).

PRACTICE

Reread Brian Arundel's "The Things I've Lost" (p. 216), a list memoir. Can you glean any wisdom from Arundel's losses? Does the piece overtly mention the wisdom, or is it something the reader takes away on his or her own? Which specifics in the essay reveal the most about the author's persona, in your opinion?

PRACTICE

Read "In My Father's Study upon His Death" by Dylan Landis (p. 161). What do you notice about the order of the items in her list? Do you think she wrote the list in this order, or do you think she arranged the order after writing the list? Which items are the most striking or sad to you? Which items are the most closely observed? What's *not* here?

PRACTICE

Review Vincent Scarpa's "I Go Back to Berryman's" (p. 65), Betsy Sholl's "Genealogy" (p. 66), George Saunders's "Sticks" (p. 304), and Adam Scheffler's "Woman and Dogs" (p. 67). Annotate the pieces, commenting on how the title helps you read the list on a deeper level and pointing to which details are the most closely observed or the most effective. In a final summary note, identify which of the four pieces you feel is the best example of a list, and why. Do you think that one of the four does not fit the criteria for a list? Say why.

Writing a List

Here is a list of prompts for list pieces. You can try them in poetry or prose.

1. Ten Things I Do Every Day. (Check out Ted Berrigan's original poem online.)

2. Things to Do at _____. (Fill in the blank with a place you know really well that most people do not know at all, like Anne's apartment, or Fireman's Field on Roosevelt Island, or the fire escape behind 4D).
3. Thirteen Things to Do While Looking at the Moon.
4. A list that uses this prompt: "I used to _____, but now I _____." How many lines long = However old you are.[2]
5. A list of things associated with your favorite season. (Make sure each item is extremely specific to you and not one of the first five items that everyone thinks of — no beaches, no first snowfall, no autumn leaves, no daffodils.)
6. A list in which each line or sentence begins with the words "My mother said . . ." or "My father said . . ."
7. A graphic/comic list, in which you show bedtime for seven nights in a row, or breakfast for seven days in a row, or seven different dates.
8. A list of twenty apologies. (The secret to success is to make each one superbly specific.) Here is an excerpt from how student writer Danielle Kraese approached the assignment, with her epigraph and a few apologies.

Danielle Kraese

From *Apologies and a Few Things I'm Sorry About*

For all the people I've wronged who probably don't realize that they have a supporting role in my Chapbook. I hope that if you ever read this, you can forgive me for my apologies.

1) To my boss: One day at work about a year ago, I was suffering from a mild sore throat that I suspected might be the onset of strep. While you were out to lunch, I needed to use your computer, like I often do. But this time, when I sat down at your desk, before putting my hand to your mouse, I made a point to lick it. I was hoping that, at the least, you might get sick enough to miss a few days of work and I would be temporarily freed from your condescending wrath. I'm sorry that it didn't work.

2) To Stephanie DiFlorio, one of my childhood best friends: The last time I was over your house was when I was eight years old. You asked me to smell your new perfume, and I had what must have looked like a psychotic episode, somehow ending up underneath your bed sobbing. At the time, I had

---

[2] From Kenneth Koch.

no idea that I was hypoglycemic, and I was actually experiencing a severe blood sugar drop. I'm sorry that our friendship had to end because the events of that day made both you and your mom afraid to have me over again (I can't say I blame you). But many years later, I realized that we would have grown apart anyway when I unwittingly stumbled upon your Facebook group, "Stephanie DiFlorio has HUGE tittays." . . .

11) To Lickity Splitz customers from the summer of 2006: I'm sorry that you all had to accept your soft-serve ice cream being presented to you upside down in a Styrofoam bowl. I told you that the hot temperatures were making the ice cream too soft to stay upright in a cone, but in truth, I just never grasped the art of swirling.

Further Reading

In This Book	Highly Recommended
• "Boys" by Rick Moody (p. 212)	• *The Glen Rock Book of the Dead* by Marion Winik
• "What Every Soldier Should Know" by Brian Turner (p. 217)	• "Going to the Movies" by Susan Toth
• "The Things I've Lost" by Brian Arundel (p. 216)	• "Jubilate Agno" by Christopher Smart
• "I Remember All of You" by Karissa Womack (p. 398)	• *Lists of Note: an Eclectic Collection Deserving of a Wider Audience* compiled by Shaun Usher
• "In My Father's Study upon His Death" by Dylan Landis (p. 161)	• "Things to Do in the Belly of the Whale" by Dan Albergotti

MONOLOGUE

Monologues are stories meant to be presented by the author or a reader onstage, on video, on the radio, or on television. Spoken word and rap are forms of monologue. In a play, when the performer talks to the audience, it's a monologue; when he talks to himself ("to be or not to be"), it's a soliloquy. Monologues can be memoir or fiction. In either case, monologues are usually character-driven, with a literary structure in which we identify with one main character, and he interacts with other people in the story through conflict. Usually a monologue has a climactic moment and a denouement, or resolution.

Contemporary writers usually avoid overt "And then I came to realize . . ." moments, but they show change—change in the main character's outlook, or development, or situation. In contemporary monologue, the main character—usually the speaker, but not always—learns something surprising, something different than what we were expecting. "That's always what we're going for, something surprising, a surprising situation—where somebody comes to a conclusion that you wouldn't expect," writes Ira Glass in *Radio: An Illustrated Guide*, his guidebook to producing stories for radio (a comic book instructional manual illustrated by Jessica Abel).

Monologue is a dramatic form. You don't have much room to preach, rant, think, emote, reflect, muse, or share feelings and memories. You're not a teller; you're a *shower*. You're up there to render a gripping, visual, fresh, evocative story. You can't go into characters' thoughts as you would in fiction or memoir. You have to show, through action, everything that is interesting—you're making a movie with your words so that the images and actions play out in your listener's mind.

Reading Monologues

You'll "read" with your ears. You might have a chance to see a live spoken word or storytelling event, or stand-up or slam. That's a wonderful way to see how this form works. Meanwhile, practice.

PRACTICE

Listen to some monologues. *The Moth* and Glynn Washington's *Snap Judgment* are excellent sources for monologues, as is *This American Life*. On *This American Life*, try "Squirrel Cop" and "Just Keep Breathing." Notice how each story is told as a sequence of actions. Not thoughts, not ideas, not commentary: actions. And the actions are framed by brief interpretation: "I didn't think it was that bad." "I just wanted to impress her." "All I wanted was to be the hero."

PRACTICE

Listen to Jenifer Hixson's "Where There's Smoke" on *The Moth* or view on YouTube. Notice what you see in your mind's eye as you listen. Then read it in print form on page 162. Make a list of five techniques she uses in order to get you to see the scenes. How does she employ reflection? How does she move between the scenes—how does she transition?

Because monologue is performed, it can be helpful to move between different kinds of scenes, to juxtapose humorous scenes, emotional scenes, beautiful scenes, with reflection or questions. And because the audience is listening, not reading, you have to be extremely clear about where things take place, when, and who is present, both in your opening and as you move through the piece. Additional monologues you might enjoy reading include those by Spalding Gray and Laurie Stone. *The Moth* and *This American Life* offer anthologies—print and audio—of inspiring monologues you can use to come up with your own story ideas and styles.

Writing a Monologue

1. Start with a series of events that are highly visual and intensely dramatic: the details before, during, and after you or your character lost her job; a trip to the doctor that does not go well; a fight in which you come to realize you are actually in the wrong.

2. A monologue is not a rant, not a confession, not a sermon, and not thoughts and feelings. It's a series of action scenes, framed by questions and insights. Write out your scenes, paying special attention to clarity: Where are we? Who is "onstage"? Because your audience is listening, you need to be especially concerned with accuracy and ease of understanding.

3. Usually, a monologue contains two turning points so that the story we think we are hearing isn't the story we are actually hearing—things change direction, and then they change direction *again*. Here are some questions that might help you deepen your story and find those key turning points:

   a. What does your speaker (and the speaker may be you or an invented character) think she wants more than anything in this moment?

   b. What does she *really* want? Attend closely to the gap between the answers to the questions in a and b—you're bound to find story juice in that gap.

   c. What are the action steps that externally show those two different levels of want?

   d. What's the worst-case scenario for this character/speaker? Set that up. Then make that happen: Show the worst-case scenario scene playing out. *Then* show us why that worst-case scenario was actually the best thing that could have happened. There are your two turns.

Record yourself reading your monologue. Most people deliver their monologues too quickly. Ask your peers to listen to your polished monologue. Have them note where they laughed, where they really saw the events you are narrating "play out" in their mind's eye, and where they were confused or unclear. Revise, and read your monologue again to the class.

Monologues are usually measured by time, not by word count or page count. It takes about two minutes to read a typical double-spaced page aloud. Five minutes is a good length for your first monologue.

Further Reading

In This Book	Highly Recommended
• "Where There's Smoke" by Jenifer Hixson (p. 162)	• In addition to the radio resources referenced above, slam and spoken word resources are listed on pages 494–95 in Chapter Twelve. Check out monologues by your favorite comedians. Also: Spalding Gray, David Sedaris, William Shakespeare, and Keegan-Michael Key and Jordan Peele.

PLAY/SCREENPLAY

A one-act play is a short play—often with only one, two, or three characters—that introduces a conflict, builds to a crisis, and resolves itself in a limited space and time. It might have one scene that takes up the whole play, or any number of short scenes. The ten-minute play, a more recent subgenre of the one-act, is very popular, especially for new actors and new writers.

Reading Plays

I think a playwright realizes after he finishes working on the script that this is only the beginning. What will happen when it moves into three dimensions?

— DON DELILLO

Almost always, a play shows a character experiencing some kind of internal change. Just as in the journey structure, which governs so much of fiction and memoir, play structure shows a central character in a conflict, going through dramatic moments of struggle that lead up to some kind of dramatic insight, reversal, or explosion. But onstage, this journey is compressed. Everything takes place more quickly than in a novel or memoir. Reading a play aloud takes much longer than reading it silently, and audiences usually don't like to sit still for very long. In a play, everything has to be crisp and exciting and dramatic. Even the opening must be powerful: In a play, especially a one-act, it's essential that a major conflict has already occurred, offstage, just before the play actually opens, and we, the audience, are plunged right into the thick of things.

The playwright will imagine the setting, the costumes, the accents, even specific types of actors or actual actors in the roles, and describe all of these before the play actually begins. Ultimately, though, when the play is performed, the playwright's vision is interpreted by many other people, all of whom have their own creative ideas. When you write your play, definitely see, in your mind's eye, all of the images as they unfold onstage—hear the sounds, foresee the lighting—every detail. And be prepared to let much of that go when your play is produced!

| PRACTICE |

Read Peter Morris's "Pancakes" (p. 274). What has already happened to establish conflict and tension offstage before the play starts? How do you imagine the stage set? Which actors (from your class, from your school, from Hollywood) would you cast in the roles? Why? What do you hear when you read? What is the atmosphere?

When you read a play on the page, you get a lot of information from the dialogue. When you read this play, where do you see the author trying to indicate or control the reader's responses? For example, in the opening paragraph, in italics, of "Pancakes," the author provides very specific direction on how he wants us to imagine the scene. If this passage of direction weren't there, what would shift for you as a reader of this play? As you reread, do you resist any passages of direction? Are you surprised by any? Do you prefer a play that has a lot of exposition and author input, or very little? Why?

Writing a Play

1. Start with characters in a setting. You can take one of your pieces from the semester—a short story or memoir—and use that as your starting point. Or you can use one of the plays in this anthology to brainstorm characters and conflicts for your plays. To write a one-act or ten-minute play, you typically start with one to three characters in immediate and fairly intense conflict, and a setting. You want to imagine the play taking place before an audience.

2. Imagine the play on a real stage. Make a list of the props, costumes, lighting effects, sounds, and anything else you need for your play. You will probably want to keep your ideas for lighting and props and atmospherics fairly simple—at first. Think in terms of a few strong "statement" props for your setting—a lamp, a chair, a stuffed animal, and a bucket of water might be all you need. Think of symbol props for your characters, too—the woman is in a tight black dress, though it's morning; the guy is in his pajamas, holding a cocktail. Make sure the props and setting are *possible* These limits—budget, time, space—actually force you to be more creative, so most writers welcome them! If you have classmates perform your play in the classroom, take those limitations into account and make them work to your advantage dramatically.

3. Work hard on your story. You will probably use classic story structure (see p. 83) to keep your audience engaged and alert, but you can consider other options. If the writing is brilliant and the images unforgettable, a ten-minute rant, with one person onstage, might work perfectly. Usually, two or three characters in conflict give you enough material for a one-act. Work out a series of escalating events, with the characters at odds with each other.

4. Write the dialogue. Keep it short and realistic. In real life, people don't listen to each other carefully, they rarely speak in complete sentences, and their character is revealed not only by what is said, but by what is *not* said.

5. Write the physical action. Show your characters moving around in space, in conflict with the setting. You need to "block" out your characters' movements and gestures. Silence, pauses, and simple sound effects create a kind of sound score for your play, a third level of potential drama and tension you will want to exploit.

6. Rehearse. Not so much for the actors, but for you. Just as the fiction writer and memoirist replay their scenes over and over in their mind's eye, honing their images, recasting the scene again and again by focusing, sketching, seeing, and reseeing, the playwright runs through the play with live actors. You don't need trained actors; friends or classmates will do a fine job. As they read their lines, you can find out what works, what feels flat, and what sounds tinny or off. Also, have the actors follow the stage directions so that you can see where the lulls are in your script and can work to hone the physical drama so that it emphasizes and underscores the verbal drama. Actors are famous for giving authors and directors (that's you for now) lots of free advice—take what's useful. Know that many plays are changed even after they open to a Broadway audience. Shown as "previews" before paying customers, many plays are revised for weeks while they are running.

7. Lighting is an important tool, though again you'll want to keep things simple for your one-act, using darkness and light, and perhaps "fading" light, to call attention to key moments. Dialogue, physical action, light, and the aural effects of sound and silence give you four different strands to script. So you can see that ten minutes of theater takes an *enormous* amount of work!

8. Format your final script (see Tips for Formatting a Play). To format a play you turn in as part of your classwork in creative writing, use the play on page 274 as an example (unless your instructor gives you other directions). At the top of the first page, list the characters by name and give a brief description of their station in life, age, and important characteristics. Then describe the setting, quickly and briefly. For each bit of dialogue, place the speaker's name on the left side of the page, in all caps. Do not use quotation

marks for dialogue, and type it all the way across the page. Tip: One page of a script is equal to about one minute of running time. If your characters are having a fight using lots of one-word sentences and back-and-forth, that's going to speed things up (a good thing!). But to maintain the tension, be sure to vary the pace, and intersperse lengthier patches of dialogue with the rapid-fire bits.

Tips for Formatting a Play

1. The name of the person talking appears in all capital letters on the left-hand side of the page. Capitalize the entire name of a character each time she or he appears. You may use the play on page 274 as a model for formatting.

2. Write a brief, tight, evocative description of each setting before that scene unfolds. You want to establish the mood, key visual cues (e.g., there has to be a window because this character flew in through a window), and any emotions that might be crucial for the actors to show onstage.

3. For scene changes, identify new settings with the details needed.

PRACTICE

To understand the difference in formatting conventions between a screenplay and a play, study the excerpt from Charlotte Glynn's screenplay "Duct Tape Twins" (p. 218) and Peter Morris's play "Pancakes" (p. 274). What differences do you notice on the page?

Tips for Formatting a Screenplay

1. The name of the person talking is centered on the page. Capitalize the entire name of a character each time she or he appears.

2. Write a brief, tight, evocative description of each setting before the drama of that scene unfolds. You want to establish the mood, key visual cues (e.g., there has to be a window because this character flew in through a window), and any emotions that might be crucial for the actors to show on-screen.

3. Identify new settings with the details that are crucial to include each time the scene changes or the camera moves in closer or farther out.

Further Reading

In This Book	Highly Recommended
• Excerpt from "Duct Tape Twins" by Charlotte Glynn (p. 218) • "Pancakes" by Peter Morris (p. 274)	• *Take Ten: New 10-Minute Plays* edited by Eric Lane and Nina Shengold • Plays by Anton Chekhov • *The Screenwriter's Problem Solver* by Syd Field • *The Compact Bedford Introduction to Drama* by Lee Jacobus

PANTOUM

The pantoum is a poem composed of four-line stanzas (quatrains); the form requires you to repeat whole lines, instead of simply rhyming words. Originally a Malayan form of poetry with Persian and Chinese influences, the pantoum has been around for more than five hundred years. John Ashbery is credited with bringing the form to the United States in the 1950s.

Instead of telling a linear story, the pantoum repeats itself and zigzags, forcing the reader to circle back and revisit. It's the opposite of classic dramatic structure; pantoums move in spirals. A pantoum is also the opposite of the conflict-crisis-resolution structure. A pantoum is devoted to circling, interlocking, unfolding. In pantoum, the journey *is* the destination. It's a perfect form for those experiences in your life you wish to write about that just don't fit into classic dramatic structure.

> *Poetry is against gravity.*
> — AI WEIWEI

Reading Pantoums

The pantoum is often clearer and more interesting when it is read aloud.

PRACTICE

Is Natalie Diaz's poem "My Brother at 3 a.m." (p. 159) a pantoum? In what ways does she take moves from the pantoum's recipe, and how does she alter the form? Do the alterations make sense to you? How so? She uses quatrains and a series of interlocking repeated lines to create a powerful portrait of a family with a very troubled brother/son. Why might the options offered by the pantoum—overlapping, interlocking, repetition—be an excellent choice of form for this topic?

PRACTICE

Read aloud the pantoums by Randall Mann (p. 302), Laure-Anne Bosselaar (p. 303), and Natalie Diaz (p. 159). Then have someone read the pantoums aloud to you. What feelings do you get as you read and then listen to these pantoums?

It's helpful to annotate the stanzas of each pantoum, paying attention to what's happening on the level of language and also carefully discerning what's happening on a practical level in the poem. In Laure-Anne Bosselaar's "Still-birth," a woman hears someone call out a person's name on a crowded train station platform. That name happens to be the name she gave her unborn child, years earlier. Chilled, she leaps into the car, and though it makes no sense, and she knows it, she can't help but search for the face of her grown daughter—impossible. But there it is, the irrational mind in all its power. In stanza 2, reality sets in: Of course her daughter, born dead (notice how the title shines a light, like a flashlight, down the spine of the poem, helping us understand what is happening), can't be on the train.

In stanza 3, the power of the pantoum form kicks in. Pantoum is a good form to use when writing about the recursive nature of memory, PTSD, difficult relationships, the things that haunt us, as the images pop up unexpectedly and keep coming back up. "No one in that car could have been you." She has told us—and herself—this before. She's trying to convince herself—to get what she knows as true to coincide with what she *feels* could be true. The speaker of the poem apparently has calculated how old the baby would now be. She confides to us—and her unborn daughter—"I sometimes go months without remembering you." Each stanza adds more detailed information. In stanza 4, we learn what she was told by the nurses and doctors: *Don't get attached*. And those powerful, chilling, terrible words repeat in stanza 5.

Bosselaar makes subtle shifts in her repeating lines. As you reread the poem, study those shifts. Here, as always, the guiding principle applies: If you are going to break the rules, you have to have a great reason. Do you think that her changes to the form improve the poem? Do they seem like mistakes or failures or wholly intentional? How can you tell?

As you read and listened, you were probably aware of the repetitions, the urgency, and the circling. Words and lines are repeated. These are poems about obsession. They keep going over certain images again and again. Whatever haunts us, annoys us, excites us—that's the province of the pantoum.

What do you notice about the "recipe" when you listen, compared to when you read the pantoum on the page? As with all structures, if the structure is truly effective, it's not the most prominent feature of the piece. The tension, the energy, the images—those are what you pay attention to. The pleasure and impact of a pantoum are in how the lines recur and surprise us when they fit together in unusual ways. So don't worry if you don't notice the structure right away. That's always a sign the poet has been successful!

It's important always to both see and hear a pantoum—to see the structure and hear its effect. Having heard a few pantoums aloud, now read them silently and examine the lines carefully. Can you label the lines that echo, placing corresponding letters by them, so that you see the pattern very clearly?

Writing a Pantoum

The pantoum *repeats whole lines* rather than words. So, as in a song, a pantoum is made up of a sequence of *refrains*, or lines that are repeated. The following pattern shows you where lines repeat. The lines can be of any length.

Line 1	A
Line 2	B
Line 3	C
Line 4	D
Line 5	B (same as line 2)
Line 6	E
Line 7	D (same as line 4)
Line 8	F
Line 9	E (same as line 6)
Line 10	G
Line 11	F (same as line 8)
Line 12	H
(and so on)	

The greatest thing a human being ever does is to see something and tell what he sees in a plain way.
— JOHN RUSKIN

So the second and fourth lines of the first stanza are repeated exactly to become the first and third lines of the second stanza. This same pattern is used to complete the entire poem. You can end whenever you like—some pantoums are *pages* long. However, a four-stanza pantoum is common, and in the final stanza, you could simply repeat lines 1 and 3 from the first stanza, or you can write new lines. You have options. Rhyme is optional but usually follows *abab, bcbc, cdcd,* and so on.

This all sounds very complicated, but it's not. It's easier to write a pantoum than to think about it. Choose a topic and just get started. It will all come together as you write.

For your subject, choose something that is inherently repetitive, something that bores you out of your mind: a bad lecture, a tedious summer painting houses, your car that constantly breaks down. Write about swimming laps. Teaching kids to write the letter "a." Watch the pantoum turn your boredom or despair into something humorous, weirdly fascinating, or beautiful. The pantoum gives you a lens for looking at repetition; you might be surprised at what you discover about the same-old, same-old. What images, in your heart of hearts, deep inside your secret self, do you turn over and over and over day and night? That's a good topic for a pantoum.

1. To get started, make a list of twenty-five things that cause your mind or body to go over the same ground, again and again. Work quickly—take no more than ten minutes to work on this list. With three minutes left, if you don't have twenty-five items, press yourself to come up with *anything*. If the last items don't "fit," just write them down anyway.
2. Pick a subject from your list that has a lot of *energy* for you.
3. List the *images* you see when you look closely at this subject. Then write two lines. These first two lines, which will give birth to all the other lines in the pantoum, affect what the pantoum does to the reader: It makes the reader feel edgy, nervous, a bit boxed in. Many poets begin with "cast-off" lines from other poems, so as to not start with a blank page. When you write a pantoum, you need only two lines you like to get going.

For your first pantoum, follow the recipe above, exactly. It's okay to get a little frustrated when you first start writing your pantoum. Learning a new dance step or a new guitar lick is hard at first, but then you have a feeling of "breaking the code." Know that once you get your two basic lines, the pantoum *will* bow to you.

Once you have tried the traditionally structured pantoum, use the basic recipe to make your own kind of pantoum. Break the rules, invent your own structure to support what you want to say. Use the pantoum's interesting back-and-forth structure to inspire you in a new creative direction. Sometimes when you break the rules, that breach becomes the most interesting part of the pattern. Musicians do this frequently. Consider a live performance, where a singer will substitute another word, maybe a rhyme, or maybe something else altogether, into a part of the song everyone knows by heart. This is part of the fun—the surprise, the play. And it calls the listener's (or reader's) attention to something important.

> *I like using forms like pantoums because I feel a set form, far from being restrictive, is very liberating and forces your imagination to explore possibilities it might not otherwise consider.*
>
> — SOPHIE HANNAH

Alternative pantoums are inspired by the pantoum form but deviate in interest-ing ways. So try at least one pantoum that loosely follows the recipe, breaking out of the form at several key points; for example, allow the pantoum to break out of the form when you yourself are breaking out of your obsession.

Further Reading

In This Book	Highly Recommended
• "Pantoum" by Randall Mann (p. 302)	• "Parent's Pantoum" by Carolyn Kizer
• "Stillbirth" by Laure-Anne Bosselaar (p. 303)	• "Poem of the Great Depression" by Donald Justice
• "My Brother at 3 a.m." by Natalie Diaz (p. 159)	• "Lower Manhattan Pantoum" by Elaine Sexton
• "Another Lullaby for Insomniacs" by A. E. Stallings (p. 335)	• "Pantoum in Wartime" by Marilyn Hacker

SESTINA

The sestina is a poem that uses six stanzas of six lines each, with the end words in each line repeating in a specific pattern throughout the poem. The Italian poets Petrarch and Dante made the form famous (and Dante gave it its name). As with the pantoum, poets often write sestinas when they want to tackle topics involving obsession. When you land on the right topic, you render a haunting experience, the kind of feeling and worry that are very hard to talk about in regular conversation.

Reading Sestinas

Read the sestina "Liner Notes for an Imaginary Playlist" by Terrance Hayes (p. 113). Read silently, and then have someone read the sestina aloud while you just let your mind take in the images. Read this long poem once more, and notice the pattern, the way words are repeated. You will notice that the poem has six stanzas, each with six lines, plus a little ending stanza of three lines, like a P.S. on a letter. If you want to read additional sestinas, you will find an excellent collec-tion at *McSweeney's Internet Tendency*, including "To My Friend, the Christian Pop Star in Nashville" by K. Judith Mowrer, "O Light, Red Light" by Cathy Park

Hong, "How to Build a Sestina Template in Microsoft Excel" by Daniel Ari, and "I'm Obsessed with My Wife" by Nicole Steinberg, along with dozens of others.

The sestina adds a slightly more intricate pattern of words to the brooding, worrying, obsessive feeling that you get from a pantoum or a ghazal. Safe to say, if you like Sudoku or Mad Libs, you will love the sestina. Writing a sestina is like a filling-in-puzzle-pieces project.

A sestina uses six different words as the end words for the lines in each stanza. However, each stanza uses the end words in a different pattern. All the lines in the poem end with one of those six specified words. The order is dictated by the recipe:

STANZA 1	STANZA 2	STANZA 3	STANZA 4
a	f	c	e
b	a	f	c
c	e	d	b
d	b	a	f
e	d	b	a
f	c	e	d

STANZA 5	STANZA 6	FINAL STANZA	
d	b	ab	
e	d	cd	
a	f	ef	
c	e		
f	c		
b	a		

The final stanza uses all six words in half the amount of space—three lines. You will be surprised at the things you are able to say; limiting your word choices actually increases your creativity. Your lines do not need to be long. Poet Ciara Shuttleworth wrote a sestina titled "Sestina" that consists of one-word lines, following the pattern.

In a good sestina, the pattern isn't completely obvious; it's supposed to be subtle, a little hidden. If the poet is doing her job, being super-specific, using enjambment, and adding new information in each stanza, the reader notices the images and the feelings the poem creates, not the overt pattern. Only upon close rereading does the structure, or recipe, become clear.

PRACTICE

Label the sestina in this book (or use others you've found that you enjoy) with the corresponding letters from the recipe above. Do you notice any variations? Do they add anything to the meaning of the poem?

Writing a Sestina

John Ashbery, a famous poet, once said that writing a sestina is like riding downhill on a bicycle and having the pedals push your feet. Keep your sense of play and your sense of humor as you explore this form.

1. Make a list of six solid end words, words that leave you some flexibility: *code, mean, shallow, mist, body, read.* Hayes chose solid, simple, clear, concrete words that punch out his theme. And, he plays with the language, punning and bending, adding surprise and music: *red* and *reed* work with *read. Man* and *Amen* resound. He goes for subtle rhymes and echoes: *code, cold, coat, coast.* Hayes uses the form as a scaffolding, but he plays within its strictures and keeps the form fresh and new.

   Avoid words that will work in only a few situations, like *hasenpfeffer.* Choose words you won't mind hearing over and over. Words that do double duty, like *read* and *sail* (a noun and a verb) give you more flexibility. To come up with a collection of good, usable end words that will work in many different situations, you can draw from your own poetry. Or you can use the end words used by other sestina writers as you learn the form. Remember that plain, clear, concrete words are easier to work with as you knit your stanzas together.

2. Next, choose for your topic something that weighs on your mind, something that you go over again and again: failed love, running track, worrying about the future.

3. Study the pattern, and place your end words on the page. Remember: The capital letters stand for the word at the end of each line. Note the logic of the pattern: Stanza 2 takes the *a b c* end words and intersplices *d e f* end words in reverse order. If all this patterning gives you a headache, don't worry about it. Just follow the guide above, and write your lines to fit those end words.

4. For the final stanza, you can follow the recipe above and write three lines. When a poem recipe shows two letters, as above, it means that you put the *a* word (the word that ended your first line in stanza 1, your second line in stanza 2, etc.) in the middle of the line, and your *b* word (the same word you used in *b*, above) at the end of line 1 of this final stanza. Line 2 of the final

stanza, *c d*, puts the *c* word in the middle of the line and the *d* word at the end; line 3, the last line of the whole poem, places the *e* word in the middle of the line, and your poem ends with whatever word you have been using in the *f* slot. Or you can make your final stanza just one line long, as Wesli Court does in "The Obsession" (easily found online).

The challenge of the sestina is to draw attention *away from* (not toward) the end words (the repeating words). So poets often break their lines so that the phrases with the repeating word flow down into the next line.

> *You can't eat language but it eases thirst.*
> — BERNARD MALAMUD

After trying a classic sestina, play a little and fudge the rules. Sometimes, for example, poets omit the final three-line stanza. That is okay. Other poets use closely related words to make patterns—*light, night, enlightened,* or *sun, son, sunned.* Try a strict sestina first; then play with form, breaking the rules in interesting and fresh ways.

Further Reading

In This Book	Highly Recommended
• "Liner Notes for an Imaginary Playlist" by Terrance Hayes (p. 113)	• "To My Friend, the Christian Pop Star in Nashville" by K. Judith Mowrer
	• "The Buffy Sestina" by Jason Schneiderman
	• "Spring Break Sestina" by Alison D. DeJesus, Allyson M. Miller, Amanda M. Kiscoe, Daniel A. Hoyt, Shawn R. Gaines, and Thomas C. Lill
	• "Sestina" by Ciara Shuttleworth

SONNET

The sonnet is a fourteen-line poem, usually composed of lines that are ten syllables in length. Enduring topics for the sonnet are politics, love, and religion, but poets have written sonnets on every imaginable subject. The sonnet is one of the most well-known and best-loved forms of poetry in the Western world. Shakespeare, Milton, and Wordsworth are well known for their sonnets, along with literary superstars such as Dylan Thomas, Gerard Manley

> *Life has been your art. You have set yourself to music. Your days are your sonnets.*
> — OSCAR WILDE

Hopkins, and Elizabeth Barrett Browning. But many contemporary poets, including Kim Addonizio, Terrance Hayes, and Denis Johnson, also write exciting and innovative sonnets. The form isn't stuffy or dusty; it's powerful and compressed yet allows great range.

The word *sonnet* comes from an Italian word, *sonetto* (a "little sound" or "song"), from the Latin root *sonus* ("sound"). That etymology is important because when you read sonnets, you will notice that the poet pays close attention to the sounds of the words, certain kinds of rhymes, and the patterns of vowels and consonants. The rhythm in a traditional sonnet is the meter of iambic pentameter—five feet, which is ten syllables in every line, and every other syllable is accented. Traditional rhyme schemes for the sonnet vary greatly, but the most popular is the one that William Shakespeare used: *abab, cdcd, efef, gg*. Contemporary sonnets may not follow the rhyme scheme or syllable count; however, they almost always have fourteen lines and two strong turns. Some poets create interlocking sonnets, where the last line of the first sonnet is used as the first line of the second sonnet, and so on. Interlocking sonnets often contain fourteen poems, and this is called a crown of sonnets.

The sonnet requires a poet to look at things in a specific way and to develop a concept with a particular focus. Sonnet writing is not simple—but it is very rewarding, once you practice a bit.

Reading Sonnets

In addition to its special focus on sound, the sonnet gives both the poet and the reader an interesting way to look at anything. The sonnet is basically a *way of thinking.* You introduce your thoughts and feelings about a topic in the first eight lines; then you look at it in a different way in the last six lines. Make a strong turn between the first section of the sonnet and the second section. The last two lines, usually called the couplet, provide a surprising resolution to the two competing ideas presented. Phillis Levin writes that the sonnet is "a meeting place of image and voice, passion and reason."

Every mood of mind can be indulged in a sonnet; every kind of reader appealed to. You can make love in a sonnet, you can laugh in a sonnet, you can lament in it, can narrate or describe, can rebuke, can admire, can pray.

— LEIGH HUNT

When you read sonnets, pay attention to the rhyme, the turn, and the final couplet. Those three aspects of the sonnet create the rich layers and meanings in the poem. Here are the basic rules of the form:

- The sonnet consists of fourteen lines.
- It is often written in iambic pentameter (ten syllables per line).

- The rhyme scheme varies but is often *abab, cdcd, efef, gg* or *abba, abba, cdcdcd.*

If you want to read more contemporary sonnets for inspiration, you can easily find many online. Try works by Kim Addonizio, Molly Peacock, Denis Johnson, Gail White, Rhina Espaillat, A. E. Stallings, and Cornelius Eady.

David Livewell

Fatigues

I stood in oversized fatigues to pose
For him, my oldest brother off in Nam.
The bedroom trapped his aftershave, a bomb
Exploding daily memories of those
Rides on his back across our creaking rooms.
His stare in photos dug a trench, a ring
That wrapped a wild-eyed medic carrying
His friends and enemies down open tombs.
And though he clawed back home, the nightmares changed
His eyes, malaria his family blood.
We couldn't see what he was fighting for
Or when the bullets ceased. He rearranged
His past for those he dragged through jungle mud.
A man at home must save the boy at war.

> *Ending is stopping without sucking.*
> — GEORGE SAUNDERS

In David Livewell's sonnet "Fatigues," you discovered the rhyme scheme *abba, cddc, efg, efg.* If you weren't aware of the subtle crafting of sound the first time you read the poem, it's a sign that the poet was very successful. Each line that rhymes is connected, powerfully, through sound. *Tombs* and *rooms* emphasize and inform each other. *Nam* and *bomb* hit hard on the ear, as do *blood* and *mud.* Do you notice other sound patterns in this sonnet, besides the end words in the rhyme scheme? Notice how the technique of enjambment—ending lines at various places in the sentence rather than placing a period at the end of the line—helps the music in the poem.

The first part of the poem, written in striking visual and sensory images (oversized fatigues, aftershave lotion, memories of riding on the brother's back), records an emotionally complex and visually straightforward moment: posing in an older brother's fatigues, as that same brother, though the brother isn't present—he is in Nam. Notice the turn: "And though he clawed back home. . . ." Up until now, the brother has been away, and the speaker has been reflecting on memories and photos of this young man at war. Then in line 9, where the sonnet typically turns, we learn tragically that "the nightmares changed / His eyes." The boy who went to war doesn't come home the same person at all. He looks different. It's clear the war is still going on in the beloved brother's head. Those last three lines are so potent, so moving— Livewell pulls back in the final two lines to make a third move, a large statement about how memory and survival are intertwined for war veterans. You might want to discuss your reaction to these final lines with your classmates.

Writing a Sonnet

Because the sonnet is especially useful for more difficult topics—unrequited love, political statements, religious questions—it's often hard to write at first. Stay with it. It's better to write four or five sonnets before you decide whether you like this form. Be patient with yourself, and allow plenty of time. Most poets work on demanding form poems in a series of short sessions, writing by hand for twenty to thirty minutes, stepping away, and coming back.

1. Start by listing topics in three categories—love, politics, religion (or spirituality). Because sonnets are about ideas, you may be tempted to just start writing. But it will be easier if you work from images. Make lists of *objects or people.* Try for ten items in each of the three categories. Here's a sample of one student's sonnet topic list, in progress:

Love	Politics	Religion
USA	Transgender	Cross misused?
First-grade crush—can't remember name; redhead	Snowden	Sunday hikes in dunes—nature is my church
	Why no one votes	
	Campus election for homecoming king—stupid	Prayer in school debate?
Current girlfriend, K.		
Ex-girlfriend, A.		
Love for my dad	Suite mates fighting over borderlands	Next-door neighbor was a minister— Mr. Goodword. For real his name.
Grandfather		
Charlie—dog (?)	CNN, weirdly addictive	
Love for nature—kayaking	If I ran for office	Boyfriend took me to synagogue
	The 25-year-old mayor	Fake Christmas stuff

After you make your lists, ask a classmate which ones he or she would like to know more about. Circle those. Then circle the three that are most interesting to you.

2. Now, for one of your topics, create a list of images that you associate with that topic.

3. Using the drawing technique, begin with a specific place and a specific time, and start your sonnet in action.

4. Writing a sonnet is similar to doing a puzzle with words. You have ten syllables per line to spend, so you might want to make a little fill-in-the-blank. (Tip: It's easier to do this work by hand than on the computer.) Make a grid with fourteen lines, ten blanks on each line. Then turn your first image into a line. Remember: You can spread the words in your first image into the next line (enjambment). At this point, it's less important that you worry about the rhythms of your lines—but do adhere closely to the *ten-syllable maximum* rule. Your instructor may introduce you to iambic pentameter—the *da dum, da dum, da dum* emphases on syllables found in Shakespeare's sonnets. However, you will notice that if you stick to exactly ten syllables, your lines will have a natural rhythm.

5. Play out your first image. You can use online rhyming dictionaries to help you work out the rhymes suggested by the end words you have established in your first lines. If those words are too hard to rhyme, then simply go back and fiddle around with your lines. It can be frustrating and time-consuming. But it's always a great way to practice creative focus and

concentration. Writing sonnets is exercise, and while not always pleasant, exercise is good for you.

> *He is a fool which cannot make one sonnet, and he is mad which makes two.*
> — JOHN DONNE

The sonnet will force you to come up with images, word choices, patterns, and thoughts that would not have occurred to you otherwise.

As you go over your sonnet and work on the words, make sure you send your poem in one direction in the first eight lines, and then in another direction for the next six lines. Perhaps in the opening of your sonnet you have argued that Tinder is mind candy, harmless, fun — a good way to relax at the end of the day. Then in the second part of the poem, you must *turn*. Moving in the opposite direction, you say that Tinder isn't really fun, relaxing, helpful, or harmless at all. In fact, you may conclude something very surprising about your Tinder addiction, something you would have never thought of without the sonnet as your guide. A sonnet provides *a way to think*.

Further Reading

In This Book	Highly Recommended
• "First Poem for You" by Kim Addonizio (p. 112)	• *The Making of a Sonnet* edited by Eavan Boland and Ed Hirsch
• "Fatigues" by David Livewell (p. 455)	• Poetry Foundation Web site: search for sonnets

VILLANELLE

> *Poetry is not an expression of the party line. It's that time of night, lying in bed, thinking what you really think, making the private world public; that's what the poet does.*
> — ALLEN GINSBERG

The villanelle is a nineteen-line poem with a pattern of repeated lines and two rhymes. Poet Annie Finch says, "The villanelle is one of the most fascinating and paradoxical of poetic forms, quirky and edgy yet second to no other European form but the sonnet in importance; prone to moods of obsession and delight; structured through the marriage of repetition and surprise."

Developed in Italy, where it was the basic pattern for folk songs, the villanelle became quite popular in France in the seventeenth century.

The nineteen lines of this form are presented in five tercets (three-line stanzas), completed by a quatrain (a four-line stanza).

Reading Villanelles

Without studying the form or reading ahead, take a moment to read aloud the villanelle on p. 302 by Gregory Orr, "The River." Online, take a look at Theodore Roethke's famous example,"The Waking."

PRACTICE

What do you notice about the patterns in the two villanelles you just read? What appeals to you about the sounds and music in the poems? What are the most striking differences in these two poems? If it's helpful, write down the "recipe" at the end of each line, annotating the poem so that you see the repetition and rhyme scheme clearly.

After you have read the villanelles, familiarize yourself with the following recipe. The nineteen lines can be of any length. The villanelle must have five tercets (three-line stanzas), one quatrain (four-line stanza), and two rhymes, plus two refrains.

STANZA 1	STANZA 2	STANZA 3
A^1—refrain	a	a
b	b	b
A^2—refrain	A^1—refrain	A^2—refrain

STANZA 4	STANZA 5	STANZA 6
A	a	A
b	b	b
A^1—refrain	A^2—refrain	A^1
		A^2

In the table, a capital letter indicates that the whole line is repeated; a lower-case letter indicates that a word is rhymed or repeated. In the villanelle recipe, the symbol A^1 indicates the first line of your poem, and each time it's repeated, you use *the exact same line* again — the poem truly writes itself. The symbol A^2 indicates a new line, but the end word *rhymes* with the end word in A^1.

Sandwiched in between those repeating lines is also a rhyme scheme: *aba* for the tercets and *abaa* for the quatrain. As you read, you probably won't overtly notice the structure, if the villanelle is doing its job. As always, it's easiest to begin a form poem by reading an example and then labeling the lines so you can see the form. The notation is confusing and frustrating until you practice writing a few. Be patient.

The successful villanelle has refrain (repeated) lines that blend and flow into the poem. As you read, the lines change meaning in their varied contexts.

Writing a Villanelle

> *Pay attention only to the form; emotion will come spontaneously to inhabit it. A perfect dwelling always finds an inhabitant.*
> — ANDRÉ GIDE

Like the pantoum, the villanelle almost writes itself, once you have settled on two lines that you think are interesting enough to repeat (and that rhyme). The two lines need to go together but also be wholly independent of each other so that at the end, when they show up side-by-side, the reader will be both surprised and satisfied. Be patient with yourself as you write your villanelle—you are building new writing muscles as you work in this form, and you will surely feel some resistance, annoyance, and frustration. Let that be part of your writing and learning process. Most students find that in each case—pantoum, ghazal, sestina, villanelle—learning *about* the poem is difficult, much more difficult than actually writing it. Try taking older, failed poems and reworking them into one or more of these forms. And allow yourself to break the rules and reinvent the forms—to claim these techniques for yourself.

Keep your lines about the same length. For topics, try writing about sisters, brothers, a river, or a job one of your parents had when he or she was young, titled "My Mother the _____" or "My Father the _____."

Further Reading

In This Book	Highly Recommended
• "The River" by Gregory Orr (p. 302)	• "One Art" by Elizabeth Bishop
	• "The House on the Hill" by Edwin Arlington Robinson
	• "The American on His First Honeymoon" by Rita Mae Reese

THE WRITING LIFE

The main reason for rewriting is not to achieve a smooth surface, but to discover the inner truth of your characters.

SAUL BELLOW

[Revision is the] refusal to let the fiction go until it has proved itself a closed and self-sustaining system.

JOHN GARDNER

The secret of good writing is to strip every sentence to its cleanest components.

WILLIAM ZINSSER

CHAPTER ELEVEN

REACHING READERS

You've written. You've created, revised, edited, proofread, and polished—it's been fun, and it's been frustrating and hard, too—but now you have a body of work to share with others. An incredibly rich and rewarding part of creative writing is taking your work to an audience. How do you know if you are ready to present work in this way? You are probably ready to share your work with an audience after you have completed several pieces, working with your teacher and peers to improve them to the best of your ability.

When you turn your work over to an instructor, in a sense you "go public"—you are finished working on the piece for the time being, and you are sharing it with someone else as a finished (for now) piece. The work is in the best shape you can possibly get it into at this point. You are saying to your reader, "Here's my best effort." When you present or turn in or publish a piece of writing, you change your relationship to the work. It's not just your personal project anymore. The experience becomes a shared one. Taking your work to readers is in part an evaluation, but it's also a celebration of your efforts, and a kind of community-building conversation, too.

Piano students play for audiences at recitals. Photographers and designers create portfolios. Football teams build all season to playoff and bowl games. Painters work on series of paintings to show to the public in gallery openings. Playwrights dream of opening night. Chefs open restaurants and invite other chefs to dine while they work out the final kinks. A start-up company works years and then "goes public." In creative writing, sharing your efforts with the public is a wonderful opportunity to continue learning your craft because the experience allows you to further focus and shape your writing life as well as your writing. Keeping the audience (or the customer) in mind trains you to make good choices as you work. When you take your work to an audience outside of

> *Publication is to thinking as*
> *childbirth is to the first kiss.*
> — KARL WILHELM FRIEDRICH
> SCHLEGEL

your peer reading group, you start to think about your readers in a different way. More than ever, perhaps, you care deeply about more than self-expression: You want your audience to be entertained, deeply moved, intrigued, or all three. Learning how to take work before an audience and come away with valuable information on your writing's strengths and weaknesses is the foundation for sustaining a lifelong writing habit.

You have a number of ways to take your work to readers. Here are the three main ways:

1. Give a live reading of your creative writing (in class, at a coffee shop, etc.).
2. Publish in a digital or print format.
3. Create a print or digital chapbook or portfolio of your work.

Performing, tweeting, blogging, and creating and distributing limited print editions of your work are all forms of publication. And publication—showing and sharing your work—is important for a number of reasons. Publication helps you stay in touch with the importance of revising your work. Publication gives you a deadline, and deadlines focus your energy and help you improve your craft and measure that improvement. Publication is a way for you and a community to celebrate hard work and creative effort. Publication lets others experience your view of the world and perhaps appreciate your craft and technical ability. Audience members untrained in the art of creative writing might simply say, "I was on the edge of my seat the whole time." You'll know—and so will the other writers in the room—just how much work went into calibrating tension, going cold at just the right moment, and creating a series of riveting scenes; your audience probably does not know. And that's what we want. We want our readers and listeners to have a fantastic experience, and we want the writing to be so polished that to the audience the performance looks effortless.

However, it's important to approach publication as a professional writer. Recitals, playoffs, performances, and publication are celebrations of *work-in-progress*. Most artists, athletes, and creators aren't ever truly *finished* with a piece—chefs perfect their béarnaise sauce over a lifetime, the backdoor pass always needs work. But there comes a time when showing, revealing, celebrating, saying "finished for now" is a necessary part of the process of evolving, of improving. Notice what worked for your readers, if you are able to. Pay attention to the feedback you get: Everyone liked the funny poems, but no one commented on your favorite, the long, dark prose poem about smoke. Good to know. Whether it's published or not, you can *always* make your work better. In the service of learning your craft, at some point (usually toward the end of a course), it's a good idea to take stock of what you have done, hone one or more strong pieces, stand back, and see how they are received by the readers.

PUBLIC READINGS

Many writers say that nothing allows them to see their work more clearly than reading it aloud before an audience. When you read your work to a live audience, all the flaws in a piece of writing can suddenly show up—if only to you—and new ways back into the piece might become obvious to you. Consider this situation: There's a sentence in your story you love, you adore it, it's your favorite. When your piece is discussed in class, everyone loves the line. It's not until you read the work aloud in front of a group of people that you realize the truth: The sentence has nothing to do with your story. Out it goes (maybe it's the first line of a new piece). A public reading helps you revise with a clear, fresh eye and a sensitive ear. And during the reading, you'll be able to see things about your writing that you can't see any other way. Sometimes you will read aloud a sentence slightly differently than how it appears on the page, and you'll realize that you've landed on a smoother syntax. You'll see readers sometimes making little marks as they read. Reading aloud transforms your relationship to your work.

> A person who publishes a book willfully appears before the populace with his pants down. If it is a good book nothing can hurt him. If it is a bad book nothing can help him.
>
> — EDNA ST. VINCENT MILLAY

Some writers feel they should wait until they are really, really good before they attempt some form of public presentation. However, presenting your work after writing intensively for even just a few months is a great way to educate yourself about your writing process—again, nothing else gives you quite this experience. Keep in mind the main mantra of this book—it's not about you, it's about your reader. You are not performing in order to have a cathartic emotional experience, to show off, or to have everyone adore you.

It's one thing to sit at your desk late at night fussing with word order, last lines, titles, and tiny details. But when you present your work for others to see and hear—not just your group, your instructor, and your friends, but a true *audience*—it greatly increases your ability to both focus and revise. Reading aloud formally lets you grow as a writer. It gives you a chance to celebrate creativity and a process. People will clap; it will feel great. And, most importantly, you will return to your work smarter, wiser.

> The secret to being a writer is that you have to write. It's not enough to think about writing or to study literature or plan a future life as an author. You really have to lock yourself away, alone, and get to work.
>
> — AUGUSTEN BURROUGHS

Before you read your own work aloud, try to attend some live readings by professional authors so you can see what you like and what you want to avoid (saying "uh" a lot, going over the time limit, reading something hard to follow or in which very little action occurs).

Readings by accomplished writers usually last about one hour. Sometimes several well-known writers will share the stage. We writers, just like music fans, will drive hours to hear a live reading by Richard Blanco, Jorie Graham, A. Van Jordan, Gish Jen, Li-Young Li, or Ross Gay. Just as established comics try out new material in tiny clubs, writers sometimes read from a new piece or even a work-in-progress in order to try it out, to get information about what is working in the piece and what is not. Again, nothing reveals the sweet spots and the weaknesses in a piece of writing more than reading it aloud before a live audience. You are urged to watch and listen to poets, writers, speakers, and performers giving readings of their work and presenting their material. Try Web sites and podcasts such as *This American Life*, *The Moth*, TED Talks, and YouTube, especially if the area where you live doesn't offer a lot of live literary readings. Search for your favorite authors or the ones in this textbook, or for the specific types of work you want to be exposed to, such as poetry slam and hip-hop at the Nuyorican Poets Café (www.nuyorican.org). Or try a search for "best spoken word performances."

New writers interested in publicly reading their own work attend as many readings as they can. They listen for what is interesting, what falls flat, what

Tips for Attending a Live Reading

1. If possible, do some background reading on the authors who are presenting.

2. Arrive early. Take notes on the setting. Eavesdrop. What kind of people are attending? What do they talk about before the reading?

3. Listen with your pen in hand. Take notes on images you like, lines you like.

4. Listen as a fellow writer: What does this reader do onstage that is particularly compelling? Does he or she have any tics that are distracting?

5. It's okay to space out . . . to mentally drift. It's really hard to concentrate continuously, especially if you are someone who does not regularly go to live readings. Gently bring yourself back to the performance when you notice that your mind has wandered.

6. When the author is finishing up, try to think of a question or a comment for him or her. You might jot it down in your notebook. During the question-and-answer period or afterward at the book-signing table, you can ask the question or make the comment.

presentation techniques work, and how the author's comments add to or detract from the work itself. We take notes to learn from the example of others. Usually, writers read aloud their more accessible works. Reading aloud dark, deeply disturbing, intricate, hard-to-follow pieces, or pieces that depend on the written page for their meaning, will probably not be as successful. Some writers have a "read aloud" version of their work that differs from the published or printed version. In the "read aloud" version of your own work, you may need to change the use and placement of speech tags ("he said," "she said"), placing them ahead of the dialogue lines and repeating characters' names more frequently.

Audiences have a hard time listening for more than one hour—listening to creative writing read aloud is more difficult than viewing a popular film. If you aren't used to being read to, you may need to go to a few live readings before you are comfortable sitting back and letting creative writing make a movie in your mind. When we were children, parents or caretakers read or told us stories. And when we listened, we "saw" the story, we experienced it, we were *there*. But most of us haven't been read to in quite a long time. We may have to remind our brain how much it loves this pleasure, this mixture of relaxing and focusing that constitutes an exquisite kind of concentration. Listening to a live reading is a skill you practice and develop.

When you give readings, stick closely to your time limit: Going over is completely out of bounds. For new writers, quick readings—five-minute, three-minute, two-page, or poem-and-a-page-of-prose readings—work best. Practice extensively to rehearse your "off-the-cuff" remarks, to work out your timing, and to figure out the best pieces to read.

Many coffeehouses around the country have open-mic nights; research the venues in your area. People aren't used to listening to poets and writers read out loud, so don't be alarmed if you don't feel entirely *listened to*. When you are out with friends, it takes effort and practice to concentrate on creative writing. It helps when the writing is exceptionally good.

When you read, you will likely be able to sense what parts hold the audience's interest and what parts may be too long, too slow, or too obscure. You may suddenly see how you could apply one or more of the tools—energy, images, tension, structure, pattern, insight—to a passage in your piece. After a live reading, you will probably be excited to revise your piece. After they leave the stage, many writers take a moment to make a few notes on the page, while it's still fresh in their mind.

Take reading aloud for what it is: a chance to "publish" your work, to give it an airing out, a good shake, to see what sticks—a rehearsal. No other experience with publishing your work gives you the kind of feedback—instant, laser-sharp, dead accurate—that reading aloud to an audience does. It's like stand-up comedy. The vibe in the room doesn't lie. You'll know. And after you read, you'll be able to make your best work even better—that's what every writer wants.

A class reading is a friendly, effective way to practice sharing your work. Some classes hold live readings at the end of the semester, and students invite friends, teachers, and family. If you are not nervous at first, you might not be normal. You will gain confidence as you continue to give live readings. With practice you'll get better; you will probably even come to *love* the experience and the insight into your work that you gain.

Classes can decide on the format. Students who enjoy reading in front of groups might read excerpts or short works by students who are terrified of reading aloud. Short-shorts and narrative poems work very well for class readings, which can be held in your classroom or at the campus coffee shop—snacks and literature have a long history of complementing each other nicely.

Some authors memorize their work. Others practice in front of a mirror or with a friend and then read from their phone or a paper copy when they take the stage. Some authors begin their own reading with a short poem or paragraph by

WRITERS' TIPS: Giving a Public Reading of Your Work

Here are some important things to keep in mind before you read in front of an audience.

1. Plan out the order of your pieces carefully (if you are reading more than one short piece).

2. Plan out your comments (if you need to briefly explain the background of a poem or the context of a story excerpt). Know what you will say when you take the stage. Do you need to thank anyone? Prepare your first couple of sentences, and rehearse them.

3. Practice reading the piece aloud several times. Practice in front of someone who can tell you if you're speaking too fast (this is the most common mistake—almost *everyone* reads too fast). Read more slowly than feels normal.

4. Stick to the designated time requirements. Do not go over your time. Very bad form.

5. Make sure you have water and a readable copy of what you will present.

6. Use your anxiety to infuse your reading with energy. If you are not nervous, you may read "flat."

7. Have an exit strategy. Slow down, way down, as you read the last lines of your piece. Look directly at the audience, say "thank you," and get off the stage.

8. After the live reading, take a few minutes to make some notes on your text, marking places that you may want to consider revising—places where you stumbled, or got an unexpected laugh, or places where you could sense you may have confused the audience.

another writer, honoring and giving credit to an author who has inspired them. Prefacing your own reading with someone else's words pays homage to that person and at the same time serves to calm your nerves: You start your reading with a proven winner.

LITERARY MAGAZINES: PRINT AND DIGITAL

Editors are constantly looking for new, undiscovered writers. Every magazine wants to be able to say it published the first story by Ernest Hemingway or Flannery O'Connor, the first poem by W. S. Merwin, the first short story by Jhumpa Lahiri. New writers should explore as many of the so-called little or literary magazines as time allows, both print and digital. To get a good sense of what editors and readers are interested in, read through the pieces published in magazines devoted to showcasing new and accomplished writers side-by-side. Numerous online guides can help you find new, high-quality literary magazines. Note: Do not send money to anyone, ever, when you submit work. Some scam artists and disreputable outfits might promise to publish your work in an anthology—for a fee. Run, don't walk, from any outfit that asks you to pay money to publish or to read your work.

> *A lot of people talk about writing. The secret is to write, not talk.*
>
> — JACKIE COLLINS

Online Resources

The following resources are reputable and comprehensive guides where you can find lively, wonderful magazines, journals, and resources to read and perhaps to publish your creative writing.

WebdelSol.com Web del Sol is an outstanding directory for anything pertaining to literary magazines. From their Web site: "Beginning in late 1994, WebdelSol.com (WDS) undertook a mission to effectively utilize the Internet in the marketing and web-publishing of independent literary journals. WDS was the second organization to place a literary journal on the web—the first being *Mississippi Review*. Since that time, WDS has served content to millions of readers worldwide, and links lead to WDS content from over 40,000 other Web sites." This is your go-to site for learning the workings of the literary magazine world.

> *I just try to warn people who hope to get published that publication is not all it is cracked up to be. But writing is. Writing has so much to give, so much to teach, so many surprises. That thing you had to force yourself to do—the actual act of writing—turns out to be the best part.*
>
> — ANNE LAMOTT

clmp.org The Community of Literary Magazines and Presses is also a directory that catalogues independent literary publishers. Like independent bookstores or independent record labels, these publishers focus on publishing indie poetry, fiction, and creative nonfiction, and they are mission-driven, meaning that their main concern is long-term, quality relationships with authors and small but devoted audiences, not ads, dollars, or fame. Contemporary literature thrives in these small magazines and literary journals: They celebrate emerging voices and hybrid and experimental art forms that are overlooked by mainstream magazines. *The CLMP Directory* helps you find these indie and alt publications so that you can determine what their preferences are before sending work to them.

writersmarket.com and writersdigest.com *Writer's Market* and *Writer's Digest* offer a lot of free content online, but to obtain the detailed directories for literary magazines and markets that pay writers to write, you must subscribe or go to your local library and peruse the hard copies. *Writer's Market* is a large reference work, printed each year in several volumes: One volume is devoted to the novel and short story markets, another to the children's literature market, and another to the poetry market. It is updated annually and also includes listings, as in *The CLMP Directory*, of magazines looking for new writers as well as submission requirements. In addition, helpful articles on how to write attention-getting queries and effective cover letters precede the actual listings. Your library's reference section will likely have access to these volumes.

pw.org *Poets and Writers* is a fantastic resource for new writers. Online you'll find an excellent search engine for literary magazines specifically looking for writers; the site also offers a bimonthly magazine that is beloved by creative writers at all levels. This is a practical, thoughtful, inspiring, and invaluable resource for those interested in researching grants for writers, summer workshops, writing conferences, and contests.

awpwriter.org and *The Writer's Chronicle* Both the Association of Writers and Writing Programs Web site and the information-packed monthly periodical are core resources for those interested in creative writing as a discipline, submitting work to new and outstanding journals, and interviews with writers alongside in-depth articles on reading and writing literature.

newpages.com NewPages is a respected Web site that provides information on literary journals and the publishing world. The site's call-for-submission page is updated regularly.

lithub.com Literary Hub has a lively and ever-changing Web site and daily emails for literary news, insider tips, insights, and interviews.

Visit two of the resources listed here and spend some time exploring the sites. Write a brief reaction: What are two or three things that surprised you as you dug deeper into the sites? Then make a brief list: In what ways are the two sites you chose different from each other? Did you like one better than the other?

Research a Wide Range of Publications

Magazines are like shops at the mall—each one has its own personality, its own look and feel. Reading literary magazines is empowering. You'll find some authors who knock you out. And you may also say, "Hey, I can write this well." Look up some of the following publications and see what you think of the work inside. In addition to online versions, you may find interesting versions of these literary magazines in your library and in most bookstores shelved alongside periodicals.

The following magazines often make the "best of" lists, and most have both print and digital versions:

Tin House	*The Gettysburg Review*
Zoetrope: All-Story	*Creative Nonfiction*
The Sun	*The Paris Review*
The Believer	*Granta*
Fourth Genre	*Glimmer Train*
Mississippi Review	*Callaloo*

Online, look at *Fugue, Pleiades, The Rumpus, Hobart, Ruminate Magazine, BOAAT, Guernica, Diagram, Blackbird,* and *Brevity.* If you search for "best literary magazines," "top ten literary magazines," or "best new literary journals," you will find that some titles keep appearing; check those out and read the work they are publishing to get a good feel for what the editors are looking for.

Explore an online literary magazine, one listed above or one that you find on your own. Write a mini-review of the magazine, and share it with your class so that others can decide if they want to explore this magazine or possibly submit work to it in the future. Your instructor may bring in an array of print publications for you to peruse as well.

When you travel, you can find magazines with limited distribution—rare, local, and intriguing journals tucked away in unlikely places. Visit locally owned, independent bookstores, college bookstores, and art galleries, and look for local authors in arts journals and literary magazines.

Using the directories of literary magazines listed on pages 469–70, do your research before publishing. You might not be able to publish a work in a print journal after publishing it on a Web site or to publish work more than once. Read your contracts carefully. There are prestigious online journals that you will be proud to publish in; however, don't give away your best works to journals that may not be around in six months. Make sure you know the history of the Web site, as well as its reputation—your instructor can help you analyze the quality of the publication you are considering. This is important because you are permanently and irrevocably linked to a magazine that publishes your work.

Submit Your Work

Before you submit your work for publication, take it through as many rounds of workshops, writing groups, and editing as you can. The manuscript must be without error—many editors simply won't read past the first line if they spot grammar mistakes, typos, missing page numbers, or any failure to follow the magazine's submission requirements. Magazines receive hundreds of manuscripts a week. Many of these are quickly discarded, without being read from beginning to end; experienced editors often know instantly whether the answer is "maybe" or "no." Editors may glance at the first page of a story or the first lines of a poem and decide immediately that the work does not have enough energy, pattern, or tension to keep reading. Editors won't do your work for you. Editors edit *magazines*. You edit your work. Your piece must be absolutely perfect before you send it.

Again, *never* send money to anyone to read or publish your work. Unscrupulous organizations prey on young writers' desire to publish, and no one will take your publication seriously if you had to pay for it. You should be paid for your work, even if only in contributor copies. Many small magazines will send the author copies of the magazine instead of a check—budgets are tight at these nonprofits. Don't pay to publish.

Decide Where to Send Your Work.   Read sample issues of the magazine so that you don't end up sending your sexiest, rawest love sonnets to a magazine edited by clergy who are looking for uplifting short stories about overcoming hardship through prayer. Make sure that your work is of the same quality as the pieces you see in that publication. And be familiar with the magazine's submission guidelines.

Some writers suggest that you have at least six pieces of submission quality before you start submitting your work. It's always a good idea to have a couple of pieces circulating so you aren't completely devastated when one is rejected. Work on your writing; that's the whole point of reaching readers—to celebrate your hard work and to keep you working, focused on improving as a writer and continuing to learn. When a piece comes back, look at it gently but carefully. Can you improve it? Often, a rejection note changes your relationship to the piece. You read with a colder eye and are more willing to cut weaker parts. You read like an editor, asking editor-type questions: *What's the experience of reading this like? Why would my subscribers be interested in this? Where's the energy, the tension, the insight in this piece? Is it smooth, fresh, creative, evocative, polished?*

Start with your school's literary magazine. If your school doesn't yet have a literary magazine, maybe it's time for you and your friends to start one online. Next, research local and then regional markets for creative writing. Visit locally owned bookstores for zines and journals with a regional focus. Be realistic about which publications might be a good fit for your work, stay creative, and have fun choosing where to submit your work. Most writers start small and close to home, steadily building a résumé of publications.

After you have written and revised a body of work (and perhaps read aloud in front of an audience)—three to five good poems or about ten pages of prose—you are ready to prepare a submission packet, sending your work off to an editor. Remember that this process is lengthy and slow. Do not expect to get published the first time you try. Editors usually take weeks, even months, to reply. Use the submission process as a way to learn the field of creative writing, to improve your work, and to discover exciting new authors in the literary magazines you encounter.

PRACTICE

Read every piece in two or three issues of a literary magazine you really like. Consider if you have a piece of writing that would be a good fit for this magazine.

How to Send Your Work Out. First, obtain the magazine's submission guidelines from its Web site. Before submitting, carefully read these guidelines, which tell you exactly what to do and which vary for each publication. Many publications have specific reading periods. Some do not accept unsolicited work at all. Most journals use Submittable.com for online submissions. Magazines and journals that require hard copy and snail mail will ask you to include a self-addressed stamped envelope (SASE). They use the envelope to return your acceptance letter or rejection note. Plan on waiting anywhere from two weeks to six months. Don't eschew print journals and hard-copy submission processes—consider your odds.

Most magazines are struggling to make ends meet, and because they receive so many submissions, they can't afford to subsidize the time and money it would cost to deal with extensive correspondence. You'll likely receive a form rejection, freeing you to resubmit the work to the next magazine on your list. Don't pester editors with questions about how to improve your work; that's what your writing group is for.

Finally, if you have published your work online — even on your own blog or in another digital format — you may be disqualified from submitting that work to a literary magazine. Read their policies carefully. If your work is available to the public in another format, make sure your editor knows this, and follow the magazine's guidelines carefully.

Embrace Rejection

To build a career in the arts (or any career, for that matter), you must find creative strategies for dealing with inevitable rejection.

Professional author Chris Offutt has said that when he first started writing fiction, he didn't send out his short stories because the idea of rejection scared him. A poet friend told him that sending out work was part of his job as a writer, so Offutt set up a file labeled "100 Rejections" on his computer and made it his goal to fill the file with rejections. As the rejection letters for his early stories came in, one after another, he filed them, and it felt as though he was accomplishing a part of his job. He almost filled the file before he got an acceptance.

All writers get rejected — it's part of what we do. We submit our work, and most of the time editors can't use it. Perhaps the magazine just published a short story featuring aliens in coveralls, free-range chickens gone wild, or a bunch of pantoums. (Once you've carefully studied sample issues of the journal, you will know what the magazine has published recently.) Perhaps the editor likes your work but sees some rough edges. If an editor asks to see more work, follow up immediately with your next-best piece.

Many editors want to see whether you have two, three, or five stories, or twenty decent poems, before they invest valuable pages in you and your writing. That's harsh, but fair. You must have some depth as a writer in order to break into print. Often, editors are looking for authors, not just poems and stories and plays.

Publication is a process that *includes* rejection. So thinking through how you are going to feel when you get rejected (which you will) is useful if you plan to one day be a published author (which you will). Working on a magazine as an editor can be a great way to gain insight into the publishing process.

Many nonwriters think they would never be able to handle rejection. But as all musicians, athletes, actors, and people in the dating scene know, rejection is part of the deal. It means at least you are in the game. You will not get every part you audition for. Acceptance — publication — is a process. Rejection is part of that process. Plan on being rejected. If you can't make friends with rejection right away, practice seeing rejection as arbitrary—it doesn't have anything to do with you personally. Magazines publish a tiny percentage of what they receive (1 to 6 percent). Magazines receive hundreds of manuscripts each week. Some receive hundreds of poems *each day*. Rejection might indicate that you are sending your work out too early—it needs more revision, more attention. Rejection of a piece might mean that a particular editor just doesn't like this kind of piece, even though your

> *Close the door. Write with no one looking over your shoulder. Don't try to figure out what other people want to hear from you; figure out what you have to say. It's the one and only thing you have to offer.*
> — BARBARA KINGSOLVER

writing is fantastic. You don't like everything you read. Some published works—perhaps in this very textbook—might make you wonder, *What is so great about this? I don't get it.*

Not all editors need to adore your work; just one editor does. Don't give editors, and rejection, more power than they really have. Just because an editor likes or dislikes your work doesn't mean it's good or bad. Great works go unpublished. Flawed works find publishers and readers. Don't pay too much attention to that human aspect of the process. You can't do anything about taste, but you can control two things: your commitment to always improving your craft and your persistence. You'll resubmit your work (revising and improving along the way) many times before it finds a good home—that's how publication works. Rejection actually means you are a *successful* writer: working, submitting, fine-tuning, paying attention, studying markets. The people who get published are the ones who keep on submitting, again and again and again. When you submit a piece of work, you can plan on getting between ten and twenty rejections before you might want to consider doing another revision. If you give up after one, two, or three rejections, you do not yet have a realistic sense of how the marketplace works. Get friendly with rejection. Your path to publication is paved with dozens of rejections.

Your best strategy for rejection is, in a word, revision.

CHAPBOOKS AND PORTFOLIOS

In composition classes or other writing classes you have taken, you may have turned in a portfolio of your best work. In art classes, the end of the semester provides an opportunity to show the body of work you have created, shaped, and polished, so that others can see what you do. Your instructor evaluates your growth by examining this portfolio, and you gain valuable insights into your strengths and weaknesses and can take stock of where you want to go next.

A portfolio is a sampling of your best work — your best poems, short-shorts, a short play, an outstanding essay. Sometimes a portfolio contains an artist's statement or other reflective writing in which you discuss your process and your habits of mind as a writer. Portfolios can be copied for each class member or simply discussed with your instructor. Portfolios present a collection of polished, professional work.

Many creative writing classes design their own literary magazine; a class literary magazine is the perfect introduction to publication. The entire class can serve as an editorial board, selecting a piece from each class member, working from portfolios of submitted works in either print or digital formats. Or small writing groups can publish print or digital literary magazines, each with its own vision and mission.

Creating a Chapbook

Another way to collect your best work is to create a chapbook. A chapbook is a small book, like a pamphlet, stapled and photocopied and sold or given away. The name derives from "cheap books," popular in Great Britain in the eighteenth and nineteenth centuries, where "chapmen" (peddlers) made up inexpensive publications — often just a single sheet of paper folded to make eight, sixteen, or twenty-four pages — to sell to the literate.

Simplicity and economy are hallmarks of the chapbook, and for poets, especially, chapbooks remain the most popular and widely respected mode for distributing new work. Chapbooks can be sold or given away at live readings. Some creative writing classes ask each participant to create enough copies of their individual chapbooks so that all students have one. If you would like to look at some excellent examples, search for publishers who specialize in chapbooks. Main Street Rag is one famous example. Also explore Yellow Jacket Press, Slapering Hol Press, the Poetry Society of America, and Tupelo Press. Check out the Center for Book Arts in New York, the Minnesota Center for Book Arts in Minneapolis, and Printed Matter (printedmatter.org) in New York for samples and resources. For additional information regarding the history of the chapbook, read Noah Eli Gordon's "A Brief History of the Little Book" in *Jacket* and Sam Riedel's "Chapbooks: A Short History of the Short Book."

A chapbook that is made into a high-quality, professionally printed book is called an artist's book; examine the Center for Book Arts (centerforbookarts .org) for more information on how writers turn their work into art, taking the publishing process into their own hands.

The type of chapbook most often submitted in creative writing classes usually has a simple cover on regular paper or card stock and may include illustrations by the author, clip art, or other graphic design elements. The chapbook also has a table of contents and often, in the back, a short biographical note about the author. A chapbook can be printed on 8½ × 11 inch paper with a landscape orientation so that the pages can then be folded and saddle-stapled.

> *You write about the thing that sank its teeth into you and wouldn't let go.*
> — PAUL WEST

Using the search term "bookletize," search online or in your word processing program for directions on how to create multiple copies of chapbooks. The article "DIY: How to Make and Bind Chapbooks," on the *Poets and Writers* Web site (pw.org), is a good introduction to making chapbooks.

A class chapbook — essentially a joint portfolio to which each student contributes one of his or her best pieces of writing — is a wonderful way to publish your work. The class decides on the guidelines. For example, each person might submit up to three pages of creative writing. Students decide who will organize the selections, who will proofread, and who will prepare the table of contents. Depending on the budget, the class can print extra copies so that each class member, the instructor, and friends and family have a chance to read this work.

If you continue with creative writing, you can hand out chapbooks of your work (or your writing group's work) at your live readings, just as musicians may offer copies of their music at live performances.

Publishing your own work in a portfolio or chapbook helps you maintain high standards for revision and editing. While the process is time-consuming, it provides invaluable information to you as a writer. When you prepare work for public consumption, you learn to let go of things that were hard to cut during earlier revisions. That long poem has to fit onto one page? You might decide that the last four stanzas simply aren't needed. Or you choose to start your story in the middle because you see that the beginning is merely preface. You discover links and connections in your work that you never noticed before.

PRACTICE

Examine some chapbooks online by searching for "best chapbook publishers" or "poetry chapbooks." Your instructor may bring a set of chapbooks to class for you to peruse. Can you imagine making a chapbook of your own work?

Finally, some instructors ask students who assemble chapbooks to gather quotations from other classmates, other instructors, or peers to include on the back of the book, just as commercially published books have "blurbs." (Blurbs are those quotations on the back of a book that say things like "Luminous! Enchanting! The best new writer of this generation!") These quotations encourage people to look inside. Simply pass around drafts of the pieces you will include in the book to some friends, and ask them to write a few sentences about what they notice. Include this praise on the back of your chapbook, if you like.

Writing an Artist's Statement

At the end of the semester, it's a good idea to take stock of what you have learned, how far you have come. Much literature of interest to creative writers — interviews, essays, biographies, letters, autobiographies such as Eudora Welty's *One Writer's Beginnings*, books on craft such as Flannery O'Connor's *Mystery and Manners* — is in fact a kind of artist's statement: an extended piece of non-fiction where the writer explores process, inspiration, and artistic progress. A written essay or statement of this kind is an important bookend to the semester.

When you reread your writing from a few months ago, take notes. Pay attention to what makes you cringe or wince. Were you trying to sound writerly? Confident? Intrepid? Teacher-pleasing? What does your four-months-ago voice sound like? How has it changed? Did you say things back then that were false but seemed true at the time? Things that make you laugh now? Myths you subscribed to, now debunked? Things that were true then and are now truer than ever?

What were your preoccupations back then, and what are they now? Did the course turn out as you thought it would? It's helpful to track your learning, so the first section of your artist's statement might be a reflection on this earlier version of you. Write a reflective reaction to your earlier writing. What have you changed your mind about? Try to notice at least ten things.

Your instructor may ask you to create an artist's statement. Or you may mull over these questions on your own. You may choose to use these questions to construct an artist's statement, which you can hand out at a live reading, post on a Web site, or include as an introduction or afterword in your portfolio or chapbook. You may wish to pull out just a few lines from your artist's statement to include in your class literary magazine or chapbook.

> *I don't have much interest in writing if there are not opportunities to crack open the inherited forms. The writing I love to read most does this as well. I'm a form junkie.*
> — LIDIA YUKNAVITCH

If you struggle with an artist's statement or if you are interested in what other writers have to say about the writing process, where great ideas come from, and creativity in general, the resources in Chapter Twelve will guide you to the best books on these topics.

Good luck. Keep writing. *Everyone* who wants to gets to be a creative writer. You don't need fancy tools. You don't need to be weird or artsy. Every human being on the planet is allowed to sing, to dance, to play, to draw, to make stuff, and to write. Humans are meaning-making creatures, and making art is one way we know we are alive. Making art is how we make sense of the world. Shaping experiences so that we can look at them more closely, and laugh and cry and understand, and, ultimately, see ourselves more clearly—that's creative writing. Creative writing is something you can do for the rest of your life. You have the tools—energy, tension, images, insight, pattern, structure. You have the equipment—paper, a pencil, and ten minutes.

QUESTIONS TO ASK: Writing an Artist's Statement

Consider the following questions when writing about your own work, whether for self-reflection or to include as an artist's statement to submit at the end of the term.

1   Will you take another writing class?

2   Have your goals as a writer changed?

3   What's the most important thing you have learned?

4   What do you wish you had learned that you didn't?

5   What do you want to say about your work?

6   What would you write if you had the time and talent to write anything? Will you?

7   What have you learned about your writing habits?

8   Do you see yourself as part of a writing community? Do you prefer to work in isolation, focusing on the work and reading?

9   What's the most important thing you learned about getting and giving feedback about work-in-progress?

10   What techniques, authors, or exercises have been most useful to you?

11   What insights have you gained into the practice and art of creative writing?

12   Has your voice changed? Is your writing truer, deeper, better?

13   What authors do you want to read now? Has that changed from when you started the course? Do you have writer role models?

14   What's your most successful piece from the semester? Why is it successful?

WRITING PROJECTS

1. Give a live reading of your work. Ask a friend to take some notes for you: What did you do really well? Is there one area where you can improve? After you read, make a few notes: Do you see anything in your piece differently now? Will you make any changes?

2. Take one of your most successful pieces of writing and go over it one more time. Then submit this work to your school's literary magazine or to another local magazine. Before submitting, make sure you have carefully studied several issues of the magazine.

3. Create a chapbook or a booklet of some of your favorite pieces of writing. If you have the resources, make copies to give to classmates, family, or friends.

4. Start a magazine. Using your favorite works from this course, create a digital or a do-it-yourself print booklet and distribute the book at a live reading. Ask whether your school's bookstore or library will display copies.

CHAPTER TWELVE

GOING FURTHER

Instagram for up-and-coming authors, books on how to write your novel in thirty days (and lose weight in the process), Web sites listing calls for manuscripts from high-power literary agents, magazines promising publication and lucrative possibilities in "Six Quick Steps"—information for writers is abundant. How do you sort through the screens and pages of material? How do you find trustworthy, high-quality information on building a writing life? It's not easy. This chapter serves as a guide to digital and print resources you can use as a jumping-off place. The resources listed here are ones that other writers and teachers of creative writing have cited as helpful. You will also certainly find additional valuable resources on your own.

As a writer, your best resources are always your dedicated daily writing practice—the ten minutes or two hours you spend at your craft—and your writing group. To supplement your daily writing habit, you may want to collect writing books for further study, use YouTube and Facebook to create community after your writing class ends, or locate publishing markets open to new writers. Remember: Do not send money for any reason in order to publish your work, have it edited, or enter a contest that requires fees unless your instructor has assured you it is a reputable and worthy venue.

Rather than rushing to publish, you might want to purchase a few good-quality books on writing and select some discerning blogs or feeds to monitor regularly. Keep in mind that if you self-publish your work digitally, you may not be able to publish it elsewhere. Do your research.

In this chapter, you will find many valuable resources that offer specialized instruction, spark inspiration, and help you navigate the publishing world, as well as resources to consider if you plan to teach creative writing to elementary, secondary, or college students.

> *Don't be seduced into thinking that that which does not make a profit is without value.*
> — ARTHUR MILLER

Often, the best writing advice is hidden away in used or out-of-print books—you may want to search abebooks.com or powells.com for some of these titles or consult a local independent bookseller and the library. As you take advantage of all the riches social media offer, remember to also consider print sources. If you buy a classic, tried-and-true title, you might save money in the long run; a new, hotly marketed writing guide could seem tired and worn just a few months later. Because many digital sources aren't edited or fact-checked, writer beware.

SMART SEARCHING

A quick Google search will reveal thousands of writing Web sites on the Internet. So how are you supposed to know what is good and what is garbage? By developing good searching skills. A few tips will help you refine your search and separate the good, the bad, and the ugly.

The "Advanced Search" feature on Google lets you narrow down your results. Try limiting the search to domains ending in .edu or .org—these sites are affiliated with reputable, noncommercial enterprises. Use quotation marks in your search to find exact phrases (e.g., "daily writing prompts," "creative writing MFA programs," "contemporary sonnets," "flash fiction," or "slam poetry in Arkansas"). In the example shown in Figure 12.1, a student wanted to find daily writing prompts for fiction or nonfiction writing. He wanted a .org domain but didn't want to be linked to a blogspot site.

To find good advice on writing, search for interviews with your favorite author. Literary magazines often publish excellent interviews with authors, and these interviews frequently appear online. For example, the Web sites for *The Paris Review* and *The Believer* have excellent archives of author interviews. *Brevity*, the online-only journal for flash nonfiction and micro-memoir, has a section devoted to craft essays. Also, check out podcasts such as *Fresh Air*, *Longform*, and *How to Be Amazing* to hear authors and artists in conversation.

To hear great storytelling and spoken word, download podcasts from *The Moth*, *Snap Judgment*, *Radiolab*, *This American Life*, *Serial*, and *The Story*. Search for "TED Talks to Inspire Creativity" and discover TED talks by brilliant and motivating authors from around the world, such as Elizabeth Gilbert, Young-ha Kim, Amy Tan, Isabel Allende, and Chimananda Ngozi Adichie.

Google

Advanced Search

Find pages with...		To do this in the search box
all these words:		Type the important words: tricolor rat terrier
this exact word or phrase:	DAILY WRITING PROMPTS	Put exact words in quotes: "rat terrier"
any of these words:	FICTION NONFICTION	Type OR between all the words you want: miniature OR standard
none of these words:	BLOGSPOT	Put a minus sign just before words you don't want: -rodent, -"Jack Russell"
numbers ranging from:	to	Put 2 periods between the numbers and add a unit of measure: 10..35 lb, $300..$500, 2010..2011

Then narrow your results by...

language:	any language	Find pages in the language you select.
region:	any region	Find pages published in a particular region.
last update:	anytime	Find pages updated within the time you specify.
site or domain:	ORG	Search one site (like wikipedia.org) or limit your results to a domain like .edu, .org or .gov
terms appearing:	anywhere in the page	Search for terms in the whole page, page title, or web address, or links to the page you're looking for.
SafeSearch:	Show most relevant results	Tell SafeSearch whether to filter sexually explicit content.
file type:	any format	Find pages in the format you prefer.
usage rights:	not filtered by license	Find pages you are free to use yourself.

Advanced Search

Figure 12.1 Google Advanced Search

High-quality Web sites are often connected to universities, writing programs, and nonprofit writing projects. Check out the Web sites for top writing programs such as the Vermont College of Fine Arts, the Iowa Writers' Workshop, Bennington College, the University of Michigan, the University of Arizona, and the UCLA Extension Writers' Program. Many of the official sites for these programs will link you to their own publications and other excellent writing sites.

In addition to a Google search, go to your school's library and use academic databases to find the most reputable writing resources. Reference librarians are your best resource for help with your search. Most colleges and universities have access to a selection of academic databases, which require a subscription. Academic databases tend to provide results from scholarly journals. You will discover fewer articles from popular magazines and more articles geared toward serious writers. Two particularly useful databases are Project MUSE and JSTOR. Project MUSE gives access to several literary magazines, including *Callaloo* and *Prairie Schooner*. JSTOR is more academic than Project MUSE, but it is a good resource for finding articles on authors. As with Google, the advanced search features are extraordinarily helpful. You can browse by discipline, journal, author, title, keyword, or date of publication.

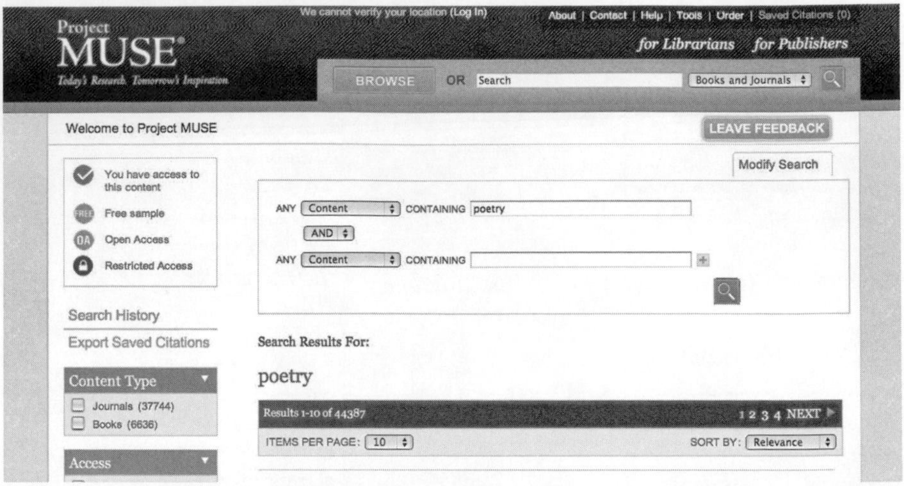

Figure 12.2 Project MUSE Advanced Article Search

SOCIAL MEDIA

> *You will feel insecure and jealous. How much power you give those feelings is entirely up to you.*
> — CHERYL STRAYED

You've probably already considered the numerous resources on Twitter, Facebook, Instagram, and other digital venues. Most major journals, presses, and literary organizations are active on social media. Here are some suggestions for useful hashtags to search to get you started:

#askagent (agent questions and answers)

#author

#editing

#fridayflash (flash fiction Friday)

#nanowrimo (National Novel Writing Month)

#novels

#poets

#poetry

#pubtip (publication tips)

#scifi

#vss (very short story)

#wip (work-in-progress)

#writegoal

#writequote
#writer
#writers
#writing
#writingtips (writing advice)
#wrotetoday

The following hashtags are chats used as meeting places:

#journchat
#kidlitchat
#litchat
#scifichat
#storycraft

Here are a few helpful Web sites:

post-mfa.tumblr.com
poetryprompts.tumblr.com
www.litcristic.com

Facebook Groups

On Facebook, you can quickly find specialty groups for your particular interests. If you are brand-new to the field, keep in mind the following two groups:

- **Indie Author Group**
  In this space, authors come together to share advice and help one another become better writers.
- **Writers Helping Writers**
  "A collection of unique resources devoted to descriptive writing. For authors, students, screenplay writers, and anyone else looking for help in this area."

Twitter Accounts

- @theoffingmag
  The Twitter account for *The Offing*, an online journal from the *Los Angeles Review of Books*, actively updates its followers on issues in writing and craft. This feed shares articles and creative essays from its own journal and other online sources that can be used in the creative writing classroom.

- @NarrativeMag
  Follow this account to stay up-to-date on the latest publications by *Narrative Magazine*. Founded in 2003, *Narrative* aims to advance online literature.
- @mcsweeneys
  McSweeney's Quarterly Concern, Internet Tendency, and *Books* are all discussed on this feed. The *Internet Tendency* articles are regularly posted to provide comic relief and writing inspiration.
- @submittable
  This account for Submittable, a submission manager tool, tweets open submission calls for writers.

Mobile Apps

- Brevity's Nonfiction App
  Brevity's blog can be accessed through this easy-to-use app, which arranges posts in a scrollable list of captions and images. Posts contain news about publishing and nonfiction writing.
- WordPress App
  This app allows writers to blog right from their phone.
- Dragon Dictation App
  This tool lets users dictate notes and ideas, hands-free.

GENERAL RESOURCES
Creativity and Inspiration

If you are interested in increasing your creative powers, or you just want to read about artists, writers, and how they work, many resources are available. Each book and Web site on this list is accessible, lively, fascinating, and packed with useful information on what it is to "be creative." If you are stuck, these resources are extremely useful in helping you work through a block. Many of them have specific exercises that you can try in order to develop new creative muscles.

In Print

Ayan, Jordan E. *Aha! 10 Ways to Free Your Creative Spirit and Find Your Great Ideas.*
Baldwin, Christina. *Life's Companion: Journal Writing as a Spiritual Practice.*
Barry, Lynda. *Syllabus.*
Bayles, David, and Ted Orland. *Art and Fear: Observations on the Perils (and Rewards) of Artmaking.*
Brande, Dorothea. *Becoming a Writer.*

Edgarian, Carol, and Tom Jenks, eds. *The Writer's Life: Intimate Thoughts on Work, Love, Inspiration, and Fame from the Diaries of the World's Great Writers.*

Gilbert, Elizabeth. *Big Magic: Creative Living beyond Fear.*

Gourevitch, Philip, ed. *The Paris Review Interviews.*

Maisel, Eric. *Fearless Creating: A Step-by-Step Guide to Starting and Completing Your Work of Art.*

Metcalf, Linda, and Tobin Simon. *Writing the Mind Alive: The Proprioceptive Method for Finding Your Authentic Voice.*

Palumbo, Dennis. *Writing from the Inside Out: Transforming Your Psychological Blocks to Release the Writer Within.*

Perry, Susan K. *Writing in Flow: Keys to Enhanced Creativity.*

Rico, Gabriele L. *Writing the Natural Way: Using Right-Brain Techniques.*

Tharp, Twyla, and Mark Reiter. *The Creative Habit: Learn It and Use It for Life: A Practical Guide.*

Ueland, Barbara. *If You Want to Write.*

Online

Duotrope [www.duotrope.com]

> This resource aids writers in the submission process. It provides a searchable aggregate of information on literary journals. Users disclose statistics from their submitting experience. This information allows Duotrope to provide insider information, such as expected response time. The site charges a monthly membership fee.

Writer's Digest [www.writersdigest.com]

> *Writer's Digest* magazine hosts this comprehensive site—slanted more toward popular writers rather than literary writers, but with good nuts-and-bolts information for everyone. Look for their annual feature, "One Hundred Best Sites for Writers." The sites are selected by reader-writers and are grouped into subsections: inspiration, fantasy writers, technique, finding a writing group, and so on.

Images: Seeing More Closely

The books listed here present different approaches to the "images" method presented in this textbook. In *How to Use Your Eyes*, James Elkins explains in great detail his philosophy of seeing—the art of looking more closely at the world and the people in it—with numerous visual examples to support his points. In *Zen Seeing, Zen Drawing*, visual artist Frederick Franck teaches how to enter that focused state in which you can see the aliveness in the image. Although Franck is talking to visual artists, his principles also apply to the work creative writers do.

In Print

Barry, Lynda. *What It Is.*
Cassou, Mitchell. *Point Zero: Creativity without Limits.*
Elkins, James. *How to Use Your Eyes.*
Franck, Frederick. *Zen Seeing, Zen Drawing: Meditation in Action.*
Ganim, Barbara, and Susan Fox. *Visual Journaling.*

Self-Expression and Personal Writing

The assignments in this textbook are designed to help you write more effectively for others. Many creative writers also enjoy writing for themselves in a journal, in a blog, or as an informal daily practice. The following books and sites can help you go further with the writing you do just for yourself.

In Print

Adams, Kathleen. *Journal to the Self: Twenty-Two Paths to Personal Growth.*
Aronie, Nancy Slonim. *Writing from the Heart: Tapping the Power of Your Inner Voice.*
Badonsky, Jill Baldwin. *The Nine Modern-Day Muses (and a Bodyguard): 10 Guides to Creative Inspiration for Artists, Writers, Lovers, and Other Mortals Wanting to Live a Dazzling Existence.*
Cameron, Julia. *The Right to Write: An Invitation and Initiation into the Writing Life.*
Cerwinske, Laura. *Writing as a Healing Art.*
Goldberg, Natalie. *Writing Down the Bones: Freeing the Writer Within.*
Heard, Georgia. *Writing toward Home: Tales and Lessons to Find Your Way.*
Hughes, Elaine Farris. *Writing from the Inner Self.*
Joselow, Beth Baruch. *Writing without the Muse: 50 Beginning Exercises for the Creative Writer.*
Metzger, Deena. *Writing for Your Life: A Guide and Companion to the Inner Worlds.*
Raab, Diana M., ed. *Writers and Their Notebooks.*
Sher, Gail. *The Intuitive Writer: Listening to Your Own Voice.*

Online

750 Words [750words.com]

> 750 Words is an online journaling site aimed to keep you writing 750 words every day. It has an interesting point system and many analysis tools that can tell you all about your writing.

Amherst Writers and Artists [www.amherstwriters.com]

> From the site: "AWA is an international community of writing workshop leaders committed to the belief that a writer is someone who writes and that

every writer has a unique voice. AWA trains writers to become workshop leaders so that they affirm that commitment in every AWA workshop, with novice writers who have been led to believe they have no voice and with experienced writers who want to hone their craft."

Literary News

A key to writing is to immerse yourself in the literary world around you, not only by reading ferociously but also by keeping up-to-date on literary news. The following Web sites are great resources for headlines, reviews, interviews, and tips.

Arts and Letters Daily [www.aldaily.com]

A news service collecting articles of interest to writers and artists from around the world. It's like subscribing to one hundred newspapers, but you get only the section you care about.

Arts Journal: The Digest of Arts, Culture, and Ideas [www.artsjournal.com]

Articles on art, dance, literature, music, and more, with well-written, interesting blogs in every area.

Guardian Books [www.guardian.co.uk/books]

The books section of the *Guardian*, a British newspaper. This is an excellent place to find headlines, interviews, reviews, and articles on the contemporary literary scene.

Literary Hub [lithub.com]

A Web site devoted to curating in one place the vast amount of literary news available online. Partnering with publishers, presses, and booksellers, Literary Hub provides original content, excerpts, and the latest news from the book world.

NewPages [www.newpages.com]

A guide to the world of the independent press. NewPages provides news and reviews on publications, bookstores, and periodicals, as well as resources for writers, such as a list of MFA programs and a list of blogs by published writers.

> *A writer who waits for ideal conditions under which to work will die without putting a word on paper.*
>
> — E. B. WHITE

Poets and Writers [www.pw.org]

The Web site for *Poets and Writers Magazine*. The magazine itself is a must-read for creative writers interested in literary publishing. Both the magazine and the Web site are portals into the world of writing, providing news and trends, features on small presses, interviews with famous as well as up-and-coming writers, and articles on how to write and what to read—all of the very highest quality.

INSTRUCTION IN SPECIFIC GENRES

This semester, you had a chance to practice writing in several different genres. If you want to study a specific genre more deeply, the resources in this section will guide you in mastering a single genre—the short-short, the novel, the form poem, and so on. Some of the books listed are textbooks, but most of these resources are guides designed for the individual writer working independently.

Fiction

In Print

Baxter, Charles. *The Art of Subtext: Beyond Plot.*

Baxter, Charles. *Burning Down the House: Essays on Fiction.*

Baxter, Charles, and Peter Turchi, eds. *Bringing the Devil to His Knees: The Craft of Fiction and the Writing Life.*

Bell, Madison Smartt. *Narrative Design: A Writer's Guide to Structure.*

Bernays, Anne, and Pamela Painter. *What If? Writing Exercises for Fiction Writers.*

Block, Lawrence. *Writing the Novel from Plot to Print.*

Brady, Catherine. *Story Logic and the Craft of Fiction.*

Browne, Renni, and Dave King. *Self-Editing for Fiction Writers: How to Edit Yourself into Print.*

Burnett, Hallie. *On Writing the Short Story.*

Butler, Robert Olen, and Janet Burroway. *From Where You Dream: The Process of Writing Fiction.*

Carlson, Ron. *Ron Carlson Writes a Story.*

Gardner, John. *On Becoming a Novelist.*

Hemley, Robin. *Turning Life into Fiction.*

Koch, Stephen. *The Modern Library Writer's Workshop: A Guide to the Craft of Fiction.*

Lamb, Nancy. *The Art and Craft of Storytelling: A Comprehensive Guide to Classic Writing Techniques.*

Le Guin, Ursula K. *Steering the Craft: Exercises and Discussions on Story Writing for the Lone Navigator or the Mutinous Crew.*

Lukeman, Noah. *The Plot Thickens: 8 Ways to Bring Fiction to Life.*

Maass, Donald. *Writing the Breakout Novel.*

Madden, David. *Revising Fiction: A Handbook for Writers.*

Stern, Jerome H. *Making Shapely Fiction.*

Online

National Novel Writing Month [www.nanowrimo.org]

> National Novel Writing Month is November, and there is a thriving movement made up of novel writers who push hard to get a full first "down" draft done in November of each year. The site offers instruction, guidance in forming the necessary support team, and excellent tips for completing a novel (and what to do next). One of the best features at NaNoWriMo is the community that forms among working writers.

Science Fiction and Fantasy Writers of America [www.sfwa.org]

> Science Fiction and Fantasy Writers of America features contests to enter, publications, writing instruction, and member discussion forums.

Flash Fiction and Micro-Memoir

If you search for "nano fiction," "six word memoirs," and "Rose Metal Press," whole new worlds will open up. Look for the *Southeast Review*'s "World's Best Short Short Contest." Check out the New Zealand online magazine *Sport* and the well-respected *New Flash Fiction Review.* Explore NPR's "This I Believe" audio essay feature.

In Print

Allen, Roberta. *Fast Fiction: Creating Fiction in Five Minutes.*

Kitchen, Judith. *Short Takes: Brief Encounters with Contemporary Nonfiction.*

Masih, Tara, ed. *The Rose Metal Press Field Guide to Writing Flash Fiction: Tips from Editors, Teachers, and Writers in the Field.*

Moore, Dinty, ed. *The Rose Metal Press Field Guide to Writing Flash Nonfiction: Advice and Essential Exercises from Respected Writers, Editors, and Teachers.*

Stern, Jerome, ed. *Micro Fiction: An Anthology of Fifty Really Short Stories.*

Online

Brevity [brevitymag.com]

Edited by Dinty Moore, *Brevity* is an online publication featuring work in the extremely brief essay form. Though *Brevity* publishes award-winning work by accomplished authors, it is also dedicated to publishing new writers.

Gulf Coast Barthelme Prize [gulfcoastmag.org/contests]
Hobart [www.hobartpulp.com]
NANO Fiction [nanofiction.org]

Poetry

In Print

Addonizio, Kim. *Ordinary Genius: A Guide for the Poet Within.*
Addonizio, Kim, and Dorianne Laux. *The Poet's Companion: A Guide to the Pleasures of Writing Poetry.*
Behn, Robert, and Chase Twitchell, eds. *The Practice of Poetry: Writing Exercises from Poets Who Teach.*
Davis, Todd, and Erin Murphy, eds. *Making Poems: Forty Poems with Commentary by the Poets.*
Drake, Barbara. *Writing Poetry.*
Oliver, Mary. *A Poetry Handbook.*
Orr, David. *Beautiful and Pointless: A Guide to Modern Poetry.*
Wooldridge, Susan G. *Poemcrazy: Freeing Your Life with Words.*

Online

The Academy of American Poets [www.poets.org]

In addition to featuring numerous poems, the Web site for the Academy of American Poets also offers biographical glimpses of some of the world's most renowned poets. Among the site's best resources are articles on and definitions of important poetry terms and forms.

Favorite Poem Project [www.favoritepoem.org]

The Favorite Poem Project showcases videos of Americans reading and talking about their favorite poem and includes valuable resources for teachers, too.

Fooling with Words [http://billmoyers.com/content/fooling-with-words-part-i/]

> The companion site to the Bill Moyers PBS show has video clips, a teacher's guide, lesson plans, and many other resources, including interviews with poets.

The writing begins when you've finished. Only then do you know what you're trying to say.
— MARK TWAIN

Lannan Podcasts [podcast.lannan.org]

> This highly regarded series by the Lannan Foundation features poetry readings and conversations with well-known poets.

Naropa Poetics Audio Archives [archive.org/details/naropa]

> The archives contain readings, performances, lectures, and workshops from respected avant-garde poets.

Poetry Daily [www.poems.com]

> This Web site emails you a poem every day. The site is devoted to many topics of interest to writers (in any genre), including interviews with authors, background information on featured poets, and lively discussions of contemporary poetry.

Poetry Foundation [www.poetryfoundation.org]

> The online companion to the publication *Poetry*, this Web site features thousands of poems, as well as a wealth of interviews, essays, and news articles on both well-established and up-and-coming poets.

Poetry International Web [www.poetryinternationalweb.net]

> This site features poets from around the world writing in languages other than English, with English translations, as well as valuable articles, interviews, and links to other organizations.

Poetry Out Loud Project [www.poetryoutloud.org]

> The National Endowment for the Arts and the Poetry Foundation sponsor a national contest for young poets, and the associated Web site features lesson plans, writing activities, and a blog that poets and teachers find invaluable.

Poet Vision Webcasts [www.loc.gov/poetry/media/poetvision.html]

> This Library of Congress site features ten poets, including some former U.S. Poets Laureate, reading and discussing their work.

Form Poetry

In Print

Boland, Eavan, and Mark Strand, eds. *The Making of a Poem: A Norton Anthology of Poetic Forms.*

Dacey, Philip, and David Jauss. *Strong Measures: Contemporary American Poetry in Traditional Forms.*

Finch, Annie, ed. *A Formal Feeling Comes: Poems in Form by Contemporary Women.*

Finch, Annie, and Kathrine Varnes. *An Exaltation of Forms: Contemporary Poets Celebrate the Diversity of Their Art.*

Oliver, Mary. *Rules for the Dance.*

Padgett, Ron, ed. *The Teachers and Writers Handbook of Poetic Forms.*

Turco, Lewis. *The Book of Forms: A Handbook of Poetics.*

Online

McSweeney's [www.mcsweeneys.net]

> This literary magazine and publishing house maintains a comprehensive Web site. If you visit mcsweeneys.net/columns/sestinas, you will find hundreds of interesting sestinas.

Spoken Word

City Lights Bookstore [www.citylights.com]

> This Web site contains many resources; of particular interest is the "Events and Readings" section, with the *Live from City Lights* podcast series.

Get Lit [getlit.org]

> Get Lit advocates for teen literacy by sponsoring spoken word and poetry events in cities around the country and on YouTube.

Nuyorican Poets Café [www.nuyorican.org]

> The Nuyorican Poets Café Web site features a calendar of upcoming events and showcases esteemed alumni such as Benjamin Bratt and Savion Glover. The site also offers educational links.

Poetry Slam, Inc. [www.poetryslam.com]

> Here you will find resources for slam poets from the official governing body of poetry slams worldwide, as well as SlamMasters support, news, a slam map, and links to tournament information.

Nonfiction

In Print

Baker, Russell. *Inventing the Truth: The Art and Craft of Memoir.*
Bly, Carol. *Beyond the Writers' Workshop: New Ways to Write Creative Nonfiction.*
Gornick, Vivian. *The Situation and the Story: The Art of Personal Narrative.*
Gutkind, Lee, ed. *Keep It Real: Everything You Need to Know about Researching and Writing Creative Nonfiction.*
Karr, Mary. *The Art of Memoir.*
Ledoux, Denis. *Turning Memories into Memoirs: A Handbook for Writing Life Stories.*

Online

Creative Nonfiction [www.creativenonfiction.org]

> This online companion to the magazine of the same name includes access to several articles from each issue. It's a highly respected site where writers of creative nonfiction discuss craft.

Write Nonfiction in November [writenonfictioninnovember.com]

> Created in response to National Novel Writing Month, Write Nonfiction in November is a new enterprise encouraging authors to create a work of nonfiction in one month. This site offers helpful advice both on the craft of nonfiction and on the publication process. Writers working on nonfiction can also use this space to discuss their problems and their successes.

Plays and Screenplays

In Print

Downs, William Missouri, and Lou Anne Wright. *Playwriting: From Formula to Form.*
Field, Syd. *Screenplay.*
Hagen, Uta, and Haskel Frankel. *Respect for Acting.*
Horton, Andrew. *Writing the Character-Centered Screenplay.*
McKee, Robert. *Story: Substance, Structure, Style, and the Principles of Screenwriting.*
Sossaman, Stephen. *Writing Your First Play.*
Stanislavsky, Konstantin. *Building a Character.*
Vogler, Christopher. *The Writer's Journey: Mythic Structure for Writers.*
Voytilla, Stuart. *Myth and the Movies: Discovering the Mythic Structure of 50 Un-forgettable Films.*
Walter, Richard. *Essentials of Screenwriting: The Art, Craft and Business of Film and Television Writing.*

Online

BAFTA Screenwriters on Screenwriting [www.bafta.org]

The British Academy of Film and Television Arts put together this site in order to help educate writers in the art of screenwriting. This high-caliber site features videos of professional screenwriters talking about the art.

BBC Writersroom [www.bbc.co.uk/writersroom]

Straight from the BBC comes this online resource for writing for television, cinema, and radio. With an excellent writing tips section and a constant flow of contests and opportunities for publication, the BBC Writersroom fuels an interest in script writing.

> *The culture is telling you to hurry, while the art tells you to take your time. Always listen to the art.*
> — JUNOT DÍAZ

Script Magazine [www.scriptmag.com]

This site is dedicated to screenwriting techniques. *Script Magazine* offers detailed film analysis, news, reviews, and interviews. Famed writing instructor Robert McKee frequently contributes.

Children's Books

In Print

Lamb, Nancy. *The Writer's Guide to Crafting Stories for Children.*
Trotman, Felicity, and Treld Pelkey Bicknell, eds. *How to Write and Illustrate Children's Books and Get Them Published.*

Graphic Narratives and Comics

In Print

Abel, Jessica, and Matt Madden. *Drawing Words and Writing Pictures.*
Eisner, Will. *Comics and Sequential Art.*
Madden, Matt. *99 Ways to Tell a Story: Exercises in Style.*
McCloud, Scott. *Making Comics: Storytelling Secrets of Comics, Manga and Graphic Novels.*
McCloud, Scott. *Reinventing Comics: How Imagination and Technology Are Revolutionizing an Art Form.*
McCloud, Scott. *Understanding Comics: The Invisible Art.*

Online

Fantagraphics [www.fantagraphics.com]

> The online home of the publishing house Fantagraphics gives author bios and news on the graphic novel industry. Most useful is the interview section, in which many of the world's premier cartoonists talk about their work.

Teaching Creative Writing

If you are thinking about teaching after you leave college, you will rely on these resources on why art is necessary in schools; how students can be taught to make original, true art; and the role of the artist/writer as teacher.

In Print

Donnelly, Dianne. *Establishing Creative Writing Studies as an Academic Discipline.*
Drew, Chris, David Yost, and Joseph Rein. *Dispatches from the Classroom: Graduate Students on Creative Writing Pedagogy.*
Elkins, James. *Why Art Cannot Be Taught: A Handbook for Art Students.*
Flynn, Nick, and Shirley McPhillips. *A Note Slipped under the Door: Teaching from Poems We Love.*
Koch, Kenneth. *Making Your Own Days: The Pleasures of Reading and Writing Poetry.*
Koch, Kenneth, and Kate Farrell. *Sleeping on the Wing: An Anthology of Modern Poetry, with Essays on Reading and Writing.*
Leahy, Anna, ed. *Power and Identity in the Creative Writing Classroom: The Authority Project.*
London, Peter. *No More Secondhand Art: Awakening the Artist Within.*
Moxley, Joseph M., ed. *Creative Writing in America: Theory and Pedagogy.*
Myers, David Gershom. *The Elephants Teach: Creative Writing since 1880.*

Schneider, Pat. *Writing Alone and with Others.*
Stafford, William. *You Must Revise Your Life.*
Vanderslice, Stephanie. *Rethinking Creative Writing in Higher Education: Programs and Practices That Work.*

Online

ArtsEdge [artsedge.kennedy-center.org/educators.aspx]

Run by the Kennedy Center, ArtsEdge is a comprehensive online database with great resources on teaching creatively. ArtsEdge has lesson plans, how-to guides, and articles for families, students, and teachers.

Assay: A Journal of Nonfiction Studies [www.assayjournal.com]

This online journal from Concordia College offers practical classroom resources, including a syllabi bank, essays to teach, and reading lists.

Creative Writing: Teaching Theory and Pedagogy [www.cwteaching.com]

This journal features many peer-reviewed articles on the theory of teaching creative writing in school. An excellent place to study teaching methods, *Creative Writing: Teaching Theory and Pedagogy* also links to other online articles discussing the theory of teaching.

National Council of Teachers of English [www.ncte.org]

The Web site for the NCTE publishes lesson plans, news articles, suggestions for teaching English, and a forum for teachers of English to swap tips and share successes and failures. Specialized features are available depending on what grade level you are teaching.

New Writing: The International Journal for the Practice and Theory of Creative Writing [www.tandfonline.com/loi/rmnw20]

New Writing, a peer-reviewed journal, publishes both critical and creative work. Critical articles cover a range of topics, such as pedagogy and the analysis of creative works. The journal is also available in print format.

Read Write Think [www.readwritethink.org]

Associated with the NCTE, this Web site lists resources and ideas for assignments. An exceptional search engine allows you to sort activities by grade, subject, and learning objectives.

Teachers and Writers Magazine [www.twc.org/magazine/]

> The Teachers and Writers Collaborative produces this free magazine, home to a variety of resources for teaching kindergarten to college. The Web site contains teaching tips.

The Business of Writing: Agents, Freelancing, Book Proposals, and Publishing

You can find dozens of books on the business aspects of writing. Consider the 80/20 rule, and spend 80 percent of your writing time working on your craft and the remaining 20 percent on exploring markets, agents, and publishers. Here is a selection of the most useful resources devoted to helping you publish your work.

In Print

Banks, Michael A. *How to Become a Full-Time Freelance Writer: A Practical Guide to Setting Up a Successful Writing Business at Home.*
Begley, Adam. *Literary Agents: A Writer's Guide.*
Community of Literary Magazines and Presses. *The CLMP Directory of Literary Magazines and Presses.*
Herman, Jeff, and Deborah Levine Herman. *Write the Perfect Book Proposal: 10 That Sold and Why.*
Higgins, George V. *On Writing: Advice for Those Who Write to Publish (or Would Like To).*
Lerner, Betsy. *The Forest for the Trees: An Editor's Advice to Writers.*
Lyon, Elizabeth. *Nonfiction Book Proposals Anybody Can Write: How to Get a Contract and Advance before Writing Your Book.*
Lyon, Elizabeth. *The Sell-Your-Novel Tool Kit: Everything You Need to Know about Queries, Synopses, Marketing, and Breaking In.*

Online

Agent Query [www.agentquery.com/default.aspx]

> Often recognized by *Writer's Digest* as one of the best Web sites for writers, Agent Query is an online database of hundreds of literary agents. In addition, Agent Query offers several helpful guides on the world of publishing, as well as a list of the best places to send your work, both in print and online.

The Association of Writers and Writing Programs [www.awpwriter.org]

> The Association of Writers and Writing Programs is a useful guide to schools, programs, and writing conferences—a must for those wanting to continue their education after undergraduate studies. The Web site for the

AWP offers many useful databases for discovering writing programs and conferences. The organization also offers a useful print publication. Student discounts are available.

The Authors Guild [www.authorsguild.org]

Members of the Authors Guild receive legal support, including contract reviews and health insurance discounts. Though membership is required for those benefits, nonmembers viewing the Authors Guild Web site will get the latest legal news in the publishing world.

Community of Literary Magazines and Presses [www.clmp.org]

The Community of Literary Magazines and Presses Web site is an excellent resource for those interested in independent literary publication. The site lists Web sites for all of its member publications.

The Internet Writing Workshop [www.internetwritingworkshop.org]

The Internet Writing Workshop is a formal, online creative writing workshop that allows users to read and critique one another's works. The IWW has many subcategories and genres—a writer can sign up for a workshop in fiction, nonfiction, the novel, poetry, or other genres.

NCW Literary Magazines [mockingbird.creighton.edu/NCW/litmags.htm]

This list, compiled by the Nebraska Center for Writers, contains hundreds of publications and links to each publication's Web site. This list might seem a bit daunting, but it's a superb way to see just what is out there.

P&W Literary Agents Database [www.pw.org/literary_agents]

Agents are listed with contact information and submission guidelines and are organized according to what sort of literature they are interested in representing.

Writers Guild of America [www.wga.org]

This site is a very useful introduction to the business side of creative writing, with links where you can "ask the expert," learn to write for television, and connect with other writers. Especially helpful is the guide to Internet developments of special interest to writers, which is updated monthly.

APPENDIX: TERMINOLOGY FOR CREATIVE WRITERS

Creative writers use a specialized vocabulary when talking about work-in-progress and when reading other writers' works, both student and professional. Here are some of the key words that you will hear frequently this semester and in your future writing and literature classes.

Alliteration: Repeated consonant sounds. Example: *Bring back baby*.

Assonance: Repeated vowel sounds. Example: *Oh no, don't let go, Jo-Jo*.

Backstory: Information about the characters' pasts that enriches the reader's understanding of the story's present.

Beat: A moment when something happens.

Block: A fear-based "freeze" reaction stemming from a lack of understanding of how the human brain engages with a writing process, as in "writer's block." See Practicing Focus (p. 18).

Cliché: Predictable choices—familiar words, stereotypical characters, and formulaic plots—that should be avoided in creative writing. To avoid clichés, try taking the fifth exit on the highway, not the first.

Complication: The practice of ordering beats so the situation gets more intense as the piece progresses. For example, imagine that you're late to class and you can't find a parking space. If you then hit a golf cart, that's a complication.

Conflict: The opposing elements in a piece of writing; without conflict, a piece usually lacks tension. (See Chapter Six.)

Couplet: A two-line stanza. See "We Real Cool" (p. 101) and "Hustle" (p. 112).

Creative Nonfiction: True stories written with the dialogue, characterization, scene, and conflict common to fiction. Though these strategies are borrowed from fiction, they are used to present real situations instead of invented stories.

Direct Dialogue: The conversation of a character who is talking in real time. Direct dialogue is indicated by quotation marks. Example: *"I just published six poems," Emily Anne said.*

Enjambment: A poetry technique in which lines are wrapped so that they don't end with periods. See "First Poem for You" (p. 112).

First Person: The "I" point of view. See "How to Touch a Bleeding Dog" (p. 250).

Free Verse: A type of poem written without rhyme, with no rules for counting syllables, line length, or rhythm.

Genre: A type of writing. There are many different genres, including poems, flash fiction, plays, detective novels, graphic novels, comic books, monologues, radio plays, and so on. (See Chapter Ten.)

Green Line: To cut a certain amount of a piece of writing before publication. (In decades past, a green-colored pencil was used to strike out words and sentences.) Example: *Green line 10 percent of this story* or *We need to green line fifty words.*

Indirect Dialogue: Summarized dialogue. Indirect dialogue does not use quotation marks. Example: *The student said that she had writer's block and that it was cray-cray.*

Memoir: Personal writing about one's own life, using scenes, dialogue, and insight.

Metaphor: A comparison between two unlike things in order to make a point about a character, setting, or deeper insight. Example: *She's such a sunny person.* This person isn't actually being called the star at the center of our solar system but is being described as bright and warm.

Monologue: A story or speech spoken or delivered by one speaker. Comedians such as Jim Gaffigan and Wanda Sykes perform monologues, as do characters in plays and in other kinds of stories.

Narrator: The person telling the story.

Omniscience: A point of view in which the narrator is able to go into any character's perspective and make comments about the world of the story from an all-knowing perspective. In one of his novels, Tolstoy even went into a dog's point of view.

Point of View: The person or perspective from which a story is told. In addition to omniscience, types of points of view include first person ("I"), second person ("you"), and third person ("he," "she," or "they").

Prose: Works of fiction and nonfiction written in sentences and paragraphs, as distinct from poetry and drama.

Prose Poem: A poem where the lines extend over to the right margin. It is more like a paragraph than a traditional poem, where the lines may vary in length. Prose poems often make heavy use of images and sound work and are less concerned with narrative drive, tension, conflict, and character. See "af•ter•glow" (p. 67).

Protagonist: The main character of a story, usually the one to whom the most happens in a story, the one who tells the story, or the one with whom we identify most closely.

Scene: A combination of visuals, action, dialogue, and setting. A scene creates a movie in the reader's mind: a box of space with time passing inside it. Something happens in the box, and the scene concludes.

Second Person: The point of view from the "you" perspective. Example: *You walk in. You sit down. You can tell she's upset. You don't know why.*

Setting: The place where the piece happens in space and time. "Cat in the Rain" (p. 337) is set in a hotel shortly after World War I.

Stanza: A group of lines in a poem, set off by space breaks from the other groups of lines. "We Real Cool" (p. 101) is written in four stanzas.

Submittable: A popular online management tool for submitting work to literary magazines for publication.

Subtext: The meaning beneath the surface. Subtext is not overtly stated but is quite clear. For example, in a scene where a woman is chopping carrots harshly and speaking to her husband, the subtext may be that she is angry with her husband.

Summary: A technique used to move through time quickly or give background information efficiently instead of painting a detailed scene.

Third Person: A point of view that uses pronouns such as "he," "she," and "they." Example: *He walked in. He could see she was upset. He didn't know why.*

Voice: A writer's style, including types of sentences, vocabulary, and tone—essentially, how a writer writes. A writer might have a very informal, edgy, conversational, in-your-face voice or might have a very mannered, detached, formal voice.

Acknowledgments

Kim Addonizio. "First Poem for You." Copyright © Kim Addonizio. Used with permission.

Brian Arundel. "The Things I've Lost." Copyright © Brian Arundel. Used with permission.

Laure-Anne Bosselaar. "Stillbirth" from *A New Hunger*. Copyright © 2007 by Laure-Anne Bosselaar. Reprinted with the permission of The Permissions Company, Inc., on behalf of Copper Canyon Press, www.coppercanyonpress.org.

Gwendolyn Brooks. "We Real Cool." Copyright © Brooks Permissions. Reprinted by consent of Brooks Permissions.

Jericho Brown. "Hustle" from *The New Testament*. Copyright © 2014 by Jericho Brown. Reprinted with the permission of The Permissions Company, Inc., on behalf of Copper Canyon Press, www.coppercanyonpress.org.

Raymond Carver. "Cathedral" from *Cathedral* by Raymond Carver, copyright © 1981, 1982, 1983 by Tess Gallagher. Used by permission of Alfred A. Knopf, an imprint of Knopf Doubleday Publishing Group, a division of Penguin Random House LLC. All rights reserved.

Gregory Corso. "Marriage" from *The Happy Birthday of Death*, copyright © 1960 by New Directions Publishing Corporation. Used by permission of New Directions Publishing Corp.

E. E. Cummings. "(Me up at does)." Copyright © 1963, 1991 by the Trustees for the E. E. Cummings Trust, from *Complete Poems: 1904–1962* by E. E. Cummings, edited by George J. Firmage. Used by permission of Liveright Publishing Corporation.

Michael Cunningham. "White Angel" from *A Home at the End of the World*. Copyright © 1990 by Michael Cunningham. Reprinted by permission of Farrar, Straus and Giroux, LLC.

Natalie Diaz. "My Brother at 3 a.m." from *When My Brother Was an Aztec*. Copyright © 2012 by Natalie Diaz. Reprinted with the permission of The Permissions Company, Inc., on behalf of Copper Canyon Press, www.coppercanyonpress.org.

Brian Doyle. "Two Hearts" from *Leaping: Revelations and Epiphanies*. Copyright © 2013 Loyola Press. Used with permission of Loyola Press. To order copies of this book, call 1-800-621-1008 or visit www.loyolabooks.org.

Javier Etchevarren, trans. Jesse Lee Kercheval. "Unemployed." Copyright © Jesse Lee Kercheval. Used with permission.

Carolyn Forché. All text from "The Colonel" from *The Country Between Us*. Copyright © 1981 by Carolyn Forché. Originally appeared in Women's International Resource Exchange. Reprinted by permission of HarperCollins Publishers.

Katie Ford. "Still-Life" from *Blood Lyrics*. Originally in *The New Yorker* (September 30, 2013). Copyright © 2013, 2014 by Katie Ford. Reprinted with the permission of The Permissions Company, Inc., on behalf of Graywolf Press, Minneapolis, Minnesota, www.graywolfpress.org.

Amy Fusselman. "The Pharmacist's Mate." Reprinted by the permission of Lippincott Massie McQuilkin as agents for the author. Copyright © 2001 by Amy Fusselman.

Charlotte Glynn. "Duct Tape Twins" pages 1–4. Copyright © Charlotte Glynn. Used with permission.

Jessica Greenbaum. "A Poem for S." Copyright © Princeton University Press; permission conveyed through Copyright Clearance Center, Inc. Used with permission.

Terrance Hayes. "Liner Notes for an Imaginary Playlist," from *Lighthead* by Terrance Hayes, copyright © 2010 by Terrance Hayes. Used by permission of Penguin Books, an imprint of Penguin Publishing Group, a division of Penguin Random House LLC.

Ernest Hemingway. "Cat in the Rain." Reprinted with the permission of Scribner, a division of Simon & Schuster, Inc., from *The Short Stories of Ernest Hemingway* by Ernest Hemingway. Copyright © 1925 by Charles Scribner's Sons. Copyright renewed © 1953 by Ernest Hemingway. All rights reserved.

INDEX

Abecedarius, 406, 409–412

Abstract words, 194

Accuracy, 314–316
  of dialogue, 315–316
  of gestures, 315

Action, layering dialogue and, 240–242

Action verbs, 195–196

Addonizio, Kim
  First Poem for You, 112

Adjectives, 194, 207

Adverbs, 207

af•ter•glow (Jordan), 44–45, 67

Alliteration, 284

Anaphora, 281, 406, 413–416
  reading, 413–415
  writing, 415

Annotations, 43

Another Lullaby for Insomniacs (Stallings), 320, 330, 335–336

Apologies and a Few Things I'm Sorry About (Kraese), 438

Art as a sensory experience, 11

Articles, 98

Artist's books, 476

Artist's statement, writing an, 478–479

Arundel, Brian
  The Things I've Lost, 216–217

Assonance, 284

Audience, 465

Backstory sentences, 85, 86

Beats, 101–102

Big, going, in cultivating insight, 326

Block. *See* Writer's block

Bodies (Shattuck), 263–274

Bosselaar, Laure-Anne
  Stillbirth, 303–304

Boys (Moody), 212–215

Braids, 406, 416–420
  reading, 417–418
  writing, 418–419

Breaks, 202

Brooks, Gwendolyn
  We Real Cool, 101

Brown, Jericho
  Hustle, 112–113

Building blocks, 83–130
  conflict as, 86–87
  projects in, 109–110
  readings in, 112 130
  scenes as, 87–90
  sentences as, 85–86
  workshop in, 111

Bureaucratic writing, 289

Buying Wine (Matthews), 69–70

Camera work, 202–207

Cartoons, 52

Carver, Raymond
  Cathedral, 119–130

Cathedral (Carver), 119–130
Cat in the Rain (Hemingway), 337–340
Chapbooks, 476–478
Character sentences, 85, 86
Characters, working with, in maintaining
    tension, 228–232
Chase, David
    The Sopranos, 191
Children's books, resources for, 497
Class readings, 468
Clichés, 324
    action, 242
    avoiding, 242
Close reading
    creative reading as, 38–45
    of literature, 41–45
    of own work, 39–40
    of work by peers, 40–41
Close up, writing from, 231–232
Cold, going, in cultivating insight, 185,
    322–323
Collective point of view, 206
The Colonel (Forché), 185–187
Comics, 45, 52. *See also* Graphic narratives
    and comics
Conflict-crisis-resolution, building
    narratives with, 90–93
Conflicts, 51, 84, 86–87, 208
    starting with, 90–91
Consonance, 284
Consonants, 283–284
Contemporary narratives, 46
Conversation, 207
Copywork, practicing, 42
Corso, Gregory
    Marriage, 114–117
Couplets, 236
Course, reversing, in cultivating insight,
    325
Creative nonfiction, 47–48
    responding to, 48
Creative reading, 35–82
    as close reading, 38–45
    curiosity of reader, 36

personality of reader in, 36–38
projects in, 62–64
readings in, 65–82
tolerance of discomfort of reader, 37–38
Creative writers, 2–3
    comfort zone and, 137–138
    cross-training of, 45
    focus of, on practice, 8
    as free-range readers, 35
    questions asked by, 3–4
    reading and, 7
    sharing of work by, 7–8
    working with other writers, 7
    writing by, 4–7
Creative writing, 1–8
    comparing to photography, 2
    components of
        energy in, 6
        images in, 5–6
        insight in, 6
        pattern in, 6
        revision in, 6–7
        tension in, 6
    defined, 3
    dialogue in, 243–244
    experimental, 53
    field guide to, 45–53
    fine-tuning, 193
    five senses in, 320
    insight in, 312, 313
    as interdisciplinary, 1
    moving images as difference in, 134
    parts of, 4–7
    patterns in, 280
    process of, 3–4
    pursuit of, 1
    resources in teaching, 497–499
    structure in, 83
Crisis, building to a, 91
Cummings, E. E.
    (Me up at does), 287
Cunningham, Michael
    White Angel, 341–354
Curiosity, in creative reading, 36

Dashes, 202
Desire as element in tension, 227
Dialogue
    accuracy of, 315–316
    in creative writing, 243–244
    direct, 240
    disembodied, 242
    energy in, 187, 192, 193
    layering action and, 240–242
    leaps in, 190–191
    sustaining tension in, 241
Diaz, Natalie
    My Brother at 3 a.m., 159–160
Dimension, layers in adding, 237–242
Direct dialogue, 240
Direct speech, 241
Discomfort, tolerance of, 37–38
Distance, 208
Distractions, 19, 23–24
    external, 23–24
    internal, 24–25
Do Not Go Gentle into That Good Night
    (Thomas), 117–118
Doyle, Brian
    Two Hearts, 340–341
Drama, 50–52. *See also* Plays/screenplays
Dramatic poetry, 49
Duct Tape Twins, excerpt from (Glynn),
    218–221

Echoes, 281–283
    sound, 283
Editing, 356, 389–392
    defined, 357
    distinguishing between proofreading,
        revision and, 356
    for flow, 390
Embellishment, 207
Emotional shorthand, 242
End-stopped line, 99
End words, 98
Energy, 6, 183–221
    camera work and, 202–207
    conflict in, 208

dialogue in, 187, 192, 193
distance in, 208
focus and, 207
guidelines for increasing, 187–188
leaps in, 183, 189–193, 208
manipulating, 199–207
pace in, 199–202, 208
point of view in, 208
principles of, 183–184
projects in, 209–210
readings in, 212–221
sentence variation in, 208
subjects in, 183, 184–186, 208
troubleshooting, 208–209
words in, 184, 193–199, 208
workshop in, 210–211
Enjambment, 100
Essays
    expository, 197
    literary, 47
    lyric, 48
Experience, in cultivating
    insight, 318–319
Experimental pieces, responding to, 53
Expository essays, verbs in, 197

Façade, 242–245
Facebook, 38, 484, 485
Fantasy, 46
Fatigues (Livewell), 455–456
Fiction, 45–46, 83
    flash, 45, 46, 49–492, 83, 91, 406, 426,
        491–492
    micro, 46, 91, 426
    nano-, 426
    realistic, 45–46
    resources for, 490–491
    responding to, 46
    revising, 370–375
    science, 46
    speculative, 45
Fill-in-the-blanks, 56, 327
Filters, 43–44, 196, 197–198
Finished forms, 408

First drafts, 193
  reading aloud, 40
First person, 203, 204
First Poem for You (Addonizio), 112
Flash fiction, 45, 46, 83, 91, 406, 426–429
  reading, 427–428
  resources for, 491–492
  writing, 428
Flashlight technique, 283
Flow
  editing for, 390
  in focus, 21
Focus, 11–34
  distractions in, 23–24
  flow in, 21
  judgment in, 25–26
  lack of, 22–26
  mind's eye in, 11–16
  practicing, 18–21
  projects in, 26
  readings in, 27–34
  subject and, 16–18
  writing rituals in, 20
Forché, Carolyn
  The Colonel, 185–187
Ford, Katie
  Still-Life, 158
Form poetry, resources for, 494
Forms, 405–460. *See also specific types*
  defined, 405
  experimenting with, 407–408
  finished, 408
  poetry and, 408–409
  types of, 406–407, 409–460
Free association, 50
Free verse, 291
Fusselman, Amy
  From *The Pharmacist's Mate*, 76–82

Gaps, power of, 189–193
Gardner, John, 462
Genealogy (Sholl), 61–62, 66–67
General, avoiding the, 188
Genre, 45. *See also specific*
  defined, 45

Gestures
  accuracy of, 315
  patterns of, 295–296
Ghazals, 235–236, 406, 430–432
  reading, 430–431
  writing, 432
Glynn, Charlotte
  Excerpt from *Duct Tape
    Twins*, 218–221
Google search, 482–484
Graphic histories, 52
Graphic instruction manuals, 52
Graphic literature, 52
Graphic memoirs, 48
Graphic narratives and comics, 45, 52, 83,
    406, 420–425
  reading, 420–423
  resources for, 497
  responding to, 53
  writing, 423–425
Graphic novels, 52–53
  responding to, 53
Greenbaum, Jessica
  A Poem for S., 335
Guided practice, 54–56

Haiku, 96
Hard copy, reading from, 40
Hayes, Terrance
  Liner Notes for an Imaginary Playlist,
    113–114
Hemingway, Ernest, 6,
    328, 426, 469
  Cat in the Rain, 337–340
Hicok, Bob
  A Primer, 74–75
Hixson, Jenifer
  Where There's Smoke, 162–166
Hopler, Jay
  That Light One Finds in Baby Pictures,
    158–159
Horror, 46
How to Touch a Bleeding Dog (Kessler),
    250–251
Hustle (Brown), 112–113

Iamb, 289–291
Iambic pentameter, 101, 289–291, 454
I am not Batman. (Ramirez), 70–74
I, as narrator, 226
Ideas, 154–156
I Go Back to Berryman's (Scarpa), 65–66
Images, 5–6, 133–182
    as active, 134
    creating with, 142–154
    defined, 132
    focusing on people in action, 142–143
    generating, 140–142
    ideas and, 154–156
    layering, 238
    moving, 13–15
    moving around in, 147–148
    one sentence, one action in, 148–150
    as the opposite of thought, 137
    orienting yourself in, before writing, 141
    principles of, 133–142
    projects in, 156–157
    reading and viewing of, 134–137
    readings in, 158–182
    resources for, 487–488
    sliding and, 152–154
    specifics in, 145–146
    summary, 151–152
    thinking from within, 143–145
    trusting, in cultivating insight, 320
    workshop in, 157
Imitation, 54–62
    types of, 56–62
Improvisation, 50
Information, providing interesting, 187
In My Father's Study upon His Death
    (Landis), 161–162
Insight, 6, 311–354
    accuracy in, 314–316
    asking questions in cultivating,
        320–322, 327
    avoiding overwriting in, 329–330
    avoiding preaching in, 329
    avoiding stating the obvious in, 330–331
    creating subtext in cultivating, 327–328
    experience in cultivating, 318–319

generosity in, 316–317
going big, in cultivating, 326
going cold, in cultivating, 322–325
projects in, 331–334
readings in, 335–354
reversing course in cultivating, 325, 327
surprising yourself in cultivating,
    326–327
trusting images in cultivation, 320
workshop in, 334
Instagram, 484
Iowa Writers' Workshop, 483
I Remember All of You (Womack), 398–402

Jordan, A. Van
    af•ter•glow, 44–45, 67
Journaling, 4
Journeys, 406, 433–435
    reading, 433–424
    writing, 434–435
JSTOR, 483
Judgment, 25–26
Juxtaposition, power of, 232

Kessler, Rod
    *How to Touch a Bleeding
        Dog*, 250–251
Kraese, Danielle
    From *Apologies and a Few Things I'm
        Sorry About*, 438

Landis, Dylan
    In My Father's Study upon His Death,
        161–162
Law briefs, 289
Layering of patterns, 298–299
Layers, in adding dimension, 237–242
Laziness, 19
Leaps in energetic writing, 183, 189–193,
    208
Limericks, 96
Line break, 99
Liner Notes for an Imaginary Playlist
    (Hayes), 113–114
Lines, 99–101
    polarity in, 100

List poems, 436
Lists, 202, 281, 407, 436–438
    reading, 436–437
    writing, 437–438
Literary essays, 47
Literary Hub, 470
Literary magazines, 38, 469–475, 482
Literary news, 489–490
Literature, close reading of, 41–45
Live reading, tips for attending, 466
Livewell, David
    Fatigues, 455–456
Lyric essays, 48
Lyric poetry, 49, 95, 228
Lyrics, rap, 288, 291

Magnolia (Shipley), 160–161
Mann, Randall
    Pantoum, 302–303
Marriage (Corso), 114–117
Matthews, Sebastian
    Buying Wine, 69–70
(Me up at does) (Cummings), 287
Memoirs, 47, 52
    graphic, 48
    micro, 427–429, 491–492
Memorizing, 43
Memos, 289
Michigan, University of, 483
Micro-fiction, 46, 91, 426
Micro-memoirs
    reading, 427–428
    resources for, 491–492
    writing, 428–429
Miller, Brenda
    Swerve, 118
Mind's eye, 11–16
Minnesota Center for Book Arts, 476
Modulation, 207
Monologues, 51, 407, 439–442
    reading, 440–441
    responding to, 52
    writing, 441
Moody, Rick
    Boys, 212

Moore, Dinty, 297
    Son of Mr. Green Jeans, 305–310
Morris, Peter
    Pancakes, 274–279
My Brother at 3 a.m. (Diaz), 159–160

Nano-fiction, 426
Narrative poetry, 49, 50, 95, 96, 228
Narratives
    building with conflict-crisis-resolution,
        90–93
    conflict in, 86–87
    graphic, 83
    parts of, 84–95
    scenes in, 87–90
    sentences in, 85–86
    writing scenes for, 93–95
Narrative scaffolding, 60–61
Narrator, "I" as, 226
The Neighbor (Roselló), 27–34
New journalism, 48
NewPages, 470
The New Year (Painter), 69
Noncreative writing, 142
Nonfiction, 47
    creative, 47–48
    resources for, 495–496
    revising, 379–389
Not-writing, strategy for overcoming, 19
Nouns, 194
Novellas, 45, 46
Novels, 45, 46
Nursery rhymes, 291
Nye, Naomi Shihab
    Wedding Cake, 336–337

Objective approach, 205
Objects, pattern of, 292–295
Obstacles in tension, 227
Omniscience, 204
Online resources, 469–471
Opponents, matching your, 229–230
Orr, Gregory
    The River, 302
Overwriting, avoiding, in insight, 329–330

Pace, 208
    in manipulating energy, 199–202
Paged words, 298
Page, Jimmy, 96
Painter, Pamela
    The New Year, 69
Pancakes (Morris), 274–279
Pantoum (Mann), 302–303
Pantoums, 407, 446–460
    reading, 446–448
    writing, 448–449
Passive verbs, 196, 198
Patterns, 6, 280–310
    consonants and vowels in, 283–284
    in creative writing, 280
    defined, 280
    echoes in, 281–283
    gestures as, 295–296
    layering, 298–299
    meter in, 289–292
    objects as, 292–295
    on the page, 296–298
    projects in, 299–300
    readings for, 302–310
    rhyme in, 281–283
    rhythm in, 288–289
    word order in, 285–288
    workshop in, 300–301
Peers, close reading work by, 40–41
Pentameter, 290
Personal story, 47
Personal writing, 488–489
Person, as element in tension, 227
The Pharmacist's Mate, from (Fusselman),
    60, 76–82, 299, 312
Place, picking a, 94–95
Plays/screenplays, 51, 83, 407, 442–446
    formatting, 445
    reading, 442–443
    resources for, 496
    responding to, 52
    writing, 443–445
Plot sentences, 85, 86
Plural point of view, 205

Plutarch, 138
A Poem for S. (Greenbaum), 330, 335,
    410
Poems, 83, 408–409. *See also* Ghazals;
    Pantoums; Sestinas; Sonnets;
    Villanelles
    defined, 49
    dramatic, 49
    line length in, 102
    lines in, 99–101
    list, 436
    lyric, 49, 95, 228
    narrative, 49, 50, 95, 96, 228
    parts of, 95–109
    playing with, 108–109
    prose, 49, 83, 101
    resources for, 492–495
    responding to, 50
    revising, 375–379
    scaffolding, 57–59
    speakers in, 204
    stanzas in, 107–108
    turns in, 103–107
    words in, 96–99
Point of view, 202–207, 208
    collective, 206
    plural, 205
Polarity, 94
Pontificating, 329
Portfolios, 475–476
Preaching, avoiding, in insight, 329
Pretty Ice (Robison), 166–170
A Primer (Hicok), 74–75
Procrastination, 19, 22, 24–25
Proofreading, 389–392
    defined, 357
    distinguishing between editing, revision,
        and, 356
    for grammar errors, 391
    for presentation, 391
Prose poems, 49, 83, 101
    responding to, 50
Publications, 464, 474
    researching, 471–472

Public readings, 465–469
Publishing, 4

Questions
    asked by creative writers, 3–4
    asking writing, 367–369
    in cultivating insight, 320–322, 327

Ramirez, Marco
    I am not Batman. 70–74
Rap lyrics, 288, 291
Read aloud, 40, 42, 51
Readers, reaching, 463–480
Reading, 4
    close, 38–45 (*See also* Close reading)
    creative, 35–82 (*See also* Creative
        reading)
Realistic fiction, 45–46
Rejection, embracing, 474–475
Relationship sentences, 85, 86
Repairing the House (Ridl), 396–398
Repetition, 280–281. *See also* Patterns
Researched work, 48
Resolution, ending with, 92
Resources
    for the business of writing, 499–500
    for children's books, 497
    for fiction, 490–491
    for flash fiction, 491–492
    general, 486–500
    Google search in, 482–484
    for graphic narratives and comics, 497
    for images, 487–488
    for micro-memoirs, 491–492
    for nonfiction, 495–496
    for plays and screenplays, 496
    for poetry, 492–495
    social media in, 484–486
    for spoken word, 494–495
    for teaching in creative writing, 497–499
Reversing course in cultivating insight,
    325, 327
Revising, 4, 6, 355–404
    asking questions in, 367–369
    choosing beginning point in, 366

conquering writing blocks in, 359–362
defined, 357
deleting versus fixing in, 367
distinguishing between editing,
    proofreading, and, 356
editing and proofreading
    in, 389–392
effectiveness in, 362–369
of fiction, 370–375
by hand, 366
limiting time in, 363
of nonfiction, 379–389
of poetry, 375–379
projects in, 392–393
readings in, 395–402
reading to get unstuck in, 365–366
sketching scene in, 363–365
steps in, 369–389
strategies for creative writing in, 358
workshop in, 393–394
Rhymes, 281–283
Rhythm, 288–289, 296
Ridl, Jack, 367
    Repairing the House, 396–398
The River (Orr), 302
Robison, Mary
    Pretty Ice, 166–170
Roselló, Jarod
    The Neighbor, 27–34

Saunders, George
    Sticks, 304
Scaffolding, 56–59
    narrative, 60–61
    of a poem, 57–59
Scarpa, Vincent
    I Go Back to Berryman's, 65–66
Scenes, 84, 87–90
    writing, for narratives, 93–95
Scheffler, Adam
    Woman and Dogs, 67–68
Scholl, Betsy
    Genealogy, 61–62
Science fiction, 46
Screenplays, 51. *See also* Plays/screenplays

Second person, 203, 204
Seinfeld (TV show), 314
Self-expression, 488–489
Sentences, 84, 85–86
    backstory, 85, 86
    character, 85, 86
    plot, 85, 86
    relationship, 85, 86
    short, 202
    single-word phrases at the end of, 200
    variation in, 208
Sestinas, 407, 450–453
    reading, 450–452
    writing, 452
Sharma, Akhil
    Surrounded by Sleep, 171–182
Shattuck, Jessica
    Bodies, 263–274
Shipley, Ely
    Magnolia, 160–161
Short-shorts, 45, 46
Short stories, 45, 46
Silver, Marisa
    What I Saw from Where I Stood, 251–263
Sliding, 152–154
Social media, 484–486
Sonnets, 96, 407, 453–458
    reading, 454–456
    writing, 456–457
Son of Mr. Green Jeans (Moore), 305–310
Sound, 296
    patterns of, 284
Sound echoes, 283
Sound repetition, 283
Specificity
    in images, 145–146
    tension and, 230–231
    of words, 193–195
Speculative fiction, 45
Speech. *See also* Dialogue
    direct, 241
Spoken word, 50
    resources for, 494–495
Stakes, as element in tension, 227

Stallings, A. E., 455
    Another Lullaby for Insomniacs, 320, 330,
        335–336
Stanzas, 107–108
Steinbeck, John, 133, 285
Sticks (Saunders), 304
Stillbirth (Bosselaar), 303–304, 447
Still-Life (Ford), 96, 158
Storyboards, 425
Story line, 92
Structure, 83
Subjects, 16–18
    in energetic writing, 183, 184–186, 208
Subtext, 192
    creating, in cultivating insight, 327–328
Summary, 230
Summary images, 151–152
Surprising yourself, in cultivating insight,
        326–327
Surrounded by Sleep (Sharma), 171–182
Swerve (Miller), 118
Syntax, 286, 296

TED Talks, 466, 482
Tension, 6, 222–279
    characters in maintaining, 228–229
    close-ups and, 231–232
    decreasing and increasing, 233–237
    defined, 222
    elements of, 225–228
    façade in, 242–245
    layers in, 237–242
    maintaining, 228–232
    manipulating, 232–245
    matching opponents in, 229–230
    point of view and, 225
    principles of, 222–228
    projects in, 246–248
    readings in, 250–279
    specificity in, 230–231
    workshops in, 248–249
Text on page as pattern, 296–298
That Light One Finds in Baby Pictures
        (Hopler), 158–159

The Things I've Lost (Arundel), 216–217
Third person, 203, 204
Thomas, Dylan, 453
    Do Not Go Gentle into That Good Night,
    117–118
Thoughts, images as opposite of, 137
Time, tightening up, 94
Tolerance of discomfort, 37–38
Triangles, layering with, 238–240
Turner, Brian
    What Every Soldier Should Know, 217–218
Turning, 103
Turning points, in monologues, 441
Turns, 103–107
    words that signal, 106
Twitter, 38, 484, 485–486
Two-column lists, 188, 198
Two Hearts (Doyle), 340–341

Unified pattern of imagery, 292

Verbs, 195–197
    action, 195–196
    passive, 196, 198
    strong, 202
Verses, 103, 104, 107
Villanelles, 407, 458–460
    reading, 459–460
    writing, 460
Vowels, 283–284

Wedding Cake (Nye), 336–337
We Real Cool (Brooks), 101
What Every Soldier Should Know (Turner),
    217–218
What I Saw from Where I Stood (Silver),
    251–263
Where There's Smoke (Hixson), 162–166

White Angel (Cunningham), 326, 330,
    341–354
White space, 296
Womack, Karissa
    I Remember All of You, 398–402
Woman and Dogs (Scheffler), 67–68, 96,
    106
Word choices, 98, 208
Word order, 285–288
    inversion of, 287–288
Word packages, 193
    avoiding, 97
Wordplay, 50
Words, 96–99
    abstract, 194
    in energetic writing, 184, 193–199, 208
    paged, 298
    specificity of, 193–195
Writer's block, 19, 22–23
    conquering common, 359–361
Writer's Market, 470
Writing, 4. *See also* Creative writing
    exploring through, 17–18
    as habit, 19
    between the lines, 56–57
    noncreative, 142
    for others, 5
    resources for the business of, 499–500
    rituals in, 20
    signs of lazy, 242
    submitting your, 472–474
    what you know, 16–17
    what you see, 12–13
    for yourself, 5

Yellow Jacket Press, 476
YouTube, 466

About the Author

Heather Sellers is professor of English at the University of South Florida, where she teaches creative nonfiction and poetry in the undergraduate and MFA writing programs. Born and raised in Orlando, Florida, she earned her PhD in English/Creative Writing at Florida State University and then went on to teach at the University of Texas–San Antonio, St. Lawrence University, and for almost two decades, Hope College, where she was elected Teacher of the Year. A recipient of a National Endowment for the Arts Fellowship for Fiction and a Barnes & Noble New Discovery Writers Award for her short story collection *Georgia Under Water*, she has published widely in a variety of genres. Recent essays appear in the *New York Times*; *O, the Oprah Magazine*; *Good Housekeeping*; *Reader's Digest*; *Parade*; *Real Simple*; and the *Sun*. Her most recent book is the critically acclaimed memoir *You Don't Look Like Anyone I Know: A True Story of Family, Face Blindness, and Forgiveness*. Other publications include *Drinking Girls and Their Dresses: Poems*; *Spike and Cubby's Ice Cream Island Adventure*, a children's book; and *Page after Page* and *Chapter after Chapter*, both books on the craft of writing. She lives in Saint Petersburg, Florida.